Certain special effects have the razzle-dazzle of a performance by a master magician, conjuring up visions of the never-before-seen, the dreamlike, the fantastic. Others are so subtle that they are impossible to detect. This is true of the work of master matte artist Albert Whitlock, who is so good at what he does that millions of filmgoers have seen his paintings without knowing that they were looking at anything but real life. For the Peter Sellers remake of *The Prisoner of Zenda,* Whitlock used his matte-painting technique to transform a street scene in Austria into a picturesque view of nineteenth-century London. *Top:* First, the live-action scene was shot on location in Austria. *Center:* Next, the unwanted portion of the scene was matted out. *Bottom:* Finally, Whitlock's glass painting of London, with Big Ben in the distance, was combined with the live-action element to produce the composite that appears on screen.

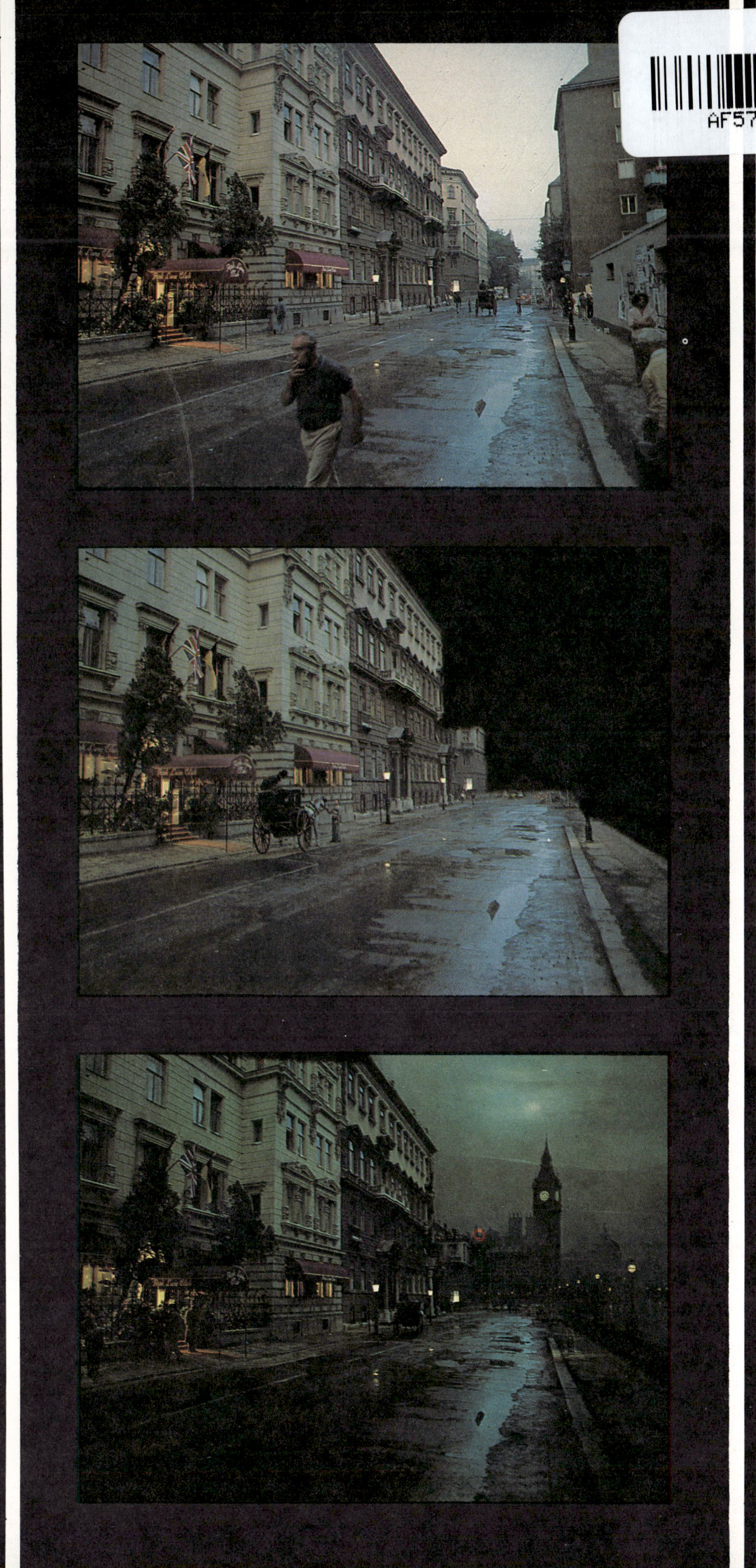

For the opening moments of *Mary Poppins* matte artist Peter Ellenshaw painted a panoramic bird's-eye view of turn-of-the-century London on a sheet of glass, leaving a small section of the glass unpainted in the upper right-hand corner. Footage of Julie Andrews was then projected onto the clear portion of the glass to produce this magical scene.

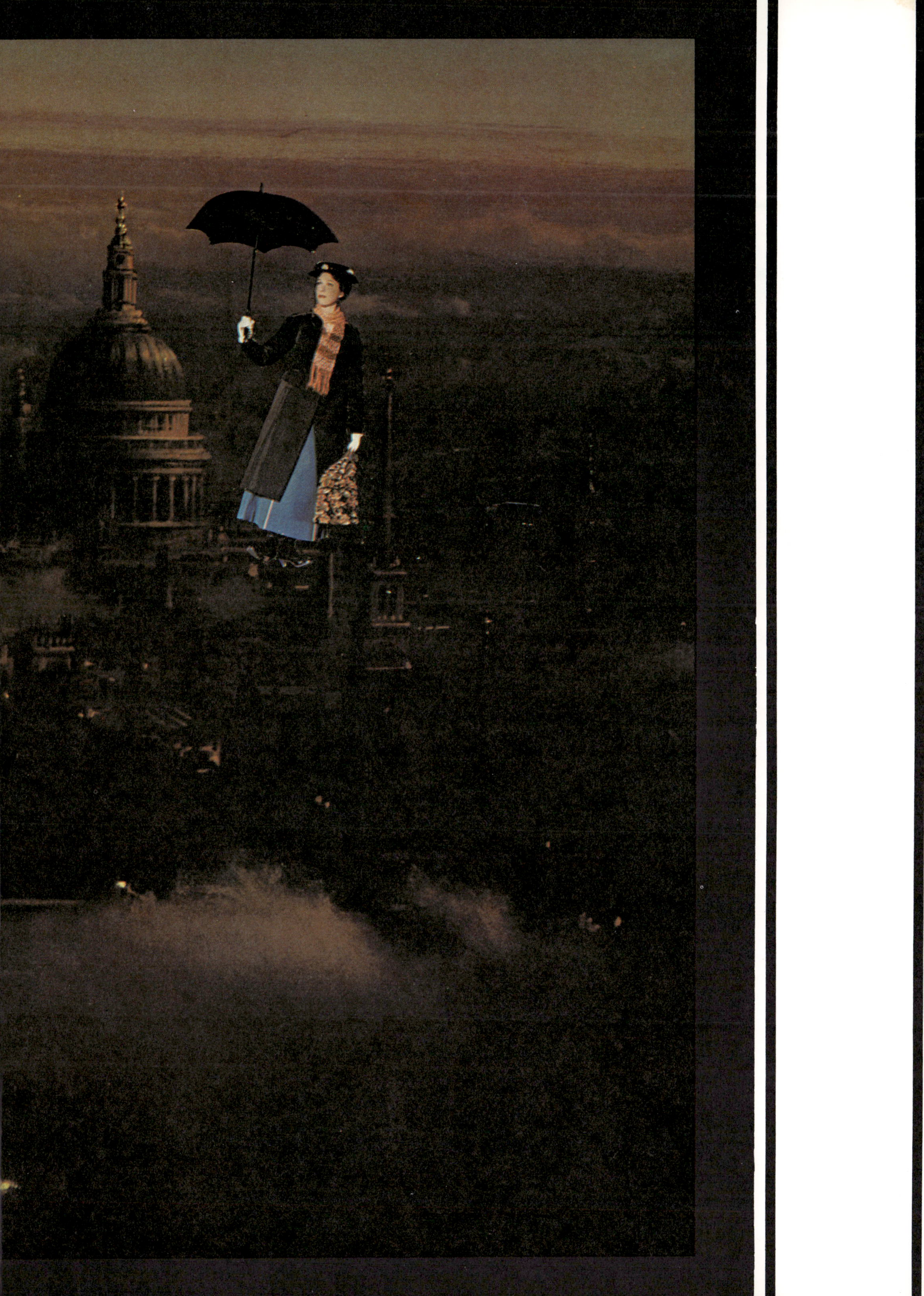

Makeup/effects artist Tom Savini created this gruesome scalping sequence for the horror movie *Maniac* by using a trick scalpel with tubing glued to its underside through which fake blood could be pumped; to simulate her flesh, mortician's wax was applied to the actress's forehead; and a latex scalp with additional blood-tubes attached to its bottom was used. To make the actress's head beneath the scalp look suitably gory, Savini applied pink and white makeup, clots of artificial blood, and a coating of Vaseline.

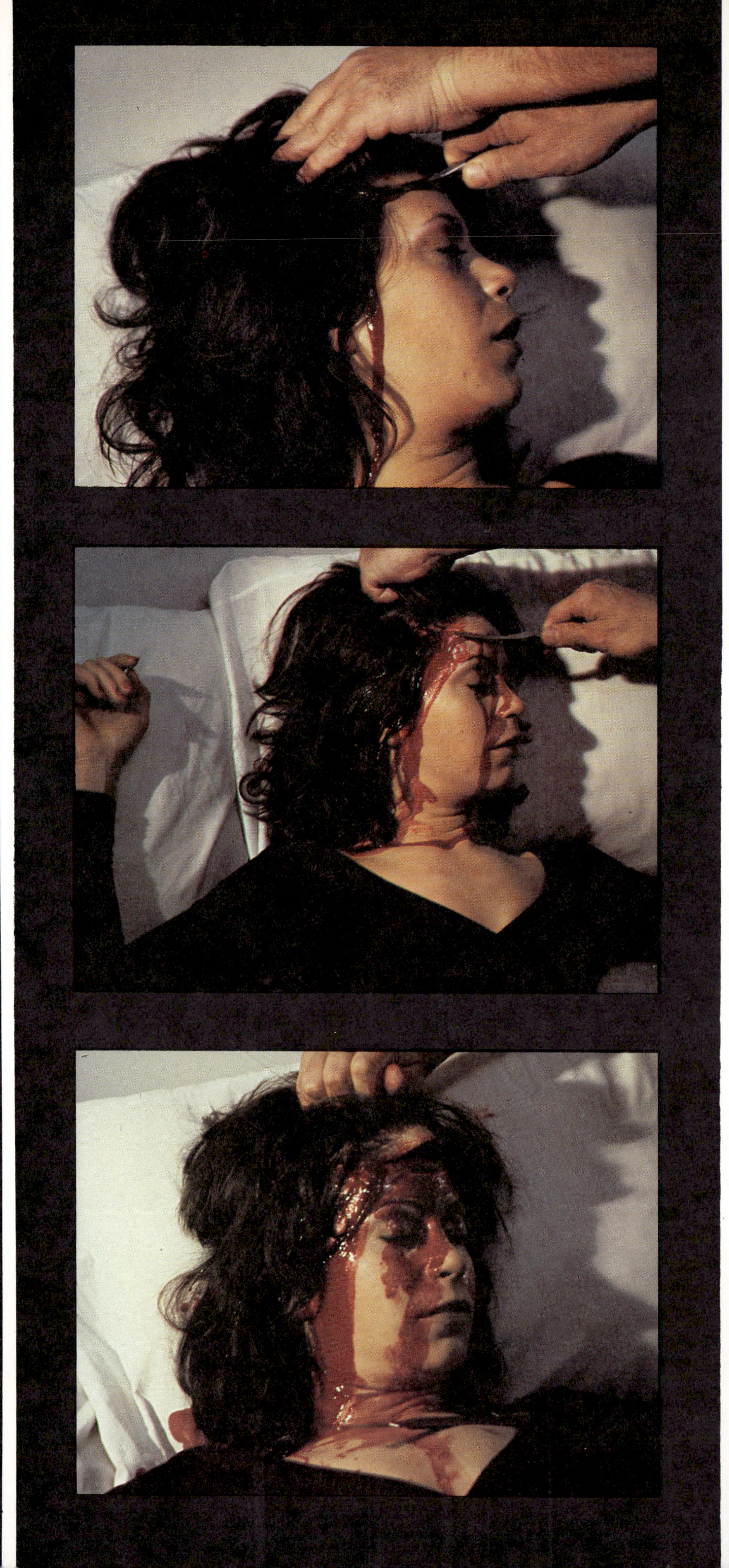

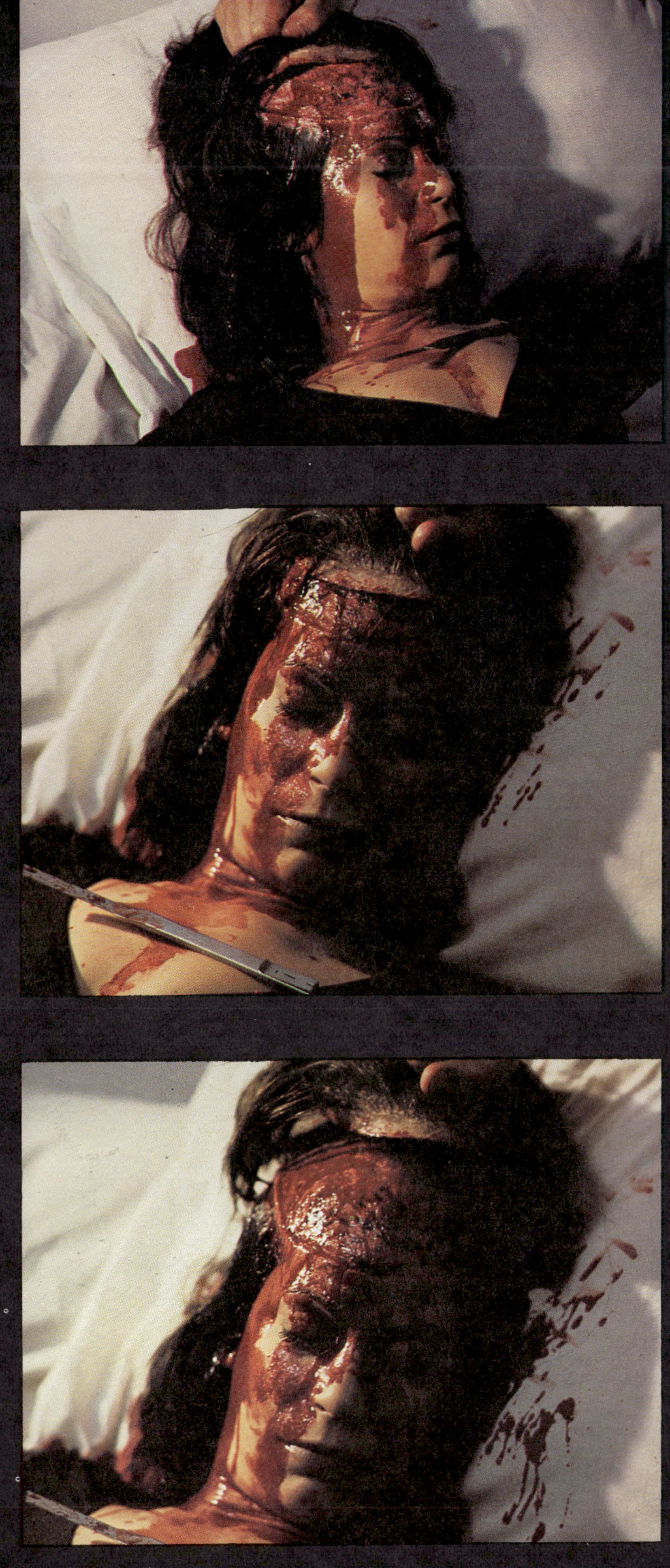

The skeleton fight from Ray Harryhausen's *Jason and the Argonauts,* combining live actors with models brought to life through stop-motion photography. One of the most brilliant pieces of dimensional animation ever done for a film, this sequence took nearly five months to complete, though it lasts less than five minutes on screen.

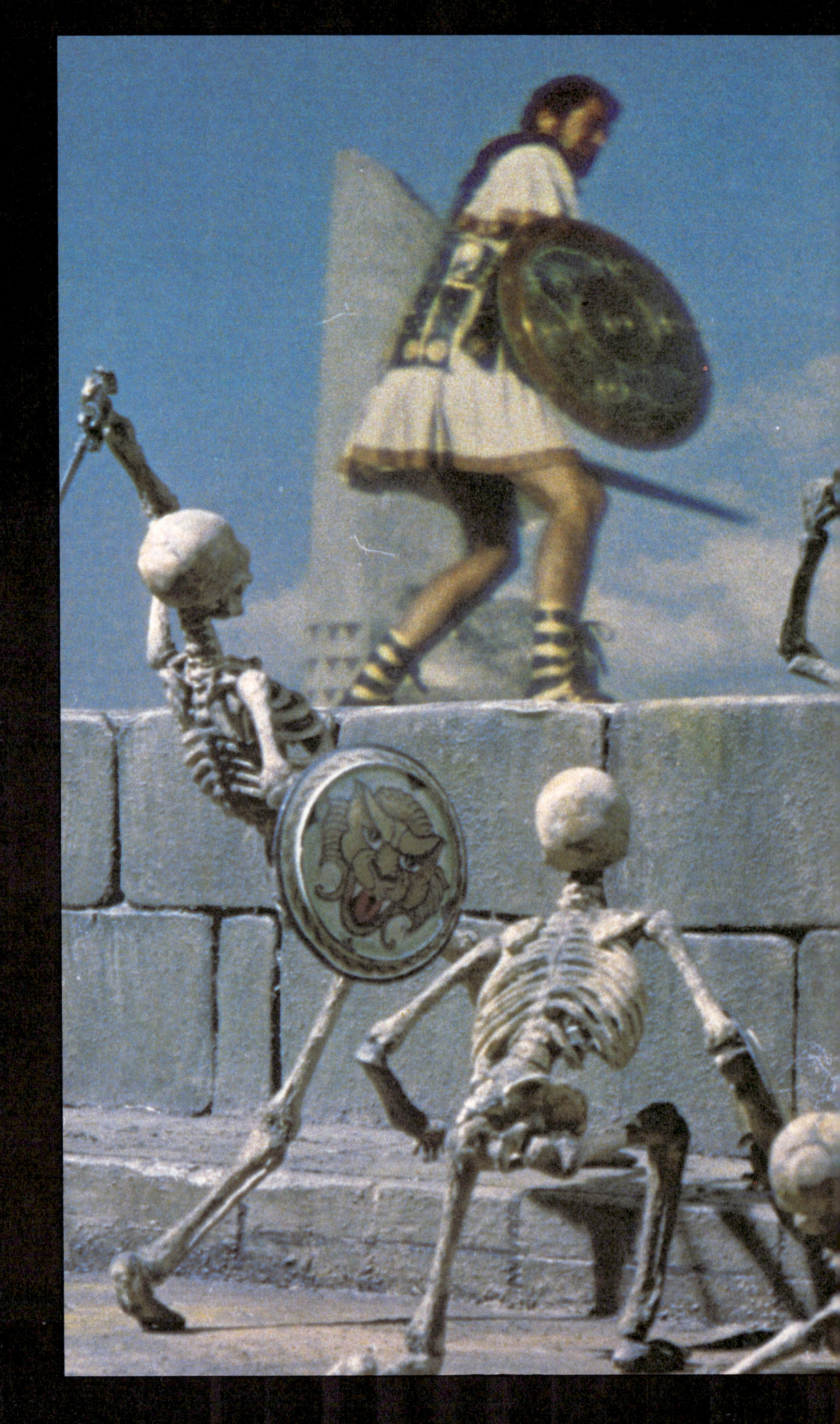

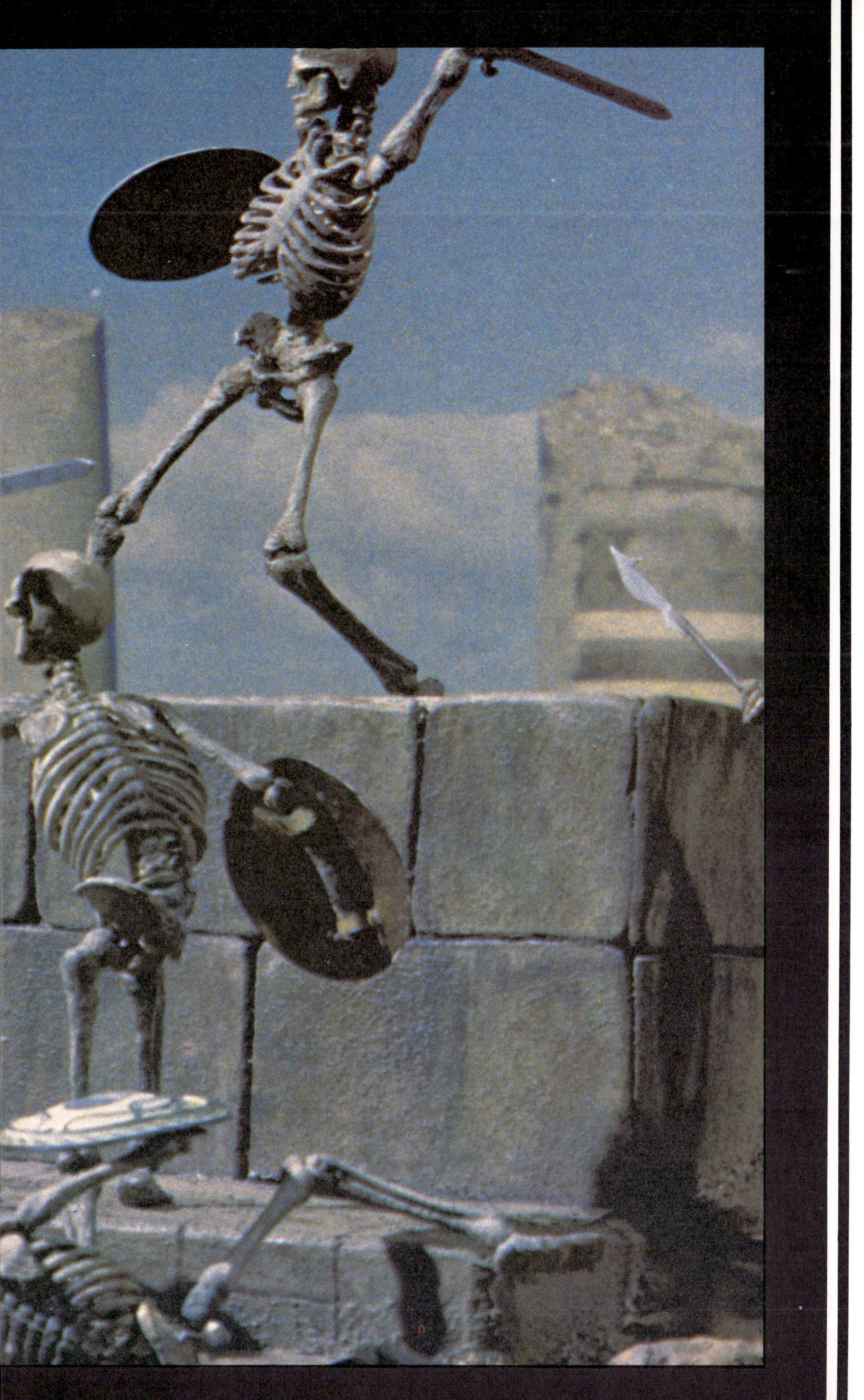

Top: Animator Gene Warren Jr. at work behind a tabletop set of the prehistoric world from the TV series "Land of the Lost."
Center: Another miniature set from "Land of the Lost" with a painted backdrop in progress.
Bottom: James Aupperle animates a horned dinosaur model in front of a rear-projected image of the live-action footage for *Planet of Dinosaurs.*

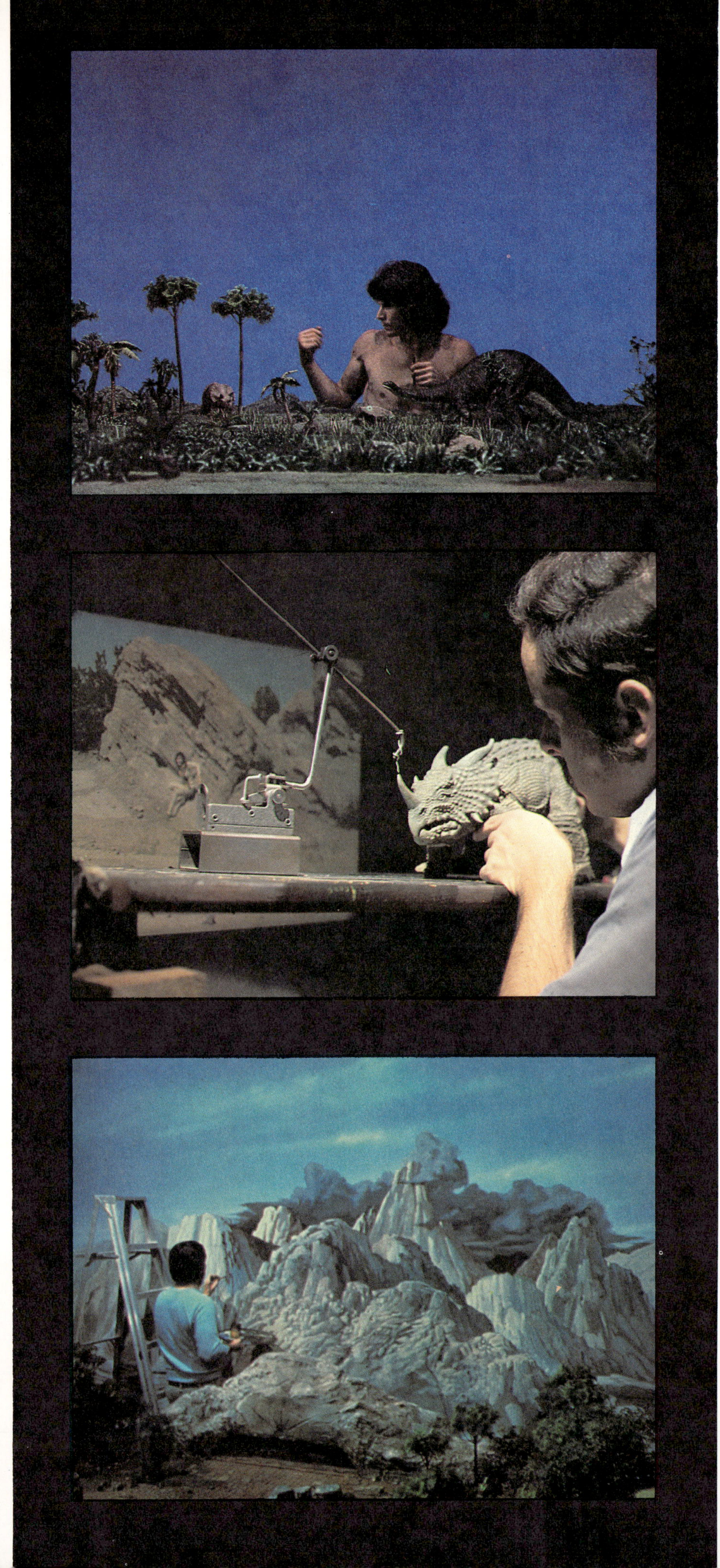

FILM TRICKS

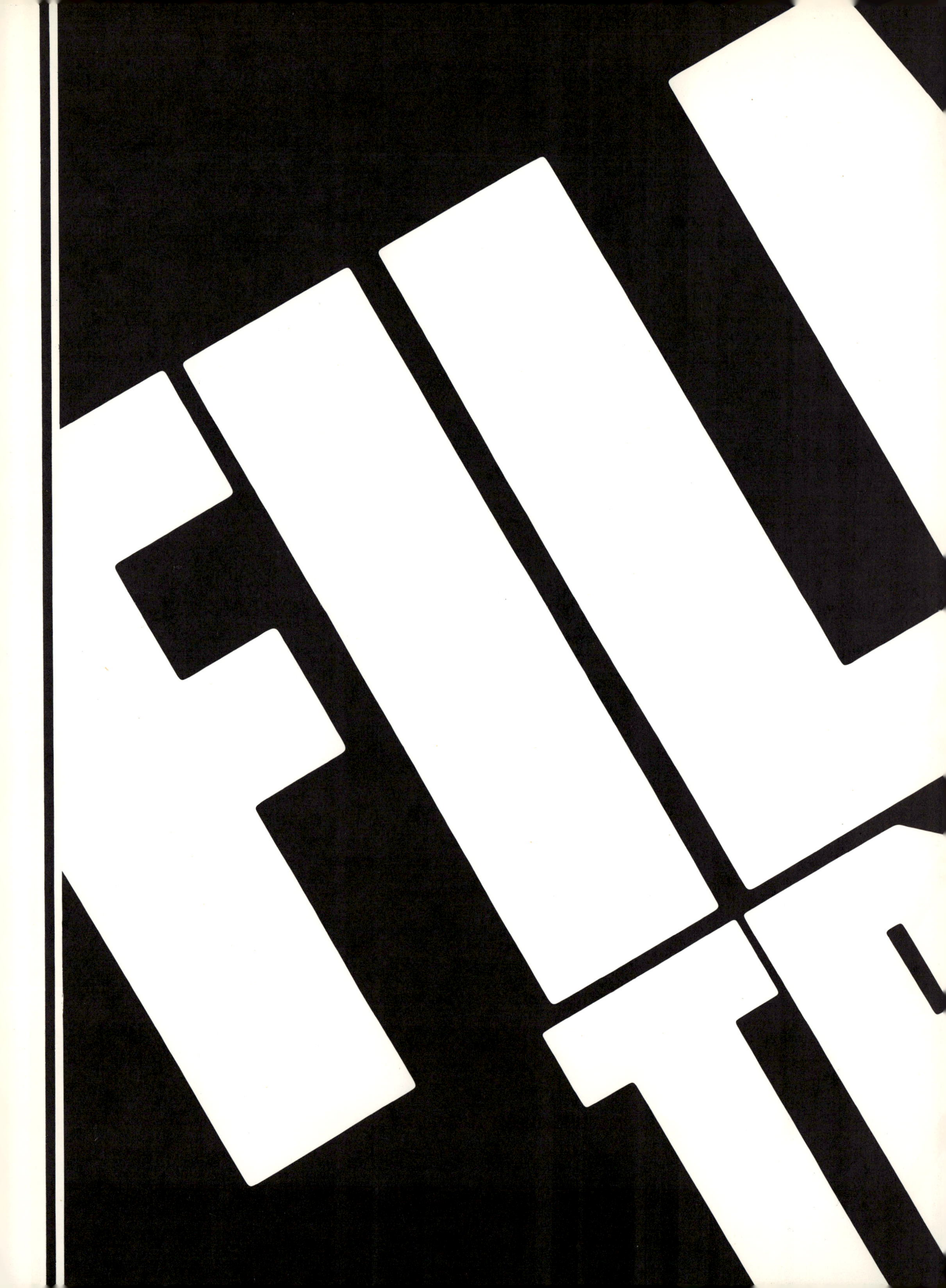

M
ICKS

SPECIAL EFFECTS IN THE MOVIES

BY HAROLD SCHECHTER AND DAVID EVERITT

Another Harlin Quist Book

A Harlin Quist Book.
Distributed by Dial/Delacorte Sales.
One Dag Hammarskjold Plaza,
New York, New York 10017.

Manufactured in the United States
of America. First printing.
The line drawings were created
by David Prestone.

Library of Congress Cataloging in Publication Data

Schechter, Harold.
Film tricks.

Includes index.
1. Cinematography—Special effects.
2. Cinematography, Trick. I. Everitt, David, 1952- joint author.
II. Title.
TR858.S34 778.5'345
80-16965
ISBN 0-8252-2599-X

TABLE OF CONTENTS:

INTRODUCTION:
PAGE 7

CHAPTER 1
CAMERA MAGIC:
MELIES AND
THE BEGINNINGS
OF SPECIAL EFFECTS
PAGE 15

CHAPTER 2
MIRACLE WORKERS:
PIONEERS
OF SPECIAL EFFECTS
PAGE 27

CHAPTER 3
GRAND ILLUSIONS:
SPECIAL EFFECTS
IN MOVIE SPECTACLES
PAGE 39

CHAPTER 4
DELIGHTFUL
DECEPTIONS:
SPECIAL EFFECTS
IN COMEDIES
AND MUSICALS
PAGE 61

CHAPTER 5
MANUFACTURED
NIGHTMARES:
SPECIAL EFFECTS
IN HORROR MOVIES
PAGE 87

CHAPTER 6
IMAGINARY FUTURES:
SPECIAL EFFECTS
IN SCIENCE FICTION
MOVIES
PAGE 109

CHAPTER 7
DREAM WORLDS:
SPECIAL EFFECTS
IN FANTASY MOVIES
PAGE 151

CHAPTER 8
UNNATURAL
CATASTROPHES:
SPECIAL EFFECTS
IN DISASTER MOVIES
PAGE 181

CHAPTER 9
SYNTHETIC DEATH:
SPECIAL EFFECTS
AND VIOLENCE
PAGE 193

CHAPTER 10
CHEAP TRICKS:
THE WONDERFUL WORLD
OF SCHLOCK
PAGE 209

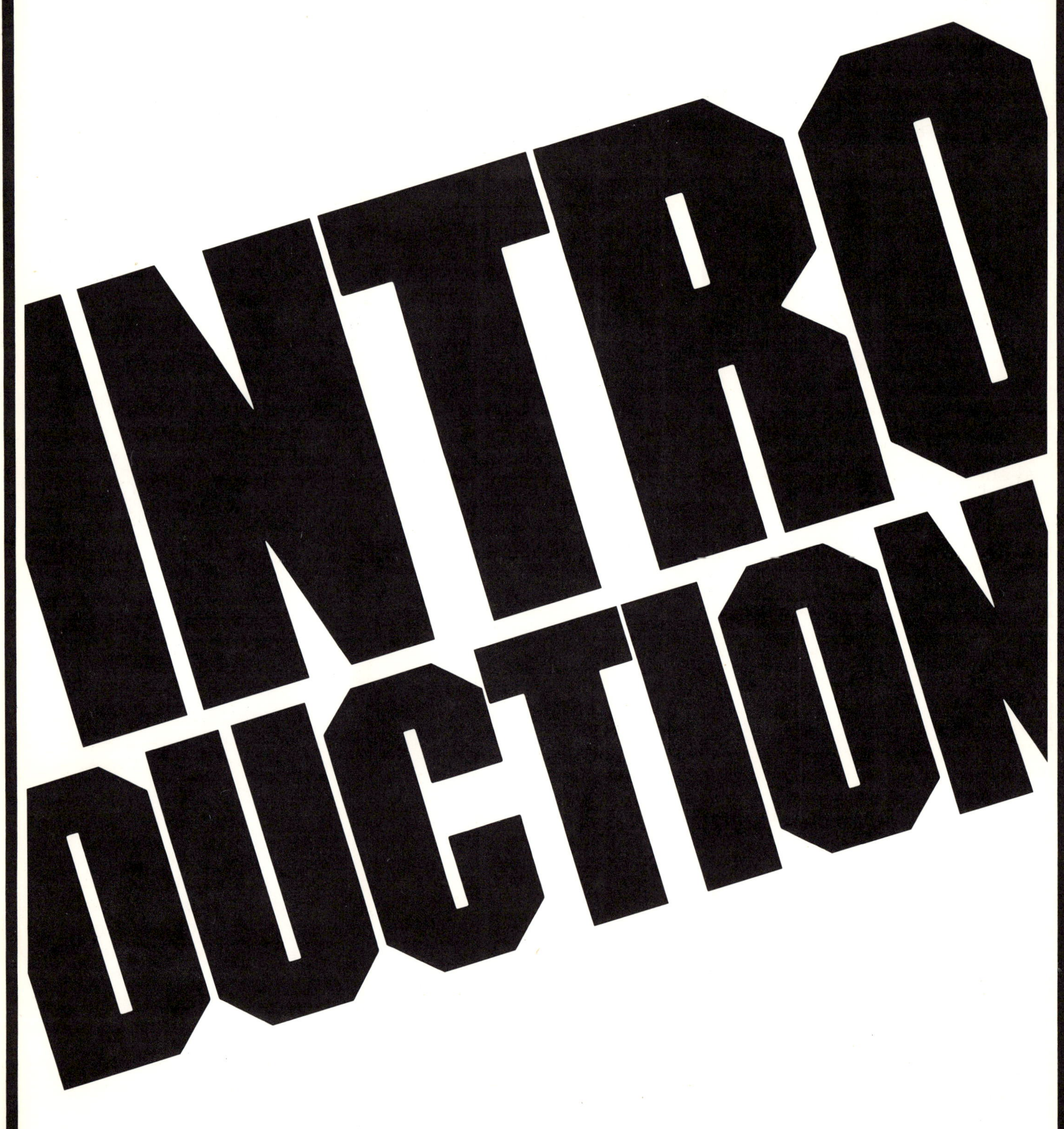
INTRO
DUCTION

Ever since the acrobatic spacecraft of *Star Wars* first soared across the screen and the movie's box office receipts blasted off into the stratosphere, America's filmgoers have been treated to a dazzling array of special effects: a rollicking fleet of UFOs whizzing around the midwestern flatlands, a celestial city of light rising majestically over a mountain, a crystal fortress erupting from beneath the arctic ice, a costumed superhero taking his girl friend for a late-night glide high above the streets of Manhattan. The blockbuster movies of the past few years—*Star Wars, Jaws, Close Encounters of the Third Kind, Superman, Alien, Moonraker, Star Trek*—have all been, to one degree or another, special-effects showcases. We are living at a time when audiences can't seem to get enough of interplanetary dogfights, mechanical monsters, and epic disasters. Dino De Laurentiis, Italy's answer to P. T. Barnum, obviously understands this widespread hunger for sensational effects, and sought to exploit it during the selling of his bungled remake of *King Kong* by telling the public that his giant gorilla was a miracle of modern technology when in fact, except for one fleeting sequence, it was merely a man in a monkey suit.

What exactly is behind the current boom in special-effects movies? Why are filmgoers flocking to see them? What satisfactions do they supply? Partly, it seems, people enjoy motion pictures in which a great deal of money has obviously been lavished on special effects (or *sfx,* as the phrase is sometimes abbreviated) precisely because these pictures cost so much to make. Just as in the good old days, when movies were marketed on the basis of how much time and trouble it took to film them ("Five years in the making!"), today's producers know how profitable it can be to publicize their movie's budget. In a guest-spot on the *Today* show, which was billed as a feature on " how the special effects of *Moonraker* were created," producer Albert Broccoli offered very little information beyond the cost of his effect-filled extravaganza, which he estimated at $250,000 per minute of film.

The fact is that, at a time when most Americans are feeling financially pinched, millions upon millions were spent to convince us that Christopher Reeve could fly does not fill us with indignation; on the contrary, it makes us feel better. In an age of economic crisis and national self-doubt, the big-budget effects film is a reassuring sight, comforting us with its air of abundance and its visible proof of America's technological superiority. The Arabs may have the oil, but we're the ones with the good old Yankee know-how, and here's a space station as big as Cleveland being blasted into subatomic particles to prove it! In these technologically oriented times, the flashy, expensive effects movie has the same kind of appeal that the lavish musicals and overblown historical romances of the 1930s had for Depression-era audiences.

Another reason for the present popularity of films like *Superman, Star Wars,* and *Close Encounters* is suggested by the colorful terms often used to describe special effects: "movie magic," "cinemagic," "sorcery of the screen," "visual wizardry," "camera trickery." Special-effects movies supply their audiences with a welcome shot of wonder, offering us a brief vacation from the routine and banal—a "cinematic trip," as the ads for Kubrick's *2001* put it. They revive in us, however temporarily, the sense of awe and delight which we have all known as children and which, as adults living in a frequently depressing world, we desperately need to recapture from time to time. Everybody needs some magic in his life, and Hollywood, "The Dream Factory," "The Magic Store," has from its earliest days been America's prime supplier of the marvelous. There is something inherently magical about the motion picture itself: a movie is, after all, an optical illusion, a string of still photographs which we are made to perceive as alive. When motion pictures were first invented, a film of anything at all (so long as the subject moved) could bring an astonished gasp from the audience. The earliest films by the Lumière brothers had titles like *Arrival of a Train, Workers Leaving a Factory,* and *The Demolition of a Wall.* After a while, of course, audiences grew fairly blasé about films showing waves breaking on a beach and babies eating dinner; such simple records of everyday events could no longer satisfy their hunger for the marvelous.

And so the special-effects movie was born. It's no accident that the father of the trick film was a French magician, Georges Méliès, who turned his talents from making ladies vanish and reappear onstage to creating miracles of another kind, dazzling moviegoers with such cinematic sleight-of-hand as *The Impossible Voyage, A Trip to the Moon,* and other film fantasies. Given this close connection between magic and special-effects movies, it's no surprise that they are as successful as they are today, when audiences seem far less interested in works dealing with the realities of everyday life than in those which promise to transport them to worlds of fantasy and wonder. In this respect, the boom in special-effects films is just one part of a much larger trend, evident in the current craze for "sword-and-sorcery" fiction like J.R.R. Tolkien's *The Lord of the Rings;* the popularity of picture books about gnomes, elves, and fairies; and the fascination with astrology and the occult.

The professional magician amazes us by creating the illusion that he is not subject to the same natural laws that keep the rest of us poor mortals shackled and earthbound. If he wants to, he can turn a tiger into a dove, float a person ten feet in the air, make an elephant vanish, or saw a lovely lady through the midriff and then put her back together. Special-effects movies astonish us with the same impossible tricks. Before our very eyes startling transformations take place: a handsome young doctor turns into a hairy monster, a Transylvanian count changes into a bat. Mouths agape, we watch as an adolescent girl, possessed by the devil, levitates to the ceiling of her bedroom, or as a scientist swallows a potion which makes him transparent, a piece at a time. Until very recently, when advances in medical technology have endowed certain surgeons with what seems like supernatural skill, only sorcerers and special-effects men could restore a severed limb. One of the earliest trick films ever made, for example, is a French short called *The Accident* in which a weary drunk decides to take a little snooze on a cozy-looking stretch of road. A cab comes tooling along, runs over him, and cuts off both his legs, which causes him a certain amount of dismay until the passenger, who happens to be a doctor, hops out and reattaches them.

Creating such marvels, however, makes up only one part of special-effects work. Fantastic films which rely on spectacular effects to bring our dream visions (and nightmares) to life are exciting for the audience to see and fun for the effects artist to do, since they give him an opportunity to show his stuff, to wow viewers with his virtuosity. But while flashy things like nose-diving rockets, rampaging dinosaurs, and incredible shrinking humans are what most people automatically think of when they hear the term "special effects," there is another area of effects work which is no less important, though it is often less obvious and not as well known to most filmgoers.

Linwood Dunn, one of the most prominent effects artists in Hollywood, who has worked on countless movies in the course of his distinguished career, from *Citizen Kane* and *King Kong* to *Hawaii, Airport, West Side Story,* and *Taxi Driver,* defined for us during an interview several different categories of special effects, the two most important of which are "fantasy" and "reality." Fantasy effects are the kind we are all familiar with because in general they are the most outstanding part of any movie in which they appear. As eye-catching as Raquel Welch is, the real stars of *Fantastic Voyage* (a movie about a miniaturized submarine on an urgent mission inside a man's body) are the giant antibodies, red blood cells, and vital organs. "Reality effects," on the other hand, generally call less attention to themselves. Instead of conjuring up the never-before-seen, the dreamlike, or the imaginary, reality effects recreate the world we know, simulate events which are, as Frank P. Clark puts it, "too difficult to film for reasons of safety, convenience, or cost." The special-effects artist may be called upon to reproduce natural phenomena (earthquakes, volcanic eruptions, avalanches, dust storms, cyclones, hurricanes, blizzards), historical events (the attack on Pearl Harbor, the charge of the Light Brigade), or exotic locales (African jungles, tropical islands).

Several good examples of reality effects works can be seen in the movie *Hawaii,* which was pitted against *Fantastic Voyage* for the 1966 Academy Award for Special Visual Effects. Linwood Dunn was responsible for *Hawaii*'s optical effects, which include a spectacular storm sequence and panoramic vistas of beaches and harbors. Interestingly, Dunn told us that as soon as the nominations were announced, he knew he didn't stand a chance, because in a contest between fantasy and reality the former invariably wins. This situation is undoubtedly frustrating to people like Dunn, and it is certainly unfair, but it is not difficult to understand.

A good fantasy effect of the kind found in *Star Wars* will always seem more brilliant and breathtaking, more of a technical tour de force, than even a very impressive reality effect. Although both must seem convincing and real if they are to succeed, fantasy effects are meant to be amazing ("out of this world"), while reality effects are limited to the actual, the visible, the well known. Ironically, fantasy, though it certainly requires a great deal of expertise and ingenuity, is, in some respects, easier to bring off than reality. After all, only the doctors in the house will complain if a thirty-foot blood corpuscle looks inaccurate, and no one has ever seen a Wookie, so there is a certain amount of leeway for error and imprecision. But if a storm looks unrealistic, the whole illusion is killed.

While some special-effects

work has the razzle-dazzle of a performance by a master magician, much of it bears very little resemblance to magic at all. It is significant that the only effects people we spoke to who saw their work as a form of legerdemain were the ones involved in the current spate of science-fantasy films. When we mentioned to Brian Johnson, a special-effects supervisor on both *Alien* and *The Empire Strikes Back,* that part of the appeal of visual effects seemed to be their magical quality, he agreed emphatically and admitted that he enjoyed "tricking people." On the other hand when we asked Albert Whitlock if he thought his work was similar to magic, he looked surprised, shook his head, and said, "No, it's the very opposite."

Whitlock is Hollywood's master of matte painting, a special-effects technique which consists of combining a piece of live-action footage with a background scene (usually painted on a relatively small sheet of glass) and coming up with a shot that looks totally convincing. One of the fascinating things about the work Whitlock does—and this is true for other kinds of special effects as well—is that the better it is, the harder it is to detect, and it achieves perfection when nobody notices it at all. Millions of people have seen hundreds of Whitlock's paintings without knowing they were looking at anything other than real life.

Such skill has its disadvantages. Whitlock likes to tell of the time he worked on a made-for-TV movie set in various exotic locations across the globe, although the film was shot entirely in and around Los Angeles. The foreign scenery was all furnished by Whitlock in the form of matte paintings that were so absolutely authentic that they earned him a nomination for an Emmy Award. The prize, however, went to an artist who had done some showy illustrations for another program. Naturally enough, Whitlock was a bit disappointed: "I couldn't help it, because there had been so much talk about this film and how it had all been shot locally. So I asked one of the guys at work who's an art director and who was on the committee. And he said, 'Yeah, but the trouble was, when we looked at the film, we couldn't tell what you had done,'" a comment which might not seem very consoling but which is in fact the highest compliment certain kinds of effects men can receive. "That was better than the Emmy," says Whitlock.

Most artists thrive on audience recognition; they want as many people as possible to see and admire what they've created. The average effects artist, however, has the very opposite attitude toward his work: if filmgoers can see it, then it's a failure, like a poorly made toupee. This attitude is perfectly summed up in a remark by Harrison Ellenshaw, another well-known matte painter: "If people come up to see me and say how much they enjoyed my work in such and such a movie, I get worried." In others words special effects don't always explode off the screen. Many of them are meant to be totally invisible, and there is one category of effects work that is so fine and subtle that most people outside the movie industry (and indeed quite a few people within it) don't even know it exists. This is the type of work which Linwood Dunn, one of the masters of it, calls "fixing up," and it consists basically of using the techniques of special effects to repair a botched scene which has already been filmed and cannot, for one reason or another, be reshot.

Dunn described several fascinating examples. The first concerned an onscreen fistfight. When two actors slug it out in a movie, they don't, of course, really hit each other. Rather, one of them tosses a punch which comes close but doesn't connect, while the second throws back his head at the instant of supposed contact, and if the whole thing is done with skill and conviction, the illusion of a resounding right hook to the jaw is achieved. When this particular fight scene was developed and viewed, however, the filmmakers saw to their horror that, in Dunn's words, "the first actor's punch fell short about six inches, and the second actor's head snapped back before the first guy's fist even came close." What made the situation even more depressing was that one of the actors had left town right after the scene was shot and couldn't be called back to redo it. Dunn, however, was able to step in and save the day. Using a device called an optical printer, he enlarged the shot, removed the gap separating fist from face, and brought the two together. Moreover, since the guy getting hit still reacted prematurely, Dunn slowed down the side of the film containing the actor's head and held it until the punch caught up with it.

He used the same technique to salvage key scenes in other movies, too. In an airplane melodrama called *Ace of Aces,* a thrilling sequence in which a pilot is nearly burned alive when his plane bursts into flames upon crashing turned out to be disappointing because the flames did not appear quickly enough after the crash, making it look as if the pilot had plenty of time to get away. With the aid of his optical printer Dunn was able to speed up just that segment of the footage containing the fire and come up with an extremely dramatic shot of the pilot barely escaping as his downed aircraft explodes all around him. In a later film, *It's a Mad, Mad, Mad, Mad World,* an overeager crewmember came close to completely spoiling an elaborate and carefully planned sight gag in which Jonathan Winters backs his pickup truck into a water tower, which then topples over onto a service station and demolishes it. To make sure the building collapsed convincingly, wires were attached to it and these were held offscreen by several crewmembers. One of them, however, got "trigger-happy" (in Dunn's words) and tugged too soon, so that the walls of the service station came tumbling down before the tower ever touched it. Once again Dunn came to the rescue with his optical printer, splitting the screen and delaying the collapse of the building until the tower hit it.

What happens when a fierce struggle onboard a speeding passenger train ends up looking dull and anemic? Here is the story as Linwood Dunn tells it:

The sequence took place on a train with sleeping compartments. These two fellows got into a fight and they were slamming each other around into the compartments, and they would fall down and fight all over the place. But when the editor cut it, it had nothing; it wasn't vicious at all. So I took the work print and put it in the Moviola, and I went through and eliminated certain frames—just certain ones. Say a fellow threw a punch. I would take out one frame while his fist traveled. Then I'd take one out as the other guy fell. And it would snap then—the punch would go like that*! And the other guy would* fall *and hit hard. And I went through the scene and put a little grease pencil* x *on the frames I wanted to remove, then I stuck it in the optical printer and had the operator go through and take out the* x *frames.*

Every now and then Dunn is called upon to do some tricky postproduction cosmetic work on a movie. When censors threatened to slap an X rating on *Taxi Driver* because its climactic bloodbath was so extreme, he helped win the film a more acceptable rating by toning down the color of the gore. And once, in those simple, faraway days when such anatomical features were regarded as tasteless if not actually immoral, he managed to satisfy the censors by removing the hairs from some shots of a barechested actor—a job which, however ridiculous it may seem, required a great deal of skill to perform.

Clearly special-effects men have been the unsung heroes of many a movie, coming in, helping to get a project out of a tight spot, and then retreating into the background with no more acknowledgement of their contribution than an inconspicuous credit line generally located, as effects artist Les Bowie once said, under the name of the hairdresser. Of course in recent years, when some of the big space-fantasy films have become objects of fanatical devotion, certain effects artists like Doug Trumbull and John Dykstra have achieved a degree of celebrity. But even they are not likely to make the cover of *People* magazine, and for the most part, special-effects men do their work as they always have: out of sight, behind the scenes, and (at least as far as the general public is concerned) anonymously.

In the end the special-effects artist is neither a black magician nor a space age scientist. And in spite of the last-minute rescue work he is sometimes called in to perform, he is not the Lone Ranger either. For one thing he gets rewarded very nicely: the top effects men in Hollywood are a highly paid bunch of professionals. Albert Whitlock, for example, has been thinking about retiring for years, but Universal Studios keeps making him offers he can't refuse. But if the average special-effects man does not really fit very comfortably into any of the colorful costumes people are always trying to dress him up in—conjuror, visionary, "master of dreams"—then exactly who or what is he? What is the precise nature of his profession?

These questions are not easy to answer, largely because special-effects work encompasses so many different kinds of crafts. As the person responsible for creating everything from a simple breakaway bottle to a lunar landscape to a convincing replica of San Francisco at the time of its famous earthquake (with buildings rigged to collapse on cue), the effects man must be, in the words of Frank P. Clark, "a happy combination of artist, mechanic, carpenter, gadgeteer, and inventor." In addition, says Clark, "he might also be an explosives engineer, a crack shot, a skin diver, and a daredevil. He must have a healthy imagination and be willing to experiment with new ideas." But this is not all. "The special-effects man should be a diplomat and a good businessman as well," Clark counsels, since he will not only be "required to deal with other members of the motion-picture industry" but also to act as "a liaison man with the public."

Clark, whose description appears in a how-to book for effects technicians published by the Society of Motion Picture and Television Engineers, provides a highly detailed list of the equipment required by the average worker in this field:

He must have carpenter's tools, electrician's tools, mechanic's tools, and plumber's tools. He should also have scissors, needles, a blaster's crimping tool, a broom and dust pan and glazier's tools, to mention but a few. He should have access to, and a working knowledge of, machine tools, power woodworking tools, and welding equipment. His supplies should include tools, nails, screws, spikes, nuts and bolts, string, thread, electric wire, piano wire, paste, glue, brads, putty, Scotch tape, Mystic tape, masking tape, and a number of colored felt-tipped pens, to start the list. . . .

Though descriptions of special-effects men as "movie magicians" sound nice and are generally more interesting to read than hardware-store inventories, Clark's checklist, plain and prosaic as it is, actually comes closer to capturing the essence of effects work than perhaps any other piece of writing on the subject. Special-effects movies *are* often magical; as we said ourselves, a large part of their appeal comes from their ability to fill us with wonder and awe. But there's no magic involved in producing these wonders—just hard work, expertise, and perhaps most important of all, inventiveness.

Americans have always had a special place in their hearts for the inventor, the man of imagination, mechanical skill, and ingenuity who can tinker together a miracle out of the commonplace materials at hand. Maybe this is another reason for our fascination with the special-effects man: he is the heir not of Houdini, but of Edison, Franklin, and Bell. It was Edison, in fact, who invented the first practical movie-viewing apparatus, a coin-operated device called the Kinetoscope, the grandaddy of today's porno shop peep show machine. And among the assorted fifty-foot filmstrips Edison's company produced for use in his invention was the world's first special-effects motion picture: an 1893 short called *The Execution of Mary, Queen of Scots* which, true to its title, consisted of nothing more than a quick scene (the whole thing lasted less than thirty seconds) of a costumed actress being led to the block and decapitated. Though the action, as the viewer saw it, appeared to be continuous, this illusion was accomplished during the shooting of the scene by the very simple trick of stopping the film before the ax came down, substituting a dummy for the actress, and then starting the camera again.

With all the advanced computer technology that has begun to be applied to filmmaking, it's easy to envisage today's effects men as white-frocked technicians fiddling with knobs and dials in futuristic laboratories. But the fact is that except for the heavy concentration of cameras and other photographic equipment, the average effects studio more closely resembles a household handyman's basement workshop: a busy, cluttered place whose long wooden worktables are covered with tools and blueprints, rulers and glue, plywood, paint, and plaster of Paris—a place where the sounds of hammering and sawing are heard at least as often as the soft whirr of movie cameras. Moreover, in spite of all the money that producers have begun pouring into the big science fiction and fantasy films, the people we spoke to were, without exception, proudest of the effects they had managed to pull off not with unlimited resources at their disposal, but with the use of nothing more than their wits and a few inexpensive supplies.

Albert Whitlock likes to recall a shot he did for the sequel to *The Exorcist* in which a tiny airplane makes its way through a spooky, cloud-filled sky. With what he calls "seat-of-the-pants ingenuity," he and his helpers assembled the scene out of the most ordinary materials: black velvet, wooden blocks and dowels, cotton, a light bulb, and an airplane painted on a piece of glass. "And it was a completely convincing thing," says Whitlock. "We did it for nothing, we did it in an hour, and the whole thing worked. It was a totally convincing shot, and it was nothing more than tabletop photography." Similarly Linwood Dunn takes satisfaction in remembering the time he saved the producers of *The Great Race* a small fortune. One scene in the movie featured the destruction of the Eiffel Tower. Dunn's company, Film Effects of Hollywood, was commissioned to put together (and then convincingly destroy) a sixteen-foot miniature, which would have cost a great deal of money. Instead Dunn managed to find a seven-dollar plastic model kit and produce a perfectly acceptable effect. And then there is the well-known case of the late A. Arnold Gillespie, who created an extremely realistic locust attack for the film *The Good Earth* by pouring a can of coffee grounds into a glass tank filled with water and shooting the action with the camera placed upside down. When the resulting footage was turned rightside up and superimposed over a scene of a farmer's fields, it looked exactly like a swarm of insects rising ominously over the horizon.

This talent for improvisation—for finding simple, clever, and dollar-saving solutions to difficult problems—is a source of great pride to the effects man. Few things are more frustrating to him than to see a filmmaker throwing money away on a shot that could have been done much more cheaply and efficiently with special effects. One effects artist told us of his astonishment when he found out that the producers of a big-budget war movie made in the late 1960s had spent hundreds of thousands of dollars to find, refurbish, outfit, and operate a fleet of genuine B-52 airplanes for a relatively minor bombing sequence, when perfectly satisfactory results could have been obtained by using miniatures and matte paintings. Sometimes this kind of wastefulness seems to occur because the filmmaker simply doesn't realize what can be accomplished with special effects. Ask any effects artist, though, and he will tell you that nothing is beyond the bounds of possibility—an attitude summed up in a favorite saying of one of Linwood Dunn's former colleagues: "It can't be done, but here it is."

Like the professional magician the special-effects man deals in the impossible; but one of the main differences between them is that the conjurer closely guards his secrets, since his very livelihood depends on making people believe he is the possessor of supernatural power. The effects man, on the other hand, justifiably proud of his resourcefulness and skill, generally enjoys explaining the tricks of his trade. He has the same attitude toward his work that a certain young photographer whom Al Whitlock knew years ago used to have. This young man worked as the chauffeur for one of England's leading silk manufacturers. Another of his duties, however, was taking the advertising photographs of his employer's fabrics, since he did a better job of it than the professionals. Whitlock asked to see some of the young man's work and was astounded at its quality: "He'd take these pictures where you could see the hairs on the fabric—not just the weave, but the hairs on the individual threads." How, Whitlock wondered, did he get such marvelous shots? "It's simple," said the young man, very matter-of-factly. "He gives me the fabric, and I wait for a foggy day. Then I tack it up on the garage door, drive the Rolls-Royce around, shine the headlamps upon the fabric, set up my camera, and shoot." Whitlock asked him how he felt about using such an unorthodox technique. "Well," the young man replied, "they tell me I can't do this and I can't do that, but I go ahead and do it. And it works!"

It would be hard to think of a more fitting motto for the men who make special effects.

A publicity painting for the original *King Kong*.

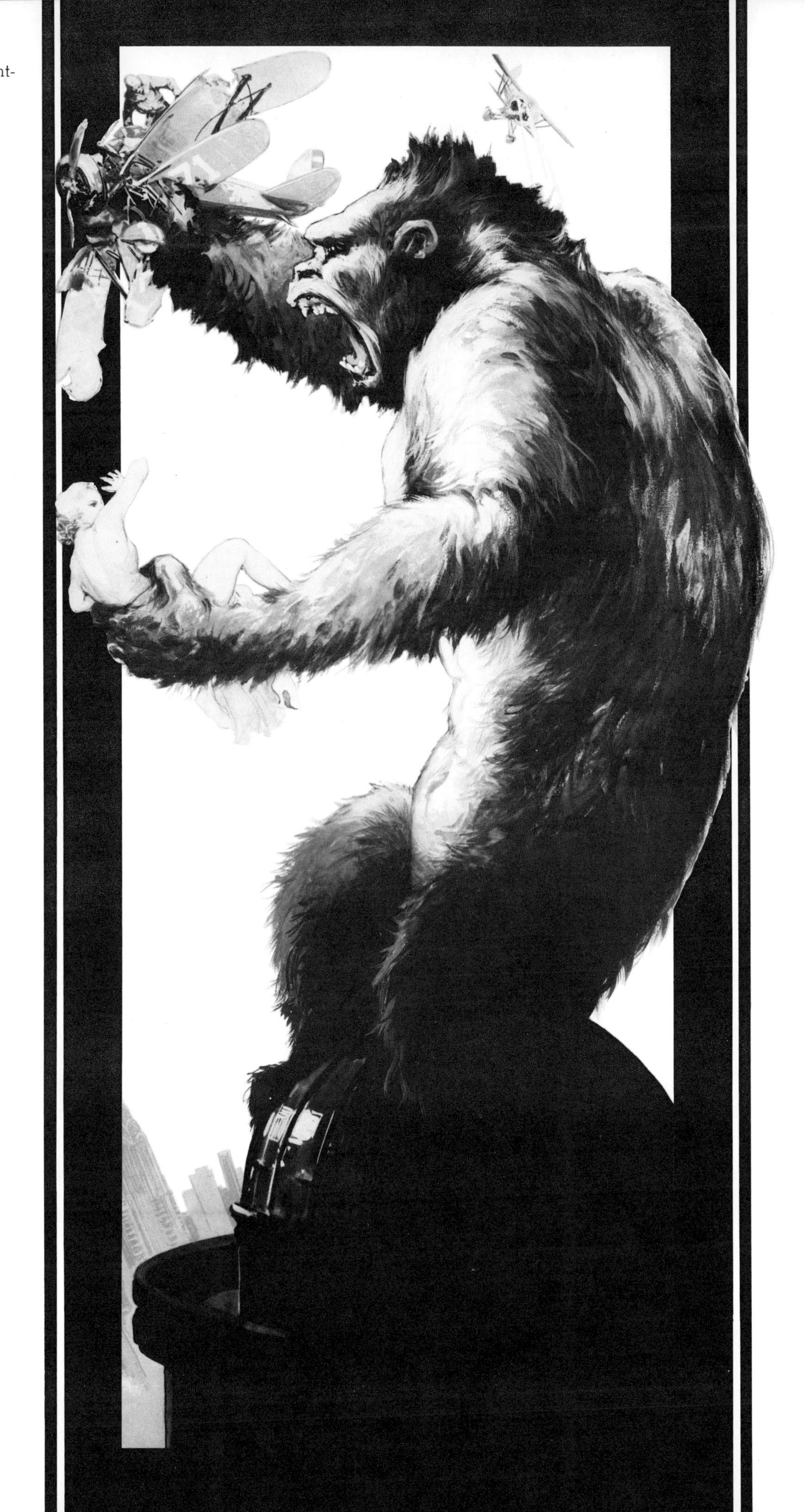

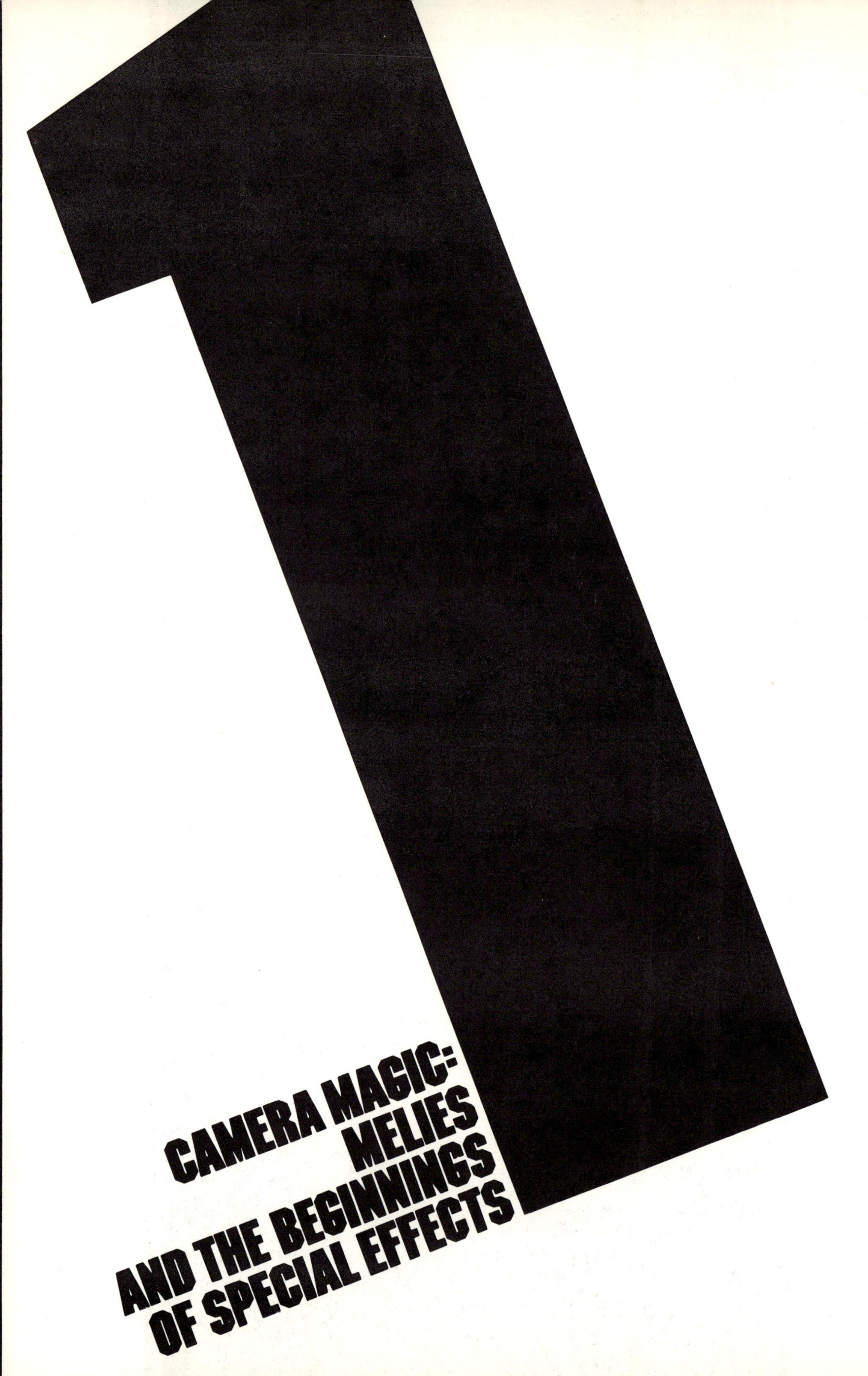

1 CAMERA MAGIC: MELIES AND THE BEGINNINGS OF SPECIAL EFFECTS

Magicians are always keeping an eye out for new inventions and discoveries which they can put to use in their acts, for though it's nice to pretend every once in a while that certain people really do have supernatural powers at their command, the disillusioning fact is that stage magic, like almost everything else in our lives, depends on machines. Here stands the mighty conjurer, keeping a woman afloat in midair! Take a peek backstage, however, and there, like the con man Dorothy and her friends discover hiding behind a curtain in the throne room of the great Oz, stands a perfectly ordinary human being operating a winch. As a result advances in technology can be as important to a magician as they are to an engineer: with a little ingenuity a new and sophisticated machine can be used to produce a strikingly original effect.

It is not surprising, then, that when a young prestidigitator by the name of Georges Méliès got his first glimpse of a startling invention capable of projecting moving pictures, he immediately saw in it an exciting new way to make magic.

Born in Paris in 1861, Méliès grew up to be a gifted painter and caricaturist, and early in his life, he had hopes of becoming an artist. His father, however, objected so strongly to this plan that Méliès was forced to abandon it and take a job in the family shoe factory. Though the kind of work he found himself doing was a far cry from the creative life he had originally dreamed of, the experience was not completely worthless for the imaginative Méliès. On the contrary, he came away from it with mechanical skills which, in his later career, proved to be invaluable.

During a year-long stay in London in 1884, Méliès became fascinated by the sleight-of-hand performances he saw at a theater called Egyptian Hall and decided to take up conjuring as a hobby. Returning to Paris, he began to take lessons from the owner of a magic shop. His interest continued to grow. It wasn't long before he was performing himself, first for his friends, then before schools and clubs, and finally at various theaters around Paris. When Méliès's father retired from business, leaving the factory to his children, Georges promptly sold his share to his two brothers and used the money to buy the Théâtre Robert-Houdin, named after the legendary French magician whose shows had been the sensation of mid-nineteenth century Paris. At the age of twenty-seven Méliès's career as a professional conjurer was underway.

In order to appreciate the nature of Méliès's achievement as a film pioneer, it's important to understand the tradition he was working in. Stage illusions were remarkably complex and sophisticated in the late nineteenth century. In 1898 Albert A. Hopkins, the editor of *Scientific American,* published a book called *Magic: Stage Illusions and Scientific Diversions, Including Trick Photography,* which describes the workings of some of the more sensational theatrical effects of the day. These included full-size ships which sailed across the stage, "freighted with harmoniously grouped spirits and . . . with fairies and graceful genii" swimming in the ocean below; thrilling races with actual horses which galloped "upon the stage without going out of sight of the spectators" while meadows and hills flew by in the background; Samson's destruction of the Temple of Dagon; the "Burning of Moscow," in which the Kremlin was consumed by a huge conflagration and reduced to a pile of "charred remains"; and the slaying of a giant fire-breathing dragon by the young hero Siegfried. All of these spectacles were achieved by means of highly complicated mechanisms operating below, above, or behind the scenes.

The shows put on by Georges Méliès at the Théâtre Robert-Houdin featured similarly spectacular illusions. Houdin himself had presented elaborate magic shows featuring machinery, lighting effects, and music. When Méliès assumed the ownership of the theater he followed the master's lead, presenting not a string of disconnected tricks but rather meticulously mounted sketches with story lines and supernatural themes. These uncanny little dramas combined conventional magic with extremely clever machinery, most of which was devised and constructed by Méliès himself.

In *La Decapité Récalcitrant* for example, a magician, driven to distraction by the endless speeches of a particularly long-winded professor, cuts off the latter's head and sticks it in a box, where it continues to lecture as though nothing has happened. The headless body meanwhile takes the opportunity to leave and dashes off the stage, pursued by the magician and his assistant. While they are gone, a living skeleton (actually a life-size marionette operated by an ingenious four-wheeled mechanism running along an overhead rail) sneaks in and steals the box containing the professor's head, setting off a series of crazy complications which, however, are all sorted out in the end.

If one major turning point in Méliès's career occurred

on the day he wandered into Egyptian Hall in London and saw a man working miracles onstage, another took place on the evening of December 28, 1895, when, along with thirty-four other people, he sat in the basement of a Paris café and watched the world's first motion-picture show—a demonstration of the Lumière brothers' Cinématographe, a revolutionary machine capable of photographing, printing, and projecting moving pictures. The program the world's first filmgoers saw consisted of little more than a collection of home movies: workers leaving a factory, a baby eating its dinner, a train pulling into a station. The audience, however, couldn't have reacted more emotionally if they had been watching *The Exorcist.* As the locomotive engine came hurtling straight toward them, women shrieked, men ducked under their seats, and a few people even fainted. But it was all just an illusion, and Méliès, who had spent years equipping the Théâtre Robert-Houdin with the most ingenious machines he could devise, realized as soon as he saw the first image come to life that here was an invention with more potential for producing wonder than all his other mechanical marvels combined.

As soon as the show was over, he rushed up to Antoine Lumière, the father of the two inventor-brothers, offering to buy the machine at any price. The old man advised him to save his money, telling him, in a remark that has to rank as one of the world's most shortsighted predictions, that the motion picture "may be exploited as a scientific curiosity, but apart from that it has no commercial future whatsoever."

Undaunted, Méliès traveled to London, where he purchased a motion-picture projector from another inventor and film pioneer, Robert W. Paul. With the help of his mechanics from the Robert-Houdin, Méliès succeeded in converting Paul's apparatus into a camera and began his career as a moviemaker. His earliest films were very much like the Lumières': straightforward recordings of such everyday subjects as a group of men playing cards, a ship leaving port, a gardener burning weeds. Then he decided to film one of his pet presentations at the Théâtre Robert-Houdin, a trick called "The Vanishing Lady," in which he transformed a seated woman into a skeleton. Méliès soon discovered, however, what many subsequent magicians have found: that illusions which appear absolutely astounding when they are performed live often don't survive the transition to the screen. The premiere of his first magical movie, *Escamotage d'une Dame chez Robert-Houdin (1896),* was a flop. "The whole thing appeared childish on the screen," Méliès later wrote. "The audience could only see a lot of smoke and flames. They did not get the idea." Although Méliès had instantly recognized the magical potential of motion pictures, he apparently still did not know how to exploit fully their unique capacity for creating illusions. He had yet to learn that the secret of creating successful visual effects is not to make magic in front of the camera, but to make magic *with* the camera.

The story of how he arrived at this discovery has been told many times; it is one of those charming anecdotes, probably untrue, that attribute significant discoveries to lucky accidents. As Méliès himself told it, he was at the Place de l'Opera in Paris one day in 1896, filming the busy street scene with his new camera. Suddenly the camera jammed. By the time he got it working again, a minute or so had passed, and later, when he developed the footage, he was startled by what he saw: a bus change into a hearse, and a man become a woman while crossing the street. According to this story Méliès had accidentally hit upon the principle of *stop-motion photography,* which is simply to start filming a scene, stop the camera, make a change in the scene, then begin shooting again. In this case, for instance, there had been a bus on the street when Méliès's camera broke down. When he resumed filming a few moments later, the bus had driven away and a hearse was parked in its place. What the projector showed, however, was one vehicle miraculously turning into another. A single glimpse of this startling transformation, so the legend goes, was all it took to set Méliès on the road to inventing special effects.

This is a pleasing story, though it has the oversimplified quality of a comic strip. The truth is undoubtedly a bit more complex. For one thing, although it's entirely possible that some such cinematic accident did play a part in Méliès's discovery of stop-motion photography, it's not strictly true that he invented the technique, since the Edison company had used it as early as 1893 in its film *The Execution of Mary, Queen of Scots.* Moreover, many of the special-effects techniques pioneered by Méliès were adaptations of camera tricks still photographers had been making use of for years, such as multiple exposures, mattes, and black backgrounds. It seems unlikely that Méliès wouldn't have known something about these methods. Certainly this knowledge was readily available to him: Hopkins's manual of magic contains a lengthy illustrated section explaining the principles of trick photography in detail, and since Méliès read and spoke English perfectly, it is quite possible that he was familiar with this book.

In any event what we know for certain is that by 1897 Méliès had built a motion-picture studio on his estate at Montreuil-sous-Bois and had begun making movies in earnest. The studio resembled a cross between a greenhouse and a magic theater: to permit the use of natural light for filming, its walls and roof were constructed of glass, while its interior was rigged with all the mechanisms and fixtures found at the Robert-Houdin. There were trapdoors, capstans, winches and pulleys, sliding floor panels, and special dollies, plus a well-stocked carpentry workshop and, of course, all the necessary cinematic equipment. At first Méliès's trick movies were based almost entirely on acts he had staged: the finest illusions from the Robert-Houdin were recreated for film. Now, however, thanks to the miracle of motion-picture photography these illusions could be made to seem more astonishing than ever. For example, instead of making a lady disappear by setting off a smoke bomb onstage and having her descend through a trapdoor while the billowing cloud concealed her exit, Méliès could now use the far more effective device of stop-motion. *The Conjuror* (1899) is a good example of his early trick films. A magician (played by Méliès himself) places a cloth over a lady assistant seated to his left and instantly yanks it away. She is gone. He turns around to a nearby table with a barrel standing on it, raises the barrel, and reveals his assistant underneath. He lifts her off the table and she dissolves into a cloud of confetti. He climbs onto the table, leaps off, and changes into the woman in midair. She climbs onto the table, leaps off, and changes back into the magician. He vanishes in a puff of smoke, and the movie is over. All of these disappearances and transformations were achieved by the very simple method of stop-motion. To make his assistant vanish from her seat and rematerialize under the barrel, for instance, Méliès had only to stop the camera after covering her with the cloth. The woman would then get up from her chair and climb under the barrel, whereupon Méliès would give the signal to start the film rolling again. Even today this exuberant display of stop-motion magic is a delight to watch.

Strictly speaking, Méliès was not a cinematic pioneer in the same sense as, say, the great American director D. W. Griffith. There was no conscious effort on Méliès's part to explore the expressive possibilities of the new medium. His primary interest was filmed prestidigitation, not film as an art form. Throughout his career he remained a professional conjuror, a modern Merlin, the "Sorcerer of the Screen," who saw the motion-picture camera as the most exciting magic apparatus ever devised by man, as well as a means of reaching a far wider audience than he ever could from the stage of the Robert-Houdin. But essentially his movies were theatrical performances recorded on film. However, his great achievement, whatever his intentions, was that he managed to develop or successfully adapt from other art forms (primarily theater and still photography) techniques which form the basis of nearly every type of cinematic effect, including today's highly sophisticated wonders. To a large extent the history of special effects consists of the constant refinement, as motion picture technology has become increasingly advanced, of methods introduced at the turn of the century by Georges Méliès.

In Méliès's movies, for instance, we find for the first time in cinematic history the extensive application of two separate categories of effects: mechanical and visual. This distinction still exists today; in fact, strictly speaking, the term "special effects," when it appears on the credits at the end of a movie, refers solely to the mechanical kind: illusions produced during the actual filming of a scene by means of some type of mechanism, specialized material, or prop. This type of effect, derived directly from the theater, includes such things as fog, rain, wind, explosions, breakaways, trapdoors, wires (to make people or objects fly), and assorted mechanical creations (robots, dragons, giant insects, etc.). Since so many of Méliès's screen effects came straight from the stage of the Robert-Houdin, his films are full of such illusions. One of his most spectacular mechanical effects appears in the movie *The Merry Frolics of Satan* (1906). At one point in the film, in an attempt to get as far away as they can from a haunted house, the hero and his servant jump into a horse-drawn carriage and begin to drive off. Before they can get anywhere, however, the Devil appears and transforms the horse into a literal night-mare: a spooky, skeletal creature that flies off into the air and takes the terrified travelers on a crazy ride across the cosmos. This supernatural steed, which even today remains one of the screen's most imaginatively macabre creations, was actually a life-size marionette attached to wires and manipulated by stagehands standing on a catwalk overhead.

Top: The Frost Giant from *The Conquest of the Pole.* *Center:* A sketch showing how the Frost Giant was operated. *Bottom:* The uncanny coach from *The Merry Frolics of Satan.*

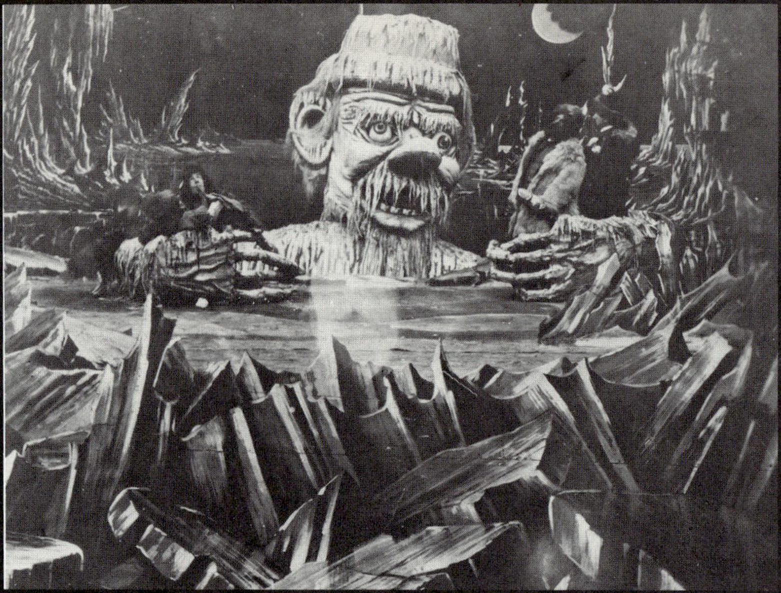

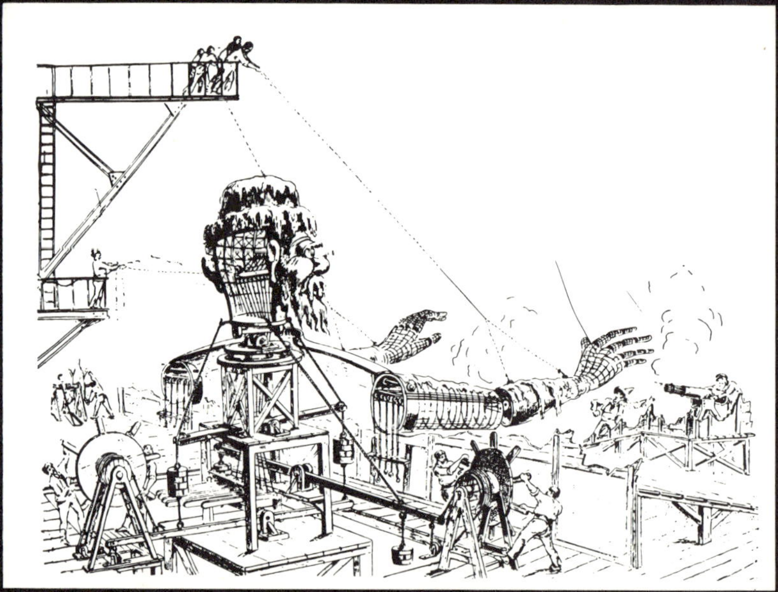

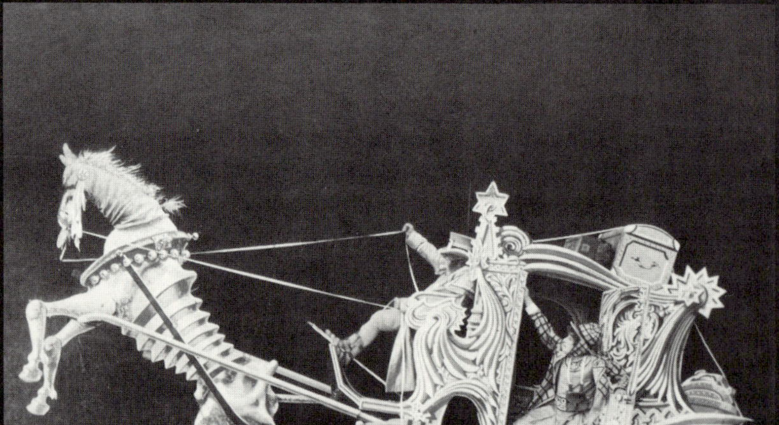

Another of Méliès's mechanical marvels is the Frost Giant from his film *The Conquest of the Pole* (1912), a cannibalistic creature that rises up out of the ice and begins gobbling down a group of explorers. Like the spectral horse this monster was essentially a marionette, an immense puppet constructed of plaster, cardboard, and wood and operated by a complicated system of windlasses and cables.

Méliès's main contribution to special-effects technology, however, lies in the area of optical (as opposed to physical) illusions: in other words, tricks that are performed not with mechanical props but with photography itself. Although most moviegoers use the term "special effects" very loosely to refer to the whole range of cinematic wonders, this second type of effects work is known technically in the film industry as special *visual* (or *optical,* or *photographic*) effects. Its roots are in nineteenth-century still photography. Trick photos—of a woman holding a doll-size duplicate of herself in her hands, of a dinner guest having his own head served to him on a platter, of a boxing match between two fighters who, on closer inspection, turn out to be the same man—were popular novelty items in the late 1800s. These "photographic diversions" were accomplished by the comparatively simple techniques of *multiple exposure* and *split screen* (or what was known in those days as "duplex") photography.

Hopkins, for example, prints a trick shot of an artist in his shirt-sleeves seated at an easel in his studio, working on a portrait of a top-hatted gentleman who sits to his right. What is tricky about this shot is that both the painter and the model are the same person. To achieve this surprising effect, an opaque card, known technically as a *matte* (the French word for "mask"), is placed in front of the camera lens so as to block out the right side of the painter's studio. Only the left half of the scene, containing the painter and his easel, is recorded on the film (or at that time, the plate). The right hand portion of the plate remains unexposed. At this point the artist gets up, puts on a hat and coat, and poses himself like a painter's model on a chair beside the easel. The opaque card is now switched around, blocking out the left half of the scene; the right side is photographed, and the result is a striking composite picture of a painter using a clone of himself as a model.

Méliès's great innovation was to apply this and other methods drawn from still photography to the creation of highly imaginative motion pictures. In several of his early trick films, for instance, he made use of the basic matte technique described above (which, as we will see, was soon to develop into the single most versatile tool in the effect man's kit) to allow him to act with himself in the same scene. He would simply have himself filmed on one side of the frame while the other was blocked off (or "matted out") with a piece of black cardboard positioned in front of the lens. After rewinding the film and shutting out the portion of the scene already shot, he was photographed again on the part that had been left unexposed.

Multiple exposure was another gimmick Méliès took from still photography and added to his repertory of cinematic tricks. One of his most famous short films, *The Man with the Rubber Head* (1897), tells the story of an oddball chemist (played, as most of these roles were, by Méliès) who takes a living, smiling replica of his own head, places it on a table in the center of his lab, and, using a bellows hooked up to a hose, begins to pump it up to giant size. When the colossal head comes perilously close to exploding, he shrinks it back to normal size by opening a valve on the connecting tube and letting out the air. His bumbling assistant, who is eager to give this exciting new discovery a try, gets carried away and works the bellows so hard that the head explodes like an overinflated balloon. Two clever effects, were combined to create this entertaining short. First, the fanciful lab set (which, like all of Méliès's whimsical scenery, was designed and painted by the filmmaker himself) had a completely darkened doorway located directly behind the table. Once the live-action antics of the chemist and his assistant were shot, the incredible expanding head was added to the footage by simple superimposition—that is, by rewinding the film and photographing the head in the black, unexposed space surrounding the table. The way the filmmaker managed to make the head swell and shrink was this: Méliès sat in a boxlike contraption resembling an old-fashioned steambath, which left only his head exposed. This box had wheels on the bottom and was mounted on an inclined platform with rails on it and a movie camera standing on the opposite end. Both the box and the backdrop were covered with black fabric. When the box was moved up the platform toward the camera, the head would appear, to the camera's eye, to be getting bigger and bigger; when the box rolled back down, the head would seem to shrink.

Multiple exposure played an important part in a

Three engravings based on nineteenth-century trick photographs. From Albert A. Hopkins's *Magic: Stage Illusions and Scientific Diversions, Including Trick Photography* (1898).

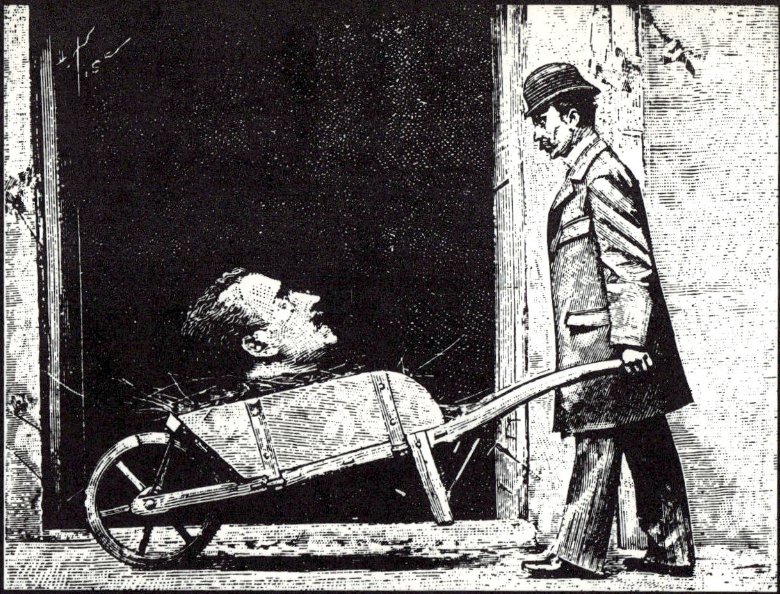

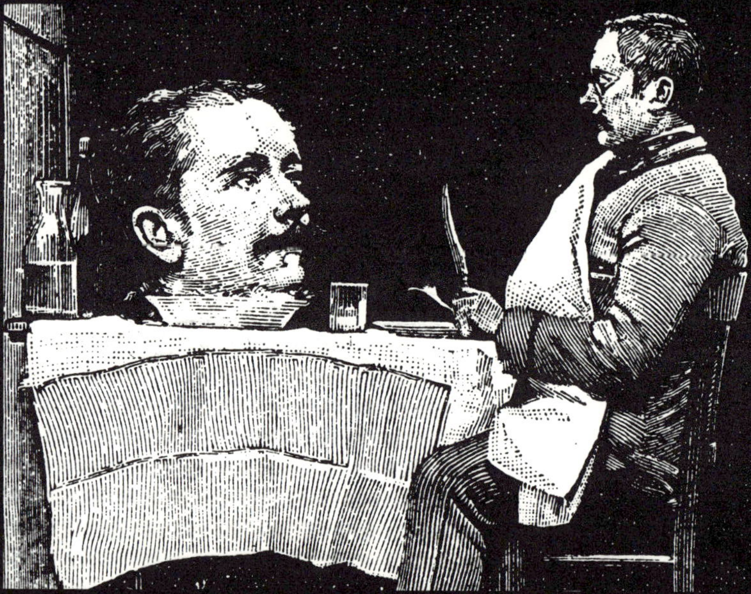

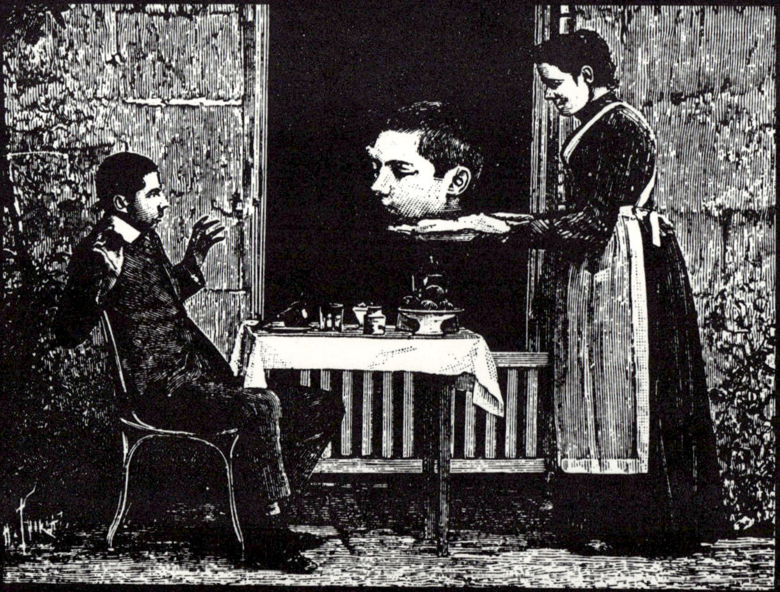

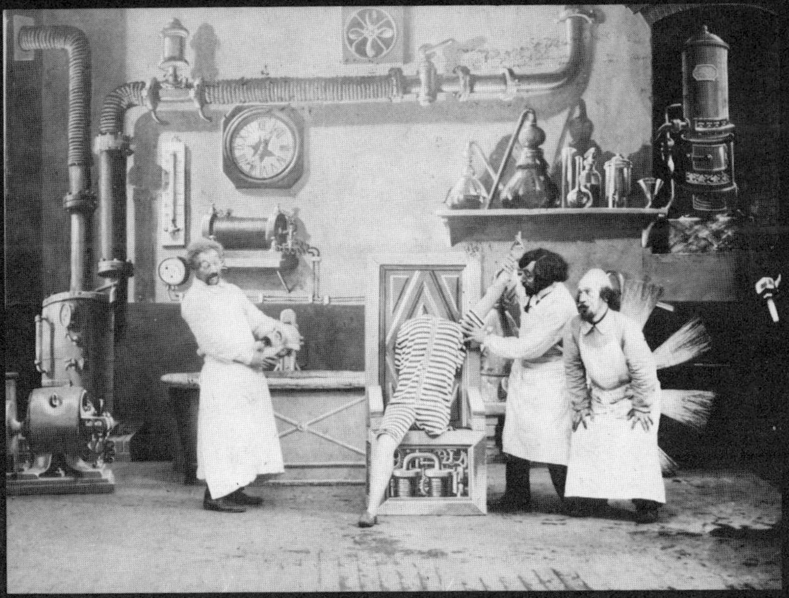

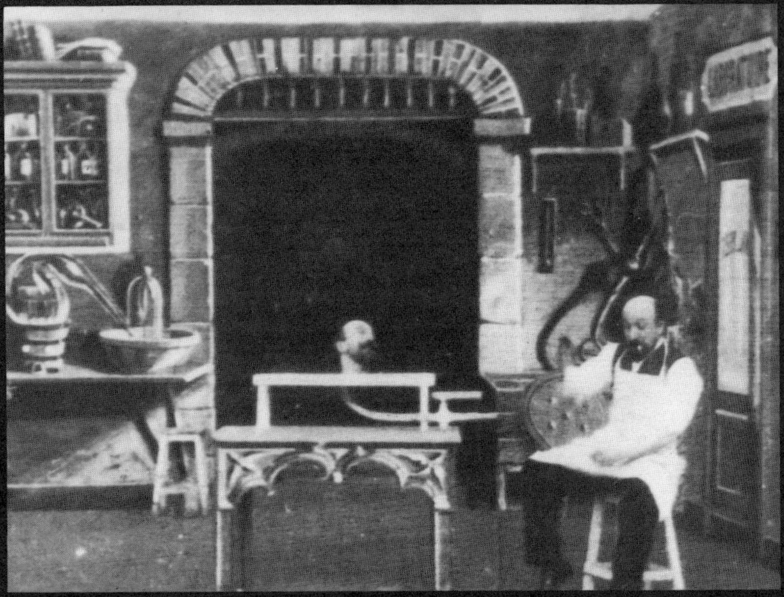

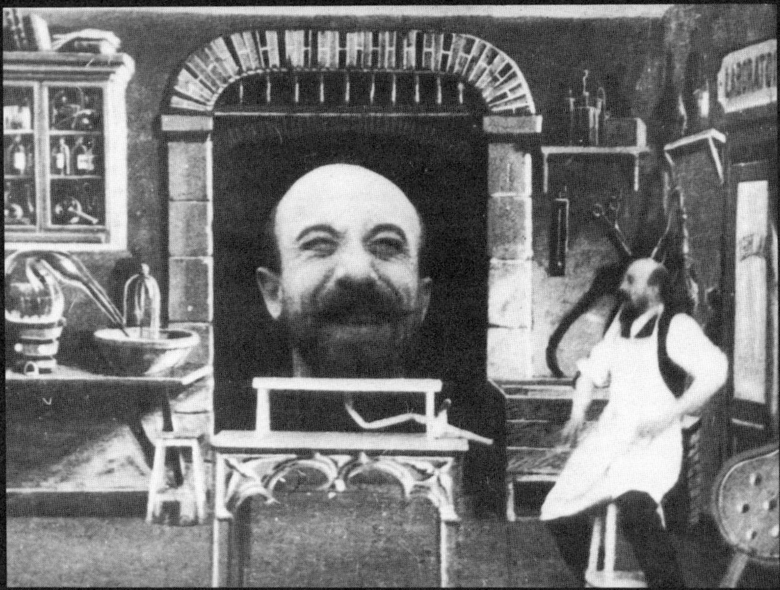

Top: A trio of bumbling physicians reassembles a patient who has gone to pieces during treatment. From *L'Hydrothérapie Fantastique. Center and Bottom:* Méliès uses a bellows to inflate his own head in *The Man with the Rubber Head.*

number of Méliès's magical movies. In *The One-Man Band* (1900), for example, he appears on screen as every member of a seven-piece ensemble. Seven separate exposures (one of himself playing a clarinet, one of himself playing a violin, and so on) were combined to create this clever illusion. (Twenty-one years later another master of the humorous effect, Buster Keaton, would use the same sight gag in his film *The Playhouse.*) In *The Melomaniac* (1903), Méliès's most famous musical fantasy, six different images of his own head are strung across five parallel telegraph wires to create a living piece of sheet music with a chorus of singing notes. Though some of Méliès's multiple exposures are marred to an extent by what is known as a "phantom effect" (in *The Melomaniac,* for instance, the background wires are visible through the superimposed images of the head), his visual jokes are so playful and inventive that they are more fun to watch than many later, more technically polished movie tricks.

The decapitation effect Méliès uses in *The Melomaniac* (in which he turns his head into musical notes by lifting it off his shoulders and tossing it up into the telegraph lines, a trick he is able to repeat six times because his head—besides being detachable—has the amazing power to regenerate itself) appears in a number of his films. Fake beheadings were a favorite illusion of still photographers and professional conjurers in Méliès's time. Hopkins's book on magic contains more trick shots of chopped-off heads than *The Texas Chainsaw Massacre,* and a number of the illusions Méliès staged at the Théâtre Robert-Houdin featured miraculous decapitations.

The Edison company's crude recreation of the execution of Mary Stuart contained the world's first cinematic beheading, accomplished by a primitive stop-motion technique which allowed a dummy to be substituted for the actress. Méliès did the Edison people one better by performing trick decapitations which left the headless body alive and kicking. He did this by combining stop-motion with a gimmick borrowed from still photography: the black backdrop, sometimes referred to in those days as "black magic."The way Méliès was able to remove his own head from his body in *The Melomaniac,* for example, was really very simple. Standing face forward in front of a black velvet backdrop, he would lift his hands to his head. At that moment the camera would stop. Without changing positions, Méliès would cover his head with a black velvet hood, then take a dummy head painted with his features and hold it up in front of his camouflaged face. When the camera started rolling again, he would move the fake head forward and down as though he were detaching it from his shoulders and toss it up into the air. Since the black velvet hood he was wearing couldn't be seen against the black velvet background, his real head was completely invisible to the camera, creating a convincing illusion of a truly topless performer. Méliès used this simple device for producing other striking fantasy effects, including a chorus line of dancing skeletons (from the 1905 film *The Palace of the Arabian Nights*), which he conjured up by dressing some men from top to toe in tight-fitting black velvet suits with skeletons painted on the front and having them perform against a black background so that only the bright white bones showed up on the film. In this way he created the screen's first *danse macabre,* anticipating both Walt Disney's 1929 cartoon *The Skeleton Dance* (the first of his famous "Silly Symphonies") and the living skeleton sequences in the sword-and-sorcery fantasy films of animator Ray Harryhausen.

Méliès is credited with the invention of many other special effects. He was, for instance, the first to use fades. For a *fade-out,* the lens aperture of the camera would be closed up by degrees until no light reached the film. On screen, the resulting image would gradually disappear into darkness. For a *fade-in,* the opposite process would be used to produce the effect of an image gradually emerging out of the blackness into full definition. *Dissolves* were produced by superimposing the two types of fades—that is, by fading out the first scene, winding back the film a few feet, then fading in the next. By cranking the camera more slowly than usual while shooting a scene and then running the resulting footage through the projector at normal speed, Méliès created the illusion of *fast motion.* For *slow motion* the reverse procedure—shooting at an accelerated rate, then projecting the printed film at the regular speed—was used. Méliès's also pioneered the use of *miniatures*—that is, small-scale models built to represent full-size reality. In *The Conquest of the Pole,* for example, the explorers' marvelous "aerobus"—a fanciful flying machine with airplane wings, helicopter blades, and the head of a fabulous bird—is a detailed miniature which travels over the arctic wastes on invisible wires. In *20,000 Leagues Under the Sea* (1907) Méliès devised the screen's first underwater illusion by shooting through a tankful of water containing

Sketches showing the secrets behind three of Méliès illusions. *Top:* The setup used to perform the inflatable head trick in *The Man With the Rubber Head.* *Center:* An underwater scene created by placing an aquarium between the camera and the actors. *Bottom:* The mechanical skeleton from the stage illusion *La Decapité Recalcitrant.*

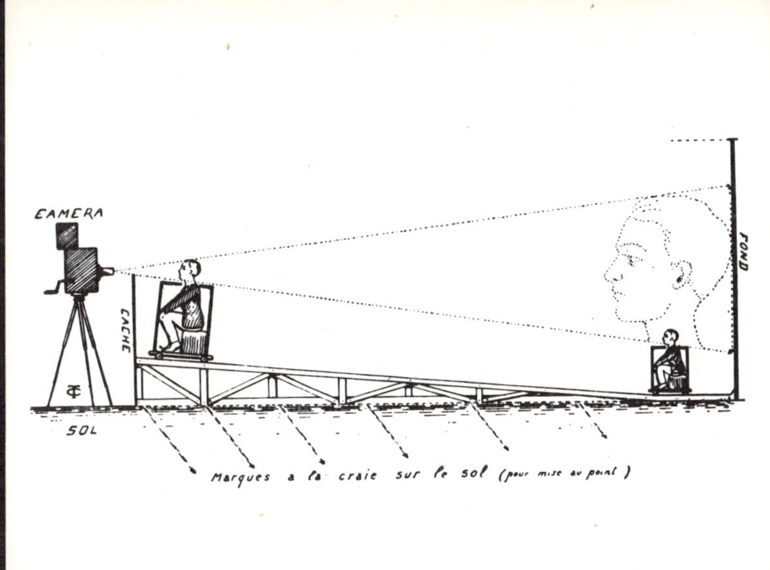

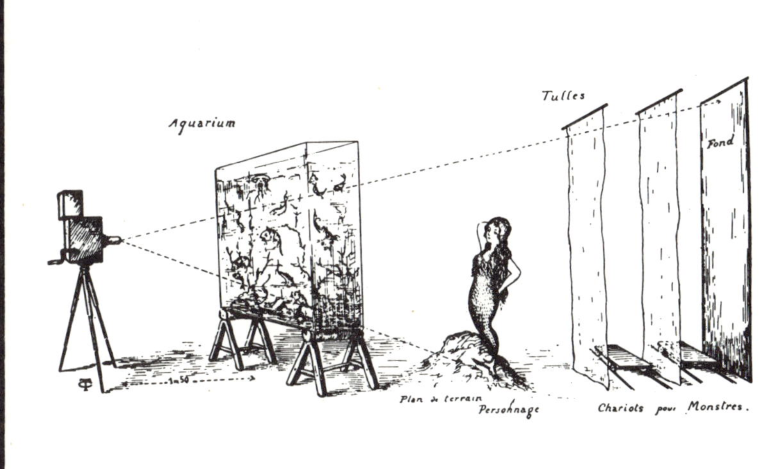

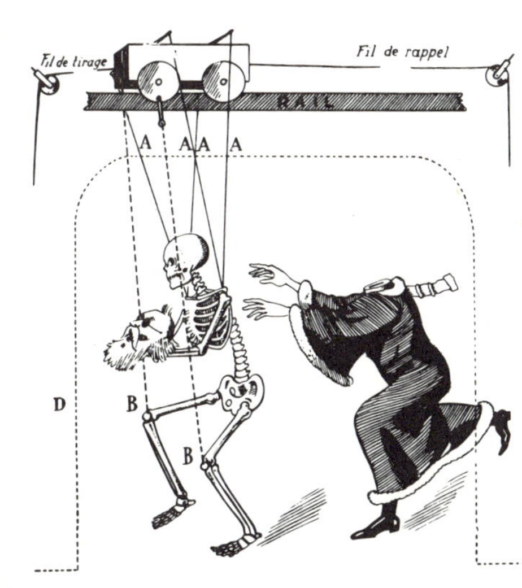

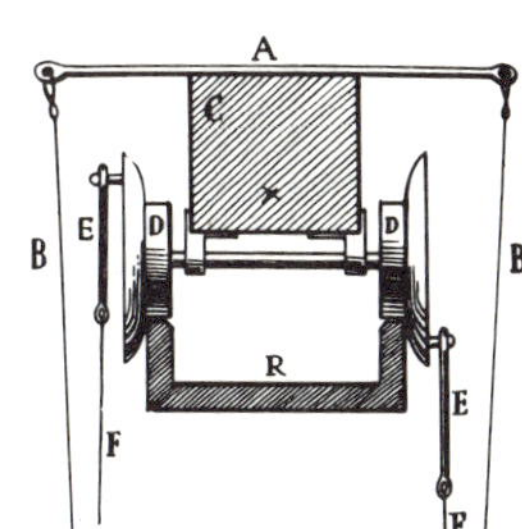

LA TÊTE COUPÉE

A, Barre de fer.
R, Rails.
BB, Fils d'acier fixés à cette barre et suspendant le squelette par les épaules.
C, Chariot roulant chargé de sable.
DD, Roues à joues en bois de 30 centimètres de diamètre.
EE, Bielles montées sur les joues des deux roues *D*, en sens inverse.
FF, Fils d'acier qui, par le mouvement des bielles, produit le mouvement de course des jambes.
Ces deux fils sont attachés un peu au-dessus de la rotule.

seaweed and fish. He even invented a few early disaster effects, the kind of cinematic castastrophes that were to become such a popular attraction seventy years later in pictures like *The Poseidon Adventure* and *Earthquake.* These appeared in something the filmmaker called "reconstructed news." In addition to trick movies Méliès's company, Star Films, produced a series of simulated documentaries which recreated some of the more sensational current events of the day. Among these were *The Explosion of the Battleship Maine* (1897), for which Méliès blew up an authentic scale model of the battleship in a detailed set of Havana harbor, and *A Volcanic Eruption on Martinique* (1902), which had a plaster-of-Paris volcano spewing flour over a miniature fishing village.

The works Méliès is best remembered for, however, are neither his trick shorts nor his reconstructed news but his elaborately produced "enchantments"—films like *Cinderella, The Palace of the Arabian Nights, The Impossible Voyage, The Conquest of the Pole, Twenty Thousand Leagues Under the Sea,* and the most famous of them all, *A Trip to the Moon.* Though these movies—with their stationary camera, painted background scenery, visible trapdoors, wires, and other theatrical props—are in many ways as stagey as his shorter films, they are nonetheless regarded as an important contribution to the development of the cinema, since they were the first sustained, imaginative narratives ever made for the motion-picture screen. Composed of what Méliès called "artificially arranged scenes," they were comparative extravaganzas. Méliès pulled out all the stops for these productions, filling the screen with spectacular trick effects, fantastic scenery, and (canny showman that he was) as many scantily-clad bathing beauties as he could manage to work in.

A Trip to the Moon (1902), loosely based on Jules Verne's *From the Earth to the Moon* and H. G. Wells's *First Men in the Moon,* is generally acknowledged to be Méliès's masterpiece. Though it is the first science fiction movie ever made, it is anything but a serious prediction of the future. On the contrary, it would be hard to conceive of a more playful lunar expedition than the one Méliès imagines here. Dressed as if they were off for a stroll on the Champs Elysée, the four explorers, members of a Parisian astronomers' club, climb into an oversized bullet which is loaded by a bevy of plump, smiling cuties into a colossal cannon mounted on the rooftops of the city. The gun is aimed at the sky and ignited. We see the Man in the Moon draw nearer and nearer; then, with a silent splat, the bullet hits him smack in the eye (the single most famous image from all of Méliès's films). Once on the moon, the explorers are set upon and captured by a bunch of bug-eyed monsters called Selenites (actually a group of acrobats from the *Folies Bérgère* dressed up in bizarre insect costumes). Luckily for the earthlings—who, though they seem not to have brought along any food, medical supplies, or scientific equipment, *did* come prepared for rain—these evil aliens have an Achilles' heel: they explode when they are hit with umbrellas. Escaping from their subhuman captors, the Frenchmen make their way back to the space capsule, which has somehow ended up perched precariously on the edge of a cliff. With some Selenites clinging to its sides, the capsule topples over and plummets back to earth, where it makes a pratfall splashdown in the ocean.

The wild, dreamlike atmosphere of Méliès's work has frequently been described as surrealistic; but its surrealism is that of *Alice in Wonderland,* not *Un Chien Andalou*. His movies bear very little resemblance to the bizarre fantasies of a Dali or Magritte. Watching them, one is reminded instead of Orson Welles's famous comment that a motion-picture studio is the best toy a boy could ever have. Old as they are, Méliès's movies remain eternally childlike, and if he is the father of anything at all, it is not the science fiction but the fantasy film: the movie of magic and enchantment which is meant to appeal, as the saying goes, to the child in all of us.

Unfortunately Méliès's own career did not have the shape of a fairy tale. His life ended sadly. Competition from other producers and a decline in the public's taste for his brand of fantasy film drove him into bankruptcy. When World War I broke out, his studio was commandeered by the military. Unable to afford a move to new facilities, Méliès sold the bulk of his films to a junk dealer; they were melted down and converted into a chemical used in the manufacture of shoe heels. Méliès faded into obscurity. Years later, in 1928, a journalist recognized him as the owner of a tiny kiosk located near a Paris subway station, where he was eking out a living selling newspapers, tobacco, and candy. He was honored by the French filmmaking community with medals and retrospective showings of his surviving films, but plans to have him serve as supervisor on a remake of one of his movies somehow never materialized. He died of cancer in 1938, in a home for destitute actors.

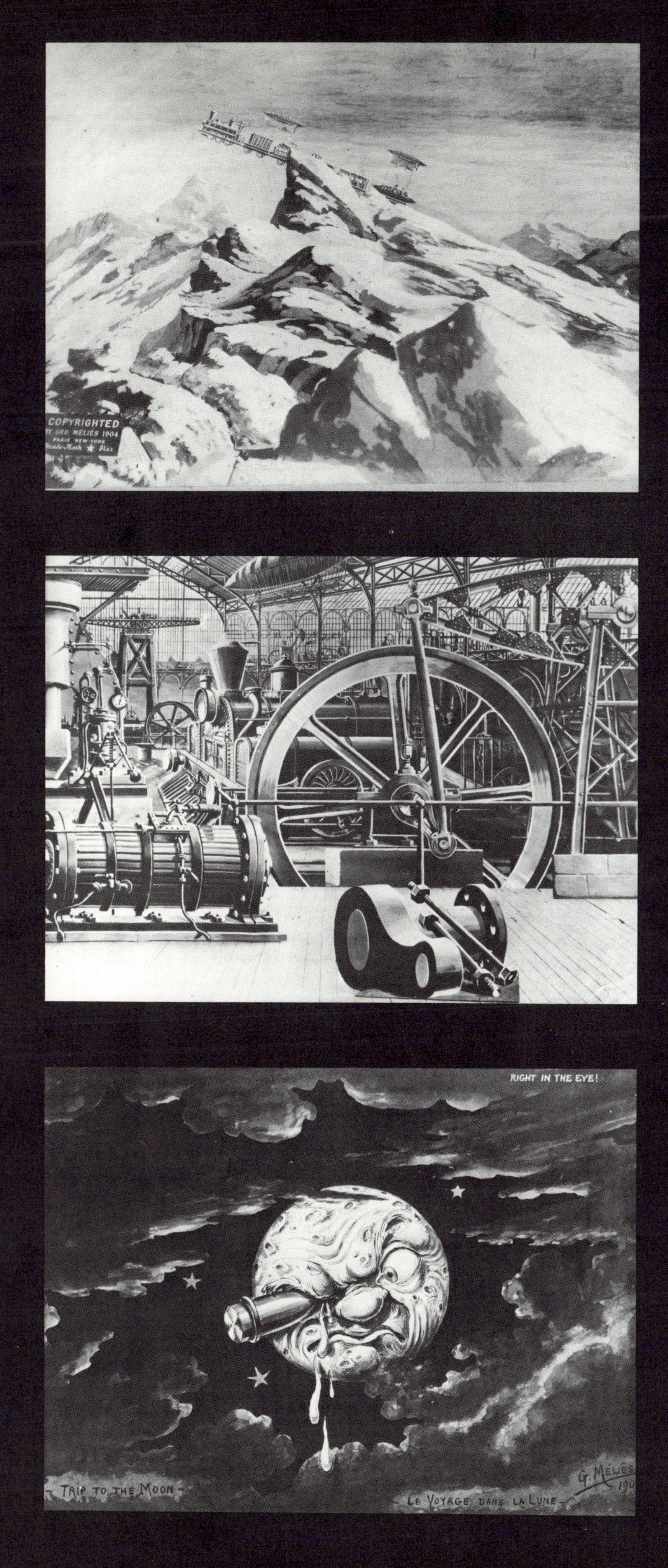

Top: The flying train takes off for the sun in *The Impossible Voyage.*
Center: One of Méliès's elaborate painted backdrops.
Bottom:A Trip to the Moon (1902): a preproduction sketch by Méliès of the most famous scene in his movies.

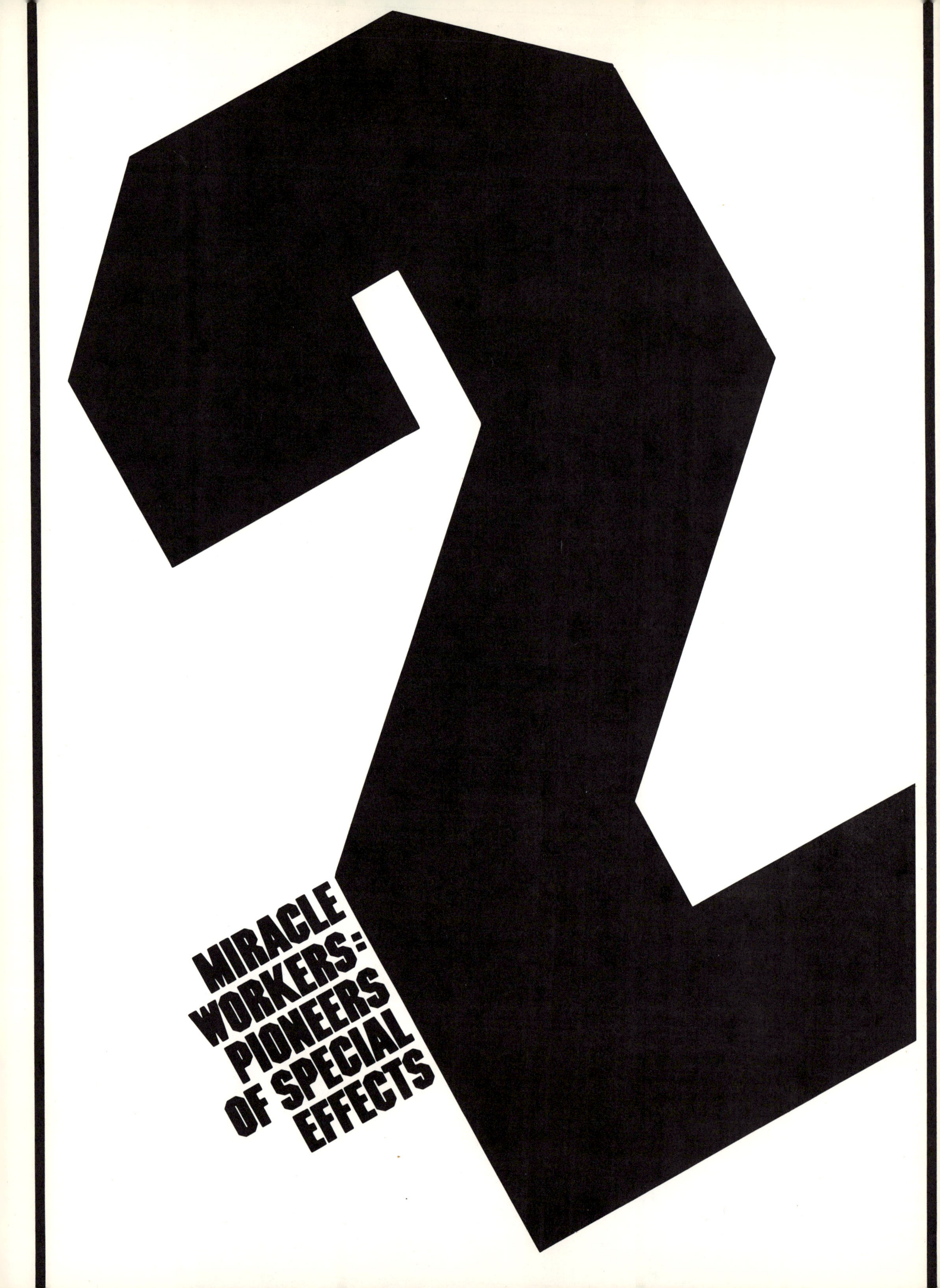

2 MIRACLE WORKERS: PIONEERS OF SPECIAL EFFECTS

For several years, before the combination of war, competition, and shifting public taste drove him out of business and ultimately into the poorhouse, Méliès's magical movies were famous on both sides of the Atlantic—so famous that they were pirated, duplicated, and sold by American manufacturers who released them under their own names. Not surprisingly Méliès's influence on fellow filmmakers during the early years of the twentieth century was immense. In France, Ferdinand Zecca, Emile Cohl, and Jean Durand followed in his footsteps, producing a string of trick movies which were often straightforward imitations of the master's "fantastical fantasies."

Except for the comparative crudeness of its effects, Zecca's *The Seven Castles of the Devil* (1902), for example, could easily have been made by Méliès. The story is a religious allegory about a penniless young man who sells his soul to the Devil. In exchange Satan showers him with riches, transforming his hovel into a glittering mansion called "The Castle of Envy" and his rags into a magnificent suit of clothing. To achieve this metamorphosis and other miraculous conversions and disappearances, Zecca relied on Méliès's oldest cinematic trick, stop-motion photography.

The movie takes our essentially good (if misguided) hero on a tour through a series of supernatural tableaux, each representing one of the Seven Deadly Sins: there is "The Castle of Avarice" (a dungeon filled with pots of gold), "Anger Castle" (a battlement demolished by gunfire), "The Castle of Luxuriousness and Idleness," and so forth. These scenes are fashioned out of the same materials Méliès used, including elaborate painted backgrounds and giant mechanical props. The spirit of "Gluttony Castle," for instance, is a grotesque, swollen monster with a great frog's mouth bristling with teeth. Like Méliès's Frost Giant, though not nearly as impressive, this creature is essentially an oversize puppet, that devours a gargantuan meal of mammoth papier-mâché roast pigs, French breads the size of tree trunks, and for dessert, a couple of naughty children. At the end of the movie we see our hero ferried across a subterranean river toward Hades; at the last moment he is saved from the pit by the love of his wife and transported, in the climactic scene, to a picture-postcard version of heaven.

Méliès's trick movies also influenced the work of Emile Cohl, who has been called the father of the cartoon. Cohl used the technique of stop-motion to animate clever little line drawings which he would then set into a live-action framework. In *The Joyous Microbes* (1909) for example, a scientist proudly displays his new microscope to a skeptical friend. Through the lens we see a series of simple but very ingenious cartoons in which clusters of tiny black specks arrange themselves into caricatures of the personality disorders they supposedly cause. The drunkard germs, for instance, combine themselves into the figure of a lush; the mother-in-law germs turn into an overweight scold; and the politician germs become a blustering demagogue.

Cohl's most delightful movie, however, is not a cartoon at all but a magical chase film called *The Pumpkin Race* (1908). Unlike Méliès's trick films, with their exaggeratedly unreal settings, *The Pumpkin Race* achieves a large part of its effect by having the impossible suddenly erupt in the everyday world. Most of the film takes place in the side streets of turn-of-the-century Paris. The action begins when a peasant leaves a cart full of giant pumpkins parked for a moment on a steep hill and a gang of mischievous boys tips the wagon over. The pumpkins go bouncing down the cobblestone street, but instead of stopping, they actually pick up speed, leading the farmer and a bunch of frantic pursuers on a rollicking wild-gourd chase around the city: down alleys, up walls, through the window of a wealthy couple's apartment, across the dining room table, up the chimney, over the rooftops, into a manhole, through the sewers, and finally back up the hill and into the cart, where they neatly rearrange themselves in their original order.

Whereas Zecca and Cohl relied heavily on stop-motion photography, another of Méliès's contemporaries, Jean Durand, exploited the trick possibilities of fast motion in his comic short *Onésime Horloger* (1910). Upon hearing that he is to inherit a dead uncle's fortune in twenty years, the goofy hero speeds up the hands of a magical clock to make the time pass more swiftly. The film consists of a string of outrageously accelerated scenes: carriages and pedestrians zoom around the streets, ballroom dancers spin across the floor at a crazy pace. The funniest bit compresses the marital history of a young couple into the space of a few seconds. We see the man and the woman courting; then they are married; then the new wife, still in her bridal gown, carries a baby out to the proud papa, who begins bouncing it up and down very rapidly. As he does so the child grows

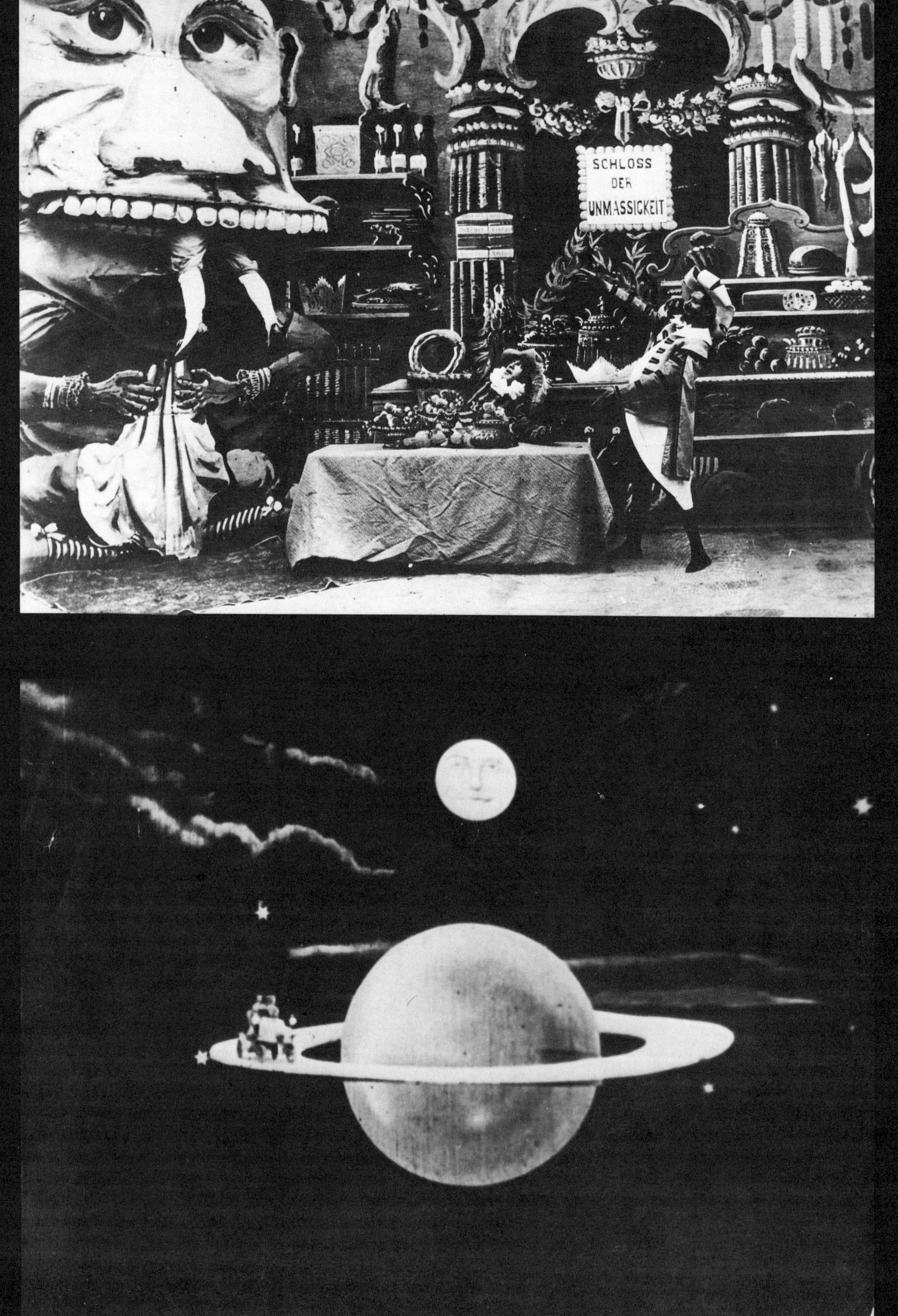
SCHLOSS
DER
UNMASSIGKEIT

larger and larger with every bounce until Daddy is holding a big ugly gorilla of a man, still dressed in a diaper and baby bonnet.

The French were not the only people producing trick films. Across the Channel significant contributions to the development of special-effects techniques were being made by a small group of men: R. W. Paul, G. A. Smith, Edgar Rogers, James Williamson, and an American expatriate named Charles Urban. While Méliès was unquestionably the single most influential of the special-effects pioneers, some writers (generally Englishmen themselves) have put forth the claim that many of the camera tricks he is credited with having originated were actually invented by these early British filmmakers. It's true that in 1897 Smith took out a patent for double exposure, a technique he used in a film called *The Corsican Brothers,* and that he made a movie of the Cinderella story, complete with trick photography, in 1898, a year before Méliès's version. It's also true that in 1898 R. W. Paul produced a film in which a man walked across a ceiling and that several years later the same illusion showed up in a 1902 Méliès movie called *The Human Fly.* Still it's impossible to establish with any precision who invented what and when. All that really can be said is that trick motion-picture photography was obviously an idea whose time had come, and that talented moviemakers in different parts of the world were working along similar lines, sometimes making the same discoveries independently of each other and at other times drawing on the innovations of their rivals.

Top: The Castle of Gluttony from Zecca's *The Seven Castles of the Devil.* *Bottom:* R. W. Paul's *The ? Motorist* ends with an automobile ride around the rings of Saturn.

Another early innovator, Robert William Paul, a successful manufacturer of scientific instruments, knew nothing about motion pictures until he was hired by some Greek showmen in 1894 to provide them with a half-dozen copies of the Kinetoscope, the peephole viewer invented by Edison and his assistant, W.K.L. Dickson. Like Antoine Lumière, Edison had grossly misjudged the commercial possibilities of the movies. Regarding them as little more than an entertaining novelty, he had decided to save the $150 which the English and European patent rights would have cost and failed to patent his invention. As a result Paul's piracy of Edison's invention was perfectly legal, and after finishing the commissioned Kinetoscopes, he manufactured sixty more for himself. When an indignant Edison refused to supply Paul with filmstrips to show on the pirated machines, the Englishman simply built a movie camera and started to shoot his own. Along with the Lumière brothers and several other inventors in Europe and America, Paul also turned his talents to the problem of projecting motion pictures onto a screen, and in the race to invent the world's first practical projector he came close to beating out the Lumières. Just a few months after the Frenchmen gave their first, historic demonstration in the basement of the Grand Café, Paul was in London exhibiting his own machine, an apparatus he called the Theatrograph.

Like Méliès, who came to London to buy one of Paul's projectors after the Lumières refused to sell him theirs, Paul built his own motion-picture studio—England's first—and began producing movies. Most of these were trick films along the lines of Méliès's; they featured giant devils, living skeletons, undersea adventures, and spectacular disasters. His most famous movie, which some film historians think is better than anything his French competitor ever made, is a 1906 comedy with the peculiar title of *The ? Motorist,* in which a couple in a speeding automobile, after eluding a pursuing policeman, go shooting up the side of a building and out into space, where they end up tooling around the rings of Saturn.

In spite of his important contributions to the development of the British film industry, however, Paul seems to have thought of himself less as a filmmaker than as an engineer: throughout his career, his main interest seemed to be the technology, not the art, of entertainment. One of his projects, conceived in collaboration with H. G. Wells but which never got off the ground, was the world's first multimedia show, in which a complicated system of rocking floors, moving walls, projected slides, blinking lights, and whirring motors were to work together to give theatergoers the sensation of traveling through time. In 1910, after deciding that film production was too financially risky, Paul sold his studio, burned his stock of negatives, and took up his former profession of instrument making. He died in relative obscurity in 1943, and though his obituaries ranked him with Edison as a film pioneer, his name remains known mostly to specialists.

Another important figure in the early days of special effects was Charles Urban, an American businessman whose career was closely linked with Edison's inventions. Following a stint as a phonograph salesman, he ran a Kinetoscope parlor in Detroit and later moved to

London to assume the management of Maguire and Baucus, the English distributor of Edison's films. After quadrupling the sales of the firm, which he renamed the Warwick Trading Company, he broke away to form his own business and began producing and distributing various types of motion pictures, including travelogues, advertisements (for whiskey, soap, and cigarettes), and nature and science films. The latter consisted mainly of a series of short movies under the general title of "The Unseen World," which used microcinematography to film assorted biological subjects. The 1903 catalogue for the Charles Urban Trading Company, for example, advertises a movie with the catchy title of "American Blight and Green-Fly," offering magnified views of two garden pests "crawling about in search of food." "The American Blight, or Woolly Aphis," the blurb enticingly continues, "presents a very curious, untidy appearance, with bits of woolly matter, which it has formed itself, stuck about its legs and body."

Urban also produced a number of impressive trick films, the most famous of which is *The Airship Destroyer* (1909), known variously as *Aerial Warfare, Aerial Torpedo, Battle in the Clouds,* and *The Possibilities of War in the Air.* A futuristic melodrama about an air attack on England by a sinister dirigible, this short movie seems quaint (or crude, depending on one's point of view) by today's standards. Considering when it was made, however, its mechanical effects are really quite sophisticated. These include a breakaway armored car destroyed by enemy bombs, a miniature city in flames, models of the attacking warship and defending airplanes, and realistic explosions. One of the most impressive moments in the movie shows a defending fighter plane flying across the screen in the foreground, then circling around in the distance to come in for an attack on the invader. This sequence was achieved through a skillful combination of live-action and model work: a close-up of a full-size airplane moving in front of the camera was added to a special-effects shot of a matching scale-model plane making a strafing run on a miniature blimp. The film ends happily when the young hero saves the day by shooting down the invader with a propeller-driven ground-to-air torpedo which buzzes around the blimp like a dragonfly, hits, and sends the enemy crashing down into a lake in a miniature set of the English countryside.

Like R. W. Paul, Urban was not primarily a film artist; rather, he was a first-class businessman-producer whose movies owe their superiority to the talent of the men he employed. One of these was George Albert Smith, who, according to some film historians, was making trick movies even earlier than Méliès. Smith's fantasy films include *Aladdin and the Wonderful Lamp, Santa Claus, Faust and Mephistopheles,* and *Photographing a Ghost,* the last two of which make use of the double exposure technique he patented in 1897. Smith, in collaboration with Urban, also developed the first color motion-picture process to work by mechanical means, Kinemacolor. Before this, color movies had to be painstakingly produced by hand. (Méliès, for instance, employed a staff of fifty women to hand-tint his movies frame by frame.)

Edgar Rogers was another of Urban's employees credited with several special-effects innovations, including some early glass shots (paintings, generally of background scenery, which are done on glass and combined with the main action during filming) and one of the first aerial effects, which he produced by setting up a phony airplane section on a rocking platform and filming it against the sky. For a number of years Urban also distributed the work of James Williamson, another British motion-picture pioneer, who specialized in chase movies and comical, Méliès-style trick films like *The Clown Barber* (1899), in which the scatterbrained title character accidentally decapitates one of his customers while giving him a shave. This minor mishap does not faze the barber in the least, however; he just goes ahead and finishes up the shave, then reattaches the head to the customer, who gets up, pays the bill, and strolls away.

As entertaining as the trick movies of Méliès and his imitators are, it's easy to see how early twentieth-century filmgoers could grow tired of them after a while, just as they had eventually grown bored some years before with simple scenes of moving objects such as trains, sea waves, and dancers. Even the most astounding illusion will start to seem commonplace if it's repeated often enough, and there are only so many funny ways of chopping off somebody's head before the magic begins to wear thin. Thus the next important step in the evolution of the cinema was the introduction of movies with lots of realistic action and fast-paced plots. Though Williamson and another Englishman, Cecil Hepworth, are often given credit for having made early narrative movies with dramatic story-lines (Williamson's *Fire,* 1901; and Hepworth's *Rescued by Rover,* 1905), the title of "father of the story film" is generally accorded to an American, Edwin S. Porter, who began his career as a cameraman for the Edison Company.

Porter's most important contribution to the history of film was his innovative use of editing. For all the camera tricks and acrobatic stunts they contain, Méliès's fantasy narratives remain essentially static because he conceived of a motion picture as a succession of "moving tableaux" or "artificially arranged scenes." As he himself put it, his intention was to "set the cinema on the path toward theatrical spectacle." Obviously this is a misguided notion of what a motion picture should be, and it was Porter who pointed movies in the right direction by combining shots in a uniquely cinematic way to tell an exciting story. He did this first in *The Life of an American Fireman* (1903), in which a brigade of fire fighters races to the rescue of a mother and child trapped in a burning house. Later in the same year came his masterpiece, *The Great Train Robbery,* the early Western classic which elevated Porter to the position previously held by Méliès—that of the world's most influential director.

The Great Train Robbery is important for another reason: It was the first film to make skillful use of a "reality effect." Like almost every other moviemaker of his time, Porter was deeply impressed by the trick films of Méliès and imitated Méliès's style in a number of fantasies, most notably *Dreams of a Rarebit Fiend* (1906). Based on a popular comic strip by the American cartoonist Winsor McKay, the movie uses some of Méliès's favorite gimmicks, including stop-motion and double exposure, to portray the extravagant nightmare of a man who has overdosed on a bedtime snack of Welsh rarebit and ale. As is true of so many fantasy films, the real star of this movie is the trick photography; the story is little more than an excuse to trot out a bunch of showy effects. In *The Great Train Robbery,* on the other hand, the story is foremost and the special effects are used very subtly and sparingly to make the action seem more realistic and believable.

The first scene takes place inside a telegraph office. Through a window we see a train arrive outside. Though some film historians have claimed that the scene was filmed on location, the truth is that it was done by means of a clever but comparatively simple matte technique. The telegraph office was constructed and filmed inside a studio. When the scene was shot, a piece of black cloth was hung behind the window, blocking—or "matting out"—this portion of the set and therefore leaving a part of the film unexposed. The film was then rewound and a "countermatte" was made. This was a completely opaque card with a small rectangular hole cut out of it, corresponding to the area of the window. Soon after, the camera with the rewound film in it was set up beside some railway tracks near Dover, New Jersey, and with the card positioned in front of the lens, a passing train was shot, recording the image in the blank space left for it inside the window frame. A similar matte shot was used later in the movie to show the landscape rushing by outside the doorway of a moving express car. What makes the fairly rudimentary trick photography in *The Great Train Robbery* so noteworthy, then, is precisely the fact that it was not meant to be noticed at all. For the first time in the movies visual effects were used not as a form of spectacle, but as a way of

Following page:
Fantasy and reality.
Top: A flying bed takes its owner on a midnight tour of New York City in Edwin S. Porter's *Dreams of a Rarebit Fiend.*
Bottom: For this scene in *The Great Train Robbery,* Porter used a simple matte shot to show the train arriving outside the telegraph station window on the right.

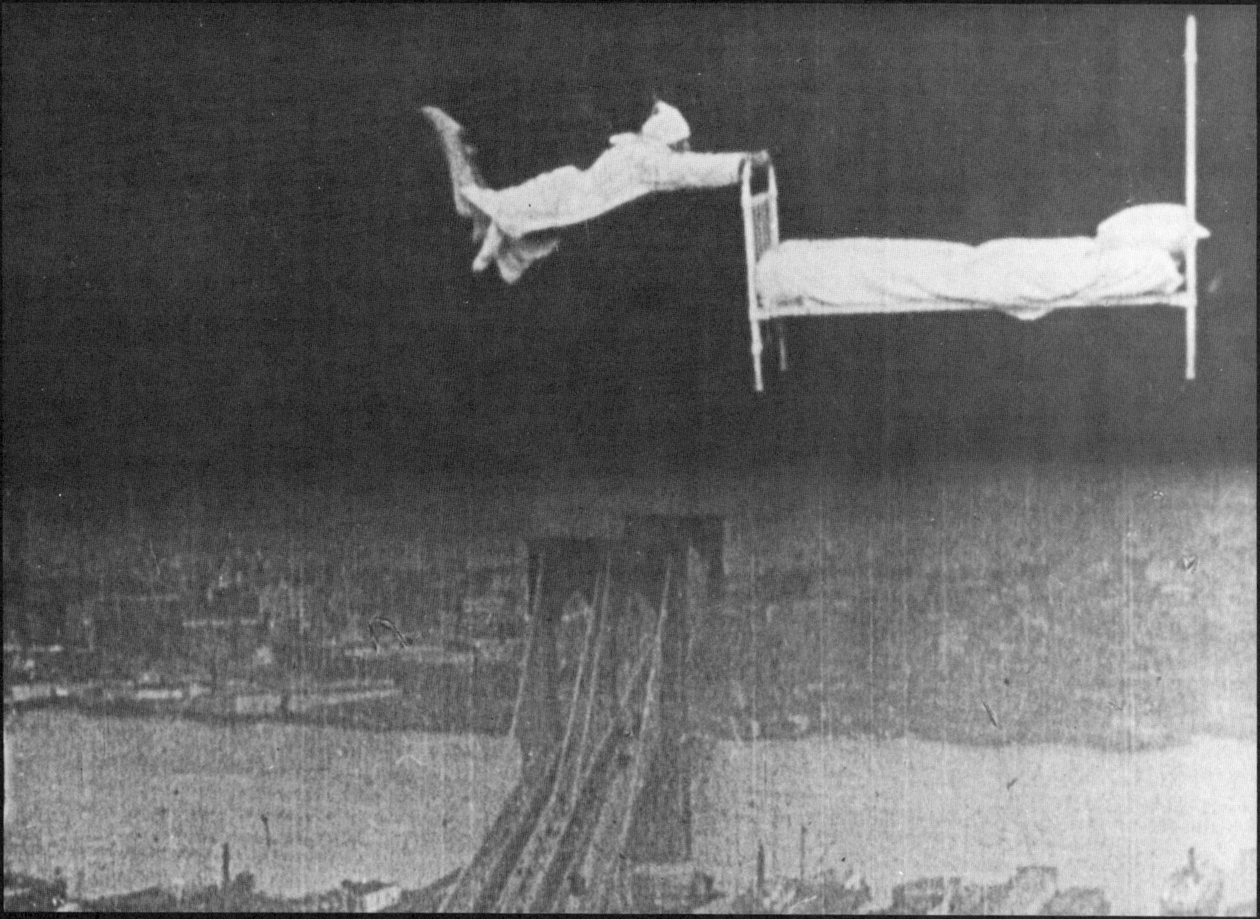

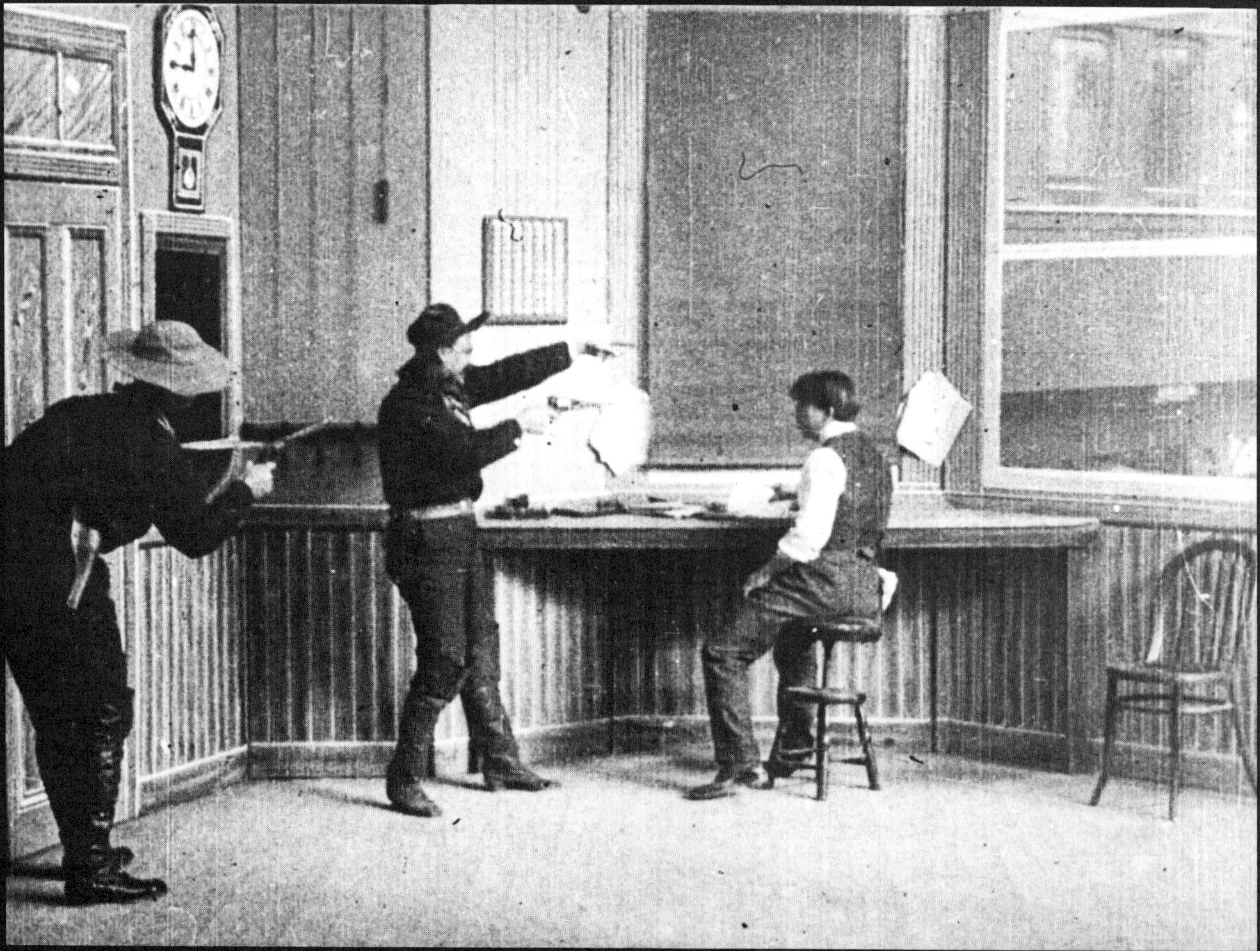

making scenes in a film look natural and lifelike.

It was not Porter, however, but another American film pioneer who was the great innovator of camera tricks used to fake reality. This man's name was Norman O. Dawn. Very few people have heard of Dawn, partly because he made so many unmemorable movies: *A Tokio Siren* (1920), *The Adorable Savage* (1920), *Lure of the Yukon* (1923-24), *Typhoon Love* (1924), *Orphans of the North* (1938), and more. But in the paradoxical way of special-effects work, his obscurity is also partly the result of his technical genius: the illusions he created for the screen were so skillful that audiences took them for the real thing. Dawn, in short, was the first in a long line of anonymous effects experts whose talent guarantees that their work will go unseen. That he has come to be acknowledged as one of the outstanding figures in the history of special effects is due mainly to the efforts of Professor Raymond Fielding of the University of Iowa, who detailed Dawn's achievements in a lengthy 1963 article published in *The Journal of Motion Picture and Television Engineers.*

Like many other special-effects techniques, several of Dawn's inventions had their origin in still photography, a field he entered professionally at the age of nineteen when he went to work for a Los Angeles engraving firm. Besides being a first-rate photographer, he was also a talented painter, and in 1906 he traveled to Paris to study art. It was during his stay there that he met both Méliès and the Lumière brothers and was introduced to the fascinating new art of motion-picture photography. When he returned to the United States in the spring of the following year, he brought a motion-picture camera with him.

Soon after his return Dawn undertook to make a short documentary film called *Missions of California* (1907), which, as its title suggests, was a cinematic sightseeing tour of the Spanish missions at San Gabriel, San Juan Capistrano, San Diego, San Fernando, Ventura, and Santa Barbara. What makes this otherwise insignificant film noteworthy is that in it Dawn used, for the first time in his motion-picture career, a camera trick he adapted from still photography, a technique called a *glass shot.*

Dawn had used this process several years earlier when he worked for the engraving company and was given the assignment of taking pictures of some architectural scenes around Los Angeles. At that time Dawn had discovered that not all the buildings he was asked to shoot were located in particularly photogenic settings; some, for example, had telephone poles directly in front of them. His solution to this problem was ingenious: he used his skill as an artist to improve on reality. First he positioned a large sheet of plate glass in front of the camera. Onto this glass he painted a few picturesque details—bushes, trees, and so on—which blended naturally with the actual scene while blocking out its undesirable features. The final step was to photograph the scene through the partially painted sheet of glass, thereby producing a picture of a building surrounded by cypress trees instead of one half-hidden by wires and poles.

When, several years later, he set about shooting his documentary on California missions, he encountered a similar problem. He found that some of the buildings he wanted to film had fallen into such an extreme state of disrepair that only sections of them remained standing. By painting the missing parts onto a sheet of glass and using great care to match the painted image with the real scene, Dawn was able to make a movie in which the dilapidated missions looked as good as new.

For many years this technique was used extensively by Dawn and other filmmakers since, as *Missions of California* showed, it was a handy way of accomplishing one of the prime purposes of the movies: to make life look better than it actually is. The glass shot had other uses too. Like later techniques that evolved from it, it was an important way of saving money on set-construction costs. For example, instead of erecting a vast, multi-tiered temple for a movie set in the Orient, a filmmaker had only to construct the ground floor, where the live action would take place, and combine this with a painting of the remaining levels to come up with a perfectly convincing illusion of the entire structure. It was also an effective way of conjuring up dramatic landscapes. Westerns requiring a background view of the Rockies, for instance, could be shot in a Los Angeles park by filming the actors through a sheet of glass on which a distant mountain range had been painted.

There are, however, limitations to the glass shot technique. First it takes an extremely talented artist to produce the glass painting in the first place, since its details, perspective lines, and tonal values have to correspond so precisely to the real scene that the camera won't be able to tell the difference between the two. Setting up and painting such a picture also takes time, even for an experienced matte artist, and this is a second disadvantage since Benjamin Franklin's old saw that "time is money" holds especially true when it comes to making movies. On location, filming has to stop entirely while the artist does his job. As a result the savings in set-construction costs may be partially or even largely offset by the money lost during the delays in the production. Even after the painting is finished, this method poses problems, the most serious of which is that the movements of both the camera and the actors are severely restricted. Unless the camera remains more or less stationary, the relationship of the painted image to the live-action element will shift, thereby destroying the illusion. And if an actor accidentally makes a wrong move, he may end up disappearing behind a piece of the painted image.

Dawn, however, was nothing if not resourceful. Méliès may have been the father of special effects, but he was, first and foremost, a magician. Norman O. Dawn was the prototype of the modern effects technician, the motion picture craftsman who brings artistry, engineering skill, and boundless ingenuity to the task of performing the impossible. In 1911, after spending several years as a globe-trotting cameraman shooting travel shorts and newsreels, Dawn devised a new and superior way of producing composite images called an *in-the-camera matte shot.*

Méliès, Porter, and other early moviemakers had used mattes to combine separately filmed images into a single shot. These early matte shots lacked flexibility, however, because they relied on opaque cards to block out part of the film, leaving this part unexposed so that another visual element could be added later on. For splitting the screen in half or placing a second image within a clearly defined area of the first (as Porter did twice in *The Great Train Robbery*—once when he matted the arriving train into the window of the telegraph office and again when he matted the moving landscape into the open doorway of the express car), this technique could be very effective. But more complicated composites were hard to achieve. The process was also very time-consuming. To do the train-through-the-window scene, for example, Porter first had to shoot the footage inside the telegraph office set, then take the same camera with the same roll of film inside it, place it by some railroad tracks, and wait for a train to come by. And if something had gone wrong—if the matte card had been misaligned or the exposure was off—the whole shot would have been ruined and he would have had to go back and do the whole thing over again, starting with the scene in the telegraph office.

The improved matte process Dawn used for the first time in 1911, in a two-reeler called *Story of the Andes,* overcame many of the drawbacks of the earlier method as well as of his own glass shot technique. Dawn's new matte process also began with a sheet of glass set up in front of the camera. However, instead of creating a picture right on the glass, he now covered its surface with opaque black paint, blocking off everything but the area through which the live action was to be filmed. For instance, if Dawn needed to shoot a scene located in Tibet, he might set up his camera in a Los Angeles park and position a sheet of glass between the lens and the costumed actors who stood on a nearby hill. Then he would take his black paint and quickly apply it to the glass, leaving only the hillside visible; everything surrounding it would be blocked from the camera's view. Unlike his earlier method, which required him to create a detailed, highly realistic picture on location, this process only required that he apply a layer of black paint. As a result the live-action footage could be shot with little delay. What Dawn now had was a piece of film on which only the foreground area had been recorded; the rest remained unexposed, having been matted out by the black-painted glass.

The remainder of the process took place inside a studio laboratory where a special camera had been set up. This camera was mounted on a massive concrete base to keep it from vibrating. Facing the lens was a brightly illuminated easel, known technically as a *matte-board.* It was on this board that Dawn would paint the background scenery he wanted to combine with the live action. In the example we've been using, the painting would consist of an exotic Asian landscape. Dawn's first step was to develop a strip of the live-action footage and insert the negative into the camera. Using a specially designed viewfinder, he was able to look into the camera and see the matte-board through the clear, unexposed portion of the negative, the part surrounding the image of the hill. With a light pencil he would carefully draw the outline of the hill onto the easel. (A later, alternative method using a device called a rotoscope lamp made this step in the process much easier by allowing the effects artist to project a frame of the negative directly onto the easel and simply trace the boundary line between the live-action component and the unexposed section of the film.) Dawn would then take black paint and fill in the area occupied by the hill, thereby producing a *counter-*

Top:
GLASS PAINTING: Early "glass shot", as employed by Norman C. Dawn in 1907. Camera (A) records painted areas of sheet of glass (B), which "replace" ruined portions of buildings (C). Stage upon which camera rests (D) is solidly built so as to prevent movement of camera. (Such a stage would generally have a canvas cover or roof to prevent reflections of the camera into the glass sheet.)

Bottom:
IN-THE-CAMERA MATTE SHOT: Banks of lights (A) illuminate easel (B) upon which is mounted a painting of a Buddhist temple. The bottom of the painting is blacked out. Camera (C) combines live-action footage (D), which has been filmed on a studio soundstage, with the painting to produce the final composite shot (E).

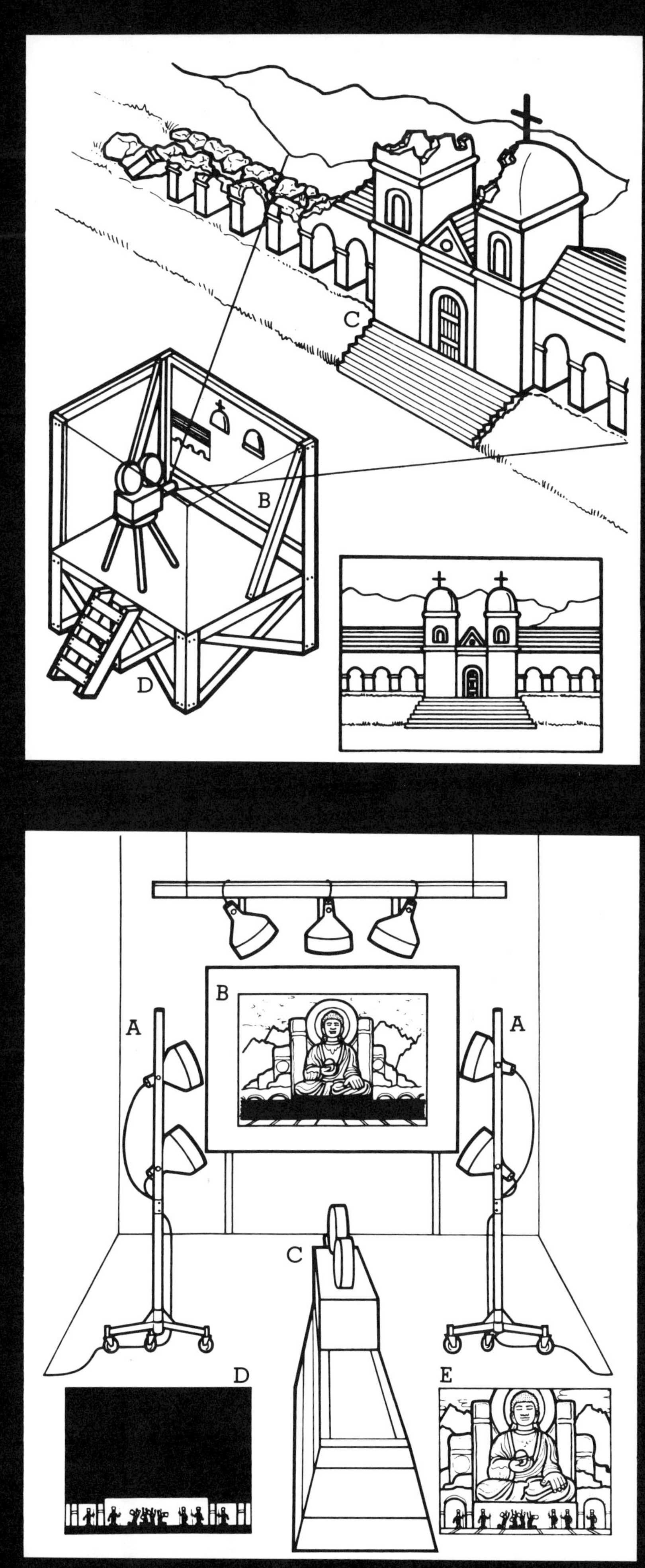

matte which blocked off the part of the picture that had been filmed during the live-action shooting. Though this procedure obviously required patience and precision, it did not, as his earlier method had, hold up production of the movie, since filming could continue in the studio or on location while Dawn took as much time as he needed in the lab to create a good painting. With the bottom portion of the board matted out, Dawn would then go ahead and fill in the blank space around it with whatever Tibetan details he desired: mountains, Buddhist temples, strange-looking foliage. While he did this he would regularly check the viewfinder to make sure that the painted image taking shape on the easel blended perfectly with the scene already recorded on the film. Finally, when he was satisfied with his work, he would run the original footage through the camera, adding the art to the live action and ending up with a fake shot of the Himalayas which, as far as audiences were concerned, looked exactly like the real thing.

During the next few years Dawn refined this technique until he could make it perform a variety of complicated optical tricks. Besides combining a real scene with a painted one, he could put together several live-action images, as he did, for example, in *The Right to Happiness* (1919), in which the actress Dorothy Phillips, playing a dual role, bends down at one point and kisses her twin self on the cheek. In a film released the following year, *The Firecat,* he used his matte process to place a crawling tarantula on the face of a very sensible actor who demurred from playing the scene live. (More than forty years later a much simpler method was used to film a similar scene in the first James Bond movie, *Dr. No.* As Bond lies in bed, a large hairy spider, placed there by one of Dr. No's henchmen, makes its way with agonizing slowness across 007's body. In this case a large sheet of glass was placed over Sean Connery and the spider simply crawled across its surface while the camera filmed the scene from above.) Dawn could also create composites by matting together miniatures and live-action scenes. For a 1919 movie called *Two Men of Tinted Butte,* for example, he combined a shot of a miniature canyon flooded with water with a scene of people running for their lives.

Hollywood producers were deeply impressed by Dawn's effects, which were unlike anything they'd ever seen before, and from 1911 onward his services were in great demand. However, he soon began to run into resistance from directors who didn't like seeing somebody else have so much control over the shooting of key scenes in their movies. Dawn's solution to this problem was to become a producer and director himself, and in his very first production, *The Drifter* (1913), he experimented with still another innovative effects technique: *rear projection.*

Basically rear projection is a way of shooting an outdoors scene inside a studio. The actors perform in front of a large translucent screen. As the name of the process indicates, background scenery is projected onto this screen from *behind* it, a method which insures that the actors will not cast any unwanted shadows onto the screen. In *The Drifter* Dawn used a stereopticon to project landscape photographs onto a ground-glass screen set up in back of his performers. The quality of the image, however, was not very good. Dissatisfied with the results, he abandoned the method, but it became extremely popular in the thirties and forties when technological advances made it possible to produce brighter and sharper images and to make the background itself move by using a motion picture projector behind the screen synchronized with the camera in front.

As important as Dawn's methods were, they were not by any means the last word in special effects; on the contrary, they were only the start of a process that is still going on today: namely, the continuing quest for new and better ways of combining various visual elements into a single, seamless, natural-looking image. The need for good composite work became especially important when talkies were introduced and the filming of actors was forced to move indoors, where dialogue could be recorded under the strictly controlled conditions which early sound equipment required.

It fell to the special-effects men (who, by the early 1930s, were assembled into distinct departments within virtually all of the major studios) to develop ever more efficient ways of conjuring up reality through cinematographic tricks. They were also under continual pressure to come up with techniques equal to the demanding illusions screenwriters and directors were constantly dreaming up for them. Special effects had begun as a way of imitating the marvels of professional magicians. As early as the 1920s, however, effects men were being asked to duplicate miracles previously performed only by God.

A matte shot from the 1939 version of *The Hunchback of Notre Dame.* *Top:* To create a view of fifteenth-century Paris, the facades of some buildings were constructed on the studio's back lot. A matte was then used to block off the upper portion of the scene. *Bottom:* The final composite, with panoramic background view added by the matte artist.

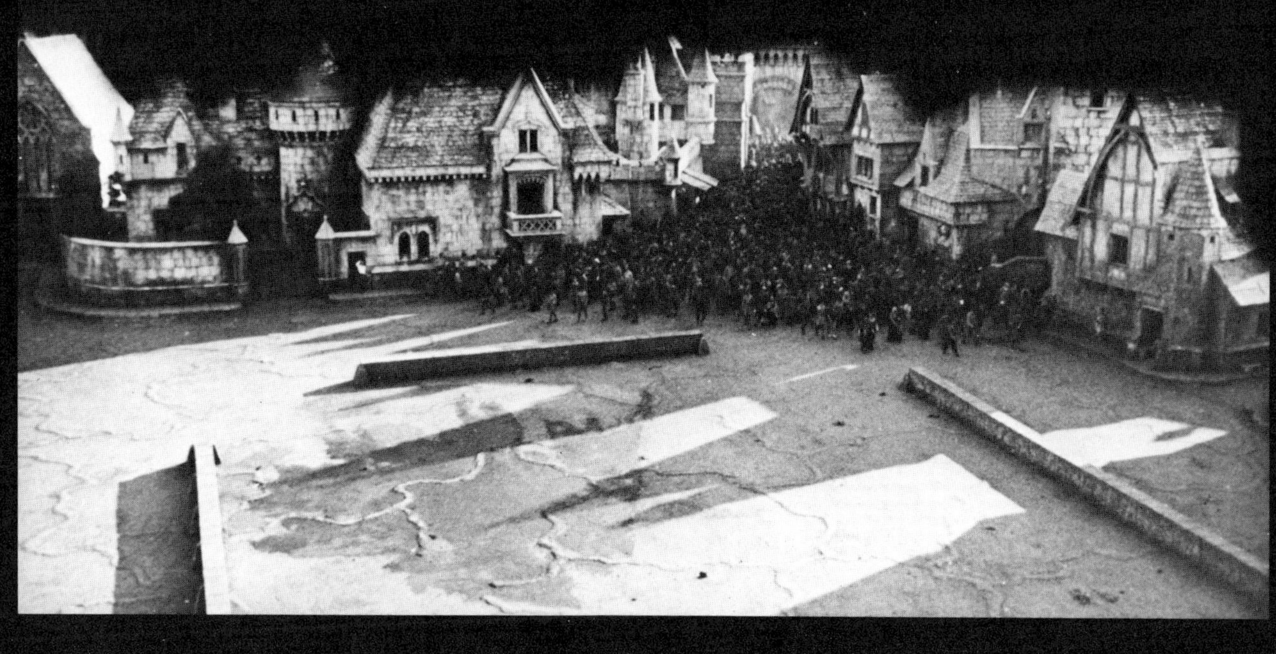

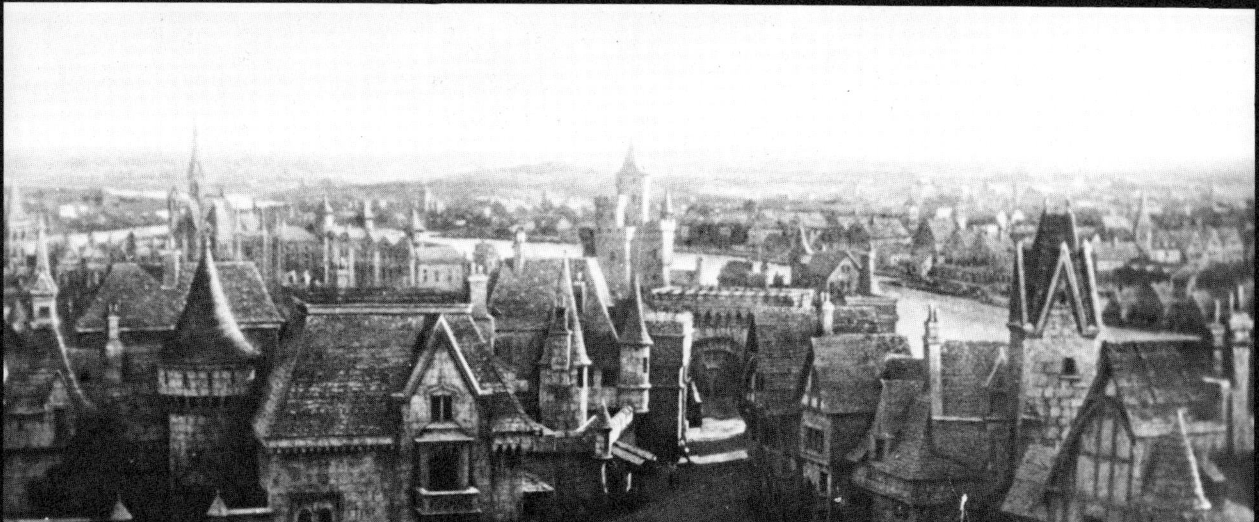

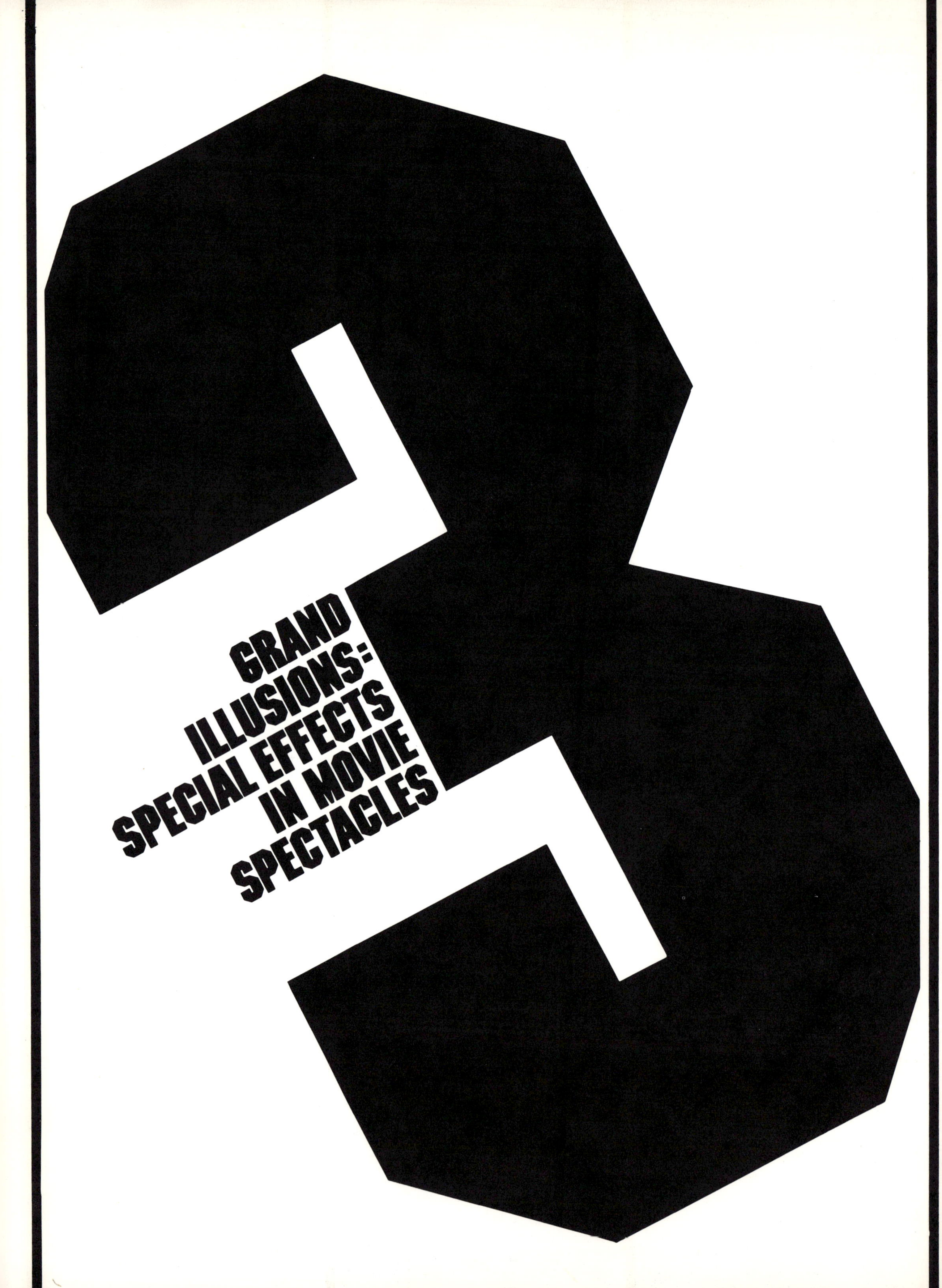
3
GRAND
ILLUSIONS:
SPECIAL EFFECTS
IN MOVIE
SPECTACLES

Motion picture spectacles derive from the stage. Nineteenth-century theatergoers thrilled to awesome sights such as Samson's destruction of the Temple of Dagon, a scene Cecil B. De Mille would later use as the climax of one of his cinematic extravaganzas. When the movies came into existence, they were quick to take aim at the public's desire for pageantry and splendor.

The very first feature-length film was an Italian production of the biblical saga *Quo Vadis?* (1912), a nine-reel epic lasting an unprecedented two-and-a-half hours. The following year the Italians released a two-hour version of *The Last Days of Pompeii* which, film historian Lewis Jacobs reports, was advertised as "having 10,000 people, 260 scenes, and costing $250,000 to produce."

In an attempt to outdo the Italians, D. W. Griffith made America's first epic movie, *Judith of Bethulia,* in 1913. The film featured an impressive set of the biblical city of Bethulia, hordes of extras, and spectacular battle scenes, but these were trifling in comparison to the grandeur of the Babylonian sequence of his 1916 masterpiece *Intolerance,* for which Griffith built a set of monumental proportions. Covering a ten-acre tract of land in Hollywood, this full-size replica of the ancient city had massive hundred-foot walls, towers that rose even higher, and eight soaring columns topped by colossal statues of rearing elephants. However, although Griffith made enormous contributions to the development of the movies, he is not a particularly important figure in the history of special effects, since he shied away from using them, apparently believing that they were a form of cinematic cheating.

It was Cecil B. De Mille who first made extensive use of effects work to bring spectacle to the screen. Inspired by the Italian epics and the masterworks of Griffith (not only *Intolerance* but also *Birth of a Nation*), De Mille devoted himself to making the most sumptuous and monumental movies he could. The "central ambition" of this type of film, writes critic Michael Wood in his book *America in the Movies,* "is simply to do the biggest thing there is to do," and De Mille spent enormous sums to get the grandeur he was aiming for, lavishing fortunes on magnificent costumes, armies of extras, and gargantuan sets. Some of the best moments in his movies, however, could only be provided by special-effects experts, and this was particularly true of those dramatic scenes of destruction which are generally the most sensational and exciting part of epic movies. As Wood points out, the highlight of virtually every cinematic spectacle, whether biblical or historical, is something he calls "the great crash," a colossal disaster from the past: apocalypse then. This might be the burning of Rome or Atlanta, the destruction of Pompeii by volcano or San Francisco by earthquake, or the annihilation of the Pharaoh's army by the raging waters of the Red Sea.

In 1923 Cecil B. De Mille, who liked to believe that everything he did, no matter how crass or commercial, was motivated purely by his deep concern for the welfare of the public, hit upon a plan to generate interest in his next project before the project even existed. As he later wrote in his autobiography, he cooked up a publicity stunt thoughtfully designed "to let the people choose the subject" of his new production. De Mille's gimmick was a contest: a $1,000 first prize to the person who supplied him with the best idea for a motion picture. Thousands of suggestions poured in, but the letter that won the award was from a man named F. C. Nelson, a lubricating oil manufacturer from Lansing, Michigan. Its first sentence proclaimed: "You cannot break the Ten Commandments—they will break you!" The movie that evolved from De Mille's decision to film the Ten Commandments proved once and for all that there was nothing the Hollywood effects men couldn't do.

De Mille's 1923 version of *The Ten Commandments* is split into two parts which have only the most tenuous connection to each other. The second half, the major portion of the film, is a modern-day melodrama intended to illustrate what happens to a man when he flies in the face of God's law. The story concerns two brothers, whom we first see seated at a kitchen table in their home in San Francisco, listening to their pious, white-haired mother read to them from the Bible. One brother (played by Richard Dix) is a dutiful son who takes his mother's religious instruction to heart, but the other (Rod La Rocque) is a true heel who mocks the Bible as old-fashioned, leads a despicable life, and ends up contracting a well-deserved case of leprosy from his Oriental girl friend. Even at the time of its release, this section of the movie was hooted at by critics. But the first and far more impressive half of the movie received the respectful notices it deserved. This was a biblical prologue, a grand-scale recreation of the Book of Exodus, covering the story of the children of Israel from their bondage in Egypt to their worship of the Golden Calf.

To reproduce the kingdom of the Pharaohs, De Mille became a kind of ancient-empire builder himself, leading 2,500 people and 4,500 animals out into the desert, requisitioning a hundred war chariots ("the largest order for chariots in 1,700 years," according to contemporary publicity releases), and overseeing the construction of a mammoth replica of the city of Ramses II, complete with an approachway lined with two dozen sphinxes, each weighing four tons.

However, to reproduce the parting of the Red Sea required more than big money and manpower; it called for the kind of miracle special-effects men get paid so well to produce. Roy Pomeroy, head of Paramount's special-effects department, solved the problem by having thousands of gallons of water dumped down either side of a large, U-shaped steel tank. As the water came crashing together, a motion picture camera recorded the scene. When the shot was run in reverse, the effect was of a large body of water miraculously splitting apart into two churning halves. The separated walls of the Red Sea through which Moses and his people pass unharmed are somewhat less impressive since they look like two quivering mounds of Jell-O, which is essentially what they were. Pomeroy, according to his assistant, T. K. Peters, set up a large gelatin mold on a table, parted it in the middle, and subsequently matted a shot of the fleeing actors into the blank space in between. To show the Pharaoh's army being swallowed up by the Red Sea, Pomeroy simply ran the water-parting scene forward, showing the sea crashing together over the heads of the matted-in Egyptians, and then cut to a shot of some submerged dummies photographed through the glass wall of a tank.

The success of *The Ten Commandments* prompted several Hollywood filmmakers to make their own biblical extravaganzas. One of these, *Noah's Ark* (1929), also featured a centerpiece scene of evildoers being drowned by a vengeful God. In this case, though, the director, Michael Curtiz, decided to outdo De Mille by shooting the scene in which a crowd of sinners is inundated inside a heathen temple without optical trickery. For heightened realism he planned instead to dump 600,000 gallons of water directly onto the teeming mob of idol-worshipers, only forty or fifty of whom were trained stunt people. The rest were down-at-the-heels extras, willing to do anything for a day's pay but completely unprepared for such dangerous work. Ignoring the objections of his principal photographer, Hal Mohr, who quit in protest over the scheme, Curtiz went ahead and unloaded several tons of water on the heads of the hapless actors, producing a biblical catastrophe whose authenticity was achieved at the cost of severe injuries and, reportedly, three drownings.

For another flooding scene, in which the city surrounding the temple is washed away by God's wrath, Curtiz was obliged to rely on effects work. One big difference between a natural disaster (such as a cyclone, flash flood, or fire) and a cinematic one is that a real disaster always happens very suddenly and spontaneously, whereas the motion picture kind must be set up with painstaking care. In real life if a major earthquake, for example, hits a big city and the buildings miraculously escape destruction, the people rejoice in the unexpected saving of human life and money. In the movies the very opposite is true: if a massive earthquake doesn't succeed in knocking over everything in sight, gloom settles over the studio and the sequence has to be repeated at tremendous expense.

To make sure that their ancient city would be completely wiped away by the flood, Curtiz's head effects man, Fred Jackman, assembled miniature buildings out of prebroken shards held together by clay. For good measure he also rigged them with small charges of dynamite. Two networks of pipes, one located in the ground beneath the minature city, the other set up overhead, supplied the deluge, and fifteen cameras recorded the scene, which was made even more spectacular with the help of wind machines, used to churn the water into a raging storm. The cataclysm came off nicely, though Jackman needed four days in bed to get his nerves back in order.

Meanwhile a second effects man, Hans Koenekamp, was busy creating various optical tricks for the film. Several scenes in the picture, for example, show a large assortment of animals assembled in the same place. Actually these are composite shots filmed at a number of different zoos. Instead of bringing together a bunch of animals that might not have gotten along very well in a studio, Koenekamp used an in-the-camera matte technique to produce the illusion of a congregation of beasts. One of the most complicated of these shots consisted of eighteen separate exposures on a single piece of film. The Ark itself was only partially constructed, the bulk of it being filled in with matte paintings.

For the makers of biblical epics in the 1920s, certain disaster sequences had a way of turning into genuine, out-of-control calamities. This seemed to be particularly true when the disasters took place around water. The 1926 version of *Ben-Hur,* considered by many critics to be the best

Top: An article in the March 1924 issue of *Science and Invention* explained how special-effects experts parted the Red Sea for De Mille's *The Ten Commandments.* *Bottom:* A glass shot from *Noah's Ark,* combining a live-action foreground with a painting of the partially constructed ark.

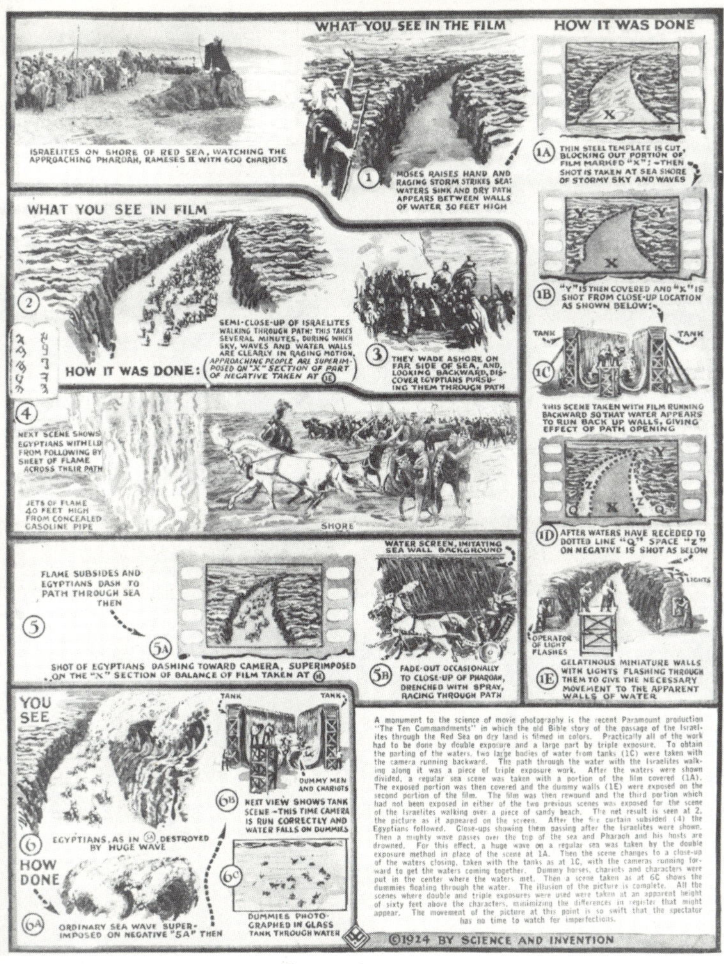

Parting of Red Sea Filmed

Spectacle Shows Israelites Passing Through Sea On Dry Land.

WHAT YOU SEE IN THE FILM

HOW IT WAS DONE

ISRAELITES ON SHORE OF RED SEA, WATCHING THE APPROACHING PHAROAH, RAMESES II WITH 600 CHARIOTS

(1) MOSES RAISES HAND AND RAGING STORM STRIKES SEA: WATERS SINK AND DRY PATH APPEARS BETWEEN WALLS OF WATER 30 FEET HIGH

(1A) THIN STEEL TEMPLATE IS CUT, BLOCKING OUT PORTION OF FILM MARKED "X": —THEN SHOT IS TAKEN AT SEA SHORE OF STORMY SKY AND WAVES

WHAT YOU SEE IN FILM

(2) SEMI-CLOSE-UP OF ISRAELITES WALKING THROUGH PATH: THIS TAKES SEVERAL MINUTES, DURING WHICH SKY, WAVES AND WATER WALLS ARE CLEARLY IN RAGING MOTION.

HOW IT WAS DONE: (APPROACHING PEOPLE ARE SUPERIMPOSED ON "X" SECTION OF PART OF NEGATIVE TAKEN AT (1E))

(3) THEY WADE ASHORE ON FAR SIDE OF SEA, AND, LOOKING BACKWARD, DISCOVER EGYPTIANS PURSUING THEM THROUGH PATH

(1B) "Y" IS THEN COVERED AND "X" IS SHOT FROM CLOSE-UP LOCATION AS SHOWN BELOW:

TANK

TANK

(1C) THIS SCENE TAKEN WITH FILM RUNNING BACKWARD SO THAT WATER APPEARS TO RUN BACK UP WALLS, GIVING EFFECT OF PATH OPENING

(4) NEXT SCENE SHOWS EGYPTIANS WITHELD FROM FOLLOWING BY SHEET OF FLAME ACROSS THEIR PATH

JETS OF FLAME 40 FEET HIGH FROM CONCEALED GASOLINE PIPE

SHORE

(1D) AFTER WATERS HAVE RECEDED TO DOTTED LINE "Q" SPACE "Z" ON NEGATIVE IS SHOT AS BELOW

(5) FLAME SUBSIDES AND EGYPTIANS DASH TO PATH THROUGH SEA THEN

(5A) SHOT OF EGYPTIANS DASHING TOWARD CAMERA, SUPERIMPOSED ON THE "X" SECTION OF BALANCE OF FILM TAKEN AT (1E)

WATER SCREEN, IMITATING SEA WALL BACKGROUND

(5B) FADE-OUT OCCASIONALLY TO CLOSE-UP OF PHAROAH, DRENCHED WITH SPRAY, RACING THROUGH PATH

LIGHTS

OPERATOR OF LIGHT FLASHES

(1E) GELATINOUS MINIATURE WALLS WITH LIGHTS FLASHING THROUGH THEM TO GIVE THE NECESSARY MOVEMENT TO THE APPARENT WALLS OF WATER

YOU SEE

(6) EGYPTIANS, AS IN (5A) DESTROYED BY HUGE WAVE

HOW DONE

(6A) ORDINARY SEA WAVE SUPERIMPOSED ON NEGATIVE "5A" THEN

TANK

TANK

DUMMY MEN AND CHARIOTS

(6B) NEXT VIEW SHOWS TANK SCENE —THIS TIME CAMERA IS RUN CORRECTLY AND WATER FALLS ON DUMMIES

(6C) DUMMIES PHOTOGRAPHED IN GLASS TANK THROUGH WATER

A monument to the science of movie photography is the recent Paramount production "The Ten Commandments" in which the old Bible story of the passage of the Israelites through the Red Sea on dry land is filmed in colors. Practically all of the work had to be done by double exposure and a large part by triple exposure. To obtain the parting of the waters, two large bodies of water from tanks (1C) were taken with the camera running backward. The path through the water with the Israelites walking along it was a piece of triple exposure work. After the waters were shown divided, a regular sea scene was taken with a portion of the film covered (1A). The exposed portion was then covered and the dummy walls (1E) were exposed on the second portion of the film. The film was then rewound and the third portion which had not been exposed in either of the two previous scenes was exposed for the scene of the Israelites walking over a piece of sandy beach. The net result is seen at 2, the picture as it appeared on the screen. After the fire curtain subsided (4) the Egyptians followed. Close-ups showing them passing after the Israelites were shown. Then a mighty wave passes over the top of the sea and Pharaoh and his hosts are drowned. For this effect, a huge wave on a regular sea was taken by the double exposure method in place of the scene at 1A. Then the scene changes to a close-up of the waters closing, taken with the tanks as at 1C, with the cameras running forward to get the waters coming together. Dummy horses, chariots and characters were put in the center where the waters met. Then a scene taken as at 6C shows the dummies floating through the water. The illusion of the picture is complete. All the scenes where double and triple exposures were used were taken at an apparent height of sixty feet above the characters, minimizing the differences in register that might appear. The movement of the picture at this point is so swift that the spectator has no time to watch for imperfections.

©1924 BY SCIENCE AND INVENTION

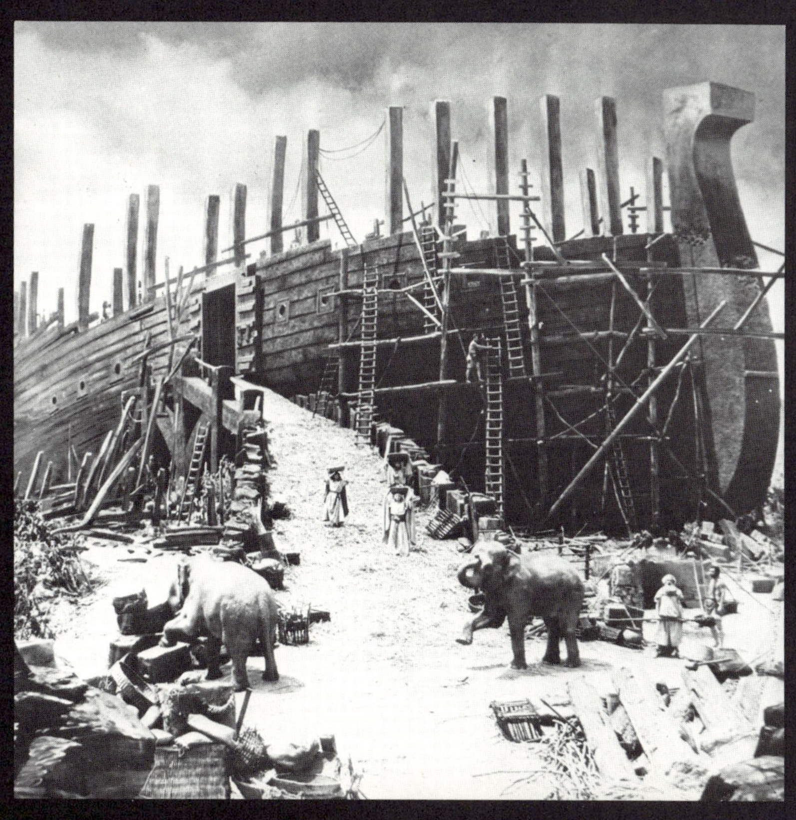

Top: For the silent version of *Ben-Hur,* only the bottom portion of the Circus Maximus set was built in full scale. *Center:* The upper section was a hanging miniature positioned between the camera and the background set and filled with thousands of tiny, mechanical figures. *Bottom:* BI-PACK CONTACT MATTE PRINTING: A simplified, cutaway drawing of a process camera loaded for bipack printing. Duplicating negative raw film stock is loaded into chamber A of the camera. A master positive roll of film is loaded into chamber B. The exposed dupe negative film is taken up into chamber C, the master positive roll of film into chamber D. The two strips pass through the intermittent movement, emulsion to emulsion, with the raw stock to the rear. A white matte board (E) is set up in front of the camera and the lens of the process camera is focused on this board

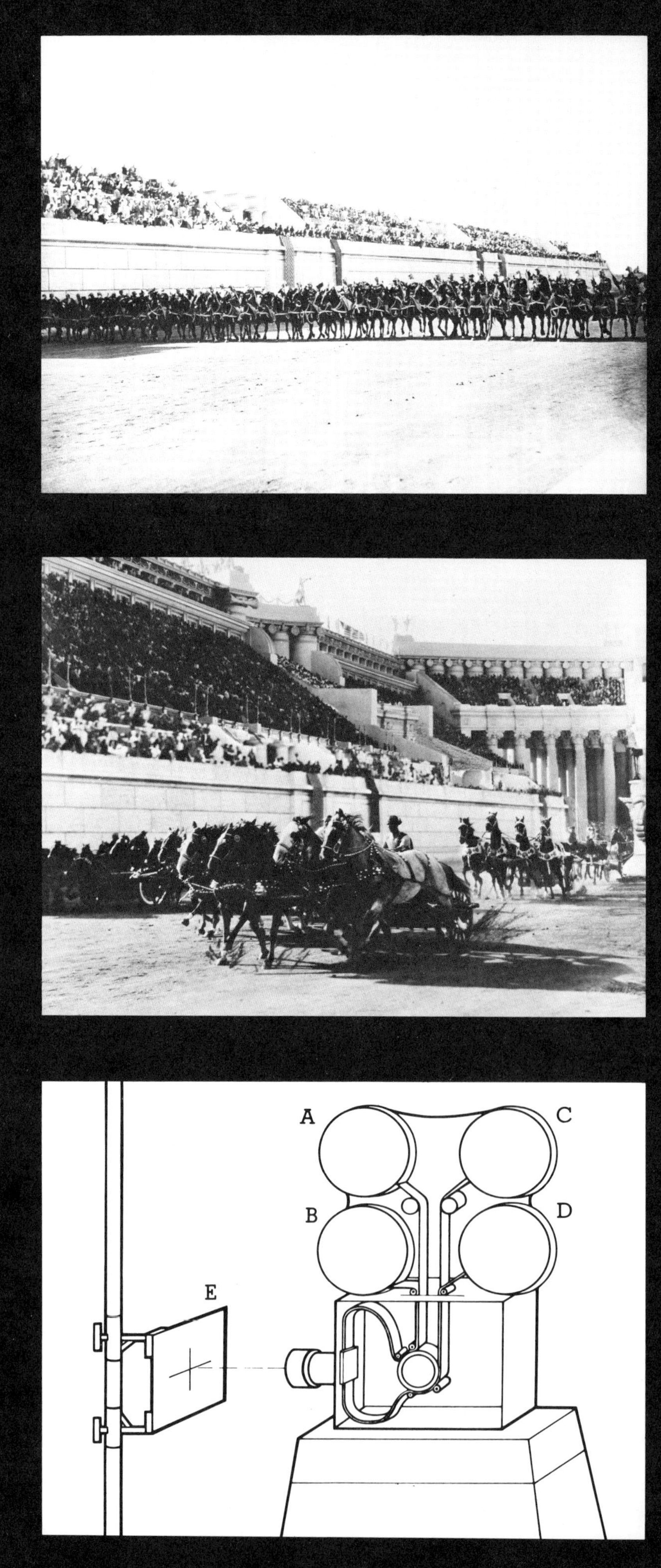

movie of its kind ever put on the screen, contained a spectacular death-by-water scene which, like the temple-flooding episode in *Noah's Ark,* ended up being a good deal more calamitous than anyone had counted on.

For years Hollywood moviemakers had been itching to get their hands on the rights to *Ben Hur;* indeed, in the early years of the American film industry, General Lew Wallace's biblical story was the hottest property around, having sold more copies than any other book in history except for the Bible itself. In 1899 it was turned into a major theatrical production, a Broadway hit containing a host of spectacular scenes, including a dramatic chariot race in which real horses thundered over a treadmill while a painted backdrop of the Circus Maximus revolved behind them. As early as 1907, filmmakers tried to cash in on the enormous popularity of *Ben Hur.* In his invaluable book about the silent movie era, *The Parade's Gone By*, Kevin Brownlow recalls the case of an enterprising director named Sidney Olcott. Hearing of a chariot race that was going to be staged as "an added attraction to a fireworks display at Sheepshead Bay," Olcott got hold of a cameraman and a couple of actors, went down to the track and filmed the race, then added a few interior scenes and came up with the screen's first *Ben-Hur,* modestly advertised as "positively the most superb motion picture spectacle ever made." Olcott's company was immediately sued by the publishers of the book and the producers of the play and ended up paying a settlement of $25,000. When the movie rights to the story were finally sold in 1921 (for $600,000), the people in charge of making the film insisted on shooting it in Italy, where, they argued, the spirit of the Roman Empire could be captured more faithfully than on a back lot in Hollywood.

The production was plagued by trouble from the start: labor problems, inadequate facilities, cheaply constructed sets, an incomplete script. The biggest fiasco, however, occurred during the filming of the famous sea battle, in which a fleet of Roman galleys is attacked by pirate raiders. Full-size, highly detailed, and perfectly seaworthy ships had been constructed for the scene, and these were packed with hundreds of Italian extras decked out as galley slaves and soldiers. Like the men and women in *Noah's Ark* who had been willing to risk their lives for a day's work in a movie, these extras were poor people, natives of the countryside around Livorno, where the sequence was shot; all of them had claimed—not very accurately, as it turned out—to be first-rate swimmers. The scene began with the ramming of the Roman flagship by one of the pirate vessels which was hooked up to a high-powered speedboat that pulled it across the water and sent it crashing into the side of the Roman ship. As soon as the collision occurred, however, pandemonium broke out on board: "The extras were seized by panic," reports Brownlow. "Many of them, appalled by their plight, dropped to their knees and implored the saints for help."

While it's fairly amusing to imagine a shipload of Roman soldiers reduced to hysteria at the first bump of their boat, the comedy soon turned deadly serious. The climax of the sea battle occurs when the Roman flagship, after some savage fighting, is set on fire by the pirates. Barrels of flammable chemicals had been placed on board the galley, but the fire, which was supposed to be limited to the flagship's forward section, was fanned into a wild blaze by a draft blowing through the oarholes. In a moment the whole ship was in flames and the panic-stricken extras, many of them dressed in heavy armor costumes, plunged overboard. Rescue boats were launched to retrieve them, but though accounts of the casualties differ, several men were apparently drowned.

Since the shooting of the sea battle had ended so disastrously, the filmmakers turned to miniature work to complete the sequence. MGM gave up on its ill-fated efforts to make the movie in Italy and the production company returned to the states, leaving behind in Rome a number of sets, including an impressive reproduction of the Circus Maximus. A new one was constructed in Culver City for the filming of the movie's most thrilling sequence: the chariot race between Ben-Hur and his archfoe, Messala. Eight hundred men worked for four months on this massive coliseum, the biggest movie set ever built up to that time. On screen it seems awesome. What is most impressive about this set, however, is not its actual size but the fact that a large part of it is really a *hanging miniature.*

A hanging miniature serves the same function as a glass painting. In the case of *Ben-Hur,* instead of spending a great deal of money to build a complete coliseum, only the bottom half (required for the race) was erected. The upper section was a small scale model built by effects artists and carefully positioned between the camera and the partially constructed full-size set. On film the two components blend together seamlessly, producing a perfect illusion of a colossal amphitheater. The main advantage of this method over the glass shot is that it allows the camera the freedom to pan over the model. Designed by Cedric Gibbons and A. Arnold ("Buddy") Gillespie, a legendary figure in the field who was to go on to become head of MGM's special-effects department, the Circus Maximus miniature was further distinguished by a brilliant touch which made it seem uncannily real: its galleries, supposedly packed with wildly cheering spectators, actually contained 10,000 tiny mechanical figures that could be made to stand up and wave.

Like most epic movies, *Ben-Hur* also contains an example of the type of scene Michael Wood calls "the great crash": in this case, the collapse of the Roman senate building onto a crowd of people. Gillespie, along with optical expert Frank Williams, created this catastrophe by means of a special-effects method known as a *traveling matte,* a much more sophisticated way of producing composite images than any previous matte technique.

Thanks mainly to the contributions of Norman O. Dawn, matte work in the 1920s was considerably more practical than it had been in the days when Edwin S. Porter made his trick train-arrival shot by first filming the interior of a telegraph office set, then carrying his camera to some tracks in New Jersey and filling in the blank space outside the office window with a shot of a passing freight train. Dawn's innovative in-the-camera matte method made it possible to do all the composite work with a separate, specially designed apparatus set up inside a studio lab. But this technique also had its disadvantages, the main one being that a single piece of film still had to be exposed at least twice, once when the live action was filmed and again when the matted-in element was added to the scene. Combining the different elements on the same roll of film in this way was a tricky affair; if anything went wrong during the second exposure, the original, live-action footage would be ruined and the whole scene would have to be shot over again from scratch at great cost and inconvenience.

The next noteworthy step in the development of this area of optical effects was the introduction of a technique with the daunting name of *bipack contact matte printing,* which was designed to overcome the drawbacks of the in-the-camera method. The bipack process, as its name suggests, uses *two* rolls of film. The first step in the procedure is to record the live-action element on one of these rolls. Let us say, for example, that a busy street scene is being shot on a soundstage inside a studio. A fake sidewalk lined with the façades of office buildings and fancy boutiques has been constructed. For economy's sake, however, only the lower story of each of these phony structures has been put up. Above the set, completely visible to the camera, is the usual studio paraphernalia: lights, ladders, microphones, catwalks, and so on. It is the filmmaker's intention to use a matte painting to create the illusion that the sequence is taking place amid the towering skyscrapers of downtown New York City.

After the live-action scene has been shot on the set, the film is developed into what is known as a *master positive.* The next step is to load this print into a special camera (called a *process camera*) along with a second, undeveloped roll of raw film, the technical name for which is a *dupe* (duplicate) *negative.* The point of the procedure is to transfer only the lower part of the live-action scene (showing the crowd of extras hurrying along the make-believe street) onto this second roll of film. The top part of the original print (containing the exposed studio equipment) will not be transmitted to the dupe, a blank space will be left on the dupe into which a painted image can be inserted like the missing piece of a jigsaw puzzle. As in Dawn's method, this is accomplished by setting up a white board or easel in front of the camera. Using black paint or ink, the artist blocks out the part corresponding to the unwanted section of the master positive, in this case the upper area of the easel. The two rolls of film, which actually come in contact with each other, are then run simultaneously through the camera. Since no light is transmitted by the black matte, this part of the image will remain unexposed on the duplicate roll of film. In short, what the effects man ends up with at this point in the process is a new negative containing the live-action scene with a clear space above it. A matte painting of the upper stories of the buildings is now prepared on a second easel, the dupe negative is run through the camera again, and the artwork and live action are fitted together to produce a single image. The big advantage of this method is that should anything go wrong and the composite shot be ruined, the live action does not have to be staged and photographed all over again, since the first roll of film (from which the master positive is printed) remains untouched and another print can simply be made from it.

There is, however, one major limitation to this method. While the performers have complete freedom of movement within the live-action area, there is no possibility of any interaction between this part of the scene and the added background image. The boundary separating the two, while it might be totally invisible to the naked eye of the filmgoer, is fixed and inflexible. In the hypothetical case we've been using, for example, a fire engine might come to a screeching halt by the curbside and unload a team of firefighters, who send a ladder shooting up the side of one of the buildings. As soon as the ladder passes the first story, however, it will abruptly disappear; it cannot possibly cross the matte line into the painted portion of the scene. There are times, however, when it's necessary for just this kind of crossover to take place, and in cases like these what's called for is a matte line that moves—in other words, a traveling matte.

Let us say, for example, that a movie about the harmful effects of nuclear radiation on the arachnid population of Pennsylvania features a scene of an immense spider chasing a panic-stricken crowd down the main street of a town. This effect might be created by filming a spider in an extreme close-up (to make it appear very large) and then matting this image together with a shot of a mob of extras fleeing through a small town set. To fit the giant bug into the scene with the actors would require an entire series of individual mattes: spider-shaped silhouettes which would change position from frame to frame in accordance with the creature's movements. One way of doing this would be to draw each of the mattes by hand, the method Gillespie and Williams used in *Ben-Hur* to show the crowd of Romans being buried by the falling debris of the senate building.

Though the hand-drawn matte technique is very versatile, it is also extremely tedious, time-consuming, and expensive. An early attempt to create traveling mattes by photographic means was introduced in the late 1920s by C. Dodge Dunning and Roy Pomeroy. Known as the "Dunning-Pomeroy self-matting system," this method made use of a bipack camera loaded, as always, with two rolls of film in contact with each other. In this case, however, the background scenery was shot first and the resulting master positive was dyed orange before being loaded into the process camera along with a roll of raw negative. On the set the actors performed in front of a screen illuminated with blue light, while they themselves had an orange light trained on them. Inside the camera two things took place simultaneously during the filming of the live action. First, light from the orange-lit actors passed through the master positive and exposed their image on the dupe negative. At the same time the blue light from the screen caused the background scenery on the master positive to be printed directly on the dupe. Wherever the actors moved, their bodies would block out the blue light behind them, permitting them to function as their own traveling mattes.

Though the Dunning-Pomeroy self-matting process was popular for a number of years, it was not particularly practical and could only be used for black-and-white movies. By the 1930s it had been abandoned, replaced first by new, improved rear projection techniques and later by more efficient (though even more complex) ways of producing traveling mattes through color photography. Even though it is now obsolete, this process is worth remembering as an important early stage in the quest which effects men have pursued from the start: the attempt to find the technological means of manufacturing perfect optical illusions.

Clever optical effects were the specialty of Gordon Jennings, head of Paramount's special-effects department from the mid-1930s until his death in 1953. In 1933 Cecil B. De Mille, whose most recent film, *Four Frightened People,* had died at the box office, received some helpful advice from movie mogul Adolph Zukor: "Better do another historical epic, Cecil, with plenty of sex." De Mille took Zukor's suggestion to heart and decided to produce *Cleopatra* (1934), a property which lent itself perfectly to his talent for cinematic excess and which turned out to be a tremendous hit. Given the following description of one of its scenes from Gabe Essoe and Raymond Lee's book *De Mille: The Man and His Pictures,* the movie's success is not hard to understand:

Claudette Colbert in the title role and a variety of Paramount contractees appear in the briefest of gowns and togas in some remarkable sets. The Royal Barge, for example, is an incredible fabrication, from its banks of oars, each surmounted with a ram's head, to the pillowed dais on which Cleopatra seduces Marc Antony. At her signal, an inexhaustible supply of slave girls bursts out of every door to perform a series of exotic dances, a garlanded ox is led in, to be caressed by semi-naked girls, one of whom in the second before fade out assumes a pose of sexual surrender before the animal; a nude group is whipped into submission by a huge slave; a net-full of girls, clad only in sea-weed, is dredged up to sprawl out wriggling on the deck and offer seashells full of jewels. When Antony succumbs to her wiles, Cleopatra gestures to the slaves and, as veils rise around her bed and singing girls strew them with flowers, the cadence drummer strikes up the rhythm that sets the oars moving, and the barge moves slowly out to sea.

For long shots of the Egyptian queen's barge entering and leaving port, Jennings and his effects team constructed one of the most sumptuous models ever to grace the screen. To call this glittering, swan-shaped vessel a miniature is almost misleading, since it was twelve feet long and weighed several tons. It was fitted with 300 oars which made perfectly realistic rowing motions by means of a complicated mechanical system powered by an electric motor. For added authenticity Jennings built tubes into the bottom of the barge which shot jets of compressed air up through the water, creating the effect of spray from the stroking oars. Seeing the movie, a viewer has no way of knowing that this glorious vessel is actually a model ship propelled across a studio tank by offscreen stagehands pulling ropes attached to the underside of the boat.

This miniature was also used, in slightly disguised form, in a scene containing one of the most ingenious illusions Jennings ever produced. The action highlight of *Cleopatra* is the famous Battle of Actium, a naval engagement involving two large fleets of enemy ships. In reality only a single pair of model boats was used for this scene: the Royal Barge, modified to look like a war galley, and a second, slightly less-detailed miniature built expressly for the battle. These two ships were turned into an entire fleet by means of what Jennings described as "the old, familiar trick of parallel mirrors," an illusion known to anyone who has ever stood in between a pair of facing mirrors and seen his image repeated into infinity. This phantom fleet was then multiplied again into two opposing armadas by split-screen double exposure.

Since ancient naval warfare involved extensive use of catapulted fireballs to incinerate the enemy's fleet, and since Jennings and his crew had only two ships to work with, they took the economical step of fireproofing their models with nonflammable chemicals and asbestos fabric, a precaution which allowed them, as Jennings put it, "to burn the ships daily for several weeks." Jennings also saved money in the filming of the land battle by intercutting shots of fighting actors with stock footage of horsemen and chariots made fourteen years earlier for De Mille's *The Ten Commandments.*

Though epics about the ancient world continued to be made in the thirties (another example is the 1935 version of *The Last Days of Pompeii,* whose fiery, climactic disaster was the work of Willis O'Brien, the effects wizard responsible for the marvels of *King Kong*), audiences of the day seemed to prefer spectacles which took place in more recent times: sweeping historical romances generally set in the late nineteenth or early twentieth century and featuring at least one good catastrophe per picture. It's easy to see why the average Depression-era filmgoer would find such escapist entertainments appealing, with their glamorous, richly dressed stars living in a storybook version of the past and caught up in thrilling, momentous events. It's somewhat less easy to understand why audiences demanded that movies such as *San Francisco* (1936), *The Hurricane* (1937), *Suez* (1938), *In Old Chicago* (1938), *The Rains Came* (1939), *Gone With the Wind* (1939) and others include a major catastrophe. Perhaps the sight of so much expenditure and waste was oddly comforting to people who in real life didn't have a penny to spare. In general, filmgoers in the thirties seemed to find temporary relief from their own financial woes in the extravagant fantasies of the Hollywood dream factory, in overblown productions with impossibly lavish sets and casts of thousands. As images of conspicuous consumption, scenes of large-scale devastation could be even more effective than the average Busby Berkeley musical in drawing audiences and satisfying their desire for spectacular effects. As Michael Wood observes in his discussion of the obligatory "great crash" in epic films, "the idea of waste in these movies receives its fullest expression here.... This is visible expense, like crowds of extras, only more startling. This is money being burned."

It's also possible that Depression-era audiences took comfort from the feeling of sharing some misery with the beautiful people on the screen, from the notion that no one, no matter how rich or glamorous, is immune to disaster. Or perhaps, since so many of these films were made at the tail end of the Depression, in the period just before the outbreak of World War II, their preoccupation with cataclysmic events (images of terrifyingly destructive storms, earthquakes, and conflagrations) reflected the public's growing anxieties about the forces of destruction that were about to be unleashed on the world. Whatever the reason for the appeal of these scenes, their creation fell to the studio effects specialists, who found themselves using all their considerable technological skills to simulate convincing natural disasters.

According to legend, the earthquake engineered by A. Arnold Gillespie and his assistant, James Basevi, for

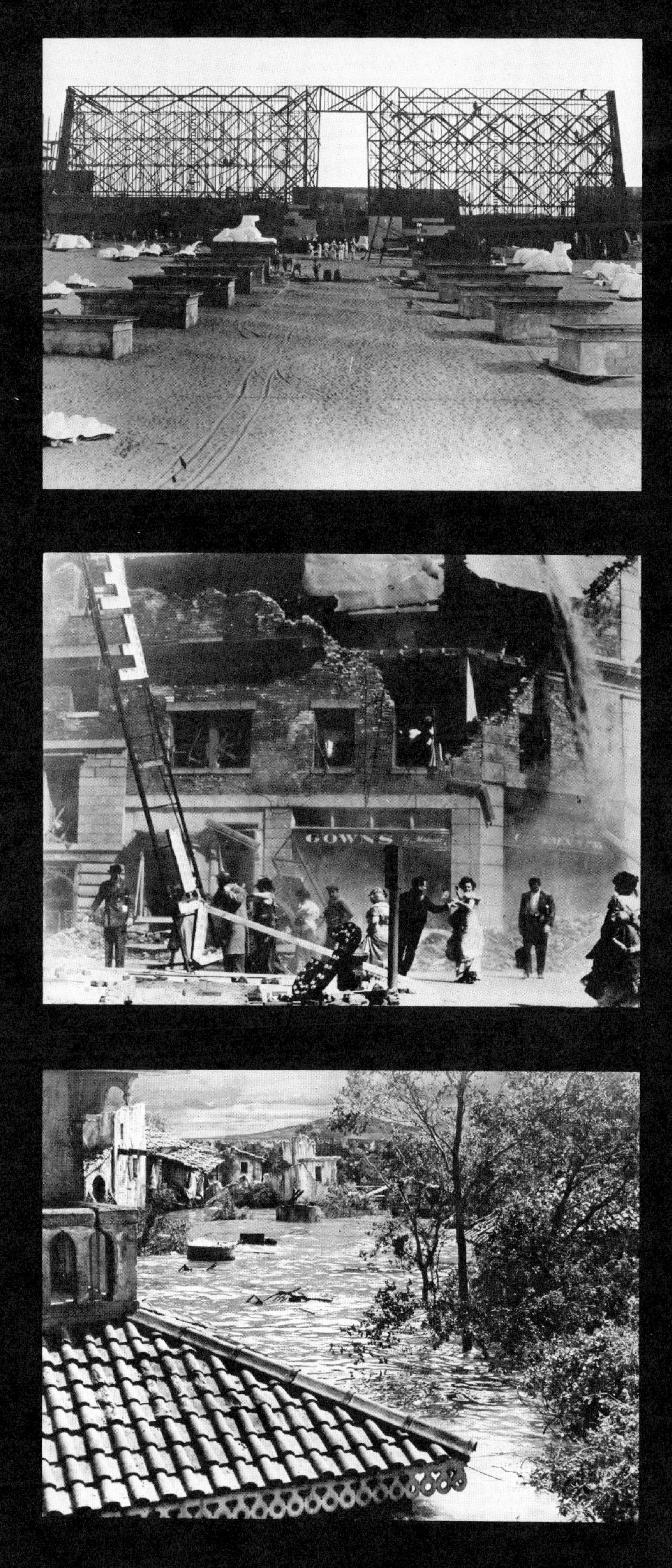

Top: The colossal city gates of Per-Ramses under construction for the 1923 version of De Mille's *The Ten Commandments.* *Center:* The cataclysmic earthquake engineered by A. Arnold Gillespie and James Basevi for *San Francisco.* *Bottom:* A simulated flood on an indoor set. From *The Rains Came.*

MGM's 1936 movie *San Francisco* was so convincing that some of the extras fled the studio in fear when the first tremors hit the set. They needn't have worried, however: unlike the original upheaval which devastated the city in 1906 (and unlike some of the accident-prone epics of the past, such as *Noah's Ark* and *Ben-Hur*), this cinematic cataclysm left nobody injured. This in itself was a tribute to the skill of Gillespie and Basevi, since the effects they designed for the movie did include a few potential hazards. Instead of relying on miniatures, they constructed full-scale buildings on top of hydraulically operated rocker platforms. During filming, the whole set shook in an authentic imitation of a massive quake: walls crumbled, houses toppled, bricks rained down, and balconies crashed.

One of the interesting features of any decent earthquake is the instant chasm: the giant crack which suddenly, and very inconveniently, appears where a nice paved street used to be. After consulting with some earthquake experts at the California Institute of Technology, Gillespie designed what he later described as a "simple, mechanical" effect to simulate the splitting of the earth. First he took some columns, which he'd found in a studio storage room, and laid them lengthwise on the floor. On top of them he built his set: a fake street with a hidden crack running down the center. Since the set wasn't secured to the columns, it could be moved back and forth with little trouble. Beneath the concealed crack was a large piece of sheet metal covered with rocks and dirt and mounted on a hydraulic ram. For the scene in which the street splits in half, Gillespie and his crew simply pulled the set apart and opened up the crack, at which point the hydraulic ram drove the rocks and dirt up through the break, creating the impression that the street had been ruptured by the violent upheaval of the earth.

After finishing his work with Gillespie on *San Francisco,* Basevi left MGM for Sam Goldwyn's company, Samuel Goldwyn Productions, and soon found himself involved with another historical romance, John Ford's *Hurricane,* whose climactic disaster easily deserves the title of the most fearsome rainstorm ever to take place entirely indoors. On a soundstage Basevi and his assistant, Stuart Heisler, constructed a 600-foot-long miniature set of an island village, with native huts, a church, palm trees, and a sandy beach leading down to a large tank made to look like a lagoon. For the tempest itself the two men used some standard special-effects equipment plus a great deal of water. Wind machines fed by fire hoses lashed the spray into a driving storm; wave machines churned the lagoon into a frenzy; and to top it all off, dump tanks unloaded a 2,000-gallon tidal wave onto the island. The resulting scene of destruction is a perfect example of the kind of epic waste Michael Wood describes as one of the central features of the cinematic spectacle, since Basevi spent four months and $150,000 to build the miniature set, only to spend another quarter of a million dollars to wash it away as soon as it was done.

Effects men don't aspire to extravagance; on the contrary, they take a great deal of pride in their ability to find low-priced ways of producing high-quality results. In the case of onscreen catastrophes, this means creating sensational scenes of destruction which aren't nearly as costly as they look. One of the most famous disaster scenes in the movies was not only relatively inexpensive to bring off but actually ended up saving the producer a great deal of money. This was the Burning of Atlanta sequence from David O. Selznick's *Gone With the Wind* (1939).

Originally Selznick had planned to shoot this sequence toward the end of the production, when the sets that had been built for the movie weren't needed anymore and could be conveniently destroyed. The problem was that the studio back lot on which he intended to construct his sets was already overcrowded with the remains of old movies, including the great wall from *King Kong,* the barrier which protected the natives of Skull Island from the fifty-foot ape. However, William Cameron Menzies, who designed the production for Selznick, came up with a solution that was sublime in its simplicity. Instead of shooting the conflagration last, he reasoned, why not shoot it *first,* using the old sets redecorated to look like Civil War Atlanta? In this way Selznick could kill two birds with one stone, getting one of the movie's major scenes out of the way, while at the same time clearing off the back lot without spending unnecessary time and money to dismantle the outworn sets.

After being disguised with some false fronts, the obsolete wooden structures were set on fire by Lee Zavitz, the movie's "powder man" (trade lingo for an effects expert who specializes in explosives and pyrotechnics). Zavitz installed two networks of pipes among the sets, one containing the fuel to feed the blaze, the other containing a mixture of water and extinguishing solution to control it. Selznick himself operated the small keyboard which regulated the flow of the liquid through the pipes.

Top: An early wind machine from the silent movie era. *Center:* A more up-to-date model, here being used to blow a boxful of artificial snow into a blizzard. *Bottom:* The Great Wall of Skull Island goes up in flames during the burning of Atlanta sequence from *Gone With the Wind.*

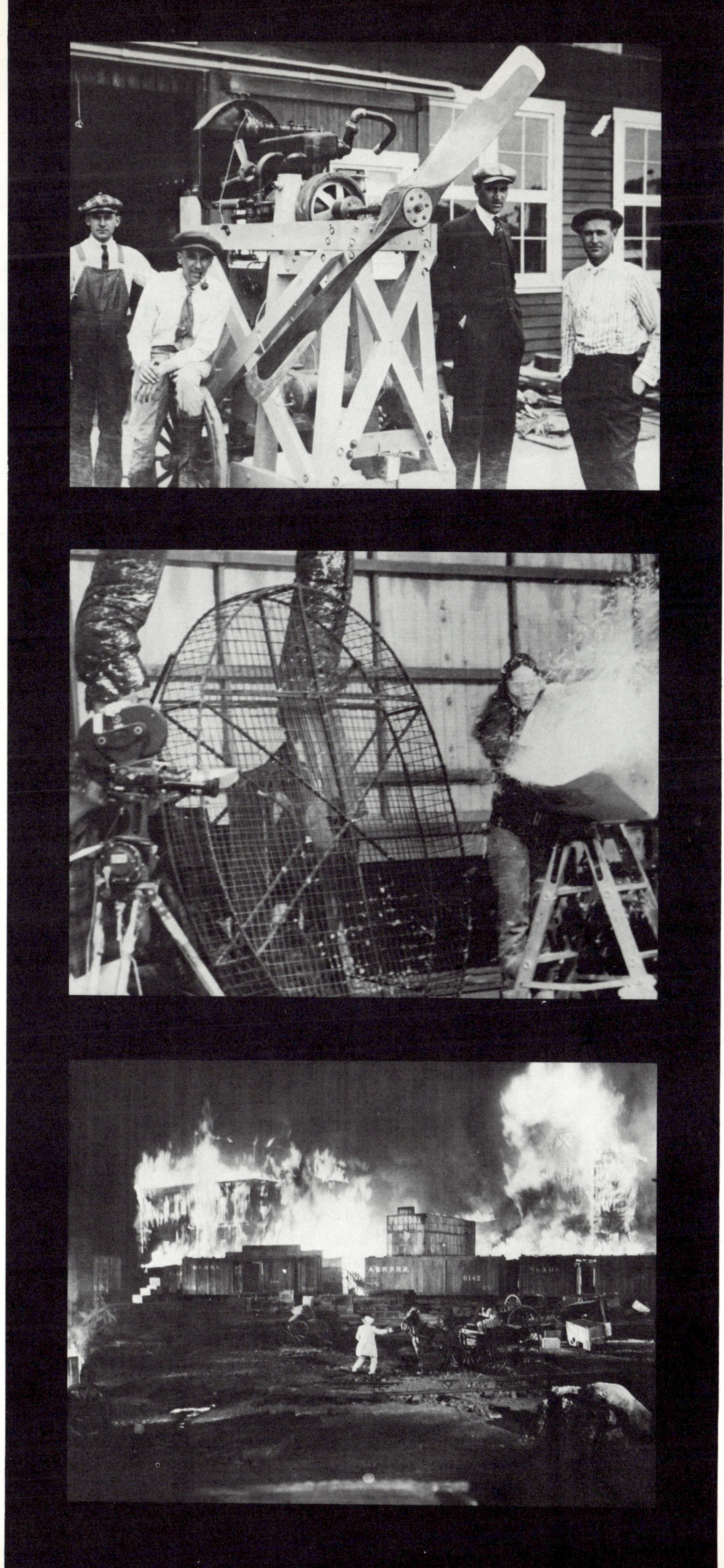

The resulting fire was the biggest ever filmed up to that time, with the set from *King Kong* collapsing in a particularly spectacular blaze. Contrary to popular belief, then, the great wall of Skull Island was not demolished by a rampaging giant gorilla; in reality it went up in flames when Sherman razed Atlanta.

Given the steady decline in the public's desire to see actors dressed in togas, it's no surprise that during the late thirties and forties De Mille also turned his attention from the ancient world and began making big-budget historical epics set in America's legendary past. These films included *The Plainsman* (1937), a colorful, highly romanticized Western about the exploits of Wild Bill Hickok (Gary Cooper), Buffalo Bill Cody (James Ellison), and Calamity Jane (Jean Arthur); *Union Pacific* (1939), a typically colossal account of the building of the transcontinental railroad; *Reap the Wild Wind* (1942), a deep-sea adventure yarn set in the Florida Keys in the early 1840s; and *Unconquered* (1947), a frontier saga about indentured servants in colonial America. Each of these films contains fancy effects, which were provided by Paramount's crack team of technicians headed by Gordon Jennings and a man named Farciot Edouart.

Edouart, whose specialty was rear projection, developed a device known as a *triple-head process projector,* which enabled him to beam a very intense background image onto a transparency screen set up behind the actors. This machine worked by combining three separate optical systems synchronized to cast three identical images onto the background screen at the same time. One projector was pointed straight at the screen, while the other two were located on either side of—and at right angles to—the first. Tilted mirrors positioned in front of these two lateral projectors bounced the beams onto the screen where the three scenes from the triple-head projector converged, producing an extremely bright image. Edouart's innovation made the background projection of moving scenes a workable method, and throughout the thirties and forties it was Hollywood's favorite method of bringing the outside world inside the walls of the studio.

The Plainsman, for example, contains an exciting scene in which a band of Indians charges into a river, only to be cut down by Wild Bill and a bunch of fellow sharpshooters, who are concealed behind a barrier on a little island in midstream. The Indians were filmed on location, galloping into a river and tumbling from their horses as they approached the island. Some weeks later, inside the studio, this scene was rear-projected onto an eight-by-twelve-foot transparency screen. On the floor in front of it lay Gary Cooper and the other actors, firing blanks at the footage of the oncoming Indians. The same method allowed Cooper to canoe over a waterfall in perfect safety in De Mille's *Unconquered.* This time Cooper, along with his costar, Paulette Goddard, crouched in a boat floating in a studio tank. Behind them, rear-projected onto a screen, was some dramatic footage of a raging wilderness river. While technicians churned up the water in the tank, the photographed river rushed along on the screen behind the two actors, creating the illusion that they were caught up in a deadly stretch of rapids drawing them inexorably to their doom.

Edouart's work earned him a number of Oscar nominations and Academy Awards, including one for his contributions to De Mille's *Reap the Wild Wind,* a prize he shared with Gordon Jennings. As impressive as this film's rear-projection scenes are, the most outstanding effect is the mechanical squid which attacks John Wayne and Ray Milland in the ruins of a sunken ship, lashing out with its thirty-foot tentacles until Milland dispatches the creature by driving a large cargo hook between its eyes. This malevolent mollusk, a precursor of the giant sea monster that Walt Disney's studio was to create twelve years later for *20,000 Leagues Under the Sea,* was made of red sponge rubber and brought to life by electric motors. Cables, activated by hydraulic pistons, ran through the length of its tentacles, whose movements were controlled by a twenty-four-button electric keyboard, which also operated the creature's large, repulsive eyes. The scene was shot underwater in Paramount's 800,000-gallon tank. De Mille actually went down along with his actors, directing them through telephone wires which ran from his deep-sea diving helmet to theirs.

Since these cinematic excursions into America's past were highly profitable and even garnered some respectful reviews, it took De Mille close to fifteen years to get back to making the kind of film his name is most closely associated with: the biblical extravaganza, "gingered up," as he put it in his autobiography, "with large infusions of sex and violence." *Samson and Delilah* (1949) turned out to be a rather lumbering spectacle, and even contained one glaring technical gaffe, a rarity in a film by De Mille, who, whatever his other weaknesses as a director, generally went to great lengths to get the best effects he could. The mistake can be

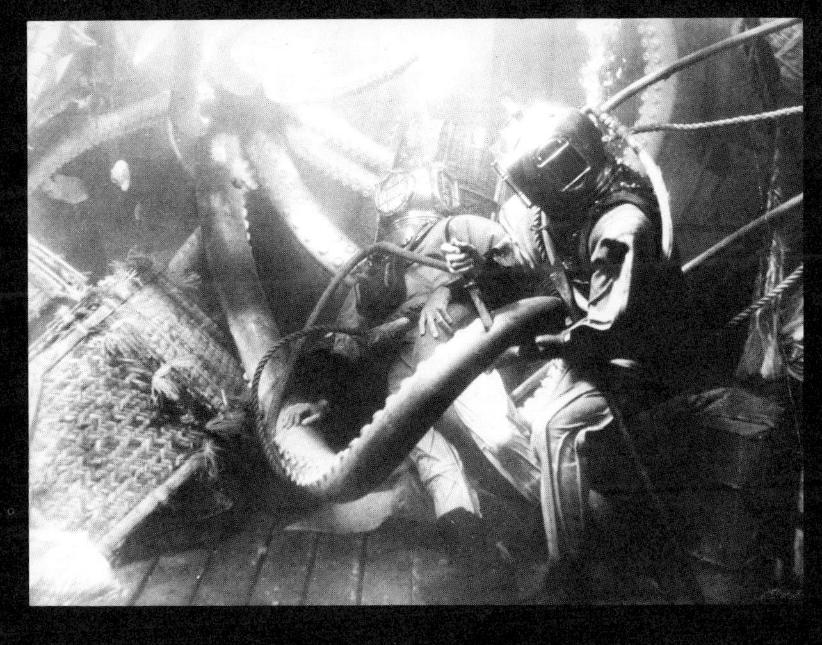

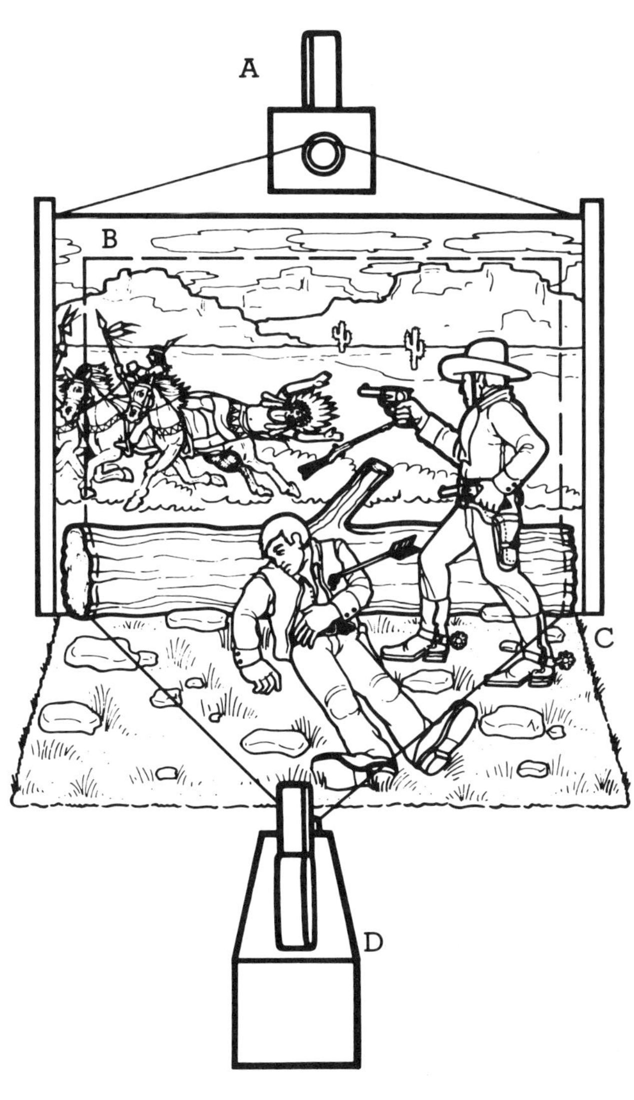

Top: John Wayne and Ray Milland do battle with a mechanical squid in De Mille's *Reap the Wild Wind.*
Bottom: REAR SCREEN PROJECTION: A typical studio setup for a rear screen projection shot. Projector (A) projects an image of Indians on horseback on a translucent rear projection screen (B). Actors in studio (C) interact with images on the screen and both are filmed by camera (D).

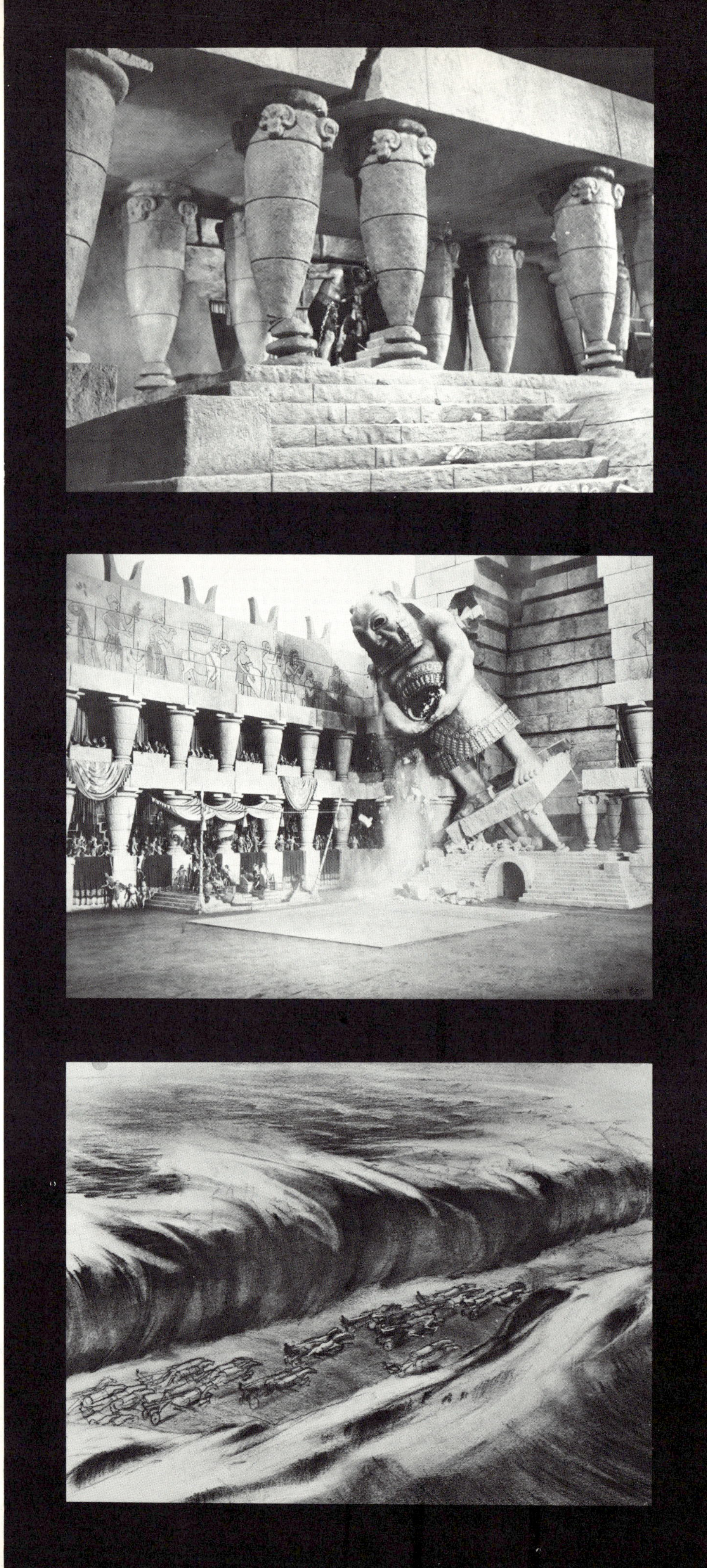

Top: Victor Mature as Samson strains against a pair of lightweight plaster pillars on a full-scale section of the Philistine temple. *Center:* The collapsing temple was actually an imposing forty-foot miniature. *Bottom:* A storyboard sketch for the 1956 remake of *The Ten Commandments.*

seen when Samson (Victor Mature) wipes out a platoon of Philistine soldiers with the jawbone of an ass. At one point in the battle, the biblical strongman grabs one of the soldiers, lifts him high overhead, and hurls him away. Unfortunately this thrilling moment is inexplicably marred by the clearly visible piano wires holding the soldier up in the air.

Another technical problem with the filming of *Samson and Delilah* was ultimately surmounted, but at great expense. When the mighty Samson pulled down the Philistine temple, its pillars were not actually made of stone. Mature was filmed on a full-size section of the temple, constructed on a sound stage. He was chained to a pair of fake, easily toppled columns, made of lightweight plaster disguised to look like carved stone. This part of the scene was then matted together with a very impressive model: a one-third scale, carefully researched replica of an ancient Minoan temple standing forty feet high. Built into its back wall was an imposing thirty-foot statue of the pagan god Dagon with a sacred fire blazing in its belly. Gordon Jennings had rigged the model with a small charge of dynamite. At the push of a button the explosives were to dislodge the statue from its base and simultaneously cause the rear wall of the temple to collapse, bringing down the house around the heads of Samson's tormentors. The great crash did not come off as planned, however: on the first take, the detonating device misfired, while on the second, the back wall failed to fall. It wasn't until the third try (by which time De Mille had already spent an extra $40,000 in delayed-production costs) that the director got the catastrophe he was looking for.

Partly because of De Mille's success with *Samson and Delilah,* biblical blockbusters came into fashion once again in the 1950s. Another reason for their renewed popularity was the threat posed by television. With more and more people staying home to watch TV and box office receipts dropping fast, Hollywood decided that the best way to lure people back into the theaters was by offering them the kind of pageantry and splendor they couldn't get from a tiny black-and-white screen. As a result, throughout the fifties and up until the mid-sixties, when the fad fizzled out, filmgoers were treated (or subjected, depending on one's point of view) to Hollywood's glamorized conception of ancient history in movies like *Quo Vadis* (1951), *The Robe* (1953), *Demetrius and the Gladiators* (1954), *The Egyptian* (1954), *King of Kings* (1960), *Spartacus* (1960), *The Fall of the Roman Empire* (1964), and *The Greatest Story Ever Told* (1965). Some of these were remakes of earlier spectacles, including two films which are among the best of the bunch and one which, if not the worst, was at any rate the most colossal failure: respectively, De Mille's 1956 retelling of *The Ten Commandments,* the climactic film of his career, William Wyler's widely admired version of *Ben-Hur* (1959), and Joseph Mankiewicz's *Cleopatra* (1963), one of Hollywood's most costly mistakes.

At the age of seventy-two, De Mille could spend as many millions as he wanted on a movie and was prepared to pour a fortune into his remake of *The Ten Commandments,* the film he conceived of as his crowning achievement, his gift to future generations of mankind. This time, the City of the Pharaohs would be built not in the desert outside Los Angeles, but on the site of the biblical story itself: on location in Egypt. Accordingly, on the sands of Beni Youseff, several miles southwest of Cairo, De Mille's company erected a massive replica of the city gates of Per-Ramses. Standing 107 feet high and spanning nearly a quarter of a mile, this awesome set was reportedly the largest single construction job since the building of the Suez Canal. For the stirring Exodus sequence, when Moses leads the Israelites out of Egypt, 12,000 extras and 15,000 animals surged down the great sphinx-lined avenue leading away from the city gates while De Mille directed the scene from the top of a crane, issuing his orders through a huge public-address system.

But even with the staggering financial and human resources he had at his command, De Mille was not, after all, as rich and powerful as a Pharaoh, nor could he manage the miracles recorded in the Book of Exodus, in spite of the nasty rumors that the role of God in the movie was going to be played by C.B. himself. Most of the film's visual highlights, therefore, were the product of special effects. These were the work of John Fulton, who became head of Paramount's effects department when Gordon Jennings died in 1953. Fulton, who had held the same post at Universal (where he'd been responsible for some of the best optical illusions ever put on screen, including the marvels of the 1933 film *The Invisible Man)* was held in exceptionally high regard by his colleagues. "Anything God can do," an associate of his once commented, "John can do better." His work on *The Ten Commandments,* however, proved that this remark, besides being slightly blasphemous, was also a little overstated, for as good as they are, the special effects he did for De Mille fall far short of perfection.

Early in the film, for instance, we see an army of slaves at work in the Pharaoh's "Treasure City," an awesome complex of sphinxes, temples, soaring gateways, and monumental statues raised by Prince Moses in honor of his adoptive father, Sethi I. Since no one—not even De Mille—could possibly afford to construct a set of such magnitude, it became the responsibility of Fulton and his special-effects team to create it by means of trick cinematography. The basic method was to combine live-action foregrounds with miniatures and matte paintings. For example, to show a mass of groaning slaves dragging a colossal statue of the Pharaoh through the city, De Mille's crew constructed a huge wooden platform on wheels. Hundreds of half-naked extras, playing the part of Hebrew slaves, strained at ropes attached to this platform as if it were weighed down by something enormously heavy, though in fact it was completely empty. The massive, multi-ton statue it supposedly carried was actually a miniature figure inserted into the scene by means of a traveling matte. Unfortunately the composite printing in this sequence is not as skillful as it should be, since the place where the miniature has been jigsawed into the picture is clearly visible as a black fringe surrounding the statue.

A similar problem mars the parting of the Red Sea, which was intended to be not merely the most breathtaking scene in the movie, but (to quote the characteristically modest claim of De Mille's publicists) "The Single Most Spectacular Sequence Ever Filmed!" It was certainly one of the most complicated composites ever created, costing a million dollars and including as many as twelve separately filmed elements assembled into a single image. The early parts of the scene, which show Moses and his followers trapped at the edge of the water while the Pharaoh's army approaches from behind, were filmed at the Red Sea itself. (Ironically, after going to a great deal of trouble to stage this sequence on location, De Mille ended up removing all the references to the Red Sea from the movie's script because, as he reports in his autobiography, the water was such a deep blue that he was afraid audiences would laugh if they heard it described as red.)

For the miracle itself, Fulton built an immense concrete tank in Hollywood. This structure was so huge that Paramount's back lot wasn't big enough to accommodate it, so De Mille simply tore down the wall separating Paramount from RKO and borrowed the extra space he needed. Technicians dumped 300,000 gallons of water down either side of this tank, creating two opposing waterfalls which crashed together in a tremendous wave. To show the water opening, the action was run in reverse. The wall of the sea, held back by God's power while the Israelites make their way to the opposite shore, was actually a large tilted ramp with a thin sheet of water cascading down it (a considerably more convincing illusion than the quaking mound of gelatin that appears in the original version). These water effects were then matted together with the on-location footage and various other visual elements, including miniature storm clouds (created from a special effects compound known as Britt Smoke), matte paintings of the floor of the sea, and additional live-action scenes shot on Paramount's sound stages.

The entire sequence took six months to complete. Even so, the job was a little rushed, partly because the movie had been booked into theaters for a certain date and De Mille was hurrying to meet the deadline, and partly because he had suffered a heart attack while shooting in Egypt and apparently felt his time was running out. In any case the results of this haste are visible onscreen in the clumsy patching-together of the different pieces of the sequence. Matte lines can be seen everywhere.

Other effects in the movie are also disappointing. Both the Pillar of Fire, which descends from the sky like a flaming tornado, and the Finger of God, which burns the Ten Commandments into the rock of Mount Sinai, are animated cartoons and leave a good deal to be desired as images of divine miracles. Unfortunately when it came to visualizing miracles, De Mille's imagination tended toward the mundane. In his autobiography, for instance, he describes how he solved the problem of showing "the Burning Bush as the Bible describes it, burning but not consumed." A friend of his, De Mille reports, "happened to see in a shop window a clock, shaped like a fireplace, with wavy light from a hidden source playing over small artificial logs." This nifty little decorator item corresponded perfectly to De Mille's conception of the biblical miracle, so he turned it over to Fulton, who, De Mille writes appreciatively, "immediately caught the effect I wanted and produced it on the screen." However, in spite of the movie's many flaws and some stiff competition from what many people consider a far better film (the science fiction classic *Forbidden Planet*), Fulton took that year's Oscar for special effects.

The updated versions of *Ben-Hur* (1959) and *Cleopatra* (1963) also won the Special Effects Oscar in the years they were released, though in both cases the originals were more impressive achievements. The full-size set of the Circus Maximus in the second *Ben-Hur,* for example, was very similar to the giant amphitheater built for the first; but instead of creating another elaborate hanging miniature for the upper galleries, A. Arnold Gillespie (who worked on both versions) relied on a relatively inexpensive matte painting. Moreover, the big sea battle was staged not with full-scale replicas of Roman ships and pirate raiders, but with remote-controlled models floating around a studio tank. The resulting scene isn't nearly as impressive, though this time no one drowned.

The Special Effects Oscar for *Cleopatra,* however, is completely baffling, since Hollywood producers at the time it was made were convinced that special effects "fakery" wasn't good enough anymore; they demanded the real thing in the apparent belief that the best way to bring in money at the box office was to spend as much as they could on their films. Movie mogul Samuel Bronston went broke reconstructing Rome on a Spanish plain for *The Fall of the Roman Empire* (1964) and sinking a real five-thousand-ton ship for *Circus World* (1964), while the producers of the 1962 remake of *Mutiny on the Bounty* built a completely seaworthy 118-foot replica of the H.M.S. *Bounty* and sailed it 7,327 miles to Tahiti so that audiences could catch a few glimpses of authentic Pacific Ocean water.

Such extravagance, however, was nothing compared to the excesses of Joseph Mankiewicz's $40,000,000 white elephant, *Cleopatra,* in which Elizabeth Taylor wore a crown of pure gold (cost: $6,500), floated around in a real, full-size royal barge (cost: $250,000), and held court in a sprawling reconstruction of the ancient capital of Alexandria covering twenty acres of land in Italy and decorated with palm trees flown in from Hollywood. For all the expense, however, the effects in the movie were not very impressive. The naval engagement at Actium, a pitched battle between two fleets of toy boats, was especially disappointing. The only plausible explanation for the Special Effects Oscar is that Twentieth Century-Fox spent a lot of money to convince Academy voters to give the movie as many Oscars as possible in a desperate attempt to drum up some business at the box office.

Spending money on increasingly gargantuan movies was not the only way producers tried to lure audiences away from TV and back into the theaters during the fifties and sixties. Besides visions of fabulous wealth, filmmakers offered audiences other kinds of sights, sounds, and even smells that the tube couldn't possibly provide. One of these was 3-D, or three-dimensional movies.

Stereoscopic pictures have been around for a long time. One film historian, Kenneth MacGowan, traces them as far back as 1600, to the 3-D drawings of Giambattista della Porta. In the late nineteenth century people could sit in their parlors and enjoy lifelike, three-dimensional scenes of faraway landscapes, viewed through hand-held stereoscopes (the Victorian equivalent of the modern-day Viewmaster toy), while 3-D motion pictures were attempted as long ago as 1922 when a process called Teleview was briefly shown in New York.

Three-dimensional photography, as MacGowan explains in his book *Behind the Screen,* "is based on the fact that each of our eyes sees a slightly different picture. The left eye sees a little more around the left side of an object and the right eye sees more around the right. To record these two different views, 3-D takes two shots of each scene at the same moment. The lens of one camera photographs what the right eye would see. The other, about two and a half inches to the left, takes the scene from the point of view of the other eye." These two separate images are recorded on the same strip of film and projected onto the screen in a jumble. The viewer, however, wears special glasses that unscramble the two pictures. Though some early processes used glasses with different colored lenses (one green, one red), the later, preferred method employed the cheap polaroid filters pioneered by Edwin H. Land.

Following page:
The effect of 3-D is demonstrated in this publicity still from *The Creature from the Black Lagoon.*

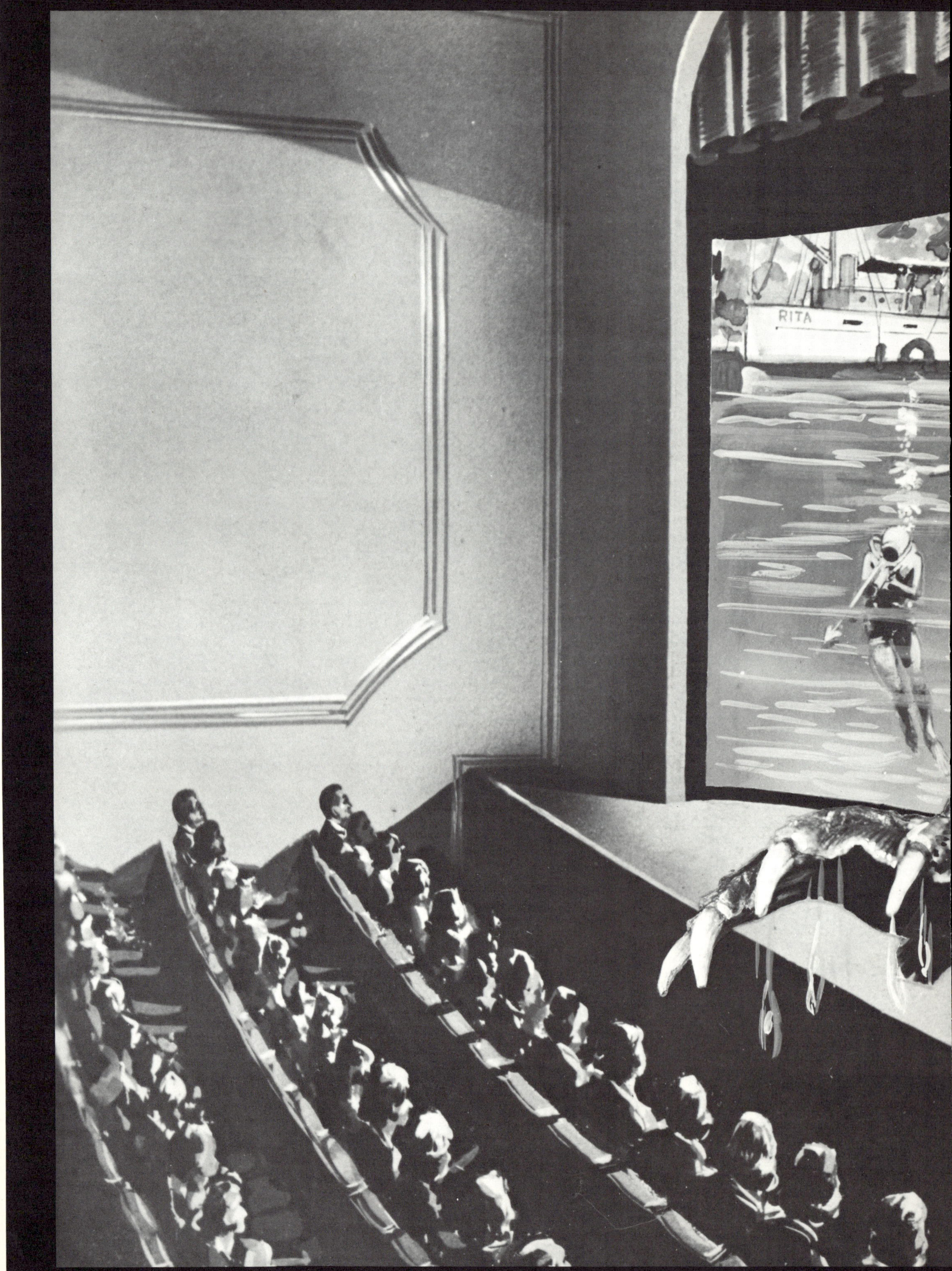
RITA

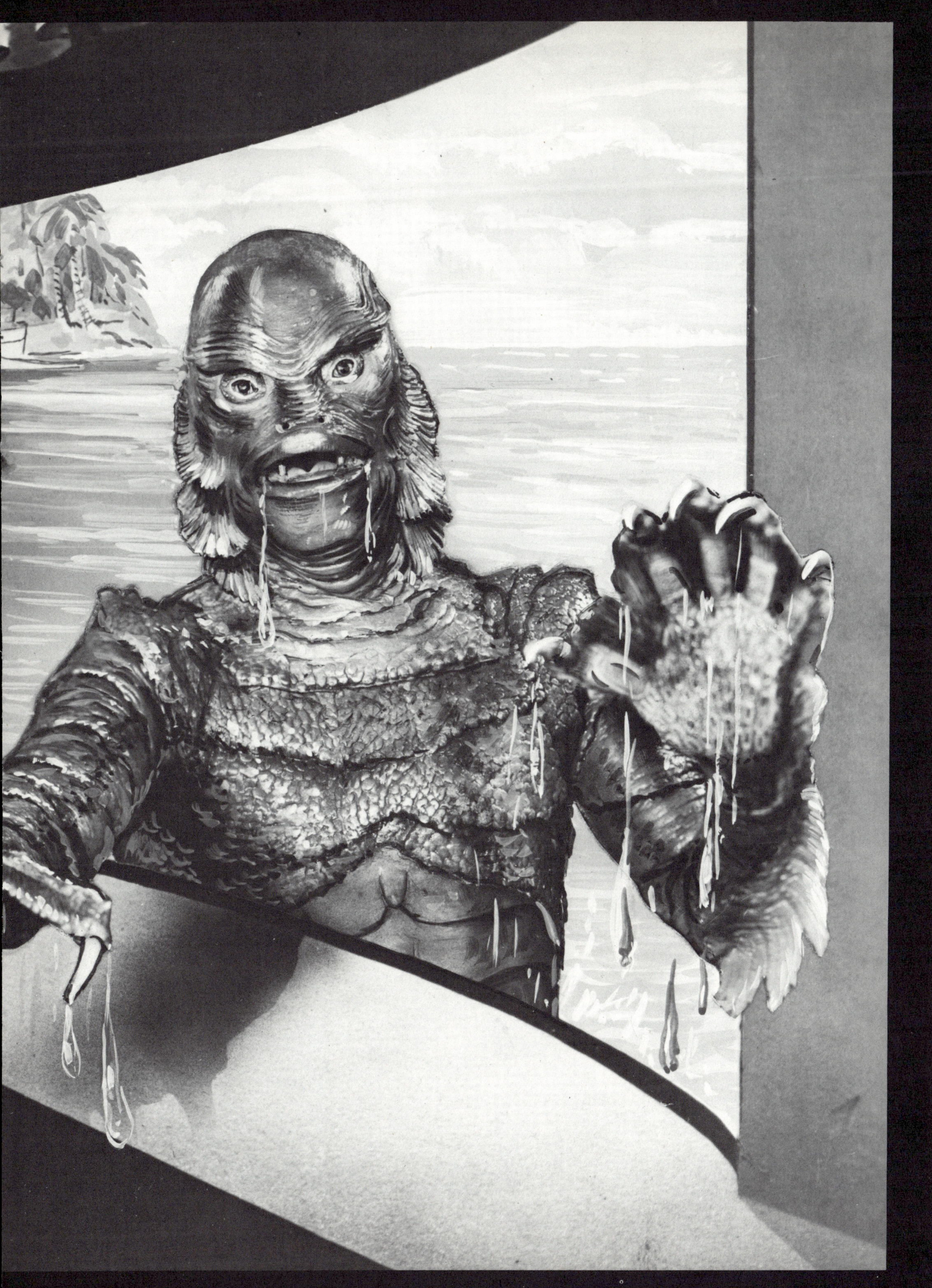

The first feature-length 3-D movie was *Bwana Devil,* released on November 27, 1952. An African adventure with rampaging lions leaping right off the screen, it became an instant sensation, and moviemakers fell all over themselves in their rush to fill the screen with stereoscopic films. In 1953 and 1954, no less than twenty-eight 3-D pictures were released, including *House of Wax, The Creature from the Black Lagoon, Murders in the Rue Morgue, Kiss Me Kate,* and *Fort Ti.* It didn't take very long, however, for serious problems to arise. Theater owners weren't crazy about the process because it required expensive alterations in their equipment. And when a fair number of filmgoers started leaving the theaters with splitting headaches, they suddenly lost interest too. Moreover, there are only so many times the average person can get a thrill from having a lion/arrow/knife/spear fly directly at his face. By 1954 the 3-D craze was dead, and several movies that were shot in the process (including Alfred Hitchcock's *Dial M for Murder*) were released as ordinary, two-dimensional films (or "flatties," as they were called in the trade).

Another gimmick which, thankfully, enjoyed an even shorter vogue than 3-D was the movie that came equipped with its own odors. In 1959 the American exhibitor Walter Reade, Jr. debuted the world's first "smellie," a China travelogue called *Behind the Great Wall,* which used a process called "AromaRama" to blow various Oriental odors through the theater's air conditioning system. Shortly thereafter, Mike Todd followed with his own slightly more complicated method named "Smell-O-Vision." Neither Todd's film (*Scent of Mystery*) nor Reade's, however, sent audiences stampeding to their local theaters.

If Smell-O-Vision was meant to be the mustard gas in Hollywood's war on television, Cinerama was its heavy artillery, its Big Bertha. The brainchild of a man named Fred Waller, who began researching the process in 1938, Cinerama essentially consisted of a huge wraparound screen—thirty-two times larger than a normal one—and triple projectors, each of which provided one third of the picture. The result was a kind of cinematic triptych: a movie composed of three side-by-side sections which, in theory at least, blended into a single gigantic image.
(In practice, early Cinerama movies were often marred by visible seams running down the right and left sides of the center picture.) By covering most of the viewer's area of sight, including his peripheral vision, Cinerama created a striking sensation of being inside the movie. Moreover, a line of five behind-the-screen stereo speakers produced a powerful wall of sound.

The first feature-length film made in the process, *This Is Cinerama* (1952), was a monumental travelogue which carried viewers along on a series of breathtaking rides, including a plunge down a roller coaster and an airplane trip over the Rocky Mountains. The movie was a box office smash, running for 122 weeks on Broadway. The next two Cinerama productions, *Cinerama Holiday,* (1955) and *Seven Wonders of the World,* (1956) offered audiences more of the same. By the early 1960s filmmakers were using the process to tell stories. Since Cinerama's super-screen format seemed tailor-made for epics, the movies which followed were all kingsize versions of the usual genres, including Western (*How The West Was Won,* 1962), comedy (*It's a Mad, Mad, Mad, Mad World,* 1963), and Sunday-school spectacle (*The Greatest Story Ever Told,* 1964). Unfortunately none of these films was very good, and though Stanley Kubrick made highly effective use of Cinerama in his science fiction classic *2001: A Space Odyssey* (1968), it wasn't long before this gimmick, too, passed from the scene.

For a while, in fact, it looked as though the motion picture epic itself, which always had something of the brontosaurus about it anyway, was doomed to go the way of the dinosaur. But the human hunger for spectacle is too deeply rooted to disappear overnight. In the early 1970s a new type of blockbuster became enormously popular, one with several significant differences from the old De Mille kind. For one thing the new brand of spectacle was set in today's world, not the world of Moses or Christ. More important, the "great crash" was no longer one of the highlights of the movie; it *was* the movie, the reason for its having been made. Catastrophe came not, as it did in *The Ten Commandments* and *Samson and Delilah,* from a wrathful God, but from an angry Mother Nature. Instead of leading the children of Israel between the parted walls of a raging sea, Charlton Heston now found himself guiding a group of survivors through the crumbling walls of a Los Angeles skyscraper. Filmmakers began turning disaster into box office gold, while special-effects men had a field day turning technology into high-gloss disaster.

The Tower of Babel from John Huston's 1966 movie *The Bible.* The set was constructed up to the midpoint of the second tier. The rest is a matte painting.

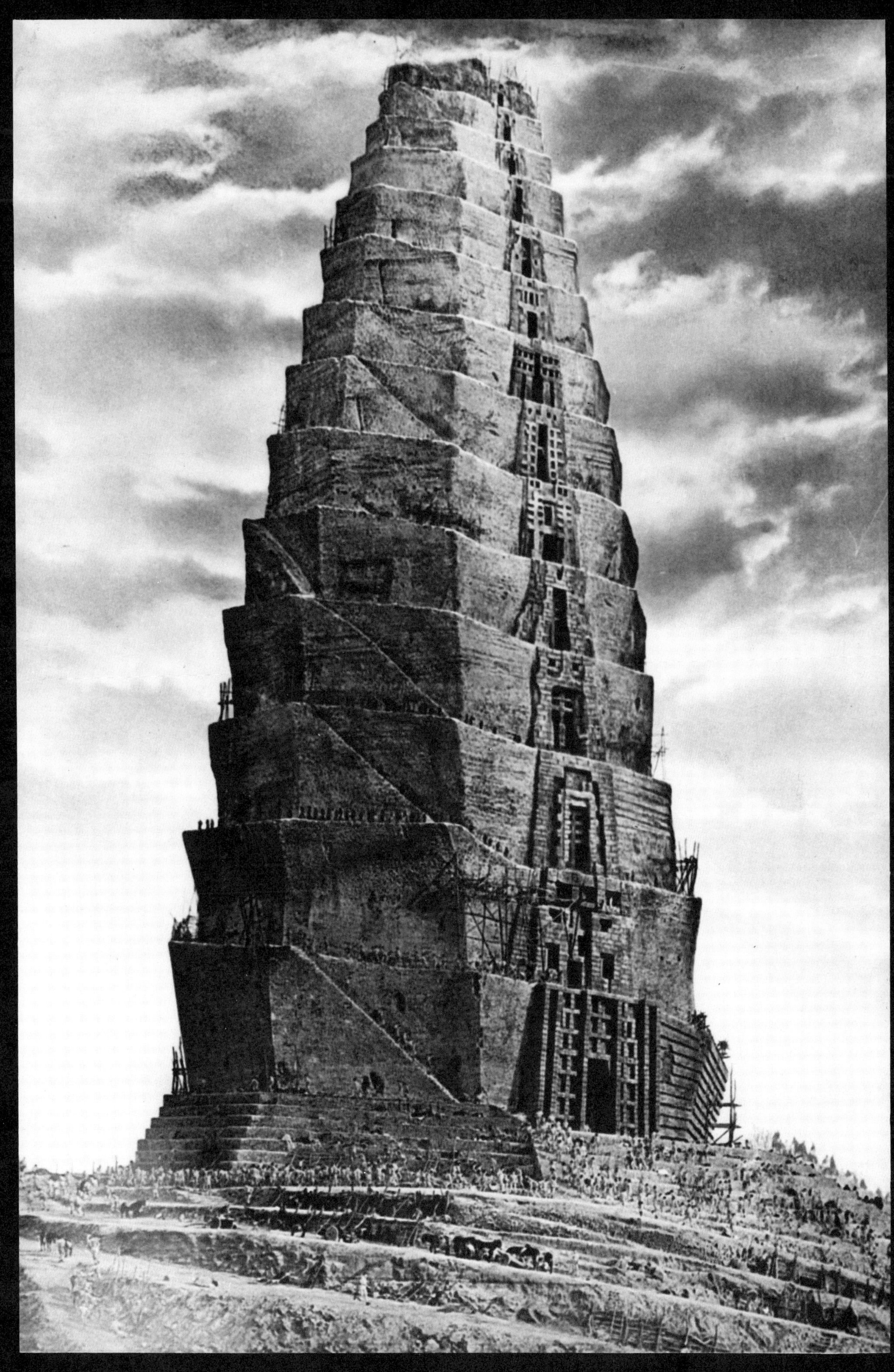

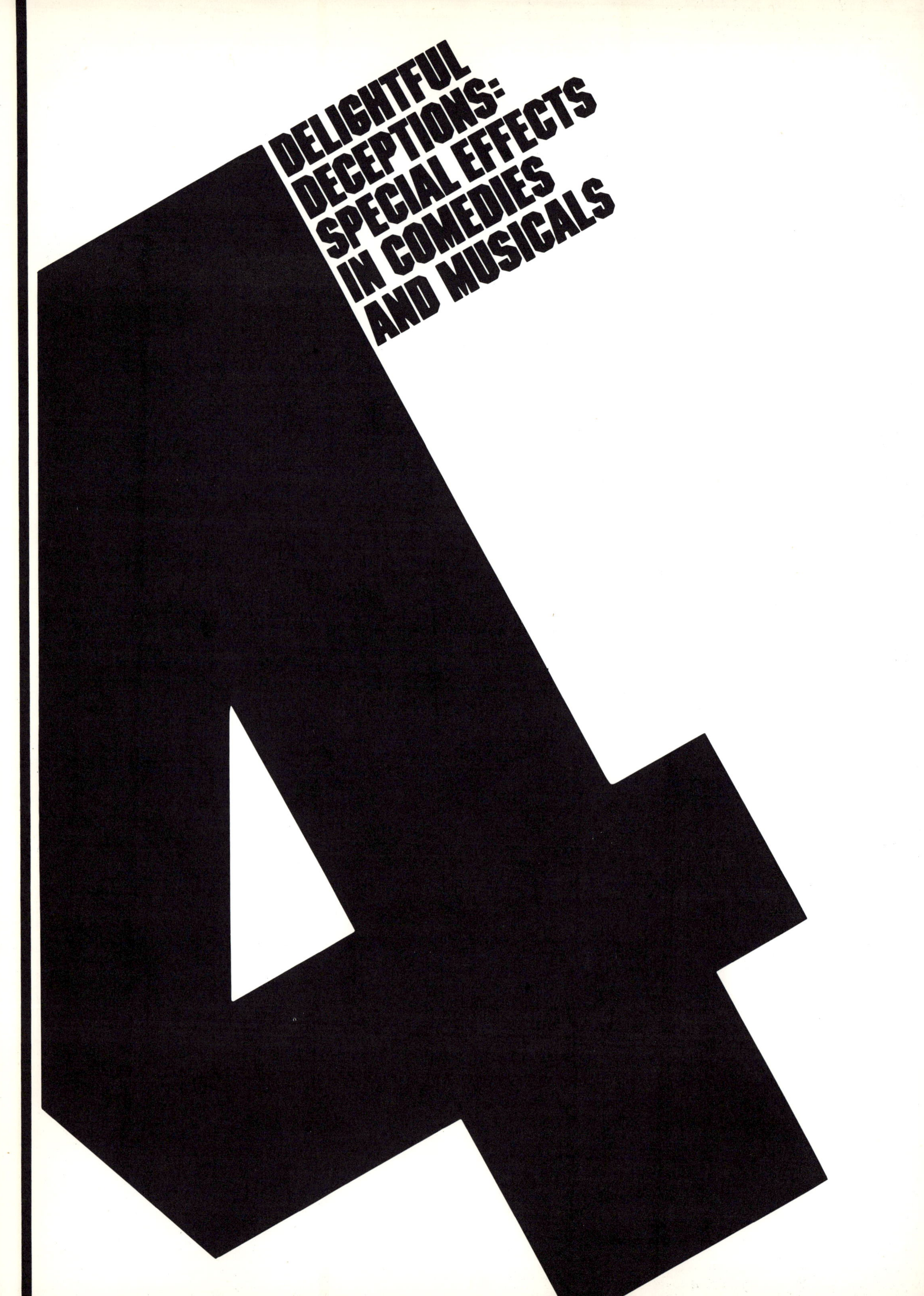

4 DELIGHTFUL DECEPTIONS: SPECIAL EFFECTS IN COMEDIES AND MUSICALS

Though special-effects men are often required to conjure up the illusion of death and destruction, there is a much lighter, happier side to their work. Since the very start of the movies, when Méliès used his own head to form a chorus of singing notes, comedies and musicals have relied on outrageous visual gags to delight filmgoers. In their tireless search for the ultimate gag or showstopper, the screen's greatest funnymen and dancers have inspired effects men to produce a host of delightful impossibilities. Buster Keaton conceives a scene in which his character, a motion-picture projectionist who dozes off during a show, steps outside his own body, strolls down the aisle, and walks right into the movie unreeling on screen. Fred Astaire plays a man so irrepressibly happy that he can't restrain himself from dancing straight up the wall and doing an upside-down soft-shoe across the ceiling. It is the responsibility of the special-effects man to make such amazing stunts come true.

Before the advent of the talkies the movies were the ideal showcase for the crazy antics of vaudeville comedians, whose slam-bang style of slapstick was tailor-made for the silent screen. The most outlandish stunts—gags that would have been unthinkable on the music hall stage—were now within the realm of possibility. If the human mind could dream it up, the effects man could bring it off.

In Hollywood's infant years Mack Sennett justifiably proclaimed himself the "King of Comedy." In the 1910s and 1920s he introduced the world to such unknowns as Roscoe "Fatty" Arbuckle, Ben Turpin, Harry Langdon, and Charlie Chaplin, and supplied theaters with a steady stream of raucous comedies that reveled in mayhem and destruction. These knockabout farces featured a broad range of effects, from rudimentary props (breakaway bottles, chairs, and walls) to complex photographic composites, all precisely synchronized with the breakneck comedy created by Sennett's stable of madcap players.

Sennett's most famous slapstick vehicles were the furious, knock-down-drag-out chases in which his unbelievably inept Keystone Kops would bring down entire city blocks. A favorite comic effect in these films was the wildly skidding car careening down the street and scattering its passengers all along the pavement. To make the ride suitably suicidal, the street (generally a Los Angeles intersection used without any official permission from the city) was coated with liquid soap, and stunt driver Del Lord would race across and spin about with the kind of reckless disregard for personal safety required of Sennett's employees. Any actor starting out with Sennett's company was tested for stamina and talent by working first as one of the Kops. Sometimes, as part of his initiation, he was required to be dragged along the street on his stomach by a speeding car. Actually the stunt wasn't quite as painful as it looks on screen, since a special prop and photographic effect were used to create the illusion. The actor would lie flat on his stomach on top of a small square skateboard and the car was filmed in fast motion, usually at eight or twelve frames per second to simulate speed. To give the scene a more frenetic look, every third or fourth frame was cut out.

Another of Sennett's trademarks was the seemingly endless parade of Kops tumbling out of the paddy wagon. The key to this illusion was stop-motion. The camera filmed the first bunch of Kops rolling chaotically out of the wagon and then the filming was stopped, by which time the first actors had moved out of camera range and were ready to be used again. They then went back inside the wagon to the end of the line, the camera was started again, and the Kops continued as before. Whenever more actors were needed to scramble out of the wagon, the stop-motion process was repeated.

In the early days of filmmaking there was no unionization and specialization; the responsibility for the special effects usually landed in the lap of the cameraman and director. For seven years Sennett's crack cinematographer was Fred Jackman, who, like many other Keystoners, moved on to greater successes: first to the Hal Roach Studio (Sennett's nearest rival), then to Warner Brothers, where he worked for ten years before leaving in the late thirties to found an independent special-effects company. While Jackman was with Sennett he worked with stunts, mechanical effects, and composites. A shot of a pack of comics caught up in a brawl along telephone wires high above a city street was a combination of the stunt work filmed on wires at the studio with a net underneath and the crowded street matted in below. Another artificially created thrill-gag was a distant shot of a horse and rider leaping from one sheer cliff to another, traversing a hundred-foot drop. The shot was actually made up of eight matched exposures. Working in-the-camera, he filmed the horse jumping off one rock in the upper half of the frame, while the rest of the scene was covered with a matte. "The rock from which the horse begins his jump is that of El Capitan," Jackman later explained in *American Cinematographer* (December

1922); "the rock on which he lands is that which adjoins Vernal Falls in Yosemite Valley, several miles away." The same procedure was used to add the steep cliffs, waterfalls, and other landscape details that make the scene look a good deal more dramatic than it actually was.

Not every silent comedian made extensive use of special effects. Some performed their most startling gags without any sort of trickery, most notably Harold Lloyd, who relied instead on daredevil acrobatics. When we watch a wide-eyed Lloyd in *Safety Last* (1923) hanging by his fingertips from a seven-story ledge, what we're seeing is not an illusion but a lot of nerve. Other silent comedians achieved their results by combining breathtaking physical stunts with ingenious photographic tricks. No one did this better than Buster Keaton, who, while just as fearless as Lloyd, also made brilliant use of special effects.

In his earliest vehicles Keaton himself supervised the effects, usually of the broad Sennett variety. An accident involving one of his most elaborate props, a speeded-up escalator he designed himself for his 1921 comic short *The Electric House,* temporarily disabled him with a broken ankle and forced him to tone down his stunts on his next picture. In the place of his usual gymnastics he concentrated on multiple exposures. The result was one of the great trick comedies of all time, *The Playhouse* (1921).

In this hilarious, dreamlike short, Keaton buys a ticket to a small-town theater, only to find, when he takes his seat, that everybody else in the place is an exact duplicate of himself. The people in the audience, the musicians in the orchestra, the stagehand, the nine-man minstrel show—all of them are Buster. For most of the audience, cutout photographs of the star were set up in the seats, but for the other scenes, to get all the different Keatons to perform with each other in the same frame, multiple exposure was used. The most dazzling and delightful illusion is the minstrel show: nine Busters in blackface perform onstage at once. The trick was done with a special lens mask designed by the comedian himself. The mask had nine separate shutters arranged from left to right that could be opened one at a time. Keaton would perform at one end of the stage in the first of his roles: the interlocutor, for instance. One of the shutters would be opened to record him on a section of the film. The film would then be rewound. Keaton would then move to the right a bit, assuming the part of Mr. Bones. The next shutter would be opened, Keaton's performance recorded, and so on, for a total of nine separate exposures. It was, of course, complicated for Keaton to coordinate nine individual performances; the task of the cameraman, Elgin Lessley, was just as tricky, since it was up to him to hand-crank the camera at exactly the same rate of speed nine separate times.

Keaton's ankle injury not only was responsible for the conception of *The Playhouse,* but also prompted an important career decision. Since the accident occurred while the comedian was fiddling with a complicated trick prop, he now saw the wisdom of hiring a technician to assist him in special-effects work. Starting with his next two-reeler, a catastrophe comedy called *The Boat* (1921), a brilliant mechanic-designer named Fred Gabourie received credit as technical director. The execution of his first major effect involving a prop in *The Boat* turned out to be as much of a slapstick comedy as the film itself. When the boat was supposed to sink, it refused to go under completely. Gabourie and Keaton tried a 1,600 pound pig-iron weight, a breakaway stern, and a series of holes bored into the wood. For all their efforts the boat did everything except sink on cue. Eventually they had to set up an underwater pulley system hooked up to an offscreen tug and then drag the thing down.

One of Keaton's funniest films, *Sherlock Jr.,* was also his most fanciful and technically ambitious picture. Playing a hapless movie projectionist, Keaton falls asleep on the job, and as his mind drifts, his transparent dream self, double-exposed on the film, leaves his body and strolls down the aisle to the front of the theater. (Later this device would be used by other screen comedians, most recently Woody Allen, who includes a scene in *Annie Hall* [1977] in which Diane Keaton steps outside her own body to regard, with complete detachment, herself and her lover in bed.) When the characters in the feature take the form of the people in his own real-life crisis, Keaton strides up into the movie's image to set things right. What follows is a hilarious interaction between Buster and the constantly changing picture on the screen. First he is kicked off the screen and back into the audience by the villain. He scrambles back only to find himself in front of a closed door. Suddenly the scene cuts again, this time to a garden, where Buster decides to sit down on a chair. In the middle of his sitting motion the background changes and he flops down into a bustling commercial street. The settings switch several times in this fashion, climaxing when

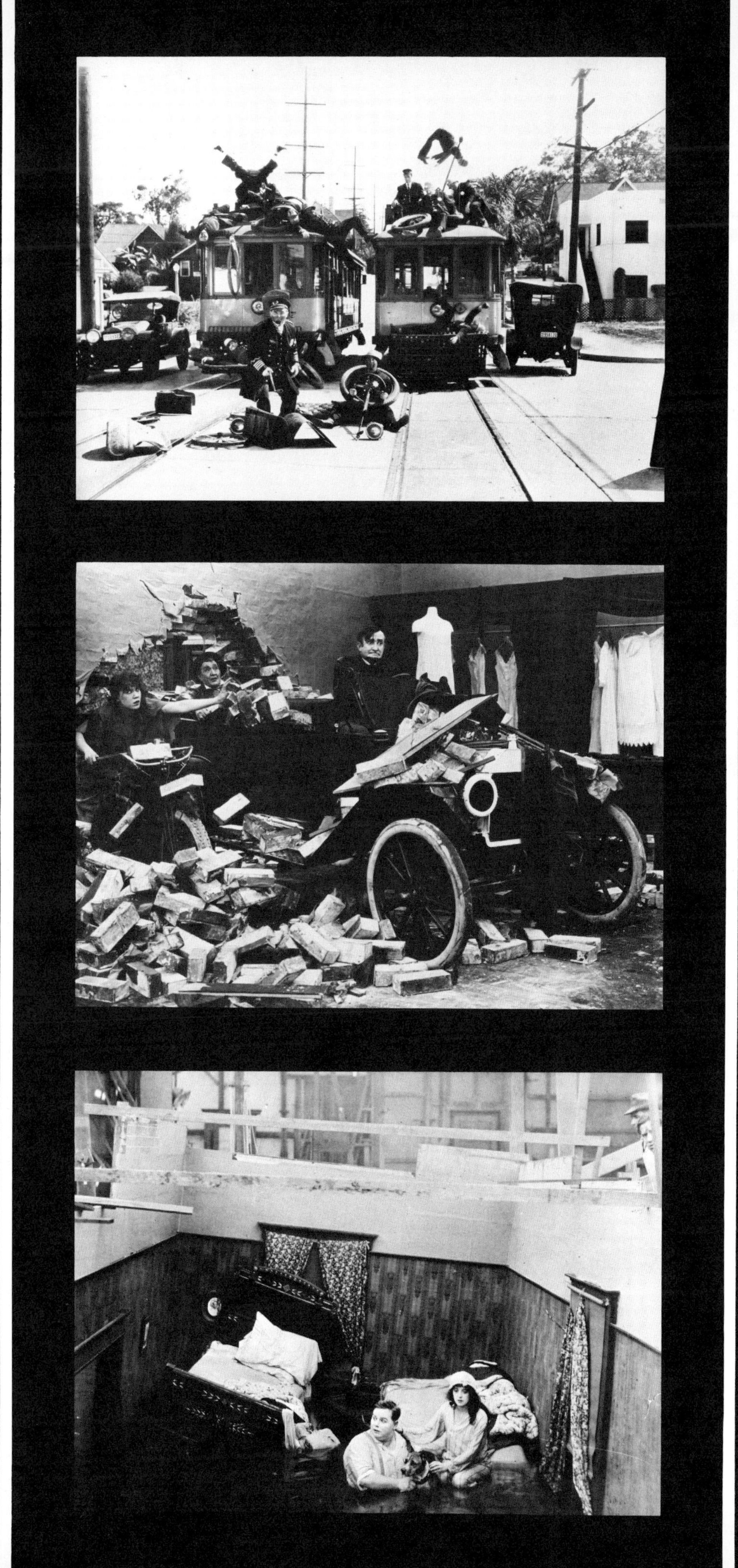

Top: Mack Sennett's wildly destructive slapsticks relied heavily on daredevil stunts and mechanical effects, such as telephone poles wired to collapse on cue.
Center: Breakaway props were a staple of the Keystone comedies. The wall through which Charlie Murray drove his Ford in this 1917 short was composed of lightweight bricks held together by wallpaper.
Bottom: In *Fatty and Mabel Adrift,* Fatty Arbuckle and Mabel Normand awaken one morning to find their little cottage floating out to sea. In reality the two stars remained safe (if somewhat soggy) on a flooded set of their bedroom.

Top: Ben Turpin's plight in this shot is less desperate than it seems, since he is being held in the air, not by the hands around his neck but by "invisible" piano wire. *Center:* Buster Keaton's car suffers a minor breakdown in *The Three Ages.* *Bottom:* Keaton (on the far right) about to step inside the fake movie screen in *Sherlock Junior.*

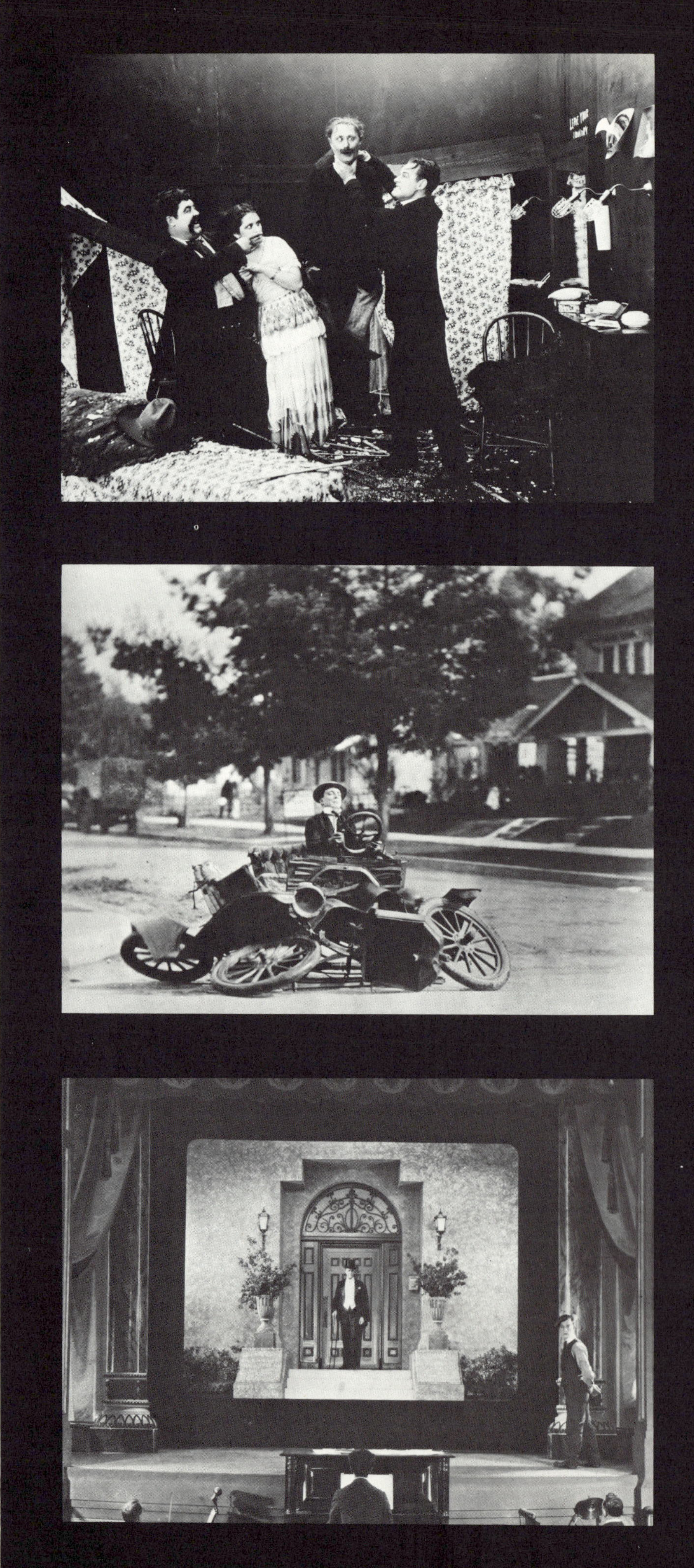

Through the looking glass: a nattily dressed Keaton checks himself out in a full-length mirror, then strolls right through it. From *Sherlock Junior.*

Keaton finds himself on an island. He dives off into a body of water, lands head first in a snowbank, then leans against a nearby tree and topples to the ground when the locale changes into the garden once more.

When *Sherlock Jr.* was released in 1924, this sequence mystified not only the moviegoing public but Hollywood technicians as well. In actuality the camera trick that made the scene possible was one of the most fundamental: stop-motion. Once again, as in *The Playhouse,* it was great precision that made the scene seem miraculous. The "movie screen" was actually a specially constructed stage. The people appearing in the movie were, in reality, actors standing on this stage. The special set appeared to be exactly like a screen because of the bright lighting it received, contrasted with the murky lighting of the rest of the theater. When the moment came for the background to switch, both the camera and Keaton stopped. Before the setting was changed, the comic's position was measured from two sides to pinpoint his spot in relation to the camera, and his height was measured with a surveyor's instrument. With these measurements his crew could place Keaton in precisely the same spot when they resumed shooting. In practice it worked like this: Keaton begins his dive into the water but stops just before leaving the ground, his crew takes the measure so that he can step away, the snowscape is substituted for the rocky island, Keaton resumes his position, and when the camera rolls again, he takes off into the snow.

Later on, during the climactic chase that takes place in Keaton's dream, Buster runs for his life with the villains of the movie in hot pursuit. Beside a barn he comes to a screeching halt, apparently with no place to run. He then sees Gillette, his faithful valet, standing with his back to the barn, dressed as a woman peddler holding a box of merchandise. In one take we see Keaton bolt for his friend, take a running dive into the raised lid of the box, pass straight through Gillette's body, and disappear inside the building. This staggering trick was a pure physical effect enacted before the camera without any photographic sleight-of-hand.

Actually Gillette was not standing with his back to the barn: he was lying on a chest-high horizontal support inside the building. A hole, hidden from the camera, allowed his head, shoulders, and arms to stick out the side of the barn while the rest of his body was concealed within. The peddler's dress hung down from his shoulders and arms and acted like a curtain, with dummy ankles and feet completing the illusion. The empty dress served to conceal a small trapdoor built into the wall of the barn. The lid on the box of merchandise was hinged and lined up with the trapdoor behind it. Though the scene seems to show Keaton passing through three solid objects (a box lid, a human body, and a barn wall) he was really diving through a hinged flap, an empty dress, and a trapdoor.

Spectacular mechanical effects are the star of the finale of *Steamboat Bill Jr.* (1928), in which Buster takes on an earthshaking tornado. While he dozes unawares in a hospital cot, the entire building around him flies into the air and Buster himself, still lying in bed, is propelled through the town. Keaton hops out of the bed, which is instantly swept away. Then comes the scene that is not only the visual highlight of the movie but one of the most daring prop effects ever put on film. We see Keaton standing in front of a building that is being battered by the vicious wind. The whole front section of the structure is torn away, teeters, and falls, with Keaton directly underneath. The front of the building comes crashing down while the comic never so much as flinches: an open window has miraculously come down around him and he is unscathed. The action was clearly photographed in one take. In this case timing and precision were necessary not only to make the scene funny, but to keep the leading man intact. Keaton later explained in an interview in *Sight and Sound* (winter 1965-66) how this astonishing feat was performed:

First I had them build the framework of this building and make sure that the hinges were all firm and solid. It was a building with a tall V-shaped roof, so that we could make this window up in the roof exceptionally high. An average second story window would be 12 feet, but we're up about 18 feet. Then you lay this framework down on the ground, and build the window round me. We built the window so that I had a clearance of two inches on each shoulder, and the top missed my head by two inches and the bottom my heels by two inches. We mark that ground out and drive big nails where my two heels are going to be. Then you put that house back up in position while they finish building it. They put the front on, painted it, and made the jagged edge where it tore away from the main building; and then we went in and fixed the

Oversize sets turned Laurel and Hardy into a pair of sweet little cherubs in *Brats.*

Following page: The spectral Kirbys (Constance Bennett and Cary Grant) lend Cosmo Topper (Roland Young) a helping hand in *Topper.*

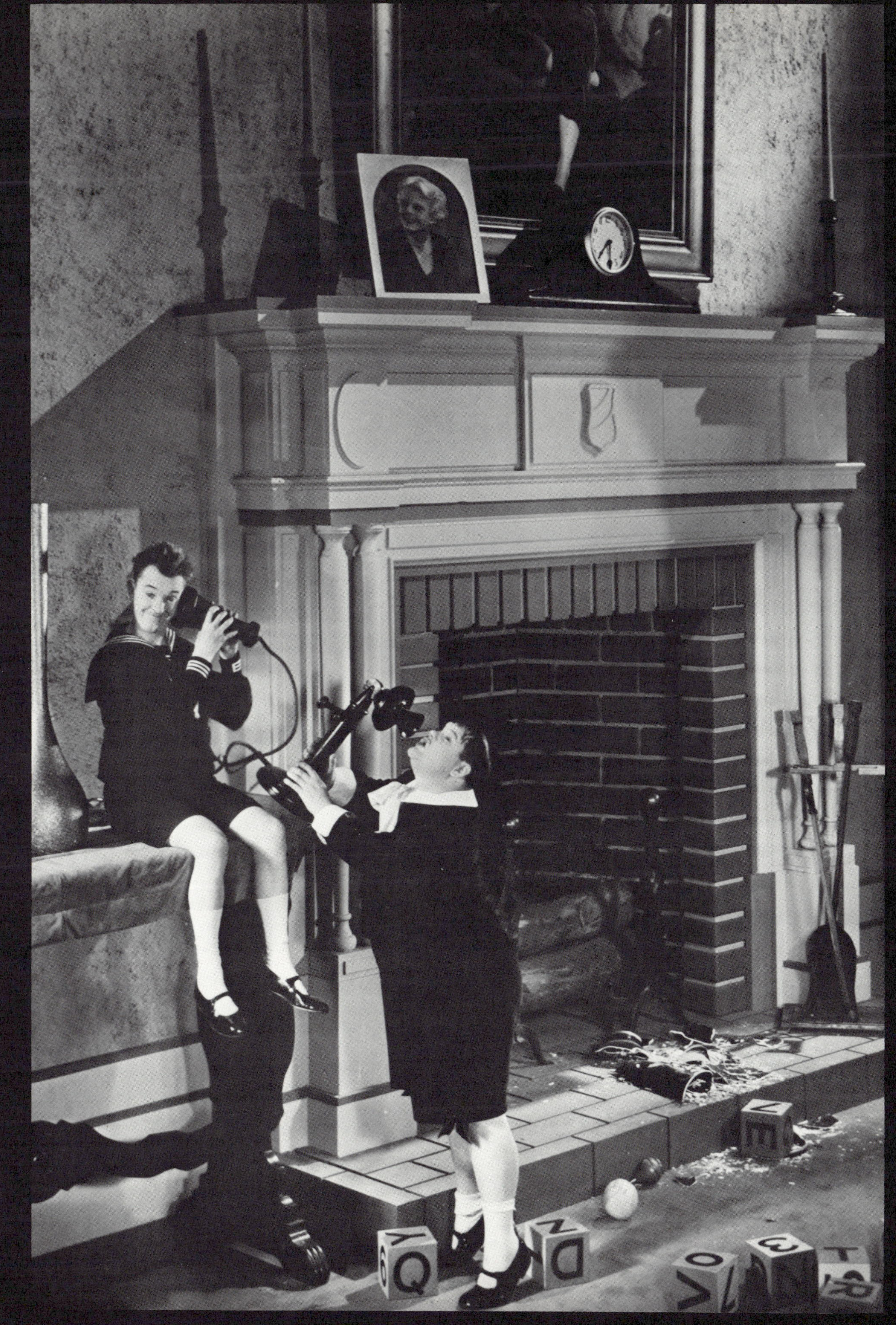

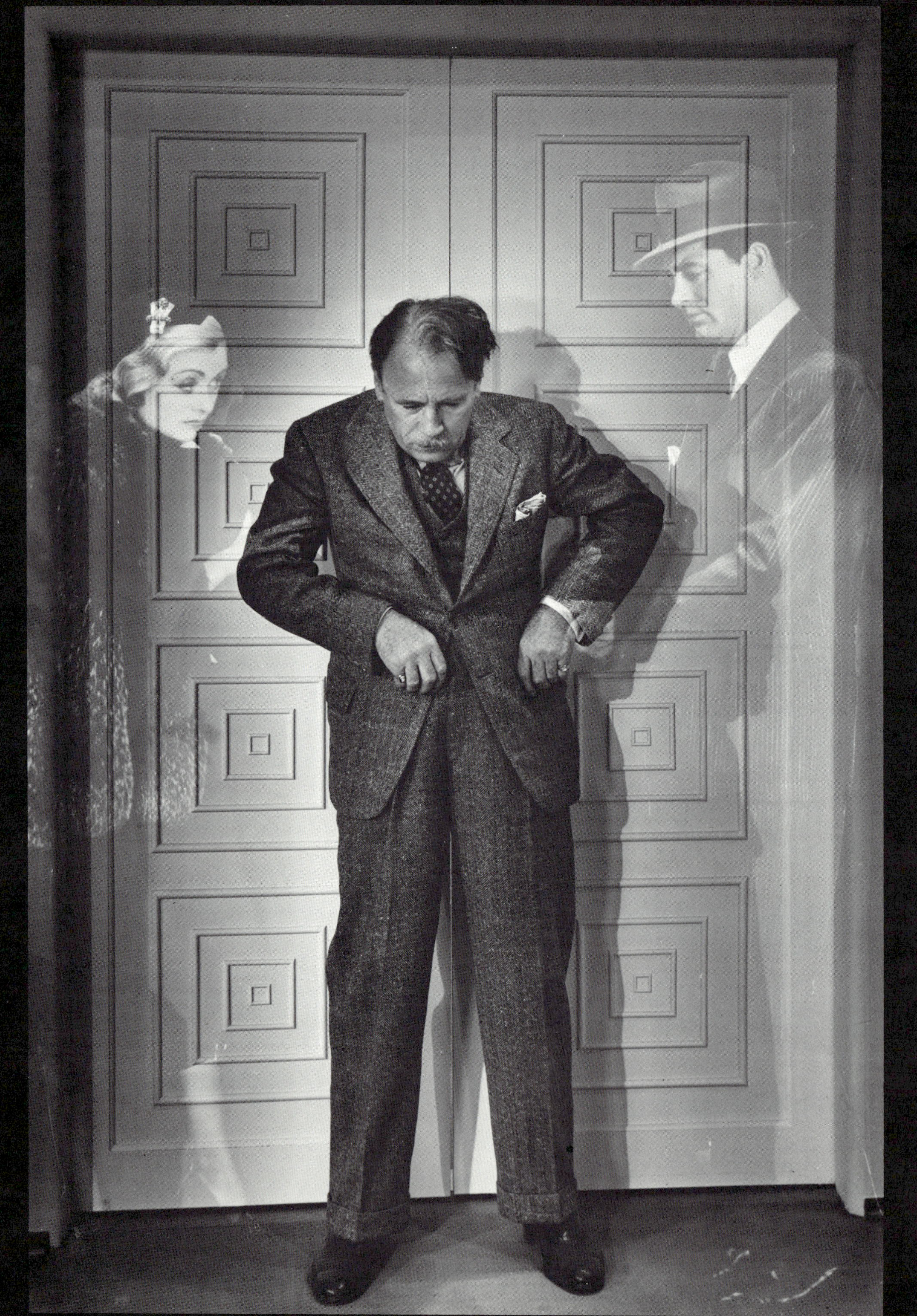

interiors so that you're looking at a house that the front has blown off. Then we put up our wind machines with the big Liberty motors. We had six of them and they are pretty powerful: they could lift a truck right off the road. Now we had to make sure that we were getting our foreground and background wind effect, but that no current ever hit the front of that building when it started to fall, because if the wind warps her she's not going to fall where we want her, and I'm standing right out in front. But it's a one-take scene and we got it that way. You don't do those things twice.

The falling building-front in *Steamboat Bill Jr.* is an example of a prop effect of the largest and most sophisticated variety. For many comedies, from the end of the silent era through the thirties and early forties, smaller-scale trick props were the bread and butter of humorous effects. Included among these props were sledgehammers made of lightweight desert yucca that could harmlessly clobber an actor, a bow tie fitted with a coil spring that spun around when the release lever was activated by the swallowing action of the actor's Adam's apple, and the irascible clam in the bowl of soup that squirted Lou Costello in the eye with the help of some offscreen tubing.

The independent company best known for this sort of work was the New York-based Messmore and Damon Company. One of the more intricate gags this firm was called on to produce was a dinner turkey that grew as it was stuffed with piles of dressing. When the gigantic bird was put under the knife at the Thanksgiving table, it popped and shrank to next to nothing. The turkey was made of rubberized fabric covering a balloon that was both filled and deflated offscreen. When the turkey was being stuffed, the dressing was actually disappearing through a hole in the table.

Laurel and Hardy made use of an especially bizarre prop in their 1937 feature *Way Out West.* Intent upon stealing back a deed from the villain, the boys sneak into his home with all the stealth of a pair of steamrollers. As they climb through a trapdoor, the flap slams down on Ollie. The fat man's head crashes through the wood, leaving him hopelessly stuck. Stan hits upon the clever idea of grabbing hold of his friend under the chin and pulling him out. Hardy's neck stretches as Laurel heaves the head up several feet. A rubberized replica of Ollie's head and neck was substituted for the real thing, resilient enough to snap back down when Laurel let go.

Photographic effects were also used by Laurel and Hardy. In the short subject *Brats* (1930), each of the comedians played two roles, father and child. There are the adult Laurel and Hardy and then an identical, pint-size pair, true chips off the old blockheads. For the scenes in which the comedians played themselves as children, giant-size props were constructed to make the actors look small. These were built to match normal-scale sets in which the adult Laurel and Hardy were filmed, and the two halves were then composited by optical experts. Using the split-screen method, the effects men placed a shot of the comics as children lying in an oversized bed on the left side of the frame; another shot of the comics as adults in a normal set was printed alongside on the right half of the picture. Great care had to be taken to make the two different sets match in such a way that they appeared to be parts of the same room. As each half of the scene was filmed, the dialogue and reactions of the performers had to be timed exactly to conform with the action that was filmed for the other half.

The Hal Roach special-effects department that worked on the Laurel and Hardy pictures was headed by Roy Seawright. Seawright, William Draper, and Frank Young created the many optical tricks for the 1937 Hal Roach production of *Topper.* This adaptation of the Thorne Smith novel spawned a series of films about the meek, baffled title character haunted by fun-loving ghosts and kicked off a trend of other comedy-fantasies that called for somewhat more subtle effects than razing buildings or squirting ink out of a pen.

As George and Marion Kirby, the best-looking pair of ghosts the world has ever known, Cary Grant and Constance Bennett had to materialize and dematerialize gradually while the flustered Topper (Roland Young) looked on in the same frame. For those times when they were invisible, objects had to move about seemingly of their own accord. To pull off these tricks, Seawright's department used some of the techniques invented by John Fulton in *The Invisible Man* and added some new ideas of its own.

The appearances and disappearances of the Kirbys were created by a technique that combined a split screen and a dissolve. In one scene Roland Young walks through a countryside set, thinking he's alone. Suddenly, much to his astonishment, two very charming ghosts appear on a nearby log. To achieve this effect, Grant and Bennett waited offscreen till Young had crossed to the left side of the shot. Then the two ghosts hurried onto the set and took a seat on a log to the right.

After allowing for the time that it would take for the ghosts to fade in, the actors played the scene normally. Extra footage of the empty set was shot at the end of the scene and the *optical printer,* the multipurpose special-effects machine introduced in the 1930s, took over from there. The screen was split on the printer so that the image on the right side of the frame could be manipulated. The footage of Grant and Bennett coming onto the set was cut out and in its place was substituted the empty set. The film of the two ghosts already seated on the log was then faded in while the empty set was faded out until the characters became opaque figures. What the audience sees are two people materializing out of thin air.

Objects being moved by invisible hands were put on the screen by several methods. In one scene Cary Grant walks toward a car disabled by a flat tire. He fades out of view and replaces the tire in his invisible form. An operator hidden inside the car opened the door and another operator, concealed in a pit below the car, was responsible for the working of the jack. Wires and stop-motion animation were used to move the tires around as they were being changed.

Stop-motion animation was also used for another very clever illusion. At one point, when Topper and his ghostly companions check into a hotel, the Kirbys dutifully stop to sign the guest register. Long shots showing the pen being lifted into the air by an invisible hand were done with wires. The close-up, however, in which we see the free-standing pen actually write out a signature, was done with stop-motion photography. The fountain pen was held upright by a special pin that was attached to its tip and stuck into the blotter holding the registration card. The pen was then animated a frame at a time until a complete signature was traced on the card.

In other cases an old special-effects standby was used: black velvet. This material has been part of the stock-in-trade of stage magicians since the nineteenth century. Méliès frequently relied on it to make things disappear. In his 1903 film *The Melomaniac,* for example, he decapitated himself by placing a black velvet hood over his head and standing against a black velvet backdrop, which left him visible only from the shoulders down. Black velvet, in conjunction with several other gimmicks, was used to create one of the most celebrated scenes in *Topper.* When an invisible Bennett takes a shower, we see the stream of water breaking against the outline of her body. At first Méliès's old method was used: a girl was dressed from top to toe in a black velvet body suit and photographed against a backdrop made of the same material. The filmmakers weren't satisfied with the results, however, so a second, more mechanical method was tried. Once again the shower was photographed against a black velvet background, but this time jets of high-pressure air were aimed at the water, causing it to fan out as though it were hitting a solid object. Steam and wire-manipulated soap were shot separately against the same background. These three elements were then printed over the set of the shower stall. (The knobs in the stall are also seen moving by themselves. The set was constructed in such a way that the dials could be manipulated from the offscreen side of the shower wall.)

The techniques used in *Topper* to bring the humorous escapades of spirits to life were subsequently employed in other comedies, such as *Blithe Spirit* (1945) and *The Bishop's Wife* (1947). Perhaps the most delightful of these comedy-fantasies was *Wonder Man,* for which John Fulton and A.W. Johns won the 1945 Academy Award for Special Effects. This film features Danny Kaye in two roles, the bookworm Edwin Dingle and the ghost of his zany comic brother Buzzy Bellew. At one point the ghost has the misfortune of inhabiting his brother's body while Edwin is "tying one on." Bellew staggers off pie-eyed and makes for a glass of bromo at the bar, only to find he can't get hold of the glass. His ghostly hands simply pass through it as he swipes at it with mounting frustration. As the hands flash through the glass, they are masked by the cloudy liquid. To achieve this effect, the effects team jigsawed the two images of Kaye's hands and the glass by making hand-drawn traveling mattes (the same technique that had been used to make the Roman senate building collapse in the original *Ben-Hur*). Earlier on, Buzzy meets his brother in Prospect Park and has a hard time convincing the prissy Edwin that he really is a ghost. The clincher comes when Buzzy casually strolls into the center of a marble post, leaving himself visible only from the chest up. He turns to his brother, gestures broadly with his hands, and cracks, "Believe what you want. What's this? Trick photography?"

A scene from *Topper.* The comings and goings of the ghostly couple were achieved by a technique that combined a split screen with a dissolve.

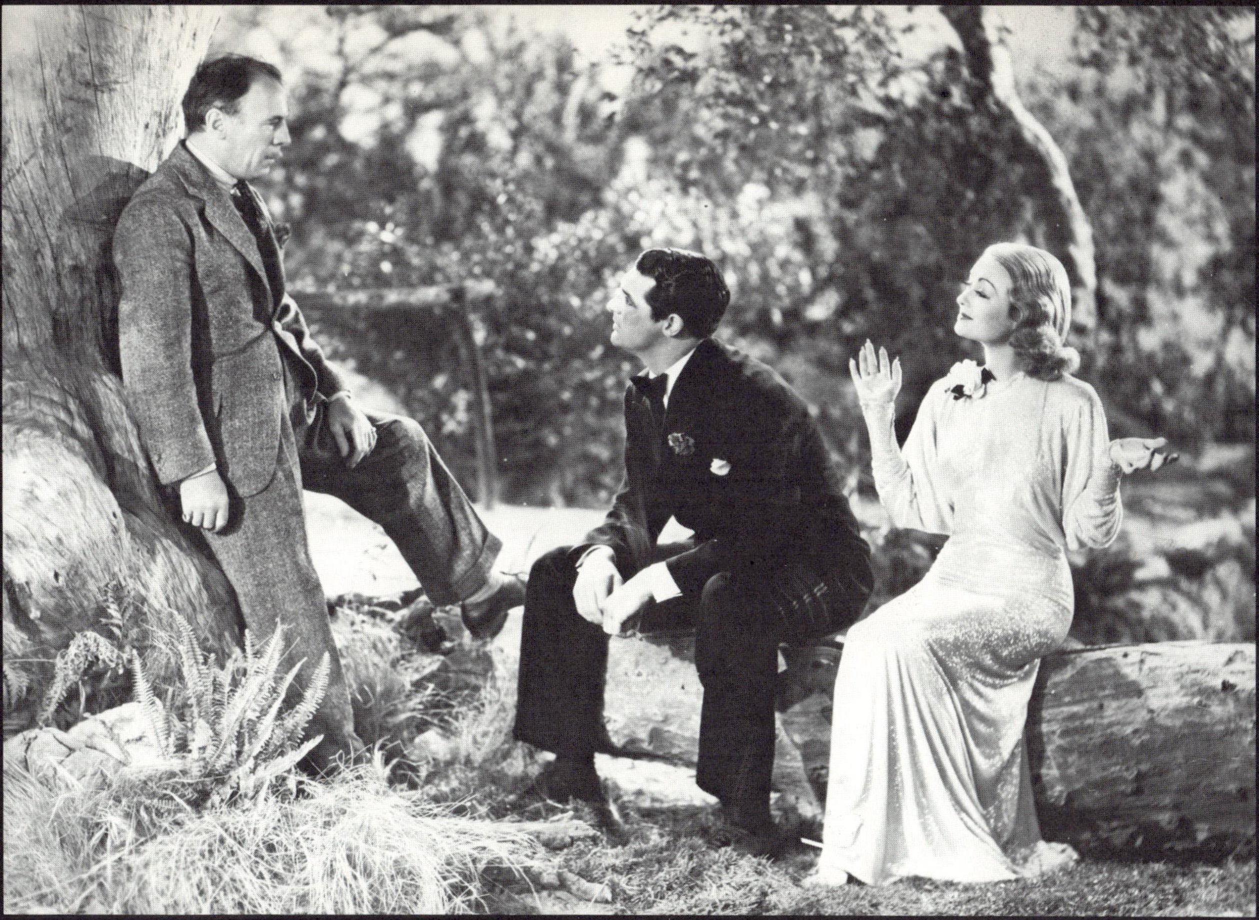

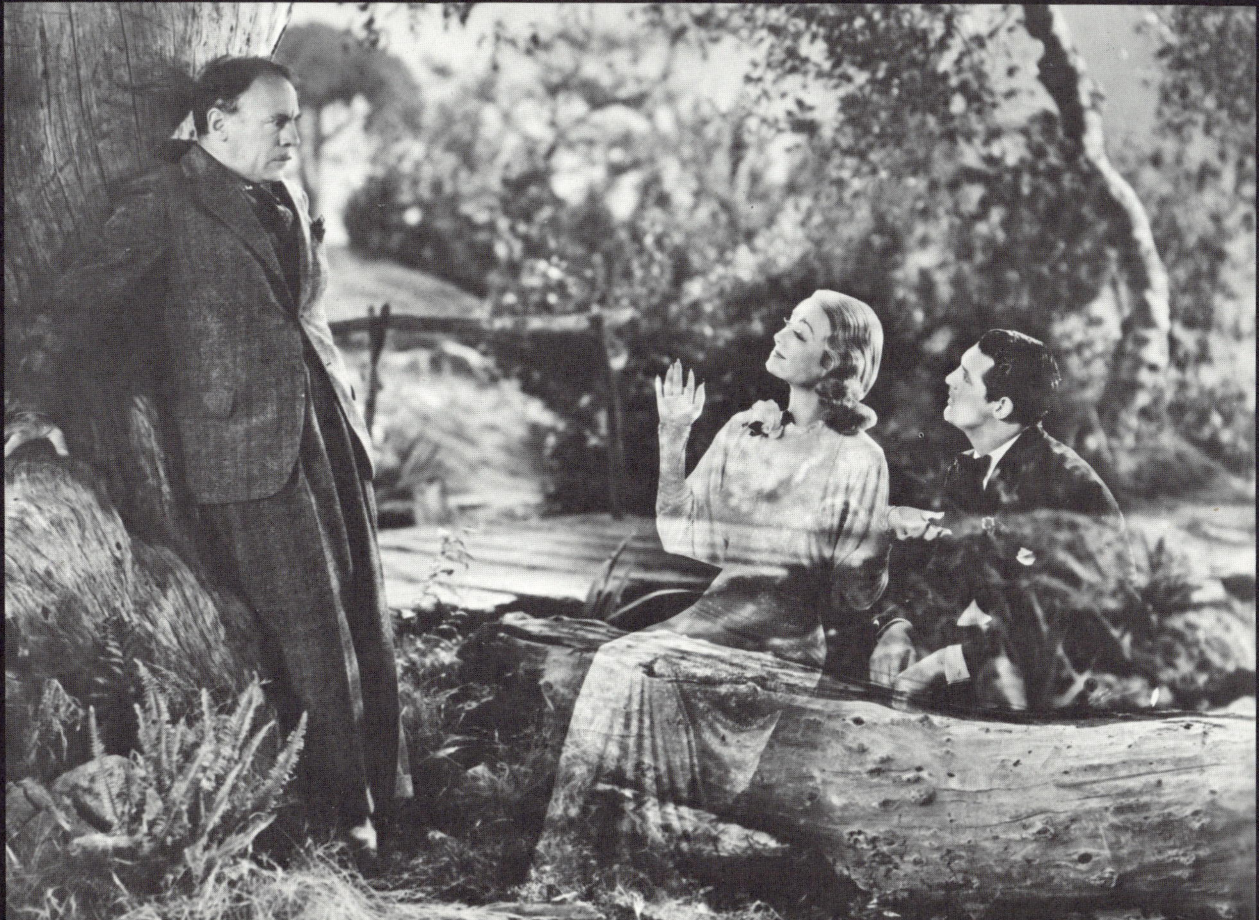

Top: Katharine Hepburn and Cary Grant come face to face with "Baby" in *Bringing Up Baby.* In reality the two human stars and the leopard were never filmed together but were combined by a sophisticated split-screen process performed on the optical printer.
Center: A multipurpose special-effects optical printer designed and constructed by Linwood Dunn's Film Effects of Hollywood.
Bottom: OPTICAL PRINTER: A simplified sketch illustrating the principle behind the optical printer.

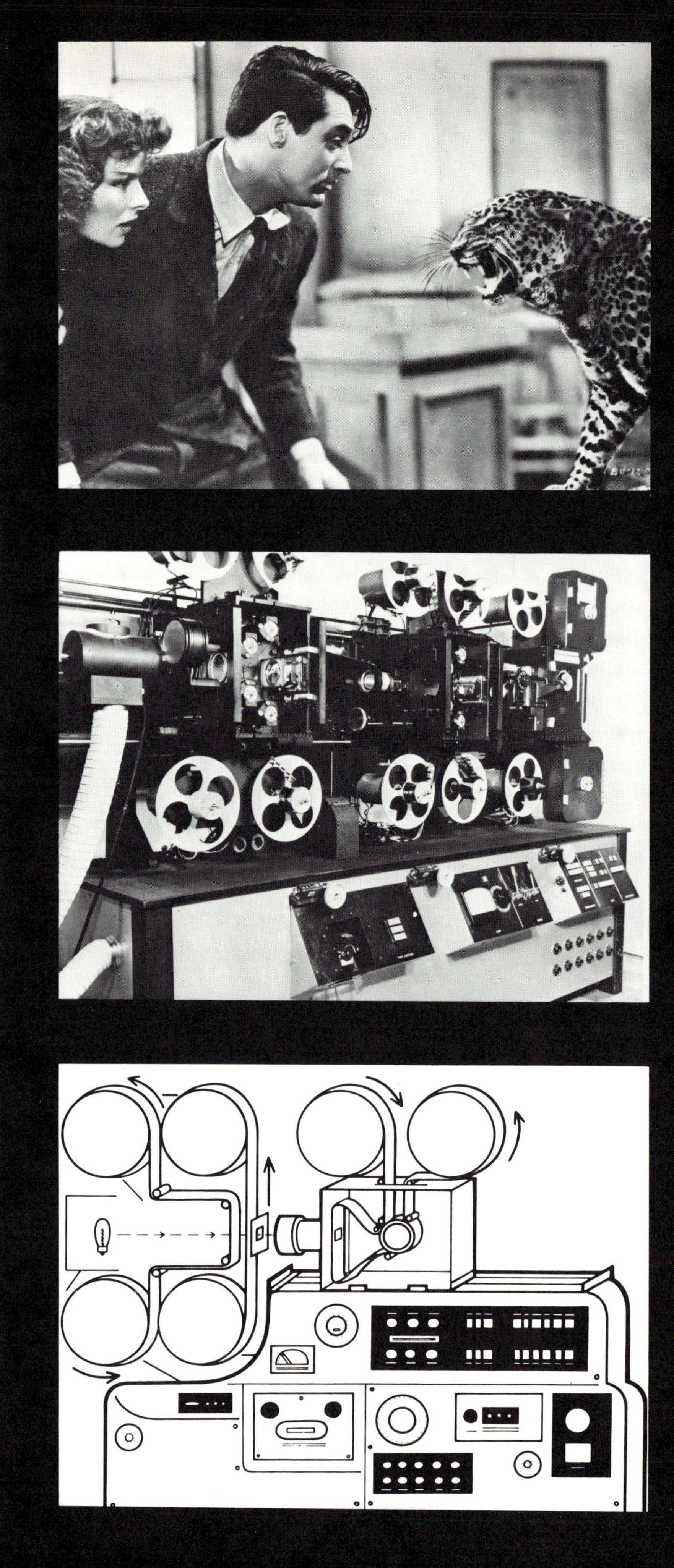

In the mid-1930s, romantic screwball comedy became the rage in Hollywood. This new sort of humor emphasized snappy repartee and tangled situations and had little use for the raucous sight gags that had been so important to the movies of Mack Sennett and Laurel and Hardy. As outrageous physical humor slowly faded in popularity, so did the mechanical effects that created that sort of gag. Although effects men weren't called on as often to collapse a breakaway wall, there was a growing need for sophisticated optical effects.

Howard Hawks's classic screwball comedy *Bringing Up Baby* (1938) is the frenzied story of a harebrained heiress who, among her other eccentricities, keeps a leopard called "Baby" as a house pet. A trained full-grown leopard was to be used in the picture, but the producers of the film discovered that the beast wasn't quite as docile as they had hoped and were quick to get cold feet about the idea of placing Katharine Hepburn on the same set with one of nature's most efficient killers. Since the script called for humans to appear alongside the big cat, the problem was to make the picture in such a way that Baby could be filmed separately. The solution was provided by Linwood Dunn and his optical printer.

The optical printer is the most versatile of all special-effects instruments, a multipurpose wonder-machine that, in the hands of a skilled operator, can create an almost limitless variety of complicated visual illusions. Though an optical printer is a highly sophisticated piece of machinery, the principle behind it is really very simple. Basically it consists of a movie projector face to face with a camera. The two are synchronized so that the camera can photograph each frame of a roll of a film run through the projector.

The idea of projecting a picture directly into a facing camera in order to make a copy of the original image goes back to nineteenth-century still photography. It wasn't until the early 1930s, however, that optical printing began to be applied to the making of theatrical motion pictures. Linwood Dunn designed the first modern special-effects optical printer in collaboration with his associate, Cecil Love, and the Acme Tool and Manufacturing Company.

The most obvious use of the optical printer is to copy a roll of film. More significantly it can be made to perform all the basic camera tricks that at one time were either done by much more complicated and laborious means or weren't done at all. During the silent era, for example, the creation of fast motion or slow was done manually by the cameraman: to make the action speed up, he would crank his camera below the normal speed; to slow it down he would do the reverse. The optical printer removed this function from the cameraman's imperfect, human hands and did the job mechanically. For fast motion the camera simply records every second or third frame of the original roll of film. With fewer frames on the duplicate negative the action speeds by more quickly. To slow movement down, the printer does the reverse: instead of skipping frames, it reprints the same frame two or three times so that the action is prolonged onscreen.

Special attachments are used to create other effects, such as split screens and multiple exposures. The optical printer can easily supply not only the usual transitions (fade-ins, fade-outs, dissolves) but also any number of flashy variations: starbursts, spirals, polka dots. It can freeze frames, reverse action, make mattes, superimpose titles, convert daytime scenes into night or color into black and white, and simulate zooms in scenes originally filmed with no camera movement at all. And that's just for starters. In short, as Raymond Fielding points out in his invaluable handbook *The Technique of Special Effects Cinematography,* the optical printer is a kind of special-effects miracle-tool, an instrument that is "capable of space, time, and image manipulations which surpass the wildest dreams of Baron Munchausen."

For *Bringing Up Baby* Dunn combined footage of the actors with shots of the leopard by using split screens, both stationary and traveling. The stationary split screen is the same technique that was used to get Laurel and Hardy to act with themselves in *Brats.* As the name of the process implies, the invisible dividing line remains fixed for the duration of the scene. (In this way, the adult Laurel and Hardy, standing on the left side of the room, could have complete freedom of movement within their half of the frame, but they couldn't possibly cross over to the right.) In a traveling split screen, however, the invisible boundary line actually moves from frame to frame. In one scene, for example, we see Baby crossing a room with Cary Grant following close behind. The actor and the leopard were filmed separately on the same set. Later, when Dunn combined the two shots, the split-screen line always remained directly behind the leopard; in other words the line that separated the leopard shot and the shot of Grant trailing behind had to "travel" just in back of the animal, following the leopard as it walked across the screen. This meant that Dunn had to move the split screen with each succeeding frame.

The films which afforded Dunn his first opportunity to show the public what his talented invention could do were two 1933 RKO musicals, *Melody Cruise* and *Flying Down to Rio*. In both these films, Dunn used the printer to create a series of dazzling transitions from one scene to the next. The most common of these optical tricks is the *wipe:* the beginning of the upcoming scene appears at the left side of the screen and replaces the previous shot by moving across to the opposite side; the moving right border of the new scene is a straight vertical line. For *Flying Down to Rio* and *Melody Cruise* Dunn achieved this effect on the optical printer with the use of something called a *wipe blade,* which acted as a matte. First the optical printer photographed the outgoing scene from a roll of film. The wipe blade gradually moved from left to right, blocking the light as a matte would. The result was a shot that ended with an unexposed area moving from left to right until the whole scene was wiped out. The upcoming scene was then recorded onto the same partially exposed roll of film; this time the blade acted as a counter-matte, blocking out the end of the previous scene so that only the unexposed area could take in the image. The finished piece of film contained a smooth wipe from left to right.

By changing the shape and position of the matte line, Dunn used the same basic method to produce many more elaborate transitions. For example, a new scene drops down from the top of the screen in a wavy, dripping line; in another instance the upcoming shot is introduced in a small area in the center of the frame and expands outward in a starburst shape. In each case the transition was timed to conform to the musical soundtrack; when a new scene comes onto the screen in a series of small expanding dots, the introduction of each circle is accompanied by a tinkling note on the soundtrack. These optical tricks are so extravagant and so frequent that one review at the time of its release called *Melody Cruise* a "rhapsody for optical printer, accompanied by Charlie Ruggles."

The optical printer also made possible a complicated dance routine by Fred Astaire in the 1936 RKO classic *Swing Time*. The "Bojangles of Harlem" sequence was a blackface number in which Astaire danced in front of and in unison with three giant shadows of himself. This Shadow Dance, a tribute to Bill "Bojangles" Robinson, was a combination of several shots. The RKO studio was a small, tightly knit corporate family that placed great importance on cooperation between departments. When working on an intricate number such as the Shadow Dance, the director, writer and special-effects artists put their heads together well in advance to map out carefully all that the scene would entail. Although the Shadow Dance was to a great extent a team effort, RKO special-effects chief Vernon Walker gave the credit for the final execution to Linwood Dunn, since Dunn was the one who put all the different elements together into one shot on the optical printer.

The first images filmed were the shadows. Astaire danced in front of a blank screen while a Sun Arc lamp cast his silhouette. Once one of the shadows was photographed, Astaire's foreground dancing could be filmed to coincide with the shadow's steps. To do this, Astaire was positioned in front of a blank screen once more; the processed footage of the dancer's shadow was projected offscreen while the camera rolled so that Astaire could keep an eye on the shadow's movements and time his new dance steps accordingly. Now the effects crew had one shot of Astaire and another shot of his shadow, the two figures dancing complementary parts of the same routine. Dunn's optical printer handled the rest. The shadow was printed three times to make a silhouette dance line and over this image was printed the foreground footage of Astaire. The different elements were precisely coordinated to create a complex interaction between the dancer and the shadows to his rear.

Throughout his dancing career Fred Astaire continued to be involved in imaginative special-effects numbers. In 1949 he thought up an "impossible" dance number for MGM's *The Barkleys of Broadway* that proved to be one of his most memorable show-stoppers. Once again the optical printer was the key to the trick, under the supervision of Irving Ries, head of MGM's optical printing department. In conjunction with Astaire, Ries worked out a way in which the dancer could interact with six pairs of dancing shoes.

After the sequence was tested in black and white, the principal live action was shot in Technicolor as Astaire danced alone on the cobblershop set. When this portion was completed, the set was covered with black velvet to prepare it for special photography. Six dancers were brought in, all of them wearing white shoes, black tights, black tops, black gloves, and black masks. Using guidemarks on the floor that corresponded to Astaire's footwork, they did their half of the dance. On film only the white shoes are seen. During the course of the routine, however, the shoes were

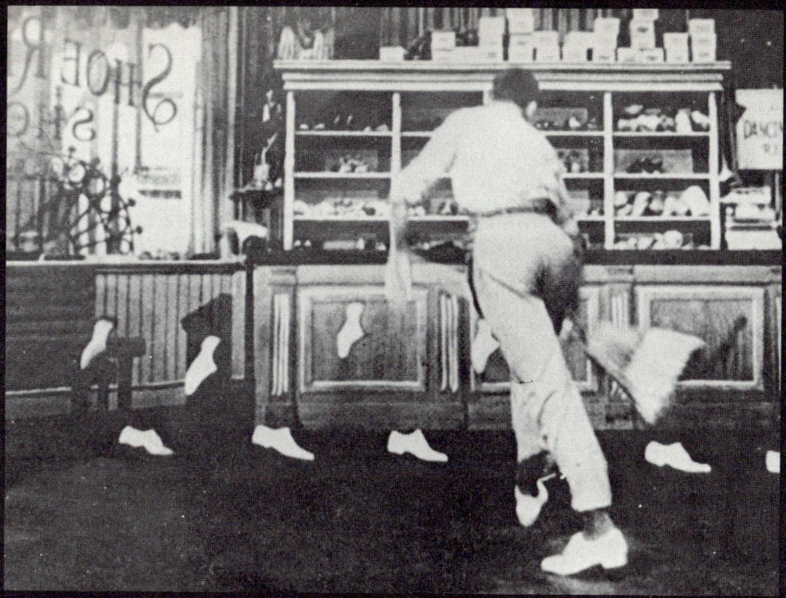

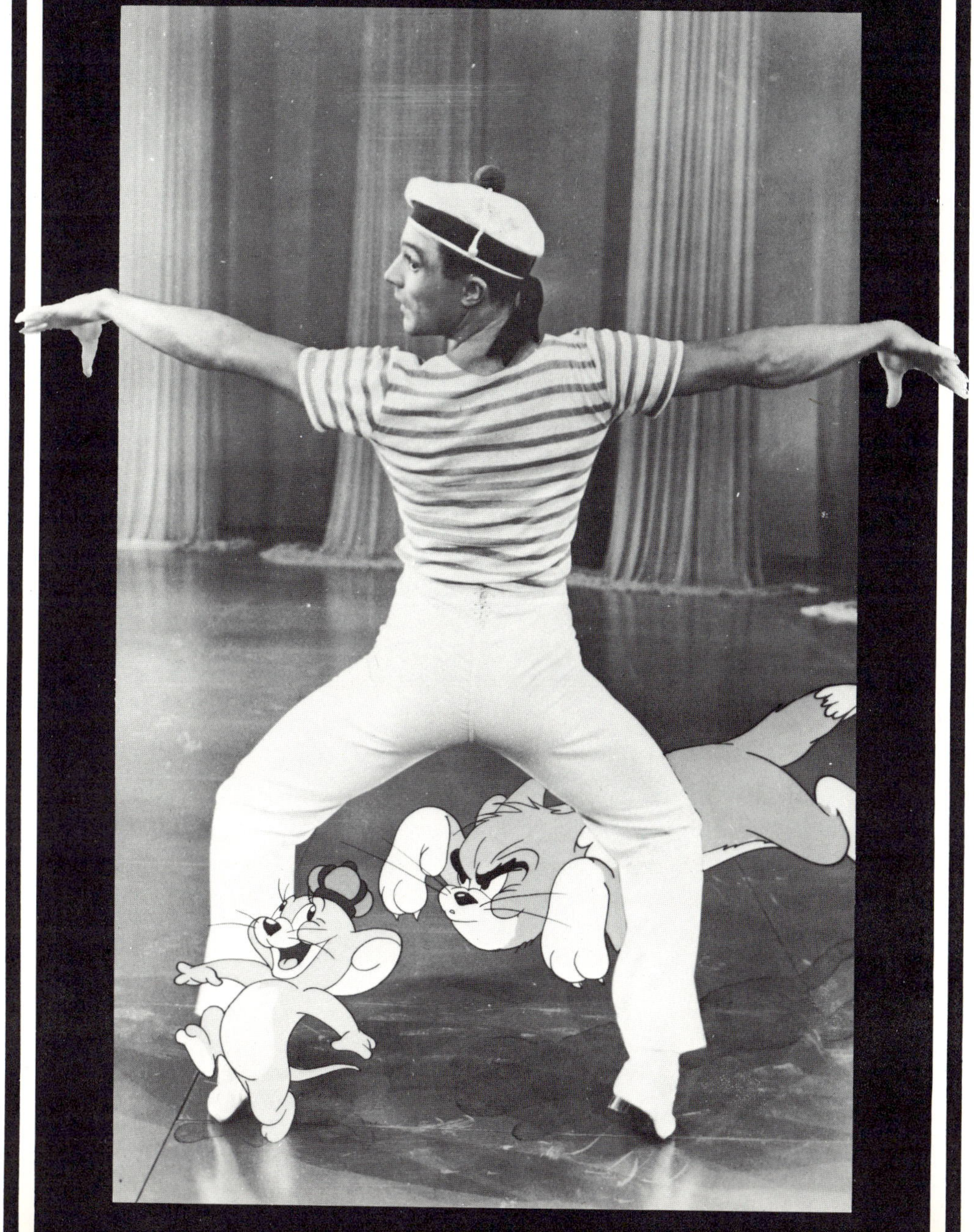

Top: The "dancing shoes" number from Fred Astaire's *The Barkleys of Broadway*. *Bottom:* A process called rotoscoping allowed Gene Kelly to dance with cartoon creatures in *Anchors Aweigh*.

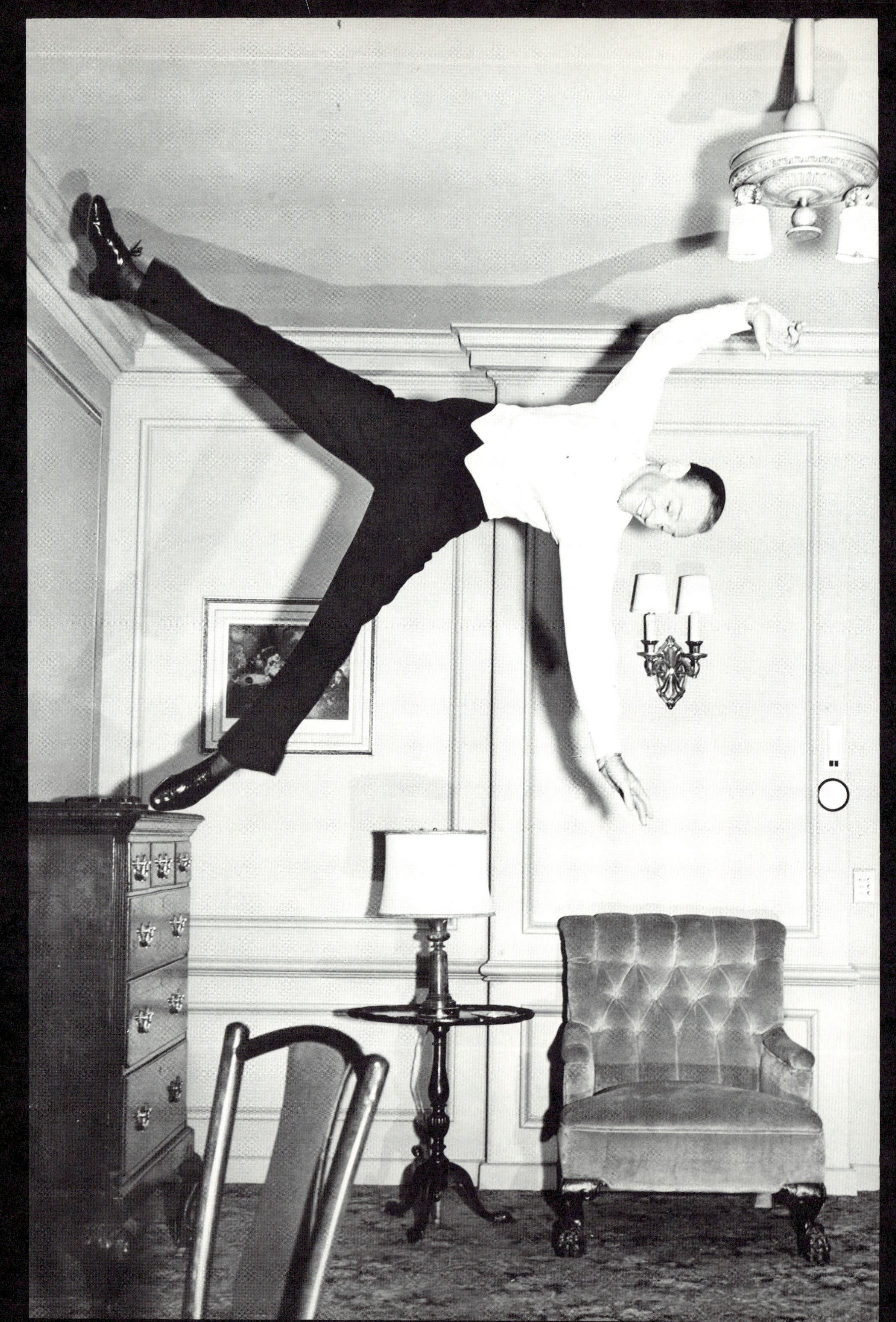

Though Fred Astaire seemed to defy gravity in this famous sequence from *Royal Wedding,* he actually remained rightside up throughout the routine; it was the room, not the dancer, that turned upside down.

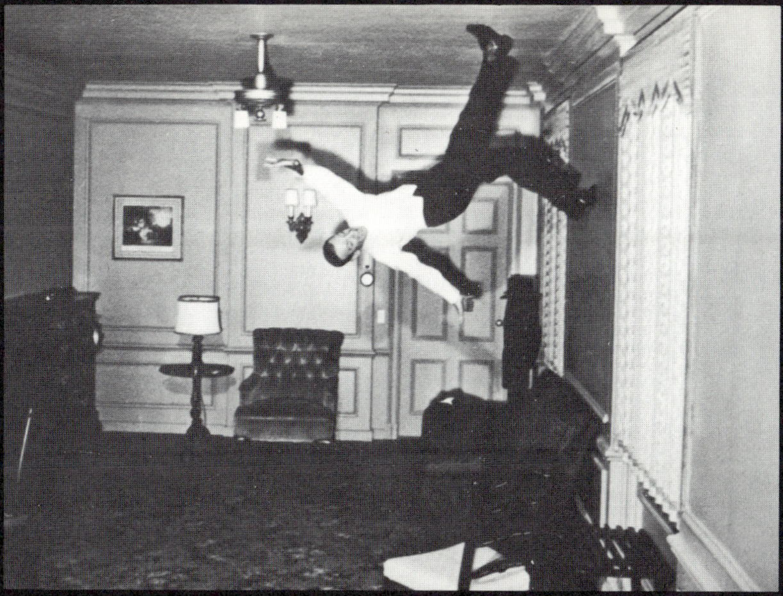

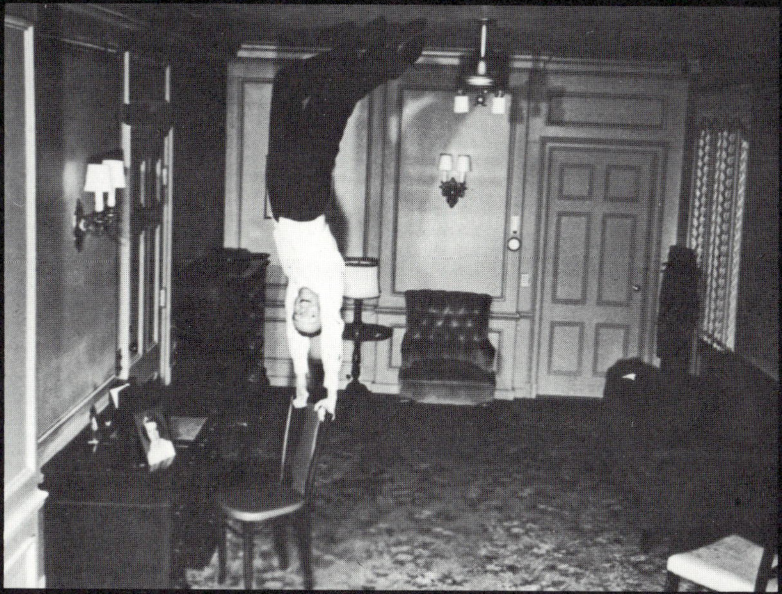

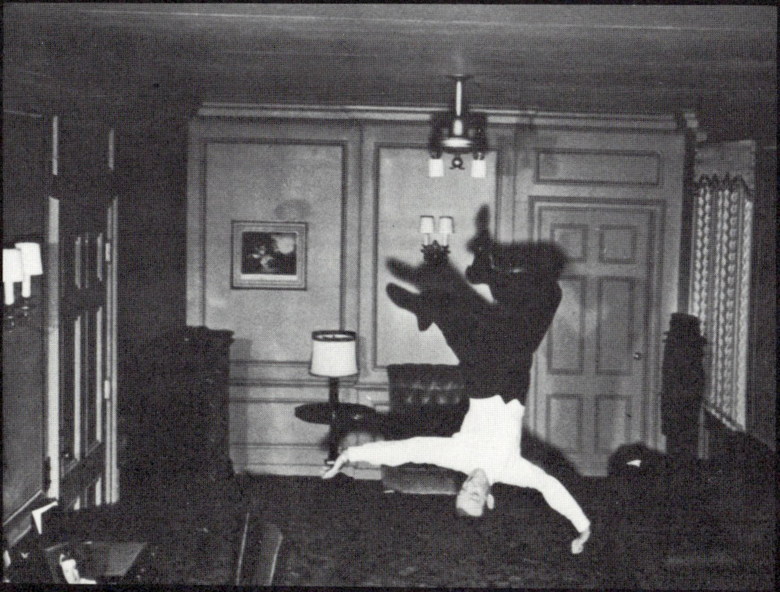

blocked from the camera each time a dancer crossed one leg in front of the other. To correct this, cartoon animation was used to supply the image of the white shoe when it was out of view. Irving Ries composited the two pieces of film on the optical printer by using photographically produced traveling mattes on a clear strip of film.

Competing with Astaire in fanciful song-and-dance acts was Gene Kelly, who performed an "alter ego" routine in which he danced with a double of himself. The picture was Columbia's *Cover Girl* (1944), and Kelly conceived of the number as a way of acting out his character's inner conflict. The technique involved was the relatively simple split-screen method. The scene is an excellent example of one of the nontechnical problems in special effects, the problem of selling imaginative effects ideas to unimaginative and unknowledgeable studio executives. The head of Columbia at the time was Harry Cohn, known by some as "His Crudeness." Cohn turned down Kelly's idea at first because he didn't think it was feasible. Even though the technical aspects were far from unprecedented, Kelly had difficulty persuading Cohn because the studio head wasn't capable of envisioning a dance number that made use of an element of psychological fantasy. It was only through great persistence that Kelly was finally able to convince Cohn to approve of what was to be one of the picture's highlights.

Kelly almost had another imaginative concept rejected the following year at MGM. For the 1945 film *Anchors Aweigh* he came up with the idea of doing a pas de deux with a cartoon mouse. When they were told about the concept, the MGM chiefs were far from enthusiastic. The technical problems that the dance would entail had never been solved before and the men at the top weren't in a hurry to risk their money on something so experimental. When producer Joe Pasternak backed Kelly's idea of combining live action with a cartoon, the studio bosses told the dancer to consult Walt Disney first to see if it was possible. Although he didn't do any work on the scene, Disney played a key role in putting it into the movie. Kelly told him what he had in mind and the animation king was impressed. At the time Disney was working on a similar mixture of elements in *The Three Caballeros* (1945), but he felt that Kelly's idea was much more advanced. Disney phoned MGM's general manager and raved about the concept, confirming that it could be done. On the basis of that recommendation Jerry Mouse made his musical debut.

First Kelly was photographed going through the carefully planned steps against a neutral background. Since Disney was too busy to commit any of his people to the job, MGM's own cartoon department got the call to add the mouse. Jerry Mouse (of "Tom and Jerry" fame) was drawn and filmed through a process called *rotoscoping,* in which the Kelly footage was projected one frame at a time onto an animation stand and the mouse was drawn to complement each of Kelly's poses. The result was a series of animation cels of the mouse, each cel corresponding to a frame of the live-action film. The cels were then printed with the Kelly footage and a cartoon background to show the two performers in perfect interaction; Jerry at one point slides across the dancer's outstretched arms and at another props Kelly up as he is about to flop backwards.

Though optically printed composites were responsible for some of the screen's most inventive dance routines, the most famous and astounding musical effects number had nothing to do with complicated opticals. Fred Astaire's dance up and down the walls and across the ceiling in *Royal Wedding* (1951) is as dazzling today as it was thirty years ago. The MGM special-effects crew made this scene possible not with intricate photographic processes, but with a variation on a trick that dates back to the beginning of movies. A well-known example of this gimmick appears in the Marx Brothers picture *At the Circus* (1939), when Groucho inadvertently talks himself into putting on suction boots and dancing on the ceiling with circus performer Peerless Pauline (Eve Arden). When shooting this sequence, the makers of the film called into service a device used at the turn of the century by Méliès in *The Human Fly* (1902) and by R. W. Paul in *Upside Down* (1898). Thus, Groucho and Peerless Pauline danced on an upside-down set with the camera also positioned upside down. In *Royal Wedding* the MGM effects crew made this relatively prosaic technique seem astoundingly new.

The room Astaire danced in was set inside a revolving drum, with the furniture bolted down and the camera fixed to turn with the set. As the set revolved, the room appeared to be always right-side up, while Astaire, who actually remained in a normal position throughout the scene, seemed to be defying gravity. The technical problems in this scene weren't as intricate as the "dancing shoes" composite in *The Barkleys of Broadway,* but the *Royal Wedding* num-

Top: Jerry Lewis unleashes a flood of champagne from a trick bottle fed by a hose in *The Errand Boy*. *Bottom:* Invisible wires (not Flubber) created the flying basketball team in Disney's *The Absent-Minded Professor*.

ber seems much more magical since it is obviously performed entirely before the camera and in a single take.

If Astaire used mechanical effects with great subtlety and a dancer's precision, funnymen like Bob Hope and Jerry Lewis used them to create the kind of broad physical comedy generally associated with Road Runner cartoons. In *The Paleface* (1948) Hope is captured by hostile Indians and prepared for the most gruesome of executions. Two supple young trees are bent inward and tied together to form twin arches with the comedian in between, one foot roped to each sapling. When the cord holding the straining trees together is cut, they are supposed to spring apart, tearing Hope in two like the wishbone of a Thanksgiving turkey. However, things do not go as planned: when the trees are cut loose, everything gets fouled up, and instead of being halved, Hope slips out of his oversize cowboy boots and is whipped up into the air. In a long shot we see a dummy of the comedian soaring over the horizon and dropping to comparative safety in a treetop. To complete the ridiculous cartoon feeling of the scene, Hope cries out for help while the words "Help me!" are superimposed on the screen as a cartoon-dialogue caption.

One of the writers of *The Paleface* was Frank Tashlin, who got his start in the industry doing animation for Porky Pig and Bugs Bunny cartoons. As a writer and director in the late forties and throughout the fifties, Tashlin continued to think up impossible, Looney Tunes gags for effects men to create. One such joke appears in the 1950 Marx Brothers movie *Love Happy* when spurts of steam rush out of Harpo's ears. Outrageous laughgetters were especially prominent in the pictures Tashlin directed for Jerry Lewis. When Lewis turned to writing and directing on his own, he followed Tashlin's lead, filling his movies with mechanical sight gags.

Lewis's manic antics always lent themselves to insane tricks. In *At War With the Army* (1951) his arms were rigged up with tubes so that they could spurt water from holes made by preinduction injections. Cartoonlike mechanical effects were common: a wired fire hose in *Rock-a-Bye Baby* (1958) wriggles about the street like a snake while the high-powered blast from its nozzle wreaks havoc all along the neighborhood; a huge champagne bottle fed by a hidden pipe explodes in *The Errand Boy* (1962) and gushes all over the honored guests; substitute elongated arms were used in *The Nutty Professor* (1963) when Lewis tries taking hold of a heavy barbell and his hands drop to the floor.

Mr. Cartoon himself, Walt Disney, added his own style to this brand of cinematic slapstick with the discovery of that amazing antigravitational substance called Flubber in *The Absent-Minded Professor* (1961). Fred MacMurray fuels his old Model T with the stuff and takes off for an aerial cruise around Washington. He also finds the time to shake up his snippy rival for Nancy Olson by bouncing his old crate on the top of the man's car. Reminiscent of R. W. Paul's *The ? Motorist,* this car in flight was put on film by combining a

Traveling Mattes for Color Movies

The traveling matte is one of the fundamental techniques of optical trick photography. It is a way of combining actors, filmed inside a sound stage, with a background scene shot outdoors. As opposed to rear projection, in which actors are photographed against a prefilmed background, the traveling matte actually "jigsaws" in the moving image of the actor into the background scene. In order to do this, it is necessary to create a contoured "hole" in the background image. The image of the actor can then be inserted into this hole, the outline of which precisely matches the shape of the actor's body. The two most common techniques used to produce traveling mattes for color movies are the *blue backing* and the *sodium light* processes.

The blue backing method, the older of the two, requires a number of steps. First the actor is shot on color film in front of a screen that is either painted or illuminated blue. The resulting negative is printed in contact with a roll of black-and-white film, filtered so that it will be exposed only by the blue portions of the scene. The result is a black-and-white color separation positive with a completely clear (because it is completely exposed) background.

The original negative is again printed with a second roll of black-and-white film; this time, however, only the red portions of the scene are recorded. Since there is no red at all in the background, the result is a second color separation positive with a completely *black* background. This positive is then printed as a high-contrast duplicate negative, producing a negative image of the actor against a totally clear background.

This negative is now printed in contact with the blue-filtered positive, which consists of a positive image of the actor against a clear background. Placed together, the two images of the actor, positive and negative, cancel each other out to produce a completely black image, while the background is clear on both strips of film. When these two strips of film are printed in bipack on a high contrast black-and-white stock, the result is a completely opaque background that is clear in the area of the actor's body. This is the traveling matte. The negative of this image is an opaque silhouette in the shape of the actor against a transparent background. This is the counter-matte.

The first of these mattes, the opaque background with the clear, actor-shaped hole in it, is run through an optical printer along with the original color negative of the actor against the blue background. Since the opaque background of the matte blocks off the blue, the result is a new negative of the actor against an unexposed background. The counter-matte, the moving silhouette of the actor against a clear background, is printed with the negative of the background scenery. The result is a new negative of the background with an unexposed area in the shape of the actor moving through it. The two negatives are then fitted together like a jigsaw puzzle to produce the final composite.

The sodium light process, which was developed in England by the J. Arthur Rank Organisation and has since become the favored method of Walt Disney Studios, was introduced several years after the blue-backing system. The main advantage of this method is that it produces traveling mattes in a single step by means of a sophisticated device called a *beam-splitting camera.*

The beam-splitting camera, as its name suggests, has a prism behind the lens that divides the light entering the camera into two identical images, which are simultaneously recorded on two separate rolls of film. In this case the actor performs in front of a bright yellow screen illuminated by sodium vapor lamps. The actor himself is illuminated with ordinary white lamps filtered to prevent any yellow light from hitting him. Because the prism is also filtered, it transmits the image of the actor to one roll of film, while on the second roll only the background is recorded. This second roll results in a print of an opaque background with a clear space in the shape of the actor's body. This print serves as the traveling matte. The final composite is produced in an optical printer, following the same steps used in the final stages of the blue-backing process.

shot of the auto with high-altitude surroundings by means of the *sodium-light traveling matte process,* which was supervised by Eustace Lycett. For close shots of MacMurray behind the wheel, the appropriate background was rear-projected. Slapstick reached new heights in this picture in the hilarious basketball game decided in favor of Flubber. Seeing his school's lightweight players getting mauled by a team of giants, the professor irons his invention onto the soles of his students' sneakers and the ninety-eight-pound weaklings bound over their tormentors' heads, erase the gigantic lead, and win the game when one of their newfound stars vaults across the court and takes the ball with him down through the basket. The high-flying players were lifted and set down by hidden wires. The technique was nothing new, but the timing of the absurd leaps in conjunction with the dumbfounded reactions of the opposite team made the scene a success.

Frantic, cartoonlike comedy has been done better, but no one has ever done it bigger than Stanley Kramer, producer of the 1963 slapstick epic *It's a Mad, Mad, Mad, Mad World.* This two-and-a-half-hour movie of continuous comic disaster was described by Linwood Dunn as the "most challenging, most extensive, difficult, as well as the most rewarding special-effects assignment I have ever had."

In charge of the demolition-derby mechanical effects was Danny Lee, a versatile technician who has worked on such diverse assignments as the bloody *Bonnie and Clyde* (1967) and Walt Disney's *Bedknobs and Broomsticks* (1971). His job in *It's a Mad, Mad, Mad, Mad World* included destroying a restaurant and a gas station. A full-size airplane rammed into the restaurant, which was a specially designed breakaway building. Lee used a strong cable as a sort of leash for the plane by anchoring one end of the cable and attaching the other end to the tail of the plane. The cable brought the craft up short and prevented it from crashing too far into the restaurant. A breakaway billboard made of balsa wood and Styrofoam was another structure demolished by a plane. Lee collapsed the specially constructed filling station in one take with the help of offscreen operators working a battery of devices that involved air rams, compressors, and electric cable-cutters. Since the action was recorded by the camera in one run-through, the timing of the work of all the operators had to be perfect. In an early scene Lee used radio control to show a furniture truck barreling down a slope, the furniture getting tossed out by the bumpy ride. The pieces of furniture were individually placed on compressed springs and triggered out of the truck by radio signals.

The most demanding sequence was the outrageous finale on a fire escape. While Spencer Tracy tries to make his getaway with a suitcase full of loot, ten of the other stars chase him down a fire escape, which gives way under their weight. They cling desperately eleven stories above the street and sweat it out while the fire department goes into action. Considering that the Three Stooges are part of this rescue team, it's just a matter of time till everything goes wrong. The eighty-foot rescue ladder gets the stars off the fire escape but then starts to whip about in the air, sending each of the characters hurtling through the sky and generally creating complete chaos. To put this precarious piece of action on film, Linwood Dunn and his crew needed three sets of miniatures and a series of optical additions and composites.

The miniatures of the ladder, actors, and buildings came in three scales: one quarter inch to the foot, one inch to the foot, and two inches to the foot. The first was used in extreme long shots. The next largest set was for stop-motion purposes. Small, flexible replicas of the actors were animated by Jim Danforth and photographed one frame at a time as they struggle on the fire escape and ladder. The largest scale, used for shots of the ladder collapsing onto some power lines, was filmed at extreme high speed to slow down the action and give the ladder the illusion of weight.

The sparks created in the power line sequence were added onto the original footage with an optical printer. Dust was also superimposed around objects when they hit the ground after a long drop. The same instrument matted actors onto footage of the miniatures and added the crowd below the building. The optical tour de force of the finale was a full shot of the plaza composed of seven different elements, including the partial set, matte paintings, animated miniatures, optical dust, and small areas of live action. Like so many great effects, Dunn's optical printing was done so well that moviegoers were willing to believe there was no trickery involved at all.

A more recent attempt at a big-budget comedy epic was Steven Spielberg's epically unfunny *1941* (1979). Airplanes speed down Hollywood Boulevard and create panic on every block; an enormous runaway Ferris wheel rolls through an amusement park and down a pier; tanks and other military equipment raze everything else in sight. This so-called comedy was an unqualified flop, but it wasn't for the lack of special-effects expertise.

As in *It's a Mad, Mad, Mad, Mad World, 1941* relied a great deal on miniatures when filming what appeared to be large-scale slapstick. The supervisor of miniature effects was Greg Jein, the model-maker who built the mothership in *Close Encounters of the Third Kind* (1977). For *1941* Jein made miniatures of airplanes, a submarine, tanks, Hollywood Boulevard, an amusement park, and various California landscapes. The term *miniatures* may be misleading in some cases, since some of the models are what are called oversized miniatures. The Japanese submarine, for instance, was twenty-five feet long. Jein's intricate craftsmanship was especially impressive in the miniature of the amusement park, Pacific Ocean Park, a set that required eleven months to build. The park was constructed on a scale of one and one-half inches to the foot and was modeled with painstaking detail. The star component of this extraordinarily authentic-looking set was the runaway Ferris wheel. Near the end of the picture the crew of the Japanese submarine off the coast of Santa Monica somehow mistakes the Ferris wheel for a military target and opens fire on the amusement ride. The enemy shell dislodges the wheel from its support. The wheel then rolls through the park, continues on along a narrow jetty, and drops off into the ocean. For this scene both a full-scale mock-up of the wheel and an oversize miniature were built. The shots of the mock-up and the miniature in motion were interspliced to create the very convincing illusion of one object in one continuous action.

The man in charge of the many mechanical effects was A. D. Flowers. Flowers's Oscar-winning contributions to man-made and natural disasters in *Tora! Tora! Tora!* (1970) and *The Poseidon Adventure* (1972) qualified him for the task of creating *1941*'s sprawling comic violence. A typically catastrophic effect that Flowers worked on in *1941* was the scene of a tank crashing into a paint factory and destroying everything inside. The construction department spent five weeks building the set for the paint factory; Flowers and his crew had to devote a week to setting up all the physical effects once the set was finished, making sure that the cans and vats of paint would split when run over, and that the buckets would fall and the shelves collapse on cue. In all, 50,000 gallons of paint were used to splatter the entire set.

At the end of the movie Flowers got the opportunity to do an effect he had never attempted before: he got to spill a two-story house over the face of a cliff. Relying on special-effects know-how that had been developed over the course of nearly forty years of movie experience, Flowers was able to rig the specially built house in such a way that it collapsed and tumbled down the cliff in one take. Any mistake in the sequence would have meant shooting the scene over, a job that would have cost two or three hundred thousand dollars.

One of the most complex effects sequences was the scene of Wild Bill Kelso (John

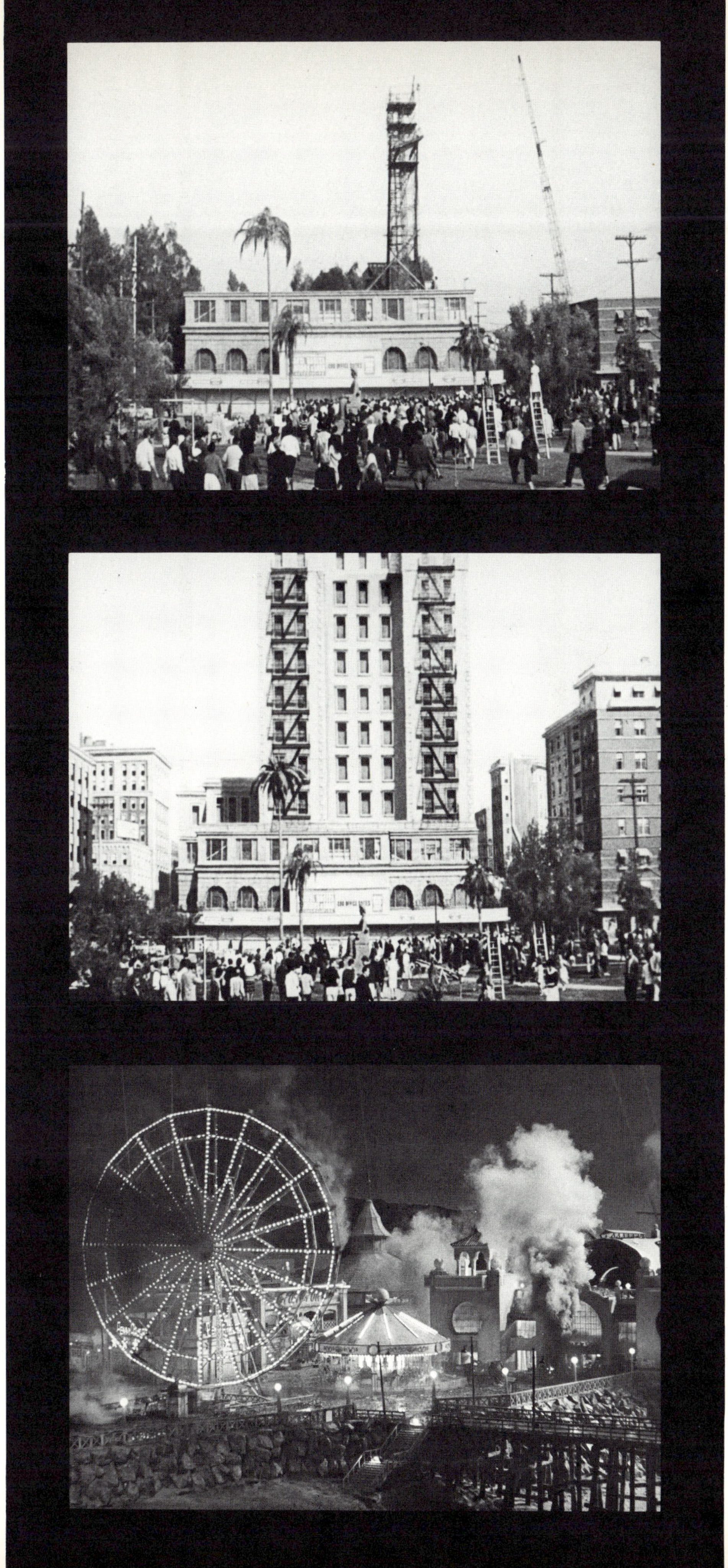

Top: The set on the Universal back lot where the climactic plaza sequence of *It's a Mad, Mad, Mad, Mad World* was filmed. *Center:* The plaza as it appears on screen. This composite shot consists of seven separate elements combined in Linwood Dunn's optical printer. *Bottom:* The marvelous miniature amusement park created by Greg Jein for *1941*.

Belushi) crash-landing his P-40 fighter plane along Hollywood Boulevard. Miniatures, full-scale mechanical effects and optical composites were used. Greg Jein built a miniature of the street and the P-40. The plane was "flown" by running the model along parallel wires that passed through the wing tips. The wires are known as "Lydeckers," named after the brothers Howard and Theodore Lydecker, who engineered plane maneuvers in such films as *Flying Tigers* (1942) and *The Flight of the Phoenix* (1965). Shots of Jein's model plane crashing into the miniature street were alternated with shots of full-scale effects supervised by A. D. Flowers; in the latter a full-size P-40 was made to dive into the full-scale set and lay waste to everything in its path by sending the plane down a specially constructed offscreen track. The third technique in this elaborate scene was to shoot the plane and the street separately and to combine them by means of a traveling matte. L. B. Abbott and Frank Van der Veer were responsible for the blue-screen system that was used for these composites.

Flowers described Spielberg's comedy as "probably the busiest show that I've ever been on. I started working with the picture in November of 1977 and finished in August of 1979. I don't think there were five days of shooting on the whole picture that effects of some sort weren't required." Flowers understandably seems to take pride in meeting the challenge of such extensive effects work, but the problem with the picture as a whole was that the special effects are too extensive. The movie is crammed with so many disaster effects that there was almost no room for development of the plot and characters. The makers of *1941* were intent upon outdoing all other comedies as far as destructive gags were concerned; they didn't seem to realize that a collapsing building is only funny if the characters involved in the collapse are funny. Stan Laurel could get more laughs out of breaking a simple trick doorknob than the tiresome Wild Bill Kelso could get out of leveling all of Hollywood Boulevard. When designed to complement a good comic personality or situation, special effects can be hilariously funny but they can't carry the picture on their own.

In *The Errand Boy* Jerry Lewis has lunch under a large painting of Samson, which comes to life and showers him with chunks of falling stone. In the first scene *(above left)* Lewis sits beside a real painting. In the next shot *(above right)*, the "painting" is really a framed alcove in the wall. Inside stands a costumed actor, pushing against a pair of lightweight pillars, which come raining down on the comedian. This trick is as old as the films of Méliès, who used it to create living paintings in several of his comic shorts.

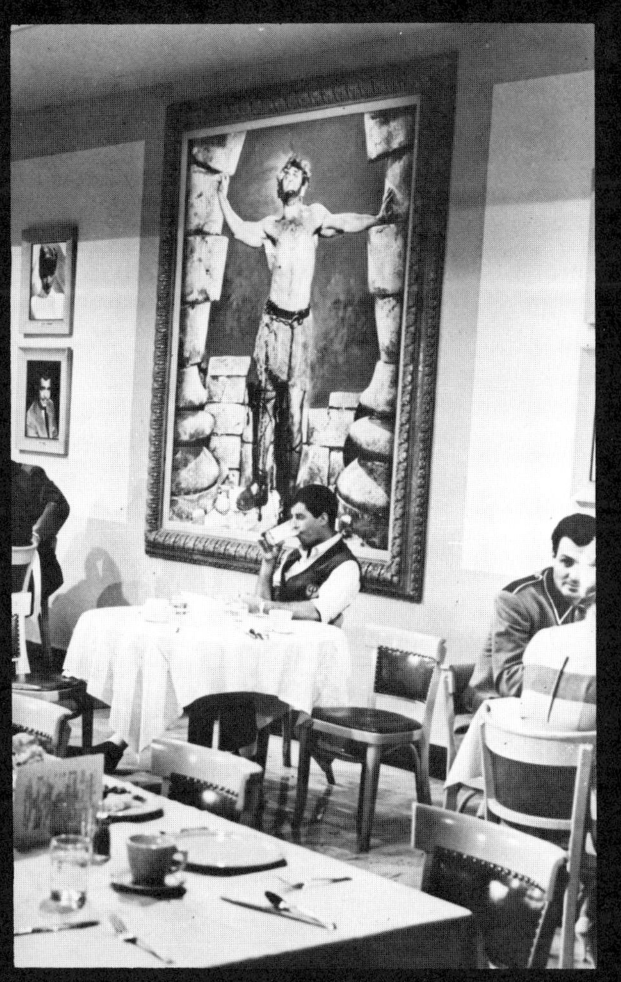

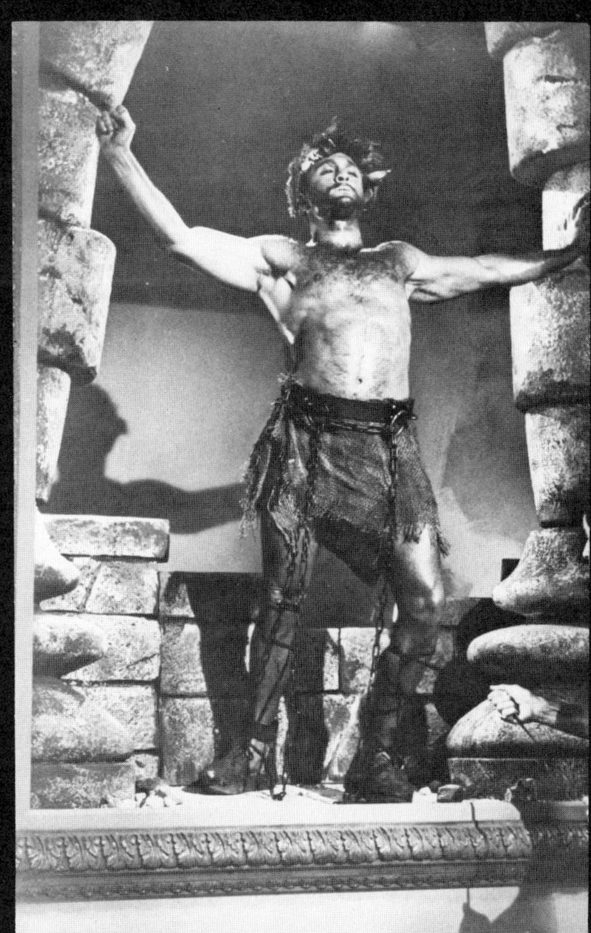

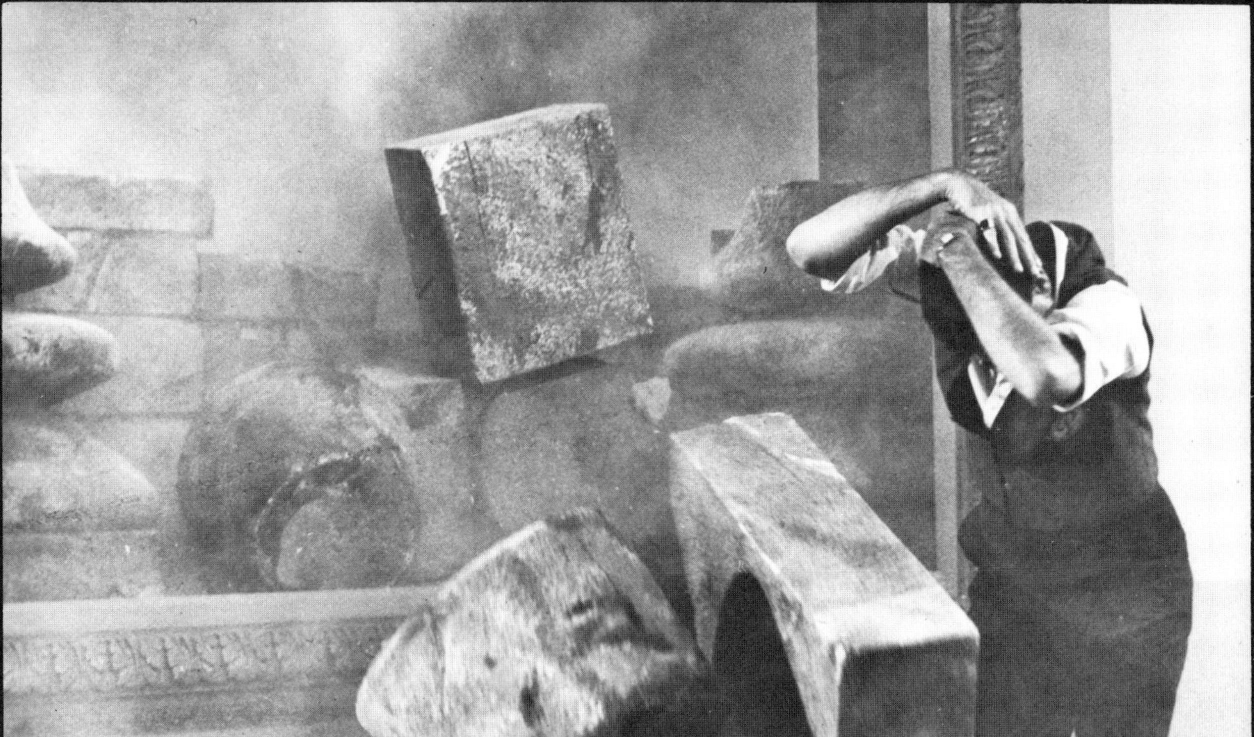

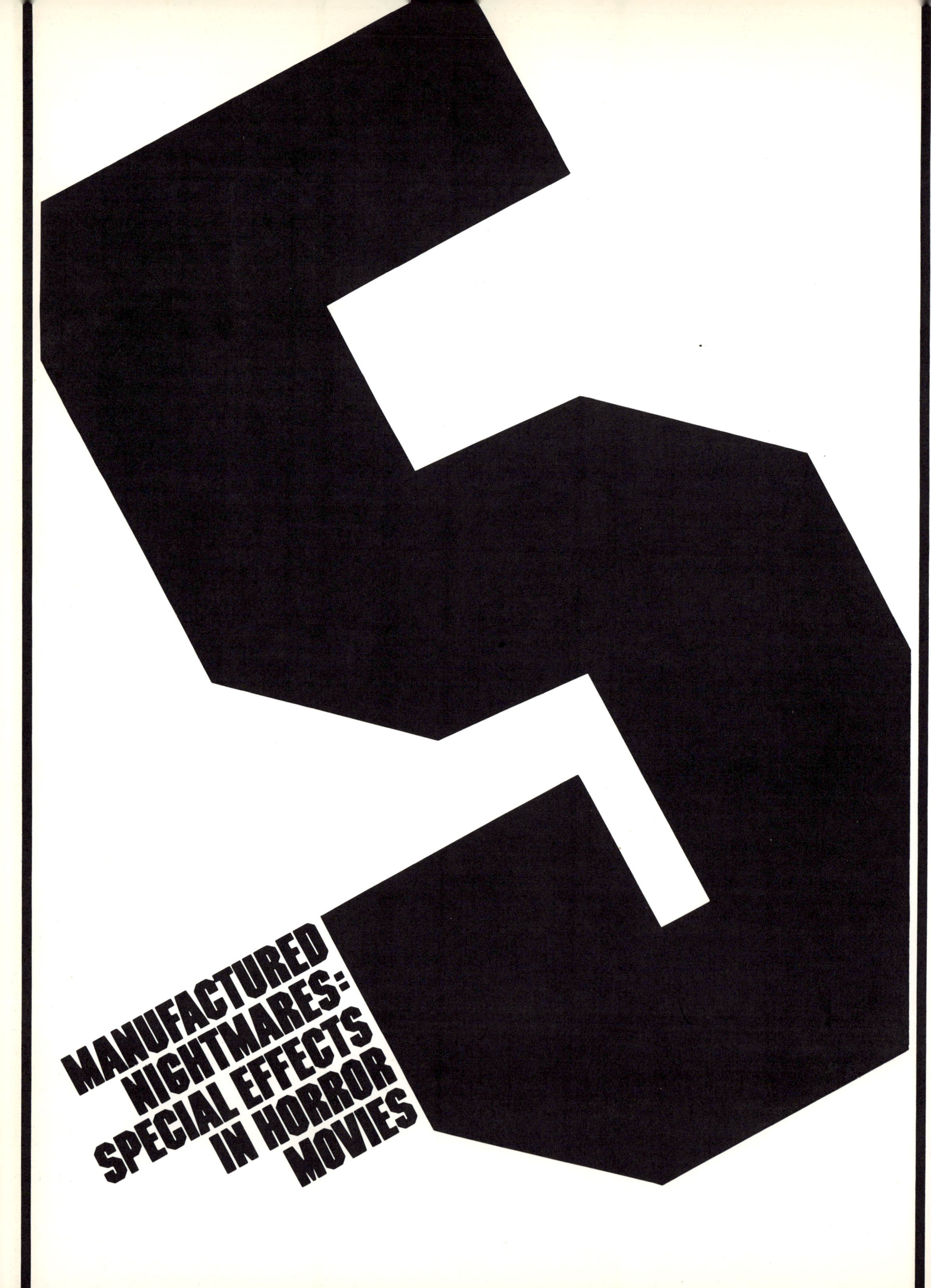
MANUFACTURED
NIGHTMARES:
SPECIAL EFFECTS
IN HORROR
MOVIES

If Hollywood is a dream factory, horror movies are its manufactured nightmares. They allow us to confront—in the security of a theater, with a box of popcorn in our hands—deep-rooted dread and ancient anxieties: nameless fears which we can safely ignore in the daylight but which plague us at times in our sleep. Often the task of the special-effects man is to recreate the outside world within the confines of a studio sound stage; in the case of horror movies his job is to give concrete shape to the phantoms that haunt the darkness of our own minds.

Hollywood horror films can be divided roughly into two periods. The more recent, which began in the fifties and has culminated in such recent blockbusters as *Jaws* and *Alien,* consists of pictures that jolt audiences with graphic blood-and-gore effects. In the earlier period, however, stretching from the twenties to the forties, horror films tended to rely less on shock tactics than on spooky atmospheric illusions like artificial fog creeping across a moonlit graveyard. Visual trickery in early horror movies like *Dracula* (1931) and *Frankenstein* (1931) was incidental to the plot line; elaborate electrical laboratories for mad scientists to tinker in and glass paintings of gloomy castles perched upon craggy hilltops constituted typical work for the effects man. The grotesque makeup for the Frankenstein monster is displayed in shocking detail and the incredible transformation of Lon Chaney, Jr., into the murderous Wolf Man is presented in full view, but the violence perpetrated by these creatures is relatively discreet. Viewers in the 1930s were horrified because they were forced to provide their own gruesome details.

When horror films first became popular in the twenties, the special effect that most often attracted the attention of moviegoers was the bizarre makeup for characters like the Hunchback of Notre Dame and the Phantom of the Opera. The great silent star Lon Chaney, Sr., both acted the parts and created the makeup for these two horribly deformed characters. From 1923 to 1930 he devised so many cinematic disguises that he became known as the Man of a Thousand Faces. His makeup work laid the groundwork for all of the grotesquely ugly monsters to come.

Chaney served his apprenticeship onstage in touring stock companies and in music halls. He worked as an actor, director, stage hand, and slapstick comedian, finding time throughout all these jobs to learn the fundamentals of makeup. In 1913 he made the transition to movie acting and started his second stage of training. He was a little-known supporting player in about a hundred pictures over the course of the next five years. He developed his acting and makeup skills with little critical or financial reward until he was cast as a villain opposite the popular William S. Hart in a Western called *Riddle Gawne* (1918). For the next five years Chaney was a respected Hollywood badman. He reached star status in 1923 when he played the misshapen bell-ringer in *The Hunchback of Notre Dame.*

There were no makeup departments in early Hollywood, so Chaney had to create the Hunchback himself. As he did with his other grotesque parts, Chaney studied anatomy and physiognomy in order to turn his face and body into an extraordinary special effect. For the Hunchback he wore a rubber hump and rigged himself with a harnesslike device that prevented him from standing erect. The apparatus was so painful that it had to be removed between takes. The bell-ringer's crooked nose and misaligned eye were sculpted by Chaney with mortician's wax. Other items in his makeup kit were putty, grease paint, lining pencils, gutta-percha (a tough rubbery substance), and collodion (a gluey solution used for sealing wounds).

His most famous monstrosity is Erik, the composer turned disfigured prowler in *The Phantom of the Opera* (1925). For half of the movie Erik's features are concealed by a mask. When a curious Mary Philbin sneaks up to him and snatches the mask away, Chaney's crazed death's-head face provided what may have been the most shocking moment of film in the 1920s. Since Chaney was so secretive about many of his techniques, the methods used for the creation of Erik as well as other characters are still a subject of speculation. According to Robert G. Anderson in *Faces, Forms, Films,* Chaney made his face seem elongated by using a built-up headpiece topped with sparse hair and taping back his ears. For the piercing sunken gaze he made his eyes seem more deeply set by blackening the sockets, then whitening the top of the lower lids to draw more attention to the eyes. Two other essential parts of Erik's living-skull appearance are his up-tilted nose with its gaping nostrils, and gaunt, skeletal cheeks. The nose was done with hairpin-shaped wires which Chaney (who was always willing to put up with extreme physical discomfort for an effect) inserted into his nostrils. Opinions differ on how his skull-like cheeks were achieved. Anderson writes that Chaney transformed his strong, full face by building up the cheekbones with putty and darkening the areas below, creating an artificial shadow. Rudy Behlmer, on the other hand, writing in *Films in Review* (October 1962), claims that Chaney created the illusion from the inside by wedging cotton wadding and celluloid discs up inside his mouth to exaggerate the cheekbones. The mouth itself was stretched into the shape of a skeletal grin by small prongs fixed to a row of false jagged teeth.

With each grotesque role that he took, Chaney confronted a new makeup challenge and furthered his reputation as a cinematic chameleon. Although he was a fine actor in straight roles as well, Chaney is most remembered for his uncanny makeup inventions. His list of disguises includes a leering bugeyed vampire, a hunchbacked apeman, a legless gangster, and an armless knife-thrower. Perhaps the greatest tribute paid him was a running joke in Hollywood reputedly started by director Marshall Neilan, who was supposed to have once said, "Don't step on it, it may be Lon Chaney."

Chaney's employer, Universal, was about to step up its horror film production when Chaney died in 1930. Without monsters there could be no horror movies; Universal had to find a makeup artist of Chaney's caliber to produce new fiends. The makeup successor was Jack Pierce who established himself with his creation of the Frankenstein monster in 1931 and went on to produce the Mummy, the Wolf Man, and a variety of hunchbacks and ghouls. For *Frankenstein* Pierce worked six hours before each day of filming to fit Boris Karloff with a flattop head, forehead scar, sunken cheeks, and electrodes that were embedded so firmly against the actor's neck that they left tiny scars that lasted for years. Pierce's work on the monster is outstanding not only because of its ghoulish detail, but also because the heavy makeup didn't interfere with Karloff's facial mobility; the actor was able to convey with great subtlety both the horrid and sympathetic qualities of the monster.

The dramatic power of the scene in which the monster is brought to life is due in great part to the eerie setting, the humming lab of shooting sparks and high-voltage arcs. The electrical wizard who built this equipment was Kenneth Strickfaden. Making the transition from electrical hobbyist to movie professional in the twenties, Strickfaden began by supplying electrical effects for the melodramas that were popular at the time. One such job was the grisly task of simulating the curling smoke and the searing sound of a man being fried in the electric chair. Both the smoke and the sound were created by shooting an electric current through a block of wood. In *Frankenstein* Strickfaden became a sort of unsung star by showing Universal how Dr. Frankenstein could harness the power of lightning. The stunning setup of transformers and gaps connected by what Strickfaden called "lightning bridges" proved to be so photogenic that it kept cropping up in later Universal comedies and serials. In the sixties and seventies Strickfaden's contraption was still in use. It appeared most recently in Mel Brooks's hilarious parody *Young Frankenstein* (1974).

Whenever a character had to monkey around with Strickfaden's high-charged gizmos, the actor would often, understandably, opt for the inventor to double for him. Strickfaden had great confidence in his contraptions, but even he had to admit that they weren't foolproof. In the 1932 Karloff vehicle, *The Mask of Fu Manchu,* the Chinese master criminal was supposed to test a sword by diverting a 1,500,000-volt arc to the blade with his long, evil-looking fingernails. Strickfaden stepped in to do the bit, and when a cable punctured, the inventor convulsed into a back flip from the jolt. His confidence was strong enough to inspire him to try the scene again when the equipment was adjusted.

With *Frankenstein* Universal started the first full-blown horror movie fad. Throughout the thirties and the early forties, effects men concentrated on producing images that conveyed an aura of the supernatural (the world of werewolves and the living dead) and the unnatural (scientifically created monsters). Of all the spooky tricks the most sensational were the hair-raising metamorphoses of a man into a monster.

Perhaps the best of these transformations occurred in Paramount's 1932 version of *Dr. Jekyll and Mr. Hyde,* starring Fredric March in the double role. The first time we see March change into the hideous Mr. Hyde, the actor's face creases and caves in at the cheeks while the camera records the sequence continuously without any dissolves or cuts. The rest of the transformation is suggested with subjective camera work: the camera makes a dizzying 360-degree spin to show the doctor's disorientation. When Jekyll recovers enough to make it to a mirror, his change into his bestial double is complete. For years the method used to produce the first few moments of the transformation, the only part that we see, remained a closely guarded secret; there was no conventional explanation for how March's face metamorphosed while the camera rolled on without interruption, with no opportu-

Man of a Thousand Faces: the legendary Lon Chaney and two of his immortal grotesques.
Top: Chaney in the characteristic act of transforming his appearance.
Center: As Quasimodo in *The Hunchback of Notre Dame.*
Bottom: The hideously deformed Erik in *The Phantom of the Opera.*

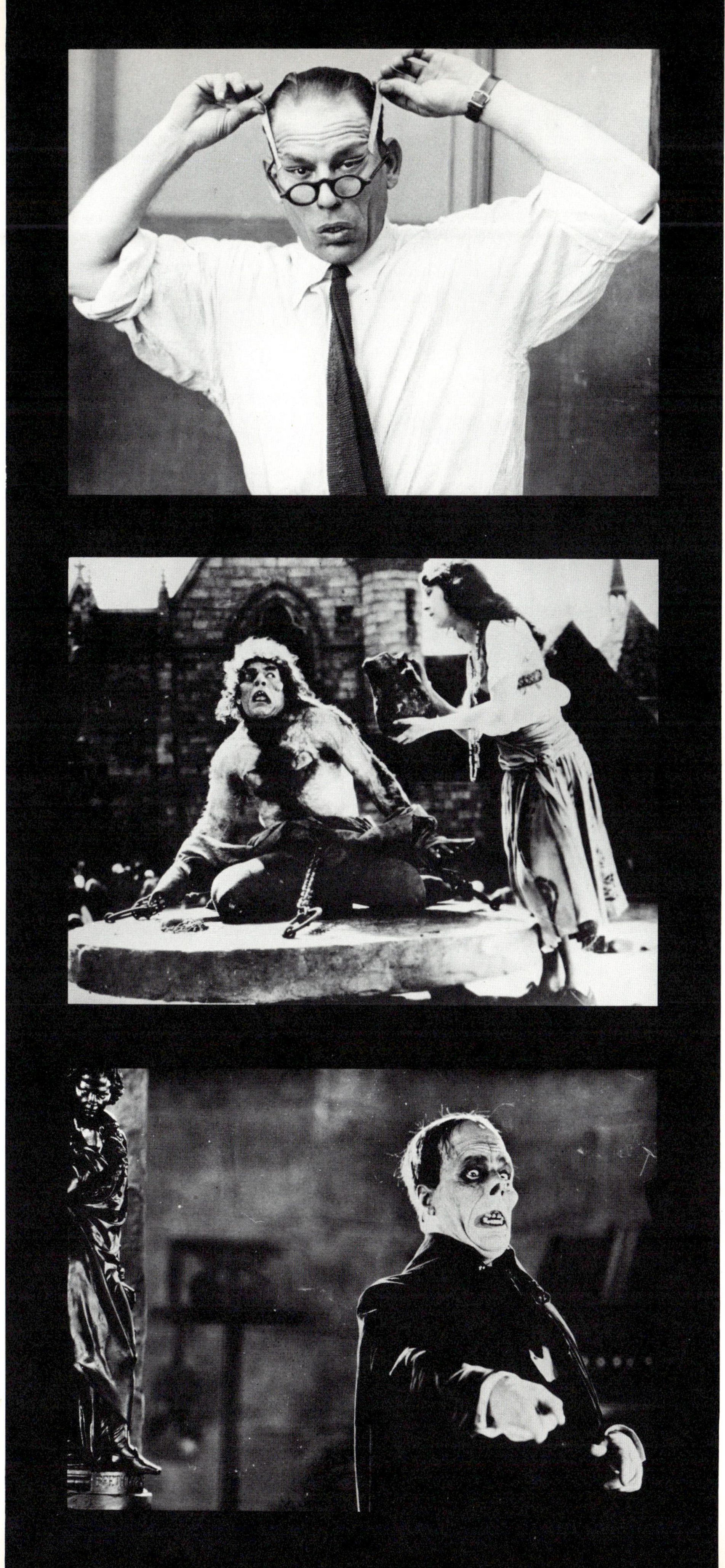

nity to add makeup. Director Rouben Mamoulian perpetuated the mystery by claiming he never would reveal the technique used in the scene. He finally broke his silence on the subject in an interview in Charles Higham and Joel Greenberg's book *The Celluloid Muse*.

Before the shot was begun, March's face was lined with red grease paint in those spots where the first changes would take place. A series of red filters placed in front of the lens prevented these markings from being recorded on film. Then, after Jekyll downs the bitter potion, the filters were removed one at a time and the lines and shadows appeared where the makeup had been applied.

Three other scenes in the picture show the entire transformation, full-face, before the camera: once from Jekyll to Hyde, and twice in reverse. The addition or deletion of hair, bestial teeth, and other major alterations in the actor's appearance had to be done by stopping the camera on a held pose, making the makeup changes in the dressing room (the work of Wally Westmore), and shooting again as before. Dissolves smoothed the transition between phases. In order to insure that each makeup stage conformed exactly to the one preceding it, March's outline was traced on the frosted glass of a Graflex still camera placed alongside the moving picture camera.

Universal performed a similar beastly transition trick in Hollywood's first wolf-man picture, *Werewolf of London* (1935). This time the victim of the full moon's curse was Henry Hull, whose degeneration into the monster was devised by the great effects man, John Fulton. Head of Universal's special-effects department through most of the first horror period, Fulton also made Claude Rains invisible in *The Invisible Man* (1933) and later won Oscars for his work in *Wonder Man* (1945), *The Bridges at Toko-Ri* (1955), and *The Ten Commandments* (1956).

Fulton used several methods to turn Henry Hull into a werewolf. In one scene we see the actor change as he runs down a portico lined with columns. Hull was photographed running against a black velvet backdrop. At various points he would stop and Pierce would apply the werewolf makeup in increasingly monstrous stages. A traveling matte was used to combine Hull's figure with the background scene. The pillars were filmed separately and matted onto this composite, masking the exact place where each makeup change took place. On other occasions Fulton worked the transformation by progressing through a series of dissolves, similar to the ones Mamoulian had used to turn Dr. Jekyll into Mr. Hyde. Unfortunately Fulton's work suffered because of Hull's refusal to wear the sort of extensive makeup Karloff had tolerated when he played the Frankenstein monster. Jack Pierce was forced to cut down on his work, and as a result, when Fulton's job was done, the lead actor looked somewhat like a hairy pixie. In 1941 the same studio produced the full-blown treatment that this kind of sequence deserved in the classic *The Wolf Man*.

The makeup job Pierce did on Lon Chaney, Jr., was perhaps his most ferocious creation, a monstrous man-beast. Full application of the makeup took six hours, during which Chaney was fitted with a rubber snout and covered with yak hair, glued on a few strands at a time. Chaney's onscreen transformation took even longer to achieve. The actor had to remain absolutely motionless while the camera shot a few frames of his face in its full werewolf makeup, which would then be completely removed. Immediately he would be newly made-up, this time, however, in a slightly less advanced stage of the transformation. He would then resume his former position in front of the camera and a few more frames of film would be shot. This procedure went on through twenty-one separate makeup changes and took twenty-two hours to complete.

More consistently popular than the mummy, the werewolf, or any other monster has been the vampire. The vampire film is particularly fascinating for two reasons: it offers the special-effects man an especially wide range of opportunities to display his skill, and because it spans the early and current periods of the horror movie, it reflects the different emphases of those two historical periods. The vampire has an imposing array of magical powers: he has the animal world at his command, he can crawl up a sheer wall like a human spider, he can change into a bat or wolf at will, or he can dematerialize into vapor. It is up to the special-effects expert to make these supernatural feats possible onscreen. In more recent movies, effects men have discovered that in addition to being magical, the vampire can also be extremely gory. In the interests of shock value, his bites on the neck can drip with blood and his supernatural strength can literally snap a man in two. The violence can be just as explicit when it is directed at this monster. A stake through the heart is rife with bloody possibilities, while the truly astute vampire hunter knows that the staking is only a preliminary; the complete destruction of the living dead requires that there also be decapitation and the cutting out of the heart.

Top: Dr. Frankenstein (Colin Clive) throws a switch on one of Strickfaden's machines, while his hunchbacked servant, Fritz (Dwight Frye), looks on. From *Frankenstein.* *Bottom:* A behind-the-scenes look at Dr. Frankenstein's laboratory, outfitted with the marvelous electrical equipment created by Kenneth Strickfaden. From *The Bride of Frankenstein.*

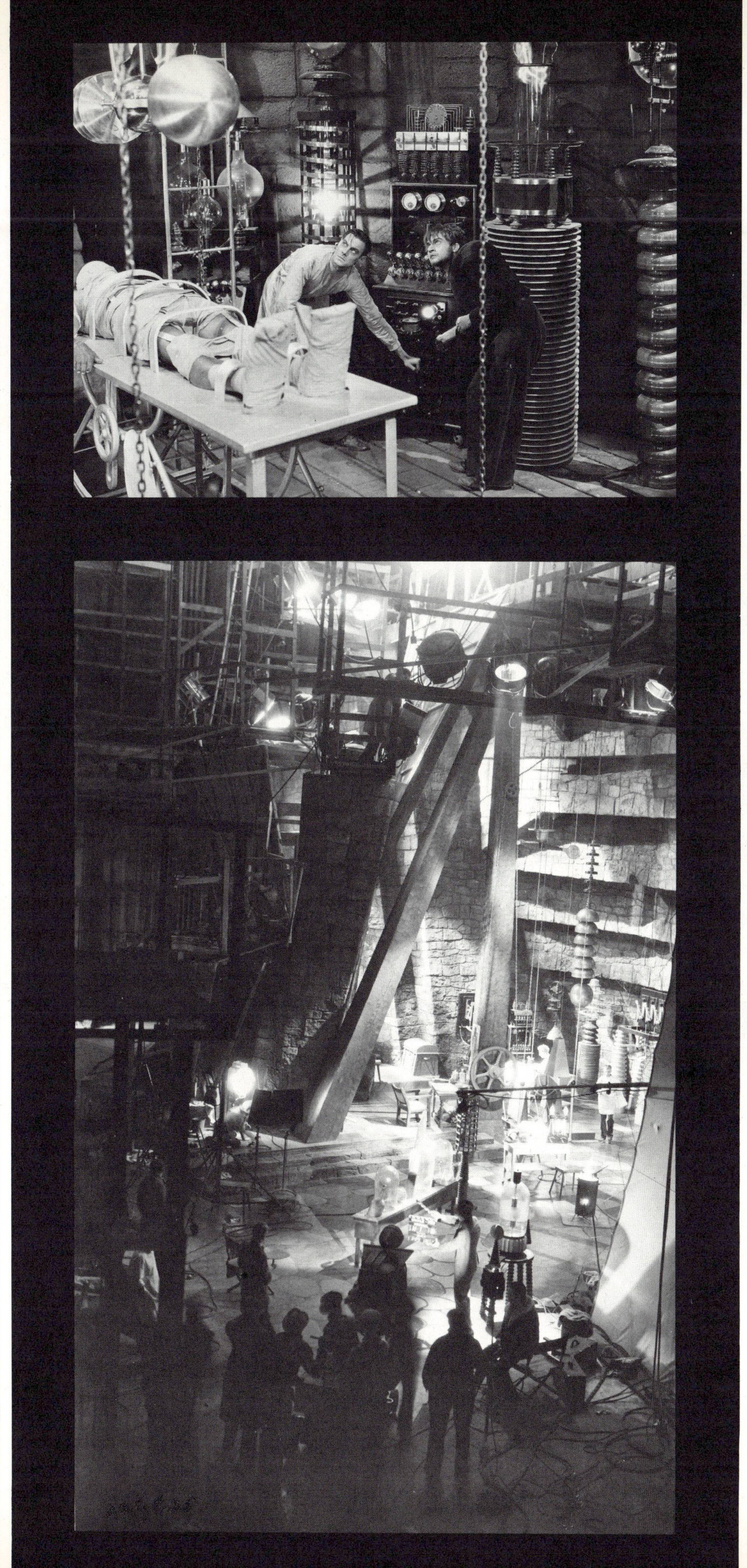

Following page: Frederic March as Dr. Jekyll turns into the hideous Mr. Hyde in Rouben Mamoulian's version of Robert Louis Stevenson's classic tale.

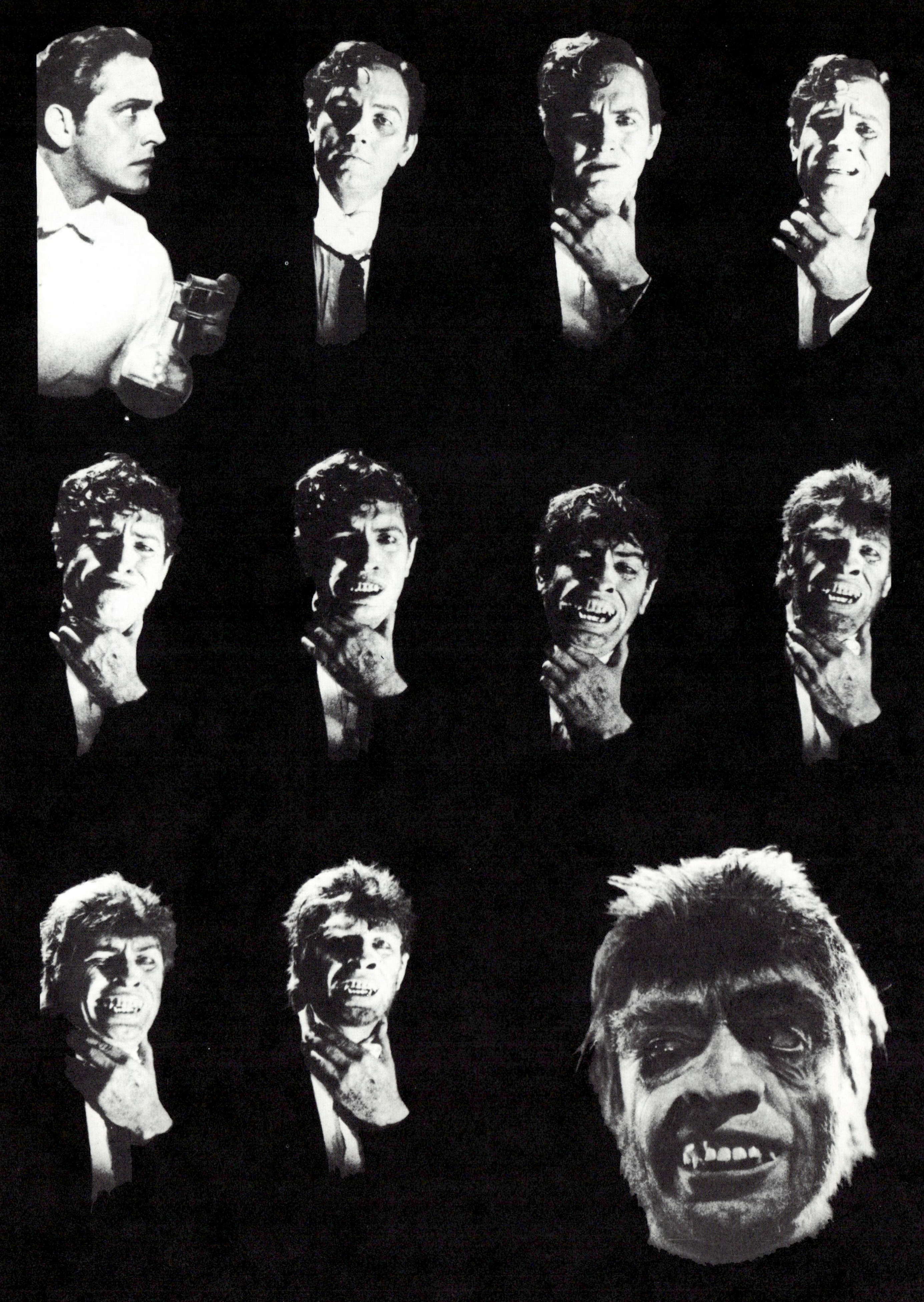

The king of vampires, of course, is the title character of Bram Stoker's famous novel *Dracula* (1897). The bloodthirsty Count first stalked the screen in the silent classic *Nosferatu* (1922). Made by noted German directer F. W. Murnau in the heyday of Germany's expressionist-fantasy period, the film is based on Stoker's book, though both the title and the vampire's name were changed to avoid copyright problems. The Prince of Darkness, here called Count Orlok, is played by Max Schreck ("schreck" is German for terror) beneath a gaunt, taloned, nightmarish makeup—a physical depiction of pure evil. In addition to makeup, mechanical and photographic effects were used to convey the eerie world of the undead. These effects are of variable quality, some of them impressive, others rather crude.

Some of the best effects are in those scenes in which the Count wills doors to open and close as he approaches and passes the entrances. Concealed wires and stop-motion were used to manipulate the doors; the techniques were fundamental even in the early twenties, but they are an effective means of showing the monster's mental power over the physical world. Perhaps the most unearthly effect is used during the coach ride to Orlok's castle near the beginning of the picture. To provide a landscape from an uncanny world, Murnau used negative film for a shot of the forest near the vampire's castle. The result is a countryside where all the proper shades of black and white are reversed.

In keeping with the restrained approach to horror at the time, the scene of Orlok's demise is absolutely bloodless. Instead of Stoker's stake-in-the-heart ending, Murnau's vampire is shown caught in the rays of morning light, fading and then disappearing completely. To accomplish this scene Schreck was filmed in front of a sunlit window while the camera's aperture was closed down until the scene was completely faded out. The camera was then rewound to the beginning of the fade and the same scene, this time without Schreck, was filmed again with the camera fading in. On the screen the overlapping scenes give the impression of a constant background seen through the disappearing form of Count Orlok. As opposed to Stoker's bloodcurdling staking scene, Murnau's climax strikes a ghostly tone.

Much less effective are the scenes in which Murnau used fast motion to show Orlok moving with demonic speed. When a visitor to the Count's castle waits for a coach to arrive, Orlok enters the scene in his own coach and zips along the country road to stop suddenly at his guest's side. Later on, the Count loads a cart with coffins in fast motion in preparation for a journey to his new home. Schreck appears to scurry back and forth like a frenzied automaton. The idea of a supernatural being moving with superhuman quickness makes sense in theory, but on the screen the speeded-up action looks more like madcap comedy than menacing melodrama.

Universal's Bela Lugosi version of *Dracula* in 1931 was not as ambitious as Murnau's film in its use of cinematic tricks. *Dracula* was a faithful adaptation of a successful stage production of Stoker's novel, and the result was a stodgy theatrical treatment that left little room for any action. Dracula's ability to change into a bat or wolf was referred to in dialogue but John Fulton wasn't given the chance to show the transformation taking place. The one memorable effect in the picture appears during Renfield's fateful coach ride to Castle Dracula. As Renfield travels along a bleak mountain road in the oncoming darkness, there is a shot of the coach laboring toward the castle in the distance. The decaying home of the Count is a glass painting matted together with the live action of the coach on the road. The darkly looming castle, matched with the murky countryside, establishes an ominous setting and foreshadows the evil presence of Dracula himself. After this film, composites of castle paintings and live action became a staple of horror movie effects, beginning with early pictures like *White Zombie* (1932) and continuing through the 1970s with the popular horror movies by England's Hammer Films.

In 1943 Universal finally gave John Fulton the opportunity to explore the magical qualities of Dracula. The Count's first appearance in *Son of Dracula* is as a vapor rising from his coffin; the mist then materializes into human form. In a similar sequence later in the movie, Dracula enters a room to confront his enemies by seeping through the crack beneath the door in his vapor form. These illusions were elementary, however, compared to the amazing trick Fulton performed for Universal's next vampire movie, *House of Dracula* (1945), in which we see the Count change from a bat to human form in what appears to be one continuous take. Lugosi had changed into a bat in the 1931 version but the audience didn't see the transition, only the end result: a flapping, wire-manipulated bat-puppet. The great supernatural power of the vampire wasn't demonstrated until Fulton devised the transformation trick for John Carradine, the star of *House of Dracula*. First Fulton photographed the wired bat in action. After cutting the shot, he then filmed a few more feet of the same setup, this time with the bat gone. The camera was stopped again, and in the spot where the bat was last seen, Carradine took his position. The actor was filmed continuing with the action, and then the reel was taken to the lab. Here a sequence of animated cartoons was matted into the middle section of the scene, where there is nothing but an empty set. Frame by frame these black cartoon forms corresponding to the bat were made to grow larger and more human in shape until the last figure exactly matched the outline of Carradine. This process was then reversed when the Transylvanian shrinks into a bat. There is really no doubt when watching one of these scenes that cartoon animation is being used, but the change is so smoothly executed that the illusion of otherworldliness is never spoiled. Three years later this effect was repeated for Bela Lugosi by Stanley Horsley and Jerome Ash in *Abbott and Costello Meet Frankenstein* (1948).

The farcical treatment Universal's formerly magnificent monsters received in *Abbott and Costello Meet Frankenstein* signified the close of an era. At the end of the forties the studio dropped its line of horror movies, and for nearly a decade, Dracula and his friends disappeared, replaced by an endless stream of oversize creatures spawned by nuclear fallout. As anyone who has ever seen a vampire movie knows, however, it takes more than a temporary shift in public taste to keep Dracula down. Drive a stake through his heart, cut off his head, disintegrate him with a blast of bright sunshine—sooner or later Dracula will rise from his grave. In 1958 a little-known British company called Hammer Films revived Stoker's charismatic creation in a movie called *Horror of Dracula*.

Hammer had experimented with low-budget fright films before with increasing success; *Horror of Dracula* turned out to be enough of a blockbuster to establish the company as the successor to Universal in the field of gothic horror. Part of the secret to the popularity of this vampire movie was a fresh, violent approach that employed what were then considered to be very shocking special effects. There were no magical transformations or fog-shrouded landscapes because, as screenwriter Jimmy Sangster has put it, the filmmakers wanted to get away from the fairy-tale aspects of the story. Instead the audience is shown a female vampire being staked through the heart, the wound bursting with blood.

The highlight of the movie, both dramatically and technically, is the final confrontation between Dr. Van Helsing, the vampire-hunter (Peter Cushing), and the Count, played for the first of many times by Christopher Lee. Nearly thirty years before, Bela Lugosi had suffered the indignity of bowing out with an offscreen groan; *Horror of Dracula* set the standard for the destruction of vampires in the second period of the horror movie by staging a prolonged struggle that climaxes with the graphic disintegration of the Count. Exposed to a shaft of sunlight during a fight with Van Helsing, the vampire crawls for the shadows, but Van Helsing crosses a pair of candlesticks and the Count is pinned to the spot by the force of the makeshift crucifix. The awful disintegration then begins. Lee's face peels away and gradually decomposes into dust. Special-effects man Syd Pearson took a day to shoot the complicated sequence.

The scene cuts back and forth between the succeeding stages of the vampire's disintegration and Van Helsing's horrified reactions. The first part of Dracula's body to be hit by a shaft of sunlight is his leg. A skeleton bone was stuck through a pants leg and into a shoe. Pearson lay on the floor out of camera range and rattled the bone to simulate the start of the vampire's death-spasms. Next we see Lee raking his hands down his cheeks in agony and terror, his face peeling away as his nails drag across the flesh. Pearson achieved this gruesome effect by covering Lee's face with dyed mortician's wax and a plastic skin that would tear away under the actor's fingers. As the disintegration progressed, Pearson himself stepped in for Lee, applying a number of claylike compounds to his face, which crumbled and fell away like dust. For the final steps of the monster's destruction a skull covered with fake, rotted-away flesh and fitted with teeth made of a sugar-and-sand mixture was placed on the floor, directly over a small hole. A rotating probe was pushed up through this hole and into the back of the head. As the instrument revolved, the teeth and the last remnants of skin collapsed into tiny particles. In the end all that is left of the Prince of Darkness is some empty clothing and a pile of dust.

The success of this film prompted a long series of vampire pictures from Hammer, beginning with *Brides of Dracula* (1960) and *Kiss of the Vampire* (1963) and continuing through the seventies with such films as *The Scars of Dracula* (1970) and *Vampire Circus* (1972). Although Syd Pearson was responsible for the special effects in *Horror of Dracula,* most of the effects work for the rest of Hammer's vampire movies, as well as most of the company's other horror pictures, was handled by Les Bowie. Just as Hammer was the successor to Universal, Les Bowie was the successor to John Fulton. Bowie became known for supplying the shocking violence for Hammer's Dracula, just as Fulton once endowed Universal's vampire king with evil magic.

Working on a free-lance basis with his own effects company, Les Bowie contributed to many pictures for companies other than Hammer, including Walt Disney's *Swiss Family Robinson* (1960), Stanley Kubrick's *Dr. Strangelove* (1964), and François Truffaut's *Fahrenheit 451* (1966). Like most British special-effects artists Bowie was experienced in all categories of effects, as opposed to the more specialized effects personnel in Hollywood. His talents ranged from model work to traveling mattes to mechanical effects, but the area which he considered himself most expert in was matte painting. While a young man working at Britain's Pinewood Studios, he devised a method of matte painting that revolutionized the art as it was practiced in England by drastically cutting down on time and, as a result, expense. Before Bowie, a live-action set would be projected and traced onto a sheet of glass with wax pencils. The painting would then be added to the outline of the set with slow-drying paints. The whole painstaking process for each matte painting might take as much as a month to complete. When Bowie was given the chance to try his own method, he proved that he could produce a painting in as little as one day.

Bowie set up the camera used for filming the live-action footage so that it could project that footage directly onto a sheet of glass. The artwork was then added to the area of the glass surrounding the projected image. In this way the same camera lens projected the image and photographed the finished composite. Before this a separate projector had been used to throw the image of the live-action scene onto the glass, and since the lens on the projector was never exactly identical to the lens on the camera that would record the final scene, the two elements of painted background and live-action footage often didn't match up. Pinewood was quick to adopt Bowie's ingenious procedure and make him its chief matte-painter.

While working for Hammer, Bowie continued with his matte-painting specialty. The painted hilltop castle was an atmospheric effect retained by Hammer from the tradition of the early thirties. Eerie faked buildings provided a fitting backdrop for the violent action that became a hallmark of Hammer's films. They also served the practical function of leading unsuspecting moviegoers to believe that they were seeing actual sets that the low-budget company could not possibly afford to construct. Bowie's paintings, however, differed from those made for the horror movies of the thirties in a significant way: his artwork was more realistic than the shadowy, gothic matte paintings used in the earlier films. In the thirties, castles always seemed to be seen at night, framed by either fog or low clouds and often besieged by thunderstorms. Bowie's painted castles were often seen in daylight, as in *Dracula—Prince of Darkness* (1966). In this picture the Count's home was shown bathed in sunshine, making the castle look pallid, like the ghostly white face of a vampire. The setting was less overtly melodramatic, but in its own way just as eerie as the traditional misty hilltop.

Another obvious Bowie trademark was the bloody destruction of vampires, the sort of scene that came to typify the gory Hammer approach. The 1963 production of *Kiss of the Vampire* added an unusual twist to the customary bloody climax. In this picture a colony of the living dead is preyed upon by a swarm of bats summoned through incantation. The bats crash through the skylight of the vampires' chateau and peck away at the monsters until they are all annihilated. Bowie engineered the scene with animation and two types of model bats. Cartoon animation was used for the shots of the bats leaving their caves and converging on the chateau. Rubber bats hung from chickenwire were used to produce shadows, while separate models, stuck onto the actors' skin and manipulated by nylon wires, created the illusion that the repulsive creatures were crawling all over the people.

With each successive Dracula movie Bowie had to destroy Christopher Lee at the end of one picture and reconstruct him in the beginning of the next. In order to get the Count back into action in his first sequel, *Dracula—Prince of Darkness,* Bowie had to start with nothing more than the ashes left him by Syd Pearson. The ghastly resurrection begins when Dracula's servant places the vampire's ashes in an open sarcophagus and hangs a recently murdered houseguest by the heels directly overhead. The throat of the victim is slit, the blood drips onto the vampire's remains, and in a smoky, unearthly chemical reaction, the Count slowly materializes. Bowie portrayed the development of the vampire's body by using a series of precisely matched photographs that showed the progressive stages of Dracula's resurrection.

In the movie's finale Dracula meets his end in a novel way when he falls through a sheet of ice and is undone by that bane of the vampire's existence, running water. For close shots Bowie used actual blocks of ice in a swimming pool, and for others he simulated the scene by pouring wax on the water, which hardened into an icelike surface. Onscreen, when Lee loses his balance on a dislodged circle of ice, he was actually standing on a specially constructed section that swiveled on a pivot, dumping the vampire into his watery grave.

In *Dracula Has Risen from the Grave* (1968) Bowie impaled Lee on a crucifix; in *The Scars of Dracula* (1970) it was lightning that did the trick; and in the final Hammer Dracula starring Lee, *Count Dracula and His Vampire Bride* (1978), the Count disintegrates while trapped in a hawthorne bush, yet another of the objects dangerous to Dracula's health. Through all of these Hammer films Bowie made the most of the small budgets allotted him; his gruesome effects and painted castles cleverly made the pictures seem more expensive than they really were. He was finally going to get more opportunity to work on a big-budget vampire movie when he was hired to do the special effects for the Frank Langella *Dracula* (1979). But Bowie died before production began and the work was turned over to other, very capable hands.

The film adaptation of Langella's Broadway stage success was ludicrous in many ways, but from a special-effects standpoint it was a brilliant example of the type of work popularized in the recent period of horror movies by the Hammer Draculas. The matte paintings were handled by the great Albert Whitlock, who supplied *Dracula* with a number of spooky settings, while the extensive physical effects were supervised by Roy Arbogast. The Langella version perfected several of the techniques used by Hammer and added a couple of exciting ideas of its own.

Whitlock contributed ten matte paintings to *Dracula*. Although the film was shot on location in Cornwall, Whitlock's artwork on glass was necessary to turn modern settings into a nineteenth-century landscape. The shot of Lucy driving off in a buggy to join her vampire-lover consisted of a triangular section of live action at the bottom of the screen surrounded by a painting, the most eerie in the movie. As Bowie often did for Hammer, Whitlock relied on elements other than fog or storms to convey a weird setting. This particular landscape, with its close border of hills and forbidding gray sky, manages to be claustrophobic and panoramic, completely naturalistic and yet distinctly uncanny, all at the same time. In no other part of the picture is the uneasy sense of nightmarishness so subtly and convincingly captured. Films like *Earthquake* (1974) and *The Hindenburg* (1975) have given Whitlock the reputation for simulating reality with tremendous accuracy; his landscape shots for *Dracula* show that he is equally capable of shading and molding reality into a dream vision.

Roy Arbogast's physical effects included a wide range of "impossible" scenes staged in their entirety before the camera. No other Dracula movie has endowed the Count with so many onscreen supernatural powers. In one scene, for example, the Count seems to transform himself into a wolf in one take as he runs across a room, crashes through a window, and comes out on the other side in the shape of the beast. The scene was actually shot in two passes with a split screen. First Langella, on the right half of the frame, was filmed going through the window. The left half of the scene was blocked off with a matte. Then, using the same camera setup and a countermatte to block out the right half of the picture, the wolf was photographed jumping out the left side of the window. The two pieces of the scene were joined perfectly to create the metamorphosis of man into wolf in one continuous motion. Actually the trickiest part of this effect was getting the wolf to dive through the window: the wolf was a timid creature who had to be nearly booted out the window.

Perhaps the most shocking moment in the movie occurs when a female vampire is impaled on a stake. As she dashes across an underground vault and is speared by the force of her own motion, the audience sees the stake plunge into her chest and come out of her back in one take. The entrance of the stake was fairly simple: when the vampire ran into the stake, the prop weapon collapsed inside itself to create the impression that it was entering her body. Some padding on the actress's chest was used to blunt the impact of the stake against her body. For the exit of the stake out the back of the vampire, Arbogast rigged a second prop made of foam rubber. This ingenious stake could be flattened against the actress's back and then inflated to its full length by an air hose concealed underneath her clothing. As soon as the telescopic stake went into the actress's front padding, the foam rubber device was instantaneously inflated to project out of her

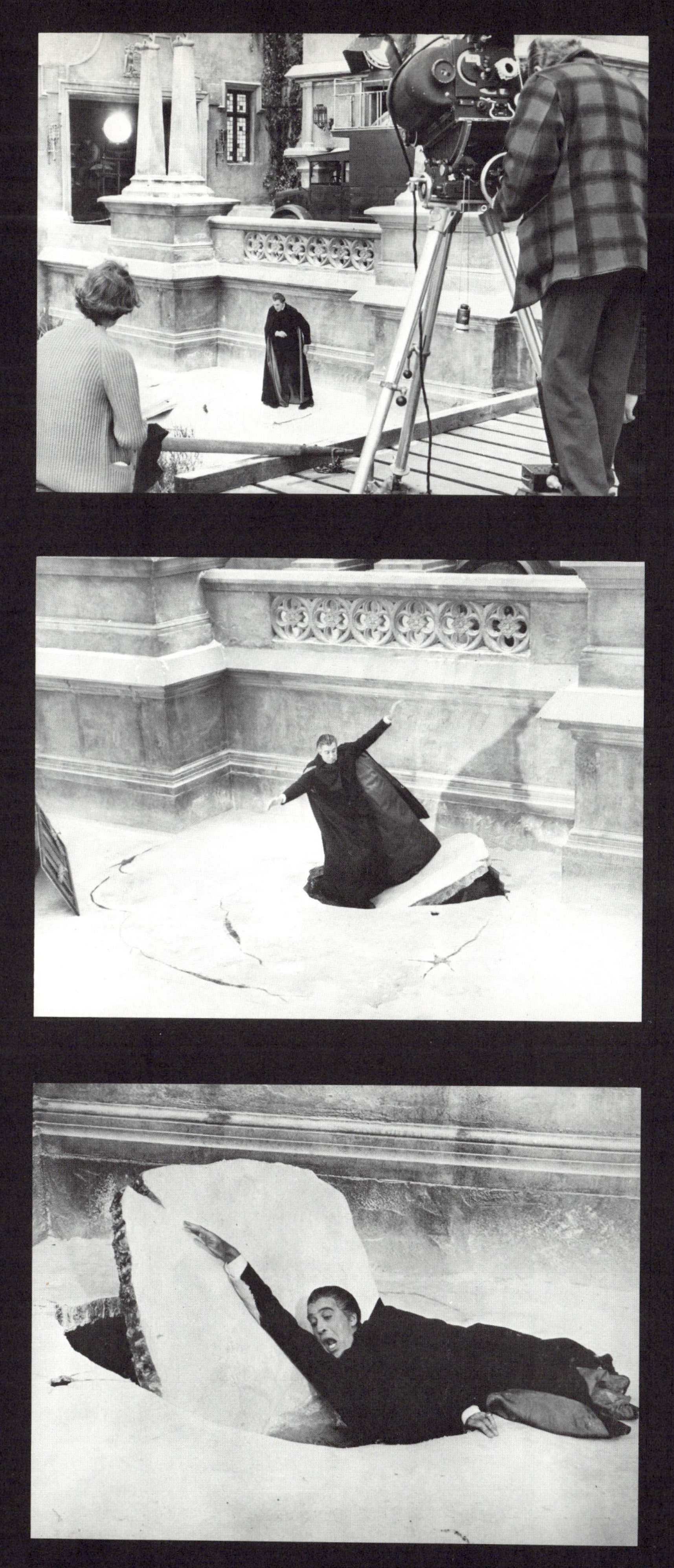

Christopher Lee as Dracula plunges to his death through a swiveling section of fake ice at the end of *Dracula, Prince of Darkness.*

back. Painted blood on the foam rubber device completed the ghastly illusion.

As was true for the specialized vampire film, the recent fashion of explicit special effects for horror movies in general had its beginning with "Hammer Horror" in the late fifties and early sixties. The British company brought back not only Dracula, but all the other familiar monsters in such films as *The Curse of Frankenstein* (1957), *The Mummy* (1959), *The Curse of the Werewolf* (1961), and *The Phantom of the Opera* (1962). Each of these pictures is highlighted by grisly effects displayed in vivid color. For the first time audiences got to see eyeballs and brains preserved in Dr. Frankenstein's laboratory and monsters dissolved in vats of acid. Shock effects helped to make Hammer a lot of money, and other filmmakers followed suit to cash in on this new approach. Among those movies capitalizing on the trend started by Hammer were *Horrors of the Black Museum* (1959), which included a scene of a girl getting stabbed through both eyes by a fiendishly designed pair of binoculars, and *Horror Chamber of Dr. Faustus* (1960), which told the story of a mad surgeon who specialized in face removal.

A more respectable thriller that made use of violent special effects in the early sixties was Alfred Hitchcock's *The Birds* (1963). As Hitchcock confessed to Charles Higham and Joel Greenberg, authors of *The Celluloid Muse,* the depiction of birds on a rampage against humans "posed so many problems that I didn't even bother bringing them up before we started the picture.... The scenes were written in and we had to discover how to do it afterwards." Once the movie went into production, the director found that he could put an army of birds on film by means of four different methods: using actual trained birds (3,200 in all), rear projection, mechanical models, and cartoon animation. At times two or more of these moving elements were printed together in one scene by means of the sodium light traveling matte process.

For the scene in which the birds stream down a chimney and swarm about a room, Hitchcock used real finches. In order to keep them from perching, as was their wont, they were prodded with air hoses. After this scene was printed, he took a shot of more birds flying around in a glass cage before a plain background. Printing these birds over the original scene made the swarm of birds look much denser. In another scene trained birds swoop down to peck at Tippi Hedren's head. A bird was photographed going into a dive, then matted together with the shot of the actress. The moment of impact was faked with a tube running through Hedren's hair. An offscreen operator shot a spurt of air through the tube and the actress's hair flew up as though it had been pecked. Rear projection and models were used in another attack sequence showing Hedren and a group of schoolchildren trying to run away from a pack of birds. In a shot of the actors running toward the camera, the birds, seen closing in from behind, were actually an image projected on a rear screen. To give more depth to the scene, models of birds were suspended on wires directly over the heads of the actors.

Although many of the special effects in Hammer movies and *The Birds* were considered shocking when the films were first released, the violence of these effects seems relatively tame by today's standards. Scenes of monsters disintegrating and birds turning vicious may still horrify, but their impact derives as much from the way the story is constructed as from the details of the effects themselves. The power of Christopher Lee's resurrection scene in *Dracula—Prince of Darkness,* for example, stems largely from the prolonged dramatic buildup leading to the Count's first appearance. Bowie's work seems no less skillful today than it did in the 1960s, but horror pictures of the seventies have revised the standards for visual shock.

The movie that raised the second stage of horror effects to a shocking new height was *The Exorcist* (1973). William Peter Blatty's best-selling novel about the demonic possession of a young girl contains many scenes of appalling feats that were unprecedented in terms of both their ghastly explicitness and the techniques needed to create them. Among the problems faced in the making of *The Exorcist* were: how to levitate a twelve-year-old girl, how to turn her face into a stomach-churning monstrosity, how to spin her head around 180 degrees, and how to make her spew a torrent of green vomit. The task of putting all these scenes on the screen went to mechanical effects man Marcel Vercoutere and makeup artist Dick Smith. According to many news reports, the work of Vercoutere and Smith was believable enough to set off a virtual epidemic of fainting and vomiting among filmgoers.

The sequence showing the young girl (played by Linda Blair) being levitated above her bed was filmed by complicated variations on an old method. Levitating a person isn't in itself a very difficult trick. As most people would suspect, it's done with concealed wires. When working for a director like

Top: Rod Taylor and Tippi Hedren under attack by a flock of malevolent finches in Alfred Hitchcock's *The Birds.* The finches were real birds, kept moving by offscreen air hoses.
Bottom: Mechanical models were used for some of the closeups in *The Birds.* Here, one pecks at Tippi Hedren's face.

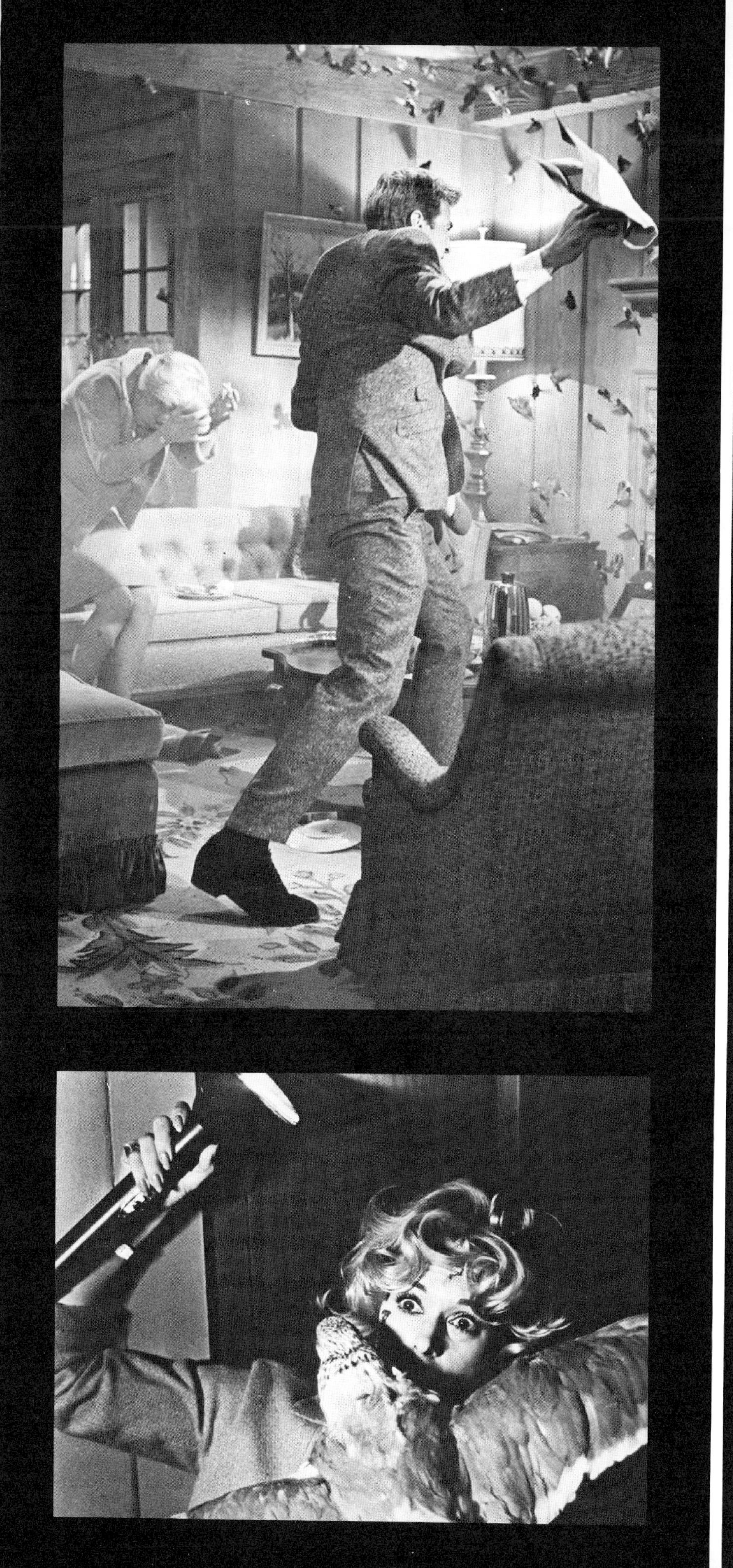

William Friedkin, who demands as much realism as possible, the stunt isn't so simple. The first problem was the placing of the wires overhead. The usual technique for filming such a scene is to keep the top of the set out of the shot so that the whole ceiling can be removed and wire rigging installed in its place. But Friedkin wasn't willing to sacrifice the low angle shot he had in mind, in which part of the ceiling would have to be seen. This meant that a special ceiling had to be constructed with an opening in the middle to accommodate the wires. The other problem was masking the wires. When shooting against a solid background, all that has to be done is match the color of the wires with the color of whatever is behind them. The conventional approach was once again overruled by Friedkin. The director insisted on the shifting background of light and shadows that was essential for creating the right foreboding feeling for the scene. There was no way that cinematographer Owen Roizman could photograph the room without wires showing when the background passed from one shade of light to another. To compensate for this, lab technicians had to perform the painstaking task of painting over the visible wires on the film itself, frame by frame, for almost the entire sequence.

Once her character is fully possessed by the demon, Linda Blair's face becomes a hideous mass of scars and welts. Previously makeup man Dick Smith had made a prominent name for himself with such work as Marlon Brando's aging Don Corleone in *The Godfather* (1972) and the uncanny transformation of boyish Dustin Hoffman into a 120-year-old man in *Little Big Man* (1970). He was able to turn wholesome-looking Linda Blair into a monstrosity by making foam latex masks of the actress. At least one new mask had to be made for each day of shooting and was applied to Blair's face in sections. Smith's demonic makeup ranks with the best creations of his idol, Jack Pierce; the contrast between Smith's work and Pierce's—between the relative restraint of Karloff's severe Frankenstein makeup and the noxious, oozing detail of Smith's prepubescent fiend—reflects the shifting styles in horror films from the thirties to the seventies. Another important difference between Smith and his predecessor is that Pierce's work was limited to disguising actors, while Smith has become directly involved in mechanical effects.

Smith was responsible for the raised welts that appear on Linda Blair's stomach to form the words "Help me." Experimenting with certain kinds of petroleum distillates, he found that these substances could make foam latex swell. By molding a false stomach appliance for Blair out of latex and writing out the words with cleaning fluid, he could form the pathetic plea on what appears to be the girl's belly. Finding a way to form the letters was tricky enough, but finding a way to make the words rise on their own posed even more of a problem. Finally Smith hit upon a cleaning fluid called Trichloroethylene. This solvent acted as a kind of invisible ink when applied to latex. Like other distillates it made the letters rise. As it evaporated, however, the letters disappeared virtually without a trace. To shoot the scene, Smith first raised the words on the fake surface of Blair's stomach. Then, standing out of camera range, he aimed a flameless heat gun (an instrument that resembles a hand-held hairdryer, though it blows a much hotter gust of air) at the writing. This caused the Trichloroethylene to evaporate very rapidly, and the letters along with it. At the same time the camera was undercranked to make the disappearance proceed even more quickly. To show the desperate plea popping out of Blair's stomach, the footage was simply run in reverse.

The head-revolving was an equally difficult problem. Smith explained his solution in the motion-picture and stage technicians' *Official Bulletin* (Winter 1973–74): "I confess I couldn't figure how to get Linda's head to turn completely around and so I had to make a dummy of her. Linda's entire body was molded in sections in a sitting-up-in-bed position, using fast-setting plaster bandages. Plaster positives were cast and refined. Then hydrocal molds were made from the casts. When we molded Linda's head, I glued on the appliances, put in her teeth and scleral contacts. We used dental alginate, timed to set in 2¼ minutes, for the mold so that Linda could keep her eyes and mouth open and smile. She did it perfectly."

This copy of Linda Blair was uncannily accurate, but in order to make it seem alive it needed movement. The head was stuck onto an axle housed in the dummy's chest. Attached to the axle was a flexible cable that ran down through a hole in the bed and was turned by an offscreen operator cranking a handle. (The dummy's hair was wrapped around the neck to conceal the separation between the two parts.) Armatures, which are flexible steel skeletons, were fitted into the arms and legs to make for some limited motion of the limbs. Marcel Vercoutere added a truly unsettling detail to the dummy by rigging up a model-airplane remote control system that moved the eyeballs in the fake head. Vercoutere's finishing touch was to make the dummy breathe.

The setting for the head-revolving scene was the child's bedroom, which in the movie had been turned as cold as the inside of a freezer by the presence of the demon Pazuzu. The set had been refrigerated to make the actors' breath come out as a frosted mist. One day, director of photography Roizman facetiously remarked, "Wouldn't it be great if the dummy had some frost on its breath?" Vercoutere immediately went to work on it. He ran a pipe for pumping steam through the rotating axle in the dummy's head and up into its mouth. When the steam shot out into the frigid studio air, it condensed and the dummy had been made to "breathe." In the short time that the dummy with the revolving head appears in the picture, the breath is the most noticeable of the lifelike effects created by Vercoutere for the scene.

The green vomit has been described by Dick Smith as his most difficult effect in the picture. He had to devise a way of concealing a tube that went across the face of the possessed child and into her mouth so that pea soup could be pumped out like vomit. Because the device Smith cooked up for the stunt was so uncomfortable to wear, a double was used for the twelve-year-old Blair. On his first try Smith inserted the plastic tube through a corner of the girl's mouth. A nozzle at the end of the tube was concealed inside and the part of the tube running along the actress's cheek was masked with foam rubber. The test film was shot so that only three quarters of the actress's face was seen, the tube concealed on the unseen quarter. The results were perfect, or so Smith thought: the hot pea soup was propelled by an offscreen pump, traveled through the tubing, and spurted out of the mouth as hoped, and there were no signs of where it came from. However, Friedkin looked at it and told Smith it wouldn't do; the director was determined to shoot the scene full-face. Smith protested that it couldn't be done, but was told to figure out a way.

The solution that Smith arrived at was to pass tubes over both cheeks; after the tubes were covered up on both sides, the resulting buildup on the actress's face would look like balanced features when the camera was positioned directly in front of her. Hiding the tubes required that Smith make Plexiglas molds of the girl's cheeks. Attached to the inside of the molds were flat tubes about three sixteenths of an inch thick. Partial latex masks covered the Plexiglas while additional makeup and a wig made the whole facial setup invisible. The tubes underneath the molds passed through both corners of the girl's retracted mouth and came together inside, forming a contrivance that resembled a horse's bit. To the front of the connected tubes was a nozzle. On the outside, behind the Plexiglas, the tubing ran under the actress's ears and were hooked up with Vercoutere's pea-soup pump. When Vercoutere started the pump, the green liquid passed around the actress's face on both sides and spewed out of the nozzle in her mouth.

Ironically Smith discovered several years after the release of the film that all his hard work on this effect had been for nothing. It appeared that the perfectionist Friedkin, unhappy about using a double for Blair, had in the end removed the footage containing Smith's vomit effect and used a different method of producing the illusion: he shot Blair as she went through the motions of lurching forward in bed and retching, then had a stream of vomit superimposed on an optical printer.

Since it was such a phenomenal box office success, *The Exorcist* inevitably spawned a host of imitations and variations that emphasized the type of graphic effects found in the Friedkin picture. The most disappointing of these followups was *The Exorcist* sequel, *Exorcist II: The Heretic* (1977). An incoherent mixture of realism, the supernatural, pulp science fiction, and a dash of jungle adventure, it even managed to squander the efforts of Albert Whitlock. Like other cheaper entries in the Demonic Possession Sweepstakes, the horror effects, even when done well, had little shock value because there wasn't a solid story to support them. One exception to this rule was *The Omen* (1976), which combined the horrific effects of *The Exorcist* with the antichrist theme first popularized by Ira Levin's *Rosemary's Baby*.

The most gruesome of *The Omen*'s shock scenes is the decapitation of a photographer (David Warner), perhaps the most convincing effect of its kind ever done. A typical example of an earlier attempt at beheading appears in the 1964 thriller *Hush... Hush, Sweet Charlotte,* in which the actual severing of the head is handled very obliquely: the action is covered in a series of quick, shadowy shots; little of the violence is clearly shown. The completion of the action, however, belongs to the post-Hammer tradition: we see the bloody, severed head bounce to the floor. The problem with the sequence is that the dummy head looks exactly like what it is—a dummy. In *The Omen,* on the other hand, when a sailing sheet of glass slices off David Warner's head, it's difficult to believe that the beheading is not real, especially because the camera lingers on it in slow motion. The sequel, *Damien—Omen II* (1978), duplicated the success of this scene by showing us a man sliced in half by an out-of-control elevator cable.

If the occult craze that began in the late sixties made Satan and his various offspring into motion-picture superstars, it also created a huge market for films dealing with such psychic phenomena as ESP and telekinesis. The best of the telekinesis pictures was Brian De Palma's *Carrie* (1976). Starting with the downtrodden Carrie's vengeful outburst at her high-school prom, special-effects man Gregory Auer was kept very busy staging one horrifying disaster after another. The violence begins when Carrie (Sissy Spacek) makes the school gym go up in hellish flames. Auer started the blaze by combining his physical-effects know-how with the work of stuntman Bobby Bass, who acted as a human torch. Bass's coat, which was dabbed with inflammable rubber cement, was set on fire by sparks flying from a microphone. Pretending to recoil in shock, Bass fell back onto a wall set-up of slotted "burner pipes" fed by a propane gas pump. The burning coat ignited the propane to create a backdrop of fire. Because Bass's skin was covered with a protective coating of sodium silicate, he was able to walk away with only a reddened hand.

Later on, when Carrie returns home, she takes revenge on her tyrannical mother (Piper Laurie) by mentally propelling a set of kitchen knives across the room and impaling her to the wall. The knives had special blades that collapsed into their hilts when something pressed against the points. These trick implements were fired across the room on wires and were rammed into the protective harnesses and breastplate worn by Laurie. Some interdepartmental planning between Auer and art director Jack Fisk helped to keep most of the wires invisible. Fisk designed the room with wainscoting in such a way that the lines of the room's paneling corresponded closely enough to the wires to help conceal them. Unfortunately, in one instance, a wire was clearly visible.

The move toward increasingly graphic horror effects was apparent not only in films of the supernatural. In 1975 Steven Spielberg showed people being eaten alive by a monster from the natural world in *Jaws*. This terrifying story of a marauding great white shark preying on summer vacationers at a resort community demanded extensive and extremely difficult special-effects work in order to put actors and a man-eater in the same scenes.

At first the producers entertained the vague notion that they might be able to use actual sharks by splicing together footage of trained great whites with shots of the actors. Before very long it became clear that sharks were not the most manageable of creatures and were not likely to take kindly to direction, even from a wunderkind like Spielberg. Although live footage could be employed in conjunction with something else, what that something else should be remained a big question mark. Spielberg wouldn't be content unless he could put the great white and the actors in the same frame. Eventually it became clear that the only logical answer was a full-scale mechanical mock-up that could swim, dive, leap, and chomp on a man. There was no precedent for such a creation.

The one movie monster that approached this sort of versatility was the giant squid in Walt Disney's *20,000 Leagues Under the Sea* (1954). This mechanical monster, a two-ton hydraulically operated contraption made of rubber, plastic, and steel, was the work of special-effects man Bob Mattey. Mattey had started his career in 1927, worked at Douglas Fairbanks Studios, engineered the camp-classic, sputtering rocket ships in the *Flash Gordon* serials, and had been one of the most valuable technicians in the Disney studio for seventeen years. He also happened to be retired. The producers of *Jaws* lured him back into moviemaking with the challenge of the shark and a very large salary.

Mattey constructed the prototypes for the mechanical fish in collaboration with production designer Joe Alves, Jr. Alves did shark research at the Scripps Institute and the California Academy of Science, talked to experts, and studied all the available literature. Working from small clay models and full-scale drawings, Alves produced a life-size sculpture of the shark. This sculpture was then used to make the mold from which the final, plastic body of the great white was cast. While the designer worked at what the shark should look like, Mattey figured out how it would operate. The effects man constructed a small-scale mechanical model and presented a successful tabletop demonstration.

In the end Mattey's plan called for not one but three separate mechanical sharks, each designed to perform a different function, each nicknamed "Bruce" (after Spielberg's attorney). Two of the mock-ups were half-sharks: they were photographed only from the left or right side; their off-camera sides were

Top: The giant squid from *20,000 Leagues Under the Sea* under construction in a Disney workshop. *Center:* Technicians set up the completed squid for its attack on the submarine *Nautilus.* *Bottom:* The mechanical squid in action.

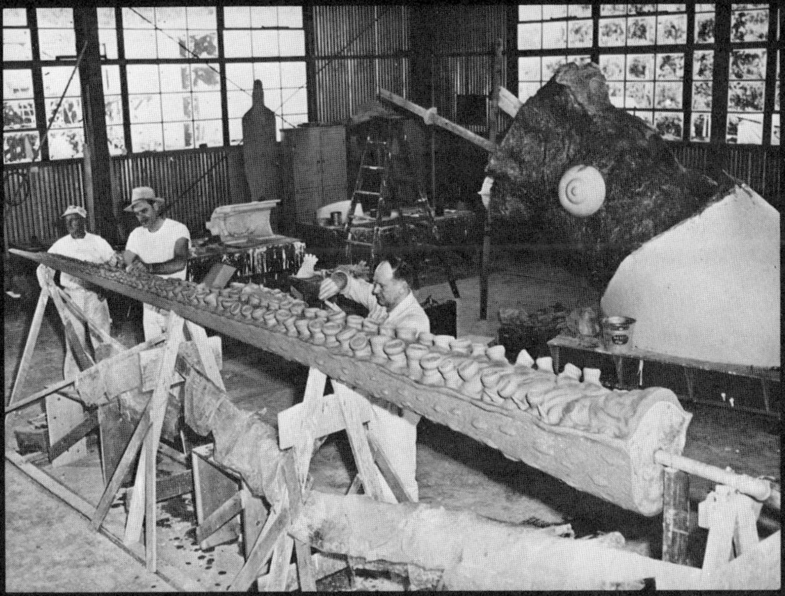

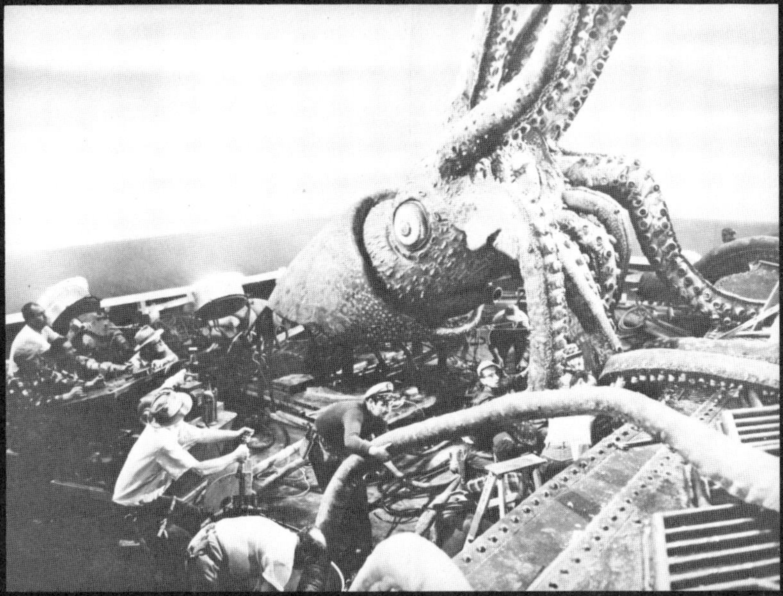

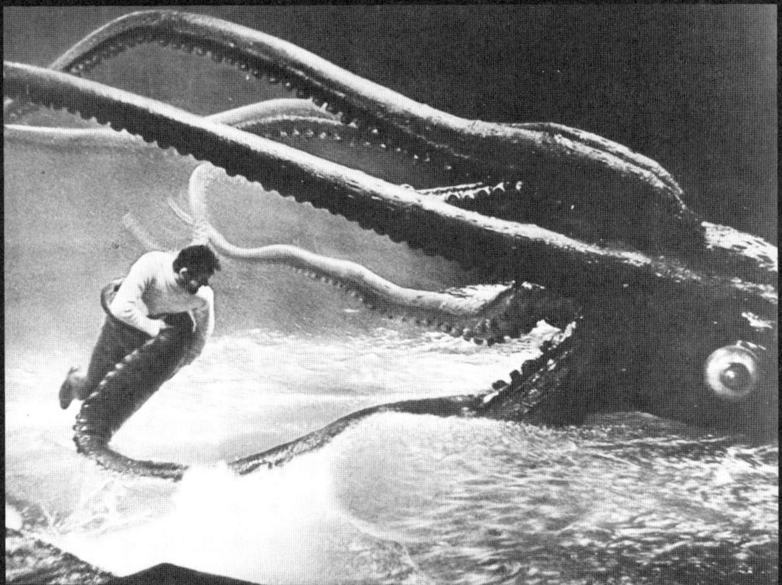

left open to allow for easy access to the machinery inside, a complex system of hydraulics, pneumatics, and electronics. Each of these half-sharks was capable of a wide range of movement, which was controlled by a mechanized steel platform connected to the models from below. The platform, which rolled along on underwater rails, could make the sharks bite, flop, or dive. The third Bruce was a full shark-body hooked up to an underwater setup called a "sea sled," which was manned by scuba divers out of camera range. The sled shark could glide along the surface and was therefore nicknamed "the floater." The three twenty-five-foot, 2,000-pound mechanical mock-ups cost a quarter of a million dollars each to produce, while the cost for making them perform has been reported at both $500,000 and $1,000,000.

Duplicating the skin of the great white was one of the more difficult assignments for the effects crew. The original paint-on-liquid-plastic mock-up skin did not have the sandpapery quality of real shark skin; to reproduce the right texture, actual sand was applied along with the paint. The all-important teeth came in two sets: one of hard plastic for general use and one of rubber for munching actors.

Once on location the effects crew found they were confronted with many problems they hadn't anticipated: the skins had to be replaced weekly because they became sunbleached and the mechanisms of the sharks were almost constantly in need of repair because of the corroding action of salt water. Even with the crew working around the clock, only one mock-up was in functioning order at any time. And when the sharks *were* working, they were hard to control, as if they had irascible, contrary minds of their own. On one occasion one of the sharks was manipulated into a dive and the crew wasn't able to steer it back up to the surface until the shark had crashed into its own platform. It was out of action for a week while its bashed-in snout was laboriously put back into shape.

In spite of all the frustrations the effort paid off. The scenes involving Bruce build to a horrifying climax as a result of Spielberg's technique of revealing the monster in progressively longer glimpses. In the first half of the film there is no clear sighting of the big shark. When Bruce finally makes his first appearance, it is only for a brief moment alongside the shark hunters' boat. A bored Roy Scheider is baiting his prey by ladling chum overboard when the great white suddenly leaps above the ocean surface to gobble up one of the chunks. The enormous size and sudden agile movements of the mock-up stun both Scheider and the audience. After this first potent glimpse Spielberg displays more of the shark in increasingly dramatic steps: he eventually shows the creature in action for a fairly extended interval when the great white hammers away at Richard Dreyfuss's shark cage, and then has it leap straight out of the water and onto the rear deck of the boat for the horrifying sequence in which Robert Shaw is eaten alive by the monstrous fish. Stretched out on the deck in bright sunshine, Bruce looks unmistakably artificial, but the image of a shark eating a man alive is so disturbing that we tend to ignore the rubber teeth and painted skin. By getting the best possible full-scale working mock-ups and putting the shark and the man in the same frame, Spielberg was able to produce a thoroughly terrifying illusion.

The phenomenal success of *Jaws,* which was essentially a high-technology remake of such 1950s monster flicks as *Creature from the Black Lagoon* (1954) and *The Creature Walks Among Us* (1956), proved that expensive effects added to a reliable old B-movie formula could produce a box office bonanza. Other filmmakers didn't take long to catch on. The blockbuster horror movie of 1979, *Alien,* was a stylish, highly sophisticated, extremely gory production whose plot was lifted virtually intact from the 1958 exploitation movie, *It! The Terror from Beyond Space.*

During preproduction on *Alien,* the key decision that would determine the success of the special effects was what the alien monster would look like. Most creatures from outer space that appeared in movies before *Alien* were usually hairy or scaley, and were obviously nothing more than men in rubber suits who were rarely frightening and always seemed too anthropomorphic to have come from another world. And the one alien that managed not to be human-looking at all was even sillier than the monster-suit variety—the flowing raspberry colored mass of gelatin in *The Blob* (1958). In order to involve the audience in their story, the makers of *Alien* had to invent a creature that looked completely extraterrestrial.

Dan O'Bannon, screenwriter for the film, was the first to hit upon the perfect visual concept for the monster. He had found a book of illustrations called *Necronomicon* by the Swiss artist H. R. Giger and was fascinated by the book's unearthly drawings. The creatures that Giger had conjured up were an obscene mixture of the organic and mechanical, a combination that the artist has described as "biomechanical." These beings were sex-

Top: Makeup artist Rick Baker transforms actor Alex Rebar in *The Incredible Melting Man. Bottom:* A close-up of Alex Rebar as Colonel Steve West, an astronaut who returns from an expedition to Saturn with a horrible disease that causes his flesh to melt.

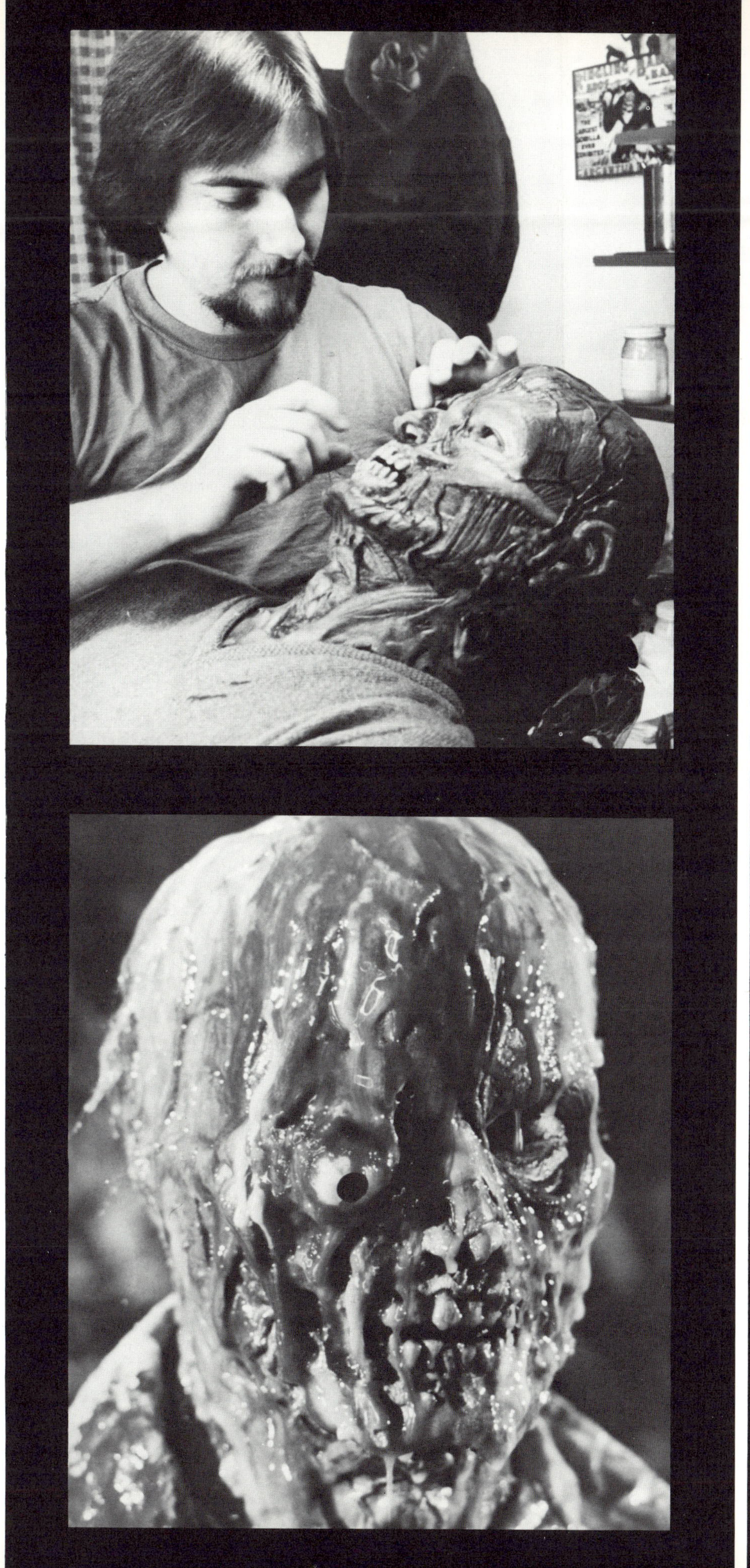

ual, slimy, elegant and repulsive in approximately equal proportions. More importantly these conglomerations of phallic tubes, rippling sinews, and skeletal-metallic features didn't look like anything from this world. O'Bannon was convinced that the Giger illustrations should be a blueprint for the monster.

Initially the producers of the movie refused to consider using the Giger drawings as models because they found them too disgusting. O'Bannon showed them to director Ridley Scott, to whom they were as much a revelation as they had been to O'Bannon; the director insisted on using them for the picture. With Scott's approval not only were the drawings used but the artist himself was hired as a designer.

Since the movie showed the entire life cycle of the alien, Giger had to design the creature in several stages of growth. Adapting his *Necronomicon* drawings to three-dimensional form, he first designed and constructed the adult alien (known as the "big chap" on the set) and then jumped back to its beginning (the egg) and worked up from there. Although the designs were all his, Giger only had the time to model the first and final stages. To construct the viscous organism that springs out of the egg (the "face hugger") and the baby that crashes through John Hurt's chest (the "chest burster"), Roger Dicken, formerly of Hammer, was called in.

Along with the creation of the monster, Giger was also involved in the design of what was the space age equivalent of the gloomy-castle matte painting used in so many earlier horror films. When the earthlings land on the mysterious distant planet, a reconnaissance party scouts the planet's surface and comes across a forbidding alien spacecraft nestled among the rocks and veiled in mist. Giger made the derelict ship as eerie as any hilltop castle by designing the craft along unearthly biomechanical lines: the horseshoe-shaped vessel has a worn, boney surface that makes it appear to be both a manufactured object and a fossilized skeleton. The reconnaissance party enters the ship through a large, distinctly vaginal opening. Unlike the usual castle scene the long shots of the spaceship establish the macabre mood through the use of models rather than paintings. A twelve-foot-wide model was constructed for the distant shots of the three astronauts approaching the mystery ship. All that is seen of the three people is the glare of the searchlights that each of them carries; in actuality the "people" are little puppets rigged with lights.

The supervisors of the picture's special effects were Brian Johnson and Nick Allder. They both received their training in gory effects with Les Bowie and Hammer, and served their apprenticeship for spaceship effects by working wonders with the meager budget of television's *Space: 1999.* According to Johnson much of *Alien*'s great success is due to the intensive preproduction planning of the effects. Many times producers and directors begin the shooting of a film without fully mapping out what will be involved with the effects; when the effects technician is finally brought in, he doesn't have sufficient time to prepare his work and coordinate it with the efforts of other members of the crew. The part of *Alien* that best illustrates the benefits of sound planning is the stupefying chest-bursting scene, in which the efforts of the mechanical-effects men, the model-makers, and the director were perfectly coordinated to create one of the most bloodcurdling moments ever put on film.

In order to get the baby alien to burst out of John Hurt, a false chest had to be molded for the actor. When the scene was set up, a table with a cutaway section was used; the mechanical-effects crew positioned Hurt in this section in such a way that most of his body was below the table. Above the table Hurt's head, shoulders, and arms were lined up with the false chest to create the illusion that he was lying on the table. The effects crew shattered the false chest from below with a system of pneumatic rams while an offscreen pump made the blood gush through the opening. The baby alien modeled by Roger Dicken was a puppet, a vicious little creature with a blind, phallic head and a gaping mouth bristling with chromium teeth. Once the chest was exploded, the alien-puppet was operated by hand. The vivid work of the mechanical-effects crew and the model-maker was made even more powerful by Ridley Scott's staging of the scene. While all the effects preparations were being made, the cast, with the exception of Hurt, was kept off the set. The filming of the scene began with none of these performers knowing exactly what to expect; when the repulsive, blood-smeared little beast popped out of Hurt's chest, the actors' shock was a genuine reaction to something authentically monstrous. Veronica Cartwright, especially shaken by the sequence, was knocked out of her seat by the jetting blood.

The "big chap" was a man in a rubber suit, but the conception, construction, and operation of this costume put it in a completely different class from the usual run of monster suits. Of all the stages of the alien the adult version was the closest adaptation of Giger's *Necronomicon* drawings, complete in all their hideous detail. The head in particular, the part that is emphasized, is especially unnerving. In an interview Giger described a problem he had in deciding how the alien would see:

In the first design for the alien, he had big black eyes. But somebody said he looked too much like a . . . what do you call it . . . a Hell's Angel; all in black and black goggles. And then I thought: It would be even more frightening if there are no eyes! We made him blind! Then when the camera comes close, you see only the holes of the skull. Now that's really frightening. Because, you see, even without eyes he always knows exactly where his victims are, and he attacks directly, suddenly, unerringly. Like a striking snake.

The actual construction of the head was handled by Carlo Rambaldi, the effects expert who built the forty-foot King Kong robot for Dino De Laurentiis's remake and the mechanical alien that appears at the end of *Close Encounters of the Third Kind.* As with Bruce, the star of *Jaws,* three separate matching props were constructed for Giger's alien: a lightweight, nonfunctioning head for long shots; a partially working head that could curl its lips into a snarl; and a truly extraordinary, fully mechanized head capable of a wide range of facial movements, all of them completely malevolent. The most remarkable feature of the alien is its obscene, slobbering mouth: whenever the monster would open wide its jaws, a thick, rigid tongue with a separate set of teeth on the end of it would shoot out to penetrate the victim. This mechanical tongue ran along a geared track and was made to protrude and retract by a powerful spring mechanism.

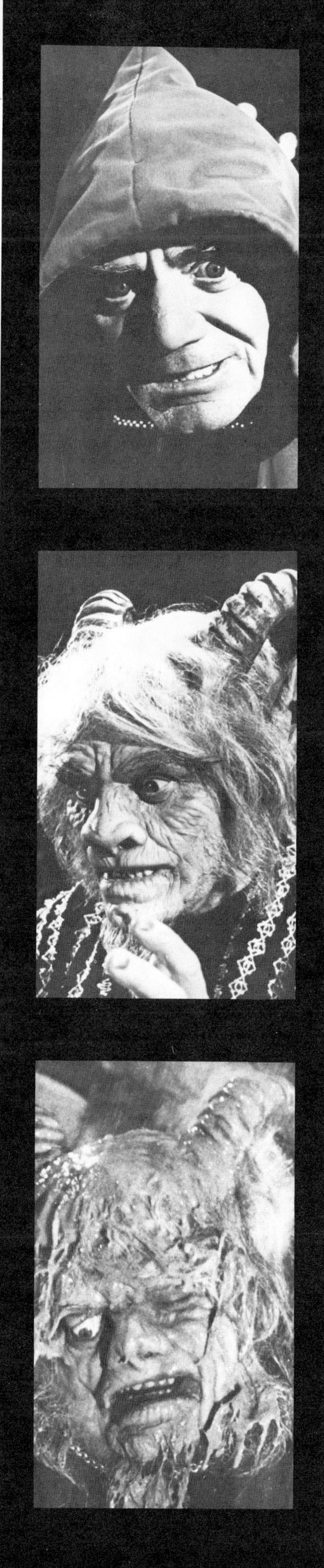

Every moving part of the head was attached to a flexible cable forty-five feet long, which ended in a hand-held lever control. To make the monster look thoroughly revolting, fluid was poured down its lips whenever it opened its mouth; its tongue was coated with K-Y jelly, and shredded prophylactics were used to simulate the membranous tendons of its jaws.

Though some of the most horrific scenes in the movie were trimmed or cut out entirely (including one episode in which a crewmember discovers the captain wrapped in a monstrous cocoon, his still-living body being slowly devoured from within by the alien larvae breeding inside it), the gory effects that remain are as disturbing as any ever put onscreen. The audience is shown, in nightmarish detail, John Hurt's chest exploding, the repulsive head of the alien closing in on its victims, and the deadly ribbed tongue of the monster boring into a blood-filled replica of Yaphet Kotto's head. In light of these images, it is tempting to claim that *Alien* is the ultimate shock-effects picture. But the standards for graphic effects do not remain constant long enough to allow such a claim to be made with any assurance. Six years before *Alien* appeared, *The Exorcist* seemed to be the last word in shocking special effects. *Alien* has demonstrated that the technology of horror is an ever-expanding field.

Ernest Borgnine undergoes a monstrous metamorphosis in *The Devil's Rain.*

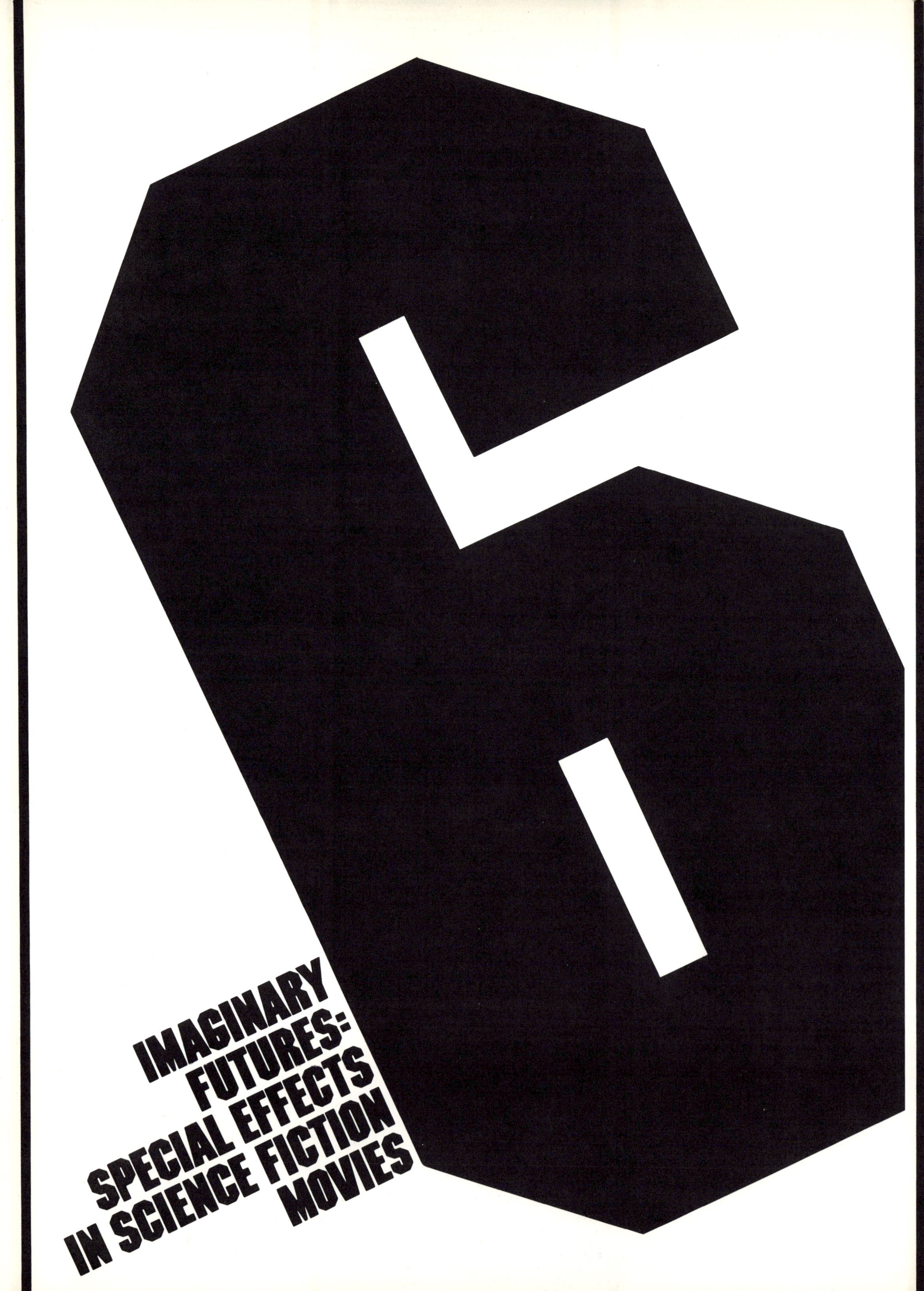
6
IMAGINARY
FUTURES:
SPECIAL EFFECTS
IN SCIENCE FICTION
MOVIES

Of all genres science fiction has been the greatest showcase for diversified, virtuoso special effects. Almost all science fiction movies have required effects of one kind or another and those effects have been of the most spectacular variety. Flying saucers, shrinking men, invisible men, giant insect mutations, futuristic cities, and swashbuckling dogfights in far-off galaxies—these fantastic visions are a sampling of the sort of work created by special-effects artists in science fiction films. To produce these visions, the effects man has to speculate on what the products of advanced technology will look like. This task demands that the effects artist draw on all aspects of his own cinematic technology. Recent science fiction movies like *Star Wars* (1977) and *The Black Hole* (1979) employed electronic computer devices that are almost as complex and sophisticated as the futuristic gadgetry seen on the screen.

More often than not, however, the technological wonders displayed in science fiction pictures are created by shrewd variations on the basic special-effects methods. Miniatures, matte paintings, and the combining of two or more visual elements to make one image constitute a sizable portion of the effects man's repertoire of techniques when staging out-of-this-world illusions. In those instances when no conventional technique seems to apply, solutions are improvised with the help of the most basic effects approach—seat-of-the-pants ingenuity. Whatever approach effects artists use, imagination and clever juggling of visual elements are indispensable in converting their effects technology into what seem to be miracles of advanced science.

Historically, ingenious use of miniatures was perhaps the first technique used to fascinate viewers of science fiction films. Fritz Lang's 1926 production of *Metropolis* dealt with the classic science fiction theme of dehumanization in a future, automated society. Filming this story meant that a technologically advanced city somehow had to be put on the screen. Since the building of an entire city set was impractical, Lang chose to create the illusion of a futuristic city by substituting a miniature. The small-scale model of Metropolis was an intricate, spectacular looking cityscape teeming with the traffic of miniature cars. To a great extent Lang's crew made the miniature convincing through detail and movement. Not only did cars cruise along the roadways at ground level, but model autos were seen traveling on elevated streets which ran past the upper tiers of skyscrapers, just below the route of a miniature airplane that glided through the main artery of the city.

The most important criterion for the believability of a miniature, of course, is whether it can be made to appear much larger than it really is. One way that Lang made his model seem like a monumental work of architecture was to use the shrewd, deceptive technique called forced perspective. The buildings further away from the camera were constructed on a smaller scale than the foreground structures. This exaggerated scale made the background buildings seem much more distant than they really were; in other words, the perspective was forced. In this way, Lang gave his miniature city greater dimension.

Another technique he used was to insert images of the actors into the miniature surroundings by use of what is called the Schüfftan process. Basically this effect involved an adaptation of an old theatrical trick in which a skeleton placed to the side of a stage could be made to appear in front of the audience by reflecting its image off of an angled sheet of glass. In *Metropolis,* actors to the side of the camera could be reflected into the doorway of a miniature by using a specially prepared mirror from which part of the silvered coating had been removed, leaving a reflective area surrounded by clear glass. The actors, standing in a mock-up doorway, were reflected off this mirrored area; at the same time, the camera photographed the miniature building which was set up behind the glass. This device allowed Lang to make the model buildings seem full-size by making the miniatures appear large enough to house his actors.

The concept of using miniatures to film futuristic cities has seen a lot of use. The immediate influence of the model work in *Metropolis* was evident in a 1930 American picture called *Just Imagine.* A hypothetical city of 1980 was elaborately constructed in miniature for $250,000. The model boasted 250-story skyscrapers, downtown canals to transport ocean liners, and landing decks for private aircraft. The set succeeded in surpassing the one in *Metropolis* in detail and scope, but unfortunately the extravagant *Just Imagine* model was wasted in an inane, futuristic musical comedy.

Miniatures also played an important part in the filming of an advanced city in the British utopia story *Things to Come* (1936). This view of the future authored by H. G. Wells envisioned an enclosed city made up of vast, multitiered interiors. Scenes of the city were assembled through composites of miniatures, live action on partial sets, and mirror-shot elements similar

The miniature city of the future constructed for Fritz Lang's *Metropolis.*

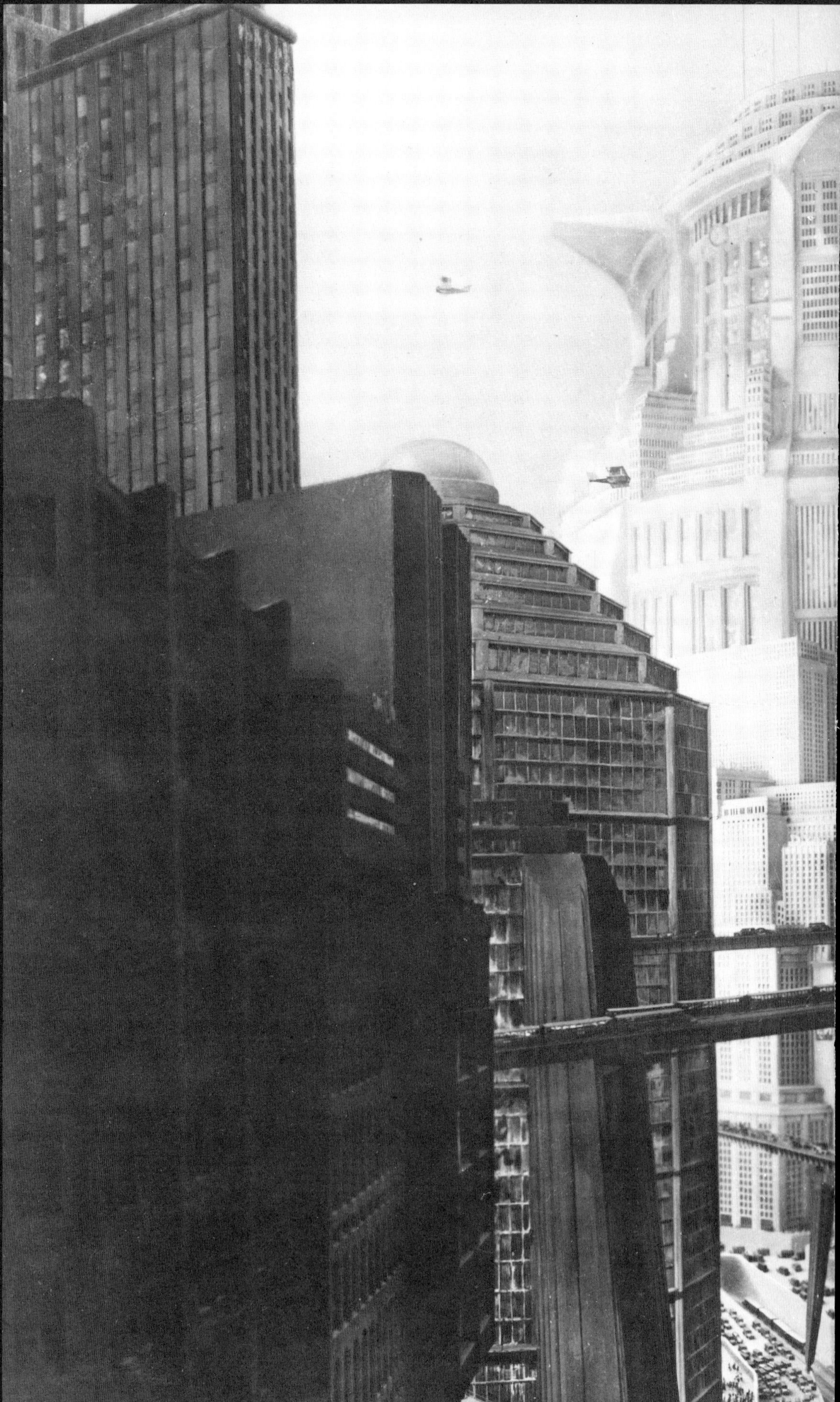

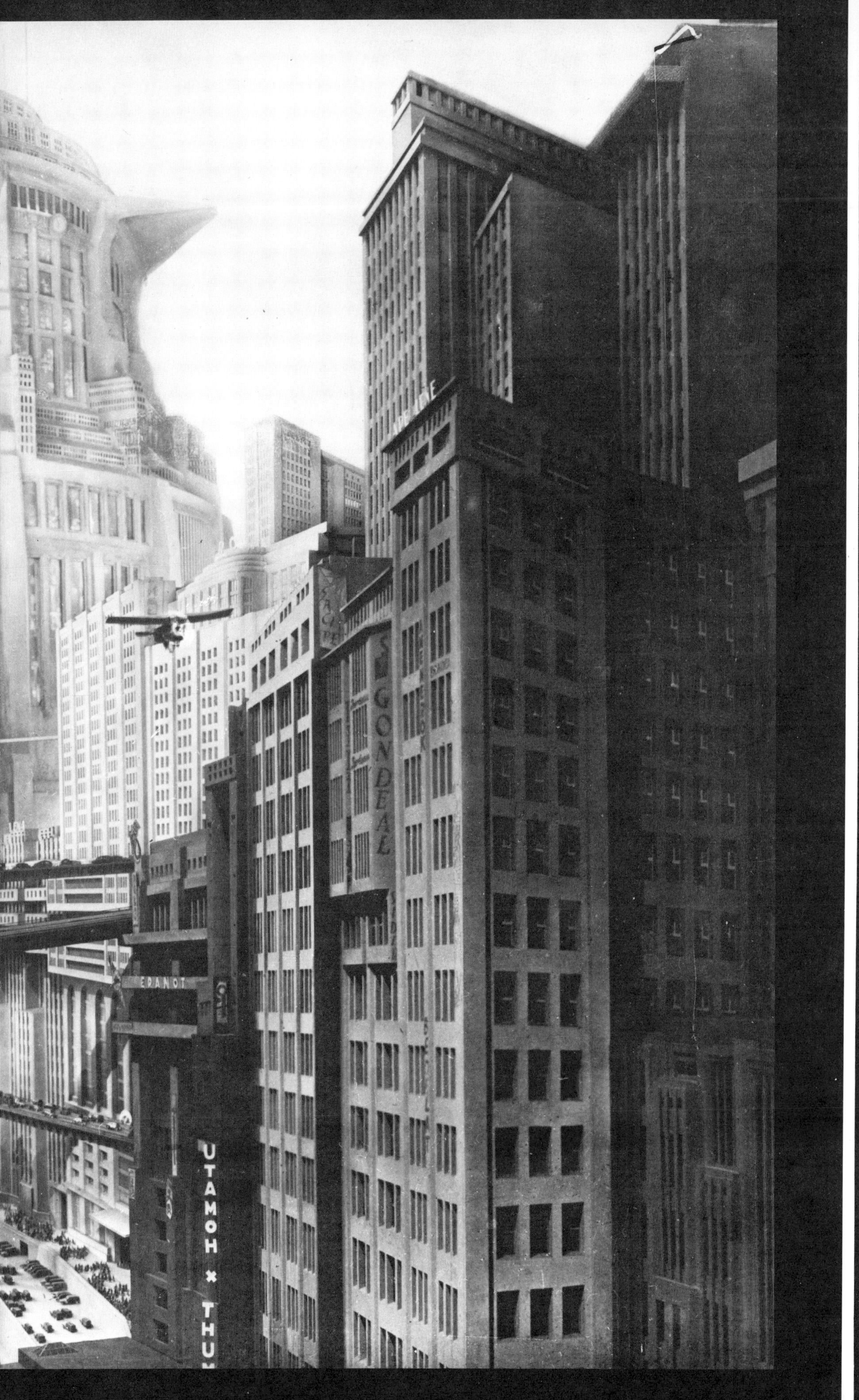
ERANOT
GONDEAL
UTAMOH × THU

Top: The awesome "domed city" in *Logan's Run* was actually a complex miniature. *Center:* With a couple of technicians standing on the set, the real size of the city becomes clear. *Bottom:* SCHÜFFTAN PROCESS: The actor (A) walks through an archway and down a flight of stairs on a studio set. This image is reflected in the silvered portion of a mirror (B) which is placed at a 45 degree angle to the camera. (The rest of the mirror's surface silvering has been scraped off.) Camera (C) photographs the reflected actor/stairs image, shooting through the cleared portion of the mirror to photograph, also, a miniature building facade (D) on a table in the studio. The result: a scene of the actor walking down the steps of a huge building of the future.

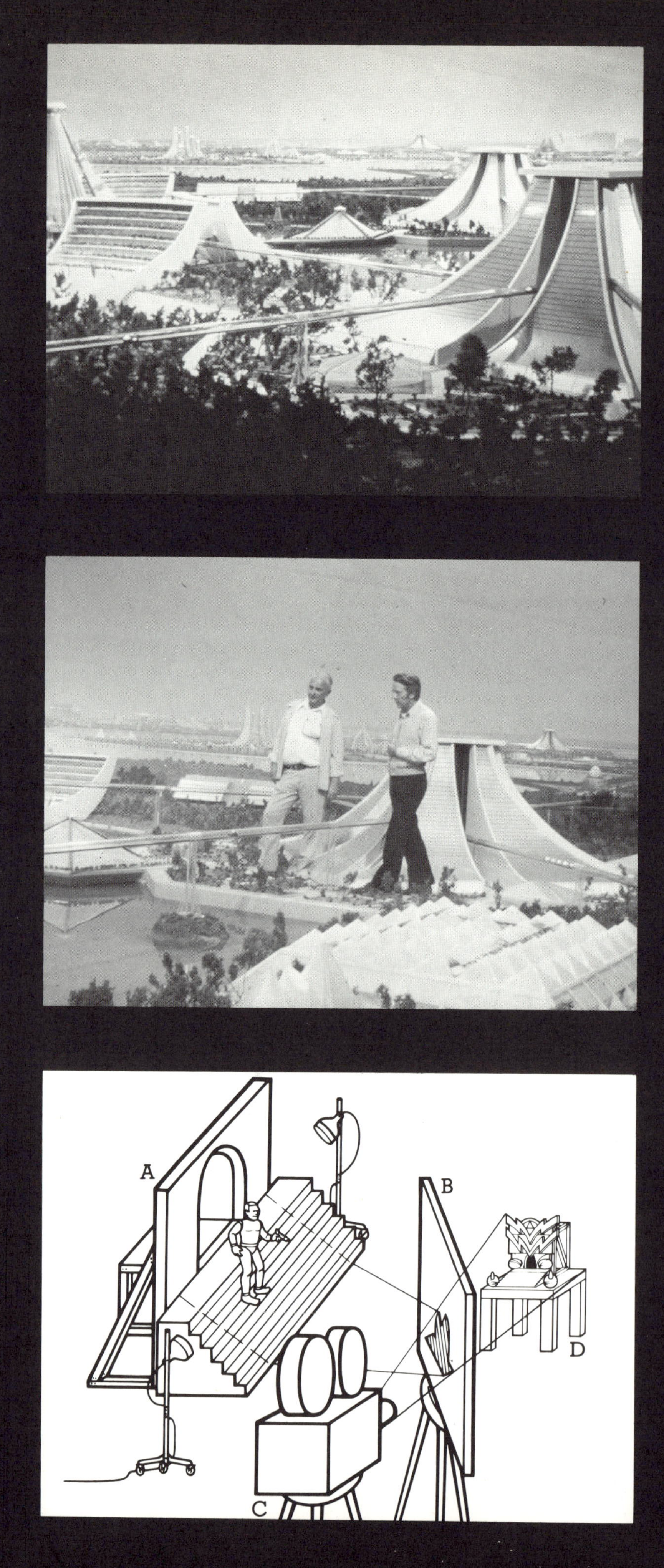

to the Shüfftan process shots used in *Metropolis*. Special-effects supervisor Ned Mann employed an unusual variation on Lang's approach by combining hanging miniatures with other elements. Similar uses of models have continued throughout the history of the science fiction cinema; the miniature domed city of the future in *Logan's Run* (1976) is a recent example of the method first popularized by Lang.

The imagination of H. G. Wells not only conjured up *Things to Come,* but supplied the concept for another movie of the thirties which dazzled audiences with perhaps the most startling science fiction effects of the decade. Universal's 1933 adaptation of Wells's *The Invisible Man* told the story of a scientist who conducts invisibility experiments upon himself. When the Invisible Man wears only a shirt, we see the shirt, as if filled by torso and arms, moving about a room with neither legs to support it nor a head above. Even more uncanny is the scene of the title character, fully dressed, unwrapping the bandages from around his head to reveal nothing but thin air. By the time Universal took on this property, the book had already been turned down by other studios because movie bosses were sure that Wells's bizarre scientific conjectures about a see-through man just couldn't be depicted on the screen. Universal could afford to take a different point of view because their special-effects department was headed by the extraordinarily resourceful John Fulton.

Fulton was able to simulate the incredible results of the Invisible Man's experiments through a clever adaptation of an old stage trick known by the particularly unscientific name of black magic. In a black magic performance, an actor dressed completely in black would stand in front of a black background in a darkened theater. If he were to spin white dishes through the air, the audience would see only the dishes "magically" moving about on their own. For *The Invisible Man* Fulton had the leading man, Claude Rains, dressed in black tights, shirt, gloves, and headpiece, and positioned the actor in front of a black velvet background. This setup of actor and backdrop reflected no light at all. When Rains was filmed wearing a white shirt over the nonreflective outfit, the film only recorded the image of the shirt; the piece of clothing appeared to be moving about of its own accord. Because of the clear contrast between black and white in this special footage, the shirt could be printed onto the normal live action scene by means of a relatively simple traveling matte. From the black velvet footage a duplicate print was made. This new print intensified the contrast between black and white and also reversed the two shades. The result was an opaque black silhouette of the shirt against a clear background. This strip of film could then be used as a traveling matte. By printing this strip of film with the normal scene, the opaque image of the shirt left an unexposed area on the film that corresponded exactly to the shirt. The original footage of the shirt could then be printed onto this unexposed portion to complete the photographic puzzle. On the screen, the viewer sees the seemingly miraculous sight of a group of men chasing an animated shirt around a room. (The same method produced the scene of the Invisible Man unwrapping his head bandages. Rains wore the character's usual clothing in front of a black backdrop. Beneath the bandages he wore a black headpiece which made his head seem invisible when the bandages were stripped away.)

The end of the picture posed a different sort of problem. The Invisible Man's spree of destruction comes to a close when he is flushed from a burning barn and forced to escape across snow-covered ground. As he runs, his footprints appear in the snow and his position is revealed to the police, who then shoot him down. To film the footprints made by invisible feet, Fulton devised an ingenious physical effect. A trench was dug along the path of the Invisible Man's run. A board was placed along the top of the trench and the footprints were cut out of the board. Cutouts were then used to plug up the footholes; securing the cutouts were pegs running from the board to the bottom of the trench. A rope was then looped around each support. Fake snow on top of the board concealed all these preparations. The impressions of the running feet in the snow appeared as each peg was pulled by the rope. The cutouts dropped one after another and the artificial snow fell into the depressions of the footholes.

Throughout the thirties the experiments of wayward scientists continued to provide special-effects men with fantastic challenges. A fiendish trick that was especially popular both with mad doctors and their audiences was the astounding feat of reducing people to miniature size. The effect of combining normal and doll-size people dates back to such pioneer trick films as R. W. Paul's 1903 fantasy *The Pocket Boxers.* In Hollywood during the thirties this trick was refined in *The Bride of Frankenstein* (1935), which featured an excellent scene of Ernest Thesiger toying with his tiny homunculi, and in the equally skillful *The*

Devil Doll (1936), which told the tale of a vengeful scientist who scales down two people in order to send them off to do his dirty work against his enemies. In 1940 a special-effects Oscar nomination went to the first full-blown Technicolor treatment of this theme: *Dr. Cyclops.*

Deep in the Peruvian mountains the bald, bespectacled, deranged Dr. Thorkel traps a group of scientists and shrinks them down with the help of radioactivity. As in all movies of this kind the illusion of minuscule people in a normal environment was created to a great extent by filming the actors among gigantic furniture props. The believability of this effect was bolstered by making the actors' voices sound unusually thin and tinny. These methods were fine for creating the impression of reduced size when the shrunken people were seen by themselves, but in order to make the predicament as convincing as possible, the miniature people had to be seen in the same frame as the normal-sized Dr. Thorkel. One technique used to achieve this effect was the old split-screen process: the shrunken scientists on an oversize set were seen on one side of the screen; the separately filmed Dr. Thorkel was printed onto the rest of the frame.

Perhaps the most inventive tricks that appear in *Dr. Cyclops* were performed with rear projection. Whereas this process was usually employed simply to provide backgrounds for actors in the foreground, Farciot Edouart altered the technique to combine two differently scaled pieces of action. In one instance the doctor is seen sitting at a table, holding one of his victims in front of him. A rear-projected background plate of the doctor's head and shoulders was matched with a live action foreground of one of the scientists being held in a giant prop of Thorkel's hand. The live action and the rear projection were coordinated to appear as a single image.

Dr. Cyclops is a smoothly executed trick picture, but it is not as memorable as Jack Arnold's 1957 thriller *The Incredible Shrinking Man.* The effects may not be as slick as those in *Dr. Cyclops,* but Arnold's low-budget illusions are more varied and deliver much more dramatic impact. As was true in the earlier film, *The Incredible Shrinking Man* is based on the premise that radiation can cause smallness, but while Thorkel's victims remained the same size, the Shrinking Man was doomed to grow ever smaller, requiring oversized sets of a constantly changing scale. The effects in *The Incredible Shrinking Man* were more impressive because they involved more imaginative action scenes. The normal setting that dwarfs the miniature people in *Dr. Cyclops* is completely prosaic but the everyday world that towers above the Shrinking Man becomes monstrous when the hero is terrorized by a relatively enormous house cat and spider.

Of the Shrinking Man's encounter with the gigantic normal world, the most hair-raising is his fight with the spider. In order to get at a piece of cake, the Shrinking Man has to lure the spider off of its web. He shakes the giant web, entices the looming black bug to scuttle down, and leads the creature on a precarious chase. When the tiny man is cornered, he grabs a straight pin with both hands and impales the spider. The Shrinking Man (Grant Williams) and the spider were filmed separately and were combined into one scene by the matte work of Clifford Stine, head of the special-effects department at Universal during the fifties. Crucial to creating the excitement of this bizarre battle was the coordination of the actions of the actor and the spider. To accomplish this close interaction, the spider was filmed first running along a window ledge and Williams's scene was then staged and shot to fit the actions of the bug. Williams performed on a matching oversize set of the window ledge. A frame from the spider sequence was inserted in the viewing mechanism of the camera so that the Shrinking Man scene could be lined up exactly with the previously filmed footage. A metronome was used to time the actor's movements. Each beat of the metronome corresponded to a certain point in the action of the spider sequence. Grant Williams then literally acted by numbers, reacting to the spider coming down the web at a certain number of beats, starting to run away a few beats later, and so on. Once the filming was completed, Clifford Stine had two perfectly matched sequences to matte together.

Jack Arnold has said that one of the most perplexing special-effects problems in the movie was finding a way to make water drops from a leaky pipe seem huge when falling on Williams's matchbox house. The solution the director came up with is a great example of a scientific wonder created by old-fashioned seat-of-the-pants resourcefulness. Arnold explained his technique in detail in an interview in *Cinefantastique* (Summer 1975):

I remembered how in my ill-spent youth I found some strange rubber objects in my father's drawer, and not knowing what they were, I filled them up with water, took them to the top of the building where we lived in New York, and dropped them

Top: A beautifully detailed oversize set from *The Devil Doll.*
Center: The film crew of *The Incredible Shrinking Man* shoots the scene in which Grant Williams clings to a pencil to save himself from being washed down the cellar drain.
Bottom: The scene as it appears in the movie.

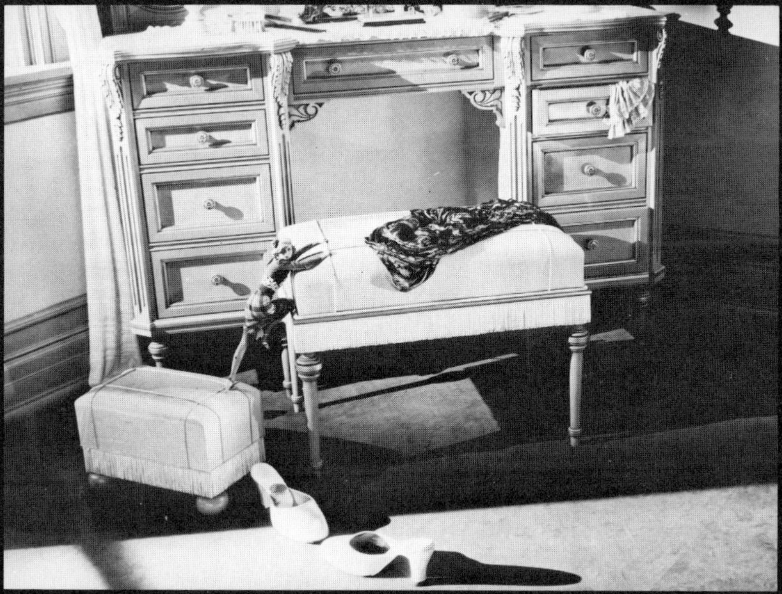

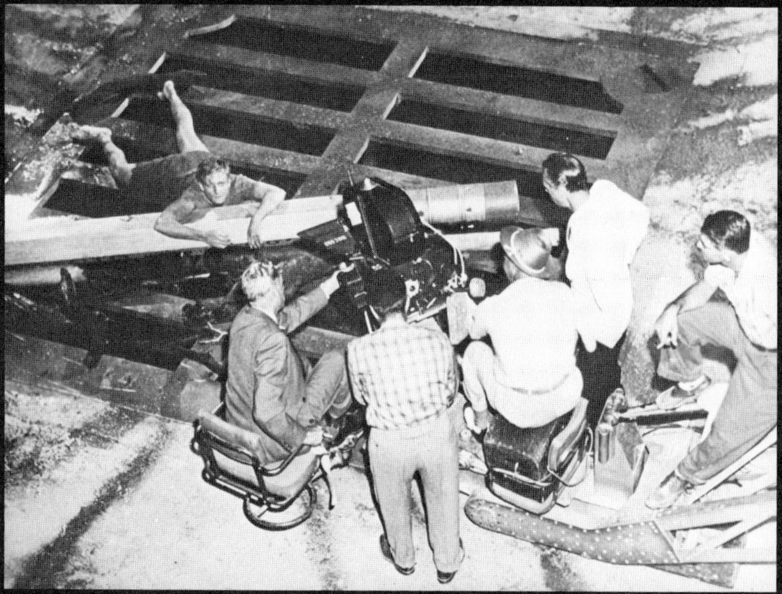

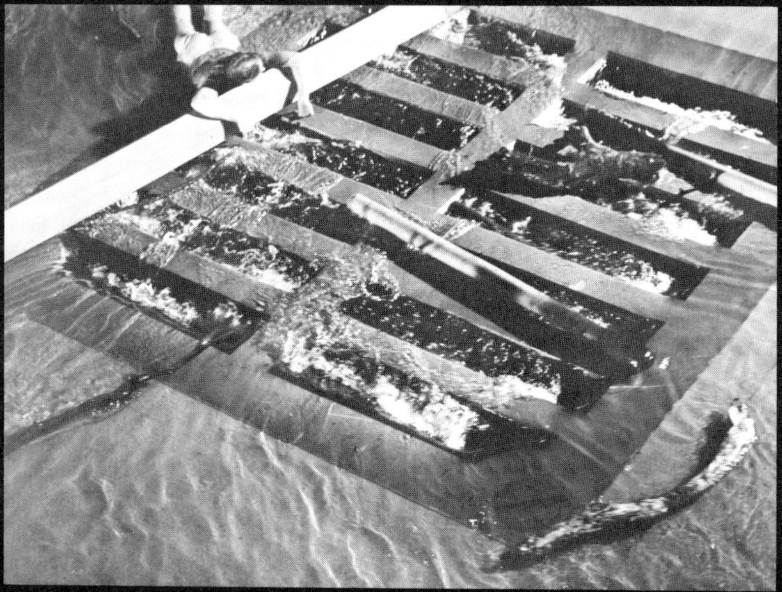

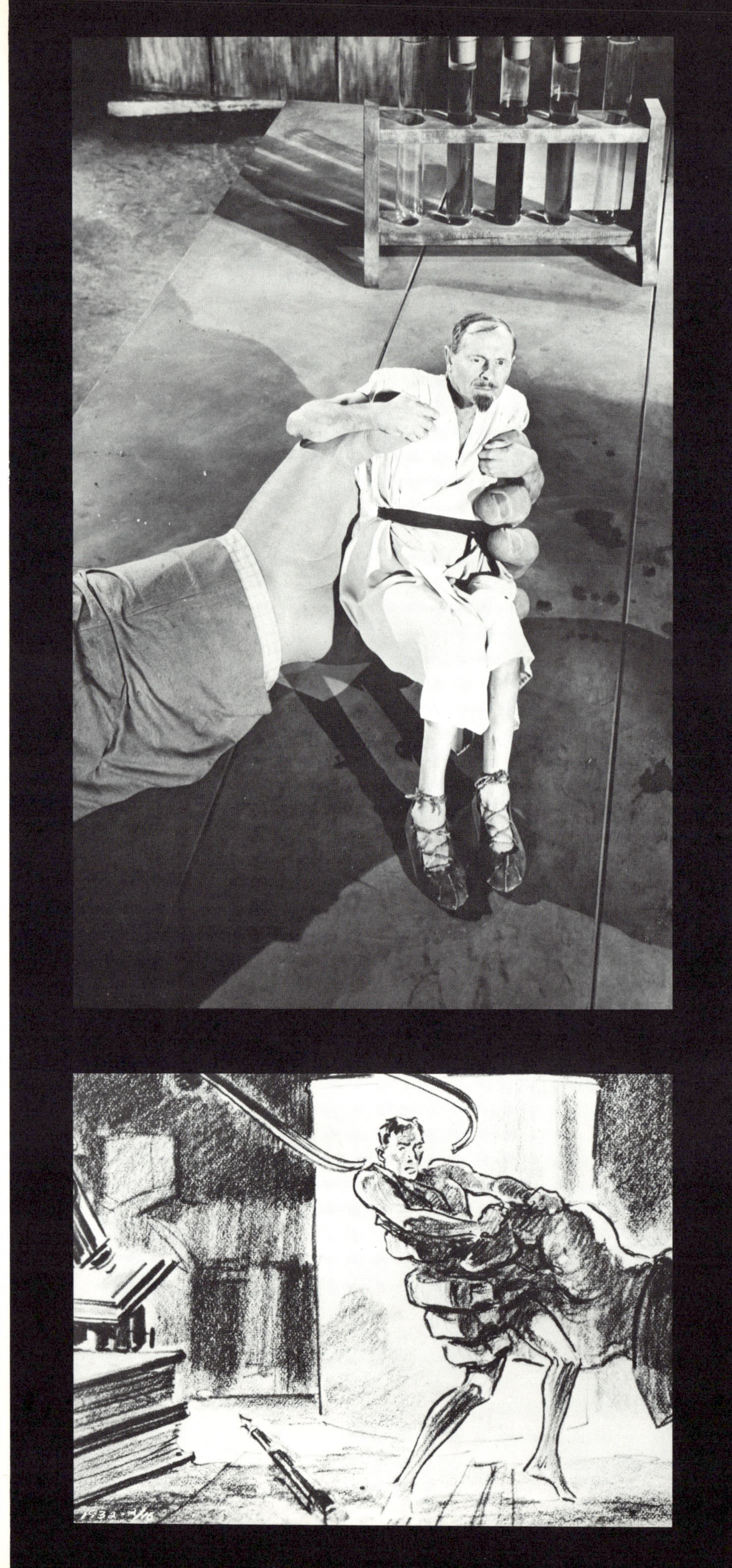

Top: Perhaps the most unsettling scene in *Dr. Cyclops* shows the evil scientist clutching one of his shrunken captives in his hand and coldly examining the helpless man with calipers. Here, actor Charles Halton is gripped by the giant prop hand constructed for the sequence. *Bottom:* A preproduction drawing of this scene.

Top: A behind-the-scenes look at the filming of this sequence. Charles Halton can be seen on the upper left, sitting in the huge latex hand, while the giant calipers hover over him. *Bottom:* Three of Thorkel's captives attempt to murder the madman in his sleep. Much of the budget for *Dr. Cyclops* was spent on the film's extremely authentic oversize props, like the ones in this scene.

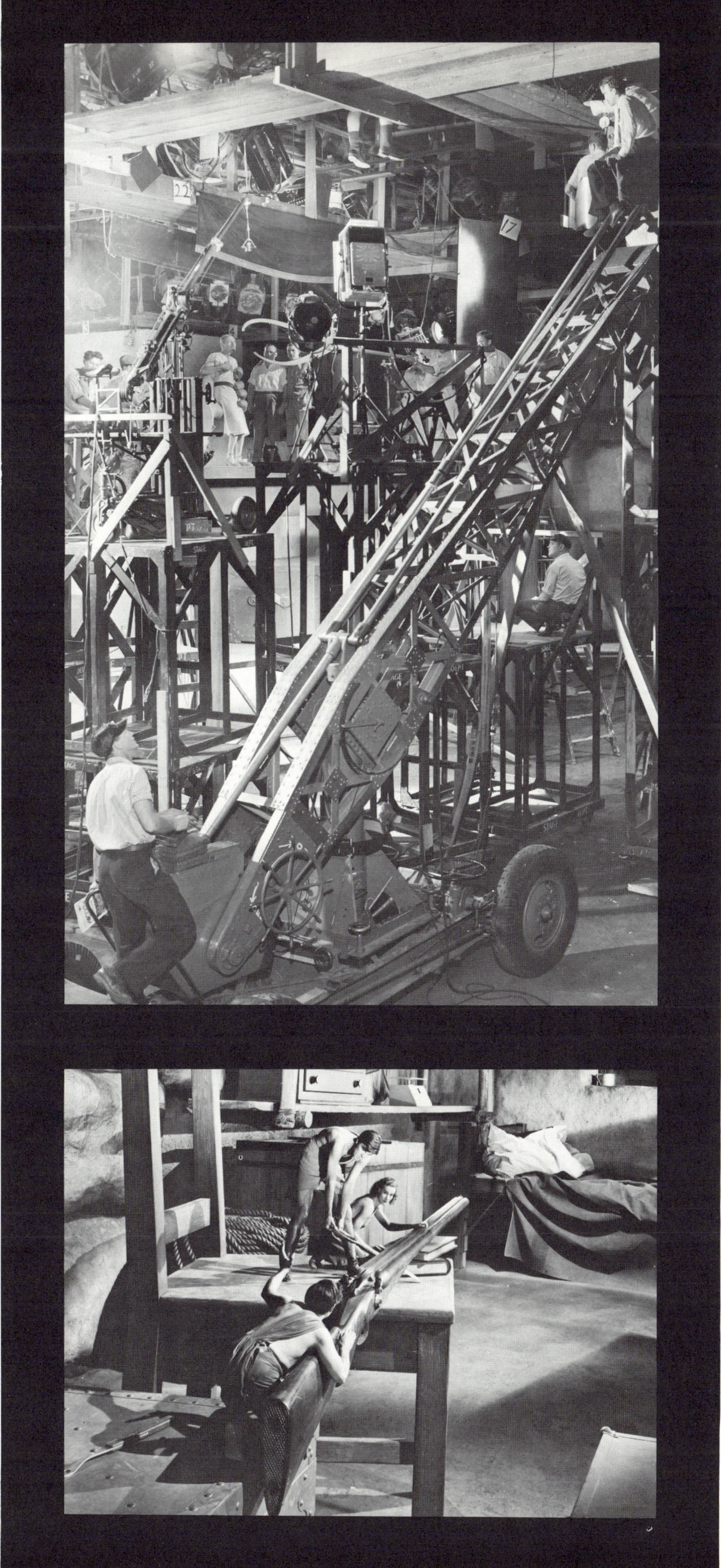

over the side. I recalled that they looked great when they hit, and that they held a tear shape. So I asked the crew, "Has anyone got a condom on him?" With much reluctance, one of the guys finally confessed that he had one. We filled it with water, tied it at the top, and dropped it. It had a tear shape, exactly in the right proportion, and it splattered on impact. So we ordered about 100 gross of them. I put them on a treadmill and let them drop until the water pipe was supposed to burst, and it was very effective. At the end of the picture, I was called to the production office. They were going over all my expenses and they came across this item of 100 gross of condoms, so they asked me, "What the hell is that for?" I simply said, "Well, it was a very tough picture, so I gave a cast party." And that was all I told them.

Futuristic cities and the fantastic pranks of mad doctors constituted the majority of science fiction effects before 1950. Up until that time science fiction was more of a novelty than a full-blown genre. However, when science fiction expanded into an active film fad in the 1950s, special-effects men finally got the opportunity to apply their know-how to simulating the technology of space travel. Although space pictures took many years to become popular, the sight of a rocket ship gliding through the galaxies or a flying saucer coasting down to the earth's surface are probably the two images most often associated with science fiction. During the fifties effects artists engineered these two images in countless space age adventures. As in the filming of vast, technologically advanced cities, enormous spaceships were depicted on the movie screen through the skillful use of miniatures.

Models suspended by concealed wires were substituted for futuristic aircraft as early as 1909, when British filmmakers staged an aerial attack on London by a futuristic dirigible in *Airship Destroyer.* Méliès used a similar technique to film the primitive flight of the Aerobus in *Conquest of the Pole* (1912). More impressive model-work was seen in Fritz Lang's 1929 space opera *Woman on the Moon*. Lang's story concerned a group of space explorers who take a rocket trip to the moon to prospect for that world's rich gold deposits. To supply what was then considered to be authenticity, Lang consulted rocket experts and hired them as technical advisors for the space flight sequences. Considering how far removed in time the makers of the film were from actual space travel, the shots of the model rocket are fairly realistic. The film, however, was not enough of a financial success to encourage other attempts at simulated rocket flights.

Interplanetary escapades garnered at least a strong juvenile following in 1936 when Buster Crabbe took on the evil might of Ming the Merciless in the first *Flash Gordon* serial. Though lavishly produced, by serial standards, the *Flash Gordon* series was made very cheaply in comparison to feature-length films. The scenes of the gyroscope saucers and the sputtering rockets had enough comic-strip exuberance to make up for their technical crudeness. The shaky effects were enough, though, to please the kids. They bought tickets week after week to see three *Flash Gordon* serials and then kept it up when Buster Crabbe turned into Buck Rogers for another serial of five-and-dime wonders.

Space travel became a box office sensation in 1950 when George Pal came out with his production of *Destination Moon*. Pal began his movie career in his native Hungary as a stop-motion animator who specialized in making films of animated puppets. He continued with this specialty in the United States by making a series of Puppetoons for Paramount in the forties. *Destination Moon,* his first of many science fiction features emphasizing special effects, was a low-key prediction of what a realistic rocket journey to the moon would look like. The movie's effects won an Academy Award but by today's standards they have dated badly. The sober, scientific effects sequences that once seemed so impressive have become inadequate today precisely because of the film's sober, scientific intentions. The toy-shop antics of *Flash Gordon* can be shrugged off as high-spirited, fantastic nonsense no matter how ridiculous they look, but when scientific conjecture is overrun historically by scientific fact, the fiction sometimes becomes embarrassing. After an actual moon flight was broadcast on television, the well-intentioned but obviously contrived rocket trip in *Destination Moon* looked completely inauthentic. The blast-off and flight of Pal's spaceship are slick-looking but hardly convincing; it is very hard to confuse 1,500 car headlights strung across black velvet for an outer space star field, and the painted backdrops of the moon's terrain look exactly like painted backdrops.

One of the tricks that was supposed to be a real eye-opener in 1950 was the sight of the astronauts working in zero gravity. Free-floating inside the spaceship was done with wires and the illusion is still good, but the shots of the astronauts walking along the walls and ceiling of the rocket with the help of magnetized

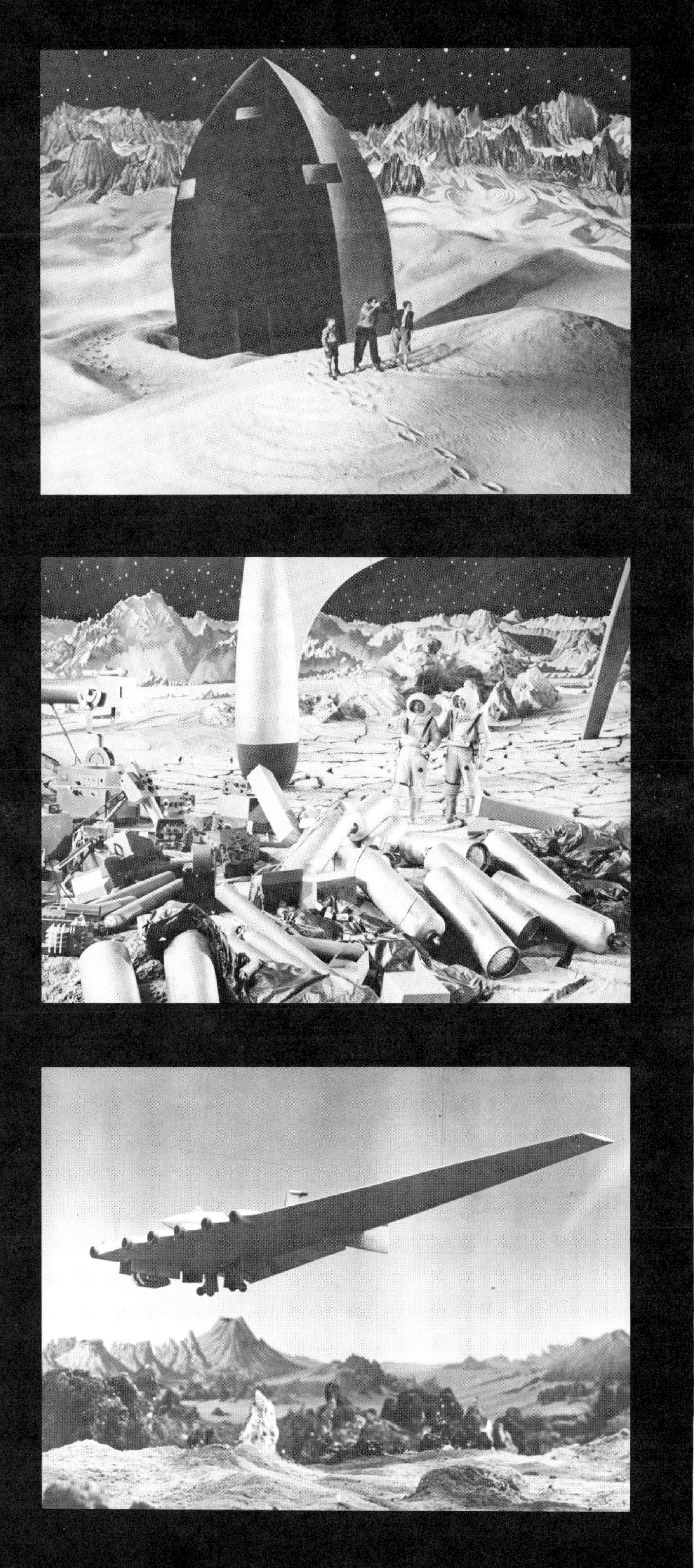

Top: Though Fritz Lang consulted rocket experts for his 1929 science fiction film *Woman in the Moon,* this scene with its bullet-shaped spaceship and explorers dressed in street clothes, is reminiscent of Méliès' fanciful *A Trip to the Moon. Center:* A scene from *Destination Moon.* The actors stand beneath a full-scale mock-up of the ship's tail section on a lunar set designed by Chesley Bonestell. *Bottom:* A model spaceship (with visible support wires) hovers over a miniature Martian landscape in this shot from George Pal's *The Conquest of Space.*

boots are very disappointing when viewed today. Basically Pal's movie revamped techniques used by Méliès and Paul. We see an astronaut walk down the wall and approach the floor. As he makes the step to the perpendicular plane of the floor, the camera position changes to show him making the shift from another angle. The walking along the wall was accomplished by rotating the set so that the wall served as the floor. The camera was also rotated to a horizontal position to create the illusion that the set was still right-side up. The disappointing part was the cut to a new angle. This change in camera position obviously accounted for the break taken to adjust the set to its normal state. (As little as a year later, in 1951, this effect became dated when Fred Astaire danced up and down the walls and across the ceiling in onc continuous take in *Royal Wedding.*)

The best effects during *Destination Moon*'s space flight sequences were the dramatic inserts. As the ship takes off, for instance, the crew grimaces against the shock and pull of the acceleration; the astronauts' faces spread as if flattened by an invisible force. To create this effect, pliable transparent sheets were molded over the actors' faces and were pulled from behind to draw back their features. Viewed today, this effect is still convincing. Later in the picture, as the crew navigates their landing, there is an impressive view of the moon's surface seen through a ship's porthole. We see the moonscape draw dramatically closer as the rocket jockeys from side to side to establish its position for descent. The painting of the moon's surface that was used for this effect seemed more realistic than most of the painted backdrops, perhaps because the motion of the shot diverted one's attention from the details of the artwork.

After the box office success of *Destination Moon,* Pal followed up with many other science fiction pictures; among them were the popular *When Worlds Collide* (1951), *The Conquest of Space* (1955), and *The Time Machine* (1960). In all, Pal's movies rated six Academy Awards for Special Effects, and with the exception of *Destination Moon,* his films are as enjoyable today as they were when they were originally released.

When Worlds Collide (1951), was based on a popular novel of the early 1930s by Edwin Balmer and Philip Wylie. Paramount had originally purchased the rights to this book for Cecil B. De Mille in 1934, but though a scenario and preproduction sketches were prepared, the project was dropped when De Mille decided to do *Cleopatra* instead. Pal picked up the rights sixteen years later while looking for a follow-up to his first highly successful foray into the field of science fiction.

The story concerns the total destruction of Earth by a pair of runaway planets, Zyra and Bellus. The first passes so close to our planet that it sets off cataclysmic earthquakes, volcanic eruptions, and massive tidal waves, including one which completely submerges New York City. Nineteen days later Bellus hits directly, blowing the earth to cosmic dust motes. Working frantically all the while to save themselves before the apocalypse comes are a group of people who hope to escape on a rocketship, a "space ark" which will carry them to Zyra, Bellus's satellite, where they plan to resettle the human race. The rocket blasts off at the very last moment, and the final scenes show the party of forty space-pilgrims arriving on their new world.

The trick photography was handled by Paramount's first-rate team of special effects experts headed by Gordon Jennings, who based his work on the superb preproduction artwork done by Chesley Bonestell. Perhaps the most spectacular moment in the movie is the flooding of Times Square by a gigantic tidal wave. Interestingly this scene was not in the original script. Someone in the publicity department, however, suggested that it would make a terrific advertising poster, so Pal agreed to put it in although he didn't have much money to spend on it. In our interview Pal described how the trick was done:

We bought stock footage from a Samuel Goldwyn movie with Danny Kaye. It was a shot of Times Square. We froze the frame and painted out the people. Then we built a replica—I would say twenty feet long—of the buildings. We painted it black and dumped water into it from two tanks. Then all we did was rotoscope it frame by frame and make hand-painted mattes. The whole sequence cost only $1,800.

Though a full-size section of the space ark was built on the Paramount sound stage, the launching scenes, in which we see the rocket taking off along a mile-long ramp, were done in miniature. A four-foot model spaceship attached to invisible wires was guided along a seven-hundred-foot ramp built on a detailed, miniature hillside.

Unfortunately Paramount was so eager to finish the film in order to cash in on the success of *Destination Moon* that Pal was pressured into releasing it before the effects were completed to his satisfaction. As a result some of the closing shots in the movie are surprisingly clumsy. In the scene in which we see the space ark blast off into the stratosphere, the model rocket

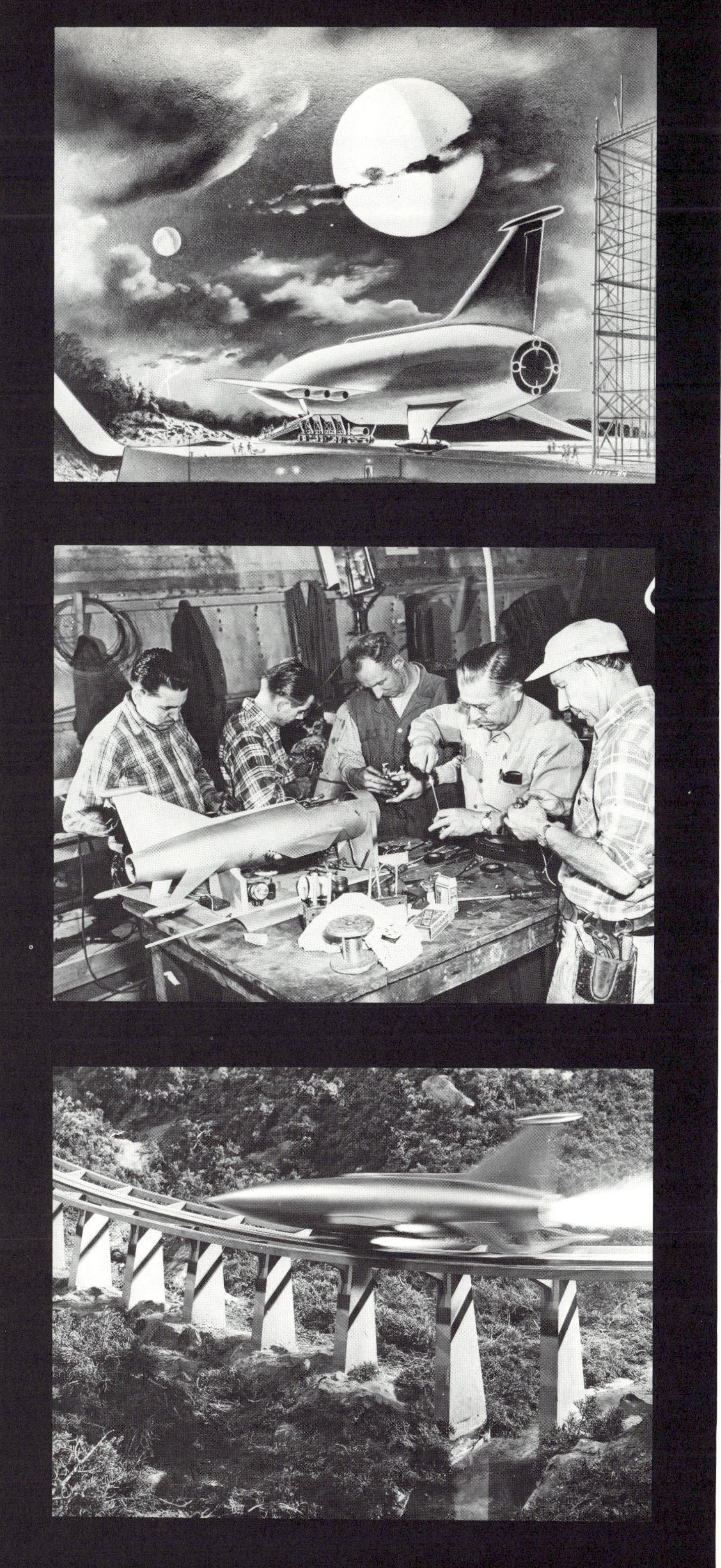

Top: A preproduction drawing of the space ark on its launching ramp from *When Worlds Collide*. *Center:* The space ark model under construction. *Bottom:* The model in action as it moves along the ramp during takeoff.

Three behind-the-scenes shots from *The War of the Worlds.* *Top:* The sleek Martian war machines were designed by art director Albert Nozaki, here shown working on a series of storyboard sketches. *Center:* Effects wizard Gordon Jennings *(right)* and technician Chet Pate *(left)* inspecting one of the war machine models. *Bottom:* Technicians setting up the models on a miniature set of the California countryside.

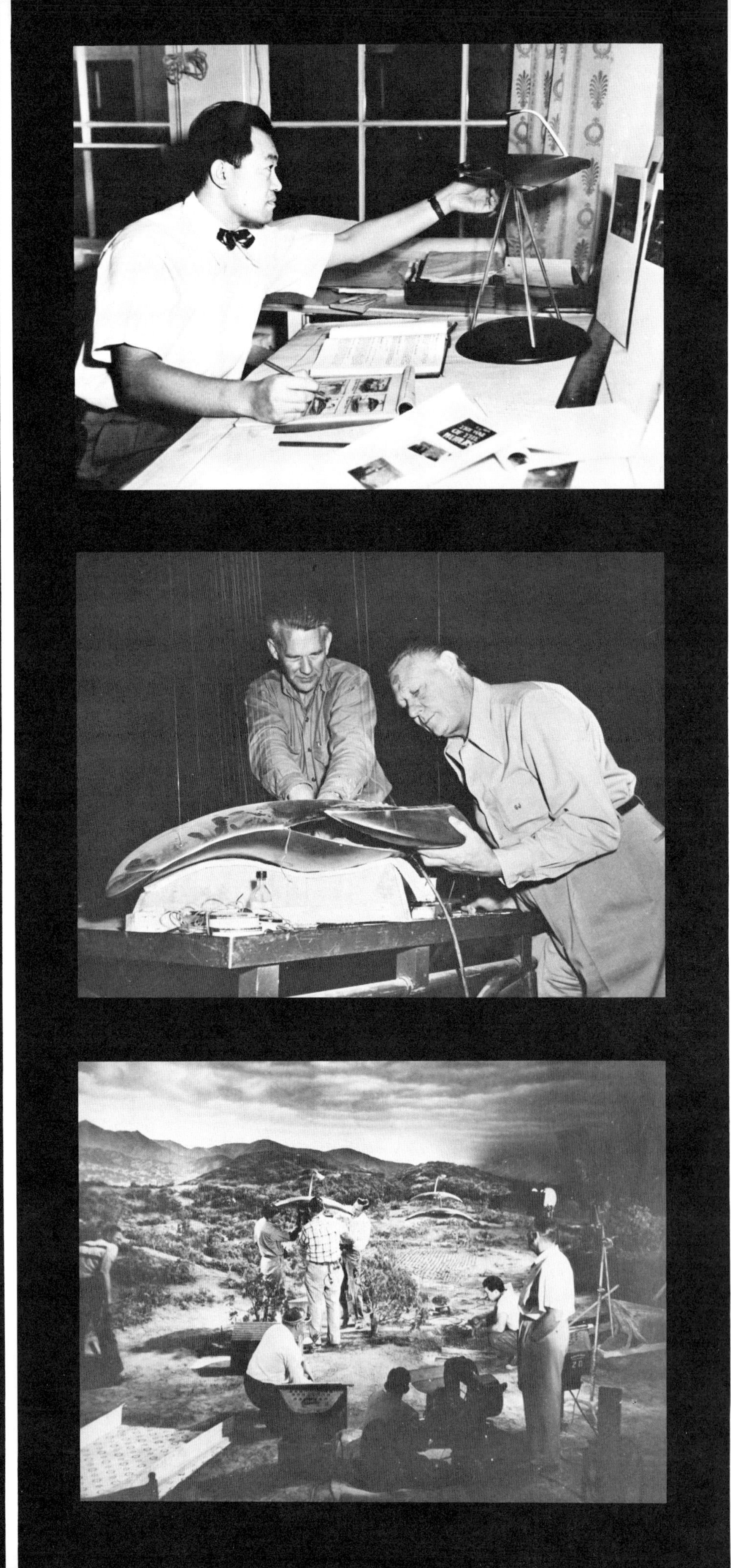

is so poorly superimposed that it is transparent: Chesley Bonestell's painting of the earth can be seen right through it. The sunrise over Zyra that greets the space travelers when they first step from the ship is also obviously a two-dimensional background painting. Nevertheless the film contains some striking images, and in spite of its flaws, it won the Special-Effects Oscar for 1951.

Although all his films from the fifties have intriguing special effects, Pal's most exciting effects picture of the decade was his version of H. G. Wells's Martian invasion of Earth in *War of the Worlds,* which was released by Paramount in 1953. Eight months of work and $1,400,000 were devoted to the special effects in this movie; the live action was shot in only forty days and at a cost of $600,000. Pal told us in an interview that he has always felt that special effects can be as big a star as any actor or actress. *War of the Worlds* bore this theory out as well as any of his productions because he was able to endow his effects with a charismatic personality, much more personality than Gene Barry and Ann Robinson were able to project as the film's leading players. No other Hollywood spacecraft models from the fifties were as graceful, menacing, and extraterrestrial-looking as the Martian warships in *War of the Worlds.* These sleek machines glide inexorably forward along cushions of energy, their slender necklike extensions spitting out devastating heat rays. They appear to be streamlined, space age dragons, a sinister combination of faultless technology and bestial violence.

With the help of his director (Byron Haskin) and art department, Pal was able to inject this distinctive character into the design of his spaceship models by developing an imaginative concept of Martian life. The models were based on the conjecture that Martians evolved from fish and amphibians and that Martian technology was a reflection of that biological inheritance. The result was a warship that resembled a manta ray, a twenty-foot-wide underwater creature whose broad-winged, monstrous form has inspired the alternate moniker of devilfish. The cobralike neck on top of the ship functioned as the transmitter of the heat ray.

The final design for the warships was made by art director Albert Nozaki. The Martian spaceships were then converted into working models by Paramount's special-effects department under the supervision of Gordon Jennings. The copper models measured forty-two inches in diameter and were suspended by wires, as was the custom with this sort of work. In addition to keeping the warships in the air, the fifteen wires per model transmitted the electricity needed for its operation. The current powered the cobra-neck, which swiveled slowly from side to side, and activated the cobra-head's eerie pulsing light. Inside of the tip of the extension was a neon bulb fronted by a fan whose rotating blades created the blinking-light effect. The cobra-neck's deadly beam was actually the glow of melting welding wire, which was disintegrated by a blowtorch and optically printed onto the scene.

The most spectacular scene of destruction by the manta-ray ships is the wholesale razing of Los Angeles. The lethal warships are relentless as they prowl the city, methodically blasting buildings into rubble. The sequence was simulated by an unusual use of miniature buildings. In order to make the small-scale city seem especially substantial, Pal had the models built relatively large. The miniature of Los Angeles City Hall, for instance, was eight feet tall. The added size of this model, with all its extra room for authentic detail, helped the cameraman make the diminutive building seem like a full-size set. When the warship supposedly demolished City Hall, the miniature was exploded by dynamite charges concealed inside. In other instances the Martians' rampage was brought to a more personal level when the war machines disintegrated earthlings and their military equipment in a glowing red flash. To make the people and weapons shimmer with intense heat and then vanish, the optical department employed the time-consuming animation process, painting glowing figures by hand for each frame and then matting them into the live-action scene. The Army loses one of its colonels in a blazing instant thanks to 144 such mattes. Paul Lerpae's optical department created more than three thousand handpainted mattes for this picture.

The malevolent personality of the warships was crucial to establishing the villainy of the Martians because the sinister machines were all that was seen of the Martian presence for nearly the entire picture. The hero and heroine get their single frightening glimpse of one of the Martians when a warship corners them in an isolated farmhouse. The alien's brief appearance was another example of a Pal effect that established a weird, distinctive character of its own. In keeping with the film's theory about life on Mars, the alien was a spindly, reptilian creature with a big tricolored eye, long tentaclelike arms, and pulsating veins close to the surface of the skin. Designed by Al Nozaki, the alien costume was constructed and worn by Charles Gamera. The outfit was made out of sheet rubber and papier-mâché and was operated by Gamera by means of wires on the inside. The creature was made to bristle with life by the heaving lungs and pulsating veins, which were worked by an offscreen pump. During the course of his walk-on performance, the bizarre Martian establishes itself as being far more interesting than any of the bland earthling actors.

Taking their cue from such successful movies as *When Worlds Collide* and *War of the Worlds,* film producers during the fifties came out with a steady stream of science fiction pictures featuring outer space special effects. Although George Pal's trend-setting films involved well-planned effects, the great majority of his imitators were content to mass-produce space operas with toy rocket ships. Standing out among the vast assortment of low-grade efforts were a small handful of ambitious ventures. The first and most financially successful of this group was Robert Wise's 1951 feature *The Day the Earth Stood Still.*

Most of the effects in this picture are concentrated at both ends of the story: the arrival of the benevolent alien's flying saucer on Earth in the first scene and the saucer's getaway in the final reel. The effects work was handled by Fred Sersen, L. B. Abbott, Ray Kellog, and Emil Kosa. The landing of the saucer on a baseball diamond in Washington, D.C., is one of the best renditions of the often-repeated sequence of Earth visited by a strange craft. The effects team made this scene memorable through the realism of the setting and the contrasting unearthly presence of the flying saucer. In order to put the two-foot-wide miniature of the spaceship into a full-scale live-action scene of Washington, the effects crew filmed the saucer separately against a black background and printed it onto the live-action scenery with a traveling matte. The seeming reality of the scene was not only established by the authenticity of a live-action setting, but also by the realistic detail of the saucer casting a shadow onto the baseball field as it hovered above the ground. Since the saucer model had been shot separately from the scene of the baseball diamond, the shadow also had to be filmed separately. For this effect the model was covered with black material and photographed on a completely white stage. Light from above created the sharply defined shadow, which was printed separately onto the final scene. The effects men made the saucer seem like a completely foreign intruder in an earthly setting by surrounding the spaceship with a shimmering white light. This eerie glow was created by photographing the model through a ground glass, which produced a diffused image. The shimmering shot of the spacecraft was then printed onto normal footage of the model.

Once the spacecraft came to rest on the ground, a full scale mock-up of the saucer was used. This replica was one hundred feet wide and twenty-five feet high. Only three quarters of the saucer's circumference was built; the remaining quarter was always out of camera range and served the functional purpose of allowing the crew easy access to the workings of the ramp that opened up on the saucer's side. The first opening of the ramp further establishes the unearthly quality of the spacecraft. Beforehand the saucer seemed to be absolutely seamless: there was no indication of any means of either entering or leaving the alien ship. The ramp seems to materialize out of a completely solid surface. To make this illusion possible, the outline of the ramp was covered with soft plastic touched up with silver paint; no cracks in the surface of the saucer were revealed until operators inside the mock-up put the hatchway in motion.

In addition to the handling of the flying saucer sequences, the great special-effects accomplishment of *The Day the Earth Stood Still* was the creation of a dignified robot. Up until 1951, movie robots usually made their appearances in weekly serials like *Flash Gordon* and *Phantom Empire,* and they always looked like garbage cans on legs. In contrast, Gort, the towering alien robot in *The Day the Earth Stood Still,* was a sleek, majestic character. His pliable metallic-looking costume was made of foam rubber painted silver. The robot's head was a metal helmet. Inside the costume was Lock Martin, a seven-foot doorman from Grauman's Chinese Theater. When threatened, Gort opens his head-visor and shoots out a powerful heat ray which can turn cannons and tanks into molten scrap. These heat ray sequences were the handiwork of matte painters Ray Kellog and Emil Kosa. Matted into the sequences were the artists' frame-by-frame paintings of the searing beams. An ingenious variation of this method was used for the scene of Gort springing his alien companion from jail by disintegrating the cell wall. Rather than actually destroying a specially constructed wall, the scene was shot with a set of the wall already blasted away. Kellog and Kosa matted in a painting of the full wall and, in a series of paintings, "melted" the side back down.

Unlike *The Day the Earth*

Stood Still, Universal's *This Island Earth* took on the extra expense and trouble of Technicolor and the more difficult task of placing much of its action on an alien world. Before the release of *This Island Earth* in 1955, most science fiction movies hadn't attempted to simulate the look of life on another planet. *War of the Worlds* was earthbound, and so were other such popular science fiction movies as *The Thing* (1951) and *It Came from Outer Space* (1953). The only previous color extraterrestrial epic had been *Destination Moon,* and that had been limited to one static moonscape. In *This Island Earth* the doomed planet of Metaluna sends an emissary to our world to tap the mental resources of Earth's top scientists in the hopes of finding a new form of energy to shore up Metaluna's protective shields. These barriers are the only things that stand between the Metalunans and total destruction at the hands of the warlike Zahgons. In an attempt to break out of their forced employment for the aliens, a pair of earthling scientists try to escape in a small plane. Instead they are hijacked aboard a Metalunan saucer and are transported back to the emissary's world. This story required that Universal's effects department find a way to film a detailed, sophisticated space flight as well as a strange, technologically advanced alien civilization beset by interplanetary warfare.

The first of the movie's spectacular effects scenes was the commandeering of the scientists' getaway plane by the Metalunan spacecraft. The plane is slowly pulled up into the bottom of the flying saucer by a misty green beam of energy. As usual the aircraft, both plane and saucer, were small-scale models. To create the saucer's powerful beam, the effects crew superimposed a cartoon-animation image over the shot of the two models. Once inside the spacecraft the two earthlings are given a tour of the ship's out-of-this-world gadgetry. These effects-created gizmos succeed in striking a believable appearance of imposing scientific knowledge. But the most impressive of the Metalunans' equipment is the device that readies the two earthlings for the saucer's acceleration to faster-than-light speed. The two scientists stand inside clear tubes which reorder their molecular configurations. On the screen we see their bodies transformed through several stages: at one point only a skeletal image of the scientists is seen; at another the outline of their vascular system becomes visible. This scientific miracle was devised by superimposing a series of images onto the figures of the two actors, with each image slowly dissolving into the succeeding stage of the transformation.

For the scenes that took place on the planet Metaluna, the special-effects crew had to create a world that bore little resemblance to anything on Earth. Since the landscape and buildings were so alien, no locations could be used as a substitute, and the construction of extensive, full-scale settings on the limited space of a sound stage would have been impractical. The solution to the problem was the one first popularized in Fritz Lang's *Metropolis:* the use of highly imaginative miniatures. Coming in for its landing, the saucer in *This Island Earth* has to coast across a Metalunan landscape strafed by meteors directed by the Zahgons. The action took place on a 110-foot model of the craggy, cratered surface. The miniature meteors were magnesium encased in plaster. They were shot down along wires to the model's surface, where electrical charges were rigged to set off gasoline for the intense white explosions their impact caused. This detailed setting is then succeeded by an even more impressive miniature of the underground Metalunan city. The city is a strange symmetrical configuration of domes, arches, and curved, elevated walkways littered with the rubble left by the Zahgon attack. The scene is given a menaced, doomed aura by sporadic meteor blasts closing in on the buildings and by the weird blue-green swirl of the backdrop, which is the underside of the enclosing ground overhead. In order to make the strikingly rendered miniature seem massive, three tiny running figures, dwarfed by the surroundings, were matted onto a distant shot of the cityscape.

Despite the first-rate effects work of Clifford Stine, Stanley Horsley, and Charlie Baker, *This Island Earth* was not enough of a box office success to warrant another big-budget science fiction adventure from Universal. Unfortunately MGM had a similar disappointment with the even more ambitious *Forbidden Planet* (1956).

Forbidden Planet was MGM's only major excursion into the science fiction genre in the fifties, but the glamor studio's expert effects department took this single opportunity to produce the most spectacular special-effects space picture of the decade. The entire story takes place on a distant planet called Altair IV where United Planets Cruiser C57D lands to rescue the survivors of a previous expedition: a man named Morbius and his daughter, Altaira, who live on top of what has been left behind by a scientifically advanced people known as the Krel. Among the marvels on Altair IV are a

Three shots from *Forbidden Planet.*
Top: The full-scale section of United Planets Cruiser C-57D stands on the set of the desolate planet Altair-4.
Center: The ship as it appears in the movie, with its matted-in dome painted by Henri Hillinick.
Bottom: Frankie Darrow, the actor inside Robby the Robot, is loaded into his costume. Darrow's face was blackened to keep it invisible behind the neon grating on Robby's chest.

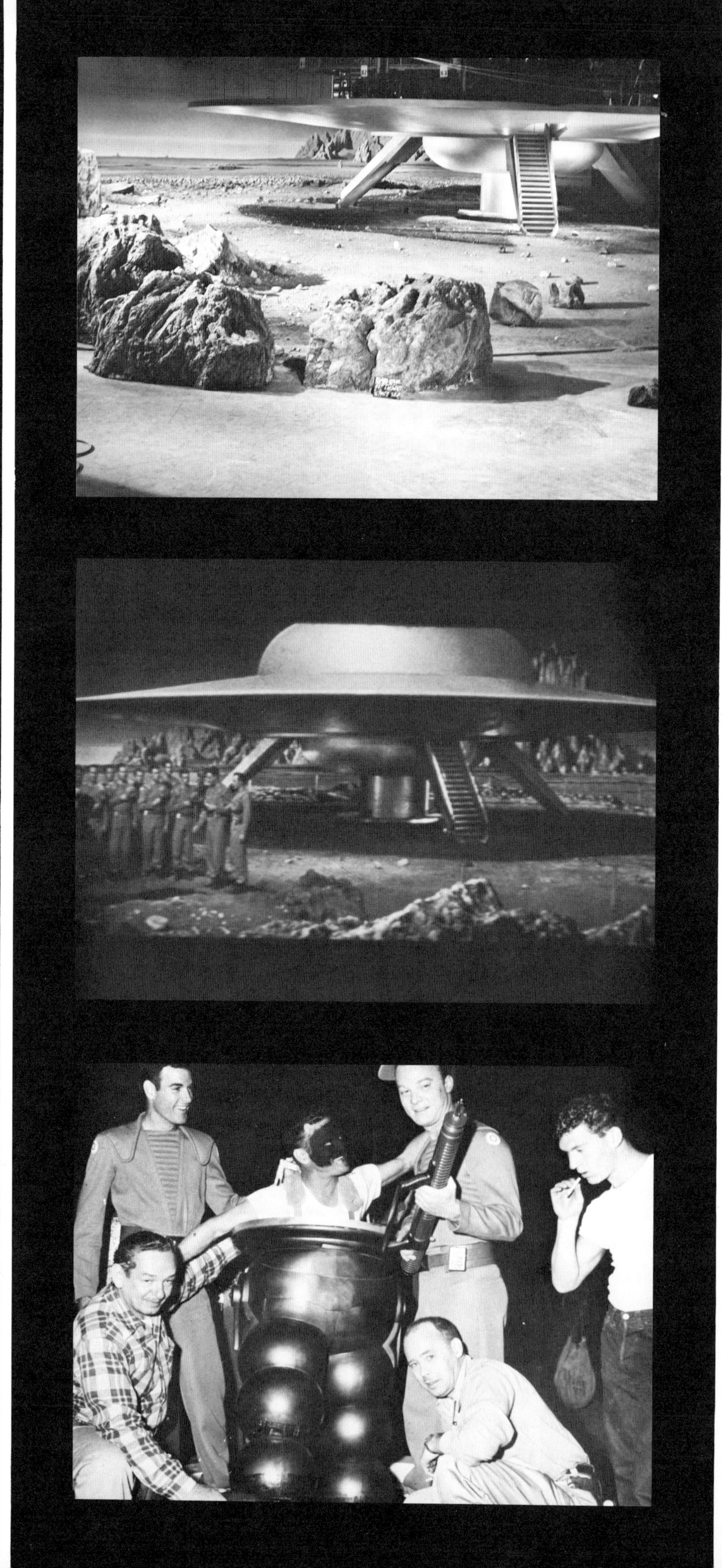

"plastic educator," which can boost brainpower and materialize images from the mind; a Krel laboratory that features a seemingly endless ventilation shaft; and Robby the Robot, who is equally capable of neutralizing weapons, manufacturing booze, and dishing out snappy dialogue.

The special-effects expertise is demonstrated as soon as *Forbidden Planet* begins, during the opening shots of the United Planets flying saucer approaching Altair IV and coming down for a landing. The model work supervised by A. Arnold Gillespie seems as colorful and graceful today as it did in 1956. One of the distinctions of this section of the film is the way in which the impression of the great expanse of space is conveyed. The saucer is seen flying in the far distance, gradually moving toward the camera and, later on in the same shot, is shown cruising across the foreground. The great distance covered in this flight maneuver actually took place on the limited space of a miniature set.

To show the progress of the saucer Gillespie made use of a technique employed around the turn of the century by Méliès and other trick filmmakers when photographing aerial models. The United Planets Cruiser was duplicated in three models: the smallest measured twenty inches across, the next larger was forty-four inches, and the largest was eighty-eight. To show the saucer approaching from the extreme distance Gillespie manipulated the smallest of the models across the background by wires attached to an overhead track. The saucer was allowed to travel off out of camera range or a shot of the interior of the craft was inserted to provide a break in the action. The next larger model could now be introduced. The second model was then filmed on the same setup. This miniature appeared to be the same spaceship, now seemingly closer to the foreground because of its increased size. When Gillespie wanted to show the saucer moving from the middle distance to the foreground, he would use the forty-four and eighty-eight inch models. The use of different-size models seemed to increase the depth of the shooting stage. As in all such model work, this scene was shot at high speed to create a slower, smoother movement. A scenic detail that enhanced the believability of these flight sequences was the convincing star field seen in the background. By this time effects men were simulating stars by piercing a black backdrop with tiny holes and then lighting the backdrop from the rear. The lighted pinholes were a great improvement over the car headlights used in *Destination Moon.*

A three-quarter section of the cruiser was built full scale for those live action scenes that took place around the grounded saucer. Unlike the mock-up in *The Day the Earth Stood Still,* one end and the top half of the United Planets Cruiser were not constructed. These missing parts were added by Henri Hillinick with a perfectly integrated matte painting. In essence Hillinick was employing the same principle used by Norman Dawn forty years before when the pioneer glass painter supplied additional floors to ruined missions. The old principles of cinematic artwork, both backdrops and matte paintings, were involved in many of the outer space wonders seen in *Forbidden Planet.* The distant barren landscape of Altair IV was actually an enormous cyclorama produced by MGM's scenic department. The curved painted backdrop posted at the outer edge of the shooting stage was 300 feet long and seventy-five feet high with cutout mountains and moons placed in front of the painted scenery to add to the impression of depth. The cyclorama was supervised by George Gibson and was painted by Ed Helms and Leo Atkinson. The huge, elaborate Krel furnace was created by matte painter Howard Fisher with three matched paintings which could be fitted together to make one image. The paintings were composited on film by Irving Ries's optical printing department.

The official credit for matte painting on this picture went to Warren Newcombe. It was typical of the Hollywood system that the name in the film's credits was not the name of the man who did the work. Instead the credit went to the man who happened to be head of the matte painting department. The co-author (with Allen Adler) of the original story for *Forbidden Planet,* Irving Block, was quoted in *Cinefantastique* (Spring 1979) as saying that Newcombe "never touched a brush.... He was my friend and I worked for him, but Warren Newcombe never did anything. He sat in his office and played around with his shortwave radio, calling his friends to play chess."

The most awesome vision in the film is the shot of the three tiny figures of Morbius and two cruiser officers crossing the walkway that spans the dizzying depths of the Krel ventilation shaft. The appearance of infinite depth was simulated by the effects crew by an ingenious combination of the basic tools of artwork and model work. An eight-foot-square, thirty-foot-long model of the shaft was constructed to represent that part of the setting that was closest to the camera. A painting from George Gibson's scenic department was placed at the bottom of the miniature to provide the image of the countless lower levels receding into the distance. The two elements were matched in such a way that the viewer is unable to discover where one ends and the other begins. As in the long shot of the Metalunan city in *This Island Earth,* the Krel ventilation shaft was made to seem like a full-scale set by the matting in of the three distant moving figures. The three people were photographed from the top of a tall building; to force the perspective, three midgets were substituted for the actors. The strip of flooring that the midgets walked on was then matted onto the image of the shaft's miniature walkway.

The savage dark side of life on Altair IV is the ferocious Monster from the Id. The abandoned Krel gadgetry has enabled Morbius to unleash this terrifying juggernaut from the primitive regions of his own mind. The Monster from the Id is an invisible creature that is only seen when it attacks the earthmen's camp; the huge snarling beast is outlined in the earthmen's force field and is bombarded by ray guns and distintegrators as it snatches up anyone within reach. This desperate battle was put on the screen by first filming the live action (the actors blasting away at an unseen menace, actors lifted by wires as if picked up by a giant hand); then the incandescent outline of the monster was added with cartoon animation. For the animation effects MGM went outside their studio personnel in order to hire the best technicians in the field, Joshua Meador's animation-effects crew fom Disney Studios. As in all cartoon animation the Id Monster was drawn frame by frame, twenty-four drawings per one second of action. The color was added by filming the artwork through filters. The soft edge of the monster's outline that was supposed to result from the vibrant light of the force field was devised by shooting through a "glow glass," a technique similar to the ground-glass method used for the glowing saucer in *The Day the Earth Stood Still.* As with all composites in *Forbidden Planet,* the cartoon image of the Id Monster and the separately animated laser blasts were combined with the live action by Irving Ries and his optical-printing crew. The final jigsaw of images was an exciting display of flashing laser lights and carefully coordinated action.

Perhaps more so than any of the actors in the picture, the star of *Forbidden Planet* was the charismatic Robby the Robot. This articulate automaton with the dome head of complex electrical units proved so popular that he appeared a year after *Forbidden Planet* in a movie called *The Invisible Boy* (1957). Since then he has never been out of work for very long, appearing regularly on television in such shows as *The Twilight Zone, Lost in Space* and *Wonder Woman.* The method for making a movie robot has always been relatively simple: an actor is put inside a metallic suit of some kind. But Robby was technically many steps ahead of the majority of previous robots, including Gort from *The Day the Earth Stood Still,* for two reasons. First, rather than the usual streamlined tin-can look, Robby was rigged with complicated external gadgetry. His intricate dome and electrical chest panel featured flashes of light and moving components that made visible the robot's computations. These devices were manipulated by remote control by means of a cable which ran into the heel of either shoe and hooked up with the control on the other end. For those scenes when Robby's feet were on screen, an internal battery was used.

The second improvement made in movie robot technology was the way in which the actor inside Robby was obscured. The position of the actor was made less obvious by the design of the robot's head. Since Robby's head was transparent, the actor had to be able to see by some means other than through peepholes in a tin skull, the usual technique for previous robots. Robby stood six feet, eleven inches tall, but he was designed to be played by a man who was only five feet six. The actor saw through the voice box grating directly below the head dome, his face blackened to make him completely invisible.

No other space opera from the fifties boasted such a varied display of spaceship maneuvers, elaborate gadgetry, and alien vistas as did *Forbidden Planet.* The movie was superior to any other science fiction effects picture at the time, but it wasn't as profitable as some of its competitors. A science fiction film that was considered to be more financially successful than *Forbidden Planet* was *Earth Versus the Flying Saucers,* a low-budget feature made the same year. *Earth Versus the Flying Saucers* made $1,250,000 in box office receipts and *Forbidden Planet* garnered $1,600,000, but the expensive MGM effort was produced for well over a million and consequently made little or no profit. The low-budget space opera, on the other hand, made a sizable profit once its relatively minor costs had been taken into account. The lesson producers learned from the financial outcome of both *This Island Earth* and *Forbidden Planet* was not to bother putting in the time and money necessary to stage the special effects for an ambitious outer space project. This lesson was remembered for more than ten years.

Flourishing at the same time as the space pictures of the fifties was the popular wave of science fiction movies starring rampaging giant creatures. According to the scripts of these films, the one force that was capable of spawning the parade of special-effects monsters from the fifties was atomic radiation. Radioactivity, it seemed, rarely ever killed anything. Neither did it seem to even make anything sick. All that radiation could do was make something grow to monstrous proportions. And if radiation wasn't doing that, it was stirring up something already big by freeing the creature from the complete suspension that had preserved the beast since its golden years in the prehistoric past.

Warner Brothers started the creature craze in 1953 with the classic *The Beast From 20,000 Fathoms.* A ferocious dinosaur called a Rhedosaurus springs into action after it is revived by an atomic blast in the arctic. The beast then begins the long trek to New York City, where it wreaks havoc with every thunderous step it takes. This picture was the first feature in which the great stop-motion animator Ray Harryhausen supervised the special effects. The giant Rhedosaurus was actually a small-scale, flexible model that was animated one frame at a time. The fundamental stop-motion technique supposedly discovered by Méliès was elaborated into a spectacular vision of destruction by combining the animated model with other miniatures and full-scale live action. Harryhausen continued with his masterful technique when creating the giant octopus in *It Came from Beneath the Sea* (1955) and the reptilian-feline Venusian in *Twenty Million Miles to Earth* (1957).

Taking a different and less time-consuming tack in 1954 was Toho Studios in Japan. Like *The Beast from 20,000 Fathoms,* Toho's low-budget production of *Godzilla, King of the Monsters* was a story about a giant reptile that was sparked back into life by radiation; but unlike the Harryhausen film, the Japanese monster was not created through stop-motion. Primarily the Toho method for filming monsters on the warpath entailed photographing an actor in a rubber monster costume as he destroyed a miniature city. Eiji Tsuburaya, Godzilla's shrewd special-effects man, was able to turn this seemingly simple technique into an entertaining spectacle of science-gone-haywire through his ingenious handling of limited resources. Tsuburaya used stepped-up lighting to allow for high-speed photography; the resulting slow-motion on the screen made Godzilla's movements seem more lumbering and dramatic. Tsuburaya also alternated long shots of the man in the reptile suit with closer shots of a small electronically-operated miniature model of the creature that was built from the midsection up. Both the actor and the model were photographed in severe contrast between light and shadow to enhance the special effects with an eerie visual style. All of these elements of Tsuburaya's technique were then skillfully edited together to make a forceful illusion. The title of "King of the Monsters" may be an exaggerated claim, but Tsuburaya's resourceful effects skills made Godzilla's destruction of Japan a strong exhibition of monstrous violence.

Godzilla was quickly followed by other Tsuburaya monsters in *Rodan* (1957) and *Gigantis, the Fire Monster* (1959). *Rodan* had some lively aerial effects in its depiction of the destructive exploits of a flying dinosaur. Instead of a man in a rubber suit, Rodan was a suspended model that levels a miniature city of Tokyo. Tsuburaya's system for filming monsters has been employed in countless other Japanese films, a series of movies whose effects became less and less skillful even though Tsuburaya remained in charge. *Mothra* (1962) was the first of Toho's completely embarrassing efforts. This picture tried to make something monstrous out of an oversize butterfly and, even tougher to swallow, tried to inject pathos into the story with two doll-size girls who were forever squealing their allegiance to the misunderstood Mothra.

Perhaps the most skilled example of the Tsuburaya method of monster effects was not engineered by Tsuburaya but by Tom Howard in the 1960 British movie *Gorgo.* As in the Toho pictures the mother and baby monsters in *Gorgo* were actors in lizard suits who spent most of their time dismantling miniature sets. The effects in *Gorgo* were an improvement over Tsuburaya's effects because of a newly developed fast color film that was ideal for the quick exposure required in the necessary high-speed shooting. This new film stock produced a sharper, more richly colored image during the slow-motion effects sequences. Another improvement was the superbly detailed miniature sets. The small-scale models were built on a scale of one to thirty and included highly accurate facsimiles of such landmarks as Big Ben and Tower Bridge. The fiery destruction of these miniatures by the mother creature was all the more convincing because of the model-makers' attention to detail.

Along with enormous rep-

Top: A behind-the-scenes look at one of the giant ant mock-ups constructed for *Them!* *Center and bottom:* The mock-ups as they appear in the film.

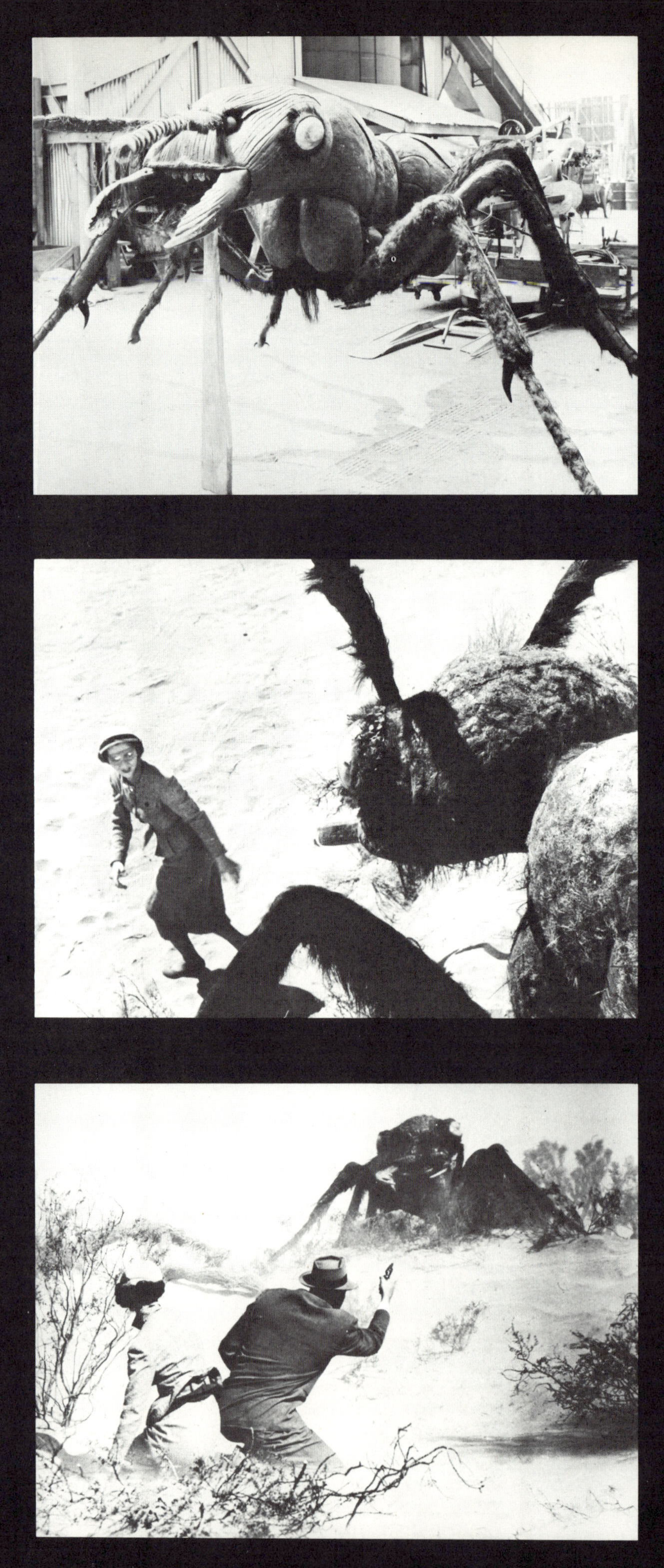

tiles, gigantic radioactively mutated insects had a field day of destruction in the fifties. A year after *The Beast from 20,000 Fathoms* stomped on New York, Warner Brothers sent giant ants out of the western desert and into the heart of Los Angeles in *Them!* (1954). This relatively low-budget thriller made great dramatic use of fairly limited full-scale mock-ups of the monster ants. Dick Smith (not the famous make-up artist) constructed the oversize insects. Only two of the mock-ups were fully mobile, and of those two only one ant was built in its entirety. The partial mock-up was of the front half of the ant and was used for close shots of a marauding insect. The other members of the giant-ant colony were primarily static mock-ups whose only moving parts were their heads and antennae, which were prodded into motion by offscreen wind machines. These ants were used as "extras" in scenes in which the audience's attention was centered on either the actors or the two working mock-ups. By skillfully diverting the audience's concentration, the makers of *Them!* were able to create the impression of many deadly mutant ants ready to pounce on human victims.

Many imitations and variations were made on the giant insect theme, usually of mediocre quality, as in *The Deadly Mantis* and *The Black Scorpion* (both released in 1957). The best of the *Them!* follow-ups was *Tarantula* (1955), which was made by the same people who produced *The Incredible Shrinking Man*. Jack Arnold's *Tarantula* used an actual spider to play the part of the enormous bug. The spider was directed with the help of air jets to spur it on. Clifford Stine combined the footage of the spider with the normal live action by means of his typically excellent matte work.

By the sixties most of the novelty of space travel and mutated monsters had worn off. New ideas in science fiction effects and themes were needed to replace the well-worn concepts of the fifties in order to sustain interest in the genre. One of the first new scientific miracles to be visualized in the sixties was produced and directed by the man who initiated the fifties science fiction craze. In 1960 George Pal put time travel onto the screen in his adaptation of H. G. Wells's *The Time Machine.* Pal's special effects team of Gene Warren, Tim Baar, and Wah Chang had to create the impression of a man traveling into the future and then faced the task of depicting a nuclear war and the post-holocaust world of 802,701 A.D. *The Time Machine*'s limited budget required that a great deal of ingenuity be employed when filming these visions.

The time travel sequences were especially resourceful. As the time traveler sits in his machine, he can see the days come and go through the skylight of his lab. The changing sunlight was staged by placing rotating four-part color wheels in front of the camera lights. Each quarter of the wheel had a different colored filter that corresponded to a certain part of the day. As the wheel rotated in front of the lights, the coloring of the scene changed. The clear portion of the wheel represented day, the pink portion denoted sunrise, the amber section dusk, and the blue section night. When the time traveler accelerated his machine, the days and nights swept by much more quickly. For this accelerated sequence an alternating black and clear color wheel was used to show the rapid succession of bright days and dark nights. Animation provided the details of time travel: the sun zipping across the sky, the stars flickering, and a tree changing through the seasons.

Ingenuity also played a part in one of the effects for the nuclear war sequence, but an oversight made the initial results backfire disastrously. For this scene Gene Warren and Wah Chang had to come up with a blanket of molten lava to flow through the streets of London. The clever solution to the problem was to shoot the scene on a miniature street and to use oatmeal as an inexpensive and realistic-looking substitute for the lava. At the end of a work week hundreds of gallons of oatmeal were cooked up and set aside for the test-shoot on Monday. The oversight was the effects team's failure to take the weather into consideration. The heat was intense that weekend, intense enough to ferment the cereal. When filming resumed on Monday, Warren and Chang unwittingly set up their high speed cameras at the end of the miniature street and waited for the trapdoor to open and release the solid flow down the chute. It flowed all right, like a fast-moving river. With their backs literally against the wall Warren and Chang could only gape in horror as the torrent of watery, foul-smelling breakfast rushed forward to engulf them.

Despite this catastrophe Gene Warren told us that he regarded *The Time Machine* as one of his most satisfying assignments. His reasons for singling out this picture were unusual because he wasn't particularly pleased with the special effects; he said that the budget was too restricted to get everything the way he would have liked. He took satisfaction in his effects work on *The Time Machine* because his effects contributed to a good film. He would rather take part in what he considered to be a mediocre effect for a strong movie than a brilliant effect for a picture that didn't hold together. The latter, as he put it, would be pointless, "like the tail wagging the dog."

Another novel showcase for special effects in the sixties was the big-budget science fiction epic *Fantastic Voyage.* The often-repeated theme of miniaturization was given an offbeat twist in this 1966 film: a group of scientists are shrunk down to microscopic size in order to perform a brain operation from the inside of a man's head. A submarine is also reduced in size to allow the scientists to sail through the patient's bloodstream. The production of this story required the building of a full-scale mock-up of the submarine that was forty-two feet long, twenty-three feet wide and fifteen feet high. Harper Goff was brought in to design the vessel, a job that was similar to the work he did for *Fantastic Voyage* director Richard Fleischer twelve years before during the preparation of Captain Nemo's *Nautilus* in *20,000 Leagues Under the Sea.* Goff's new creation, the *Proteus,* cost one hundred thousand dollars and weighed eight thousand pounds. It was fashioned as a scientifically plausible nuclear powered sub to be used for oceanic research. The layman moviegoer was less likely to notice the authenticity of the ship as he was to appreciate the *Proteus*'s smooth, sleek symmetry. The route of the *Proteus* (the patient's various inner organs) was also constructed with great accuracy and at great expense. Huge, oversize replicas were built of capillaries, lung, heart, ear, and brain; most of the sets being big enough to serve as a stage for the full-scale *Proteus.*

For all the cost and planning that went into the making of the anatomically precise sets, it was cinematographer Ernest Laszlo's ingenious use of light that ultimately made the relatively gigantic organs look convincing. Laszlo found while filming the special sets that the usual method of coloring the scene by painting the props appeared flat and unconvincing: the paint gave no impression of the pulsing life that had to be sensed while watching the inner body sequences. Laszlo's solution was to use translucent props, and then color them with colored lights, a technique he called "painting with light." This method accounted for much of the sets' vibrant quality. "Painting with light" was also used for a lifelike detail on the capillary set. A rotating color wheel was employed to show the visual effect of the intake of oxygen. The color wheel provided specks of color on the capillary walls, which changed from blue-violet to pink to correspond to the entrance of oxygen to that part of the body.

The intravascular skin diving scenes in *Fantastic Voyage* posed the problem of making the actors appear to be swimming through body fluids. Ernest Laszlo tried shooting the actors in a water tank but the footage ended up looking like a typical underwater scene instead of an unprecedented glimpse inside a man's body. As with so many wondrous effects in science fiction, the solution to the problem was an adaptation of a technique developed by pioneer trick filmmakers. As was done in Méliès's 1907 version of *20,000 Leagues Under the Sea,* Laszlo shot the fluid scenes "dry." The actors were suspended by wires on the normal set and the camera ran at the high speed of 72 frames per second to make the actor's motion slower, as if impeded by a thick liquid.

Boasting a budget of $6.5 million, *Fantastic Voyage* was perhaps the most ambitious special-effects production in science fiction at the time of its release. This was a distinction that the film enjoyed for only a short time. Just two years later, in 1968, *Fantastic Voyage* was dwarfed by Stanley Kubrick's mammoth science fiction spectacle *2001: A Space Odyssey.* Three years and $10.5 million went into the making of Kubrick's film, and unlike so many epic productions, the time and money spent on the movie were clearly evident on the screen. Realistic spaceships cruise majestically across brilliant star fields; astronauts cross richly detailed moonscapes; and a space age explorer races past mind-bending images on a breathless journey to Jupiter. *2001*'s stunning vision of the future made the special effects in the majority of previous space pictures seem completely obsolete.

Kubrick's effects team was supervised by Douglas Trumbull, who later supervised the effects for *Close Encounters of the Third Kind* (1977), and included Tom Howard, who had won Oscars for his work on *Blithe Spirit* (1946) and *Tom Thumb* (1958); Wally Veevers, an effects expert whose career began with *Things to Come* in 1936; and Con Pederson. When creating the wide-ranging special effects for *2001,* the effects crew was allowed an unprecedented freedom to experiment. Kubrick made absolute demands for realism in his effects and the techniques that could meet those demands had yet to be fully developed. The effects men were given the time and money that was needed to perfect their methods. The axiom in most special-effects work is that storyboarding and planning are crucial to producing scenes as efficiently as possible. In *2001* the effects technicians were allowed to improvise as they went along, to start composites with a single element and then gradually, piece by piece, match that first part of the puzzle with whatever element would enhance the shot. Using Douglas Trumbull's word, the effects shots were allowed to "grow." The procedure for shooting the effects was also unusually open-ended. Whereas a limited production could usually only afford to film an expensive effect from one angle, the *2001* effects team could shoot their scenes from a variety of setups. This extensive coverage of an effects sequence provided a great deal of flexibility in the editing room. The effects could be edited in the same manner as an inexpensive live-action sequence.

Letting the outer space effects shots grow one element at a time usually meant that the spaceship model was filmed first and then the star fields and planets were matted in separately later on. The problem with creating these composites was how to combine the different images without deteriorating the final visual quality of the scene. Fitting various visual elements into one scene usually involves copying the different pieces of film that contain each element. The problem with this process is that the duplication makes the image not as sharp as the original. If the effects crew on *2001* had followed this method, the scenes involving separately filmed spaceships and planets would have been of inferior quality compared to the live-action sequences. In order to maintain the highest degree of realism, the effects artists had to make the composites as vivid as the normal scenes. Ironically the solution to the problem that this sophisticated production team arrived at was to revert to a variation of the original pioneering technique of in-the-camera mattes.

The procedure for compositing in *2001* was to record as many elements as possible onto the original roll of film. As was done throughout the silent era, only one portion of the frame was exposed at one time. Each time a new element was added to the scene, the original piece of film was run through the camera again, one pass for each element. Sometimes the effects men succeeded in putting all the elements on the original roll of film by "holding" the film. A long shot during the sequence in which the scientists examine the mysterious monolith that has been discovered beneath the surface of the moon serves as a good example of holding the scene. On the first pass through the camera, the only image exposed onto the film was the set of the steel-lined excavation, the portion of the scene where the actors appear. The negative was then held for nearly a year while the other elements of the scene (the sky, the Earth, and the rest of the moonscape) were thoroughly tested. When the effects team was certain that these other parts of the scene would photograph properly, the additional elements were individually exposed on the original film to match the first exposure. The result was a jigsaw puzzle image of an alien vista in which every part of the scene was as sharp and dense as any live-action shot.

Holding negatives and improvising the effects necessitated an exacting means of keeping records of what had been photographed, how it had been filmed, and where in the movie it would end up. This crucial business was handled with an extensive filing system located in what was called the "control room."

The realism of the space flight sequences depended not only on the image quality but on impressive spacecraft models as well. The real stars of *2001,* the elaborate spaceship miniatures, were a striking departure from earlier movie spacecraft due to their originality of design and intricacy of detail. Unlike the usual streamlined rocket or saucer, the *2001* models incorporated all sorts of shapes from spheres to cylinders to octahedral forms. The detailing of these unusual models enhanced the movie's overall impression of scientific sophistication. The modelmakers were able to create the intricate and apparently scientifically advanced surfaces of the spaceships from a potpourri of common workshop items and spare parts. According to Douglas Trumbull, the detailing was made from "heat-formed plastic cladding, flexible metal foils of different textures and thicknesses, wire, tubing and thousands of tiny parts carefully selected from hundreds of every conceivable kind of plastic model kit, from boxcars and battleships to airplanes and Gemini spacecraft." The skillful arrangement of all these parts made for a surface that was so finely detailed that the cameraman could photograph as close as he wanted without betraying the illusion of an enormous spacecraft. Trumbull explained this and other effects in *2001* in an article written for *American Cinematographer* (June 1968), an effort he repeated for his spectacular effects in *Close Encounters of the Third Kind.* This willingness on Trumbull's part to explain his work seems to derive from the fact that his effects are so expert that viewers would otherwise be unable to discern exactly what his work entailed.

When the models were supposed to be seen crossing

Like Fred Astaire in *Royal Wedding,* the stewardess in this scene from *2001: A Space Odyssey* only seems to be defying gravity. In reality the actress remained on the bottom of the set, walking on a treadmill, while the rest of the room rotated 180 degrees. The camera, locked to the front of the set, rotated along with it.

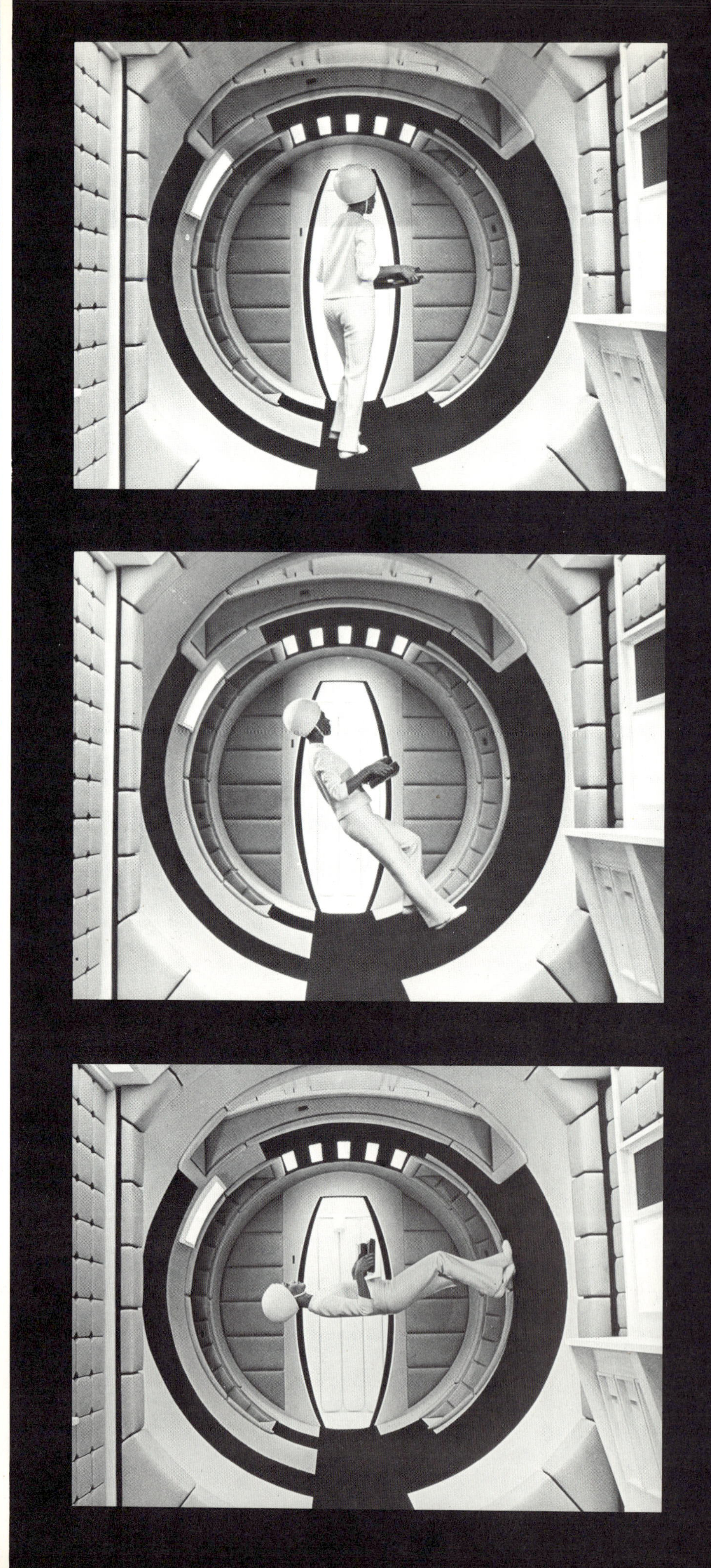

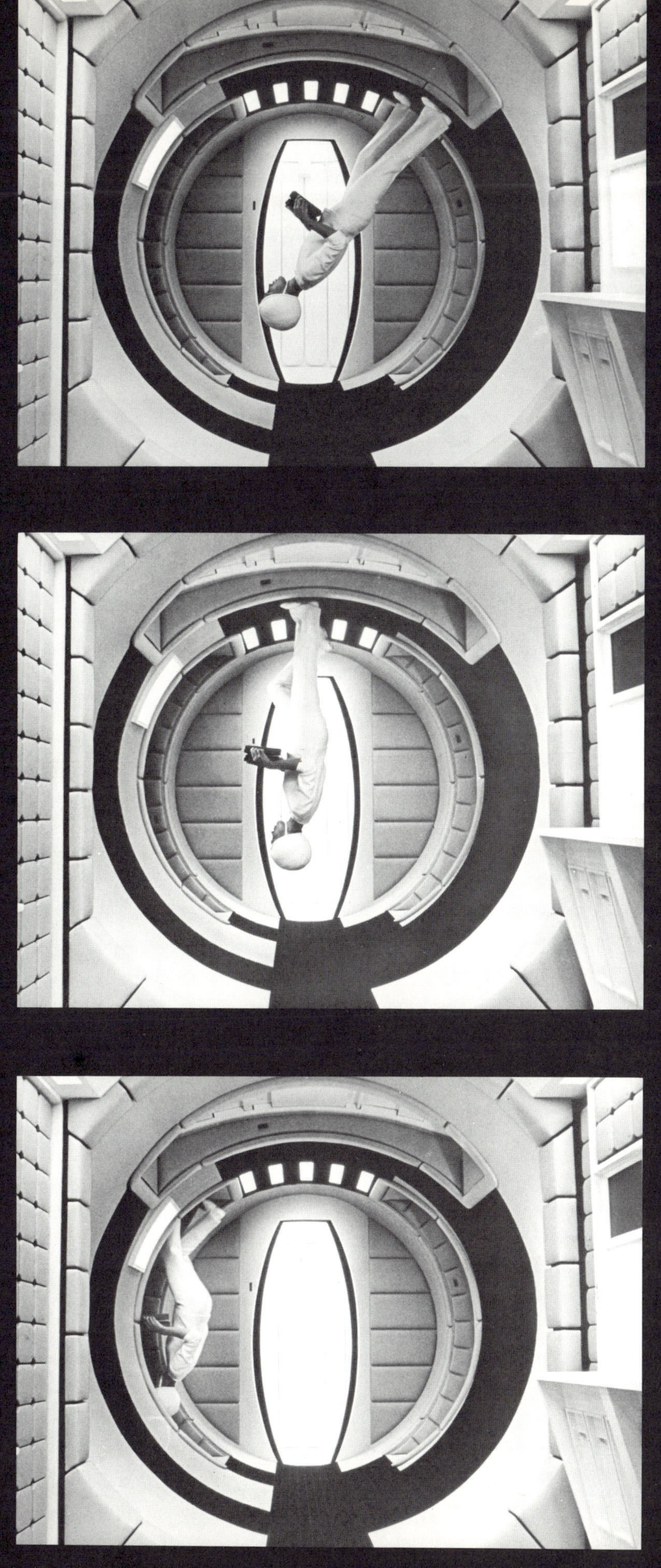

over star fields, the two separately filmed elements of spaceship and stars could not be combined in-the-camera since the moving spaceship required a traveling matte. To ensure the best possible match-up between the model and the background, the effects crew once again relied on a technique that dated back to the silent period. Rather than use the more modern blue-screen process for traveling mattes, the effects men rotoscoped the images and drew the mattes by hand for each frame. As was the case with the use of fundamental in-the-camera matting, this time-consuming technique produced perfectly matched combinations of two or more images.

Not only did the effects team of *2001* refine basic special effects processes, they also introduced some of the first innovations to appear in effects technology since the beginning of science fiction movies. One such innovation was the revolutionary *front-projection* technique used in the early Dawn of Man sequence. Kubrick was able to film a scene from the prehistoric past on an interior set by employing this front-projection technique. The actors in ape costumes cavorted about on a partial set in front of a front-projected image of a primordial landscape that was originally shot in Southwest Africa. The set and the plate were matched to create the illusion of a single exterior location.

Other novel special-effects devices figured into the psychedelic windup of Keir Dullea careening through a maze of mind-boggling light-shows. One of these surreal effects was the endless flashing corridor known as the Stargate. Douglas Trumbull engineered this sequence with a gadget called a slit-scan device. With the camera set at a very slow exposure speed, the lens took in two planes of light generated by the slit-scan. The images dashed forward from what seemed to be an infinitely distant point and formed weird streaking patterns on the film as a result of the extended time allowed for each frame to record the fast-moving colors. In essence this slit-scan technique was a clever adaptation of an old photographic trick. As Trumbull pointed out in *Cinefantastique* (Summer 1971), this process is similar in concept to "photographing car headlights at night with the shutter open—you get streaks of light. If you had the cars blink their lights on and off you'd get a pattern of streaky dots." Following the Stargate was an even more cosmic illusion laced with galactic explosions and colorful abstract visions. Surprisingly enough the whole scene was accomplished by filming chemical interactions that took place within a space comparable to the size of a deck of cards.

The standard of excellence in science fiction effects established by *2001: A Space Odyssey* was eventually to inspire such blockbusters of the late seventies as *Star Wars* and *Close Encounters of the Third Kind.* The nine years between *2001* and *Star Wars* was the amount of time it took to make big-budget, realistic space pictures practical. Ironically one of the movies made during that nine-year span that helped to make the expensive science fiction epics possible was a cut-rate porno movie called *Flesh Gordon* (1973).

This X-rated burlesque of the old Buster Crabbe serials follows the exploits of Flesh Gordon, Dale Ardor, and Professor Jerkoff as they wage their desperate battle against the minions of Wang the Impotent. These adventures involve a wide assortment of model spacecraft, which are all appropriately kinky and low-grade. Flesh pilots a penis-shaped rocket that sputters and sparks like its predecessor from the 1936 *Flash Gordon* serial; Wang's henchmen, when not ordering people to "Cyst and decease," soar through the air in space-

Effects men had been experimenting with the process of front projection for many years, but in *2001,* Stanley Kubrick's team was the first to perfect the technique in a major production. Projecting a background image from the front had the advantage of providing a brighter background than had been possible with rear projection. The obvious problem with front projection was how to mask the shadows that the actors cast onto the screen behind them.

The solution to the problem was a special screen covered with small glass beads. Light striking these beads from directly in front was reflected straight back to the light's source at about 95 percent of its intensity. With a two-way mirror positioned at a 45-degree angle in front of the camera, the projector could bounce its background from the side onto the screen while the camera, directly behind the mirror, could take in the strong projected image. This setup made it possible for the projector to beam the background image along the same axis that the camera viewed the scene. As a result, the camera could not see the actor's shadow, which was blocked by his own body. The only other problem with this process was that part of the background plate was projected onto the actors. This difficulty was solved by extra lighting directed at the actors; the illumination washed out the unwanted projected image.

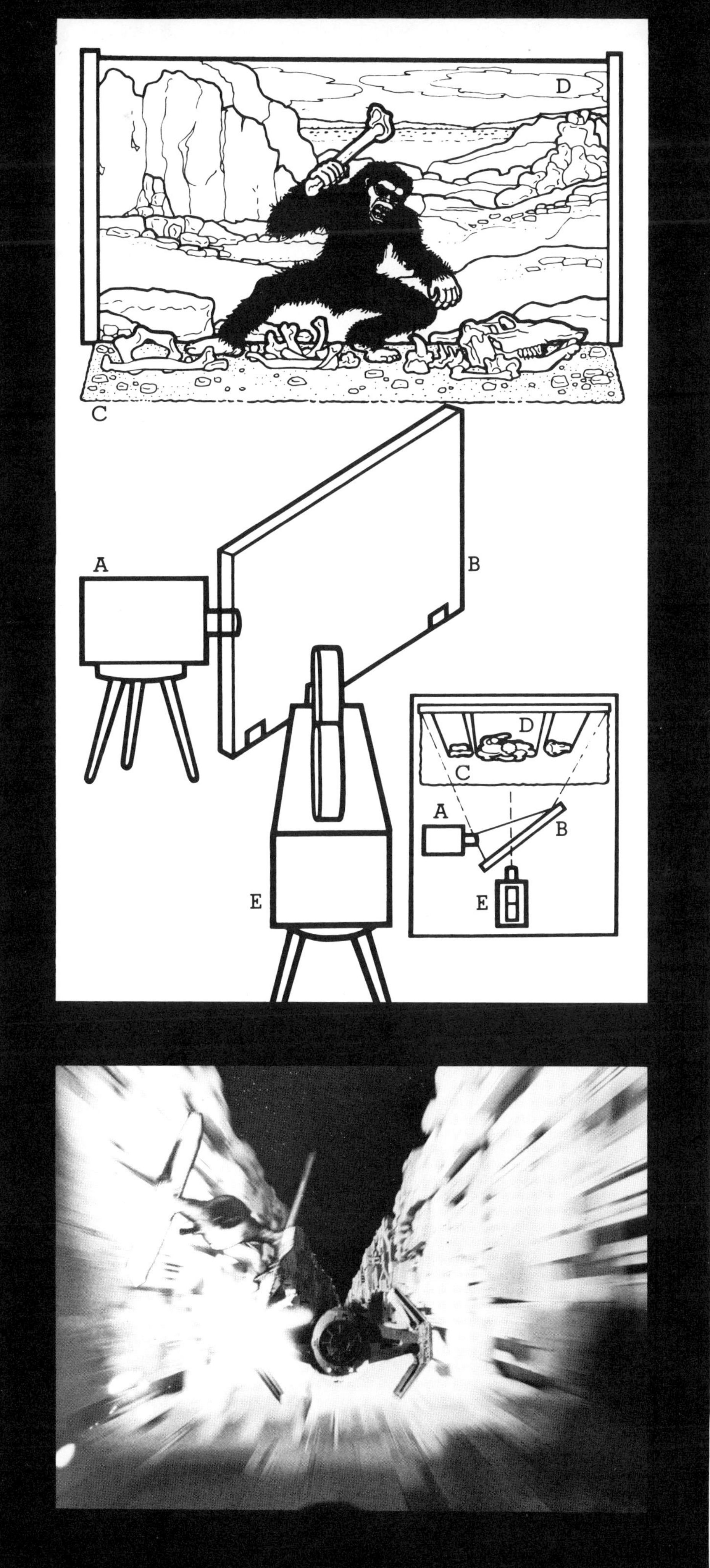

Top: FRONT PROJECTION: Projector (A) projects background image off a two-way mirror (B), which is placed at a 45 degree angle. The mirror transmits this image to the screen behind the actor in the ape costume (C). The screen (D), which is highly directional, reflects the background image through the mirror to the camera (E). Studio lighting is made bright enough so that it washes out any of the projected image which falls on the actor and set. The actor and set pieces mask their own shadows. *Bottom:* A pair of imperial TIE fighters zoom down the Death Star trench in the climactic battle of *Star Wars*.

ships that sport two painted eyes and a pair of batwings. The other model rockets include a swan ship and a fleet of ladybug spacecraft. This farcical production has come to hold an important position in the development of science fiction effects in the seventies because the film proved to be a training ground for many of today's effects experts. *Flesh Gordon*'s list of technicians, mostly unknown at the time of the movie's release, reads today like a *Who's Who* for the new breed of the special-effects field. Among them were Mike Minor, who designed the effects for *Flesh Gordon* and later did some preproduction designs for George Lucas's *Star Wars* and worked on *Star Trek* (1979); Dennis Muren, *Flesh Gordon*'s effects cinematographer, who went on to become an effects cameraman for *Star Wars* and *Close Encounters;* and Joe Viskocil, an explosion specialist for both *Flesh Gordon* and *Star Wars.* Other *Flesh Gordon* effects men to graduate to *Star Wars* were modelers Douglas Beswick, Rick Baker and Laine Liska. Greg Jein, chief model-maker for *Close Encounters of the Third Kind,* was another *Flesh Gordon* veteran. After learning their craft by working on a porno space opera, these young effects technicians have moved on to work some of the most awesome screen wizardry in science fiction.

The young effects crew assembled for the production of *Star Wars* was faced with an unprecedented task in outer space effects. George Lucas intended to project the exuberance of such swashbuckling space fantasies as the Flash Gordon comic strips and Edgar Rice Burroughs's John-Carter-of-Mars novels. As far as spaceship effects were concerned, this intention meant staging spectacular space age dogfights. Swift spaceships had to pitch, bank, and yaw with sudden grace as they tried to outmaneuver one another for a well-aimed laser blast. In order to make these fast-paced aerobatics believable, Lucas had to duplicate the realism of *2001.* The combination of frantic action and authenticity posed several problems never satisfactorily solved before. The *Flash Gordon* serials, for instance, involved lively aerial duels, but only a child could suspend his disbelief enough to accept the wobbly rockets as real.

One of the technical problems involved in filming the dogfight scenes of *Star Wars* was the question of what means of compositing would be appropriate. As much as possible, *2001* combined spaceships with backgrounds on the original film by means of a refined version of in-the-camera matting. This technique was well suited to the space flight scenes in *2001* because the elements of the shots rarely overlapped: the spaceships were usually not seen passing over a planet or crossing in front of another craft. In the *Star Wars* dogfights, on the other hand, the X-wing ships, piloted by the heroic rebels, and TIE fighters, flown by the Empire pilots, were constantly crossing over planets and each other in elaborate acrobatic displays. This complex jigsawing of elements required a more complicated system of traveling mattes.

The solution to the problem was the blue-screen traveling matte process. This technique entailed shooting the different elements on separate rolls of film and copying those pieces of film to make a composite. The next difficulty was how to maintain the image quality through the duplication stages. Since the overlapping action of the dogfight sequences ruled out the possibility of in-the-camera mattes, *2001*'s held-negative approach was consequently also eliminated as a possibility. The effects crew of *Star Wars* had to devise a method of avoiding grainy images despite duplication.

The ingenious solution to this problem was to compensate for film copying by photographing the aerial composite scenes in the previously discarded film format of VistaVision. Once used in such extravaganzas of the fifties as *The Ten Commandments,* VistaVision was a type of film stock that had eight perforations along the edge of each frame instead of the usual four; in other words the size of each frame was twice the size of regular 35mm. film. The strategy behind the use of this type of film was that although the various elements would be duplicated, on the final print the VistaVision image would be condensed into the normal, smaller frame size. The loss in image quality resulting from copying the film would be compensated by concentrating the image into a smaller area.

The most complex problem faced by the *Star Wars* effects crew was how to get the camera to move during the composite dogfight scenes. Up until the making of this film, composite shots entailed locking off the camera in a fixed position when filming each element. If an effects man was to matte in a flying saucer model onto a shot of an actual landscape, he would have to keep the camera stationary when photographing both elements. If he wanted to pan the camera to follow the motion of the saucer, he would then have to duplicate exactly the same camera motion when filming the landscape in order to make the two shots conform. Without some sort of device to regulate the camera movements on both elements of the scene,

The making of a Wookie. For the *Star Wars* Thanksgiving TV special, make-up/effects artist Stan Winston built highly sophisticated masks to be worn by the Wookie characters. These shots show three stages in the construction of the mask for the baby Wookie "Lumpy."

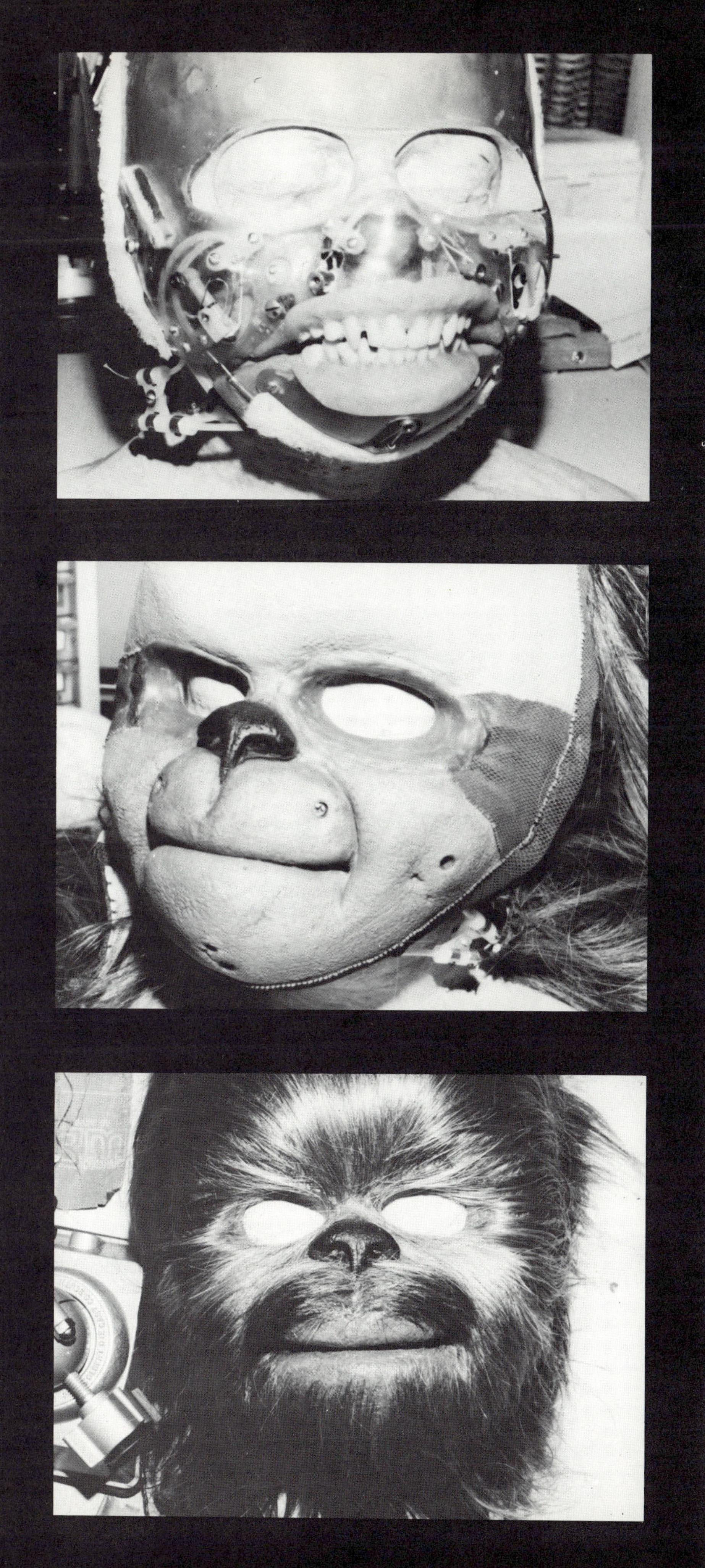

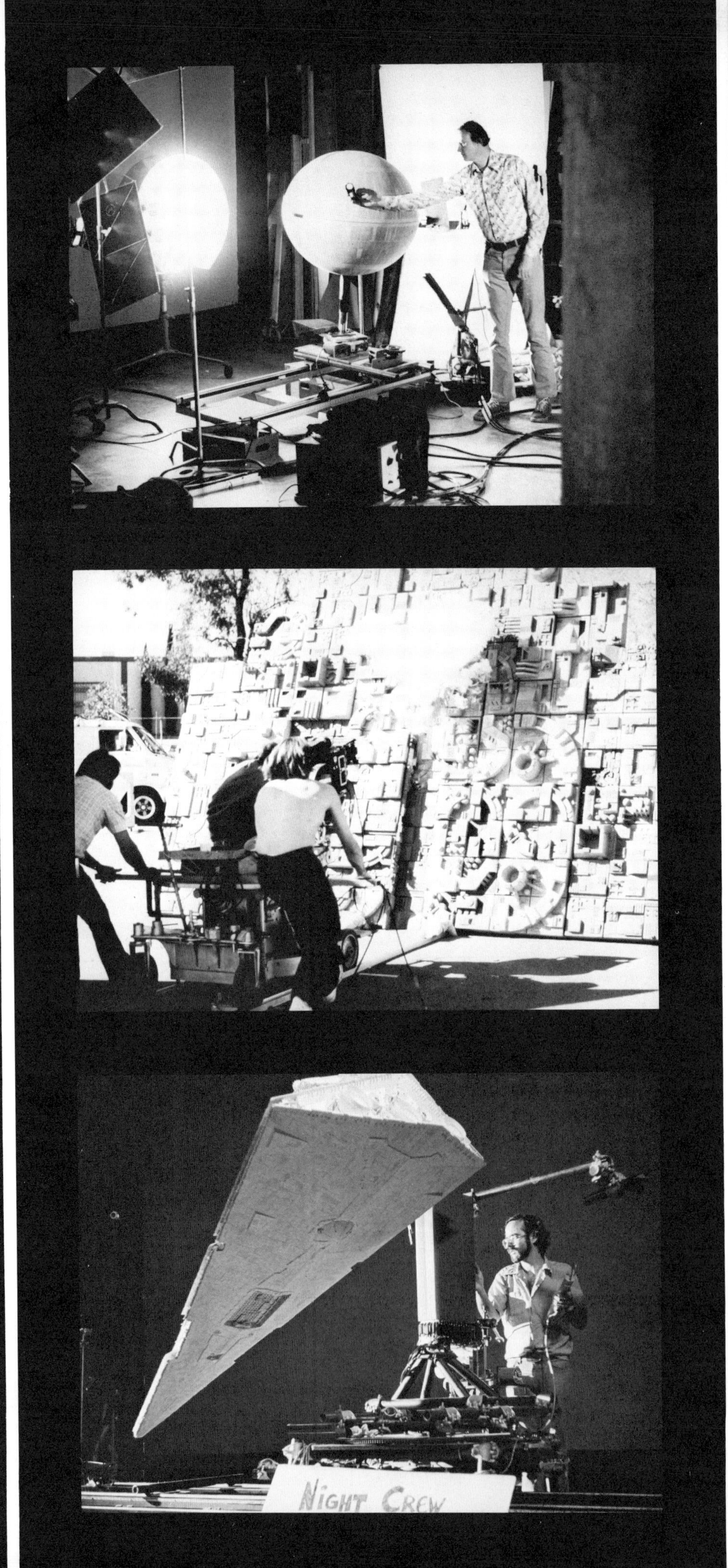

Top: A technician takes a light reading for a shot of the Death Star miniature for *Star Wars.*
Center: Filming a miniature explosion on a detailed section of the Death Star surfacc.
Bottom: An eight-foot model of an imperial star destroyer being prepared for a shot. From *The Empire Strikes Back.*

there was bound to be a discrepancy in the movements on each component. The result would be a mismatched composite. If the dogfight composites in *Star Wars* had been filmed with a locked-off (or fixed) camera, the effects shots would appear static compared to the live-action scenes filmed with a mobile camera. This difference between the effects and the live action would make the effects scenes seem less natural and consequently less convincing. For the 365 model-effects shots in *Star Wars,* a method had to be found to move the camera on one element and to duplicate that motion exactly on another visual component. The technological breakthrough that made this technique possible was a system called *motion control.* With the development of this process the technology of science fiction effects seemed to become as complex as the technology seen in the science fiction films.

By the time *Star Wars* was made, motion control for cameras was already a fairly old concept. Experiments in this technique were made as early as the forties. In 1948 Gordon Jennings used a motion-control system for a moving-camera shot in a dream sequence for a mystery called *The Big Clock.* One early motion-control prototype operated by means of an electrical system which programmed a camera to repeat movements exactly. The information that detailed the camera's movements was logged on a phonograph record. When the record player was hooked up to the camera and the disc was played back, the camera moved automatically as it followed the electrical orders received from the record. On each run-through the camera would pan or tilt up and down in the same manner. The concept of motion control was not new in 1975 when the production of *Star Wars* got under way but the practical application of the system was still to be developed.

John Dykstra was hired by Lucas to assemble the crew and equipment to shoot the miniatures for *Star Wars,* and part of Dykstra's job was to develop a motion-control system. Dykstra had gotten his special-effects training in TV commercials and industrial films, and later as an assistant to Douglas Trumbull on *The Andromeda Strain* (1971) and *Silent Running* (1972). In order to create the many effects shots for Lucas's picture, Dykstra formed a company called Industrial Light and Magic. The motion-control camera built by this outfit was called the Dykstraflex, an inside joke between Dykstra and Trumbull, who had once slipped a new box around an old camera and facetiously named it the Trumbullflex. The Dykstraflex was linked to a computer. As a result, it was capable of repeating a wide variety of moves with great precision, and it stored its electronic information on a cassette rather than a record. The spaceship model was positioned in front of a blue screen on a matching blue post. Once the model was filmed, a series of prints was made from the blue-screen footage to create photographically a traveling matte. On this setup the model was restricted in its mobility. The impression of the ship's diving and swooping was created mostly by the motion of the highly mobile camera and by the relative motion created by the sight of oncoming or outgoing backgrounds behind the model. To shoot a galactic dogfight scene, each component of the sequence was filmed separately: the fleeing spaceship, its pursuer, the spaceship engine lights, the laser shots, and the background were each photographed in a separate take. Although the basic concept of using models as substitutes for spacecraft was still part of the *Star Wars* production, the technological breakthrough of motion control put the filming of space scenes on a much more complex level.

Choreographing a shot involving an X-wing and TIE fighter was a complicated procedure. The action for the scene was first mapped out on storyboards; the reference material for the aerobatics was a reel of film clips taken from World War II movies featuring dogfights. The action of the shot was planned: the X-wing enters the frame in the foreground, zooms away from the camera, and pitches down. As it dives, the spaceship crosses the horizon line of the planet Death Star and is seen above the planet's surface. Hot on the X-wing's heels and zapping away at its tail with laser beams is the TIE fighter which follows the same path. First the X-wing ship was filmed. The model was placed on the blue post in front of the blue screen and the moves of the camera and miniature were planned out. All these movements were then made into an electronic program and entered onto a cassette. In the past, space models were usually filmed at high speed, but the *Star Wars* miniatures were often shot very slowly. The slow camera speed was used to gain greater depth of focus on the models by allowing more time for each frame to be exposed. Such an effects shot was likely to be photographed as slowly as two seconds per frame. The first programmed take of the X-wing was done in black and white to give the effects men a rough draft to examine for any possible mistakes. After necessary alterations were made, the second pass in VistaVision color was filmed.

This shooting procedure was repeated for the model TIE fighter. The electronic memory on the cassette ensured that the footage of the second model would match the X-wing shot. Then lights corresponding to the exhaust blasting out of the ship's engines were filmed. These lights were shot separately because filming them with the model would create problems in balancing the lighting of the two elements. Next to be photographed by the motion-control camera was the model of the Death Star and then the star field. All the pieces of film were then lined up in various combinations with one another in a special viewer to make sure that all the actions matched. The laser blasts and the reflections they cast upon the two spaceships were created separately by rotoscoping.

The final composite of all these images was put together after color separation prints were made of each element. With the color components of each strip of film isolated, the tone of the separately shot miniatures could be precisely controlled and matched with other elements in the scene. The first piece of film to be copied by the optical printer onto the final negative was that element which was passed over the most by all the other elements. In this case it was the star field. Once this was printed, the next most crossed-over element was printed (the Death Star). This order was followed until the scene was complete. Each color separation was printed individually with the appropriate photographic mattes. The end result of all this work was less than a minute of swift outer space action. Each outer space shot involving miniatures required a comparable amount of time and skill. In order to create all the thrilling spaceship maneuvers of *Star Wars,* the effects crew had to repeat this effort 365 times.

Many of the special effects in *Star Wars* were of a more traditional nature. The supervisor of mechanical effects was John Stears, who worked on most of the James Bond movies including *Thunderball* (1965), which earned him an Oscar. Along with Joe Viskocil and Gregory Auer, Stears engineered *Star Wars*'s many monumental explosions. These cosmic blasts were filmed both in large and small scale. Among their ingredients were magnesium, fuel oil, and dynamite caps. One of Stears's most dramatic concoctions for the picture were the luminous laser swords which figured into the climactic swashbuckling duel between Obi-wan Kenobi and the evil Darth Vader. To make this prop, the effects men coated a rotating rod with a reflective material which could beam an intense illumination into the camera lens.

Another *Star Wars* accomplishment were the robots C-3PO and R2-D2, the most endearing iron men since Robby the Robot. C-3PO, the tall fussy robot with a personality straight out of P. G. Wodehouse, was played by actor Anthony Daniels inside a metallic suit. C-3PO's small-fry sidekick, R2-D2, was a more deceptively designed robot since its small size and bullet shape didn't look anything like a costume for an actor, at least not a normal-sized actor. John Stears produced eight models of R2-D2, each one designed to perform a different sort of action. Some of these were operated by remote control, others were manned by three-foot two-inch tall Kenny Baker.

As in *Forbidden Planet,* the great space spectacle of the fifties, Lucas's epic of the seventies relied a good deal on the traditional technique of matte painting for some of its most spectacular visions. For the proposed seven matte paintings in *Star Wars,* producer Gary Kurtz recruited Harrison Ellenshaw from the Disney Studios. Ellenshaw's work turned out to be so impressive that he was asked to do thirteen paintings in all. In a scene reminiscent of the Krel ventilation shaft in *Forbidden Planet,* Obi-wan Kenobi (Alec Guinness) strolls along the edge of a seemingly bottomless power shaft. In reality Guinness walked on a platform only three feet above the ground; the dizzying depths were supplied by Ellenshaw's brush work. Just as striking and as ingenious was the invisible work Ellenshaw did for the enormous throne room ceremony attended by a cast of thousands at the close of the movie. Only 250 extras were actually on the set when this scene was filmed. The group of extras was filmed three times, each time in a different position on the partial set of the throne room. The part of the set that wasn't constructed was provided by Ellenshaw's artwork and the room was filled with his painted people.

Lucas's intention of recreating the excitement of heroic space fantasies was fully realized in *Star Wars* thanks largely to the fact that his effects crew made the story's outlandish exploits believable. The motion-control system in particular dramatically enhanced the picture by setting new standards for mobility in shooting model spacecraft. *Star Wars* made the same extravagant promises of screen thrills that *Flash Gordon* had and then delivered the excitement with a technology that had finally caught up with space fantasy concepts.

The new technology of motion-control also played an important part in *Star Wars*'s principal contender for the 1977 Special-Effects Oscar—Steven Spielberg's *Close Encounters of the Third Kind.* The nimble, streaking UFOs that Spielberg imagined for this picture necessitated a mobile camera to film the fast-moving models. The motion-control system for *Close Encounters* was developed and operated by Douglas Trumbull and his Future General Corporation effects company.

Trumbull's Motion Tracking System (MTS) differed from Dykstra's motion-control camera in that it could retain information on the movements for a shot that lasted more than two minutes while the *Star Wars* device was limited to thirty seconds. Another difference was that the MTS was to be used to combine live action with models while the Dykstraflex coordinated miniatures with other miniatures. Trumbull's approach to filming model spacecraft was also distinctive because it entailed a resourceful combination of up-to-date technology and fundamental effects methods. Instead of using a blue screen when shooting composite shots with his sophisticated motion-control camera, Trumbull and his crew filmed models inside a room lined with black velvet. By isolating an object against a black background, Trumbull was relying on a tried-and-true technique that was refined as early as 1933 in *The Invisible Man.*

Trumbull's command of basic effects methods, which contributed so much to the success of *2001: A Space Odyssey,* is equally apparent in his superb work for *Close Encounters*. The facet of Trumbull's work that seems to account for the excellent quality of his effects is his ability to take advantage of new technical developments while still extracting the most dependable approaches from basic effects technology. The filming of *Close Encounters*'s glowing flying saucers against an earthly background required the best from new as well as old techniques.

The first enthralling glimpse of the UFOs takes place at night along an Indiana hillside road called Crescendo Summit. The saucers tear along the highway, zip above the heads of dumbstruck locals, circle a McDonald's billboard, and race through the stalls of a tollbooth. Unlike previous movie saucers these extraterrestrial hot rods have no clear outline; they are defined merely by their brilliant neon glow. In order to film these amorphous balls of light, Trumbull's Future General crew made use of unusual atmospheric and photographic techniques. By filling the model set with smoke, the crew was able to create the hazy rim of light that surrounds the saucers. Normal air is usually dirty enough to cause a hazy look around an intense illumination, but the fact that the models were one twentieth full size meant that the atmosphere of the set had to be made around twenty times dirtier to induce the desired effect. The glow that was intended to emanate from the saucers was so intense that the lighting effect couldn't be recorded on film in just one take. The saucers were shot five or six times on the same strip of film, each take matching all the others. Each pass recorded a different aspect of the UFOs' glow; the models' neon lights were filmed in one take, other bulbs in the models were filmed in another, beams of light in the next run-through, and so on. The motion-control system enabled the effects cameraman to repeat the shot without variation so that the half dozen takes of the models looked like one pass through the camera.

The exterior live-action scene to be combined with the models was shot on an interior set. Interior shooting allowed Spielberg to control all the filming conditions and to make certain that the lighting and action would match the separately filmed models. The Indiana roadway on which Richard Dreyfuss and Melinda Dillon stand while gaping at the UFOs was actually a partial set in a tremendous hangar in Mobile, Alabama. The vast midwestern landscape seen in the background was a huge front-projection plate. To meet the requirements of the scene, the effects crew built a special portable front-projection screen, measuring one hundred by thirty-eight feet. Like everything else in this fabricated scene, even the image on the front-projection screen was not what it appeared to be. It was not a photograph of an actual landscape but a transparency of a finely detailed miniature constructed by Greg Jein.

Since *Flesh Gordon,* Jein had worked on the low-budget, cult favorite *Dark Star* (1974) and a handful of aborted television projects. Using the old principle of forced perspective, Jein created many miniature settings for *Close Encounters* that were commonly mistaken for actual scenery. When the saucers fly around the McDonald's billboard, for example, the model UFOs were printed over a shot of Jein's miniature section of the road. Other miniatures by Jein were the tollbooths that the UFOs streak through during the Crescendo Summit encounter and the seemingly monumental Devil's Tower seen in the final sequence. When these models were completed, Jein was asked to stay on for one more task, the ten-week job of building the miniature of the giant, gleaming mothership.

Top: Stop-motion artist Phil Tippett animates one of the dinosaur-shaped snow walkers for *The Empire Strikes Back.* On screen this model will appear hundreds of feet high. *Center and bottom:* The mothership in *Close Encounters of the Third Kind* contained a number of hidden surprises not visible on screen. Among them were this tiny graveyard and fighter plane. Others included a miniature truck and, as a tribute to *Star Wars,* a replica of the robot R2D2 the size of a pencil eraser.

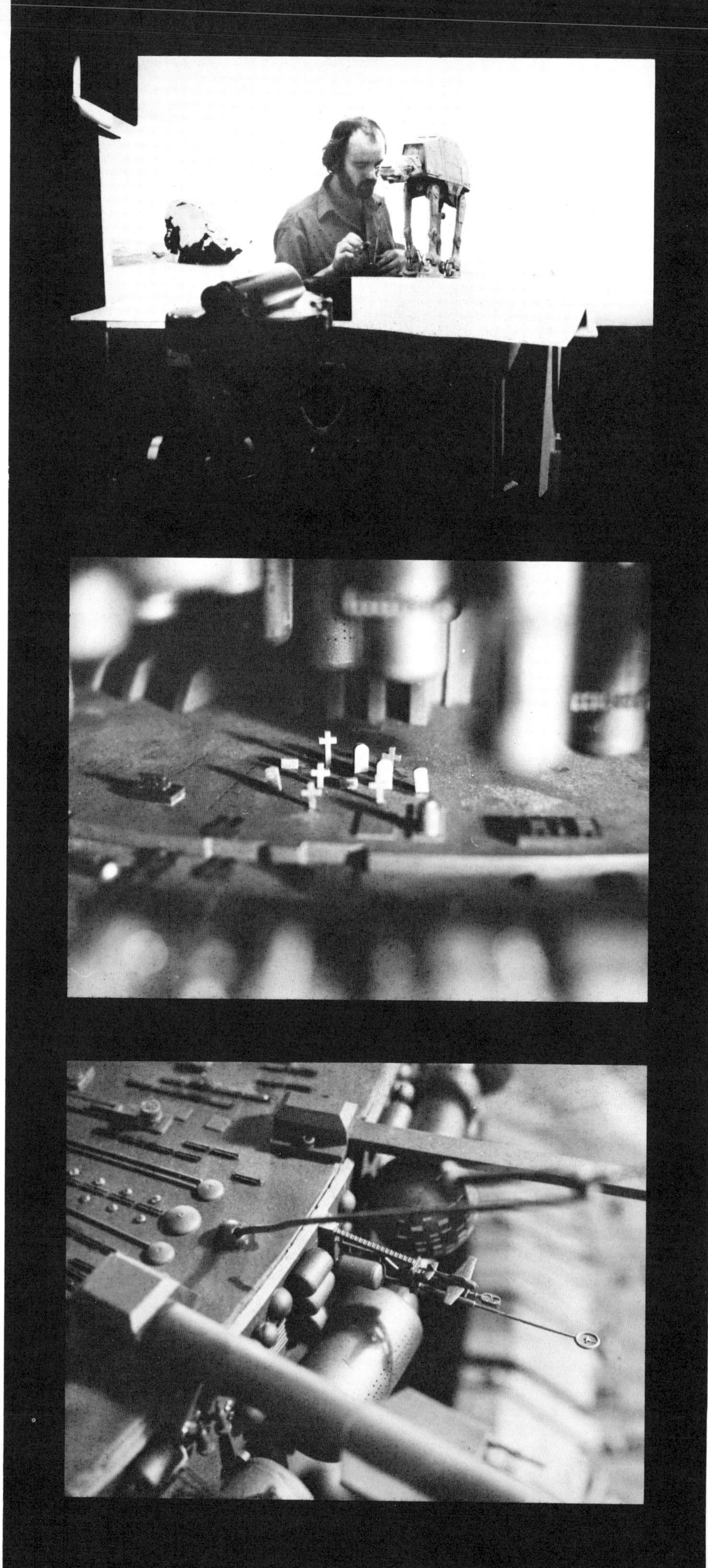

This massive spaceship, which highlights the final encounter, was originally visualized as a black, cone-shaped affair that would block out the stars as it hovered above the earthlings. Spielberg first conceived of one aspect of the final design for the Mothership as it appeared in the movie when he was shooting the India scenes for *Close Encounters.* Each day, on his way to and from the shooting site, Spielberg passed a huge oil refinery. The image of this lighted Indian refinery at night was the origin of his idea for the top half of the Mothership. After returning to California, he was then taken by another night-time sight. In a candid moment in a Fall 1978 *Cinefantastique* interview Spielberg said, "I was up on Mulholland Drive—a little stoned—and I got on my head on the hood of my car and looked out at all the lights from the San Fernando Valley upside down. And I thought that would be incredible as the underbelly of this oil refinery from Bombay." The combination of the two images was the basic idea for the concept of the Mothership as a refinery-in-the-sky/city-of-light. The final design of the spaceship was the combined effort of Spielberg, Trumbull, Jein, and illustrator Ralph McQuarrie.

The Mothership model supervised by Jein measured four feet across and two and a half feet high. Its complex lighting system was powered by 160,000 volts of electricity. This stunning, multicolored lighting setup was devised by Larry Albright and Peter Anderson under the supervision of effects project manager Robert Shepherd. The neon lights housed inside the Mothership were seen shining through thousands of tiny holes on the exterior of the model. The drilling of these holes was one of the most extensive and tedious special-effects jobs on the picture, involving everyone on hand including Trumbull, Spielberg, and the director's secretarial pool.

Dennis Muren, who had just finished his work on *Star Wars,* was in charge of the filming of the Mothership. To get enough depth of field on this intricate model, he had to shoot at extraordinarily slow speeds, sometimes ninety seconds per exposed frame, other times as long as seven minutes per frame. While some takes took eight or nine hours to film, one 150-frame shot took thirty hours. At one stage in the filming the tedium of this process was enough to inspire a taco-guacamole food fight on the special-effects stage.

When the Mothership sets down at the base of Devil's Tower, the climactic meeting between earthlings and aliens begins. To find someone to create the benevolent extraterrestrials, Spielberg went outside Future General to hire makeup artists. The aliens were first designed by Frank Griffin and constructed by Tom and Ellis Burman. The outer space visitors were conceived as little cuddly humanoids with oversize heads. The Burmans put together seamless body stockings and the rubber masks, which were worn by little girls. The casting of girls instead of boys helped to give the aliens an unisexual appearance. The heads worn by the girls featured eyes manipulated by model-airplane-style radio control. Although this concept of the aliens was used in the film, the little girls were mostly kept in the background because Spielberg decided they weren't all that he wanted. Thinking in bigger terms, he toyed with the idea of using a marionette. He approached Bob Baker, an experienced puppeteer whose film credits included George Pal's Puppetoons, some of Pal's live-action features, and such Disney pictures as *Bedknobs and Broomsticks* (1971). Working on drawings by production illustrator George Jenson, Baker built a five-foot prototype for what were to be four aliens each measuring eight feet in height. The puppet had a transparent skin that revealed "working" inner organs, a filmy cape to represent the alien's constantly recycled epidermis, and eyes that cast beams of light. The final puppets were never made. The prototype was to make only a brief walk-on in the beginning of the sequence because Spielberg hit upon another idea he liked more.

Impressed by the facial mobility of the mechanical ape masks worn by actor Rick Baker in Dino De Laurentiis's *King Kong,* Spielberg decided to try a mechanical approach to the extraterrestrials. He contacted the man who designed the ape head mechanisms, Carlo Rambaldi, and persuaded the Italian sculptor and effects artist to construct an alien for *Close Encounters.* Rambaldi's alien was a short, soft-looking creature made of polyurethane skin. Inside were an aluminum-and-steel armature and a Fiberglas skull. The extraterrestrial's operation was similar to that of the creature Rambaldi was later to construct for *Alien:* offscreen levers activated cables that ran inside the working mock-up. These devices made the face of Rambaldi's creation capable of several subtle expressions. This alien with the quizzical smile became Spielberg's favorite and was brought in for the high point of the final encounter.

With the near simultaneous release of *Star Wars* and *Close Encounters of the Third Kind,* ambitious—and finally profitable—science fiction effects movies came into their own. *Star Wars* was the winner in the contest for the 1977 Special-Effects Oscar, but *Close Encounters* was easily equal to the Lucas picture in technical accomplishments. Each of the two films marked a new advance in science fiction effects: *Star Wars* dazzled audiences with its exhilarating miniature action scenes and *Close Encounters* made people believe in bizarre spacecraft swooping down on realistic settings. To a great extent new refinements in motion-control cameras were responsible for the success of these two pictures. Since both films made a phenomenal amount of money, it was inevitable that other filmmakers would try to duplicate that success. Big-budget science fiction had suddenly become fashionable. With uneven results filmmakers tried to absorb the new sophisticated technology which seemed to be an integral part of the Lucas and Spielberg success formula.

The new technology of science fiction effects reached an apex of mismanagement in 1979 with *Star Trek: The Motion Picture*. Right from its inception this movie was a confused project. As early as 1974 the enormous, if somewhat mystifying, enthusiasm of the die-hard Trekkies had convinced Paramount to take on a movie project based on the *Star Trek* television show. The picture was set to go before the cameras at the end of 1977, but in the spring of that year the decision was made to try the project as another television series instead. After the success of *Star Wars,* Paramount about-faced once more and committed itself to making a big-budget theatrical feature. The film was first slated for a cost of $5 million, then jumped to $15 million after Robert Wise was signed to direct. The final cost was about $40 million and the picture ended up looking more like the original figure of $5 million. Despite all the time and money that went into the making of *Star Trek,* the special effects, even at their best, were never more than adequate. The rest of the time the effects work was characterized by dull model work and visible matte lines.

The story of *Star Trek*'s mismanaged effects began when Paramount hired Robert Abel to supervise the special effects. Although Abel hadn't worked on any features, his company had a strong reputation based on the dazzling television commercials made for such sponsors as Pepsi Cola and Levi Strauss. For the production of *Star Trek* Abel began developing an incredibly sophisticated computerized motion-control system that he claimed would put to shame the comparable setups in *Star Wars* and *Close Encounters.* When he was brought in in March of 1978, the budget for special effects was $4 million. At the beginning of 1979 Abel said he would need $16 million. Paramount took this into consideration along with the fact that Abel hadn't come across with one finished effects sequence and then reached a "mutual agreement" with Abel to terminate his involvement with the picture.

According to some people in the film industry, Abel had created a monster for himself in all his never-been-done-before equipment. His computerized motion-control was an extraordinarily complex system that he had yet to master and could only perfect through costly on-the-job training. Abel has said that there was another side to the story, that his problems with the picture stemmed from the unending jumble of rewrites on the script. There must have been some truth to this assertion because what finally made it to the screen still seemed like a tentative draft, and a muddled one at that. What stood out most clearly through the conflicting stories about *Star Trek*'s effects scramble was the great inefficiency of the production. Although Harold Michelson was the production art director, Abel insisted on keeping his own art director. And while Paramount supplied Abel's existing studio with new equipment for the work on *Star Trek,* the company also put up another effects facility for him in Hollywood. After Abel left the picture, Douglas Trumbull took his place and yet another studio was set up for Trumbull.

Even with Trumbull in charge of the effects there was a limit to how much could be salvaged. Too much time had been wasted on what proved to be an impractical motion-control system. Apparently realizing this, Trumbull reportedly reached a contractual agreement with Paramount about the estimated quality of his work. At the time, the studio was determined to meet their original Christmas 1979 deadline for the movie's release. Trumbull's agreement stated that if given enough time, he would provide perfect effects, but if the picture was to be finished by December, he would only have the time to make them adequate. His prediction held true, but unfortunately *Star Trek*'s story demanded special effects that were much more than adequate. The starship *Enterprise*'s momentous encounter with the alien force is a good example of adequate being inadequate. The strange gigantic object that the *Enterprise* crew finds is a huge brown mass. During the course of the film's ever so lengthy discussion on the nature of this thing, the mass is alternately described as a living organism and a machine-planet. An object that looked like both an organism and a machine-planet would have been a fascinating sight. But the brown lump shown on the screen looks like neither. If anything the *Enterprise* seemed to have tracked down a monstrous chunk of free-floating dark chocolate.

Much more satisfying effects were produced by Disney Studios for half of *Star Trek*'s budget in the 1979 production of *The Black Hole.* The movie features some first-rate motion-control model work, but *The Black Hole*'s most intriguing accomplishment is its introduction of a technological breakthrough in the filming of shots involving matte paintings. This movie was the first feature to make use of the *Matte-Scan* device, which applies the principle of motion-control to composites of live action and paintings. This computerized device makes it possible to move the camera when shooting a live-action portion of a scene and then repeat the exact same move when filming the complementary artwork. Before the development of this technique, a matte shot had to be stationary in the same way that miniatures had to be filmed with a locked-off camera before the use of the Dykstraflex in *Star Wars.*

The matte shots in *The Black Hole* were supervised and, in many cases, painted by Harrison Ellenshaw, whose mattes in films like *Star Wars* were hard enough to detect when the camera was stationary. In *The Black Hole* his paintings were filmed with the same mobility seen in the normal live-action scenes; as a result Ellenshaw's newest artwork is even more difficult to point out. His painting of the observatory dome of the tremendous spaceship *Cygnus* was a striking example of this technique. Visitors on the *Cygnus* are shown entering the dome area in a moving camera shot. When they come to a stop, they react to some spectacular sight above them. Then, as a continuation of the same shot, the camera points upward to reveal an enormous skylight fronted by glowing spheres and distant crewmembers on elevated platforms. In this scene Ellenshaw was able to turn the camera away from the normal live action to a painting of the dome. To increase the realism of the painting, he also matted small areas of live action into the artwork, showing the *Cygnus* crew members at their posts. By covering all the action in the scene in one moving camera shot, Ellenshaw made the viewer believe he was watching a scene enacted on a huge set that in reality no studio would have attempted to construct. Ellenshaw's 150 matte shots for *The Black Hole* continually created spectacular illusions of this kind. Even if the viewer is aware beforehand of extensive use of matte paintings in this film, he would have an extremely hard time trying to locate them.

The Black Hole is also distinguished by some very striking miniature work. For the giant spaceship *Cygnus,* an interplanetary Crystal Palace designed by the great matte artist Peter Ellenshaw (Harrison Ellenshaw's father), two elegant 12-foot models were built out of brass tubing, wire, plastic, and steel. The most memorable moment in the film occurs when the *Cygnus* gets caught in the meteor shower and one of the fiery red orbs hurls down the ship's power core straight toward the camera. At the last moment, three of the astronauts race across a catwalk in the foreground, barely escaping with their lives as the meteor bears down on them. The power core and meteor were miniature models, added to the live-action footage of the fleeing actors by means of the blue-screen traveling matte process.

Although motion-control of one kind or another became the fashionable technique of science fiction movies in the late seventies, not all space epics were wrapped up in computerized gadgetry. *Alien* is an example that relies on more traditional methods.

When Brian Johnson was called in for the preproduction planning of special effects for *Alien,* he advised against motion control for the space flight sequences. These scenes showed a massive spaceship moving slowly through space and involved little in the way of complicated overlapping of visual elements. With the exception of a couple of shots Johnson saw that motion control wasn't necessary at all. For those rare exceptions, the time and cost that would go into setting up such a system would have bogged down the production far more than the resulting gadgetry would have enhanced the film. Instead, whenever it was necessary to repeat a camera move, Johnson and cosupervisor Nick Allder used a specially rigged mechanical setup in which the camera moved on a track. Without computers they ingeniously developed a system that sufficiently regulated the camera's movement.

The compositing of the spaceship *Nostromo* with star fields and planets also reflected a more fundamental approach to effects. The *Nostromo* was combined with other visual elements by means of in-the-camera matting. A grid system for charting the various portions of a scene enabled the effects crew to make sure that the matting was perfectly aligned. The spaceflight scenes in *Alien* were not as complex as the aerobatics of the motion-control scenes in *Star Wars,* but Johnson and Allder's more basic methods supplied all the outer-space authenticity needed to establish the setting for the film.

Immediately after finishing his work on *Alien,* Brian Johnson moved on to become the supervisor of George Lucas's vast special-effects facility in San Rafael, California. This studio was responsible for the effects seen in *The Empire Strikes Back,* the 1980 sequel to *Star Wars.* Along with the expert effects cinematographer Richard Edlund, Johnson was responsible for supervising an effects studio that was the most complete, most self-sufficient complex of its kind, a fully-equipped space fantasy factory. Instrumental in qualifying Johnson to head such a facility was a varied and well-rounded science fiction effects background. He was a veteran of both the lavish *2001: A Space Odyssey* and television's impoverished *Space: 1999.* The Kubrick film gave him the opportunity to experiment with the most refined special-effects techniques while *Space: 1999* forced him to stretch his ingenuity in order to make the most out of the least. These diverse experiences have evidently shaped Johnson's comprehensive outlook on special effects. He believes absolutely in the importance of seat-of-the-pants savvy in combination with the most advanced electronic devices. Like Douglas Trumbull, Johnson appreciates the usefulness of both the old and new techniques when creating fantastic illusions.

Although the new computer technology of science fiction seems like a revolutionary change in special effects, in a sense it hasn't really overhauled the effects field very drastically. Motion-control systems are only tools to be manipulated by the special-effects man. The success of that manipulation depends upon the same qualities found in such classics as *The Invisible Man* and *Forbidden Planet:* painstaking care and the ability to make imaginative refinements on old techniques. The motion-control systems, though they may seem unfathomable to the average moviegoer, are actually only a sophisticated refinement on the basic principle of combining two or more separately filmed images. When it is a part of a badly organized production like *Star Trek,* space age motion-control can produce effects that seem about twenty years behind their times; when handled with good sense to illustrate imaginative concepts, as was the case in *Star Wars* and *Close Encounters,* electronic cameras can create illusions that are truly out-of-this-world.

City of Light: a close-up of some of the breathtaking detail on the mothership model built by Greg Jein.

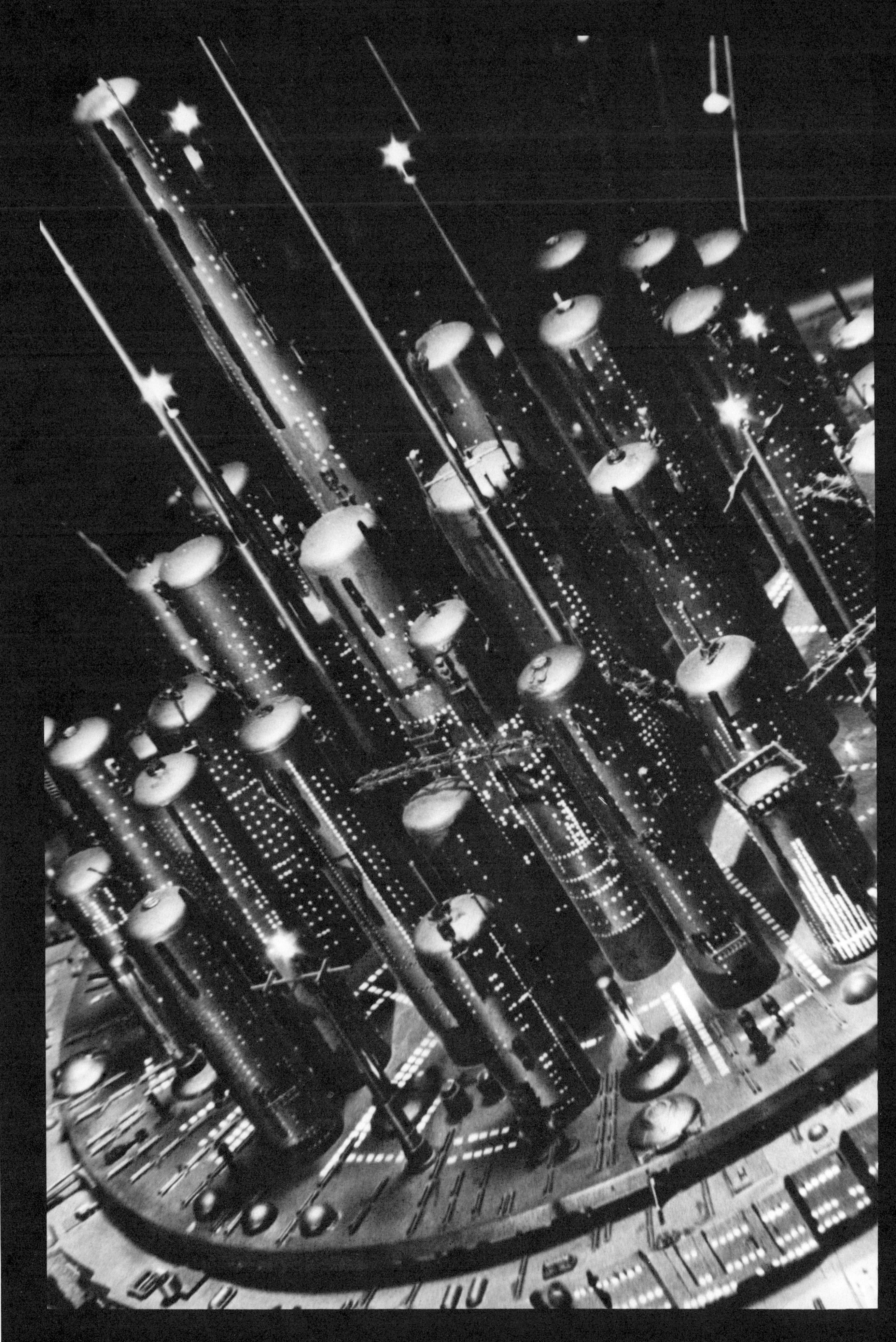

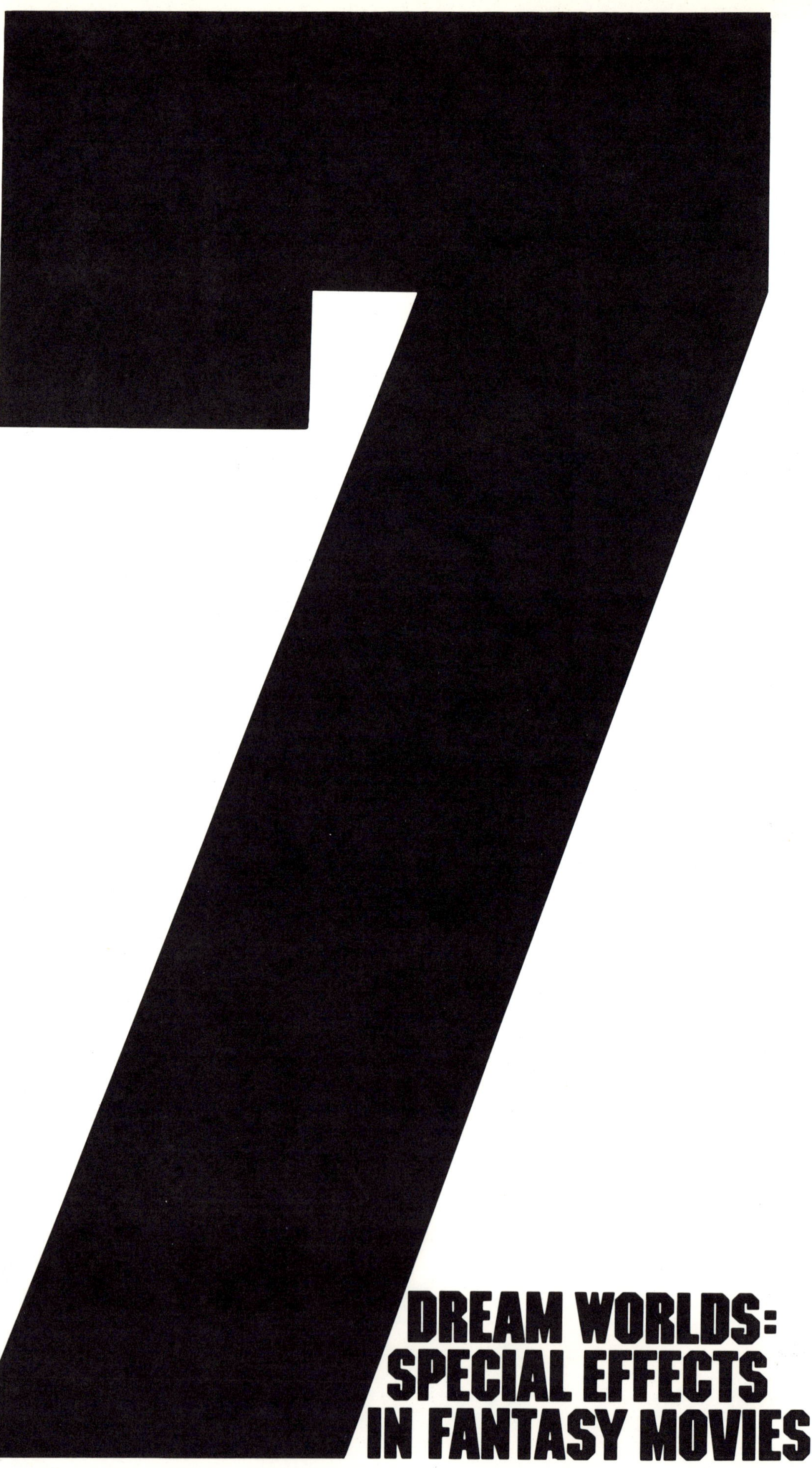

7 DREAM WORLDS: SPECIAL EFFECTS IN FANTASY MOVIES

In a sense, all movies are fantasies. For the price of a ticket we can step out of reality and live for two hours in a Technicolor dream. We can leave behind the dreariness and dissatisfactions of the everyday world and spend a delightful interlude gunning down criminals, exploring outer space, or making love on a South Pacific beach. Hollywood has always been America's most imaginative travel agency, offering instant vacations to fantasylands filled with glamor, excitement, and romance. Even the most grittily realistic movies are fantasies in the sense that they possess a shapeliness and symmetry generally missing from ordinary life.

When we speak of fantasy films, however, we're talking about a specific type of movie that appeals to our sense of wonder, which fills us with the same emotions of awe, terror, exhilaration, and delight we felt very deeply as children, when the world itself could be a wonderland. The childlike quality of fantasy is probably its most important characteristic. Fantasy films turn adults back into children by transporting us to fairy-tale worlds populated by marvelous mythical beings: sorcerers, wizards, dragons, giant apes, Munchkins, minotaurs, centaurs, and cyclopes.

Science fiction films also carry us to unknown, alternate worlds. But the point of science fiction is to speculate about the possible. There's a good chance that Jupiter really isn't the home of mysterious black monoliths with an active interest in human evolution, but *2001* makes us consider the possibility that such extraterrestrial intelligence actually exists. By contrast, fantasy deals strictly with the impossible, with experiences that only occur in a child's most extravagant dreams.

Fantasy films are pure escape. Their typical setting is not the moon, Mars, or Venus but some version of never-never land: Oz, Skull Island, the lost continent of Atlantis, Middle Earth. The very plots of these pictures often imitate the movement of daydreams: a character, leading a drab, unhappy life, leaves the real world behind and voyages into a realm of adventure and enchantment. Ann Darrow in *King Kong* is taken from the breadlines of Depression-era Manhattan to an uncharted isle, where she is carried off by a giant jungle king. Young Dorothy, in *The Wizard of Oz,* is knocked unconscious during a storm and awakens to find herself not in her colorless farmhouse on the gray Kansas prairie, but in a magical country on the far side of the rainbow.

It is the business of the fantasy film, then, to take us on a trip from the ordinary world to an extraordinary one, from the mundane to the miraculous. And it is the business of the special-effects expert to bring these motion-picture miracles to life. The task of the effects man is, first of all, to give concrete shape to something that exists solely in the imagination of the screenwriter or director. Good effects match or even outdo our wildest expectations. They enlarge our dreams. Bad effects deflate them and bring us crashing down to earth. A fantasy film with the potential for greatness can be killed by clumsy effects. On the other hand some effects are so powerful that they can create a compelling world of fantasy all by themselves, in spite of any weaknesses in the story that surrounds them.

Douglas Fairbanks's 1924 version of *The Thief of Bagdad* is a perfect example of an ambitious fantasy film that tries for a magical quality it never achieves because its special effects are so poorly executed. Fairbanks's movie was partly inspired by Fritz Lang's mystical fantasy film *Destiny* (1921), in which a young woman's quest to save her lover from death takes her to three fabulous kingdoms, where she encounters a variety of wonders. Impressed by Lang's imaginative use of camera magic, Fairbanks determined to outdo his German rival by making the most wondrous movie that the world had ever seen, a $1-million Arabian Nights extravaganza filled with as many marvels as he could pack into fourteen reels. For *The Thief of Bagdad* he constructed an incredible make-believe city, a colossal confection of towers, spires, minarets, and bazaars, where he could romp and swing like an acrobatic schoolboy on the world's most expensive set of monkeybars.

When we first meet the roguish, high-spirited hero, he is leading a free and easy life as the merriest thief in Arabia. His days consist of picking pockets, stealing purses, and climbing a magical rope to swipe freshly baked bread from the balconies of unsuspecting housewives. At the end of a long morning of vaulting, leaping, diving, dashing, and bounding around Bagdad, he returns home to count his loot. His carefree life comes suddenly to an end, however, when, with the aid of his magical rope, he steals into the royal palace, only to have his own heart stolen by the caliph's beautiful daughter. To win her hand, he is required to go on an arduous quest for a priceless treasure: a chest containing a magical powder that can conjure up anything in the world.

It is at this point in the movie that Fairbanks begins pouring on the special effects. To find the treasure, the thief must undergo a series of

Three ways to make a monster. *Top:* One of the original drawings showing the design for the mechanical dragon in Fritz Lang's *Siegfried*. *Center:* A lizard rear-projected onto a screen in *One Million B.C.* *Bottom:* A pair of animated dinosaur models locked in mortal combat from the original *The Lost World*.

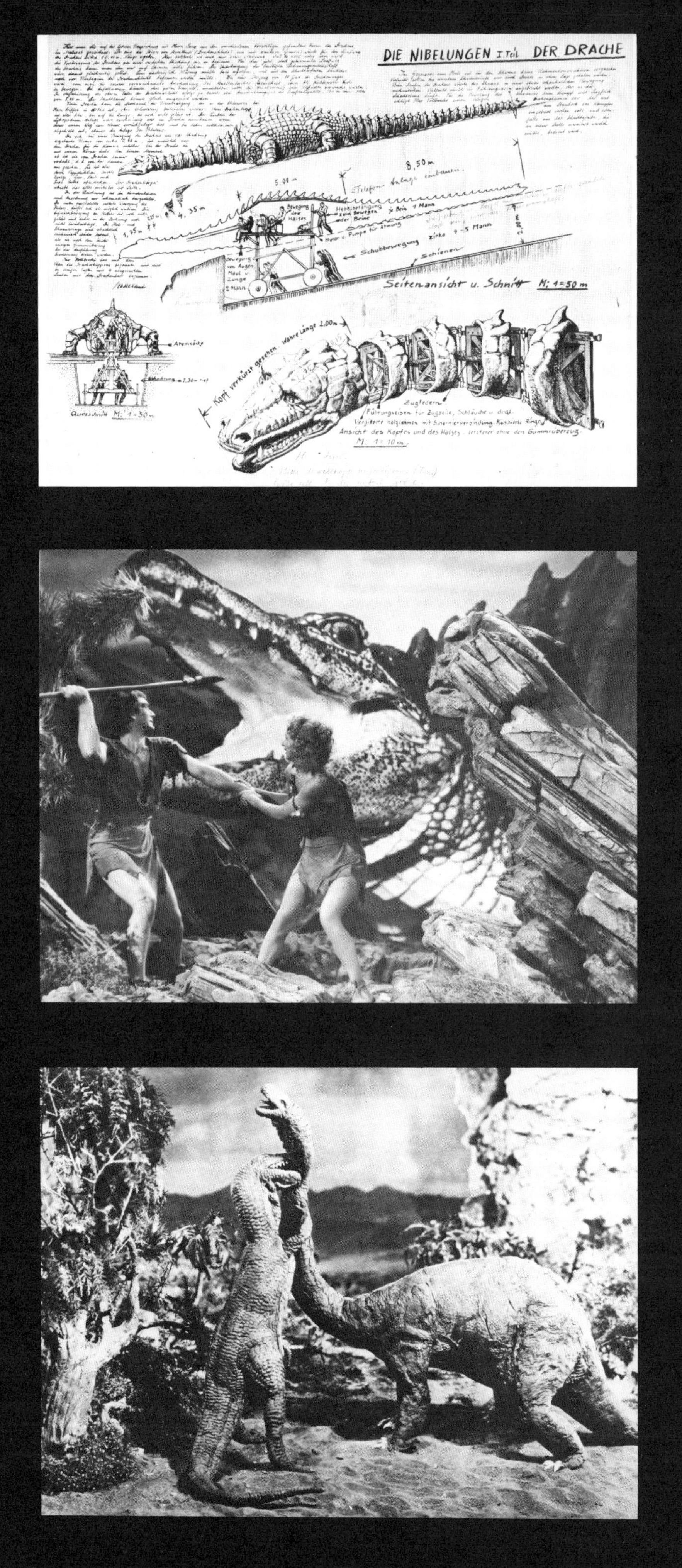

incredible ordeals. After passing through the "Valley of Fire," he fights a dragon, slays a giant bat, dives to the bottom of a stormy sea to retrieve a star-shaped key guarded by a huge, aquatic spider, and, finally, after locating the chest in the "Citadel of the Moon," returns to Bagdad on the back of a flying horse.

While each of these marvels is meant to make the audience gasp in astonishment, the more likely response is a giggle or groan. The problem is that the special effects (created by Hampton De Ruth) are surprisingly shoddy. The flying steed, for example, was simply a horse with feathered wings pasted to its back, galloping on a treadmill while superimposed clouds whiz by. The monster bat and submarine spider were both oversize marionettes. The thief's deep-sea dive to fetch the magic key is slightly more impressive. The scene was shot without any water at all, in an empty studio tank decorated to look like the bottom of the ocean. Wires were used to lower Fairbanks to the floor of the tank and also to make the kelp beds sway convincingly. At the same time the camera was overcranked to give the scene a slow-motion, underwater effect. Unfortunately the wires attached to Fairbanks and the seaweed are completely, even glaringly visible, as are the strings manipulating the giant puppets of the spider and the bat. Even more disappointing is the monster Fairbanks slays near the start of his quest. This creature is very clearly a baby alligator in dragon disguise. To shoot the sequence, the little lizard was decorated with fierce-looking papier-mâché horns and filmed in front of a miniature cavern from a distance of six feet. Since the opening of the cavern was completely dark, it served as a natural black backdrop, leaving a section of the scene unexposed. The film was rewound and Fairbanks, standing twenty feet away (to make him look tiny in comparison to the close-up image of the alligator), was added to the unexposed area. Unfortunately Fairbanks looks not like a legendary hero conquering supernatural forces, but like an overgrown schoolboy fighting his way through Disneyland.

The success or failure of a fantasy film often depends less on the strength of its story than on the quality of the mythical creatures it brings to the screen. For the true fantasy buff a well-made monster can redeem the silliest of scripts; a tacky one, on the other hand, can completely destroy whatever spell the rest of the movie has managed to weave.

One of the best mechanical monsters ever made for a movie was a representation of the dragon Fafner built for Fritz Lang's silent classic *Siegfried* (1924). When the mythological hero first comes upon Fafner, the beast is drinking from a mountain stream. Siegfried falls upon the monster, stabbing it in the eye and slashing its throat. Throughout the scene the great lizard moves with a slow, sinister grace that is particularly impressive in a creature constructed out of cardboard and wood. Four men, standing inside the body of the sixty-foot reptile, operated its neck, head, and tail, while five more, hidden in a trench underneath the dragon's body, moved it along a track built into the fake forest floor.

As good as Lang's dragon is, however, it is not entirely satisfactory as a movie monster. The problem with even good mechanical creatures is that, since they are essentially stage props appropriated for the screen, they often end up looking too stagey. In a theatrical production, with its painted backdrops and obviously mechanical effects (which we accept as real, just as we accept other dramatic conventions), a dragon made of papier-mâché and canvas can strike us as an impressive and lifelike creation. In movies, however, theatrical props and scenery always seem phony, which is one of the reasons that filmmakers generally have trouble transferring plays to the screen. Méliès could get away with a mechanically operated creature like the Frost Giant because his movies were *meant* to look artificial, like filmed theatrical performances. But most fantasy movies, even those, like *Siegfried,* that take place in weird, surrealistic settings, require more naturalistic-looking creatures—monsters which are not so obviously operated by cables and pulleys.

Significantly three of Hollywood's most successful mechanical monsters, the shark from *Jaws* (1975), the giant squid from *20,000 Leagues Under the Sea* (1954), and the great white whale from John Huston's 1956 production of *Moby Dick,* are all aquatic creatures, which look exceptionally realistic partly because we never see them very clearly. The squid attack takes place during a driving storm, which serves to obscure the monster, while Moby Dick and "Bruce" are always half-hidden under water. Interestingly the battle with the squid was originally filmed against a fiery sunset, but the footage was scrapped because the creature looked too fake. And in the one scene in which we see "Bruce" clearly (when he suddenly leaps out of the water and onto the rear deck of the shark hunters' boat), he indeed looks like a plastic fish.

The reverse problem mars a second method of producing fantasy creatures: the use of living lizards to represent monsters. This technique takes advantage of the camera's ability to make objects filmed from a short distance look enormous. A small lizard—such as an iguana, gila monster, baby croc, or alligator, with a few horns and strange protuberances pasted onto it—is placed in a miniature set and filmed in close up from an extremely low angle to give viewers the sensation that they are looking up at some gigantic creature. In addition the camera is generally overcranked; as a result the lizard appears to move very slowly and ponderously, as though it is carrying around several tons of bulk. The problem here is that in spite of all these attempts to make the reptiles appear larger than life, they always seem much too natural and familiar. Instead of looking awesome, they look perfectly ordinary (even with their exotic trimmings) and sometimes extremely silly. It is nearly impossible to get away from the awareness that what we're watching is just some pet-store reptile with a set of spikes glued to its face, a realization sure to kill the magic of any fantasy movie.

The effects method that has produced the best fantasy creatures of all is *stop-motion animation,* also known as three-dimensional or model animation. This technique exploits a type of magic that is uniquely cinematic: it can be performed solely by means of a motion-picture camera. Essentially stop-motion consists of taking a small model (generally of some awesome, nonexistent creature, either extinct or mythological), arranging it in a certain pose, shooting a frame of film, making a slight change in the position of the model, shooting another frame of film, and so on. Onscreen the rapid progression of individually photographed frames creates an illusion of continuous movement, a kind of three-dimensional flipbook effect. (The same method is used to make cartoons, only in this case each shift in the figure's pose is drawn on a transparent celluloid sheet, known as a *cel.*)

Stop-motion is one of the most fascinating areas of special effects. Since the models are highly detailed representational figures, generally designed and sculpted by the animator, it is, along with matte painting, the field most closely related to traditional art. At the same time it often seems like a branch of black magic. Myths about pieces of sculpture that miraculously come to life are at least as old as ancient Greece. It wasn't until our own century, however, that this miracle could actually be performed by a few exceptional people capable of taking a dead hunk of rubber or clay and making it live, breathe, scowl, walk, and rampage through midtown Manhattan. Among all the different types of "special-effects wizards" working in Hollywood, the model animator seems most like Merlin.

Model animation is a field with a small number of practitioners and a large number of extremely zealous cult fans who spend a great deal of their time reading, writing, and gossiping about the work of their favorite artists: Willis O'Brien, Ray Harryhausen, Jim Danforth, and the younger generation of stop-motion animators, including people like David Allen, James Aupperle, Doug Beswick, and Steve Czerkas. There is, in fact, a kind of stop-motion subculture composed of hobbyists who sell or swap rare behind-the-scenes stills, attend special showings of classic fantasy movies, and exchange information in small, privately printed "fanzines" (fan magazines). These people are true connoisseurs; they are passionately involved with Harryhausen's *oeuvre* and enjoy nothing more than a serious discussion of the skeleton army sequence in *Jason and the Argonauts* (1963) or Willis O'Brien's contribution to *Mighty Joe Young* (1949). Clearly a special-effects technique that can inspire such intense devotion must possess an unusual degree of power. After all, nobody holds rear-projection film festivals or publishes fan magazines devoted to the subject of bipack contact matte printing.

It is true that some people have no use for stop motion, which they regard as phony-looking largely because, even at their most fluid and expressive, animated models tend to move in a somewhat jerky, choppy way. But this uneven movement is like the fitfulness of a dream. There is a strange, surrealistic quality to most animated models that makes the process unsuitable for naturalistic movies but adds to the dreamlike atmosphere that is a central feature of the fantasy film. Stop motion is probably the most painstaking and demanding of all special-effects techniques, requiring prodigious amounts of patience, precision, and skill, not to mention time and money. In the topsy-turvy world of fantasy, using real creatures to make monsters is considered a form of fakery, a lazy man's way of producing an effect, while fashioning creatures out of foam rubber is regarded as the real thing.

Imparting life to inanimate objects through stop-motion photography is a film trick that goes all the way back to the work of Méliès, who used the technique to make a suit of armor do a little dance in one of his magical shorts. Two of the earliest motion pictures to animate three-dimensional figures were *Humpty Dumpty Circus,* an 1897 Vitagraph production in which toy wooden animals march around for forty seconds, and a 1907 film by Edwin S. Porter called *The Teddy Bears* featuring seven little bears cavorting on-screen. Obviously early film-makers regarded stop motion as a form of child's play, the cinematic equivalent of pretending that one's favorite dolls or toy soldiers are really alive. The man who turned model animation from an amusing little toy into an art and, along the way, made an eighteen-inch puppet into one of the Immortals was Willis O'Brien.

Before entering the movie business, O'Brien (who is invariably described in biographies as either a "two-fisted, hard-drinking Irishman" or a "soft-spoken, mild-mannered Irishman") worked, among other things, as a cowboy, prizefighter, and marble-cutter—peculiar training for a man who was to spend most of his life doing work nearly as delicate and precise as a surgeon's. He was also a talented sculptor and cartoonist. In 1913, while playing around with a pair of clay boxers he had molded, he hit upon the idea of animating them with stop-motion photography. Borrowing a newsreel camera from a friend, he shot the figurines a frame at a time, changing their position slightly with each exposure, and came up with a crude but encouraging short of a couple of sparring manikins. His next experiment was a little more elaborate: a one-minute comical film about a caveman and a dinosaur. In 1906 the American cartoonist Winsor McCay delighted audiences with his animated cartoon character Gertie the Dinosaur. O'Brien's film also features a comical Brontosaurus; unlike McCay's, however, this creature was not drawn but made of clay molded over a jointed wooden skeleton and brought to life through stop-motion photography, a method O'Brien liked to call "animation in depth." A producer who attended a screening of this film was impressed enough with it to advance O'Brien $5,000 to shoot a longer version. However, stop-motion animation is an extremely demanding form of special effects; if an animator is lucky and nothing goes wrong, a hard day's work might produce twenty seconds of usable footage. In 1914, after two months of laboring on his movie, O'Brien exhibited the result, a five-minute prehistoric burlesque called *The Dinosaur and the Missing Link* featuring characters with names like Theophilus Ivoryhead, Stonejaw Steve, Araminta Rockface, and Wild Willie, the hairy missing link of the title. The film was purchased by the Edison Company of New York. When the movie was distributed and proved a success, Edison brought O'Brien east to head a subsidiary called Manniken Films, Inc. During the next year O'Brien, who was responsible not only for the animation but also for the model-making, set construction, costume design, lighting, and camera work, turned out a series of five-minute prehistoric comedies, including *Rural Delivery 10,000 B.C., Prehistoric Poultry, Curious Pets of Our Ancestors,* and *Nippy's Nightmare.*

The success of his animated dinosaur films led O'Brien to try his hand at a more ambitious project: a sixteen-minute-long movie called *The Ghost of Slumber Mountain* (1918). Besides being longer than anything he had ever done before, the movie was significant for several other reasons. First, largely as a result of his consultation with a vertebrate paleontologist at the American Museum of Natural History, O'Brien's dinosaur models for *Ghost* were much more realistic than his previous figures. Second, the film takes a far more serious, straightforward approach to its portrayal of prehistoric times, and lacks the Stone Age slapstick of the Mannikin movies. Finally, the film uses both animated dinosaurs and live actors, though not in the same scenes. *The Ghost of Slumber Mountain,* which was made for $3,000, ended up grossing more than $100,000, a clear indication to O'Brien that the public was ready for a feature-length film starring his prehistoric monsters. His first choice for the project was Sir Arthur Conan Doyle's 1912 fantasy adventure *The Lost World.* When a producer named Watterson Rothacker, a longtime admirer of Willis's work, acquired the photoplay rights to Doyle's novel, O'Brien set about making the movie that was to become not only an immediate sensation but one of the enduring classics of the silent screen.

Doyle's novel concerns the expedition of the intrepid Professor Challenger (played by Wallace Beery) to a remote plateau deep in the Amazon jungle where time has stood still and apemen and dinosaurs roam. After a number of adventures among these prehistoric creatures, the explorers barely escape with their lives when a volcanic eruption wipes out the lost world. Challenger, however, manages to capture a Brontosaurus, which he ships back to England. Unfortunately, while being unloaded in London, the dinosaur breaks free of its cage and goes rampaging through the city, knocking down buildings,

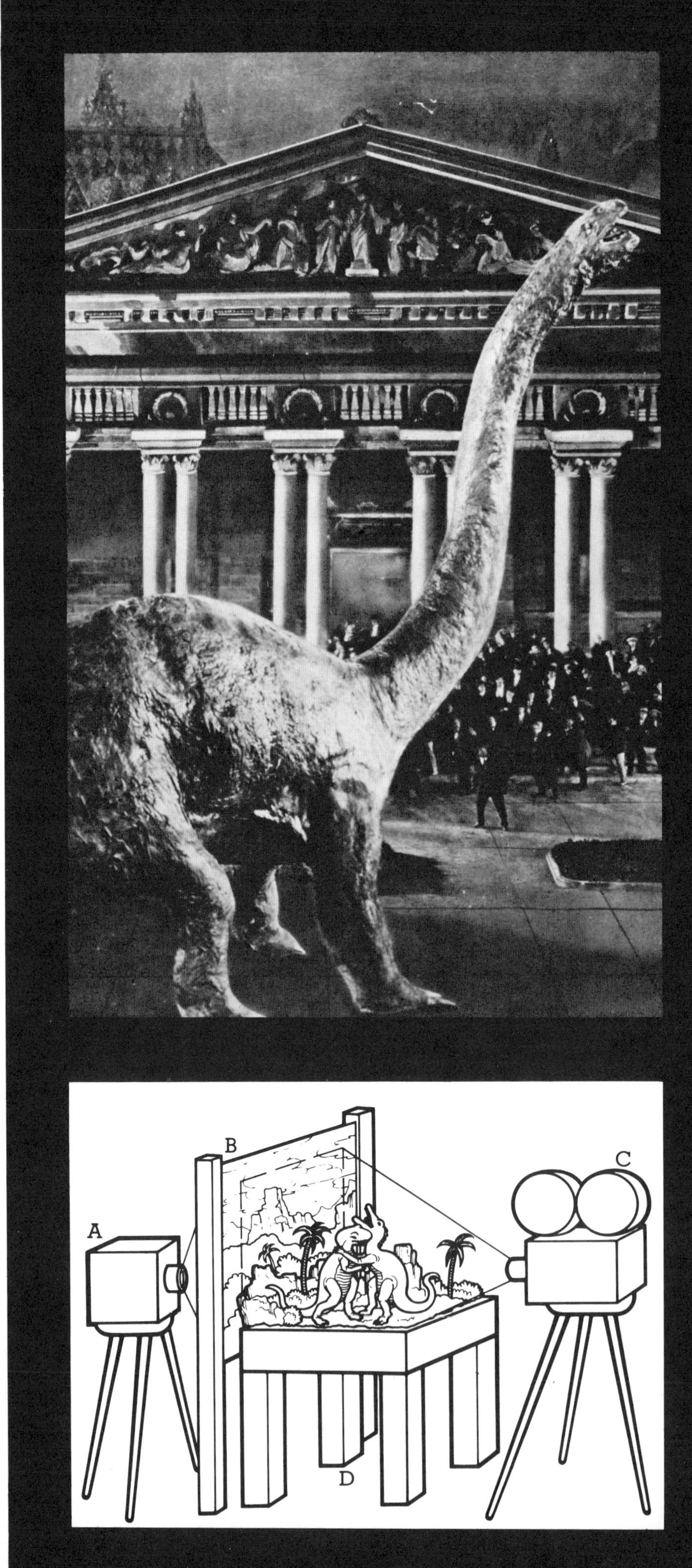

Top: An animated Brontosaurus rampages through London in the climax of Willis O'Brien's *The Lost World.* *Bottom:* STOP-ACTION ANIMATION SETUP: A typical stop-motion setup as utilized by Willis O'Brien for the silent film, *The Lost World.* Projector (A) projects a back ground image on screen (B). Camera (C) is advanced one or two frames at a time to photograph miniature dinosaurs (which are manipulated by a technician a fraction of an inch at a time) amidst small model mountains and vegetation.

trampling people, and setting off a panic. The ending of *The Lost World* is extremely unconventional for this type of movie; virtually every succeeding film about prehistoric animals on the loose in the present-day world ends with the monster's destruction by modern weaponry. *The Lost World,* however, has an uncharacteristically happy ending, at least as far as the dinosaur is concerned: after crushing an impressive number of Englishmen, the Brontosaurus wanders onto London Bridge, which collapses under its weight, and the animal plunges into the Thames and swims away.

O'Brien knew that he would need some help to do a dinosaur movie of this scope. Accordingly he started attending evening classes at the Otis Art Institute, partly to brush up on his sculpting skills and learn more about anatomy, and partly to find a person to assist him. That person turned out to be an exceptionally talented twenty-year-old named Marcel Delgado, a grocery clerk by day and art student by night. Delgado, who wasn't interested in entering the movie business, turned down O'Brien's job offer several times, but was finally persuaded.

Delgado's dinosaurs, more than forty of which were constructed for the movie, were a big improvement over O'Brien's earlier models. Instead of making the animals by placing clay over wooden frames and molding it into shape, Delgado built his monsters from the inside out. He began with intricate skeletons of tempered Dural steel, featuring articulated backbones and ball-and-socket joints for the limbs. Next came the animal's musculature. All of the sponge rubber muscles were made individually and attached to the armature with anatomical precision until Delgado had a figure that looked like a flayed dinosaur. Cotton was used to fill out the figure. The prehistoric beast was then covered with latex and rubber sheeting. Scales, spines, and plates were applied separately to give this surface a realistically reptilian texture, and electrician's wire was run just beneath the skin to simulate veins. Some of the dinosaurs even had small bladders built into them, which could be inflated and deflated by an offscreen air compressor to create the illusion that the dinosaur was breathing.

Besides being much more durable and flexible than the old-fashioned wood-and-clay kind, Delgado's dinosaurs were extremely lifelike, though no one was apt to mistake them for the real thing since they averaged only eighteen inches in length. The trick was to get them to appear appropriately gigantic. Partly this was done by placing the models in a miniature set of the fabulous jungle world, built on a very small scale to make the animals look huge.

The second trick O'Brien used to fool filmgoers into thinking that they were seeing life-size dinosaurs onscreen was to show the prehistoric monsters interacting with humans. Animated models and live actors had never appeared in the same scenes before. A typical shot in *The Lost World* might show the explorers fleeing in terror from a charging Tyrannosaurus or hiding behind a boulder while, a few yards away, a towering Brontosaurus made a meal of some trees. To work this illusion, O'Brien used a simple but effective matte technique, blocking out a portion of the animated scene, then rewinding the film and printing a shot of the actors (filmed at some distance, to make them look small) in the unexposed area.

The film's climactic sequence, in which the escaped Brontosaurus terrorizes London, was achieved by means of a slightly more complicated optical trick, an early type of traveling matte. O'Brien's first step was to create a moving silhouette of the rampaging dinosaur. He did this by animating his model against a totally white background and making up the resulting footage as a high-contrast positive. The dark-skinned dinosaur showed up on this print as an opaque black figure with clear space surrounding it. O'Brien then printed his street scene through this roll of film, producing a shot of a London thoroughfare along which moved a blank, unexposed area in the shape of a Brontosaurus. Finally the negative of the animated model, showing the figure of the Brontosaurus against a completely *black* background, was used as a counter-matte to jigsaw the dinosaur into the scene.

When *The Lost World* opened in 1925, it became an overnight sensation. O'Brien's breathing, battling, snarling monsters astounded audiences and critics alike. The movie was such a sensation that, in 1926, it became the first in-flight motion picture in history: The German Air Service Company, experimenting with the idea of on-board entertainment, screened it for a planeful of delighted passengers. Particularly impressive was the spectacular volcano sequence showing dozens of dinosaurs fleeing in panic through the jungle, an awesome feat of stop-motion photography that remains unrivaled even today.

So convincing were O'Brien's creations for *The Lost World* that, during the making of the movie, they became the center of a celebrated, if short-lived, hoax. In

1922 a test reel O'Brien had made for the film, showing a group of his prehistoric animals in action, was turned over to Sir Arthur Conan Doyle, who had been having a running battle with Harry Houdini over the issue of spiritualism. The creator of Sherlock Holmes was a devout believer in psychic phenomena, while the master magician was a dyed-in-the-wool skeptic who had toured the world giving public demonstrations in which he exposed the tricks that mediums and other pseudospiritualists use to fool their gullible customers.

When Houdini invited his esteemed adversary to a meeting of the Society of American Magicians, Doyle decided to play a little prank of his own. He brought along O'Brien's test reel, threaded it through a projector, then gave a brief, introductory speech in which he suggested that the scenes he was about to show were obtained through preternatural means. The audience, which included Adolph S. Ochs, the publisher of *The New York Times,* watched the movie in open-mouthed wonder. The next morning an article on the front page of the *Times* announced the astonishing news that Doyle had somehow managed to get his hands on moving pictures of living prehistoric beasts. DINOSAURS CAVORT IN FILM FOR DOYLE! the headline proclaimed. Having enjoyed his little joke, Doyle hurried to reveal the source of his movie. Apparently he had intended to prove to the doubting magicians that there are more things in heaven and earth than their philosophy allowed for. What he really ended up proving, however, was that of all the professional miracle workers in America, one of the very best—certainly one of the few who could mystify the great Houdini himself—was Willis O'Brien.

For a while, however, it looked as though O'Brien might never get another chance to amaze audiences with his specialized brand of magic. One scheme after another fell through: a follow-up to *The Lost World* called *Atlantis;* an adaptation of H. G. Wells's *Food of the Gods;* a version of Frankenstein with an animated monster. Finally, in 1930, RKO gave O'Brien the go-ahead on a pet project of his called *Creation,* a fantasy-adventure along the lines of *The Lost World* about a group of people marooned in a time-forgotten world inhabited by prehistoric monsters. Once again O'Brien enlisted the aid of Marcel Delgado, who immediately set about constructing a new pack of dinosaurs. As work on *Creation* proceeded, however, it became increasingly clear to the money-men at RKO that O'Brien's movie was a more expensive proposition than they had bargained for. The studio was in serious financial trouble and hard decisions had to be made. *Creation* was dropped, along with several other movies under development. Luckily the studio executive who turned thumbs down on the project was a person named Merian C. Cooper, who, as it happened, had his own idea for a fantasy film, tailor-made for a man of O'Brien's talents.

In his younger days Cooper, along with fellow filmmaker Ernest B. Schoedsack, had led a life of high adventure, traveling across the world to shoot movies in remote and exotic locales. An early investor in the civil-aviation industry, he had become an extremely successful business executive, a member of the board of directors of several major airlines, including Pan American. Sitting behind a desk in New York City, however, he continued to daydream of dangerous and unexplored lands. One dream in particular kept coming back to him: a fantasy of a mysterious, skull-shaped island in the Malay waters, where the savage tribesmen worship a living jungle god, a fifty-foot tall prehistoric gorilla. One day a daring movie producer arrives on the island to film this legendary creature, and in his company is a woman, white-skinned and blond, whose beauty touches the beast in a way he's never felt before.

When David O. Selznick took over as head of RKO, charged with the task of saving it from bankruptcy, he called on his old friend Cooper to help him reorganize the company. One of Cooper's responsibilities was to decide which properties then in production should be completed and which should be scrápped. Though Cooper put a veto on *Creation,* which he dismissed as "just a lot of animals walking around," he immediately recognized in Willis O'Brien a man with the power to make his own dream come true. It wasn't long before O'Brien and Delgado were busy on this new fantasy movie, which went through several working titles *(The Beast, The Eighth Wonder)* until Cooper opted for calling it by the name of its leading character, a movie star unlike any the world had ever seen: *King Kong.*

Thousands of pages have been written on Kong. He is a genuine folk figure, a part of our popular mythology, fully alive for millions of people in spite of the machine gun bullets and the plunge from the top of the Empire State Building. His story resonates with rich, elusive meanings. Critics see it as a fable dealing with various themes: the repression of primitive instinct by a cold, mechanical society; the devastation of the natural world by the forces of modern technology; the destructive and redemptive power of love. More simply and before anything else the movie is precisely what Cooper meant it to be: the greatest fantasy-adventure ever put on the screen, a triumph of the filmmaker's art. *The Making of King Kong* by Orville Goldner (one of the special-effects technicians who worked on the movie) and George E. Turner is the definitive book on the production of the film, a first-rate study that shows, among other things, that there is an interesting story to tell about virtually every one of the 846 scenes in the movie. *King Kong* was a special-effects tour de force, a virtuoso performance that has never been equaled. Every effects technique known in Hollywood was used to put the picture together; when a technical problem arose for which no solution existed, O'Brien simply went ahead and invented one. What makes the movie so memorable, however, is not just the effects work that went into it but the perfect matching of those effects with a marvelous, infinitely suggestive story. Unlike so many fantasy films that use their plots as a way of stringing together a series of startling effects, *King Kong* is a fully integrated work. In O'Brien's art Cooper found the perfect means of bringing his wild dream to realization.

The main technique used to bring King Kong to life, of course, was stop-motion photography. To this day rumors persist that, for some scenes in the movie—the long shot of the giant ape climbing up the side of the Empire State Building, for example—Kong was played by a man in a monkey suit. The fact is that Kong was never anything but an animated model, eighteen inches high, with a metal skeleton, sponge rubber muscles, and skin made of pruned rabbit fur (a material Marcel Delgado was never very happy with, since it tended to retain the indentations made by the animator's fingers). Actually six identical Kongs were constructed by Delgado, a timesaving ploy that permitted several different scenes to be shot simultaneously on separate tabletop sets. For some of the close-up shots a number of full-size props were also built: a giant foot for a scene later cut from the movie; a huge mechanical hand capable of clutching Fay Wray; and most impressive of all, a full-sized bust of Kong built of wood, wire, cloth, and metal and covered with forty pruned bearskins. The astonishingly expressive features of the mechanical head were controlled by levers and a compressed-air device operated by three men standing inside the bust.

O'Brien's ability to turn an eighteen-inch ape model into a living creature with a charismatic personality was crucial to the success of the film. Equally important was the brilliance he displayed in conjuring up Skull Island, Cooper's ultimate jungle dreamland. The dark, richly textured look of Kong's jungle domain owes a great deal to the drawings of Gustave Doré. One of the first things O'Brien did was to give to his assistants, Byron Crabbe and Mario Larrinaga, a series of woodcuts from the French artist's editions of the Bible, *The Divine Comedy,* and *Paradise Lost.* Using these illustrations as models, Crabbe and Larrinaga proceeded to turn out a dozen extremely dynamic preproduction drawings showing highlights of the action and establishing the movie's dramatic visual style.

The interior of Skull Island, with its lush vegetation, its huge, rotting logs dripping with moss, its chasms, caves, and murky swamps, consisted mainly of a number of tabletop sets made up of highly detailed glass paintings and miniature constructions. One of O'Brien's most important innovations involved his highly original use of glass paintings. Earlier effects men, beginning with Norman O. Dawn, would set up a single sheet of glass between the camera and the background set to add a bit of detail to the scene. O'Brien, however, might use two or even three separate paintings in a single shot, sandwiching miniature set elements—trees, roots, bushes, and the like—in between the panels of glass. A typical shot might be framed by a foreground glass painting of a dark mass of jungle foliage: dense leaves, gnarled branches, drooping tendrils. Just beyond might be a clump of ancient-looking trees—miniature constructions modeled in plastecine clay, covered with a bark made out of shellacked toilet paper, and decorated with sprigs from real shrubs. The floor of the jungle would be covered with a dense undergrowth of thick, twisting vines made of grape roots obtained from a local vineyard, exotic ferns cut from paper-thin copper sheeting, and an assortment of small living plants. Beyond this miniature section O'Brien would then place another painting, perhaps of a distant clearing. This technique produced a striking impression of depth: the illusion of a lush, mysterious rain forest receding endlessly into the unknown.

Some full-size sets of Skull Island were also required, of course. Since RKO was in such serious financial straits, ways of cutting corners had to be found. Fortunately another jungle drama, the movie version of Richard Connell's award-winning adventure yarn, *The Most Dangerous Game,* was then being filmed at RKO. A number of sets, including a dark, dismal swamp and a ravine spanned by an immense, moss-covered log, had been constructed for this film. Cooper, instantly spotting a ready-made jungle habitat for his own movie, simply borrowed jungle sets between takes on Connell's thriller. He also borrowed Fay Wray, who worked simultaneously in both pictures, appearing as a brunette in *The Most Dangerous Game* and (wigged) as "the woman of gold" in *King Kong*. The Great Wall separating the native village from the surrounding jungle was also taken from another film. This colossal construction, which, several years later, was to end its long, versatile career in a blaze of glory during the Burning of Atlanta sequence in *Gone With the Wind,* was actually a hand-me-down from Cecil B. De Mille's 1926 religious epic *King of Kings,* where it appeared as part of a sprawling set of ancient Jerusalem.

Every penny saved on set construction costs was needed for the movie's intricate special effects. One of O'Brien's biggest problems was finding convincing ways of combining the actors with his animated models. Two basic techniques were employed. The first was an improved type of rear projection utilizing a special screen invented by an RKO technician named Sidney Saunders (who was later honored by the Academy of Motion Picture Arts and Sciences for this important contribution to process photography). Unlike earlier rear-projection screens, which were made out of sand-blasted glass, a material that tended to produce a dull, gray image, the Saunders screen was fashioned out of cellulose-acetate. Stretched on a frame, it was substantially larger than the earlier kind and capable of creating a much brighter picture. O'Brien put Saunders's innovation to brilliant use. In one memorable scene Carl Denham (Robert Armstrong) and his crew dispatch a charging Stegosaurus with gas bombs, then file past the twitching carcass of the beast. To work this effect, O'Brien combined the Saunders screen with another piece of equipment: a treadmill. The actors were actually walking in place, while behind them, footage of the dying monster, with the camera panning the length of its body, was rear-projected onto the screen.

The second technique used regularly in the film was, in a sense, the reverse of the first. Instead of projecting enlarged scenes of his animated models onto a screen behind the actors, O'Brien pioneered a way of placing reduced shots of the actors within the tabletop sets. This method is known as miniature rear-projection. In one scene, for example, Driscoll (Bruce Cabot) and other members of the crew try to cross a log spanning a deep chasm. Kong suddenly appears, picks up one end of the log, and proceeds to send the sailors hurling to their deaths. (Footage of the crewmen being devoured by giant lizards, spiders, and other hellish creatures at the bottom of the gorge was shot but later cut from the film because Cooper felt that it was too gruesome and interrupted the flow of the action.) Driscoll, however, manages to escape by sliding down a vine and ducking into a small cave. Shots of Kong peering over the edge of the cliff, trying to get at Driscoll, were achieved by means of O'Brien's innovative miniature rear-projection process. The actor was first filmed in a full-size mock-up of the cave. Kong was then placed in a miniature set showing the top of the chasm with a small opening in the rock just below the edge of the cliff. A small screen made of surgical rubber sheeting was stretched across the back of the miniature cave. Finally, the prefilmed footage of Cabot was projected onto this screen and rephotographed a frame at a time while the animated model was put through its paces.

A variety of other special-effects techniques were used in creating *King Kong,* including the Dunning-Pomeroy self-matting system; another, somewhat more complicated traveling matte process invented by Frank D. Williams, which used white light to illuminate the foreground action instead of the orange light required by the Dunning-Pomeroy method; and optical printing, which was handled by Linwood Dunn.

Given the difficulty of the work involved in making *King Kong,* it's no surprise that some unusual problems arose in the course of its production. In one animated sequence a primrose plant, posing as part of the exotic jungle flora, was used in a miniature set. When the rushes of the sequence were screened the next morning, the filmmakers were aghast to see the seemingly gigantic flower abruptly burst into bloom. Unnoticed by anybody, the primrose had slowly blossomed in the course of the previous day's shooting. The resulting footage looked like one of those scientific time-lapse movies that compress the lifespan of a flower into the space of a few seconds. The whole scene, which had taken a full day of painstaking work to animate, had to be scrapped.

On a different occasion quick thinking by a clever (if somewhat careless) techni-

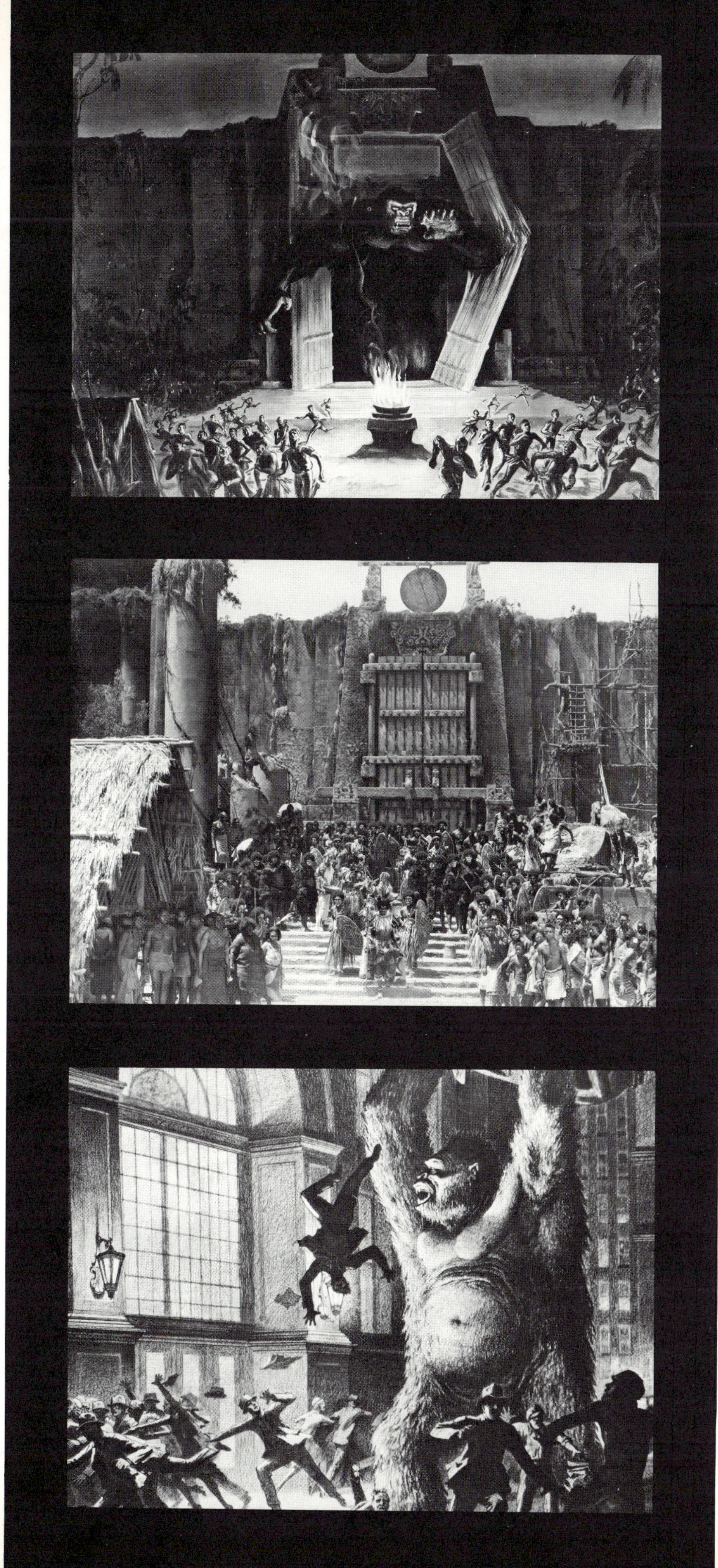

Top: Preproduction artwork from the original *King Kong,* showing the giant ape breaking through the gates of the Great Wall. *Center:* The Great Wall of Skull Island. This structure was originally built for Cecil B. De Mille's 1926 film *King of Kings* and was later used in *Gone With the Wind.* *Bottom:* One of the dramatic preproduction drawings Merian C. Cooper used to convince studio executives to go ahead with his dream project.

Top: The full-size bust of Kong under construction (from a badly damaged snapshot).
Center: A preproduction sketch of the scene (later cut from the movie) in which giant spiders devour the crewmen hurled into the chasm by Kong:
Bottom: A rare shot of the spider model built for the censored scene.

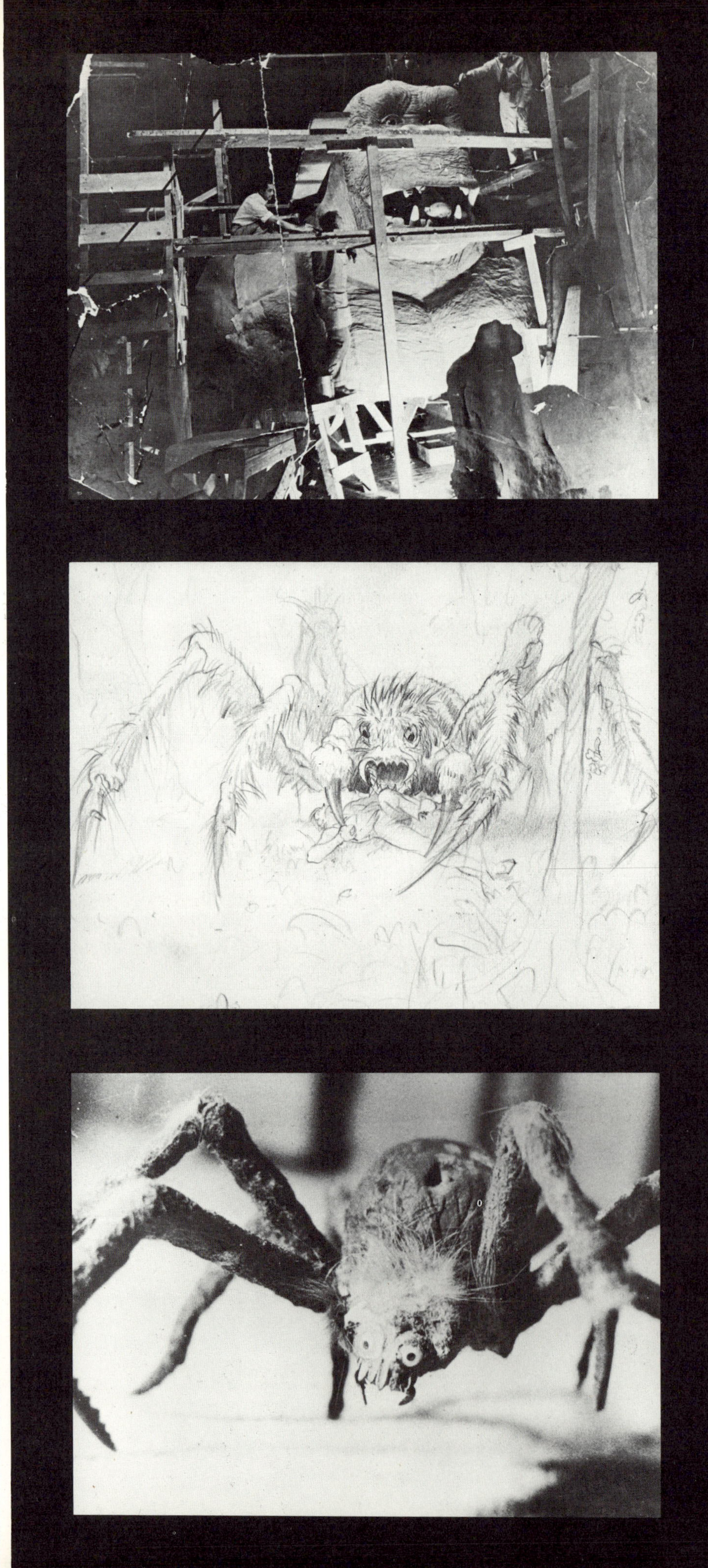

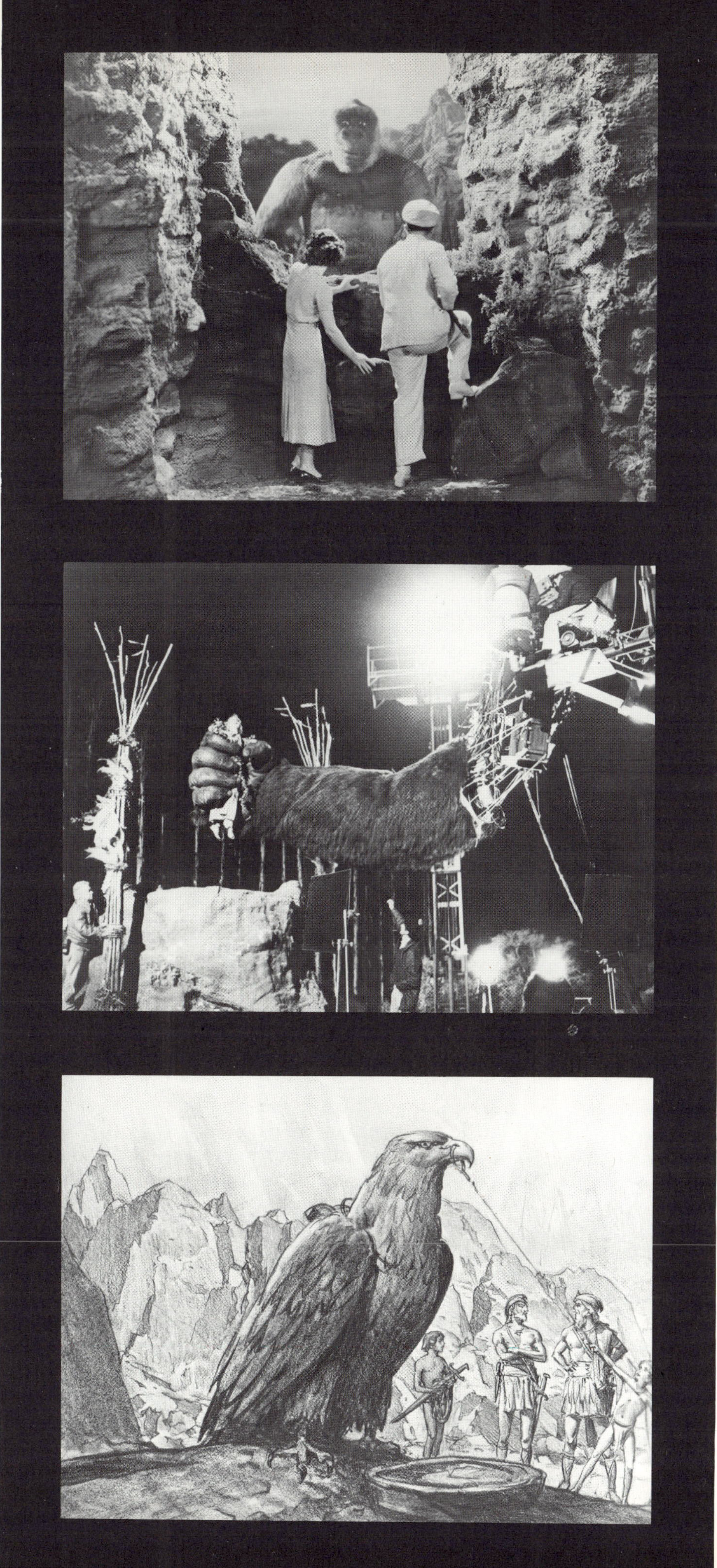

Top: Carl Denham (Robert Armstrong) and Hilda Peterson (Helen Mack) confront a rear-projected image of Kong's blond, twelve-foot baby in *Son of Kong.* *Center:* A giant mechanical arm constructed for Dino De Laurentiis's remake of *King Kong.* *Bottom:* A pre-production drawing from O'Brien's aborted fantasy epic, *War Eagles.*

cian made it possible to avoid another such costly accident. The technician had worked for hours animating a dinosaur for a particular sequence, when suddenly, like the surgeon who finishes an operation only to discover that he's left his scalpel sewn up inside the patient, he realized that one of the handles of a pair of pliers he'd been using was visible to the camera. Instead of tossing out everything he'd done and starting over, he came up with an extremely ingenious solution. He continued animating the dinosaur. At the same time he simply animated the pliers right out of the picture, removing them from the scene a frame at a time. Onscreen the living tool looks like a great gray serpent slithering into the undergrowth. However, since the pliers are off to one side, far from the center of the action, few people even notice them.

Few people notice the discrepancy in the size of Kong either. Though he is generally referred to as a fifty-foot ape, he was actually portrayed as only eighteen feet high in the jungle scenes. Cooper wanted a creature that audiences could respond to, even feel sorry for, and it's difficult to sympathize with a monster as big as an office building. For those scenes in which he actually appears alongside office buildings, Kong is shown to be somewhat larger (twenty-four feet, to be precise), since Cooper was afraid that a shorter creature wouldn't seem imposing enough among the towering skyscrapers of New York.

Kong's battle with the Navy biplanes, which finally succeed in shooting him down from the top of the Empire State Building, is probably the most famous sequence in the picture. It is certainly the most moving. For a contribution of one hundred dollars to the officers' mess fund and an under-the-table donation of ten dollars apiece for the pilots, the filmmakers got four Navy aircraft to perform for their cameras. Shots of these planes flying in formation, looping, diving, and coming in for the kill were intercut with scenes in which matching model airplanes on piano wires attack an eighteen-inch animated ape perched on a miniature of the Empire State Building mooring mast. The aerial views of New York City that form a backdrop to the action are actually highly realistic glass paintings executed by Mario Larrinaga, his brother Juan, and Byron Crabbe. For heightened drama O'Brien engineered an effect that allowed him to show strafing runs on the giant gorilla from the point of view of the pilots. He created this illusion by constructing a twenty-four-foot wooden ramp down which the camera was moved toward the animated model of Kong. The viewer is made to feel as though he's sitting in the cockpit of a plane diving straight at the maddened monster.

Close-ups of the Navy pilots and their gunners were shot inside the studio, using mock-up sections of the planes in front of rear-projected backgrounds. Interestingly the men who produced and directed the film, Cooper and Schoedsack, appear in these scenes as the flight commander and his chief observer. Cooper decided that they ought to play these parts because, as he told Schoedsack, "we should kill the sonofabitch ourselves." Clearly the man who had first imagined Kong was grabbing at a once-in-a-lifetime opportunity. Here was a chance for him to step inside his fantasy, to live out his wildest dream. O'Brien's magic had made that dream a reality—not only for Cooper himself, but for the millions of people who were to see it on-screen.

The success of *King Kong,* which singlehandedly pulled RKO out of the red, led to the production of an instant sequel, *Son of Kong* (1933). (It also led, forty-five years later, to Dino De Laurentiis's dreadful remake, about which the less said the better. This time, the title character was in fact played by a man in a gorilla suit. Though De Laurentiis spent approximately one and a half million dollars to build a forty-foot robot of Kong, and several million more on publicity hype to convince filmgoers that his monster was a technological marvel, the truth is that the mechanical ape had very little mobility and appeared onscreen for only a few seconds in a single sequence.) Though *Son of Kong* contains some impressive effects—excellent animation, beautiful glass art, elaborate miniature sets—it doesn't compare to its predecessor. The majesty and mythic power of the original are completely missing from the sequel. The main problem is the title character himself. Whereas Kong was a living legend, a towering figure who comes as close to being a tragic hero as it's possible for a gorilla to be, his son is portrayed as nothing more than an overgrown baby chimp, a blond, twelve-foot-tall monkey with a wide range of adorable mannerisms.

As it turned out, O'Brien would never again match the achievements of *King Kong*. His subsequent career was marked by a series of setbacks and disapointments: cherished projects (like his earlier *Creation*) that were planned—at times even begun—but for one reason or another were abruptly abandoned. The most spectacular of these aborted movies was *War Eagles* (begun in 1938), a fantasy epic about a group of modern-day explorers who discover a community of Vikings living in a tropical lost world somewhere near the North Pole. These hardy warriors fly about on the backs of giant snow-eagles and do battle with prehistoric monsters that eventually lay siege to New York City. MGM's decision to drop *War Eagles* was followed by another major disappointment for O'Brien when a pet project of his called *Gwangi,* a film about a group of cowboys from a Wild West show who capture a living Tyrannosaurus on a remote Texas mesa, was scuttled by RKO after nearly a year of preproduction work. Another fantasy film with a Western flavor, *El Toro Estrella* (later retitled *The Valley of the Mist*), which was to feature a showdown between an animated Tyrannosaurus and a live bull, was also dropped after extensive preparation.

With one exception all the movies O'Brien was involved with during the forties, fifties, and up until his death in 1962 (just as he was about to begin work on the animation sequence for Stanley Kramer's mammoth comedy *It's a Mad, Mad, Mad, Mad World*) were disappointments: low-budget monster movies like *The Black Scorpion* (1957) and *The Giant Behemoth* (1959), or cut-rate versions of the glorious fantasies he had once dreamed of creating. *The Beast of Hollow Mountain* (1956) used some of O'Brien's story ideas that were to have gone into *Gwangi* but none of his animation, while *The Animal World* (1956) contained only twelve minutes of the magnificent dinosaur sequences originally planned for *Creation.* The single exception was the 1949 movie *Mighty Joe Young,* which was, next to *The Lost World* and *King Kong,* O'Brien's finest piece of work and the only one to earn him an Oscar.

Mighty Joe Young is a rehash of the successful *Kong* formula. A brash, fast-talking American impresario named O'Hara (Robert Armstrong once again) comes to Africa to capture wild animals for his posh New York City nightclub, The Golden Safari. Instead of bringing hunters to bag the game, however, he is accompanied by a bunch of cowboys—a wildly unlikely situation clearly contrived so that O'Brien could indulge in his favorite fantasy (possibly deriving from his own cow-punching days) of pitting Westerners on horseback against his animated beasts. O'Hara and his cowhands come upon a king-size gorilla who seems to be a monster but turns out to be the pet of a sweet young girl named Jill (Terry Moore). Though Joe is ferocious enough to wipe out a pack of lions, he turns into a Teddy bear when Jill is around. All she has to do is sing "Beautiful Dreamer" to him and he grows weak in the knees. O'Hara convinces Jill to take Joe to New York, where he is forced to appear in a series of humiliating nightclub routines. Eventually, after being fed a few bottles of liquor by some obnoxious drunks, Joe goes berserk and demolishes the club. He becomes a fugitive from justice, but redeems himself by risking his life to rescue a baby from a burning orphanage.

When the movie first came out, ads proclaimed that its hero was "Mightier than King Kong!" However, the fact is that while *Mighty Joe Young* is a perfectly enjoyable movie, it is in every respect a much smaller, more trivial version of the original masterpiece. *Mighty Joe Young* is never anything more than an entertaining, highly polished kiddie show. Instead of an awesome ape with a woman clutched in his paw, we get a pretty girl with a giant gorilla wrapped around her little finger. It takes four Navy biplanes armed with machine guns to bring down the mighty Kong, whereas Joe can be subdued by a few bars of "Beautiful Dreamer."

Mighty Joe Young, however, is distinguished by extremely skillful effects. Six elaborate models of the gorilla were constructed, four of them eighteen inches high and two shorter ones for long shots. A technician named Harry Cunningham created the intricate metal armatures, which were so anatomically precise that they duplicated every joint found in the skeleton of a real gorilla. The hands alone each had sixty moving pieces. The muscles, made of foam rubber, dental dam, and cotton, were added by Marcel Delgado; the skin was fashioned out of the hides of unborn baby lambs, using a process devised by a taxidermist named George Lofgren. The trick photography for the movie took more than a year to complete. One fifteen-second sequence in which Joe, after being locked up in his cage, moves about very slowly and dispiritedly, took three full days to film. Interestingly O'Brien was so busy planning and supervising the complicated setups that he himself animated only four or five scenes. What is most significant about the animation in *Mighty Joe Young* is that the bulk of it, as much as eighty percent, was the work of Ray Harryhausen, a young man who would soon inherit O'Brien's position as the world's foremost stop-motion artist.

Harryhausen is one of the few real superstars in the field of special effects. Most movies are considered the work of their directors: we speak of the films of John Ford, Howard Hawks, Ingmar Bergman, Robert Altman. The movies Harryhausen has been involved in, however, always belong exclusively to him. It doesn't matter who directed them: they are Harryhausen films. He is also one of the few genuine special-effects artists. The majority of effects experts are skilled professionals who can turn out a highly specialized product on demand: a massive explosion, a miniature city, a model spaceship. In Harryhausen's hands, however, special effects become a form of personal expression. He is a filmmaker with an authentic (if limited) vision, which he embodies through the medium of stop-motion animation.

As is true of most contemporary animators, Harryhausen's career choice was settled when he saw *King Kong* for the first time, at the age of thirteen. By the time he was seventeen, he was experimenting with stop-motion home movies, using a friend's sixteen-millimeter camera and a model of a prehistoric bear made from a fully jointed wooden skeleton and a piece of his mother's fur coat. Other sixteen-millimeter movies followed, including several science fiction reels and an ambitious prehistoric epic called *Evolution,* about life in the Mesozoic Age.

After a three-year stint in the Army Signal Corps, Harryhausen returned to Los Angeles and began work on a series of charming ten-minute fairy tales done entirely with animated puppets. (Still in distribution, these films have been a favorite of schoolchildren for the past thirty-five years.) Soon after this, Harryhausen showed samples of his work to the master, Willis O'Brien, who took the young man on as his assistant on *Mighty Joe Young.* Harryhausen spent the next two years working on the picture and ended up doing most of the animation.

The first feature-length film containing effects created by Harryhausen alone was *The Beast from 20,000 Fathoms* (1953). The inspiration for this movie was a *Saturday Evening Post* story by Harryhausen's old friend Ray Bradbury, about a lonely prehistoric sea monster that responds to the mating call of a lighthouse foghorn. In the film version the monster is a dinosaur (a fictitious creature called a Rhedosaur) awakened from several million years of suspended animation in the arctic ice by an atom bomb test. This ferocious beast makes its way down the east coast of North America, causing the usual kinds of havoc, until it arrives in Manhattan, where it crushes cars, knocks down buildings, tramples pedestrians, and chews up a cop. In the film's climactic scene the monster is cornered at the Coney Island amusement park. Shot with a radioactive isotope, it crashes through the roller coaster and dies pathetically on the beach.

Given the film's shoestring budget of $200,000 (cheap even for a 1950s exploitation movie), it contains surprisingly impressive effects. These are due in large part to Harryhausen's invention of an ingenious, economical means of combining his model with live-action footage, a process that was to play a central part in all his subsequent films. Essentially this process utilizes a series of mattes to split a rear-projected image into two components, a background and foreground, allowing the animated model to be sandwiched in between. In this way Harryhausen was able to have his Rhedosaur step out from *behind* rear-projected buildings while panicked pedestrians scatter all around.

Harryhausen's basic method of placing a model into the middle of the action is this: let us say that he wants to show a dramatic scene, set in midtown Manhattan, of a group of people fleeing in terror while a maddened dinosaur follows close behind. The dinosaur model is set up and animated on a table. In back is a miniature screen extending down below the level of the table edge. Footage of the people running down Broadway toward the camera is rear-projected onto the screen. The bottom of the camera lens is masked off, blocking the table top and the lower portion of the screen. The rest of the image is recorded: a charging dinosaur with a section of Broadway behind it. The film is then rewound. On the second pass through the camera a counter-matte is used to block the upper portion of the scene, the tabletop and model are removed, and the foreground image of the panic-stricken New Yorkers, fleeing for their lives, is added to the footage. (Alternatively the foreground image may be superimposed in an optical printer.) In this way the model is sandwiched between a background and foreground that together form a single rear-projected image. The resulting composite creates the illusion that the monster is right inside the scene.

Released in "glorious sepia tone," *The Beast from 20,000 Fathoms* turned out to be the surprise money-maker of the year. Soon after, Harryhausen was approached by producer Charles Schneer, who wanted Harryhausen to do another monster movie, this one about an octopus big enough to demolish the Golden Gate Bridge. Thanks to Harryhausen's magic Schneer got his overgrown mollusk, though in somewhat truncated form. Working with another tight budget, Harryhausen decided that the best way to save money on the

Ray Harryhausen face to face with his stop-motion model of the skeleton warrior from *The Seventh Voyage of Sinbad.*

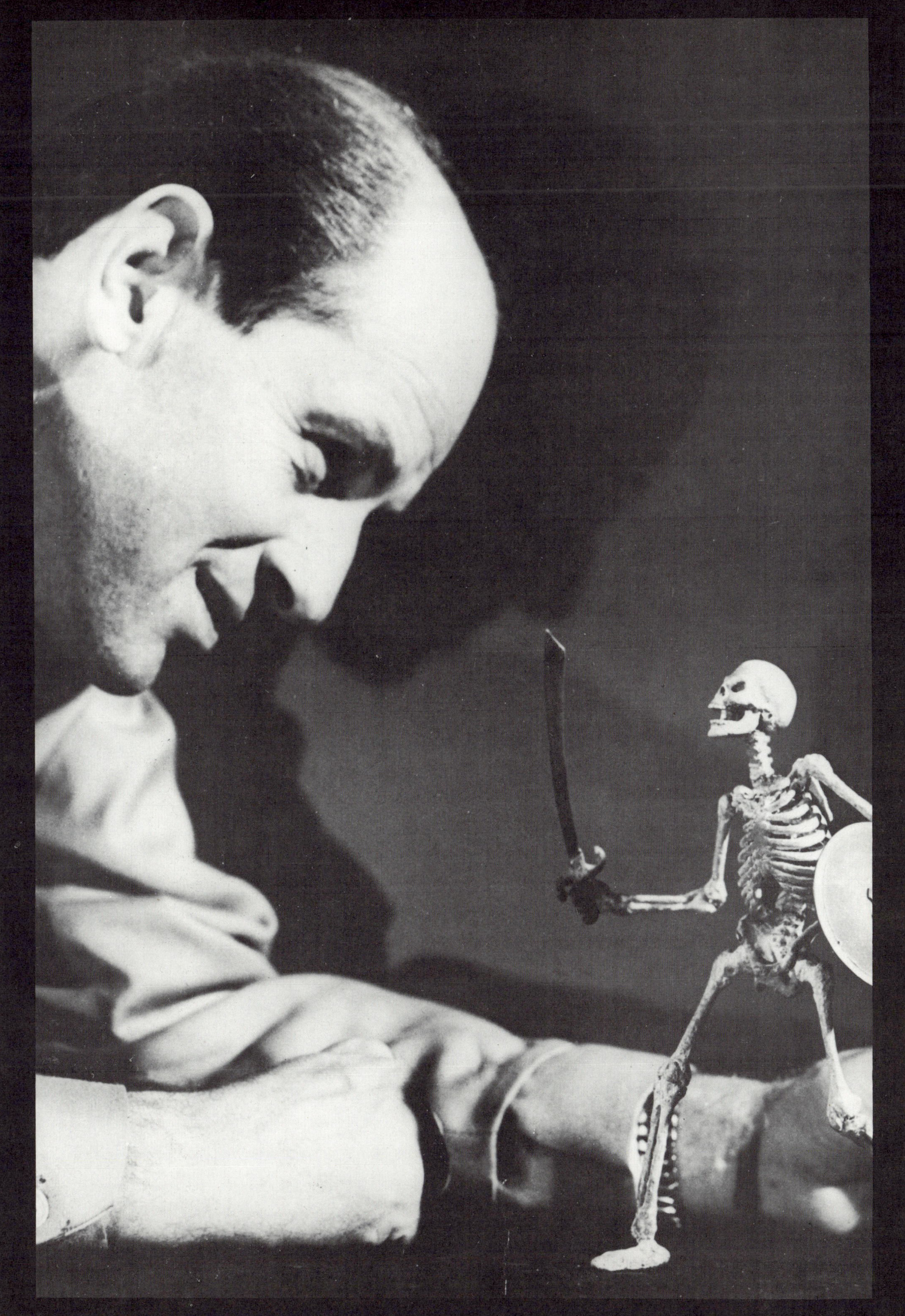

How Harryhausen works his movie magic. *Top:* First, the actor (John Phillip Law as Sinbad) is filmed as he acts out a fight with an imaginary monster. *Center:* Next, the tabletop model (a club-wielding centaur standing less than a foot high) is animated through stop-motion photography. *Bottom:* Finally, the two elements are combined through Harryhausen's rear-projection compositing technique.

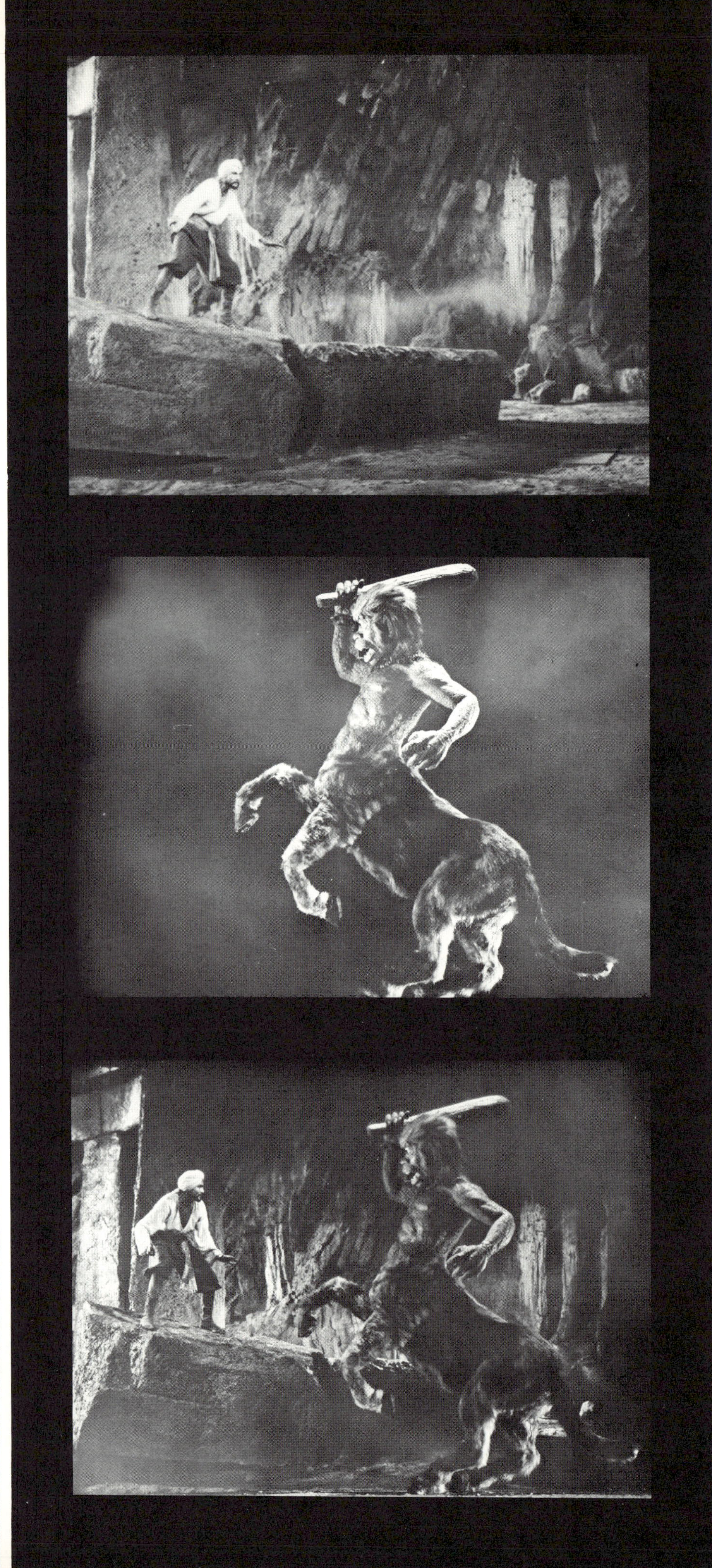

production was to reduce the number of the creature's tentacles to five. With three appendages fewer to animate, the movie could be completed that much more quickly. As a result the creature that attacks San Francisco in *It Came from Beneath the Sea* (1955) is not really an octopus at all, but the world's largest quintopus.

Like all top-flight effects men Harryhausen is a whiz at devising economical ways to work his illusions. On his third movie, *Earth Versus the Flying Saucers* (1956), limited funds compelled him once again to produce striking effects at the lowest possible cost. In the film's climactic sequence extraterrestrial spaceships attack Washington, D.C., demolishing the Capitol Building, the Lincoln Monument, Washington Monument, and other national landmarks with death rays. Harryhausen constructed miniature models of each of these buildings. The simplest way of destroying these models would have been to blow each of them up with a small charge of explosives and shoot the scene at a high speed, a technique that would have slowed down the action onscreen and made the falling chunks of miniature debris look realistically bulky. Unfortunately high-speed photography is a very costly process. As a result Harryhausen was forced to fall back on a far less efficient though ultimately cheaper technique. He actually animated the collapse of each building by means of stop-motion photography. Every single brick was suspended by a wire and its position changed a frame at a time.

Harryhausen managed this feat (one which he later admitted he would never do again) with the aid of a device called an *aerial brace.* Animation models that walk on the ground, such as two-legged dinosaurs, are equipped with threaded plates or capped nuts (called "tie-downs") that are built into the bottom of their feet. Holes are drilled into the tabletop set. To keep the creature standing upright during animation, bolts are passed up through these holes from underneath the table and screwed into the tie-downs. When a model has to leap completely off the ground or fly through the air, however, it must be supported from above. For this purpose an aerial brace is used, a rather complicated affair generally secured to the ceiling. The model, hanging from the brace by nylon thread or monofilament fishing line, can be moved up, down, forward, back, sideways, and around in the precise, incremental manner stop-motion photography demands. The aerial brace is one of Harryhausen's most important tools, since it is an inexpensive way of getting models off the ground and his movies are indeed full of flying creatures and extremely agile two-legged monsters.

Harryhausen has actually worked in a number of different modes. His first two films were of the "giant-monster-unleashed-by-nuclear-radiation" variety so popular during the 1950s. *Earth Versus the Flying Saucers* was a straightforward science fiction film, as was his fourth movie, *Twenty Million Miles to Earth* (1957), about a space-beast called an Ymir brought back to Earth by the first manned expedition to Venus. This humanoid reptile is the first of Harryhausen's truly memorable creations: though exceptionally nasty, it possesses enough personality to make audiences feel sorry for it when it meets its inevitable death in the film's climactic sequence. Other science fiction films followed: *Mysterious Island* (1961), a sequel to Jules Verne's *20,000 Leagues Under the Sea* that features a host of king-size creatures, and H. G. Wells's *First Men in the Moon* (1964), probably Harryhausen's most disappointing movie since it contains surprisingly little animation.

Another Harryhausen film with a limited amount of stop-motion photography was *The Three Worlds of Gulliver* (1960), an entertaining if juvenile adaptation of *Gulliver's Travels* that turns Swift's satirical masterpiece into the cinematic equivalent of a Classics Comic. Somewhat confusingly the movie takes the title character to only two of the fabulous worlds found in Swift's original, the miniature land of Lilliput and its polar opposite, the country of Brobdignag, which is inhabited by a race of giants. Because the movie required a large number of tricky composite shots, Harryhausen and his company decided to shoot it in England, where they could use the sodium vapor process developed by the Rank Organization and which made instantaneous mattes through the use of a *beam-splitting camera,* in contrast to the earlier blue-backing process, which required eight to ten separate steps to produce a good composite image.

As the heir to Willis O'Brien Harryhausen has also done his share of old-fashioned dinosaur movies. In collaboration with O'Brien himself he did the animated dinosaur sequence for Irwin Allen's *The Animal World* (1956), a semi-documentary movie about evolution. Thirteen years later Harryhausen resurrected his mentor's old cowboys versus dinosaurs idea. The result was *The Valley of Gwangi* (1969), set in turn-of-the-century Mexico, about a group of cowboys who come upon a "Forbidden Valley" inhabited by prehistoric beasts. The movie does contain several interesting stop-motion sequences. The highlight of the film is the scene in which Gwangi, a fierce-looking Allosaurus, is roped by four cowboys on horseback. The actors were really lassoing a fifteen-foot pole (called a "monster stick") attached to a Jeep. Later the dinosaur was inserted into this footage by means of Harryhausen's unique rear-projection compositing technique. This complicated sequence took over five months to animate.

Harryhausen's most elaborate dinosaur movie to date, however, is *One Million Years* B.C. (1968), a remake of the 1940 prehistoric melodrama *One Million* B.C. (which starred Victor Mature and Carole Landis and, for dinosaurs, relied exclusively on real lizards filmed in extreme close-up). Interestingly Harryhausen's remake also contains two optically enlarged living creatures—an iguana and a tarantula. Harryhausen later explained the reason for this unusual departure: "We felt that if we used a live animal on the first appearance it would lull the audience into the believability of the animated animals at a later time." All he really managed to do, however, was provide a graphic demonstration of the paradoxical truth that, in fantasy movies, living lizards look phonier than sponge-rubber dolls. The film's best scenes contain a wide assortment of beautifully animated Harryhausen monsters.

But of all the different types of movies Harryhausen has done, his most successful—and the ones most prized by his fans—have been his cinematic excursions into magic and myth. The first of these (and for some viewers the best) was his 1958 Arabian Nights fantasy *The Seventh Voyage of Sinbad.* The mystical East has always served as a favorite setting for fantasy films. Until Harryhausen entered the field, Alexander Korda's lavish 1940 remake of *The Thief of Bagdad,* was perhaps the best of its kind. Though his work on this film earned effects man Lawrence Butler an Oscar, its optical tricks are really quite uneven. Some, like the miniature model of the Temple of Dawn, are good; others, like the giant props of the genie's hand and foot, are passable. Still others, like the flying horse (an early example of a traveling matte done for a color movie) seem transparently phony. The movie, however, still succeeds by virtue of its visual opulence, its excellent performances, and its marvelous, adventure-filled plot.

By contrast, the performances in Harryhausen's film are for the most part merely functional, and the storyline is characteristically thin. Nevertheless the movie has tremendous power, thanks entirely to the brilliance of Harryhausen's creations. *Sinbad* was the first of Harryhausen's Technicolor films. It was also the one for which he coined the term "Dynamation" to distinguish his method from that of cartoon animation. (Later he would relabel his technique "Dynarama.") There are six different animated models in the film and each is a dream-creature made completely alive and believable by the magic of Harryhausen's art.

The first monster Sinbad meets in the film is one of Harryhausen's greatest creations: a particularly horrific horned cyclops with a devil's pointed ears, ghastly three-clawed hands, and the goat's legs and cloven hooves of the mythological satyr. Working with a restricted budget, Harryhausen found a way of saving money on the construction of this living nightmare: he stripped down the model of his Venusian space-beast, the Ymir, and reused its expensive metal skeleton for the cyclops. (A good hand-machined armature with ball-and-socket joints can cost as much as $600 an inch.) Like all of Harryhausen's really good stop-motion models, this one-eyed monster is distinguished not only by its extremely fluid, lifelike movements but also by its strong if intensely unpleasant personality. Its gargoyle face is highly expressive, which is no small achievement considering that the monster's range of emotions run from sheer malevolence to demonic rage.

In addition Harryhausen is able to make the cyclops interact with the human characters in a way that strikes many viewers as close to uncanny. At one point in the film, for example, Sinbad and his crew are inside the cyclops's cavelike "treasure trove." The cyclops comes by, removes the stone roof, reaches down and plucks out all the sailors, including Sinbad, whom he grabs by the foot and lifts high into the air. This extremely effective scene was done with miniature rear-screen projection. The actor who played Sinbad (Kerwin Matthews) was attached to invisible wires, turned upside down, and raised into the air. This footage was then rear-projected onto a miniature screen set up behind the animated model. A tiny boot, matching the one worn by Matthews, was placed in the model's hand and precisely aligned with the photographed boot on the background image. As far as the camera could see, the actor's leg went straight into the boot held by the cyclops. The animation of the model was then coordinated with the movement of the actor on the miniature screen: as Matthews moved up, frame by frame, in minute increments, Harryhausen made the corresponding adjustments in the position of the cyclops's arm.

The most riveting stop-motion scene in the movie takes place near the end, when Sinbad is forced to do battle with a sword-wielding skeleton brought to life by the evil sorcerer Sokurah. This celebrated episode, which is widely regarded as one of the masterpieces of stop-motion photography, was extremely tricky to stage. The fight was as carefully choreographed as a ballet. Kerwin Matthews rehearsed the duel with an Italian Olympic fencing master named Enzo Musumeci-Greco. Once the actor had gotten all the moves down pat, the swordsman stepped out of the way and Matthews repeated the routine for the camera, pretending that he was battling a ferocious opponent, though in fact he was slashing away at nothing. Considering that he was fighting thin air, Matthews did a commendable job of acting. His biggest difficulty was in faking blocks—stopping his sword in mid-swing as though it had just clashed against his enemy's weapon. Months later the dueling skeleton (actually an eight-inch painted rubber model with a wire armature) was animated into the scene.

The success of the skeleton sequence in *The Seventh Voyage of Sinbad* led Harryhausen to try an even more amazing version in his later film *Jason and the Argonauts* (1963), which many people, including Harryhausen himself, regard as his best piece of work to date. At the end of the film the Greek hero and two of his companions cross swords with seven homicidal skeletons that erupt from their graves when the mad king Aeetes sprinkles the teeth of a slain hydra on the ground. Originally Harryhausen had planned to conform more closely to the actual Greek myth, according to which the planting of a hydra's teeth causes the bodies of dead warriors to spring from the earth. Harryhausen wasn't very happy about the idea of animating rotting corpses, however, so he returned to the clean-picked look of the Sinbad skeleton (which actually appears in the scene as one of the seven macabre swordsmen).

Harryhausen later described this sequence as the most complicated he's ever done. As in the *Sinbad* fight the live action was filmed first, only this time there were three different performers. Later the miniature skeletons were added to the scene, an enormously complex job of animation involving seven models, each with five appendages (four limbs and a skull) that had to be animated a frame at a time in perfect synchronization with the rear-projected image of the actors. Though the scene lasts less than five minutes, it took almost five months to complete; at times, Harryhausen managed to shoot only thirteen frames of film in a whole day of work.

Next to the skeletons the film's best stop-motion creation is Talos, an awesome bronze statue that comes to life and pursues the Argonauts in a slow-moving, inexorable way. Some of Harryhausen's creatures are effective because they possess so much personality. Others, like Talos, create a powerful impression for the very opposite reason: they seem utterly soulless; they are pure, walking evil, living machines of destruction. Somehow Talos's immobile features are even more unsettling than the sadistic leers of the skeleton army. In creating Talos, who walks with a creaking, mechanical gait, Harryhausen ironically had to give his creature the kind of stiff, unnatural movements that animators are always at pains to avoid.

Creatures such as Talos appear in several of Harryhausen's later fantasy films. The success of *The Seventh Voyage of Sinbad* ultimately led the animator to do two more movies in the same vein: *The Golden Voyage of Sinbad* (1974) and *Sinbad and the Eye of the Tiger* (1977). As always the acting and storylines in these productions leave a great deal to be desired. Any deficiencies in the plot and performances, however, are more than made up for by Harryhausen's usual assortment of fabulous beings. Though both these movies did well at the box office, they received mixed notices from the Harryhausen aficionados, who pay extremely close attention to every nuance of his work.

Harryhausen's fans have put their hero in a difficult position. Like the makers of the James Bond movies, he is constantly required to go himself one better, to come up with increasingly spectacular effects for each new production. Lately his devotees have been somewhat disappointed. This is partly because Harryhausen seems content to repeat the successful formulas of his earlier movies rather than attempt anything really new and exciting. Because stop-motion fantasy films are so few and far between, an intolerable burden is placed on every new Harryhausen film: so much is expected of it, that it is almost bound to be something of a letdown.

The fact is, as Willis O'Brien's frustration-filled career shows, three-dimensional animation is an art form with few outlets for its practitioners. There are a number of extremely talented younger stop-motion artists around, but not many movies that require their services. Perhaps the most prominent of Harryhausen's potential successors is Jim Danforth, who has been called stop-motion's heir apparent. In some respects Danforth's career has been marked by the same sorts of disappointments that plagued O'Brien's. One of the first involved O'Brien himself: in 1963 Danforth took a job with Film Effects of Hollywood, hoping to work with O'Brien, who had been hired to direct the animation sequence for *It's a Mad, Mad, Mad, Mad World*; unfortunately, the master animator died just before work on the production was to get underway.

Danforth is so skilled an animator that he can make even badly built monsters look good. In *Jack the Giant Killer* (1961) the stop-motion work is far superior to the models themselves, which are embarrassingly amateurish in spite of their having been designed and constructed by two of the best model-makers in the business, Wah Chang and Marcel Delgado. In general, Danforth's effects, like Harryhausen's, are the best part of the films they appear in. He won an Academy Award nomination for his work in *When Dinosaurs Ruled the Earth* (1971), though the film itself was not very good.

As an artist, Danforth has been frustrated not only by the poor quality of many of the films he's worked on, but even more so by the failure of a whole series of pet projects to materialize.

During the past few years Danforth has supported himself largely by falling back on his considerable skills as a matte painter. Other stop-motion artists make a living doing TV commercials that feature animated models like the Pillsbury Doughboy, Swiss Miss, and the horse-drawn Conestoga that thunders across the kitchen floor in the Chuckwagon dog food ads. David Allen, another fine young animator whose own stop-motion dream-project, *The Primevals,* lost its backer a few years ago (though the movie is still in the works, with Allen now in complete control), is probably best known for his marvelous re-creation of the climax of *King Kong,* which he did for a famous Volkswagen commercial. Another stop-motion fantasy film, *Planet of Dinosaurs,* which has excellent special effects by Jim Aupperle, Steve Czerkas, and animator Doug Beswick, has actually been completed but has yet to find a distributor. Two of its creators, Aupperle and Czerkas, exercise their talents doing stop-motion work for the Saturday morning kiddie show, *Jason of Star Command.* Another children's television show, no longer in production, that relied heavily on stop-motion monsters was the prehistoric adventure series *Land of the Lost,* the effects for which were created by Gene Warren's company, Excelsior! Animated Moving Pictures.

Producer/director George Pal, who came to America in 1939 following an extremely successful career making animated advertising films in Europe, was a pioneer in the method of replacement animation, which formed the basis of his delightful Puppetoons, a series of stop-motion puppet shorts produced for Paramount between 1941 and 1947. Unlike O'Brien's brand of animation, in which a single, flexible model with ball-and-socket joints and malleable facial features is manipulated frame by frame, Pal's method employed an entire series of carved wooden figures for each character. To make a toy soldier march, for example, Pal's craftsmen would fashion a series of identical bodies, each with its legs in a slightly different position. The bodies would be changed from frame to frame until the character had gone through a complete cycle of marching steps. Similarly, making the faces of these wooden figures move required a whole set of individually carved heads, each showing a slight shift in expression. A different head would be placed on the body for every exposure. A minimum of twenty-four changes of expression were required for a single second of action. (This method is still used in the animation of such figures as Poppin' Fresh, the Pillsbury Doughboy, and Speedy in the Alka-Seltzer commercials.) The Puppetoons have a quality of Old World craftsmanship about them that is dramatically different from the slam-bang style of home-grown American cartoons like the Road Runner series. Ultimately, however, the series became too expensive for Paramount's taste (not surprisingly, since every one of the eight-minute films required approximately 9,000 hand-carved wooden figures). Pal went on to produce feature-length movies, including several that are now regarded as classics of science fiction and fantasy.

George Pal's *tom thumb* (1958) was one of Pal's most commercially successful productions. The movie, for which Tom Howard won an Oscar for special effects, used a variety of tricks to make its hero (Russ Tamblyn) look five and a half inches tall. These included a large number of giant-size props (among them a cobbler's bench built thirty-five feet high and ninety feet long, and a fifty-five foot baby's cradle) and an ingenious split-screen technique, labeled "Automotion," to combine the reduced image of Tamblyn with his full-size costars. The most delightful scenes in the movie, however, are those in which tom sings, dances, and converses with

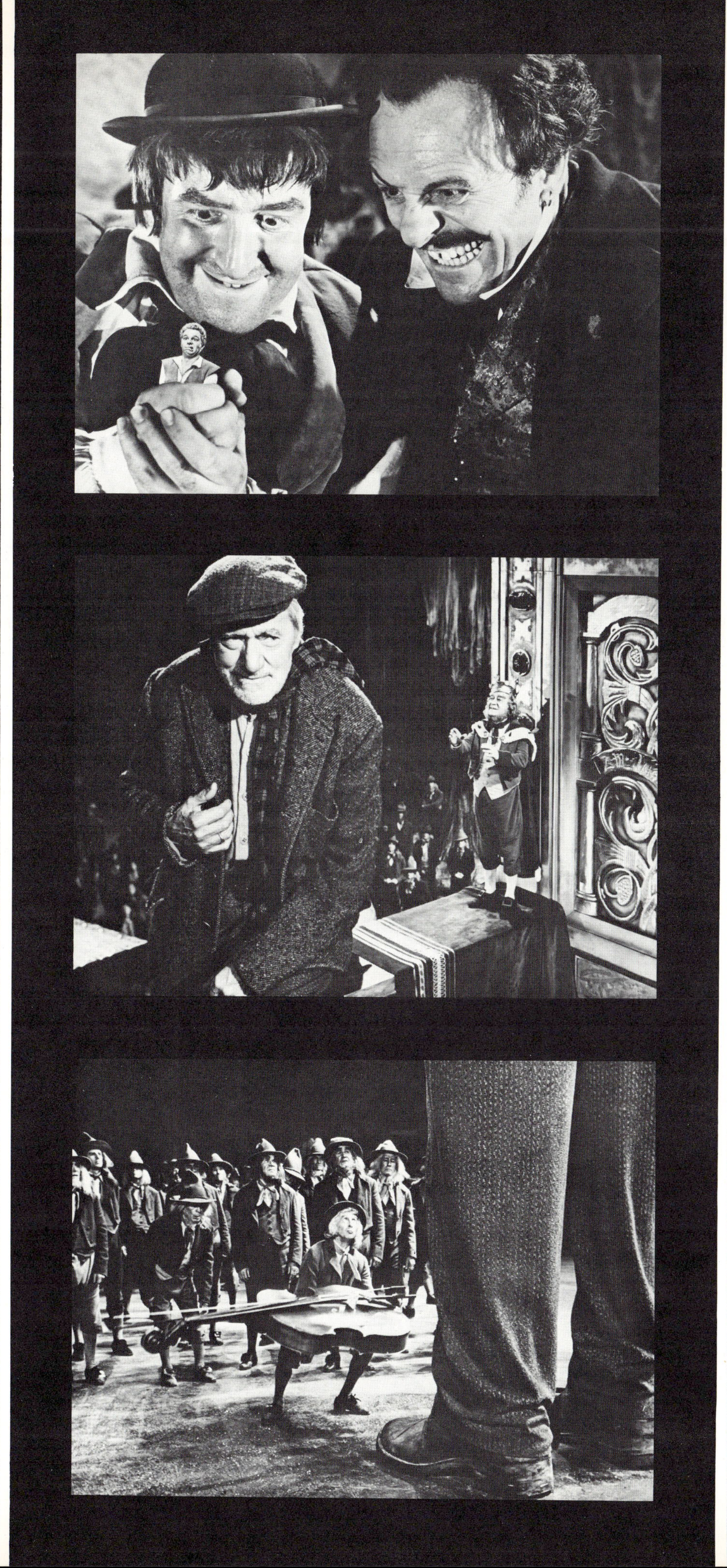

Top: Russ Tamblyn in the clutches of Peter Sellers and Terri-Thomas, the comic villains of George Pal's *tom thumb.* *Center:* An example of the outstanding split-screen work in Disney's *Darby O'Gill and the Little People.* *Bottom:* Some of the illusions in *Darby O'Gill* were achieved with mechanical, not optical, effects. The giant legs and violin in this scene were oversize props used to make the normal-size actors look like leprechauns.

his nursery companions, a virtual army of toy wooden figures that spring to life whenever the grown-ups aren't around. The Yawning Man is one of these, an endearingly dopey-looking character who can't keep his eyes open and manages to stay awake only long enough to sing tom to sleep. The figure, which was animated by Gene Warren, had a series of interchangeable wax faces sculpted by the marvelous special-effects craftsman Wah Chang.

The fabulous jewel-encrusted dragon that appears in the "Singing Bone" segment of Pal's *The Wonderful World of the Brothers Grimm* (1962) was also designed and constructed by Wah Chang. This fire-breathing monster, which looks a hundred feet long in the film, was actually a three-foot model made of foam rubber over a fully articulated steel armature and brought to life by stop-motion artist Jim Danforth. Danforth also animated the Loch Ness monster in Pal's other major fantasy movie, *The Seven Faces of Dr. Lao* (1964). In one scene a couple of local rowdies put a bullet through the fishbowl that supposedly contains the Loch Ness monster, though the creature is no bigger than a tadpole. As it flops on the ground, however, it begins to grow larger and larger until it indeed becomes a giant sea serpent, which chases the two men across the prairie. At one point the monster suddenly sprouts six additional heads, each one with the face of a mythological being: Pan, Merlin, Medusa, Appolonius, the Abominable Snowman, and the mystical title character himself. Finally a rain-making device is employed to create a storm that shrinks the Loch Ness monster back to pollywog size.

The illusion of the monster's growth was achieved by slowly moving the camera in toward the stop-motion model. Twenty separate puppets, each representing a more advanced stage of growth, were built by Danforth and substituted for one another at various points in the creature's development. To make the sea serpent shrink, the process was reversed. The animated footage was then matted in over the live-action footage. This nine-minute sequence required 12,900 separate exposures and ended up taking three months to shoot. Largely because of Danforth's work, *The Seven Faces of Dr. Lao* was nominated for a Special Effects Oscar. It lost, however, to a movie made by the man who was Pal's chief rival in the field of "family entertainment": Walt Disney.

The film that won the 1964 Academy Award for visual effects was *Mary Poppins,* the biggest money-maker in the history of the Disney studio. Dimensional animation has never been a feature of Disney movies. A certain amount of stop-motion work was used in *Mary Poppins* when the magical nanny (played by Julie Andrews) tidies up the children's nursery by casting a spell that causes the room to clean itself up. Rumpled pajamas fold themselves neatly and fly into a bureau drawer, which opens and closes under its own power; the bed makes itself; toys march obediently back to their shelves. It is a skillfully done though not particularly imaginative scene (not nearly as inventive as the animated nursery sequences in *tom thumb,* for example) accomplished primarily by means of wires and stop-motion photography. Far more impressive are the episodes involving Disney's specialty, cartoon animation, which in *Mary Poppins* is cleverly combined with the live actors.

Many fantasy movies work by taking us on a trip to incredible places. Others, like *Mary Poppins,* do the opposite: they bring magic into perfectly ordinary settings. *Mary Poppins* begins when its enchanted title character, in answer to the prayers of a pair of unhappy children, floats down from the sky (on unfortunately visible wires) clutching a carpetbag and parasol. At one point in the film, however, the main characters do in fact take a "jolly holiday" to a child's dream world when they leap into a sidewalk drawing done by the pavement artist/street musician/chimney sweep Bert (Dick Van Dyke) and find themselves in a cartoon wonderland, where they frolic and dance with a host of animated creatures. These scenes were shot with the sodium light method of producing traveling mattes: the actors performed in front of a brilliant yellow backing. Later, painted backgrounds and cartoon figures were added to create the final composite. A variety of other effects were used in the movie, including several lovely matte paintings by Peter Ellenshaw. One that appears at the very start of the film, when we see Mary Poppins hovering among the violet clouds high above London, is particularly striking. This aerial view of the city was done on a sheet of glass with a small patch of the sky left unpainted. Footage of the "floating" actress was later projected into this clear portion of glass to complete the scene.

Although *Mary Poppins* was based on a beloved series of children's books by P. L. Travers, the movie does not do justice to the richness and charm of its source. In general Disney's live-action fantasy films tend to be technically impressive, but as insubstantial as cotton candy. However, an earlier film, *Darby O'Gill and the Little People* (1959), contains virtu-

Top: One of the marvelous sets from *The Wizard of Oz.*
Center: The Wicked Witch's crystal ball was actually a hollow glass bowl with a small screen set up inside it.
Bottom: The melting of the Wicked Witch (Margaret Hamilton) was done by very simple means: the actress was lowered through the floor on a hydraulic elevator, which was concealed by her costume.

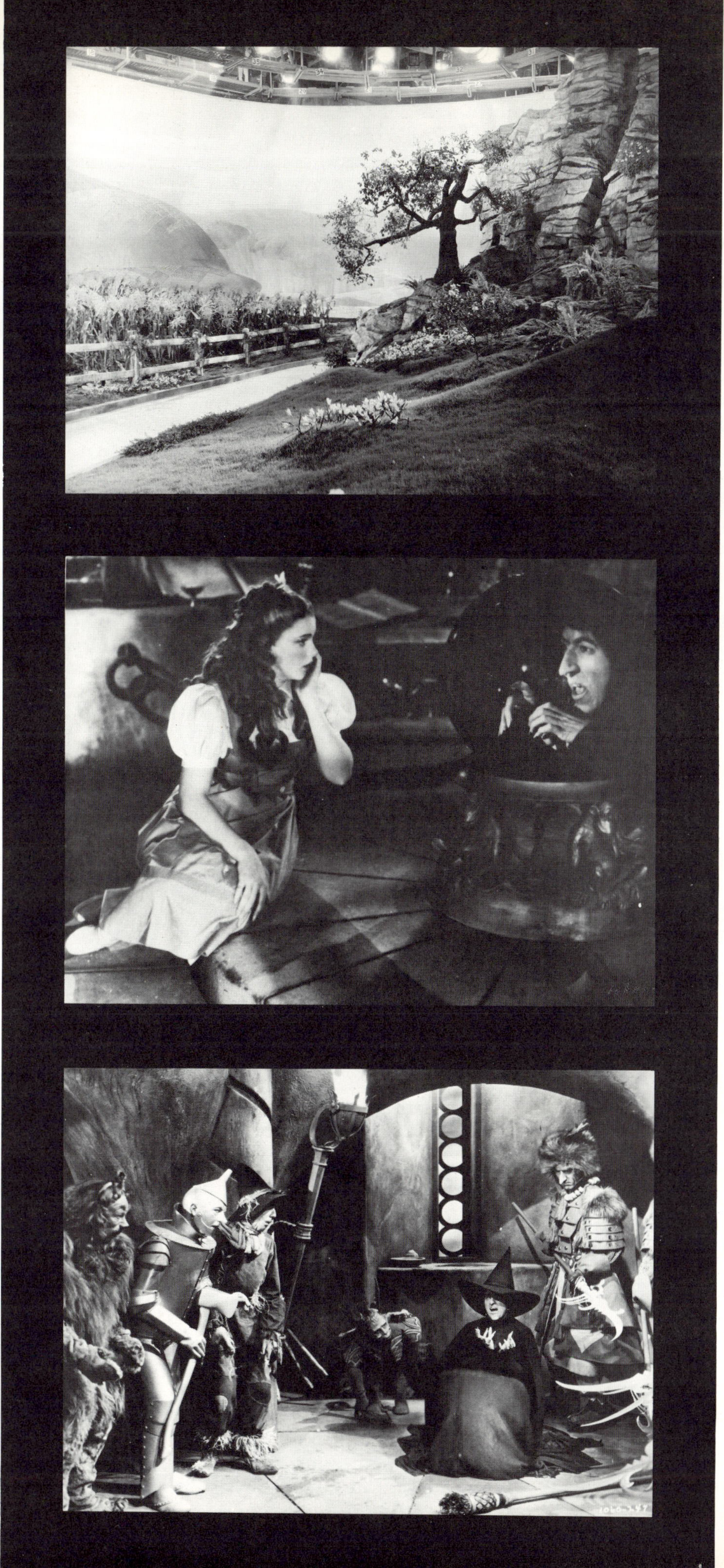

ally flawless effects. Particularly outstanding is the split-screen work. Scenes showing Darby O'Gill (Albert Sharpe), the town codger, interacting with a community of leprechauns were done by direct photography without any subsequent optical work. To show King Brian Conners, the twenty-one-inch leader of the "little people," entertaining Darby with an amusing tale, the actor playing Brian (Jimmy O'Dea) was placed on a set filled with oversize props —a large wooden table, for example, on which he strolled about while talking up to the air, as though regaling a giant several feet away. Albert Sharpe, on the other hand, was photographed on regular sets containing duplicate, normal-size props: in this case a section of the wooden table against which he leaned one arm while looking down to his left, as though paying close attention to remarks being directed at him from somewhere in the vicinity of his elbow. The two units, overscale and normal, were then matched according to mathematically determined perspective lines so that, to the camera's eye, they blended into a single set. In a few cases the blend was achieved by means of the Schüfftan process.

The trouble with *Darby O'Gill and the Little People,* however, as with Disney's other live-action films, is that it substitutes technological magic for an interesting plot and well-developed characters. The best fantasy films are not the ones with the most stunning effects but the ones that use their effects in the service of a marvelous story, that manage to find the ideal technological means of bringing the most extraordinary of daydreams to life. Few films in the history of the cinema have been able to do this. *King Kong* is one. Another is the perennial favorite that still attracts huge audiences whenever it is rerun on television, the 1939 MGM production of L. Frank Baum's classic *The Wizard of Oz.*

The magical kingdom of Oz was created entirely inside the studio's sound stages ("under roof" in the jargon of the movie industry). The dark forests and sunny fields through which Dorothy (Judy Garland) and her friends travel on their adventure-filled journey were elaborately constructed sets with scenic backgrounds painted on immense pieces of heavy white muslin. Distant shots of the Emerald City and the grim, forbidding landscape surrounding the castle of the Wicked Witch of the West were matte paintings, which were not done with oil on glass but rather with crayon pastels on four-foot-wide pieces of black cardboard.

A. Arnold Gillespie was in charge of the special effects. The most complex and costly effect in the movie was the tornado that springs from the sky and sets Dorothy's strange quest in motion. After an $8,000, thirty-five-foot rubber cone proved unusable (it wouldn't twist), Gillespie contrived an equally large, conical tornado out of muslin. Its bottom was inserted into a slot in the stage floor; its top was attached to a complicated mechanical affair suspended from the ceiling, which caused the muslin cone to move across the stage in a sinuous, squirming manner. A claylike substance called fuller's earth was fed through the porous muslin with air hoses to create the illusion of a tornado's accompanying dust cloud. To simulate a stormy, cloud-filled sky, large panes of glass with clumps of gray-painted cotton glued onto them were moved in front of the camera, while dense yellow-black smoke was released on the stage. The footage of this totally convincing man-made cyclone was then rear-projected onto a screen behind Judy Garland. Studio wind machines were used on the set to give the final touch of realism to the scene. The farmhouse, which is sent spinning up into the sky by the twister, was actually a miniature model, three feet tall. To show the cyclone lifting the house into the air, the model was actually photographed falling to the floor, and the footage was then run in reverse.

Other effects in the movie gave Gillespie less trouble than the twister. The Wicked Witch's army of winged monkeys was composed mostly of small rubber dolls about six inches in length, each one suspended by four strands of piano wire and "flown" across the stage by the same overhead gantry that moved the muslin tornado. The large crystal ball, in which Dorothy sees the image of her beloved Aunt Em dissolve into the cackling, gloating face of the Wicked Witch, was actually a hollow glass bowl with a translucent screen set up inside it onto which Gillespie simply projected shots of the two characters. The most spectacular effect in the movie, the melting of the Wicked Witch after Dorothy douses her with water, was also one of the easiest to create. In an interview he gave many years later, Gillespie revealed how this trick was performed: "It was so doggone simple. We had her on a little hydraulic lift and just lowered her down through the floor. Her black costume was fastened down to the floor. We had a little dry ice that came out to make it look as though she were melting. And she went down and down and down! Her black hat stayed on the floor and her costume just spread out and covered up the hole."

No subsequent child's fantasy film has come close to equaling the magic of *The Wizard of Oz.* The heavy-handed 1978 remake, *The Wiz,* was a major disappointment in spite of some impressive effects, including a number of remarkable matte paintings by the master of the technique, Albert Whitlock.

Even as entertaining a film as *The Muppet Movie* (1979) seems thin in comparison to *The Wizard of Oz.* Until *The Muppet Movie,* children's fantasy films starring frogs, pigs, and bears generally took the form of either animated cartoons or stop-motion puppet shorts. Jim Henson's charming creations, however, are operated more or less like hand-puppets. On TV the people who manipulate Kermit and his friends from below can easily be kept out of camera range. *The Muppet Movie,* however, required a large number of full-figure shots of its nonhuman stars. The main problem faced by special-effects man Robbie Knott, therefore, was to find ways of hiding Henson and his fellow Muppeteers.

For some of the scenes Knott had to go to incredible lengths. At the start of the film, for example, we see Kermit sitting on a log in the middle of a swamp, strumming on a banjo and singing. The scene was shot on a man-made swamp built on the back lot of Studio Center in Hollywood and decked out with forty genuine cypress trees flown in from Georgia. To operate Kermit, Henson had to be completely submerged in the water below the log. Knott managed this feat by designing and constructing a one-man aluminum bathysphere, complete with an oxygen supply, a video monitor (to allow Henson to watch the movements of the puppet overhead), and communication devices. Other scenes required the construction of elaborate sets with fake raised floors so that the Muppeteers could be concealed underneath. Toward the end of the film, for instance, Kermit and his pals are ushered into the presence of movie mogul Orson Welles. The carpeted floor of Welles's office was actually built six feet off the ground to accommodate a dozen members of Henson's team, each operating one of the Muppets.

Other effects were less involved. One of the most delightful moments in the movie was actually one of the simplest to achieve: the scene in which Kermit is shown riding a bicycle. After a radio-controlled bike that would ride by itself was tried and abandoned as impractical, Knott simply attached extremely thin monofilament wires to an ordinary two-wheeler and moved the bike along like a marionette. Kermit's feet were attached to the pedals, which rotated as the wheels went round, creating the illusion that the puppet was actually pedaling the bike.

The piece of work which Knott is proudest of, however, was his gigantic version of Animal, the snarling, wild-eyed, dangerously unpredictable drummer for Dr. Teeth's rock band who at one point in the film eats a "growth pill," which sends him crashing up through the roof of a building. Standing fifty-five feet tall, this towering puppet was worked by two men, one inside the head to operate its eyes, the second on the ground to open and close its mouth by pulling on a rope, like a medieval bell-ringer.

The success of *The Muppet Movie,* which was one of the big money-makers of the summer of 1979, points to an interesting phenomenon: the present popularity of fantasy films. Undoubtedly this has something to do with the troubled times we are living through. In periods of great stress, particularly economic stress, audiences seem to crave large doses of escapist entertainment to help them forget their woes. Pure escapism was the appeal of another big-budget movie that did very well in 1979: the cinematic version of the Superman legend.

In spite of all the time, money, and advanced technology that went into the making of *Superman,* many people found themselves disappointed by the quality, if not the quantity, of its photographic tricks. Certainly the movie contained a wealth of effects, both mechanical and optical. A variety of very sizable miniatures were built under the supervision of Derek Meddings, including a sixty-foot model of the Golden Gate Bridge, a forty-foot high replica of Boulder Dam, and the crystalline surface of the ice-planet Krypton, a plaster and Fiberglas construction that filled an entire sound stage at England's Pinewood Studios. The scene in which Superman rescues Lois Lane from a falling helicopter actually contains three different helicopters, though they are so perfectly matched it is impossible to tell that there is more than one. Shots of the whirlybird landing on the Daily Planet Building were filmed on the rooftop helipad of the Citibank building on Wall Street in Manhattan with a real helicopter. The scenes of the aircraft dangling over the side of the building after catching its skid on an electrical cable were done on a studio sound stage. A full-size set of the top of the skyscraper was constructed and a mock-up of the aircraft, built from the remnants of a wrecked helicopter weighing one and a half tons, was suspended over the side by giant cranes. Finally, for the scenes showing the helicopter actually plummeting through the air, a miniature model was built.

Hydraulic devices were used for several scenes in the movie. The destruction of the planet Krypton by a cataclysmic earthquake relied heavily on hydraulics, which shook the full-size sets and shoved huge Plexiglas crystals up through the breakaway floors. Later on in the film, when Superman smashes in the four-inch-thick steel door leading to the underground hideout of his archenemy, Lex Luthor, the feat was actually performed by hydraulic rams pounding through the metal barrier.

The most impressive trick shots in the film, however, were the flying sequences, which at times were truly exhilarating. Getting Christopher Reeve to soar through the sky realistically was, as far as the filmmakers were concerned, the key to the movie's success. Two basic methods were used: traveling mattes done with the blue-screen process (special care had to be taken to make sure that the shade of Reeve's costume was sufficiently different from that of the blue screen behind him, so that the actor wouldn't blend into the background) and an adaptation of the front projection method known as the *Zoptic* (short for "zoom optic") process, invented by a man named Zoran Perisic. It was the Zoptic process that allowed Christopher Reeve to soar high over the streets of Manhattan and straight at the audience without ever moving an inch.

Perisic's process utilizes two synchronized zoom lenses, one on the projector supplying background image, one on the camera recording the scene. When a camera lens zooms in on a subject, that subject appears to grow larger and larger. When zooming-in is done on a projector, however, the projected image grows smaller. To make Reeve seem to fly toward the audience while in reality remaining perfectly stationary, a pole was placed through a front-projection screen. Reeve, in his Superman flying position, was suspended by this pole, facing the camera with his body blocking the pole from the lens. An aerial view of New York City was projected on the screen behind him. At this point the Zoptic process came into play. The zooming-in action of the projector caused the background image of Manhattan to decrease in size. Simultaneously, however, the camera lens zoomed in on Reeve suspended in front of the background image. Since the image in the camera was growing larger and larger at exactly the same rate that the projected background image was shrinking, the view of the city, as far as the camera could see, remained constant. At the same time, however, Reeve seemed to be increasing in size. This technique produced the illusion that the actor was moving closer and closer to the camera while the background remained fixed. The faster the zooming-in was done, the faster Reeve seemed to fly. Moreover, depending on where the actor was positioned at the start of a zoom, he could be made to move in any direction: right, left, up, down, forward, or backward.

Because Reeve was not, in fact, moving at all, the special-effects people had to devise a way of making his cape flap convincingly as though it were being blown through the air. Wind machines were ruled out because they are hard to control and cannot be made to produce the kind of precisely directed breeze needed to swirl a cape. Finally effects wizard Les Bowie (who also executed nearly sixty matte paintings for the movie) came up with an ingenious solution: a battery-operated, radio-controlled flapping device, which resembled a set of motorized fishing rods built into Reeve's costume.

Since *Superman* was released, late in 1978, a number of fantasy films based on comic-strip and comic-book characters have gone into production, including a big-budget *Popeye* movie, an eagerly awaited version of *Conan the Barbarian* (whose savage hero began life in the pulp magazines of the thirties, though he has achieved his greatest popularity as the star of a series of Marvel Comics), and of course *Superman II.* Meanwhile Ray Harryhausen is at work on a $10-million stop-motion epic, *Clash of the Titans,* based on ancient Greek mythology and featuring an all-star cast. Other fantasy projects have recently been announced. In an unusual move Walt Disney Productions, which has always maintained complete independence from other studios, has agreed to finance and distribute (with Paramount) the medieval fantasy movie *Dragon Slayer.* And George Lucas is currently producing an animated feature-length film called *Twice upon a Time,* which is described by its creator, John Korty, as "a contemporary myth in which the heroes, like the heroes of classical mythology, are tricked by the villain into a devastatingly wrong act." All this is good news for the fans of special effects, though it seems to be a reflection of all the bad news that is constantly bombarding us and of a widespread desire to run away from reality and escape into imaginary worlds where problems can be solved by magic or vanquished by superhuman saviors.

Dick Van Dyke and Julie Andrews frolic with cartoon animals in *Mary Poppins.*

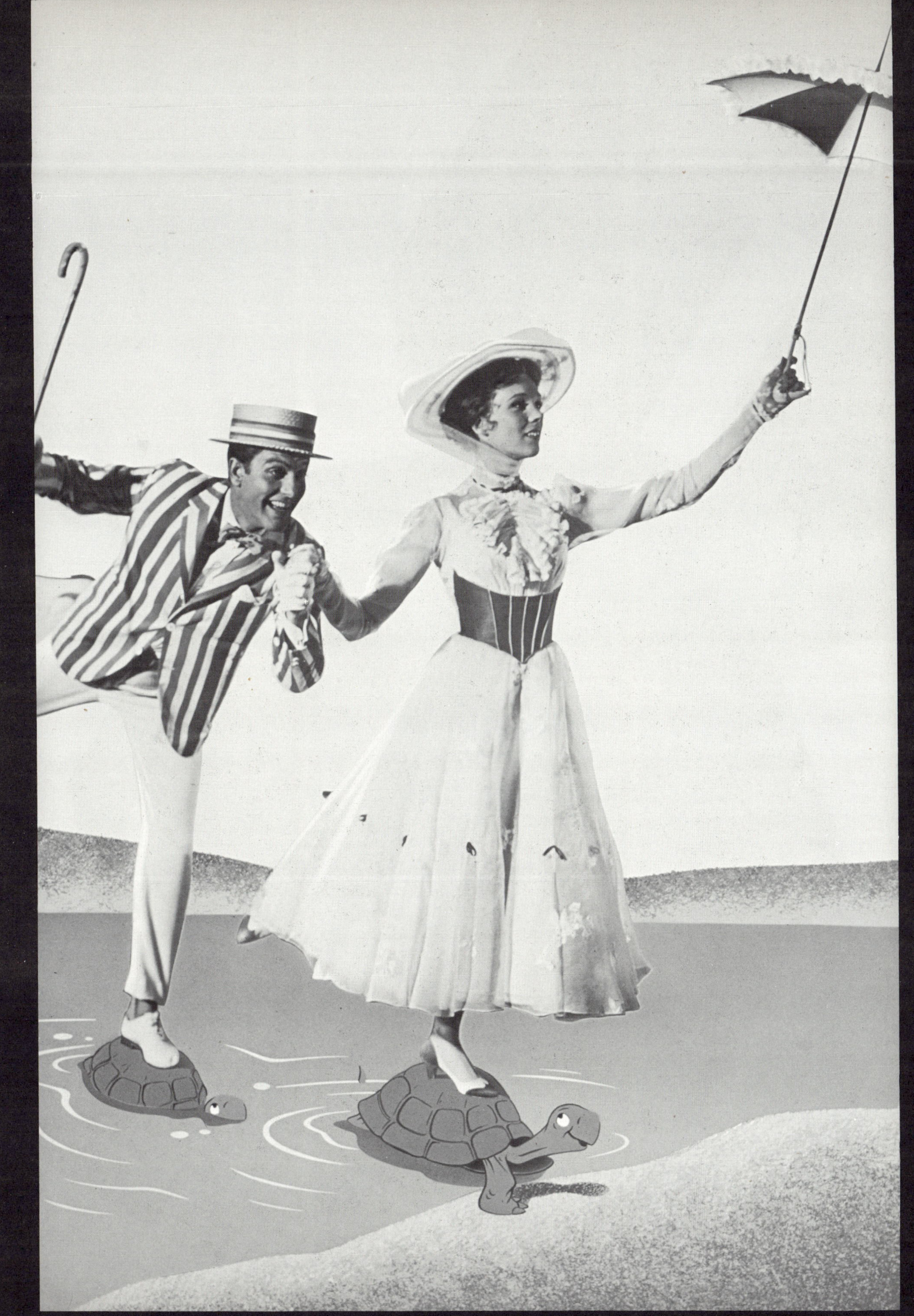

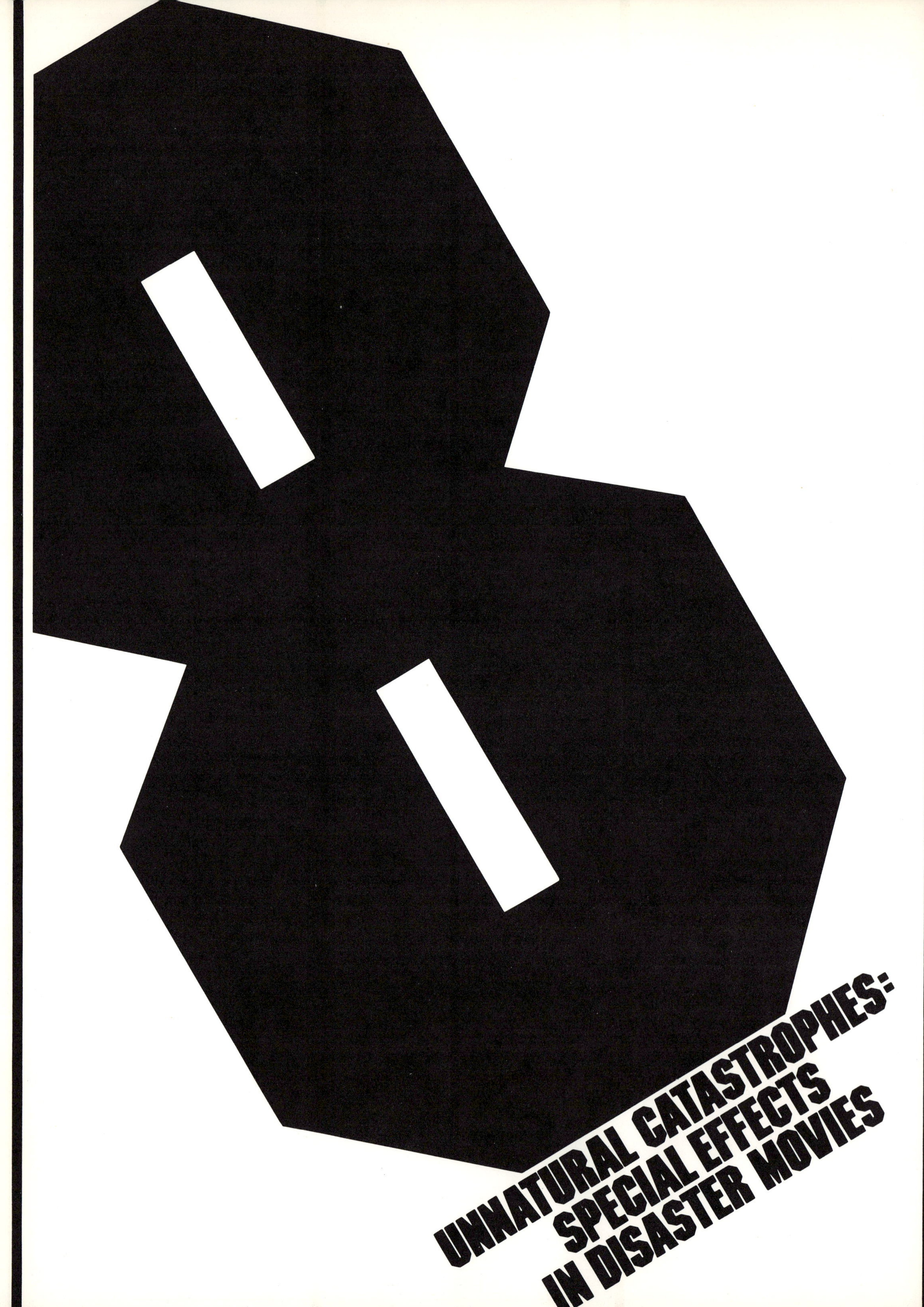
UNNATURAL CATASTROPHES:
SPECIAL EFFECTS
IN DISASTER MOVIES

Just as the Hollywood spectacles of old demonstrated what special-effects men could do to the ancient world, the more recent disaster films unleash the destructive talents of effects technicians on the contemporary world. In one sense disaster movies like *Earthquake* and *The Towering Inferno* (both 1974) are a latter-day extension of the traditional spectacle. Both spectacles and disaster movies involve a cataclysmic event visited upon a decadent and therefore deserving society. The jaded Los Angeles destroyed in *Earthquake* and the sated beautiful people who must face *The Towering Inferno* are both comparable to the wayward world that was annihilated by an irritated God during the flood in Michael Curtiz's *Noah's Ark* (1929). The corrupt American metropolis becomes the modern Gomorrah, while its colossal skyscrapers are turned into updated Towers of Babel. In other ways, however, the disaster films are significantly different from their epic predecessors.

The cataclysmic event featured in spectacles was usually the dramatic high point of the story, as in the destruction of the Philistine temple in Cecil B. De Mille's *Samson and Delilah* (1949). The raging fire in *The Towering Inferno,* on the other hand, is the *entire* dramatic point. Without it there would be no movie, just as there would be no *Earthquake* without the title event. And since the catastrophe is the centerpiece of the disaster movie, it is also portrayed in more gruesome detail than in such movies as *The Last Days of Pompeii* (1935) and *The Rains Came* (1939).

Another distinctive characteristic of the disaster movie is that the disaster is always visited upon one of man's proudest technological achievements: an unsinkable ocean liner, a fireproof skyscraper, a jumbo jet, a megalopolis. Moreover the agent of destruction is not God but the natural world, generally by one of four elements: earth, air, fire, or water. Since these movies were enormously popular in the early seventies (at the height of America's "back-to-nature" craze, when large numbers of people were seriously questioning the wisdom of unbridled technological development and celebrating the joys of natural food, clothing, and shelter), it's tempting to see the disaster film as fantasy in which Mother Nature strikes back at an industrial society that has brutally exploited her. Paradoxically, creating these pro-nature, antitechnological visions requires the use of the most complex and sophisticated special-effects technology at Hollywood's disposal.

One more important feature of the disaster film is its reliance on *Grand Hotel*-type drama to bind the various scenes of violence into a coherent story. This type of plot involves an assortment of characters, each representing a different walk of life, who are suddenly thrown together with the common purpose of facing a dire emergency and revealing their convoluted pasts at appropriately dramatic moments. This well-worn formula was successfully employed for many years in such pictures as *Stagecoach* (1939), *Five Came Back* (1939), and *The High and the Mighty* (1954) and is a main ingredient of the first disaster movie to prove a box office success.

In 1970 the 1932 *Grand Hotel* formula was dusted off for the highly successful *Airport.* Since it contains no scenes of people being burned alive or crushed by falling buildings, *Airport* is very different from later disaster films, and it hardly qualifies as a special-effects epic. One of the few spectacular action scenes in the picture involves a Boeing 707 jetliner forced to crash-land in a blizzard; the scene called for no effects trickery since it was filmed with an actual 707 in a real snowstorm. *Airport*'s story of a group of people trapped in a snowbound airfield had an important influence on disaster movies to come because it established the dramatic framework for the disaster genre: a two-hour-plus running time and a big-name cast to play a wide assortment of insipid characters.

The first producer to combine these dramatic elements with a violent catastrophe was Irwin Allen, who had previously shown a flair for special-effects production in such films as *The Animal World* (1956) and *Voyage to the Bottom of the Sea* (1961) and who continued to stage fantastic illusions for the *Time Tunnel* and *Lost in Space* television series. In *The Poseidon Adventure* (1972) he initiated the disaster craze by turning over a gigantic ocean liner and showing a small group of survivors desperately searching for a way out of the quickly sinking ship. Ship disasters had been filmed before in *Titanic* (1953), *A Night To Remember* (1958), *The Wreck of the Mary Deare* (1959) and *The Last Voyage* (1960), but Allen's high-sea calamity is much more spectacular and harrowing, even if his dramatics are best forgotten.

The scene of the tidal wave capsizing the *Poseidon* set the pattern for movie disasters to come, concentrating as it did on a violent upheaval of natural elements and wholesale elimination of extras. The first devastating moment occurs while the drunken passengers of the *Poseidon* celebrate New Year's Eve in the lavish first-class dining room. The giant wave swamps the ocean liner, drowns the crew on the bridge, and capsizes the ship. Inside the dining hall the passengers are tossed about by the sudden convulsion. The distant exterior shots of the *Poseidon* engulfed by the wave were handled by L. B. Abbott. As in most large-scale scenes of destruction, this sequence was filmed in miniature: the ocean liner was a small-scale model and the tidal wave was a relatively large disturbance in a studio water tank. The capsizing motion as seen from the interior of the dining room was devised in part by actually tilting the set. A special hinged platform was built and upon this setup a thirty-foot section of the palatial dining hall was mounted. The platform tilted at a 30-degree angle to represent the first lurching movement of the overturned ship. When Shelley Winters is seen clinging desperately to a bolted-down table, screaming for help, the viewer is watching the actress hanging on to an actual upended set. The hinged platform could be fitted with several different sections of the dining room to show more than one part of the interior turning over.

The situation inside the ship quickly becomes even more disastrous when a torrent of water explodes up through a skylight, now positioned where the floor should be. The already ravaged dining area is flooded and many of the passengers are drowned. Physical-effects expert A. D. Flowers crashed the glass with an explosion, then shot the water through the opening with water cannons and added to the deluge with pumps that spewed water at a rate of 4,000 gallons per minute. An essential factor in the success of a scene of this kind was the coordination of physical effects with the work of the stunt men. The scene of the overpowering water break involved as many as 125 stunt people thrashed about by Flowers's torrent.

The rest of the picture details the survivors' trek through the upside-down ship as they pick their precarious way to the relative safety of the bottom (now the top) of the vessel. With the bulk of the spectacular effects work out of the way, the stage was cleared for the tedious interaction between the stereotyped characters, among whom are a two-fisted priest, a tough fat cop, and a hand-wringing old Jewish couple. The intriguing bottoms-up sets designed by William Creber helped to camouflage the tiresome dramatics, as did some of A. D. Flowers's fire and water effects. The water steadily rising in the bizarre topsy-turvy interiors of the *Poseidon* helps to generate much of the dramatic tension in the movie. Creber's sets were mounted on slanted tracks that allowed the interiors to be gradually lowered into a water tank while the actors played their scenes. As the set descended into the tank, the water rose higher and higher as the characters made their way across the room.

The combination of *Grand Hotel* dramatic structure and a devastating calamity proved to be a great money-making formula. The box office success of *The Poseidon Adventure* prompted other producers to consider adapting similar ideas for a movie to duplicate or, hopefully, surpass the financial returns of Irwin Allen's disaster film. The one element of *The Poseidon Adventure* that seemed to account for its success was the disaster itself. If the disaster could be enlarged, presumably the box office pull would also be greater. This sort of thinking proved to be correct when *Earthquake* and *The Towering Inferno* (nicknamed *Shake 'n Bake* by *Variety*) were released in 1974.

Earthquake, the first of the two pictures to reach the theaters, features not one but two overwhelming catastrophes: the prolonged, monumental earthquake near the beginning of the film, and as a direct result of this natural shock, the collapse of a Hollywood dam, which floods the entire surrounding area. In between these catastrophes is the expected array of stars going through the usual tediously tangled situations.

Earthquake was one of the first movies to revive what had become the dormant special-effects field. Throughout the late sixties and early seventies, producers shied away from elaborate productions. Having learned their lesson from such colossal flops as the 1963 version of *Cleopatra,* they instead concentrated on smaller pictures that could be shot on location and required few or no special effects. By 1974 many effects men had been forced to retire because there was so little demand for their work. *Earthquake* helped to turn this state of affairs around by employing a full battery of effects personnel. One of the most important members of this team was Clifford Stine, the former head of the special-effects department at Universal, who was lured out of retirement to take charge of filming the miniatures in *Earthquake*.

Many technicians were involved in the full-scale mechanical effects, which were supervised by Frank Brendel. One of the scenes of a Hollywood street destroyed by the earthquake involved fifty-five effects men. Effects teams of this size were required by the intricate and dangerous nature of the work. In the

Top: Water explodes through the upside-down skylight in *The Poseidon Adventure.* *Center:* A film crew shoots a scene near a miniature of Los Angeles's Capitol Records Building for *Earthquake.* *Bottom:* This scene of a devastated Los Angeles is actually one of the impressive glass paintings done by Albert Whitlock for *Earthquake.*

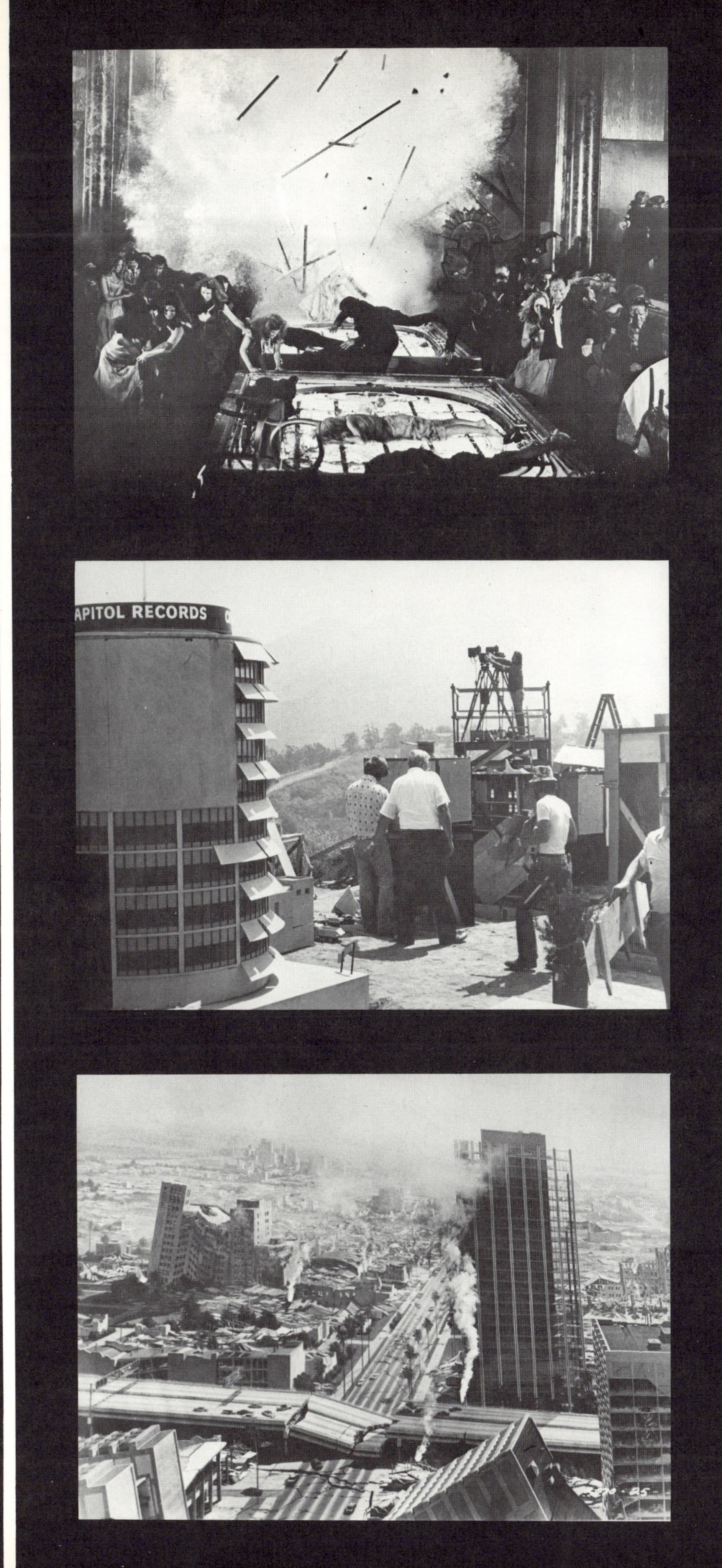

Top: A woman is struck by shards of flying glass in a scene from *Earthquake*. *Bottom:* A passenger lies with his body smoldering following the crash of the giant dirigible in *The Hindenburg*.

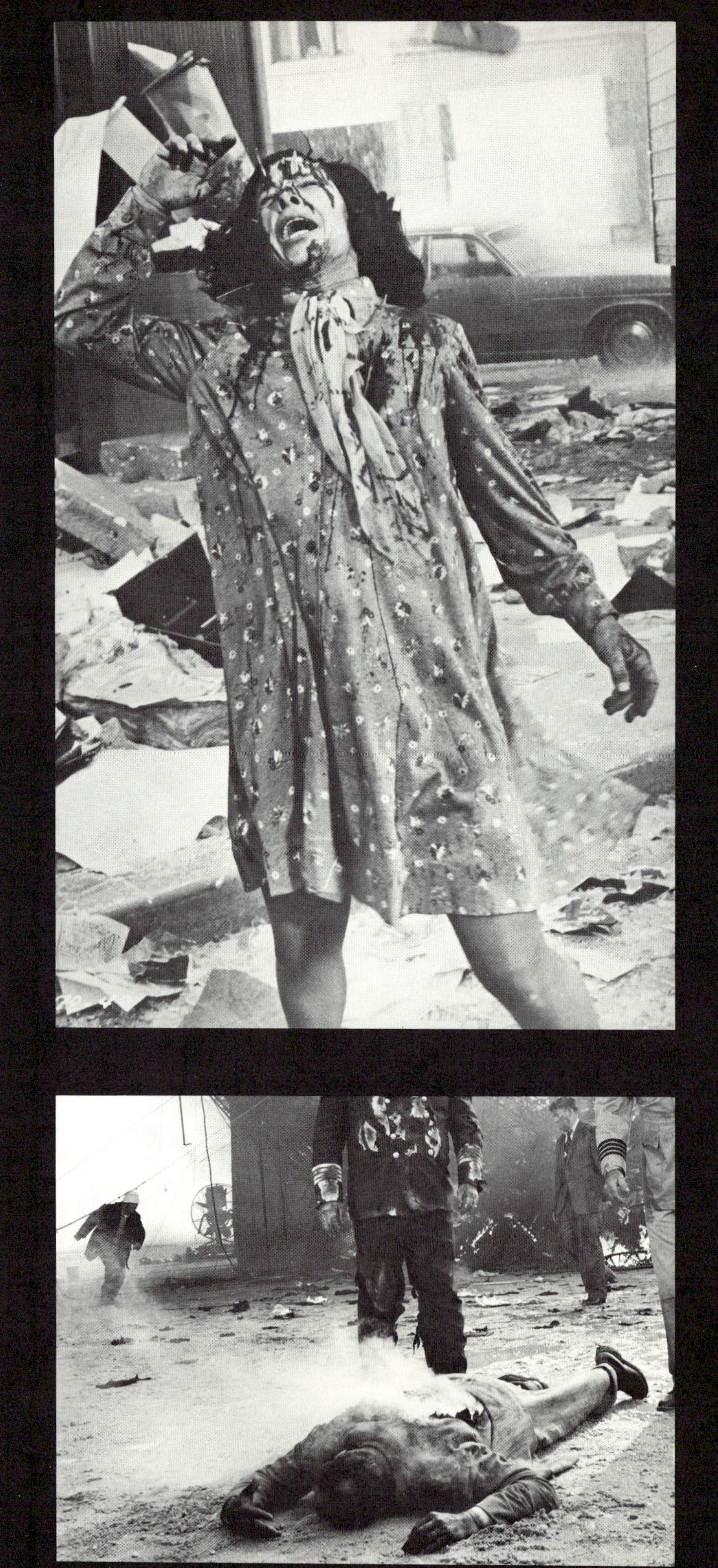

Top: In reality the woman had splinters of fake glass applied to her face by the makeup artist, while *(bottom)* the well-dressed gentleman was protected by a fireproof vest concealed under his clothes.

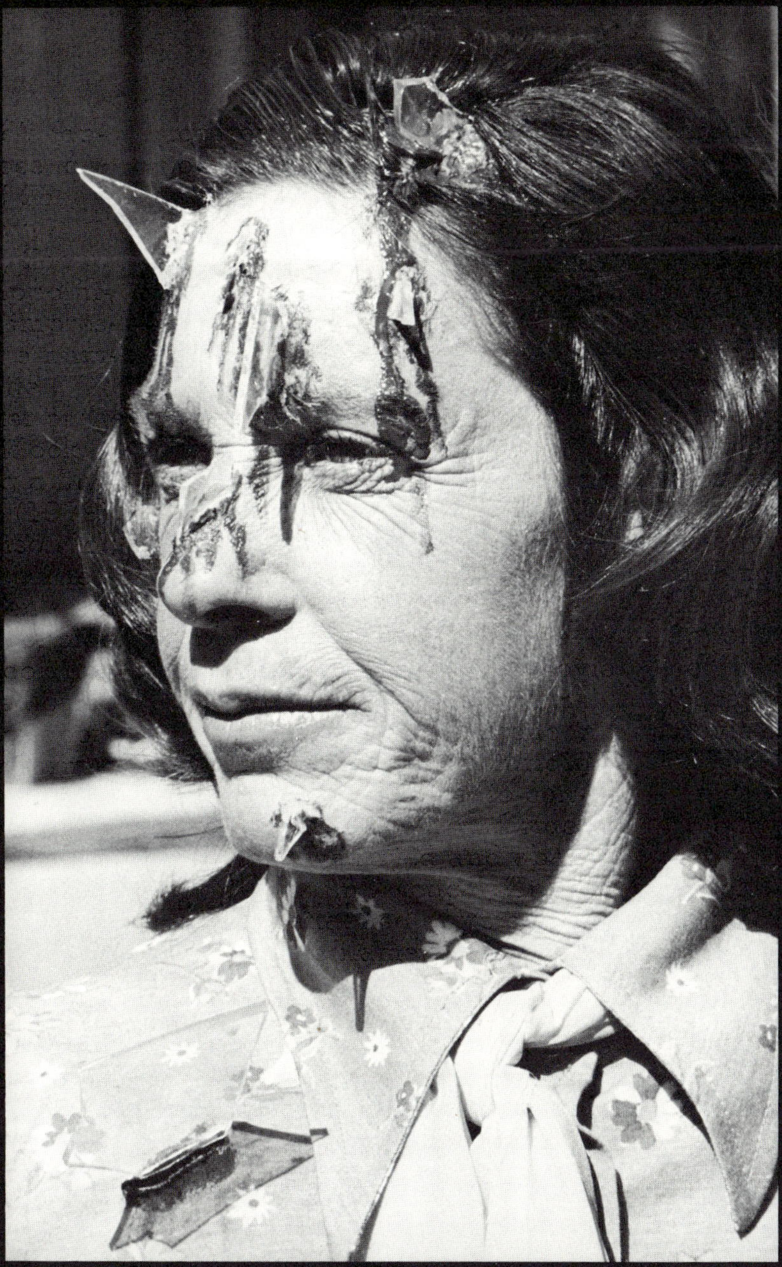

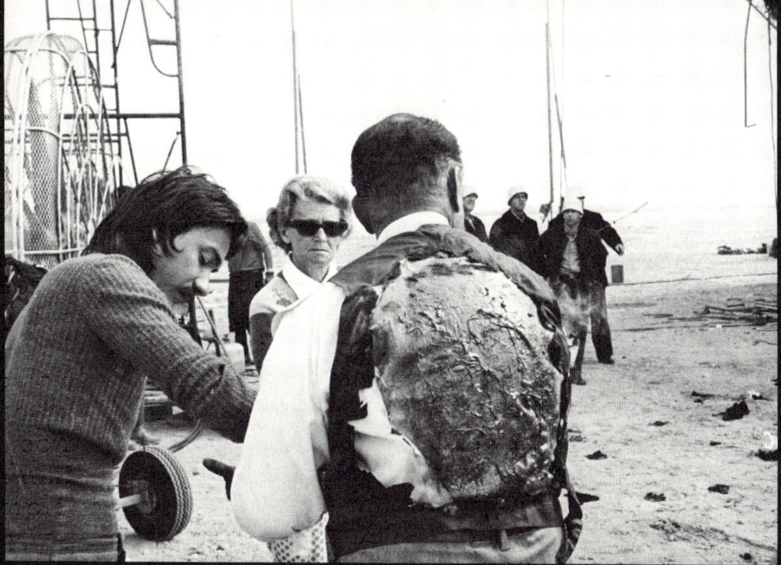

earlier earthquake epic, the 1936 *San Francisco,* the film's stars were combined with crumbling buildings primarily by shooting the performers in front of rear-projected scenes of destruction. *Earthquake* strived for greater realism by putting the actors and the falling debris on the same set. Physical-effects men on overhead platforms bombarded the actors and stunt people with chunks of the shattered buildings. Some of these chunks were made of Styrofoam weighted with steel at their cores. In many instances, though, greater realism was attained by using blocks made of concrete. To make these scenes as safe as possible, the effects men and performers coordinated their actions with great precision. Each effects man was responsible for triggering his effect only when the actor or stunt person being filmed had reached a predesignated spot. If a concrete block had been dropped before a performer reached his mark, the result would have been a very real disaster. Also involved in these scenes was the special rigging of collapsible walls and falling trees. In some cases it took four or five days to prepare one of the picture's sudden disasters. This advance planning of the precarious mechanical effects scenes paid off in the great majority of cases: only a few of the 141 stunt people who worked on *Earthquake* were injured, and those injuries were minor.

To simulate the shaking of Los Angeles when the earthquake strikes, the effects crew constructed special sets which were rocked by hydraulic rams as had been done in *San Francisco.* Director Mark Robson made only limited use of these sets because he wanted to show vast sections of the city caught in the violent tremor; building entire city blocks on hydraulic-ram platforms was impractical. Instead a device was constructed to shake the camera automatically and consequently create the illusion that the set was shaking. Robson found that the hydraulic-ram sets were most useful as a training experience for the actors. Once they had acted on one of these sets, they had a good idea of what it would be like to walk across ground agitated by an earthquake. When performing on stable ground before a shaking camera, they could then repeat the staggering movement authentically.

Many of the most spectacular scenes of destruction were filmed in miniature. One such sequence was reminiscent of the collapsing of the senate building in the silent version of *Ben-Hur* (1926). Instead of a miniature of a falling building matted into footage of the actors, the *Earthquake* scene makes use of a composite of a collapsing miniature of a Los Angeles structure and actors showered by the debris. Like the senate building scene the *Earthquake* sequence involved a complicated jigsawing of the two images of miniature and live action. In *Ben-Hur* the traveling mattes were drawn by hand for each frame of the scene. In *Earthquake* technological developments allowed the effects team to combine the two scenes by means of the less time-consuming blue-screen traveling matte process. By combining two images in this manner, the effects crew created the illusion of full-scale chunks of the building raining down on the actors.

The most elaborate miniature sequence in *Earthquake* was the breaking of the Hollywood dam. The dam and its surroundings were built as oversize models, the entire set measuring fifty-six feet wide. The bursting of the dam was filmed simultaneously from nine different positions to give the editor a variety of angles to choose from. Fortunately everything went according to plan in the first take and there was no reason to have to reconstruct the costly set.

Many of the scenes showing vast stretches of the razed city could not be practically simulated with either full-scale effects or miniatures. In order to film the unsettling vistas of a Los Angeles reduced to smoldering rubble, the makers of *Earthquake* made use of the superb talents of matte painter Albert Whitlock. For this disaster epic, Whitlock had twelve weeks to do forty paintings. As he did for such pictures as *The Birds* (1963), *The Way West* (1967), and *The Sting* (1973), Whitlock combined his paintings with live-action segments in such a way that few people were aware that paintings were used at all.

Whitlock is able to reproduce reality through the use of a painting style that he describes as impressionistic. Up close, Whitlock's paintings have an unfinished look, with roughly blocked-in areas where we expect precisely rendered detail. But when the painting is photographed and projected on a screen, it is impossible to distinguish from the real thing. Whitlock discovered this aspect of matte painting early in his career when he used a rough draft of a painting to film a test shot. When he got to see the results, he was surprised to find that his work was very convincing even though he hadn't spent any time on the realistic details of the scene. He has since found it much more important to pay attention to such optical phenomena as color and light than to strictly representational details; in *Earthquake,* for instance, he concerned himself more with the play of sunshine and shadow on a building than with each individual window and brick. If the use of light is correct in his paintings, the camera will "see" his work as something real, even though all the details aren't there.

Whitlock also makes viewers accept his paintings as live-action footage by inserting movement into his artwork. In *The Sting,* for example, he painted a broad view of Chicago that included an elevated subway track. Whitlock put life into the painting by inserting a moving subway train by means of cartoon-style animation. In *Earthquake* he added smoke and fire to his paintings of the devastated city. After a scene was painted and photographed, he placed a frame of a print of this footage into the viewing mechanism of a camera and set the camera up on a blackened stage. By looking through the viewfinder and using the frame of his painting as a guide, he could then tell special-effects men where to place fires to coincide with the details of his painting. When he photographed these fires, only the specially placed blazes were recorded on the film since the blackened stage reflected no light. This footage was then printed along with the painting to create the illusion of a burning cityscape.

The spectacular violence and vistas of destruction were part of the producers' scheme to provide the audience with the sort of entertainment that could not be found on television. Like such spectacles of the fifties as *The Ten Commandments* (1956), *Earthquake* was conceived as a project so colossal as to lure television watchers back into the movie theaters. The most extravagant part of this strategy was the process called Sensurround. Like 3-D and Cinerama, Sensurround was a theatrical gimmick that was supposed to make the audience feel a part of the larger-than-life events they saw on the screen. During the earthquake sequences special horns at the front and rear of the theater projected an overwhelming rumbling sound that made the building seem to be shaking. The wave form of the sound produced by the Sensurround horns was identical to that of an actual earthquake, though the Sensurround frequencies were not as low as an actual tremor. These artificial rumbles were engineered to vibrate the viewer's torso and diaphragm. This gimmick succeeded in enhancing the catastrophic visuals by surrounding the viewer with the approximate audio sensation of an earthquake. Since there was very little in the film's story to engage the audience, any technical embellishments were a welcome addition to the picture.

The $7.5 million devoted to the destruction of Los Angeles in *Earthquake* was quickly dwarfed by the almost simultaneous release of Irwin Allen's second lavish disaster extravaganza, *The Towering Inferno.* For the first time in Hollywood's history two major studios pooled their resources for one mammoth production. Warner Brothers had bought the rights to the Richard M. Stern novel *The Tower,* while Twentieth Century-Fox had obtained another property by Thomas Scortia and Frank Robinson entitled *The Glass Inferno.* The two books, both about buildings devastated by uncontrollable fires, were nearly identical. Rather than compete against each other, the two studios adapted the novels into one script for one disaster spectacle. Fourteen million dollars went into the filming of this picture about a San Francisco skyscraper consumed by an awesome blaze. The picture featured a huge cast of stars and superstars that included Paul Newman, Steve McQueen, and Faye Dunaway, employed four separate film crews (one for dramatic sequences, another for action scenes, a third for aerial footage, and the last for photographic effects), and made use of fifty-seven sets, a new record for any production filmed on the Twentieth Century-Fox lot.

As in *Earthquake* and Allen's trend-setting *The Poseidon Adventure,* the technical aspects of *The Towering Inferno* were the whole show. And the special effects were the most spectacular of its technical achievements. The photographic effects, supervised by L. B. Abbott, were so good that they were undetectable. Abbott, who, like Clifford Stine, was brought out of retirement by the sudden demand for effects expertise generated by the disaster craze, was primarily concerned with putting the unprecedented 138-story tower onto the screen in *The Towering Inferno.* An early shot shows the entire skyscraper in the distance, set among other actual structures of the San Francisco skyline. Abbott was able to put the fictitious skyscraper into a realistic setting by matting a painting of the tower into a live-action shot of the city. In order to make the tower seem more authentic, Abbott superimposed another painted building next to it. All the other views of the colossal skyscraper were done with an oversize 110-foot-tall miniature. When shot from a low angle, the enormous model seemed to loom above the viewer. In one instance the model was seen in the background while on a foreground, full-scale set of the roof of an adjacent building, actors were seen trying to cast a rope onto the blazing tower. Abbott matted together the full-size set and the model with a blue-screen traveling matte.

The dramatic center of *The Towering Inferno* is, of course, the action inside the hellish blaze. Although the movie features only one disaster (the fire) as opposed to *Earthquake*'s two (the earthquake and the flood), it more than compensates for the difference by making its scorching catastrophe a continuous ordeal for nearly the entire picture. The action-sequence crew, directed by Irwin Allen himself, provided the extensive scenes of the holocaust. The mechanical effects in these action sequences were supplied by A. D. Flowers, who multiplied the destructive work he performed for *The Poseidon Adventure* many times over.

The major problem in filming the fire scenes was not how to create the blaze but how to control it. Helping to supervise Flowers's propane-fed fires was a crew of thirty firemen. In order to prevent any possibility of the blaze spreading, the Los Angeles Fire Department required that the fires be extinguished after twenty or thirty seconds. To make the most of this limited time, as many as eight cameras were used simultaneously during some of the fire sequences. Stunt men who were set on fire were able to go through walls of flame with the aid of protective clothing and air devices under their coats to supply them with oxygen.

After almost two hours of fiery destruction and death, Paul Newman and Steve McQueen finally hit upon a scheme to save the lives of those still trapped inside the 138-story inferno. On the roof of the tower are huge water tanks. While the survivors of the blaze lash themselves to columns and whatever else is still standing, the two stars blow up the tanks and unleash a flood of water to douse the roaring blaze. Flowers staged the flood by emptying tanks holding 12,000 gallons of water and sending the flow down specially placed chutes.

It was to the credit of the disaster-minded Irwin Allen that even in his solution to the calamity he found yet more excuses for deadly havoc; the flood not only eliminates the fire but drowns many of the survivors and sends still more of them crashing out of upper-story windows. As always in Allen's pictures, there was no rest for his stunt people. Perhaps the greatest accomplishment of *The Towering Inferno* was that throughout all the dangerous exploits (over 200 stunts in all), not one crewmember was injured.

With the phenomenal success of both *Earthquake* and *The Towering Inferno,* the rush to capitalize on the disaster craze was on. Most of the disaster pictures were uninspired rehashes of Irwin Allen's uninspired formula. Typical of the genre were such unremarkable big-budget efforts as *Airport 1975* (1974) and *Airport '77* (1977). Probably the most contrived attempt to cash in on the disaster boom was Roger Corman's 1975 release of *Tidal Wave.* The movie was a reedited version of a Japanese epic called *Submersion of Japan,* made in 1973, a year before either *Earthquake* or *The Towering Inferno.* Like the American disaster movies, *Submersion of Japan* chronicled a great natural disaster. The Japanese film, however, was very different from American disaster movies in that it included a real human drama in addition to a violent, physical spectacle. Corman shrewdly concluded that believable characterization and human conflict had no place in the American disaster genre. When he distributed *Submersion of Japan* in the United States as *Tidal Wave,* Corman cut out virtually all the non-disaster material, reducing the film from 140 minutes to 81, and inserted scenes featuring Lorne Greene to give the movie an "international cast."

The most interesting disaster epics to follow in the wake of *Earthquake* and *The Towering Inferno* were those movies which provided variations on the catastrophe formula. The most ambitious and technically accomplished of these films were *The Hindenburg* (1975) and *Black Sunday* (1977). The dramatics on board the enormous dirigible Hindenburg fit into the customary *Grand Hotel* format, but unlike previous disaster films, the great calamity highlighting the final moments of *The Hindenburg* was the result of a plausible man-made scheme rather than a sudden upheaval of nature.

The primary special-effects problem in filming *The Hindenburg* was how to recreate the giant dirigible and its proper historical setting. A twenty-five-foot-long model of the great airship was constructed in great detail by a crew headed by Glen Robinson, the man who was responsible for the first-rate miniatures in *Earthquake.* The model was connected by four wires to an overhead track and could be operated by remote control over a 200-foot distance. The remote control system was so sophisticated that it could manipulate both the airship's rudder and elevators. Completing the illusion were three realistic backdrops for daylight, sunset, and stormy weather. For

Top: Filming the miniature model of the *Hindenburg* in front of a backdrop of the Arctic wastes.
Bottom: A miniature set from *Tidal Wave.*

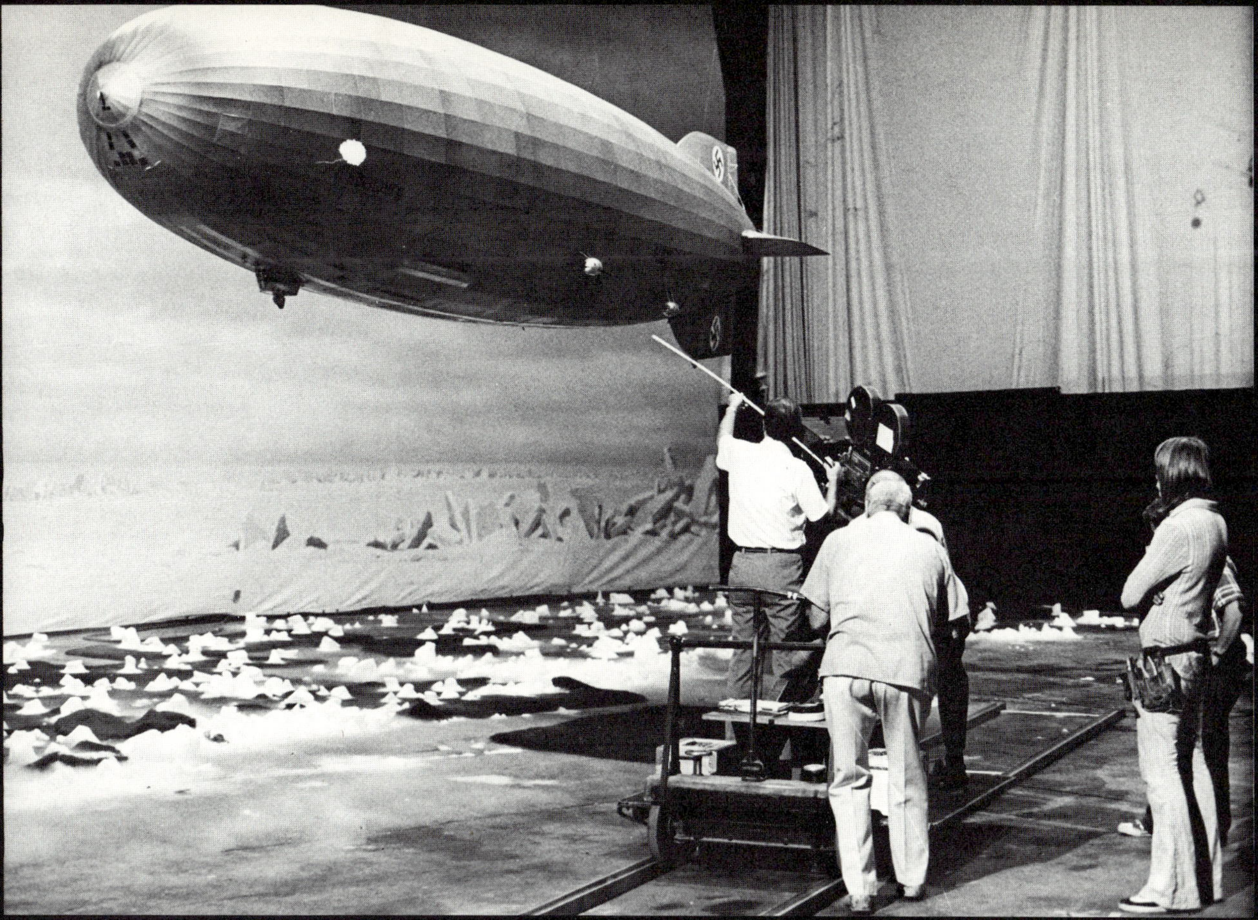

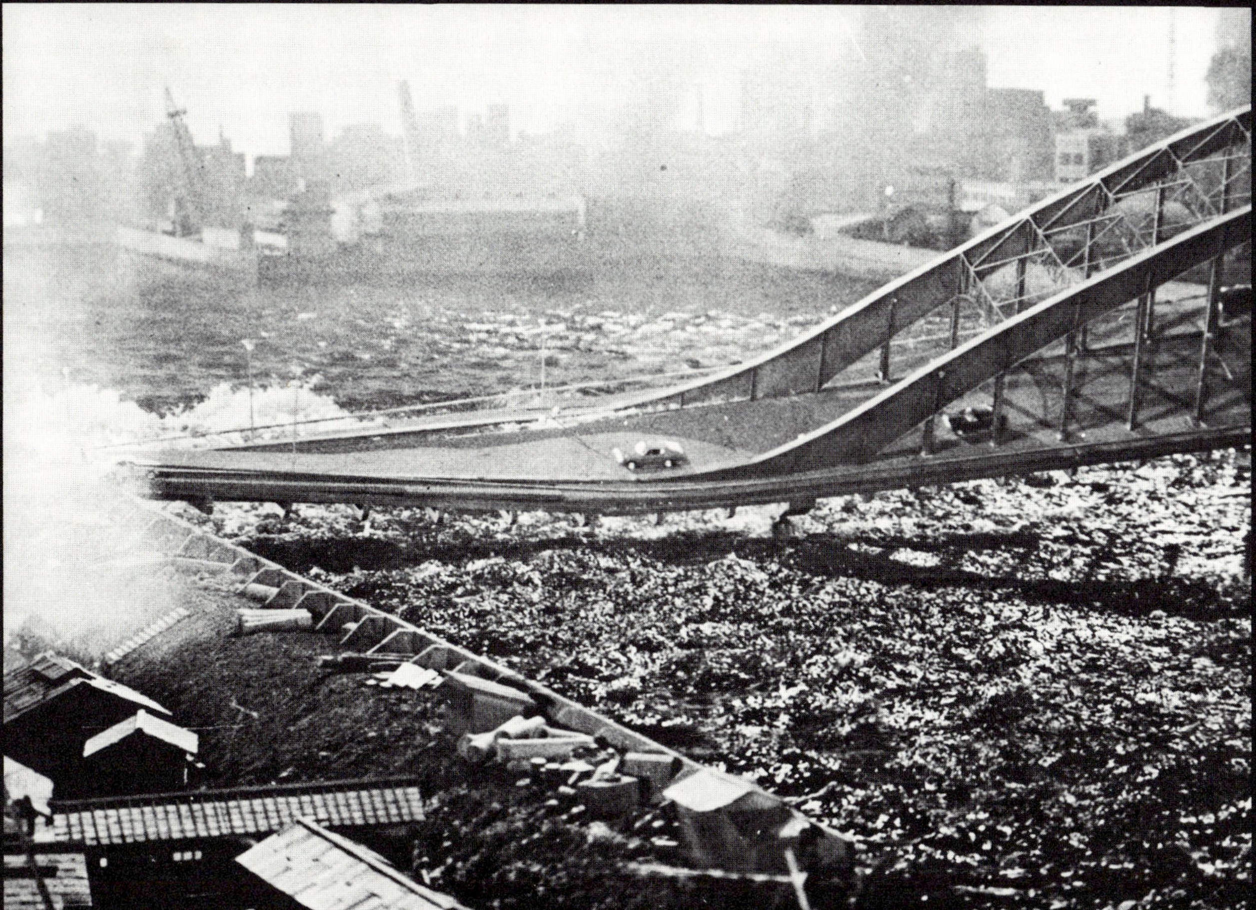

night scenes miniatures-cinematographer Clifford Stine dimmed the lights and silhouetted the model airship. For each type of background the wires were painted to blend in with the colors behind them.

Other shots of the 800-foot dirigible were simulated by Albert Whitlock, whose paintings appeared in more than seventy scenes in the picture. One of his most ingenious contributions was the view of the *Hindenburg* cruising above New York City. Since a contemporary shot of New York couldn't be substituted in a scene taking place in 1937, Whitlock painted the cityscape as it appeared at the time of the *Hindenburg* tragedy. The airship was also a painting on an otherwise clear sheet of glass. To film the dirigible passing over the city, the effects crew moved this sheet of glass across the painting of New York. This shot was characteristic of much of Whitlock's expense-saving work: without time-consuming mattes or models with intricate wire rigging, he devised a relatively simple method of film a completely convincing illusion.

An especially convincing detail was developed by Whitlock and his crew to enhance the realism of some of the flight sequences created by traveling mattes. When the blue-screen process was used, the procedure for matting in the moving airship against a separately filmed background was fairly routine. What Whitlock and his assistants were able to do was add a third layer of dimension to the scene by simulating clouds passing across the front of the dirigible. By shooting artificial clouds against black velvet, he came up with footage showing white vapor against a completely black background. Whitlock then made a reverse print of this film to create a strip of film of a black cloud against a clear background. During the filming of the airship, the footage of black, opaque clouds was positioned in a bipack arrangement in front of the unexposed roll of film. The opaque shapes blocked out all light in the areas in which they appeared. The unexposed film thus recorded the image of the airship with "holes" corresponding to the clouds. The original footage of the clouds could then be printed onto the film of the airship to fill these holes in the picture.

For the final scenes of the *Hindenburg* going up in flames, director Robert Wise felt that no Hollywood concoction could compare with the newsreel footage of the actual disaster. The use of the on-the-scene film of the tragedy made *The Hindenburg* both unusual and especially gruesome. The problem with using the original 1937 black-and-white newsreel footage was finding a way to blend it into an otherwise color movie. At first technicians tried tinting the black-and-white film to match the color footage of the rest of the picture, but the results looked fake. Wise felt that audiences were too familiar with the black-and-white *Hindenburg* newsreel to accept a doctored version. Instead new footage of stunts and effects was inserted into the newsreel to conform to the original black-and-white tones. The transition from color to black-and-white was made at the moment when the saboteur's bomb explodes. The explosion was shown in a brilliant white flash that covered the entire screen. After this flash removed all color from the screen, the horrible consequences of the explosion were seen in the original black and white.

Another man-made disaster was the highlight of John Frankenheimer's *Black Sunday,* in which a Vietnam veteran carries out a scheme by Palestinian terrorists to blow up Miami Stadium during the Super Bowl. The Goodyear blimp is loaded with a massive charge of explosives and piloted into the stadium by the ex-marine, played by a characteristically crazed Bruce Dern. The low-flying blimp topples a huge light-standard and puts the entire stadium audience into panicked flight, but the explosives are not detonated among the enormous crowd of helpless spectators. The police manage to hook up a helicopter to the blimp and haul it out of the stadium and over the Atlantic Ocean, where the explosion harms no one. *Black Sunday* was the most suspenseful of the disaster pictures because, for once, there was some uncertainty about how the movie would end.

The effects technique that enabled the *Black Sunday* crew to film the dangerous-looking action sequences in the well-supervised safety of a studio was front projection. When the Goodyear blimp is seen approaching a group of spectators from behind, the actors were nowhere near an actual airship. The separately filmed blimp was projected onto a screen behind the performers. Since the plate was projected from the front, the blimp looked as bright and vivid as the live action taking place before it. Also situated on the live-action set was the specially rigged light-standard. When the image of the blimp reached the point at which it seemed to come into contact with this structure, the standard was collapsed by the mechanical-effects crew. The most thrilling moment in the movie, however, is the shot of Robert Shaw clinging precariously to the top of the blimp as it hovers high above Miami. Though the scene makes

Shaw look like an aerial daredevil, it was actually shot entirely indoors. The actor was stretched out on top of a thirty-foot section of the blimp. Behind him a dizzying bird's-eye view of the city was front-projected onto a sixty-foot screen.

Front projection was also used in the scenes filmed with a small-scale model of the blimp, which had to be agile enough to dive and swerve. Generally aerial miniatures are manipulated by a complex system of wires. But rather than risk exposing the wires in front of the background plate, an ingenious alternate method was devised for operating the model. The miniature was manipulated by a rod inserted through the background screen. Since the miniature was between the camera and the rod, the model concealed its means of operation. (A similar technique was used to suspend Christopher Reeve before a front projection screen in the 1978 production of *Superman.*)

Although *Black Sunday* may have been the most exciting of the disaster movies, it turned out to be a disappointment at the box office. By 1977 the enthusiasm for movie catastrophes was already a thing of the past. *Black Sunday* supplied some interesting variations on the disaster theme, but the market was no longer there. Instead audiences in 1977 were becoming fascinated by a very different sort of special-effects magic in films like *Star Wars* and *Close Encounters of the Third Kind.* Although the writing was on the wall, Irwin Allen tried a story about a devastating army of bees in *The Swarm* (1978) with little success, while even worse box office results were in store for *Beyond the Poseidon Adventure* (1979) and *Concorde—Airport '79,* which tried to restore life to the dying genre by using highly advanced, computer-directed cameras for its effects. In one of the more suicidal moves ever made by a motion-picture studio, American International Pictures decided that 1979 was the perfect time to release a $20-million disaster epic called *Meteor,* which completely fizzled when it hit the theaters. With social, economic, and political problems growing worse every day, there were so many real-life disasters around that moviegoers apparently didn't want to spend their money to see more. Rather, they began to crave other, more comforting, or at least more distracting illusions—movies that would take them as far away from the real world as possible. And as always, Hollywood was only too happy to oblige.

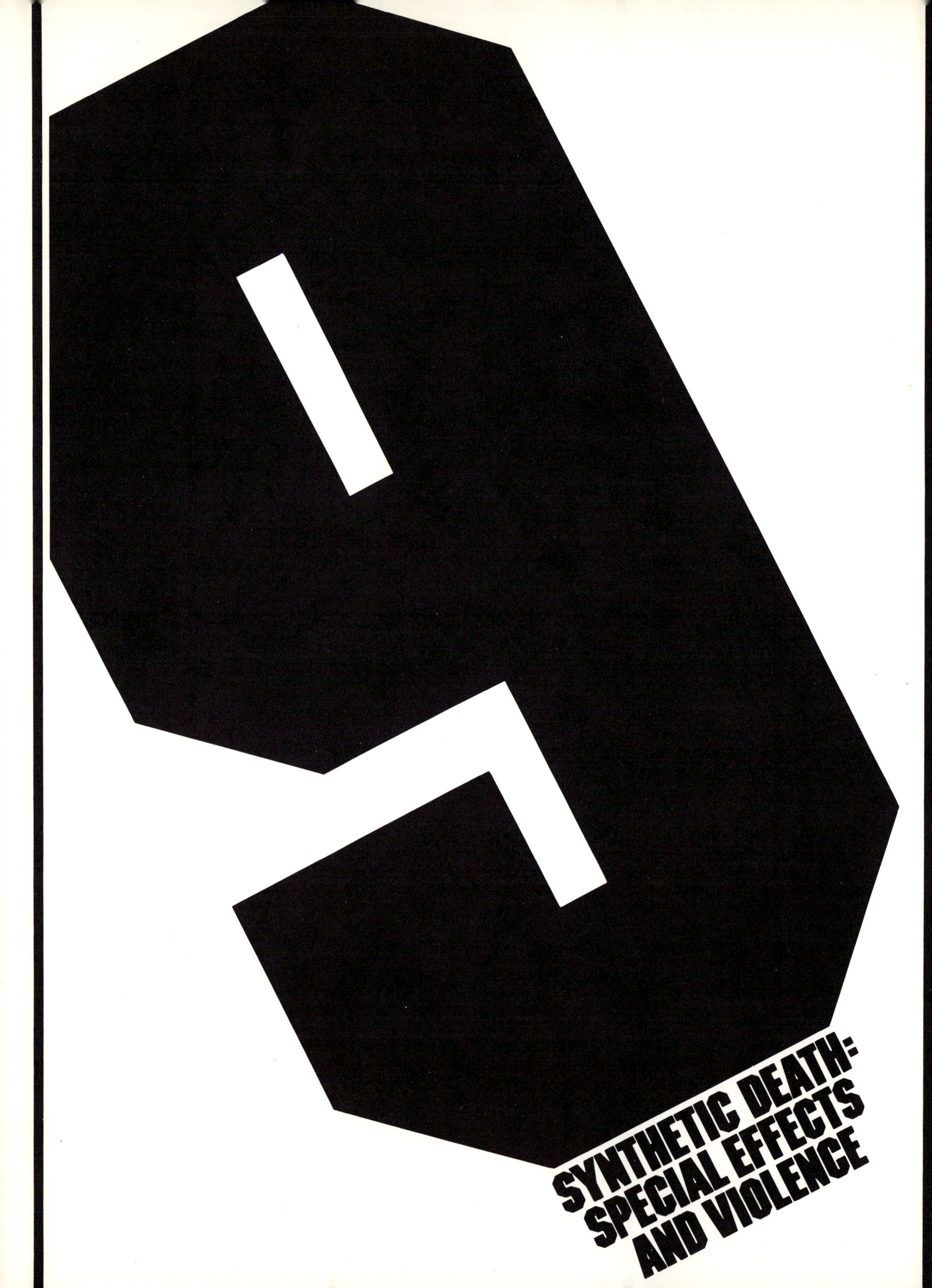
9
SYNTHETIC DEATH:
SPECIAL EFFECTS
AND VIOLENCE

It is a regrettable but inescapable fact that throughout history, torture and violence have been popular forms of entertainment. In ancient Rome gladiators butchered each other for the delectation of the crowd, while medieval peasants enjoyed nothing better than a juicy public execution. In her bestselling history of the fourteenth century, *A Distant Mirror,* Barbara Tuchman describes the citizens of the French village of Mons, who "bought a criminal from a neighboring town so that they should have the pleasure of seeing him quartered." The situation was no better in Elizabethan England. The same people who attended a performance of *Hamlet* one day might spend the next watching the public torture of a criminal convicted of high treason. For starters, the traitor would be hung from a scaffold. "Before he was unconscious," reports Shakespearean scholar G. B. Harrison, "he was cut down, his parts and entrails were cut out and burned on a fire, the body was then dismembered and dipped into boiling tar, and the pieces were displayed in various parts of the city." Public executions have always been a big draw, even in our own country. During the nineteenth century, the multiple hangings staged by Isaac Parker, the West's infamous "Hanging Judge," drew huge crowds of spectators. Therefore, if there is any consolation at all to be found in the orgies of violence that fill the movie screen today, it is that people will now settle for bloodshed that is faked and no longer demand to be entertained by the real thing.

The explicit simulation of violence, like most other forms of special effects, has its origin in stage trickery. The theater was spiced with gory effects as early as the sixteenth century. In *The Spanish Tragedy* by Thomas Kyd, a character named Hieronimo bites off his own tongue rather than divulge information to his enemies. As performed on the Elizabethan stage, this horrifying act was simulated with a piece of raw liver, which the actor kept concealed inside his mouth until the moment came for him to deliver his final lines; he then pretended to bite down hard and spat out the bloody hunk of meat.

When movies were invented, they were quick to appeal to the public's taste for violence. The Edison Company titillated viewers with *The Execution of Mary, Queen of Scots* in 1893, while Méliès's films are packed with comical beheadings and dismemberments. D. W. Griffith includes a graphic (if patently phony) decapitation shot in the Babylonian segment of *Intolerance* (1916), when one of the defending soldiers has his head sliced off by an enemy swordsman during the siege of the city.

The potential of film to create truly shocking images of violence, however, was not really demonstrated until 1928, when Luis Buñuel and Salvador Dali collaborated on the surrealistic movie *Un Chien Andalou,* which opens with one of the most unnerving scenes ever filmed. We see a man in a room, sharpening a straight razor. He strolls out onto the terrace and glances up at the evening sky. A thin cloud passes in front of the moon, cutting across its center. Suddenly the man approaches a seated woman from behind. While she sits motionlessly, he reaches around her head, separates the lids of her left eye with his fingers, and, in extreme close-up, brings the razor around and slices through her eyeball, which oozes thick, gelatinous fluid. It is difficult enough to watch this scene once; the viewer who can manage to sit through it a second time will notice that there is a quick cut at the last moment from the woman's eye to the eye of an animal, actually a dead cow. Knowing this, however, does little to blunt the shock of the image. Buñuel and Dali's intention to assault the audience with deeply disturbing images dredged up from the unconscious was more than fully realized.

Mercifully the extreme artistic notions of Buñuel and Dali were not widely shared by other filmmakers. Consequently *Un Chien Andalou* is an exception in the early history of film. In Hollywood, filmmakers were concerned with attracting moviegoers, not repelling them. Hollywood movies abounded with violence, but until relatively recently, the constant shootings and stabbings onscreen were largely devoid of gore. When a Western badman was gunned down by Gary Cooper in the middle of a frontier street, the special-effects man wasn't called upon to create gaping entrance wounds or spurts of blood; the villain simply grimaced and fell down. A good director could give such scenes great dramatic impact, but Hollywood violence remained relatively innocent for a long time of the nasty physical details of death and mutilation.

The most spectacular violence in the films from Hollywood's golden age of the twenties through the forties was featured in war movies. In order to depict combat on an epic scale, special-effects men were kept busy engineering explosions and staging sea battles and dogfights. Although death and destruction were common in these war movies, the violence was not very realistic, since war tended to be portrayed as a glamorous, swashbuckling adventure. Hollywood's notion of war as a stage for derring-do was perhaps best exemplified by those films emphasizing aerial battles between fighter planes. In such dogfight pictures as the 1930 and 1938 versions of *The Dawn Patrol,* handsome pilots took their places inside airplane cockpits like medieval knights mounting their chargers to do honorable battle against an adversary. The World War I fighter planes looped and spun gracefully through the air in a stylized joust in which no one was afraid to die heroically. What these battles lacked in gritty realism they made up for in excitement. Intricately choreographed scenes were staged by special-effects men with small-scale models of the planes manipulated by wires and full-scale mock-ups of the cockpits. An actor would sit inside a partially constructed cockpit, aiming his machine gun and firing blanks at the image of an enemy aircraft rolling and diving on the rear-projection screen set up in front of him.

During World War II, propaganda considerations allowed makers of war movies to film slightly more intense scenes of violence. Movies about the war in the Pacific, for instance, could show the Japanese doing terrible things to people in order to demonstrate how loathsome the enemy was; American soldiers could then be shown doing away with Japanese in a fairly grisly manner because that's what the "yellow-bellies" clearly deserved. This new patriotic vehemence can be seen in a film like *Flying Tigers* (1942), in which John Wayne and his fellow fighter pilots display an uncanny ability to aim their machine guns in such a way that the bullets always manage to strafe a Japanese pilot's face. The enemy pilots reflexively grab their faces while blood oozes through their fingers. The actors playing the Japanese pilots held blood capsules and made the fluid appear by breaking the capsules as they smacked their hands against their faces.

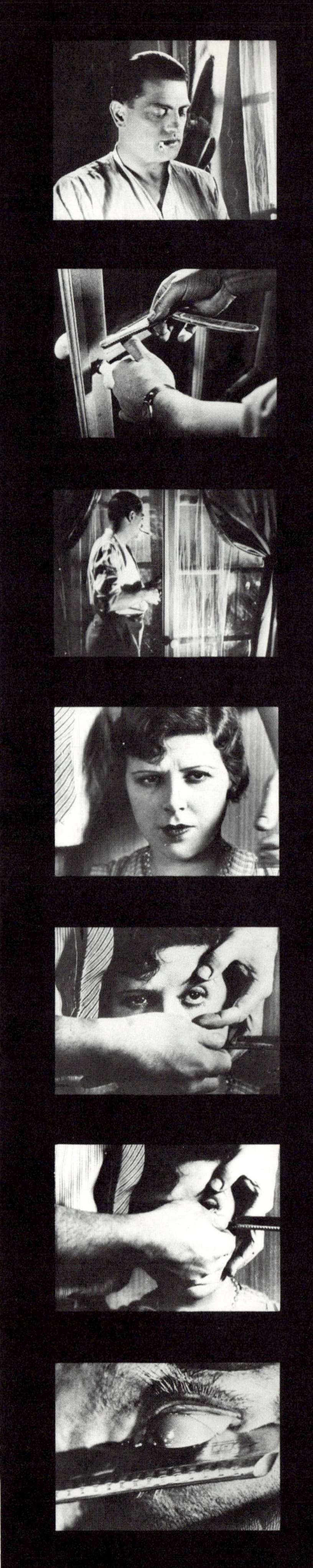

Flying Tigers was also memorable for some of the most exciting dogfight sequences ever staged for a Hollywood film. The effects were handled by the brothers Howard and Theodore Lydecker, the men responsible for the many explosions and miniature effects seen in the Republic cliff-hanger serials. In *Flying Tigers* they made use of what became known as the Lydecker method for manipulating airplane models, which involved moving the models along wires running through each wing. The miniatures were propelled either by force of gravity or by pulling the wires away from each other at the rear to shoot the airplane forward. The flight sequences are so convincing that it's hard to believe no actual airplanes were used, not even for the full-scale action on the ground. The Lydeckers' contributions to *Flying Tigers* earned them a nomination for the 1942 Special-Effects Oscar, although the Academy nominating committee was skeptical about their work. According to Theodore Lydecker, the committee thought the brothers were lying when they said there were no real planes in the film. Although the Oscar that year went to Farciot Edouart, Gordon Jennings, William Pereira, and Louis Mesenkop for *Reap the Wild Wind,* the Lydeckers must have taken some consolation from knowing that their work was so good that the Academy committee was fooled into mistaking it for the real thing.

The famous eye-slitting sequence from *Un Chien Andalou.*

Despite the occasional spattering of blood in the movies of World War II, war films of the early forties were not substantially different from previous combat movies in their presentation of violence. Just as *The Dawn Patrol* romanticized killing with swashbuckling depictions of warfare, *Flying Tigers* softened the impact of its most graphic scenes by wrapping death in the American flag. The first dramatic turning point in Hollywood violence was a short scene in the classic Western of 1953, *Shane.*

For many years the Western did more than any other movie genre to perpetuate a clean-cut, romanticized view of violence in general and gunplay in particular. Countless actors have bitten the dust on the Hollywood range, but few of these deaths were alarming in any way. When a bad guy was shot point-blank, he would grab his stomach, stagger forward, and die as melodramatically as the director would allow. The killing of Elisha Cook, Jr. in *Shane,* on the other hand, is shockingly brutal. Jack Palance played the slimy, black-clad gunfighter hired by the ranchers to frighten off stubborn homesteaders. Outside the town's lone seedy saloon Palance singles out Elisha Cook as his first victim. The hired gun taunts Cook until the homesteader can see no way out except to defend himself. The pathetically mismatched Cook is easily outdrawn by the cold-blooded gunman. Instead of falling forward to the ground, as was the custom in previous Westerns, Cook is lifted off his feet by the terrible impact of the heavy slugs and is thrown back into the mud. To show Cook hurled back by the gunfire, effects men rigged the actor with an invisible wire and tugged backward. For the first time the devastating force of a large-caliber bullet was dramatically portrayed on the movie screen.

Other techniques in the depiction of violence were developed soon after *Shane,* but for the most part they were not found in films made in the United States. The most graphic scenes of mayhem came from Japan, where audiences were ahead of the rest of the world in their taste for cinematic bloodshed. For many years the standard procedure for the worldwide distribution of such violent pictures as Hammer horror films and Spaghetti Westerns was to release the tamest edition of the movie in Great Britain, a more violent version for the United States, and the bloodiest version for Japan. During the fifties and early sixties, Japanese filmmakers explored new ways of killing people on the screen in what was their answer to the American Western, the samurai movie.

Akira Kurosawa's *Seven Samurai* (1954) was the epic adventure story that later served as the basis for the popular American Western *The Magnificent Seven* (1960). *Seven Samurai* was influential not only for its storyline but also because it was the first movie to feature a slow-motion death. Early in the film two swordsmen square off for a duel. When the fatal slash is delivered, the loser's final moment is prolonged by slow motion, a technique that forces the viewer to confront a powerful image of death. In a 1962 film called *Sanjuro* Kurosawa staged a much more shocking death. At the climax of the movie the hero (played by Toshiro Mifune) crosses swords with an enemy and drives his blade into the man's neck. The villain's jugular vein is cut, and a geyser of blood (supplied by concealed tubing) jets from his throat. These two techniques pioneered by Kurosawa, slow-motion death and spurting blood, were to become the key elements in the elaborate, effects-created violence that became extremely popular in the United States in the late sixties.

The explosion of graphic violence in American movies began in 1967, at the height of the Vietnam War. Nearly every night Americans saw men, women, and children maimed and slaughtered on the six o'clock news. The horrifying newsreels made it impossible for people to accept conventional tidy movie deaths. At the same time there was a sudden widespread hunger for increased cinematic violence, as if the nightmares produced by a particularly horrific war could somehow be purged if they were projected onto a screen and shaped into art. Exactly what influence the Vietnam War had on America's moviegoing tastes cannot be precisely measured, but the popularity of such films as *Bonnie and Clyde* (1967) and *The Wild Bunch* (1969) clearly indicates that movie audiences became fascinated by explicit gore shortly after the United States became embroiled in that brutal and widely televised conflict.

The movie that spearheaded the trend in explicit violence was *Bonnie and Clyde.* In the final scene Warren Beatty and Faye Dunaway are torn to pieces by a barrage of gunfire; the bullets riddle their bodies as they bounce and thrash about in horribly graceful slow motion. In this hypnotic dance of death the special-effects device known as the *squib* came into its own. A squib is a small cartridge encased in either paper or plastic. The black powder inside the cartridge can be detonated either by wires connected to some form of remote control or by a battery secured to the body of the actor wearing the squib. In *Bonnie and Clyde,* me-

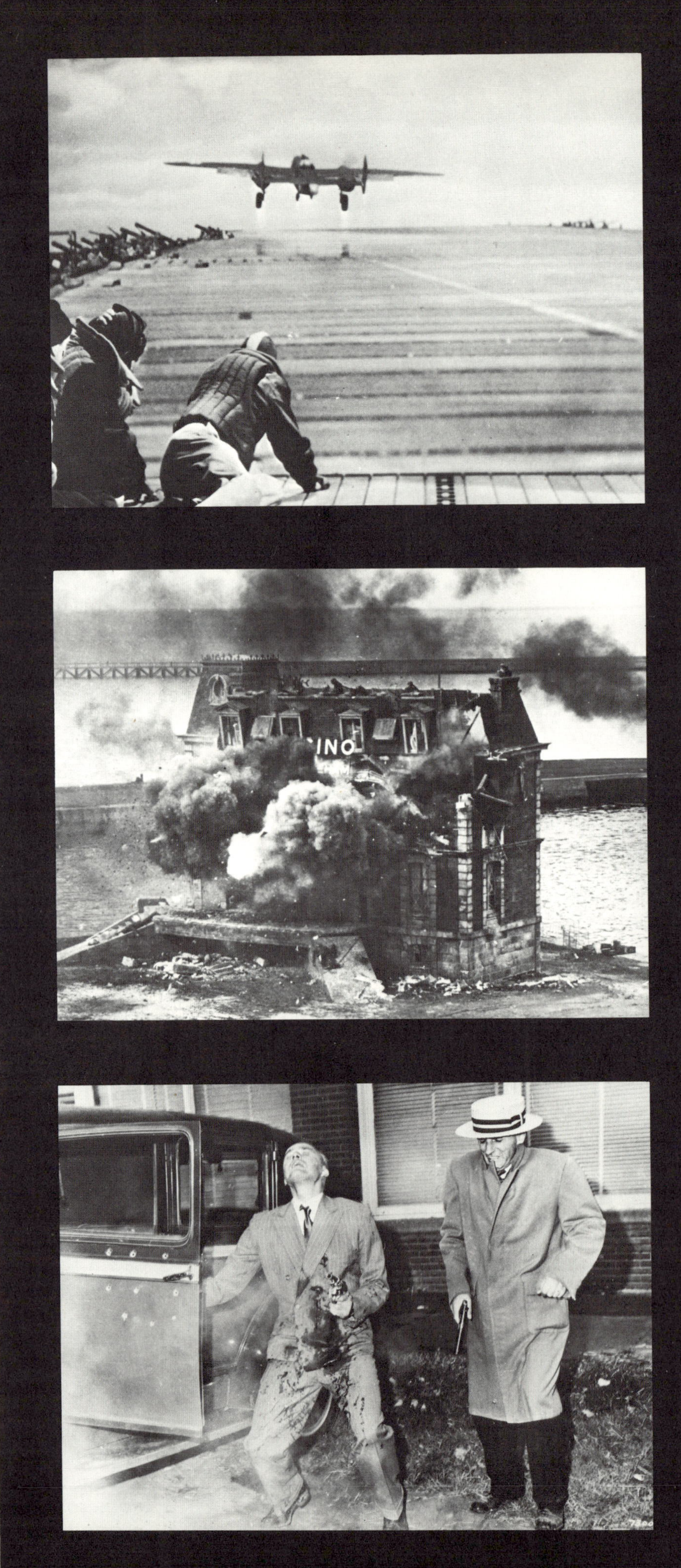

Top: The actors in this exciting scene from *Thirty Seconds Over Tokyo* are kneeling, not on the deck of an aircraft carrier, but on the floor of the studio soundstage, in front of a rear-projection screen. *Center:* Cinematic explosions come in all sizes. A large charge of explosives was used to create this dramatic scene from *The Longest Day*. *Bottom:* The graphic gunshot wounds that filled the screen in the 1970s, on the other hand, were done with tiny charges known as "bullet hits." From *Dillinger*.

chanical-effects man Danny Lee attached the squibs to the clothes and skin of Beatty and Dunaway by placing the cartridge on a small metal plate and securing a layer of foam rubber between the plate and the stars' bodies as a cushion. When the squib was detonated, the small explosion looked like the impact of a bullet, an effect that is usually referred to by technicians as a *bullet hit.*

Two years later, in 1969, Sam Peckinpah added some gruesome variations to the techniques used in *Bonnie and Clyde.* Peckinpah's masterpiece, *The Wild Bunch,* begins and ends with extended, horribly bloody gun battles. In slow motion the outlaw-heroes, their enemies, and innocent bystanders are pulverized by bullets that unleash cascading splatters of blood. As in *Bonnie and Clyde,* squibs played a central part in these large-scale slaughters. To add spurting blood to the explosive bullet hits, *The Wild Bunch* special-effects man Bud Hulburd attached condoms filled with fake blood to the top of the squibs. When the squibs exploded, the fluid splattered outward as if erupting from a bullet wound. These blood spurts were so rhythmically edited into the carefully choreographed slow-motion sequences that Peckinpah's gunfights came to be characterized as "blood ballets."

If in 1953 *Shane* chipped away at the movie myth of glamorous Western violence by showing a realistic shooting, the slow-motion bloodbaths of *The Wild Bunch* in 1969 completely exploded the myth and started a new fashion in grisly Western violence. In 1970 *Soldier Blue,* a Western with a distinctly Vietnam War-era sensibility, put the Indian Wars into a gory new perspective. In most Cavalry-versus-Indians pictures made before 1970, the most disturbing act of violence was the sight of an arrow piercing the back of a soldier. This effect was often performed by shooting a hollow arrow along a wire by compressed air. At the end of the wire, the arrow landed in a cork padding backed by a metal plate worn by the actor underneath his shirt. Violence of this sort would have attracted no attention at all in *Soldier Blue,* which featured a wide variety of bullet hits and blood spurts and was highlighted by a horrible onscreen decapitation in which a horse soldier rides up to an Indian woman and slices her head off with his saber. The scene was filmed normally until the moment when the soldier neared the woman, at which point there was a cut to a shot of the soldier slashing at a dummy of the squaw.

Bizarre, ritualized violence was depicted in great detail in the 1970 Western *A Man Called Horse.* In order to be initiated into a tribe of Sioux Indians, Richard Harris, in the role of an English aristocrat, must undergo the ordeal of the Sun Vow ceremony. Two hooks, each attached to a cord, are pierced into Harris's chest. The Englishman is then slowly raised off the ground by the two cords, the hooks pulling on his pectorals. As in the case of many explicitly gory effects, this scene was made possible by the makeup man. Makeup artist John Chambers constructed a false chest to be worn over Harris's real one. It was this artificial chest that was pierced and stretched by the hooks. The makeup work was so expert that it was impossible to see that a false appliance had been used. (Chambers's talent for simulating highly authentic body parts was originally developed during World War II, when he made prosthetic parts out of plastic and rubber for disfigured veterans.)

Cinematic gore was very popular in 1970. In addition to the atrocities seen in *Soldier Blue* and *A Man Called Horse,* grotesque gags were the highlights of Mike Nichols's big-budget black comedy, *Catch-22.* At one point in the film a soldier, sunbathing on a wooden raft on the Italian coast, begins jumping up and down to attract the attention of a buddy of his who is piloting a low-flying plane. The plane swoops down and accidentally slices the soldier in half. The top part of his body explodes in a shower of flesh and blood while his legs remain standing by themselves. Then they slowly collapse and fall into the water.

Two different techniques were used in the filming of this wildly violent scene. The actual severing of the body along the waistline was done with a specially constructed breakaway figure of the actor, equipped with hydraulic pumps to gush blood when the dummy was hit by the plane. For the second part of the effect, an actor held a sheet of a highly reflective material known as Scotchlite in front of himself. The Scotchlite had a handle attached to the back, which allowed the actor to hold it up like a shield in front of the top half of his body. The actor was standing against a bright, sunlit sky, and since the Scotchlite also reflected the sky, his upper torso was invisible to the camera; only his legs could be seen. He then went through his motions and fell into the water. At a certain point, as he tumbled backwards, the gimmick became visible, so effects man Al Whitlock simply matted out the unwanted parts of the scene during postproduction work.

The most shocking moment in *Catch-22* occurs near the end, when Yossarian (Alan Arkin), kneeling in his plane, tears open the shirt of his wounded tailgunner and the man's entrails spill out onto the floor in a slimy mound. This horrifying scene was achieved by very simple means: a fake chest was built for the actor and filled with animal offal.

Graphic violence reached a new peak of popularity in 1972 in Francis Ford Coppola's phenomenally successful *The Godfather.* The two men responsible for the gory gangland slayings in this blockbuster were mechanical effects man A. D. Flowers and makeup artist Dick Smith. The same bullet-hit techniques popularized by *Bonnie and Clyde* and *The Wild Bunch* were used to stage James Caan's grisly execution by machine-gun fire. A more unusual and highly ingenious effect appears in the scene in which the sleazy, nearsighted owner of a Las Vegas hotel is shot through the eye while getting a rubdown. The key to the sequence was a specially constructed pair of horn-rimmed glasses worn by the actor. One of the stems of the glasses housed two plastic tubes aimed at the adjacent lens. At the moment the character was supposed to be hit by the bullet, a small ball bearing was shot through one of the tubes at high speed. The ball bearing broke the glass to simulate the shattering of the lens by the bullet. The tiny steel pellet moved so fast that it couldn't be seen on the screen. And the effect was designed with great care to ensure that all of the glass broke outward instead of toward the actor's eye. Immediately after the glass broke, blood was pumped through the second tube and down the actor's face. The effect was one of the most startling and realistic in the movie.

As the film's makeup man, Dick Smith handled the simulated wounds that appeared directly on the actors' skin. One of his effects appears in the scene in which Al Pacino shoots Sterling Hayden through the forehead at a restaurant table. First Smith applied a squib on a metal plate to Hayden's forehead. For the usual body hit, a condom filled with blood could easily be concealed by covering it with clothing. Since Smith's effect took place on bare skin, there was no way to hide such a bulky device. Instead Smith covered the plate with foam rubber, making sure to leave a small air pocket between the squib and the rubber appliance. Using a hypodermic needle Smith then injected some blood into the pocket and touched up the forehead with makeup to conceal his preparations. When the squib exploded, the foam rubber burst open and the blood flowed freely out of Hayden's forehead.

Although this technique produced realistic results, Smith considered it a crude approach. Since the method involved a squib explosion, as much as an hour and a half was needed to clean up the mess and to replace the exploded foam rubber for a second take of the scene. In Coppola's *The Godfather, Part II* (1974) and Martin Scorsese's *Taxi Driver* (1976) Smith refined his technique so that it could be performed without the squib. Instead he used a removable plug which corresponded to the bullet hole and allowed the blood to flow out.

For this new technique Smith began by creating a false forehead from a mold of the actor's brow. He made the forehead appliance out of acrylic plastic, which, unlike foam rubber, doesn't absorb liquids. Next he placed a greased piece of latex over the acrylic plastic, positioning the latex so that it extended from the spot corresponding to the bullet hole up to the hairline. He then placed a second acrylic forehead on top of the first, sandwiching the latex in between. In this way the greased latex could be slipped out from the top of the appliance to create a flat cavity between the two layers of acrylic. After cutting out the bullet hole in the top plastic forehead, Smith inserted a tube into the cavity. The plastic forehead was applied to the actor, a plug attached to a monofilament fishing line was placed in the bullet hole, and the entire appliance was concealed with makeup. The impact of the bullet was simulated by pumping blood through the tube in the cavity while the plug was yanked out by the monofilament. The blood flowed out of the bullet hole realistically and the whole operation could be repeated with little waste of time, since the cavity and the tubing were still intact and the acrylic plastic hadn't absorbed any of the blood. After the blood was wiped away and the plug reinserted, the actor was ready for the next take.

This technique was further refined when Smith developed a method which didn't require a monofilament and consequently eliminated the danger of the wire showing on film. Using acrylic plastic once again, he created two concealed passageways through the forehead appliance. Air from a compressed air tank was shot through one passageway to disengage the plug while blood was pumped through the second passageway to provide the flow from the bullet hole.

For the gory conclusion of *Taxi Driver* Smith had the opportunity to stage other gruesome effects besides the standard bullet-hole illusion. At one point in the whorehouse shootout, Robert De Niro fires at a thug with a .44 Magnum and blows off the top half of the man's hand, including all four fingers. Smith's first idea was to rig a fake hand and pull off the top half with a wire, but the nature of the location ruled out this approach. The scene was shot in a narrow apartment house hallway, which left no room to hide an operator to yank off the hand. Smith's alternate solution was to blow up the top of the hand. He first constructed a stump of the hand from the middle of the palm down to the wrist. Inside were three tubes to spurt blood. The top half of the dummy hand was made of wax and contained an inner cavity in which blood and squibs were concealed. The two halves were attached, the stump half was placed over the actor's clenched fist, and the tubing and the squibs were hooked up. The squibs blew the wax section of the hand to pieces and the tubing inside the stump supplied the jets of blood.

As a result of all the carnage in *Taxi Driver,* censors threatened to slap an undesirable X rating on the film. To ensure an R rating, and consequently a larger audience for the movie, the makers of the film arrived at an unusual solution. Linwood Dunn was hired to doctor the gory scenes optically in order to "desaturate" the blood by giving it a subdued brownish tint instead of the original vivid red. This change in blood tone did the trick; it made the movie seem more acceptable to the censors.

By the time of *Taxi Driver*'s release, a peculiar development had taken place in the depiction of graphic violence in the movies. Originally, in such films as *Bonnie and Clyde,* the vivid representation of violence was a realistic reaction to the traditional, romanticized vision of death in earlier Hollywood movies. But by the mid-seventies the new "realistic" violence had, in some cases, become so extreme that it was just as fanciful as the old Hollywood mayhem. The once-shocking massacres staged by Sam Peckinpah began to seem tame as filmmakers competed to see who could pump the greatest quantity of blood out of a superficial shoulder wound. Although it was a powerful film, *Taxi Driver* contributed to this unlikely exaggeration of movie violence. Robert De Niro's opponents are hit with the overwhelming force of a bullet fired from a .44 Magnum and yet they keep on coming in order to provide more excuses for spectacular blood-spurts.

Although he has engineered some of the most explicit scenes of violence in recent movies, Dick Smith is no defender of cinematic gore and finds current blood-filled extravaganzas to be especially indefensible. Recently Smith explained his position: *I'm actually very opposed to blood and gore and violence. I don't like to see it in films. As a matter of fact I almost quit* The Godfather, *because that was the first time I was asked to do that sort of realistic stuff and I had a dilemma about should I be a party to this or not. And frankly, money won out. I mean, it was a job, and I figured if I didn't do it, someone else would. The worst I've encountered is* The Sentinel, *which I found so distasteful that I have turned down that kind of film since then.*

In *The Sentinel* (1977) director Michael Winner asked Smith to create the effects for a scene in which a ghoul is slashed across the arm with a knife, hacked in the chest, stabbed in the eyeball, and, for good measure, has the tip of his nose sliced off—by his daughter. Working from a life-mask of the actor (Fred Stuthman), Smith created an astonishingly lifelike Fiberglas replica of the man's head. The tip of the nose and the area surrounding the left eye-socket were removed from this mask. Smith then replaced these parts with a nose-end and eye-plug made of molded gelatin, a material that lends itself to easy slicing.

Although Smith, as a make-up man and a viewer, may be put off by excessive onscreen violence, there are many moviegoers who are clearly attracted to it. The grotesque ghoul scene in *The Sentinel* is a light moment in comparison to such popular shock pictures as *The Last House on the Left* (1972) and *The Texas Chainsaw Massacre* (1974). Unlike such early violent epics as *Bonnie and Clyde,* these films had no artistic aspirations beyond making audiences feel as queasy as possible.

The trend toward highly sadistic exploitation movies (a genre of film which has come to be known as horror-pornography) began in this country in 1972 with the release of *Mark of the Devil,* a German picture about the evil exploits of a cruel witch-hunter. When this movie was shown in the United States, audiences were considerately issued vomit bags on their way into the theater. A small notice on this classy item assured the viewer that the movie was "Guaranteed to upset your stomach." To further entice the filmgoer, the bag also featured a murky still from the highlight of the movie, a scene in which a woman's tongue is graphically torn out of her mouth. Later on that year an American movie, *The Last House on the Left,* told the story of a group of sadists who torture and kill two teen-age girls and then are sadistically murdered themselves by the parents of one of the victims. In the newspaper advertisements for this film, the promoters warned viewers that in order

Make-up/effects artist Dick Smith creating the Fiberglas life mask of actor Fred Stuthman for the gory scene in *The Sentinel* in which a ghoul has his eye slashed and nose sliced off.

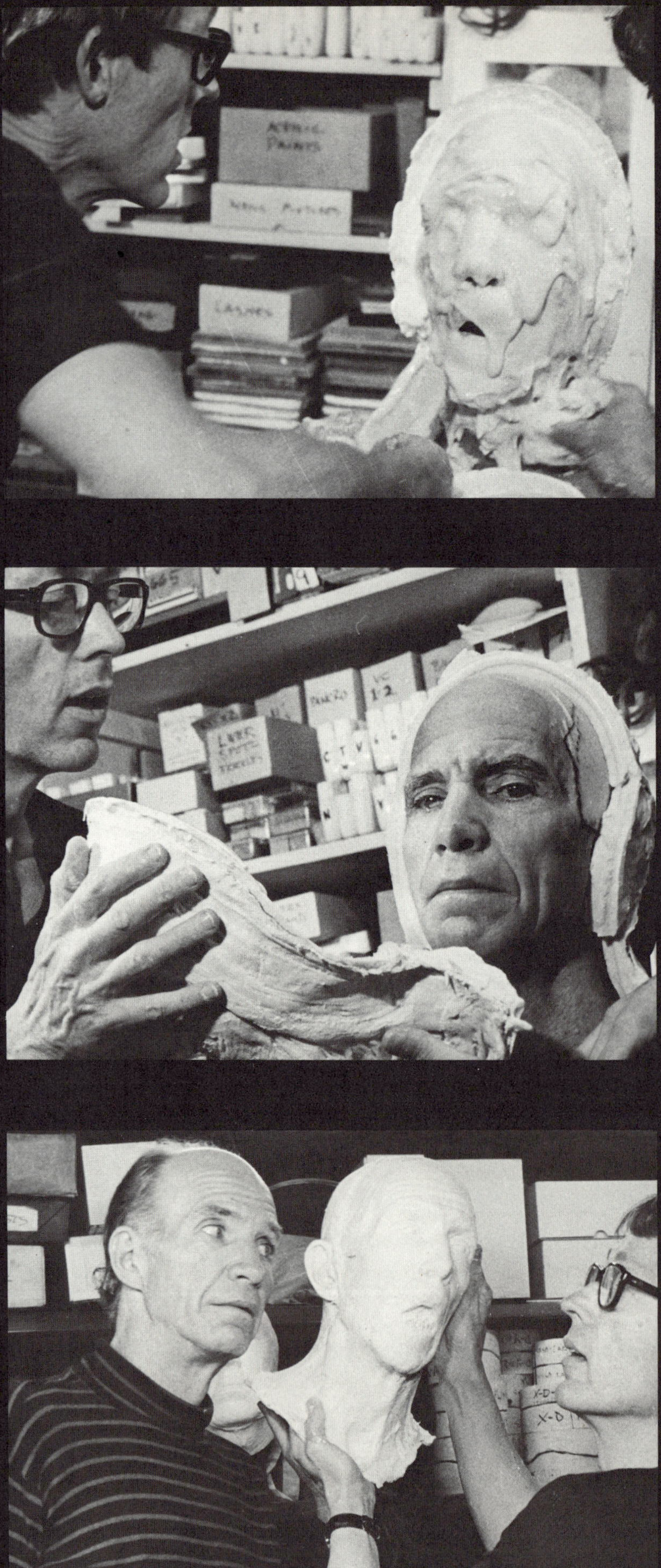

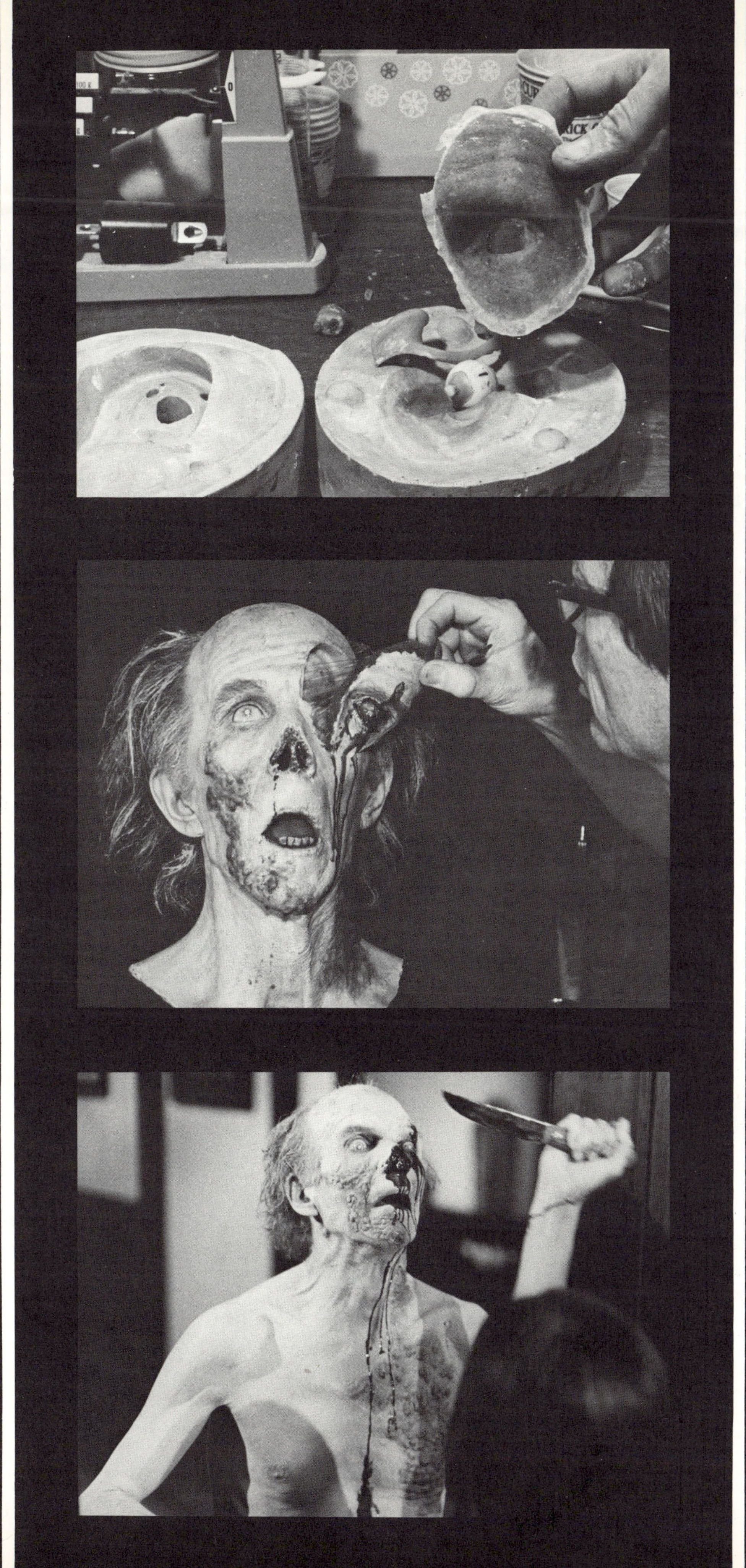

Top: The gelatin eye-plug being removed from its mold.
Center: Here, Smith removes the slashed eye-plug to replace it with a new one for a second take. The missing nose will also be replaced.
Bottom: Stuthman was filmed wearing matching makeup for some shots, which were edited together with close-ups of the mask.

to keep from fainting, they should constantly remind themselves, "It's only a movie, it's only a movie, it's only a movie. . . ." Audiences were understandably confused when the movie opened with a message informing them that the film they were about to see was based on fact. (Actually the film was a horror-porn remake of Ingmar Bergman's 1960 *The Virgin Spring.)*

The first of the horror-porn shock pictures to become a low-budget box office sensation was Tobe Hooper's *The Texas Chainsaw Massacre.* The movie was based on the multiple murders committed by a Wisconsin handyman in the late fifties, the same case that served as the basis for the novel *Psycho* by Robert Bloch. In Hooper's adaptation a group of teen-agers goes on a vacation in the Texas countryside, only to stumble upon a family of former slaughterhouse workers who have decorated their home with furniture made from bones and spare body parts. The most repulsive member of this unsavory clan is a character named Leatherface, an enormous man who wears a mask of dried human skin and communicates in piglike grunts. With his sledgehammer, meathook, and beloved chainsaw, Leatherface proceeds to turn the unlucky teen-agers into sides of human beef for the roadside barbecue stand operated by his brother.

The killings are all realistic and harrowing. Most of the gory special effects in *The Texas Chainsaw Massacre* appear in the chainsaw sequences. For some of the scenes, the teeth on the saw were filed down to a dull edge to minimize the danger involved in using a real chainsaw. In other scenes the blade could be taken off altogether, since it was spinning too fast to be seen. For the shots in which we see Leatherface slicing into a character's flesh, the sharp-toothed blade was used. The actor playing the victim was fitted with sheet metal over his body, on top of which was secured a raw steak and packets of blood. Clothing concealed the setup. Leatherface then actually sawed through the clothes and ripped apart real meat.

The Texas Chainsaw Massacre went to considerable lengths to establish itself as the most disgusting movie ever made, but five years later, in 1979, the insane violence of George Romero's *Dawn of the Dead* made Hooper's film seem practically restrained. *The Texas Chainsaw Massacre* was more realistic and consequently the more terrifying of the two pictures, but *Dawn of the Dead* was far more explicit in its depiction of spectacular gore.

George Romero first made a name for himself as the director of the cult horror film *Night of the Living Dead* (1968), which Pauline Kael has hailed as the greatest movie ever made in Pittsburgh. A low-budget black-and-white production, *Night of the Living Dead* did not feature many special effects, though it did contain a fair amount of Bosco chocolate syrup (used to simulate blood) and a nice assortment of animal entrails supplied by a friendly local butcher. The sequel to this movie, *Dawn of the Dead,* is the second part of a projected trilogy to be completed eventually by a third film called *Day of the Dead.* Unlike *The Texas Chainsaw Massacre, Dawn of the Dead* bears no relation to any actual event. When Romero was growing up in the fifties, he was a great fan of a line of comic books called EC Comics. Published by the same people who later went on to produce *Mad* magazine, these comics (*Tales from the Crypt, The Haunt of Fear, The Vault of Horror,* and several other titles) were filled with extravagant, highly explicit gore. A favorite recurring motif was the vengeful corpse that returns from the grave in an extreme state of decomposition to even the score with its murderer. *Dawn of the Dead,* which is about a small group of people fending off an army of cannibal zombies in a deserted suburban shopping mall, is a sort of cinematic EC horror comic—a strange, exuberant mixture of grotesque violence and buffoonery.

Early on in the film we learn a handy piece of information: the only way to kill a cannibal zombie is to destroy its brain. This premise allowed the filmmaker to indulge in some of the most sickening scenes of violence ever put onscreen. All of the outrageous effects in the film are performed in full view of the camera. One zombie's head is blown completely off his shoulders by shotgun fire; another zombie gets a screwdriver rammed into his ear; others bite chunks of flesh out of their victims, all in tight close-up.

Tom Savini, who created the bizarre gore in *Dawn of the Dead,* took up makeup as a hobby at the age of thirteen after seeing *Man of a Thousand Faces* (1957), a film biography of the great actor-makeup artist Lon Chaney. During the Vietnam War Savini became acquainted with real bloodshed first-hand while working as a combat photographer. In *Dawn of the Dead,* in which he served as special-effects man, makeup artist, stunt man, and actor, Savini established himself as the master of no-holds-barred cinematic violence.

When a man gets his head blown off by a trigger-happy commando in the movie's

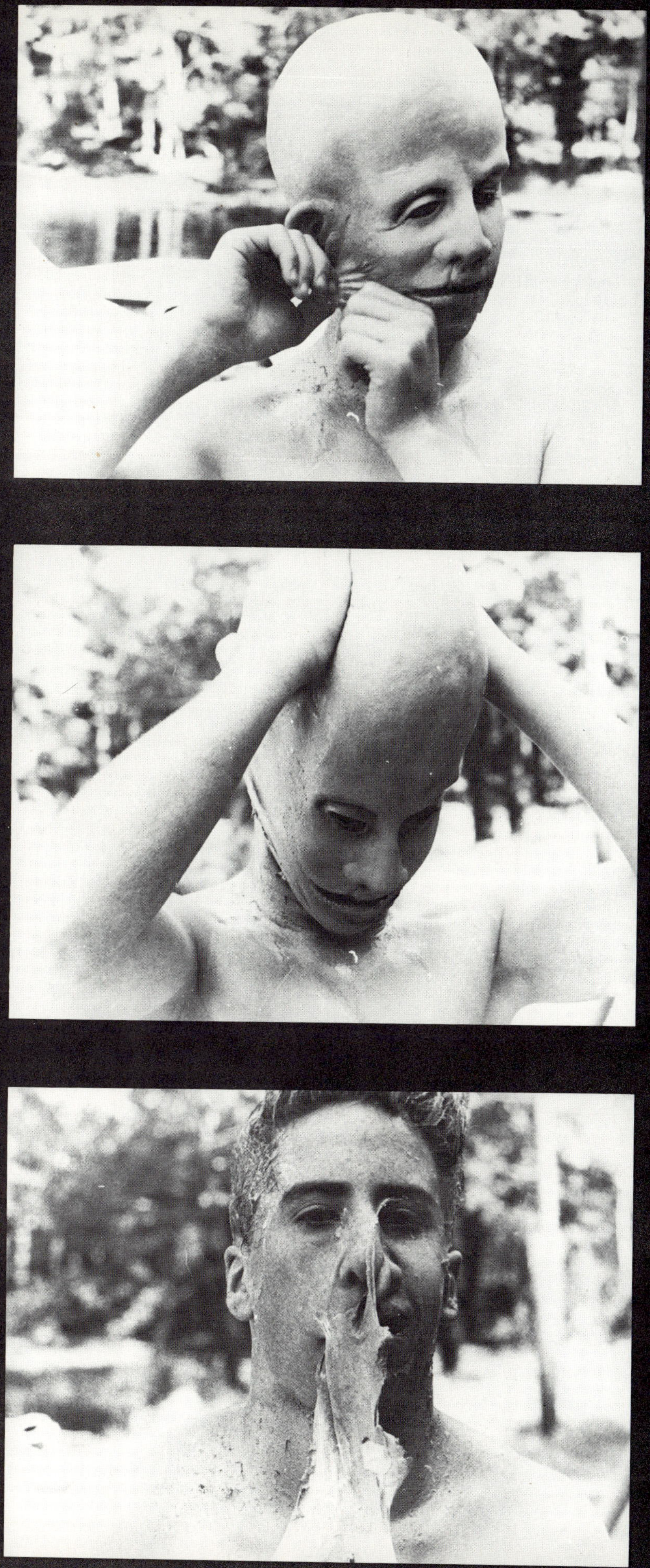

Actor Ari Lehman strips off the grotesque face mask (created by Tom Savini) that transformed him into Jason, the drowned child in the hit horror movie, *Friday the 13th*.

Top: A technician attaches a blood sack to the back of an actress playing a zombie in *Dawn of the Dead.* The sack will be covered by a jacket. When the "bullet hit"—the small explosive charge beneath the sack—is detonated, the blood will be blown out through the back of the jacket, simulating a gory exit wound. *Center:* In a gruesome scene in *Friday the 13th* a camp counselor lying in bed is killed when a murderer shoves an arrow up through his throat from beneath the mattress. *Bottom:* How the trick was done: The actor's head was resting on a foam latex neck constructed by makeup/effects artist Tom Savini.

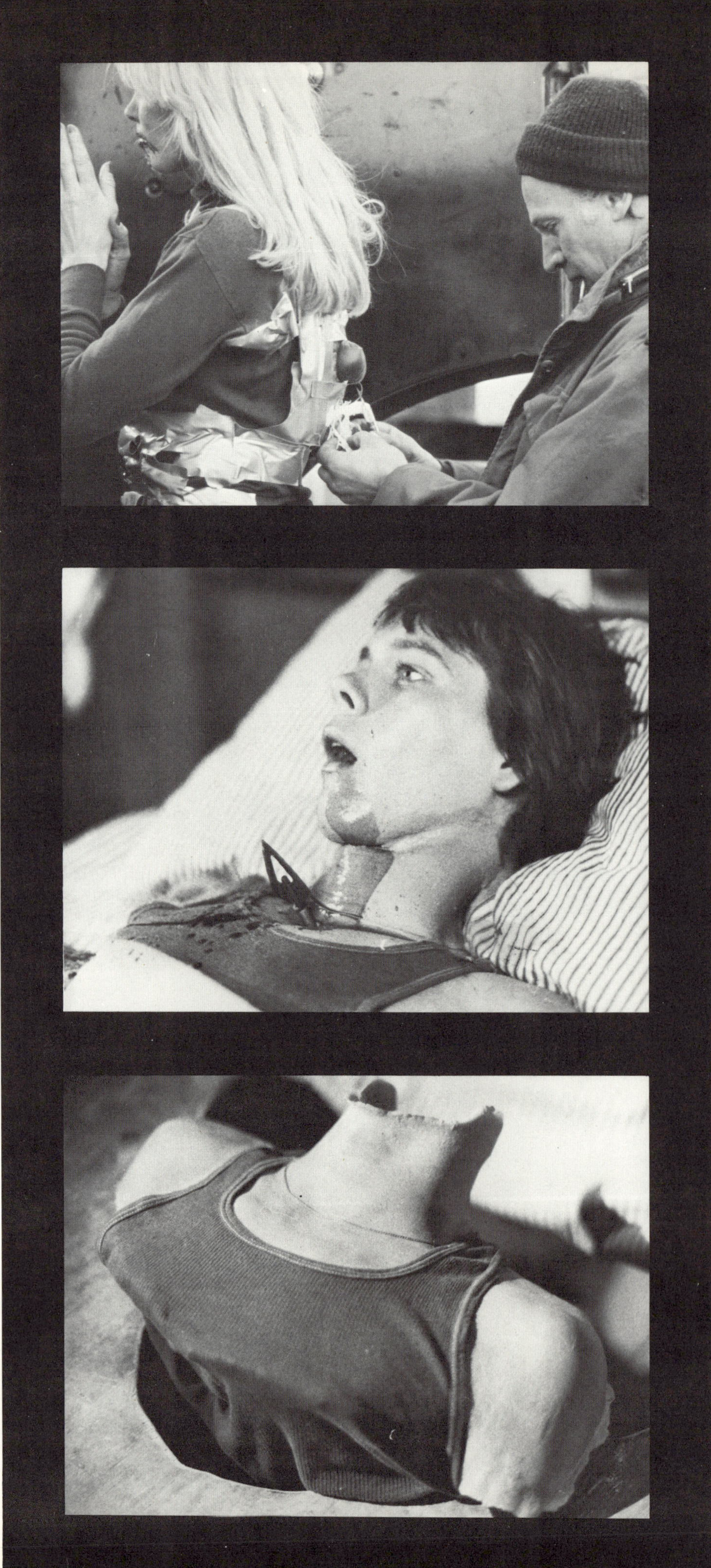

opening scene, the audience sees the victim from the waist up as the head explodes in a mess of blood and brains. Savini constructed an authentic-looking dummy (nicknamed "Boris") for this scene. Boris's head was made from a life-mask mold; plaster was used as a substitute for the skull while a latex covering gave the head a fleshlike appearance. Inside the false head were thirteen condoms filled with blood and other odd items, such as apple cores and corn chips, to supply some more bulk to the matter inside the skull. To explode the head, Savini actually fired a shotgun off-camera. By quickly cutting from the victim to the commando and then back to the dummy of the victim, Romero created the very unsettling impression that no trickery was involved at all.

From this bloody early moment on throughout the rest of the film, there is little let-up in the grotesque action. Soon after the head explosion, while the few remaining humans make their getaway in a helicopter, another zombie head gets equally rough treatment. As the helicopter starts, this creature staggers a little too close and a whirling blade slices off the top of his skull, sending yet another mess of blood and brains high into the air. This incredible feat was accomplished with a complex false section of the top of the zombie's head. Savini made this section out of foam latex and then divided it into five smaller pieces, each attached to a fishing line. This arrangement allowed the top of the head to be pulled off in pieces rather than in one fake-looking lump. Savini then fitted the entire section on top of the actor's head with artificial brain matter concealed inside and two lengths of surgical tubing running up the back of the actor's head. Since the actor had a low forehead, the build-up didn't look unnatural. The zombie was then filmed without the whirling helicopter blades in the picture. At the supposed moment of impact the head sections were yanked away by an offscreen operator, and Savini and an assistant pumped blood through the tubes from behind some onscreen crates. The helicopter blades were superimposed onto this footage later on. On the screen, the blades, the sailing top section of the head, and the jetting blood work in perfect coordination. The only flaw in the scene is the apparent shape of the zombie's skull. The false head section was a natural looking dome, but when a covering wig was applied, it wasn't slicked down properly. As a result the creature had a flattop, Frankensteinlike brow, which allows the viewer to predict, before the decapitation, that something is going to happen to the zombie's head.

Since the zombies can only be destroyed by rupturing the brain in some fashion, the head continues to be the primary focal point for violence throughout *Dawn of the Dead.* Near the end of the picture, a motorcycle gang clashes with the zombies inside the shopping mall. Savini, who appears in the movie as the sadistic leader of the bikers, does away with one of the zombies by sinking a machete halfway through the creature's skull. In this case a special prop was used instead of a special head. Savini took an ordinary machete and cut a semicircular chunk out of its blade that corresponded to the curve of the zombie's head. The effects man then fitted the machete over the head of the actor playing the zombie. When the cameras began to roll, Savini yanked the machete off quickly. The resulting footage was then printed in reverse so that the machete appears to be cleaving the zombie's skull. The action happens so fast that the hole in the blade is undetectable.

Later on in the film, one of the shopping mall zombies meets a particularly gruesome (if well-deserved) death when a policeman shoves a screwdriver into its ear and through its brain. Savini engineered this sequence with three screwdrivers and a soda straw. He cut the blade of one of the screwdrivers to half its length and another one much shorter. The soda straw was painted silver to match the color of the screwdriver's blades. First the audience sees the policeman pin the zombie to the floor and bring the full-size screwdriver toward the ear. In the next shot of the sequence the policeman slowly pushed the half-screwdriver into the silver straw, which was fitted into a wax appliance in the zombie's ear. As the handle got closer to the zombie's head, the blade appeared to be entering the ear, though it was actually going into the straw. For the final thrust of the instrument into the monster's brain, the smallest screwdriver was substituted. Tubing concealed inside the straw supplied the blood to complete the ghastly illusion.

When the zombies finally elude all these assaults on their brains and get their hands on a normal human, the violence becomes even more grisly. The cannibalistic monsters take chunks out of their victims with their teeth, the shredded flesh shown in nauseating detail. For a bite on the neck Savini made a cast of the neck of the actor playing the victim. Over this cast he applied a layer of clay and then made a mold of the clay-covered cast. When he formed a false neck from this mold and applied it to the actor, there was a space be-

Tom Savini with his creation "Boris." Boris's head was filled with blood sacks and artificial brain matter, then blown to pieces by a gunshot blast for a grisly scene in *Dawn of the Dead.*

tween the appliance and the actor's skin that corresponded to the built-up layer of clay. In this empty space he put some foam to substitute for a layer of flesh. The inside of the false neck was prepared with red paint and some tubing to supply blood. Savini then perforated the part of the neck to be bitten. This procedure served two purposes: when the zombie-actor bit this area, the perforation allowed the appliance to be ripped easily, and it made the false flesh come off in gruesome strips.

Tom Savini's work in *Dawn of the Dead* took cinematic gore to new blood-curdling extremes. More recently he has created equally ghastly effects for *Maniac* (1980), about a Son-of-Sam style murderer who scalps his victims and decorates manikins with their hair, and *Friday the Thirteenth* (1980), in which a group of teen-age summer camp counselors are killed off in various sickening ways. In the ever-growing field of bloody effects, Savini is rapidly establishing himself as the master of atrocity.

About fifteen years ago Dick Smith wrote a little "how-to" book on monster makeup for beginners. Since this manual (now a collector's item) was aimed at young amateurs, Smith tried to make things as simple as possible by recommending materials that were easily obtainable from neighborhood stores. Shopping around in a supermarket for something that would serve as fake blood, he came upon the shelf containing Karo syrup. He bought a bottle, took it home, and tried it out. The Karo, when mixed with red food coloring, worked out so well that Smith began using it professionally, first in *Midnight Cowboy,* then in *The Godfather.* During his work on the gruesome climax of *Taxi Driver,* he created a stir at his local grocery when he came in to buy eight gallons of the stuff.

The following is Dick Smith's professional Karo Blood Recipe, good for one gallon of extremely realistic fake blood.

1. *Weigh 9.9 grams Methyl Paraben in a 5 ounce paper cup. Add ½ ounce Karo and beat to a smooth cream. Stir in more Karo from the quantity in step 3.*
2. *Weigh 7.6 grams (approximately 3¾ teaspoons) D&C Red #33. Weigh 10.4 grams (approximately 5 teaspoons) FD&C Yellow #5. Add these colors to 1 pint of distilled water.*
3. *Measure out 3½ quarts (7 pints) Karo in 1½ gallon pail.*
4. *Stir Paraben mixture into the Karo in the pail. Stir in the colors.*
5. *Add 6 ounces Kodak Photo-Flo. (Makes Karo flow properly on skin and soak through cloth.)*

WARNING: *DO NOT USE THIS MIXTURE IN THE MOUTH!*

Paraben is a preservative. It is not necessary if the blood will be used in a week or two. Blood to be used in the mouth can contain Paraben but not Photo-Flo.

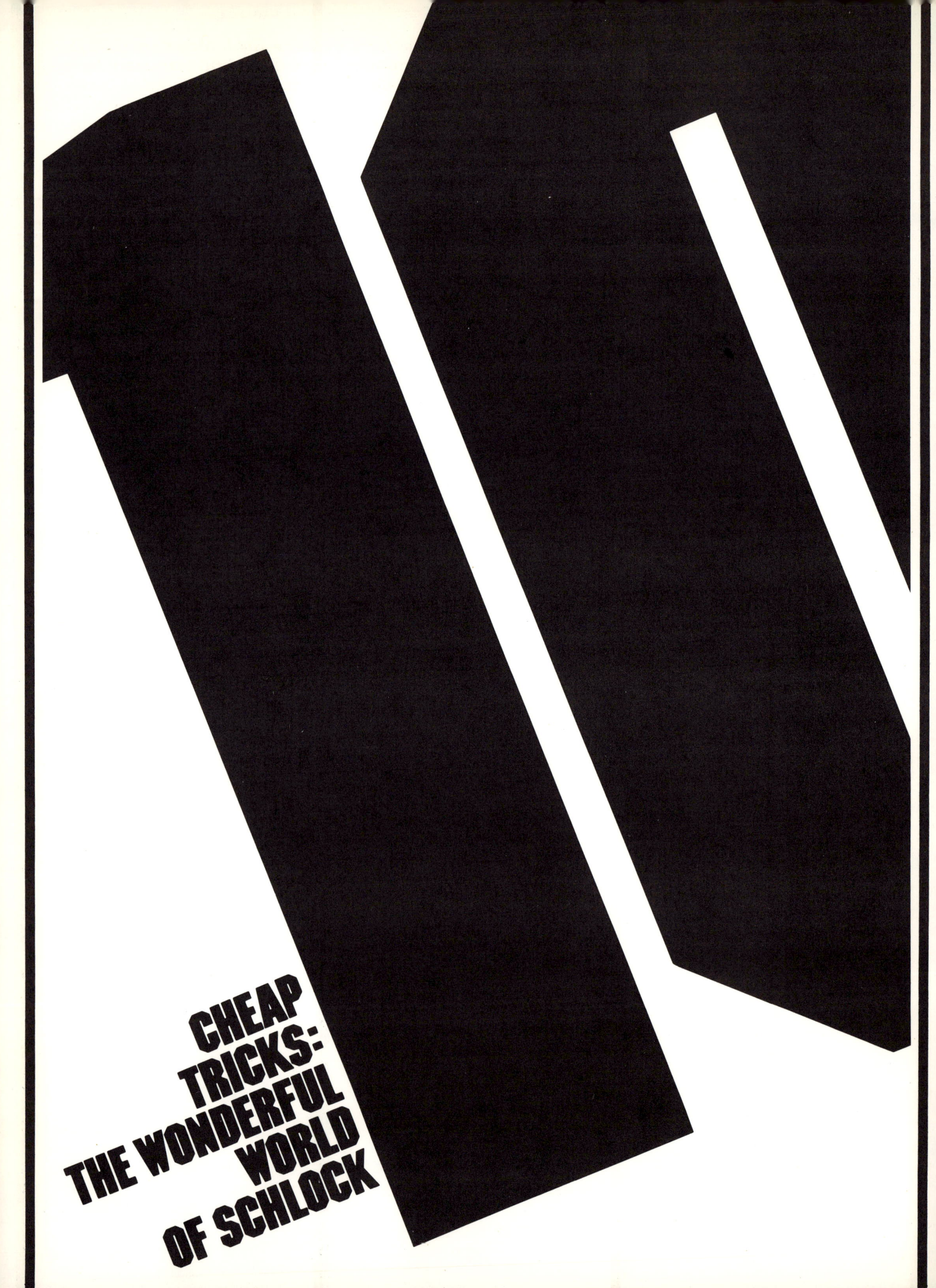
CHEAP
TRICKS:
THE WONDERFUL
WORLD
OF SCHLOCK

Schlock is American Yiddish slang for inferior, cheap or defective goods. The goods under discussion here are those schlock special effects that are far from special, the shabbiest illusions of movie history, from awesome avalanches of bouncy papier-mâché boulders to a squawking puppet-bird which can soar to Earth from the far reaches of outer space with all visible strings intact. While good special effects prompt the viewer to ask "How did they do that?", this bargain-basement magic is more likely to invite the question "Are they kidding?"

All three adjectives in the definition of schlock (inferior, cheap, and defective) apply to bad special effects, but the word that makes it all possible in the first place is *cheap.* Cheap productions have been with us for a long time, but for the serious student of schlock the heyday of absolutely atrocious special effects began around 1950.

Before the fifties, low-budget pictures were known as B movies. Although it has commonly come to apply to all low-grade films, the term B movie had an original definition that derived from a particular period in Hollywood history. The B movies were a line of inexpensive pictures produced by the studios to fill in the bottom half of double features, the "B" slot of double bills. Usually these pictures were action films like Westerns, jungle adventures, and mystery thrillers. Because B movies were part of an organized studio system, they do not qualify as total schlock. Low-budget adventure movies filmed at major studios, for instance, had access to props and sets left over from classier productions and had the benefit of the expertise of the studio's well-organized effects department. Working conditions of this kind helped the low-budget director get through some of the more complicated effects scenes with a certain amount of respectability. On the other hand the special effects in these early poverty-row productions do deserve honorable mention; no one can deny that they had their low points. Who could forget, for example, watching with bated breath as Johnny Weissmuller wrestled to death a rubber crocodile in countless Tarzan and Jungle Jim movies? The point here is that B movies did have their share of schlocky effects, but compared to the effects featured in science fiction and creature films churned out after 1950, B movies look practically dignified.

The historical development that brought about the advent of ultimate schlock in the fifties was the breakdown of the Hollywood studio system. The culprit in this breakdown was television. It was no longer profitable for studios to make movies for the bottom half of double bills when the audience preferred to stay home to watch comparable lowbrow entertainment for nothing. Since viewers could enjoy cheap shows at home for free, the popularity of B movies dropped drastically. Although B movies were quickly fading, the business of low-budget filmmaking was far from finished. It had only to be revamped and redirected.

There was still an audience that wanted to get out of the house and pay money for cut-rate entertainment: these moviegoers, most of them teen-agers, were filling up the drive-ins. According to the new breed of schlock producers, the two qualities needed to lure in the young, restless crowd were mindlessness and a complete lack of taste. The success of movies like *Cat-Women of the Moon* (1954) and *Attack of the Crab Monsters* (1957) was a vivid testament to the shrewd judgment of these new masters of schlock. The new cheap movies (called exploitation pictures for their ability to exploit the new market) were no longer geared for the bottom slot of the double feature; low-grade movies could now take the top half if they were lurid enough and featured a sufficiently sensational title. In this frantic scramble for room on programs at "passion-pit" drive-ins, the word *cheap* took on new meaning, as did *inferior* and *defective.*

The new standards in schlock could be clearly seen in a truly terrible picture called *Robot Monster* (1953). An indication of the sort of clear thinking that went into this production can be found in the various titles used for the film, which was also released as *Monster from the Moon* and *Monster from Mars.* Not only was the origin of the monster open to question, but its quantity was debatable as well, since it was also shown under the title of *Monsters from the Moon.* This kind of artistic integrity was likewise reflected in the picture's so-called special effects. In order to concoct the Robot Monster, director Phil Tucker took the usual cheap approach to creating a robot: he shopped around for an inexpensive metallic-looking costume to rent. He then found that a robot costume would cost too much. To solve his special effects dilemma, Tucker approached his friend George Barrows, who had his own gorilla suit and hired himself out to movie-makers as a stand-in ape. Since Barrows was a friend, Tucker was able to get both the performer and the costume for nothing. A diving helmet was substituted for the ape head, presumably to give the monster a robot quality. This meticulously designed crea-

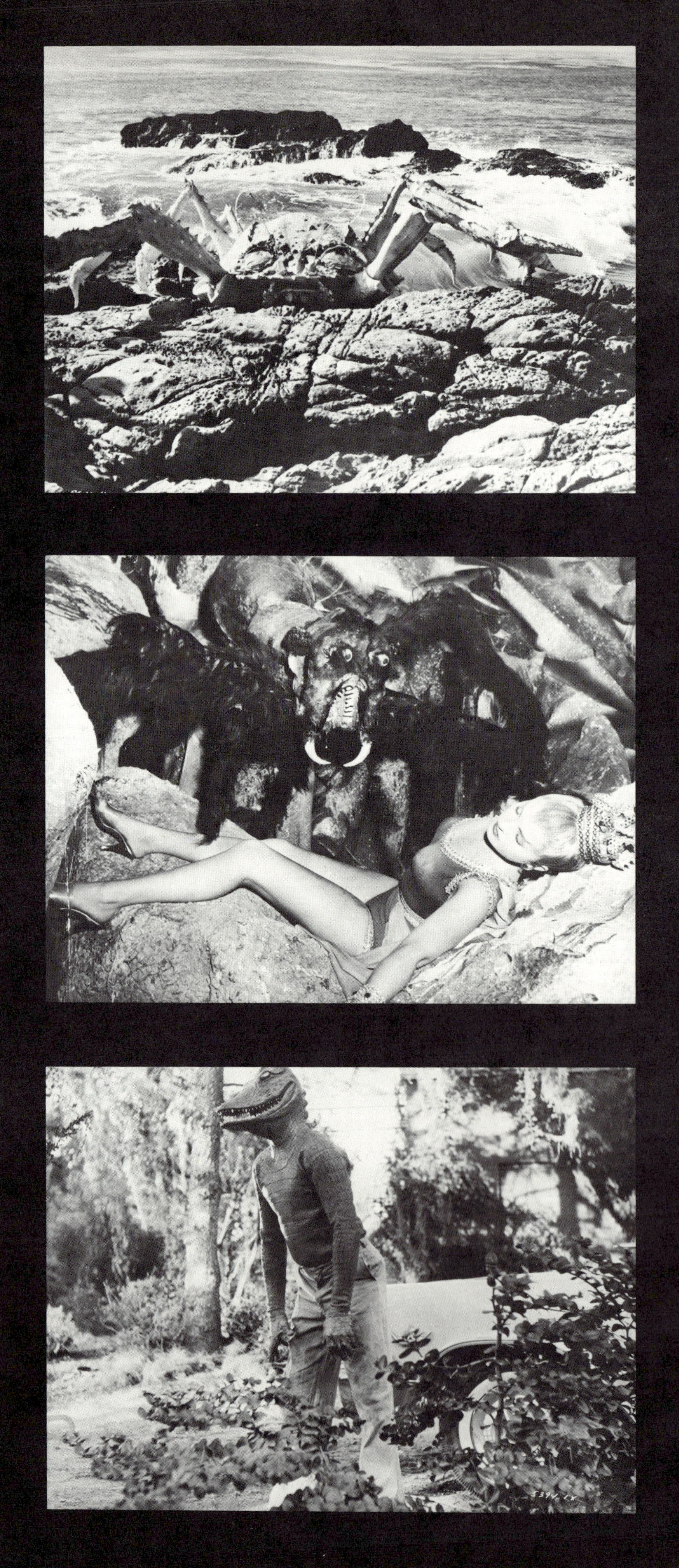

Top: Sparing no expense, Roger Corman lavished over $1,000 on the creature in *Attack of the Crab Monsters.* Two men inside the shell moved the thing around. *Center:* An effect favored by schlock film-makers is the giant puppet with visible strings. In this scene from *Missile to the Moon,* a large spider-marionette menaces an extraterrestrial bathing beauty. *Bottom:* A true schlock film always promises more than it delivers. The bloodcurdling monsters in *The Alligator People* consist of a single guy stumbling around in a lizard suit.

ture ended up as a gorilla with a steel head, who came from either the moon or Mars, depending on which set of credits had been tacked on.

The most prolific suppliers of schlock during the fifties and early sixties were two exploitation film companies called American International Pictures and Allied Artists Productions. When it came to catering to the drive-in crowd, nothing was too stupid for these two companies. (In all fairness, it must be mentioned that Allied Artists occasionally lapsed into competence; the company was responsible for the original *Invasion of the Body Snatchers* [1956], one of the best films produced in the science fiction genre in the 1950s.) Employing almost identical personnel, American International (AIP) and Allied Artists exploited juvenile delinquency in *Dragstrip Riot* (1958) and *Hot Rod Girl* (1956); explored new morality in *Sex Kittens Go to College* (1960); fashioned "hip" variations on classic themes in *I Was a Teenage Frankenstein* (1957) and its companion piece, *I Was a Teenage Werewolf* (1957); and then further catered to the youth cult they had created in *Teenage Caveman* (1958). The most ludicrously enjoyable pictures produced by these two companies were those films that attempted incredible special effects. These movies provided malevolent creatures of every shape and size to gull the viewer into suspending his belief for at least an hour and a half.

The most famous producer-director to make creature movies for both AIP and Allied Artists was Roger Corman. Much of Corman's fame is based on a series of atmospheric horror films derived from stories by Edgar Allan Poe including *The House of Usher* (1960) and *The Pit and the Pendulum* (1961). Corman's Poe adaptations inspired a cult following and many serious analyses of the director's work. During the fifties, however, critical appreciation was the furthest thing from Corman's mind. His only concerns when making films like *Monster from the Ocean Floor* (1954) and *It Conquered the World* (1956) were to make them fast, make them cheap, and to make just enough money to produce another picture very much like the one before. For sheer productivity Corman was perhaps the best schlock moviemaker of the fifties; from 1955 to 1959 he directed twenty-three movies and produced several others. Unlike most of his fellow producers of trash, Corman was able to invest many of his small pictures with an effectively moody visual style; his shoestring special effects, however, were consistently ridiculous.

Corman's first film, *Monster from the Ocean Floor,* was made for the absurdly low budget of $12,000, one hundred dollars of which was allotted to special effects. However, none of the effects money made it to the screen. Corman hired puppeteer Bob Baker to create the effects for *Monster from the Ocean Floor;* Baker did what he could to make an underwater monster and a miniature submarine with the hundred dollars. But after the effects sequences were shot in a Beverly Hills photography studio, the job was completely lost when the film was damaged. With no budget left, Corman asked Baker what could be done to salvage the picture. Baker slapped together a puppet monster out of intravenous tubing, ostrich feathers, light bulbs, and rubber cement, and set up a makeshift shooting stage in an old garage. Predictably enough the octopuslike creature that finally appeared on the screen was not very effective. From these inauspicious beginnings Corman moved on to new effects creations which were almost as bad.

Most of Corman's monsters, as well as some of the most memorable schlock creatures directed by other exploitation artists, were created by a man named Paul Blaisdell. The two met in 1955 while Blaisdell was working as an art director for a science fiction magazine. Blaisdell's first special-effects job was to build a miniature puppet of an alien and a model of the creature's spaceship for Corman's *Beast with a Million Eyes* (1955). The alien had an oversize head, batwings, no body to speak of, and generally exuded all the life-like qualities of a pet rock. Working within the usual restrictions of time and money, Blaisdell had to create the spaceship out of war-surplus parts. With this film Blaisdell began what was to be a brief but conspicuous career in the field of schlock effects. From 1955 to 1959 he worked on sixteen pictures, creating models, props, and full-scale monster outfits. He also did his share of acting: the man lumbering about inside the Blaisdell monster costumes was usually Blaisdell himself. For *The Day the World Ended* (1955) he created the costume and played the part of an atomic mutant who sported the head of a warty horned toad; in *From Hell It Came* (1957) he put together the outfit for the dreaded Nabonga, the monster-tree from beyond the grave. Since the alien in *Not of This Earth* (1957) was a normal-looking humanoid in a business suit, Blaisdell shifted from monster effects to campy special props. For this picture Blaisdell constructed the alien's suitcase that could double as a handy blood-sucking device.

Blaisdell's most spectacular schlock effect was the Venusian invader in Corman's 1956 feature *It Conquered the World.* This alien was a ribbed, cone-shaped creature with a leering maniacal face. Since the original release of *It Conquered the World* this monster has been alternately described by science fiction fans as the carrot creature and the cucumber monster. Blaisdell himself preferred to call it the psychotic mushroom. The movie seemed to be based on the notion that Venusians evolved from a highly intelligent (if somewhat depraved) race of vegetables. Although the carrot creature's appearance was enough to make the effect ridiculous, the Venusian was made to seem even more absurd by its misuse. Inside the creature's plywood frame Blaisdell could manipulate a system of wires and pulleys to make the Venusian's eyes and mouth move; he could also make the horns wiggle and the arms reach out to pluck a handkerchief out of someone's pocket. Blaisdell fitted the carrot creature with all these moving parts to make up for the fact that the script called for the Venusian to remain fixed to one spot inside a cave. Once on the set Blaisdell wasn't asked to exercise any of the carrot creature's working parts, but instead was told to move the monster out of the cave; the creature was supposed to do the one thing it wasn't designed to perform. The result was a ludicrous scene of the carrot creature rumbling about on castor wheels.

In Blaisdell's defense it should be pointed out that he was severely hampered by minuscule budgets and whirlwind schedules. The money spent on each picture was usually well below $100,000 and only 1 or 2 percent of that cost was devoted to special effects. Considering these restrictions, he probably produced the best possible results. One of his efforts, Edward L. Cahn's *The She-Creature* (1956), was actually fairly effective. The movie has some solid performances by veteran actors Chester Morris and Tom Conway, and some good eerie photography, and it was definitely one of AIP's spookier horror shows. Blaisdell's costume for the scaly, feline She-Creature, though obviously low-budget, is bizarre enough to be menacing at times; some of the scenes of the She-Creature rising out of the ocean surf at night to stalk the gloomy beach are pleasingly ghastly. But even in this relatively competent piece of schlock the cheapness of the production still caused Blaisdell some problems. In one scene the She-Creature (Blaisdell) was supposed to crash through a balsa door and strangle a man on the other side of the room. He made it through the door but tripped on his oversize monster feet halfway across the room and fell flat on his face. The retake for the scene was scheduled after lunch to give the propmen time to replace the door. When the stage and camera were finally set up once again, Blaisdell charged into the door to find upon impact that he had run into something much more solid than balsa wood. This time he flopped back on his behind. As he picked himself up, he realized he had come up against absurdly low production values once again: the propmen couldn't afford to buy more balsa wood and instead built a door out of solid pine and then left Blaisdell to figure it out for himself.

The special effects at AIP and Allied Artists weren't confined only to the monster suits and miniature puppets seen in the Corman-Blaisdell pictures. The success of such films as *Beast from 20,000 Fathoms* (1953) and *Tarantula* (1955) made the two companies anxious to exploit the gigantic-monster craze with all the slipshod ineptitude they had shown in movies like *Beast with a Million Eyes.* To produce somewhat larger-than-life effects, the schlock studios needed a cut-rate Ray Harryhausen to conjure up giants at minimal cost. In the extraordinarily economical Bert I. Gordon they found their man. A renaissance man of schlock, Gordon could produce and direct films as well as create special effects. It was clear that he approached all three functions with equal care, allotting no more time or talent to special effects than he did to either directing or producing. A man of these talents could not be overlooked by the exploitation film companies for very long.

The Gordon movie that first attracted Allied Artists' attention was a grade Z space adventure called *King Dinosaur* (1955). The picture told the story of four space explorers trapped on a distant planet where they must fight off ferocious dinosaurs. Actually the astronauts' plight isn't nearly as desperate as it might sound because there are no dinosaurs or anything resembling dinosaurs in the entire picture. What the astronauts really find on the planet is a troop of photographically enlarged lizards which the characters insist on calling dinosaurs. Rather than use stop-motion or *Godzilla*-style monster outfits, Gordon photographed lizards at close range to make them seem large, and then combined his garden-variety monsters with equally unconvincing actors primarily by means of rear projection. Gordon didn't put anything on the screen that could pass for a prehistoric monster and yet he was able to promote himself as a special-effects wizard. His reputation as an effects expert rested for the most part on his ability to produce a rough approximation of special effects on a shoestring. Also contributing to his successful self-promotion as a special-effects expert was the fact that the "trick photography" was undeniably the star of *King Dinosaur.* The story and the characters were so asinine that the effects became the major attraction by default.

King Dinosaur was made cheaply enough to be able to make a fast buck at the box office. Impressed by Gordon's moneymaking potential, Allied Artists distributed the new director's next special-effects attempt, *The Cyclops* (1957). In this picture a woman organizes an expedition to find her boyfriend, who has been lost in a plane crash in Mexico. Her search comes to an end when she finds that her boyfriend was not only disfigured by the crash but was enlarged to enormous proportions by radiation. In *The Cyclops* Gordon used economical effects techniques similar to those in *King Dinosaur* to introduce a theme he was to repeat many times: an ordinary human or animal grows to giant size and begins wreaking havoc on the normal world.

For *Beginning of the End* (1957) Gordon brought his cameras close to grasshoppers to film a story about monster grasshoppers enlarged by radioactivity. A particularly memorable scene showed a pack of the insects climbing a Chicago skyscraper. To stage the sequence at the lowest cost possible, Gordon used the resourceful method of filming actual grasshoppers walking across a photograph of the building. This method began to seem a little less resourceful when one of the grasshoppers reached the top of the skyscraper and then continued to walk up the photographed sky. In *The Spider* (1958) Gordon usually made the point of keeping his actors out of the giant spider's side of the frame in order to avoid doing anything more complicated than a split screen. In one adventurous moment, however, he came very close to doing a traveling matte when he placed the scurrying black spider on a desert road. The only hitch in his technique was that he didn't bother to use a matte. It was much less expensive to simply double-expose the spider onto the background footage. For a few moments the audience just had to settle for a temporarily transparent monster.

Perhaps Gordon's most famous giant picture of the fifties was his first AIP effort, *The Amazing Colossal Man* (1957). This time a soldier contracts a case of giantism caused by—of all things—radioactivity. Gordon exploited the picture for all its technical possibilities, displaying the entire gamut of his effects techniques, from unimaginative rear projection and split screens to unconvincing miniatures for the Colossal Man to demolish. The movie reaches a schlock-effects high point when the Army decides to end the Colossal Man's rampage by injecting him with tranquilizers. A newcomer to the cinema of Bert I. Gordon might have presumed that the safest and most efficient way to dope a giant would be to encase the tranquilizer in a bullet of some kind and tell a marksman to fire the stuff into the giant from a distance. (In *The Beast from 20,000 Fathoms,* for instance, a similar procedure was used to inject the Beast with a radioactive isotope.) But a solution of that kind smacked of logic, and for that reason had no place in a Bert Gordon production. The clever scheme hatched by Gordon's heroes is to construct an enormous hypodermic needle and send some fool to walk right up to the Colossal Man to ram the syringe into the giant's ankle. To the astonishment of everyone except the audience, the Colossal Man tumbles to the scheme, snatches up the needle, and turns it around to harpoon a nearby extra who never considered taking cover.

Gordon's gigantic antics were never more campy than the mindless exploits featured in his 1965 production of *Village of the Giants.* The basis for this movie was H. G. Wells's *Food of the Gods,* a tale about an attempt by scientists to increase the world's food supply by feeding animals a size-increasing substance. The only similarity between Wells's story and Gordon's film was the incredible substance that made things grow. In *Village of the Giants* a group of wild, thrill-seeking teen-agers eat the stuff because they regard giantism as a new kind of kick. After the sprouting adolescent girls have finished bursting out of their clothes, the teen-age giants take over the town and turn the tables on the grown-up squares. Rare moments in schlock effects history occur when a normal boy scales a pair of giant breasts belonging to an oversize, seam-lined dummy, and when an eight-foot duck does the Twist and the Jerk in the Whisky-A-Go-Go discotheque. The giants' reign comes to an end when the good kids in town, who see nothing nifty about growing big, band together to outwit the bad oversize kids.

Always the canny self-promoter, Bert I. Gordon decided to reveal all the unsought secrets behind the dubious illusions of *Village of the Giants* in a September

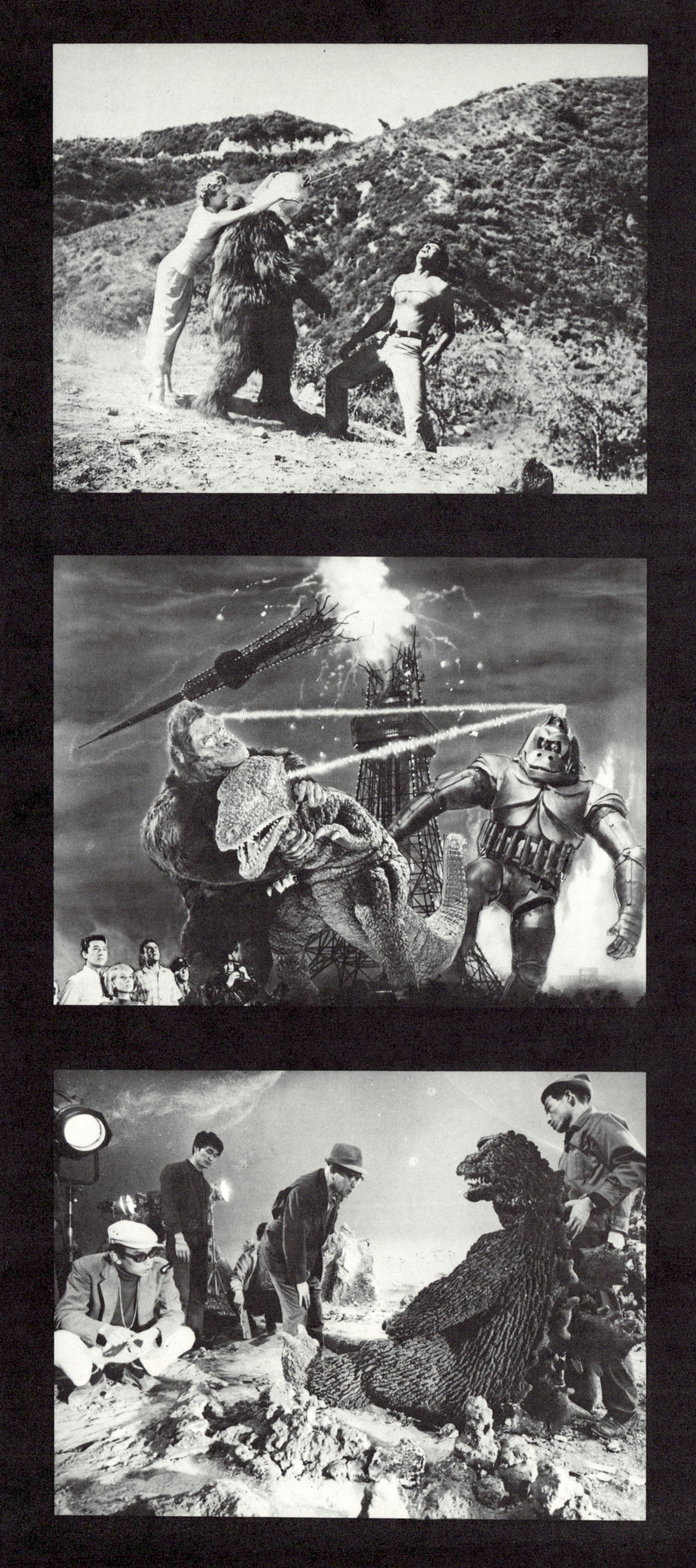

Top: When producer/director Phil Tucker found out how much a robot costume cost, he recruited a friend who owned a gorilla suit, added a deep-sea diving helmet, and came up with the legendary *Robot Monster.*
Center: This publicity still from a Japanese monster movie gives a good idea of the stunning effects work that distinguishes these films.
Bottom: Godzilla relaxes between takes on *Destroy All Monsters.*

1965 article for *American Cinematographer.* Although the movie might appear to be just an inane exercise in preposterous effects and teen-age exploitation, Gordon took the inanity a step further by pointing out that *Village of the Giants* was actually a satirical look at the way-out youth culture of the mid-sixties. For those people who thought that the goings-on in the picture were a little extreme Gordon retorted, "That's the scene, baby."

Roger Corman may have been the master of prolific small-scale effects, and Bert Gordon the king of cheap, oversize illusions, but the most outlandish schlock effects of the fifties and early sixties were the handiwork of the gimmick-mad William Castle. When he was a young play producer in the thirties, Castle once sneaked to his own theater at night, shattered the building's windows, and covered the walls with painted swastikas. Although this act might seem to be an example of insane self-destruction, there was an astute method to Castle's madness. His play starred an actress with no box office pull who had just come to this country from Nazi Germany. When Castle's late-night vandalism became shocking headlines, both the actress and the play became a hit. In the late fifties producer-director William Castle put this outrageous promotional savvy to work in such popular "spook shows" as *House on Haunted Hill* and *The Tingler* by taking special effects off the movie screen and bringing them out into the audience.

Castle's first big splash was the 1958 Allied Artists production of *House on Haunted Hill,* in which he capitalized on a gimmick process called Emergo. The name of the process was meant to suggest to the gullible moviegoer that the horrifying images in the movie were supposed to somehow emerge from the screen and haunt the theater. In actuality all Emergo amounted to was a luminous skeleton that was swung over the heads of the viewers on wires at the same moment that Vincent Price operated a skeleton-marionette onscreen. The trick was obviously cheap but it was enough to make people buy tickets.

Castle's next "process" was Percepto, featured in *The Tingler* (1959). This gimmick was more involved and was a truly enjoyable piece of schlock showmanship. The movie is an obviously contrived but entertaining thriller about a scientist (Vincent Price) conducting experiments on the emotion of fear, which, he maintained, is really a centipedelike organism located somewhere around the spine. This little creature, known as the Tingler, activates fright. According to the script the Tingler's effect on a person can only be counteracted by the release mechanism of screaming (a shrewd hint to what might otherwise have been a quiet, unresponsive audience). In order to test this principle, Price takes a deaf-mute woman and makes her an unwitting guinea pig in a cruel series of experimental situations designed to scare the hell out of her. Since she can't scream, the woman literally dies of fright. During her autopsy the creepy-crawly escapes from her body and is "released" into the theater. A few lucky viewers were sitting in seats rigged with a vibrating motor, which was occasionally turned on to fake the sensation of being tingled by the creature. As if this wasn't enough, after a number of viewers repeatedly shrieked to save themselves from the Tingler, the movie then stopped so that a woman in the audience who had obviously been hired to faint could be carried out. Vincent Price's voice then came over the loudspeaker to calm the viewers for the duration of the emergency.

In *13 Ghosts* (1960) Castle introduced Illusion-O, a gimmick that made use of special viewing glasses. Each member of the audience was issued a facsimile of the ghost viewer seen in the picture; the viewer had two filters, one red and the other blue. Whenever a ghost was to appear on the screen, the audience looked through the red filter in order to see the spirit, and if they were chickenhearted, they looked through the blue filter and were spared the "terrifying" sight. What the stouthearted saw was hardly worth the buildup unless they were particularly troubled by the sight of a skeleton on fire.

The 1961 horror film *Mr. Sardonicus* was perhaps Castle's most ludicrously transparent bit of fakery. At the end of the picture the evil Mr. Sardonicus faces certain death unless his spiteful manservant will give him his prescribed injection. Before the servant has a chance to make up his mind, the story is interrupted and none other than William Castle comes on the screen. Each moviegoer has been supplied with a "punishment" card on which has been printed a hand with an extended thumb. Castle tells the audience to take part in the movie by voting on the fate of Sardonicus. All those who want him to live are to hold their cards thumbs-up, all those who wish him to die are to hold their cards thumbs-down. While the audience members hold up their glow-in-the-dark cards, Castle goes through the motions of counting the votes, announces the result (thumbs down), and then proceeds to show the scene of the villain's death.

While AIP and Allied Artists were proving that low-grade special effects could be parlayed into box office profits, moviemakers outside the United States were exploring similar avenues of schlock merchandising. In Italy, for instance, mythical spectaculars like *Hercules* (1957) and *Hercules Unchained* (1959) put Steve Reeves in the embarrassing position of having to simulate a fight with a man-eating lion by wrestling with a growling patch of carpet. By the mid-sixties what the Italians had done to Greek mythology they were doing to the space opera in such epics as *Wild, Wild Planet* and *Planet on the Prowl* (both released in 1965). Anyone unfortunate enough to have sat through these disasters was subjected to a numbing procession of cardboard-cutout rockets coasting through planetary systems that appeared to be nothing more than a waste of good golf balls.

The country that most consistently undershot the low standards set by American exploitation producers was Japan. After a brief fling with respectable monster effects in such films as *Godzilla* (1954) and *Rodan* (1957), Toho Studios wasted little time in cutting down on production values and consequently undermined the talents of their leading effects man, Eiji Tsuburaya. By the mid-sixties Toho was churning out effects pictures comparable to any schlock productions in the world.

The early Toho monster movies were able to make men in reptile suits menacing by filming the creatures at high speed (to create the illusion of slow, lumbering movement) and shading them with stark, eerie lighting. When the intense lighting necessary for high speed photography became too expensive for Toho, Godzilla and Rodan were often filmed at regular speed, which destroyed the illusion of Godzilla's being anything other then a grown man cavorting about in a rubber costume and made the flying reptile Rodan look like a silly puppet. Substituting standard bright lighting for the early shadowy photography further betrayed the illusion of menace.

The complete degeneration of Japanese monsters was brought about by the juvenile concepts developed for the Toho pictures. After serving several years as Japan's premiere heavy, Godzilla graduated to the position of good-guy monster, ready to do battle with any new bad-guy monster born of the overworked imagination of Toho filmmakers. At first Godzilla's new capacity as monster-fighter brought him up against some fairly prosaic creatures, such as Ghidrah, a flying three-headed dragon. Toho's strained attempts to keep coming up with "refreshingly" new ideas for giant creatures became strikingly ridiculous in *Godzilla Versus the Sea Monster* (1966) in which Godzilla takes on Ebirah, the monster shrimp. The final furious bout between the two giants ends up as a monster baseball game in which Ebirah hurls boulders at Godzilla, who then bats them back with his arms. In *Godzilla Versus the Smog Monster* (1972) Japan's mammoth hero tackles a drippy-looking thing that thrives on pollution and is wont to perch on top of factory chimneys to suck up nourishment. A pair of bizarre creatures were pitted against Godzilla in *Godzilla Versus Megalon* (1976). An insidious race of underwater people known as Seatopians enlists the aid of Megalon, an extraterrestrial metallic bug, and Gigan, an outer-space chicken complete with natural protective armor plating, claws, and reptilian tail. In the final battle sequence it becomes apparent that Godzilla has been keeping abreast of recent film trends as he and his enemies exchange fighting maneuvers straight out of Bruce Lee kung fu adventures.

When Toho made it clear that absurd monster effects were no hindrance to box office success, another Japanese studio by the name of Daiei did their best to outdo the creators of Ebirah and the Smog Monster. Daiei's *Gammera the Invincible* (1966) introduced a new menace to miniature sets the world over: a giant, jet-propelled turtle. Gamera, whose name lost a letter after his first big role, starred in a series of films and, like Godzilla, eventually became a hero. Unlike Godzilla, Gamera never encountered an enemy more ridiculous than himself. The fiercesome turtle was perhaps at his most spectacularly awful in *Gamera Versus Monster X* (1970) in which he protects the Japan World Exposition from a monster who remains nameless, presumably to avoid embarrassment to his loved ones. During the final confrontation between the creatures, Monster X, a rhinoceroslike giant, lets out an ear-splitting shriek. The sound threatens to kill Gamera unless he can figure out some way to protect himself. As his final moments approach, the quick-thinking turtle snatches up a pair of telephone poles, stuffs them in his ears and, with his hearing safely cut off, takes care of the noisy upstart in short order.

The Japanese made great strides in reducing the art of special effects to a laughable state, but even though the majority of their monster pictures contained memorable low points, they failed to produce a single picture which

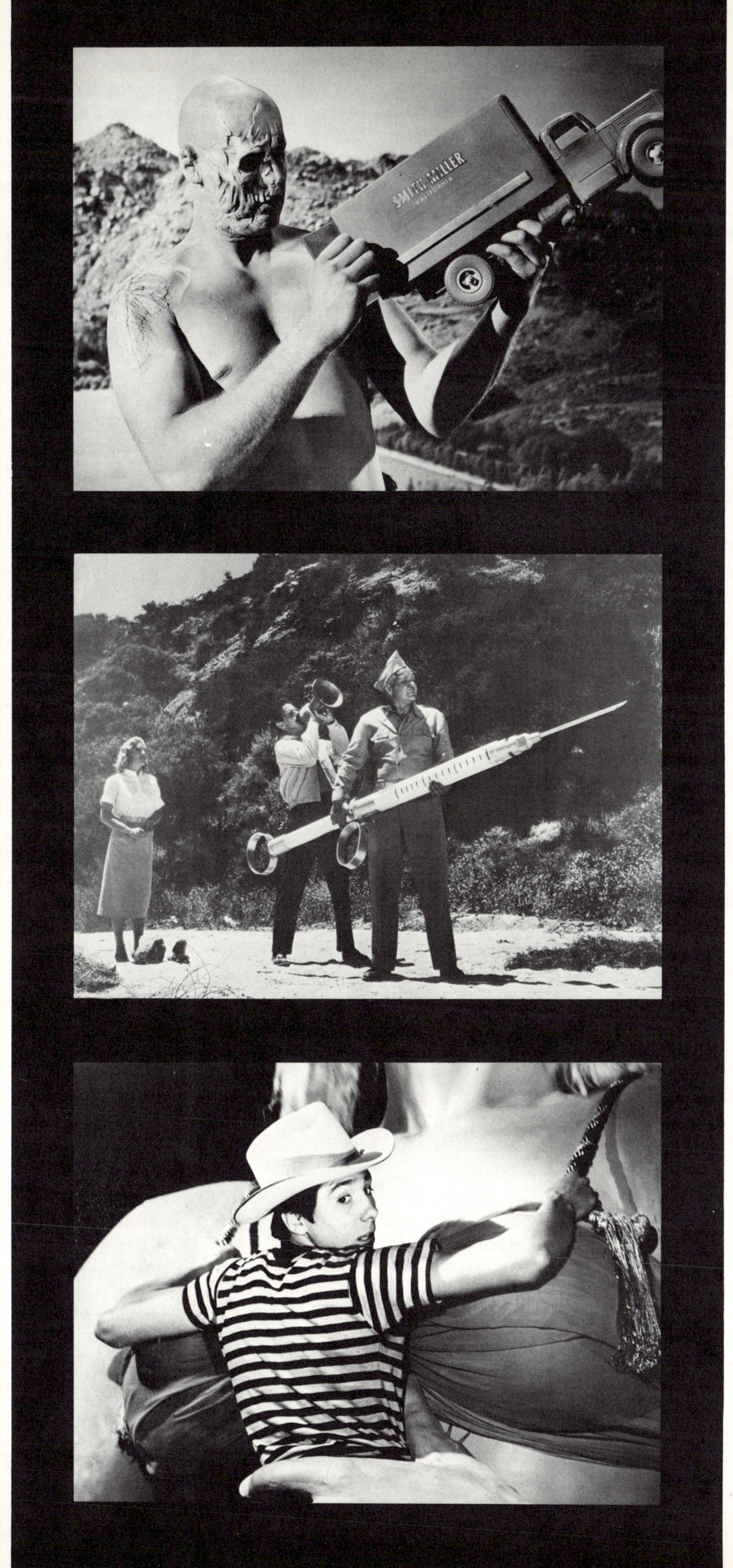

Top: The Amazing Colossal Man prepares to destroy a toy truck. From *War of the Colossal Beast.* *Center:* The Army launches its ingenious plan to subdue the Amazing Colossal Man. *Bottom:* Since optical effects cost money, schlock filmmakers avoid using them, preferring cheap, unconvincing props like the large, immobile beach bunny that has Johnny Crawford in her grip in this shot from *Village of the Giants.*

could be designated the ultimate schlock effects movie. To find the likeliest candidate for the last word in abysmal effects we have to look to America during the vintage year of 1957. The competition in trash that year was keen: Bert I. Gordon came out with *Beginning of the End* and *The Amazing Colossal Man,* Roger Corman countered with *Not of This Earth* and *Attack of the Crab Monsters,* while other shoestring producers anted up with *From Hell It Came* and *Invasion of the Saucer Men.* According to many aficionados of grade-Z effects, the one incredibly inept picture that stood out amongst this particularly unimposing array was Columbia's monster-from-space movie, *The Giant Claw.*

The man who made this bomb possible was Sam Katzman, one of the most successful producers of schlock. When it came to cinematic junk, Katzman had a considerable track record: his list of inane credits included *Voodoo Man* (1944), *Freddie Steps Out* (1946), *Zombies of Mora-Tau* (1957), *The Night the World Exploded* (1957), *Calypso Heat Wave* (1957), *Get Yourself a College Girl* (1964), and *Riot on Sunset Strip* (1967). Katzman's complete disregard for quality was instrumental in turning *The Giant Claw* into an effects movie that made *Amazing Colossal Man* seem like *King Kong.*

The absolute cheapness of Katzman's production of *The Giant Claw* was evident in the excessive use of stock footage from other films. For instance, scenes of people fleeing the oncoming monster through the streets of New York City were taken from *The Beast from 20,000 Fathoms;* one shot of panic-stricken women racing into a subway station was used twice. Another shot of a building being razed was taken from a previous Katzman picture, *Earth Versus the Flying Saucers* (1956), which in turn had taken the scene from George Pal's destruction of Los Angeles in *War of the Worlds.* Thus, *The Giant Claw* enjoyed the peculiar distinction of not only using stock footage but warmed-over stock footage.

Fortunately for schlock fans Katzman found no prefilmed scenes to use for the shots of his monster. The giant bird from outer space had to be concocted from scratch by an individual or individuals who wisely took no screen credit for their alleged special effects. The first glimpses of the creature are of an out-of-focus rectangle moving across the sky—a pathetic attempt to create an aura of mystery. Later on, this rectangle somehow becomes the extraterrestrial bird. To call this bug-eyed, squawking puppet silly would be a gross understatement; the lumpy bird with tufts of hair growing from the top if its head and visible strings sprouting from every limb was undoubtedly the worst monster ever created.

During the course of the puppet's ferocious onslaught against humanity, the bird perches on top of a cardboard Empire State Building to tear away some upper floors, and at other times proves itself to be especially rough on paper planes and Lionel train sets. The terror continues unabated because none of Earth's weapons can penetrate the bird's protective antimatter force field. Some hope survives, however, because earthmen pool all their resources in a concerted scientific effort to devise a means of deactivating the protective shield. Since this is a Sam Katzman production, the concerted effort takes the form of three scientists slaving in what appears to be a converted garage. After hours of work the scientists finally invent an anti-antimatter weapon which disintegrates the bird's force field and leaves the monster vulnerable to attack. From then on it's simply a matter of sending wobbly model planes to fire some well aimed firecrackers at the creature's vital parts. *The Giant Claw* managed to pinpoint its own place in schlock effects history when one of its characters deftly described the monstrous bird as a "turkey as big as a battleship," an apt description of the movie itself.

Although schlock fans may never see another year like 1957, the creation of horrible special effects is not a lost art. Recent effects epics like *Star Wars* and *Alien* may have spoiled moviegoers to a certain extent by showing them what fantasy looks like when it is done right, but the economic equation of "cheap plus inferior equals fast buck" is still in operation. Only a few years ago Bert I. Gordon staged a stunning comeback by underwhelming his fans with a pair of quickies called *Food of the Gods* (1976) and *Empire of the Ants* (1977), two further explorations of the giantism theme manhandled in his earlier films. Of recent newcomers the films of director Kevin Connor have shown an admirable capacity for obvious miniatures and defective mechanical effects. Such Connor films as *The Land That Time Forgot* (1975), and *The People That Time Forgot* (1977) have clearly demonstrated that there will be filmmakers to carry on should Bert Gordon become too old or too good to do so himself.

Schlock fans can be confident: as long as there are drive-ins, there will always be schlocky effects.

A pair of giant prop legs, supposedly belonging to an evil, overgrown adolescent, is lassoed by one of the good teenagers in *The Village of the Giants.*

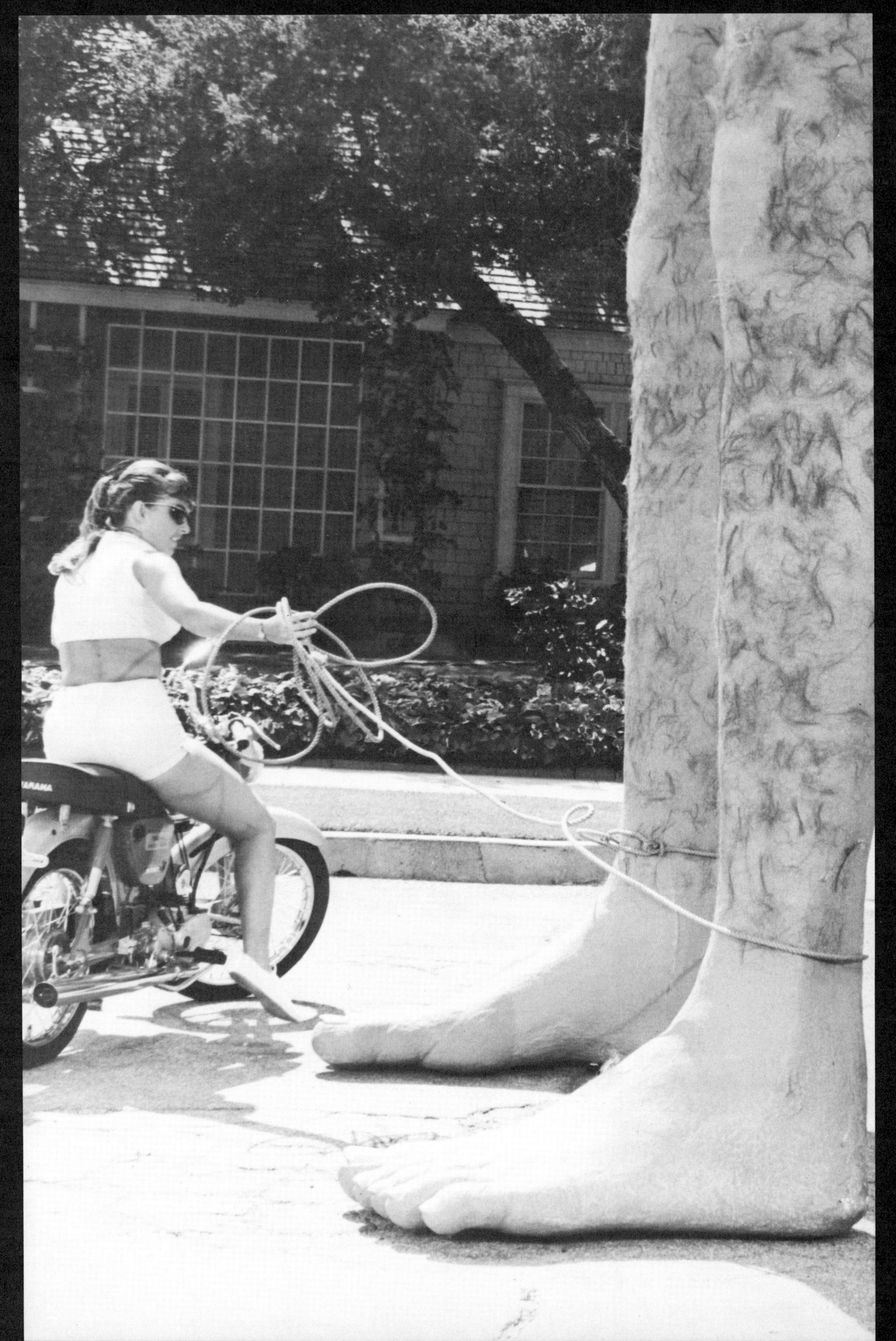

COVER CREDITS (FROM LEFT TO RIGHT):

Head explosion from *Dawn of the Dead.* Photograph: K.S. Kolbert. Copyright © 1978 Dawn Associates.

Animator Gene Warren, Jr. at work behind a table top set. Courtesy of Gene Warren.

Diorama reproduction of a scene from *When Worlds Collide,* constructed for the 1975 Filmex (the annual Los Angeles Film Exhibition). Courtesy of Mike Minor.

Actor Joe Spinell holds a replica of his head constructed by Tom Savini for *Maniac.* Courtesy of Tom Savini.

ACKNOWLEDGEMENTS

Grateful acknowledgement is made to the following studios, producers, and archives for the photographs that appear in this book: Allied Artists, Avco Embassy, American International, Columbia, Eagle-Lion, Hammer, The Laurel Group, Maniac Productions, M-G-M, Paramount, RKO, Toho International, 20th Century Fox, United Artists, Universal, Walt Disney Productions, Warner Bros., Museum of Modern Art/Film Stills Archives, National Film Archive/ Stills Library, Academy of Motion Picture Arts and Sciences/Margaret Herrick Library, and the Forrest J. Ackerman Science Fiction Archives. Photographs from *Mary Poppins* and *The Black Hole* copyright © 1964 and 1979 Walt Disney Productions. World Rights Reserved. Photographs from *Star Wars* and *The Empire Strikes Back* copyright © 1977 and 1980 Lucasfilm Ltd. Photographs from *Dawn of the Dead* copyright © 1978 Dawn Associates (photographs by K.S. Kolbert). Photographs from *Maniac* copyright © 1980 Maniac Productions.

A lot of very generous people helped us with this book, including:

Forrest J. Ackerman, David Allen, Jim Aupperle, The Cabe family, Deborah Call, Wah Ming Chang, Randy Cook, Mary Corliss, Jim Danforth, Linwood Dunn, Phil Edwards, Richard Edlund, Roy Field, Bob Gindy, Tony Iles, Greg Jein, Brian Johnson, Sid Macy, Mike Minor, Doug Murray, George Nelson, George Pal, Brick Price, Chuck Richardson, Charlie Rizzo, Tom Rogers, Larry Rothstein, D. W. Samuelson, Tom Savini, Steve Schneiderman, Wayne Schutz, Charles Silver, Anthony Slide, Dick Smith, Michelle Snapes, Al Taylor, Nat Tobin, Three Tyler, Gene Warren, Albert Whitlock, Stan Willard, and Stan Winston. We owe our thanks to all of them, and, most especially to our editor, Judy Fireman, and our research consultant, David Prestone.

GLOSSARY

This glossary contains brief definitions of the technical terms that appear throughout the book. Detailed explanations of the more important processes and techniques can be found on the pages given in parentheses.

AERIAL BRACE. A device used in STOP-MOTION ANIMATION to suspend flying or leaping models in the air.

ANIMATION. A technique used to make inanimate objects come to life on screen. There are two basic methods: cartoon animation, in which drawings done on transparent sheets (called CELS) are photographed one at a time; and STOP-MOTION ANIMATION (also known as dimensional or model animation), which involves posing a small model, shooting a frame of film, making a slight adjustment in the position of the model, shooting another frame of film, and so on. The rapid progression of individually photographed frames creates the illusion of movement.

ARMATURE. The "skeleton" inside a STOP-MOTION model. Some armatures are very rudimentary, consisting of nothing more than bent wire. Others are elaborate, hand-tooled constructions of tempered steel, with ball-and-socket joints and a large number of moving parts.

BEAM-SPLITTING CAMERA. A camera used in the SODIUM LIGHT PROCESS to produce TRAVELING MATTES in a single step. A prism behind the lens splits the entering light into two identical images, which are transmitted to separate strips of film. One strip is a standard color negative that records the foreground action; the second is a special film stock that produces a traveling matte of the same action. (See page 80.)

BI-PACK CONTACT MATTE PRINTING. A process of producing MATTE shots, involving a special camera loaded with two rolls of film that come in contact with each other behind the aperture. (See page 44.)

BLUE SCREEN. A photographic method of combining separate images (generally a live-action foreground filmed inside a studio with background scenery shot on location) into a COMPOSITE. The actors perform in front of a blue-colored screen. A TRAVELING MATTE is then produced through a series of steps involving filtered prints. (See page 80.)

BREAKAWAY. A prop, such as a bottle, chair, window, wall, or even an entire building, which is designed to be destroyed. Breakaways look perfectly realistic but are specially constructed to shatter easily and harmlessly during filming.

CEL. Each of the thousands of drawings, done on transparent celluloid sheets, used in cartoon ANIMATION.

CINERAMA. A wide-screen process, first used commercially in 1952, involving a huge curved screen and three synchronized projectors, each of which projects one third of the picture.

COMPOSITE. An image composed of two or more separately filmed elements photographically combined into a single scene.

COUNTER-MATTE. See MATTE .

CYCLORAMA. A large, curved backdrop or a cylinder with a background scene painted on it. In the silent movie era revolving cycloramas (or "cykes" as they were called) were used on sound stages to create the illusion of outdoor movement. A car, for example, might be placed in front of a cyclorama covered with a painted country landscape. The rotation of the cyclorama made the stationary car look as if it were moving.

DISSOLVE. A transition between scenes created by SUPERIMPOSING a FADE OUT over a FADE IN. While the outgoing shot disappears, the next one emerges into full definition.

DUMP TANK. A large tank used to dump quantities of water onto a set for simulated floods and tidal waves.

DUNNING-POMEROY SELF-MATTING PROCESS. An early TRAVELING MATTE technique developed by C. Dodge Dunning and Roy J. Pomeroy in the 1920s that made it possible to produce instant, in-the-camera COMPOSTES. By means of this method an actor could be photographed on a sound stage and his image simultaneously combined with an outdoors scene shot on location. A complicated process involving a BI-PACK CAMERA, orange-dyed film, orange-filtered light, and a blue-colored screen, the Dunning-Pomeroy system (which was applicable only to black-and-white movies) fell into disuse when REAR PROJECTION became popular in the 1930s. (See page 45.)

DYNAMATION. A fancy label applied to Ray Harryhausen's animated movies, beginning with *The Seventh Voyage of Sinbad* (1957). The name was coined to distinguish Harryhausen's method from cartoon animation. Later the term was changed to *Dynarama.*

FADE IN. The introduction of a new scene in which the image emerges out of blackness into full definition.

FADE OUT. The opposite of a FADE IN, a transitional device in which the on-screen image gradually disappears into darkness.

FAST MOTION. On-screen action that occurs at a frantic, accelerated pace. Generally used for comic effects, fast motion is achieved by running the film through the camera at a slower-than-normal rate. As a result fewer frames of the scene are recorded, and when the film is projected at normal speed, the action seems to happen very fast.

FRONT PROJECTION. A method of shooting an outdoors scene on a studio sound stage. More efficient than REAR PROJECTION, front projection involves filming the actors against a highly reflective screen while a background image from a slide or motion-picture projector is projected onto the screen from the front by means of a two-way mirror. (See page 136.)

GLASS PAINTING. A partial scene painted on a clear sheet of glass, which is placed between the camera and the background. Glass shots are used to add missing details to a scene or replace the existing details with other, more desirable features. (See page 33.)

HANGING MINIATURE. A small-scale model, suspended from overhead, which is sometimes used instead of a GLASS SHOT to add a missing detail to a partially constructed full-size set. The upper section of the awesome Circus Maximus set in the 1926 version of *Ben-Hur* was actually an elaborate hanging miniature carefully positioned between the camera and the full-scale, partial replica in the background. On film the two components blend together seamlessly to produce the illusion of a colossal amphitheater.

MATTE. A matte, which is the French word for "mask," is an opaque shape (cut from a card or painted on a white board or sheet of glass) that is used to block off part of a photographed scene, keeping that part unexposed so that a second element can then be inserted into the scene to create a composite image. To add this second element, a COUNTER-MATTE is used, which masks off the area of the scene already recorded and keeps the unexposed portion open for the new element to be printed in.

MINIATURE. A small-scale model built to simulate a full-size object or location.

MOTION-CONTROL CAMERA. A computer-driven camera that can repeat its movements (pans, tilts, rolls, zooms, and deceleration) with extreme precision, allowing various live-action and/or miniature elements to be combined into fast-moving COMPOSITE shots. The *Dykstraflex*, nicknamed after its designer, John Dykstra, was the first computerized motion-control camera to be used extensively in a movie (*Star Wars* [1977]). The *Matte-Scan*, a computerized camera crane designed by Disney Studios for its film *The Black Hole* (1979), uses the principle of motion control to create moving matte shots. (See pages 141 (MOTION CONTROL) and 147 (MATTE SCAN).)

MULTIPLE EXPOSURE. Strictly speaking, multiple exposure consists of several images printed on top of each other. When only two images are involved, the technique is called *double exposure*. Early trick filmmakers like Melies used double exposure to conjure up ghosts: They would shoot a background scene, rewind the film, then shoot an actor dressed in a white sheet on top of the exposed footage. Since the background could be seen through the superimposed image, the actor would look suitably ghostly. (See PHANTOM EFFECT.) Sometimes the term *multiple exposure* is used interchangeably with *multiple image*, which consists of several images printed next to each other within the same frame. An early example of a multiple image can be seen in *The Playhouse* (1921), in which Buster Keaton appears on a stage as every member of a nine-man minstrel show.

OPTICAL PRINTER. A versatile special-effects machine that essentially consists of a motion-picture camera and a projector arranged face to face. The optical printer can perform a wide variety of functions, from duplicating prints to producing such optical effects as wipes, fades, dissolves, slow and fast motion, split screens, and many more. (See page 73.)

OVERCRANK. To shoot a scene at a high speed so that when the film is projected at a normal rate, the resulting image will appear in SLOW MOTION. The term derives from the early days of filmmaking, when motion-picture cameras were cranked by hand.

PHANTOM EFFECT. When one image is printed on top of another, the background can generally be seen through the SUPERIMPOSED image, giving it a ghostlike quality.

PROCESS SHOT. Strictly speaking, process photography refers to REAR PROJECTION, although the term is sometimes applied to other optical effects, such as MATTE shots.

REAR PROJECTION. A process used to create the illusion that actors performing on a studio set are outside on location. The actors are filmed against a translucent screen while a projector set up behind the screen provides the background image. (See page 36.)

REVERSE MOTION. On-screen action that moves backward in time, an illusion familiar to anyone who has ever watched home movies run in reverse. Reverse motion is generally created by either running the film backward through the camera or creating a reverse negative in an optical printer. This technique has various uses. In the horror movie *Dawn of the Dead* (1979), for example, the shot of a zombie having his head split in two by a machete was done with reverse motion. The actor had a special machete fitted to his forehead and quickly pulled away. Running the action in reverse created the illusion that the weapon was striking the zombie's head.

ROTOSCOPE. A mechanism attached to a process camera that allows the special-effects artist to project a photographed image a frame at a time. In this way the shifting outline of a moving object can be traced onto a series of artboard easels for the production of hand-drawn TRAVELING MATTES, a process known as *rotoscoping*.

SCHUFFTAN PROCESS. A more or less obsolete technique for combining live action with model-work or paintings. The process makes use of a mirror from which part of the silvered coating has been removed, leaving a reflective area surrounded by clear glass. The live-action component is reflected off this mirrored area; at the same time the camera sees the background miniature or artwork through the glass. In this way the two elements are blended together on film, producing a convincing COMPOSITE. (See page 109.)

SLOW MOTION. On-screen action that moves at an exaggeratedly slow pace. This illusion is produced by running the film through the camera at a faster-than-normal speed. In this way more frames of the scene are recorded, so that when the footage is projected at the conventional speed of twenty-four frames per second, the action takes a long time to happen.

SODIUM LIGHT PROCESS. A refinement of the BLUE-SCREEN process. A backing colored yellow by sodium vapor lamps is substituted for the blue screen while a BEAM-SPLITTING CAMERA is used to photographically produce the TRAVELING MATTE in a single step.

SPLIT SCREEN. Two or more separate, side-by-side exposures within the same frame. Melies could act with himself in the same scene by using a simple split-screen technique: He would block off one half of the camera lens with an opaque MATTE card and film himself on one side of the frame, then use a COUNTER-MATTE to film himself on the opposite side.

SQUIB. A small, electrically detonated explosive charge used to create bullet hits. For the gruesome gunshot wounds popularized by Sam Peckinpah, squibs attached to protective metal backings and covered with "blood sacks" (prophylactics filled with artificial blood) are placed underneath the actor's clothing. When the squib is detonated, the blood explodes out through the resulting "bullet hole."

STOP-MOTION PHOTOGRAPHY. The photographic technique used to animate three-dimensional objects. The camera is operated one frame at a time. In between these single-frame exposures the object is adjusted slightly. (See ANIMATION.)

STORYBOARD. A series of drawings or paintings, often accompanied by captions, that depicts key scenes, sequences, or shots in a film. Storyboards, which resemble comic strips, are sometimes used as presentation devices (to explain the idea for a movie to potential backers, for example) and sometimes as guides to the filmmaker.

SUPERIMPOSITION. One image printed on top of another. (See MULTIPLE EXPOSURE and PHANTOM EFFECT.)

TRAVELING MATTE. A MATTE that moves from frame to frame. Traveling mattes are most often used to combine the image of an actor, photographed on a sound stage, with a background scene shot elsewhere, generally outdoors on location. A traveling matte consists of a strip of film containing the opaque shape of an actor (or other moving object) surrounded by a completely clear space. When this strip is printed in conjunction with footage of the background scene, the result is a new negative of the background scene with an unexposed area in the shape of the actor moving through it. A COUNTER-MATTE consisting of a clear silhouette of the actor against a completely black field is then used to "jigsaw" the image of the actor into the background scene.

TRIPLE-HEAD PROJECTOR. A REAR-PROJECTION device, developed by Farciot Edouart, which beams a very intense background image onto a transparency screen set up behind the performers. The triple-head projector combines three separate optical systems synchronized to cast three identical images onto the background screen at the same time. (See page 50.)

UNDERCRANK. To shoot a scene at a slow speed so that when the film is projected at a normal rate, the resulting image will appear in FAST MOTION. (See OVERCRANK.)

WIPE. An optical transition between scenes in which the outgoing image is removed by a line traveling horizontally across the screen to reveal a new picture.

ZOPTIC PROCESS. A FRONT-PROJECTION technique utilizing synchronized zoom lenses—one on the projector, one on the camera—which can be used to create the illusion that a stationary foreground object is in motion. The Zoptic process was used extensively in *Superman* (1979) to make Christopher Reeve appear to fly. (See page 178.)

INDEX TO FILMS

ABBOTT AND COSTELLO MEET FRANKENSTEIN (1948), 94
ACCIDENT, THE, 8
ACE OF ACES, 9-10
AIRPORT (1970), 181
AIRPORT 1975 (1974), 188
AIRPORT '77 (1977), 188
AIRSHIP DESTROYER, THE (1909), 30, 118
ALIEN (1979), 7, 104, 106-107, 145, 147-148
ALLIGATOR PEOPLE, THE (1959), 210
AMAZING COLOSSAL MAN, THE (1957), 213, 218
ANCHORS AWEIGH (1945), 75, 78
ANDROMEDA STRAIN, THE (1971), 141
ANIMAL WORLD, THE (1956), 165, 169, 181
ANNIE HALL (1977), 62
AT THE CIRCUS (1939), 78
AT WAR WITH THE ARMY (1951), 80
ATTACK OF THE CRAB MONSTERS (1957), 209, 210, 218
BARKLEYS OF BROADWAY, THE (1949), 74-75, 78
BEAST OF HOLLOW MOUNTAIN, THE (1956), 165
BEAST WITH A MILLION EYES (1955), 211, 212
BEAST FROM 20,000 FATHOMS, THE (1953), 129, 166, 212, 213, 218
BEDKNOBS AND BROOMSTICKS (1971), 81, 145
BEGINNING OF THE END (1957), 213, 218
BEHIND THE GREAT WALL (1959), 58
BEN-HUR (1926), 40, 42-45, 70, 186
BEN-HUR (1959), 53, 55
BEYOND THE POSEIDON ADVENTURE (1979), 191
BIG CLOCK, THE (1948), 141
BIRDS, THE (1963), 186
BIRTH OF A NATION (1915), 39
BISHOP'S WIFE, THE (1947), 70
BLACK HOLE, THE (1979), 147
BLACK SCORPION, THE (1957), 131, 165
BLACK SUNDAY (1977), 188, 190-191
BLITHE SPIRIT (1945), 70, 132
BLOB, THE (1958), 104
BOAT, THE (1921), 62
BONNIE AND CLYDE (1967), 81, 195, 197, 198, 199
BRATS (1930), 67, 69, 73
BRIDE OF FRANKENSTEIN, THE (1935), 91, 113
BRIDES OF DRACULA (1960), 94
BRIDGES OF TOKO-RI, THE (1955), 90
BRINGING UP BABY (1938), 72-73
BWANA DEVIL (1952), 58
CARRIE (1976), 102
CATCH-22 (1970), 197-198
CAT-WOMEN OF THE MOON (1954), 209
CHIEN ANDALOU, UN (1928), 193, 194
CINDERELLA (1900), 24
CINERAMA HOLIDAY (1955), 58
CIRCUS WORLD (1964), 55
CLASH OF THE TITANS, 178
CLEOPATRA (1934), 45-46
CLEOPATRA (1963), 53, 55, 182
CLOSE ENCOUNTERS OF THE THIRD KIND (1977), 7, 82, 107, 132, 133, 136, 138, 143-146, 148, 149
CLOWN BARBER, THE (1899), 30
CONAN THE BARBARIAN, 178
CONCORDE—AIRPORT '79, 191
CONJUROR, THE (1899), 16
CONQUEST OF THE POLE, THE (1912), 18, 19, 22, 24, 118
CONQUEST OF SPACE, THE (1955), 119, 120
CORSICAN BROTHERS, THE (1897), 29
COUNT DRACULA AND HIS VAMPIRE BRIDE (1978), 96
COVER GIRL (1944), 78
CREATION (1930), 158, 164
CREATURE FROM THE BLACK LAGOON (1954), 56-57, 58, 104
CREATURE WALKS AMONG US, THE (1956), 104
CURSE OF FRANKENSTEIN, THE (1957), 98
CURSE OF THE WEREWOLF, THE (1961), 98
CYCLOPS, THE (1957), 213
DAMIEN—OMEN II (1978), 102
DARBY O'GILL AND THE LITTLE PEOPLE (1959), 173, 174, 176
DARK STAR (1974), 143
DAWN OF THE DEAD (1979), 202, 204-207
DAWN PATROL, THE (1930), 194, 195
DAWN PATROL, THE (1938), 194, 195
DAY THE EARTH STOOD STILL, THE (1951), 124, 127
DAY THE WORLD ENDED, THE (1955), 211
DEADLY MANTIS, THE (1957), 131
DEMETRIUS AND THE GLADIATORS (1954), 53
DESTINATION MOON (1950), 118-120, 125, 127
DESTINY (1921), 151
DESTROY ALL MONSTERS (1968), 214
DEVIL DOLL, THE (1936), 114, 115
DEVIL'S RAIN, THE (1975), 107
DIAL M FOR MURDER (1954), 58
DILLINGER (1973), 196
DINOSAUR AND THE MISSING LINK, THE (1914), 155
DR. CYCLOPS (1940), 114, 116-117
DR. JEKYLL AND MR. HYDE (1932), 88, 90, 92
DR. NO (1962), 36
DR. STRANGELOVE (1964), 95
DRACULA (1931), 87, 93
DRACULA (1979), 96, 98
DRACULA HAS RISEN FROM THE GRAVE (1968), 96
DRACULA—PRINCE OF DARKNESS (1966), 95-97, 98
DRAGON SLAYER, 178
DRAGSTRIP RIOT (1958), 211
DREAMS OF A RAREBIT FIEND (1906), 31, 32
DRIFTER, THE (1913), 36
EARTH VERSUS THE FLYING SAUCERS (1956), 128, 169, 218
EARTHQUAKE (1974), 24, 96, 181, 182-188
EGYPTIAN, THE (1954), 53
EMPIRE OF THE ANTS (1977), 218
EMPIRE STRIKES BACK, THE (1980), 140, 144, 148
ERRAND BOY, THE (1962), 80, 85
ESCAMOTAGE D'UNE DAME CHEZ ROBERT-HOUDIN (1896), 16
EXECUTION OF MARY, QUEEN OF SCOTS, THE (1893), 11, 16, 193
EXORCIST, THE (1973), 98, 100-101, 107
EXORCIST II: THE HERETIC (1977), 11, 101
EXPLOSION OF THE BATTLESHIP MAINE, THE (1897), 24
FAHRENHEIT 451 (1966), 95
FALL OF THE ROMAN EMPIRE, THE (1964), 53, 55
FANTASTIC VOYAGE (1966), 8, 132
FATTY AND MABEL ADRIFT (1916), 63
FIRE (1901), 30
FIRECAT, THE (1920), 36
FIRST MEN IN THE MOON (1964), 169
FIVE CAME BACK (1939), 181
FLASH GORDON SERIALS, 136, 138, 142
FLESH GORDON (1973), 136, 138
FLIGHT OF THE PHOENIX, THE (1965), 84
FLYING DOWN TO RIO (1933), 74
FLYING TIGERS (1942), 84, 194-195
FOOD OF THE GODS (1976), 218
FORBIDDEN PLANET (1956), 54, 125-128, 142, 148
FORT TI (1953), 58
FRANKENSTEIN (1931), 87, 88, 91
FRIDAY THE 13TH (1980), 203, 204, 207
FROM HELL IT CAME (1957), 211, 218
GAMERA VERSUS MONSTER X (1970), 216
GAMMERA THE INVINCIBLE (1966), 216
GHOST OF SLUMBER MOUNTAIN, THE (1918), 155
GIANT BEHEMOTH, THE (1959), 165
GIANT CLAW, THE (1957), 218
GIGANTIS, THE FIRE MONSTER (1959), 129
GODFATHER, THE (1972), 100, 198, 207
GODFATHER, THE, PART II (1974), 198
GODZILLA, KING OF THE MONSTERS (1954), 129, 216
GODZILLA VERSUS MEGALON (1976), 216
GODZILLA VERSUS THE SEA MONSTER (1966), 216
GODZILLA VERSUS THE SMOG MONSTER (1972), 216
GOLDEN VOYAGE OF SINBAD, THE (1974), 171
GONE WITH THE WIND (1939), 46, 48-50, 160, 161
GOOD EARTH, THE (1937), 11
GORGO (1960), 129
GRAND HOTEL (1932), 181
GREAT RACE, THE (1965), 11
GREAT TRAIN ROBBERY, THE (1903), 31, 32, 34
GREATEST STORY EVER TOLD, THE (1965), 53
HAWAII (1966), 8
HERCULES (1957), 216
HERCULES UNCHAINED (1959), 216
HIGH AND THE MIGHTY, THE (1954), 181
HINDENBURG, THE (1975), 96, 184-185, 188-190
HORROR CHAMBER OF DR. FAUSTUS (1960), 98
HORROR OF DRACULA (1958), 94
HORRORS OF THE BLACK MUSEUM (1959), 98
HOT ROD GIRL (1956), 211
HOUSE ON HAUNTED HILL (1958), 215
HOUSE OF USHER, THE (1960), 211
HOUSE OF WAX, THE (1953), 58
HOW THE WEST WAS WON (1962), 58
HUMAN FLY, THE (1902), 29, 78
HUMPTY DUMPTY CIRCUS (1897), 155
HUNCHBACK OF NOTRE DAME, THE (1923), 87, 89
HUNCHBACK OF NOTRE DAME, THE (1939), 37
HURRICANE (1937), 46, 48
HUSH... HUSH, SWEET CHARLOTTE (1964), 101
HYDROTHÉRAPIE FANTASTIQUE, L', 21
I WAS A TEENAGE FRANKENSTEIN (1957), 211
I WAS A TEENAGE WEREWOLF (1957), 211
IMPOSSIBLE VOYAGE, THE (1904), 7, 24, 25
IN OLD CHICAGO (1938), 46
INCREDIBLE MELTING MAN, THE (1977), 105
INCREDIBLE SHRINKING MAN, THE (1957), 114-115, 118
INTOLERANCE (1916), 39, 193
INVASION OF THE BODY SNATCHERS (1956), 211
INVASION OF THE SAUCER MEN (1957), 218
INVISIBLE BOY, THE (1957), 128
INVISIBLE MAN, THE (1933), 53, 69, 90, 113, 143, 148

IT! THE TERROR FROM BEYOND SPACE (1958), 104
IT CAME FROM BENEATH THE SEA (1955), 129, 166, 169
IT CAME FROM OUTER SPACE (1953), 125
IT CONQUERED THE WORLD (1956), 211, 212
IT'S A MAD, MAD, MAD, MAD WORLD (1963), 10, 58, 81-83, 165, 172
JACK THE GIANT KILLER (1961), 172
JASON AND THE ARGONAUTS (1963), 154, 171
JAWS (1975), 7, 102, 104, 153
JOYOUS MICROBES, THE (1909), 27
JUDITH OF BETHULIA (1913), 39
JUST IMAGINE (1930), 109
KING DINOSAUR (1955), 212-213
KING OF KINGS (1926), 160, 161
KING OF KINGS (1960), 53
KING KONG (1932), 13, 158-162, 164, 165
KING KONG (1978), 7, 107, 145, 163, 164
KISS ME KATE (1953), 58
KISS OF THE VAMPIRE (1963), 94, 95
LAND THAT TIME FORGOT, THE (1975), 218
LAST DAYS OF POMPEII, THE (1913), 39
LAST DAYS OF POMPEII, THE (1935), 46, 181
LAST HOUSE ON THE LEFT, THE (1972), 199, 202
LAST VOYAGE, THE (1960), 181
LIFE OF AN AMERICAN FIREMAN, THE (1903), 31
LITTLE BIG MAN (1970), 100
LOGAN'S RUN (1976), 112, 113
LONGEST DAY, THE (1962), 196
LOST WORLD, THE (1925), 152, 155-158
LOVE HAPPY (1950), 80
MAGNIFICENT SEVEN, THE (1960), 195
MAN CALLED HORSE, A (1970), 197
MAN WITH THE RUBBER HEAD, THE (1897), 19, 21, 23
MAN OF A THOUSAND FACES (1957), 202
MANIAC (1980), 207
MARK OF THE DEVIL (1972), 199
MARY POPPINS (1964), 174, 179
MASK OF FU MANCHU, THE (1932), 88
MELODY CRUISE (1933), 74
MELOMANIAC, THE (1903), 22, 70
MERRY FROLICS OF SATAN, THE (1906), 17, 18
METROPOLIS (1926), 109-112, 125
MIDNIGHT COWBOY (1968), 207
MIGHTY JOE YOUNG (1949), 154, 165
MISSILE TO THE MOON (1959), 210
MISSIONS OF CALIFORNIA (1907), 33
MR. SARDONICUS (1961), 215
MOBY DICK (1956), 153
MONSTER FROM THE OCEAN FLOOR (1954), 211
MOONRAKER (1979), 7
MOST DANGEROUS GAME, THE (1932), 160
MOTHRA (1962), 129
? MOTORIST, THE (1906), 28, 29
MUMMY, THE (1959), 98
MUPPET MOVIE (1979), 177
MURDERS IN THE RUE MORGUE (1954), 58
MUTINY ON THE BOUNTY (1962), 55
MYSTERIOUS ISLAND (1961), 169
NIGHT OF THE LIVING DEAD (1968), 202
NIGHT TO REMEMBER, A (1958), 181
1941 (1979), 82-84
NOAH'S ARK (1929), 40, 41, 43, 181
NOSFERATU (1922), 93
NOT OF THIS EARTH (1957), 211
OMEN, THE (1976), 101-102
ONE-MAN BAND, THE (1900), 22
ONE MILLION B.C. (1940), 152, 170
ONE MILLION YEARS B.C. (1968), 170
ONÉSIME HORLOGER (1910), 27, 29
PALACE OF THE ARABIAN NIGHTS, THE (1905), 22, 24
PALEFACE, THE (1948), 80
PEOPLE THAT TIME FORGOT, THE (1977), 218
PHANTOM OF THE OPERA, THE (1925), 87, 89
PHANTOM OF THE OPERA, THE (1962), 98
PIT AND THE PENDULUM, THE (1961), 211
PLAINSMAN, THE (1937), 50
PLANET OF DINOSAURS, 172
PLANET ON THE PROWL (1965), 216
PLAYHOUSE, THE (1921), 22, 62, 64
POCKET BOXERS, THE (1903), 113
POPEYE, 178
POSEIDON ADVENTURE, THE (1972), 24, 82, 181-183, 188
PRIMEVALS, THE, 172
PUMPKIN RACE, THE (1908), 27
QUO VADIS? (1912), 39
QUO VADIS (1951), 53
RAINS CAME, THE (1939), 46, 47, 181
REAP THE WILD WIND (1942), 194
RESCUED BY ROVER (1905), 30
RIDDLE GAWNE (1918), 87
RIGHT TO HAPPINESS, THE (1919), 36
ROBE, THE (1953), 53
ROBOT MONSTER (1953), 209, 211, 214
ROCK-A-BYE BABY (1958), 80
RODAN (1957), 129, 216
ROYAL WEDDING (1951), 76-78, 80, 120
SAFETY LAST (1923), 62
SAMSON AND DELILAH (1949), 50, 52-53, 181
SAN FRANCISCO (1936), 46-48, 186
SANJURO (1962), 195
SCARS OF DRACULA, THE (1970), 94, 96
SCENT OF MYSTERY (1959), 58
SENTINEL, THE (1977), 199, 200-201
SEVEN CASTLES OF THE DEVIL, THE (1902), 27, 29
SEVEN FACES OF DR. LAO, THE (1964), 174
SEVEN SAMURAI (1954), 195
SEVEN WONDERS OF THE WORLD (1956), 58
SEVENTH VOYAGE OF SINBAD, THE (1958), 170-171
SEX KITTENS GO TO COLLEGE (1960), 211
SHANE (1953), 195, 197
SHE-CREATURE, THE (1956), 212
SHERLOCK JR. (1924), 64-66, 69
SIEGFRIED (1924), 152, 153
SILENT RUNNING (1972), 141
SINBAD AND THE EYE OF THE TIGER (1977), 171
SKELETON DANCE, THE (1929), 22
SOLDIER BLUE (1970), 197
SON OF DRACULA (1943), 93
SON OF KONG (1933), 163, 164
SPARTACUS (1960), 53
SPIDER, THE (1958), 213
STAGECOACH (1939), 181
STAR TREK: THE MOTION PICTURE (1979), 7, 138, 146-147, 148
STAR WARS (1977), 7, 8, 109, 136-143, 145-146, 148
STEAMBOAT BILL JR. (1928), 66, 69
STING, THE (1973), 186, 187
STORY OF THE ANDES (1911), 34
SUBMERSION OF JAPAN (1973), 188
SUEZ (1938), 46
SUPERMAN (1978), 7, 177-178, 191
SUPERMAN II, 178
SWARM, THE (1978), 191
SWING TIME (1936), 74
SWISS FAMILY ROBINSON (1960), 95
TARANTULA (1955), 131, 212
TAXI DRIVER (1976), 10, 198-199, 207
TEDDY BEARS, THE (1907), 155
TEENAGE CAVEMAN (1958), 211
TEN COMMANDMENTS, THE (1923), 39-41, 46, 47
TEN COMMANDMENTS, THE (1956), 52, 55, 90, 187
TEXAS CHAINSAW MASSACRE, THE (1974), 199, 202
THEM! (1954), 130, 131
THIEF OF BAGDAD, THE (1924), 151, 153
THIEF OF BAGDAD, THE (1940), 170
THING, THE (1951), 125
THINGS TO COME (1936), 109, 113, 132
13 GHOSTS (1960), 215
THIRTY SECONDS OVER TOKYO (1944), 196
THIS IS CINERAMA (1952), 58
THIS ISLAND EARTH (1955), 125, 128
THREE CABALLEROS, THE (1945), 78
THREE WORLDS OF GULLIVER, THE (1960), 169
THUNDERBALL (1965), 142
TIDAL WAVE (1975), 188, 189
TIME MACHINE, THE (1960), 120, 131-132
TINGLER, THE (1959), 215
TITANIC (1953), 181
TOM THUMB (1958), 132, 172-174
TOPPER (1937), 68, 69-71
TORA! TORA! TORA! (1970), 82
TOWERING INFERNO, THE (1974), 181, 182, 187-188
TRIP TO THE MOON, A (1902), 24, 25, 119
TWENTY MILLION MILES TO EARTH (1957), 129, 169
20,000 LEAGUES UNDER THE SEA (1907), 22, 24, 132
20,000 LEAGUES UNDER THE SEA (1954), 50, 102-103, 132, 153
TWICE UPON A TIME, 178
TWO MEN OF TINTED BUTTE (1919), 36
2001: A SPACE ODYSSEY (1968), 7, 58, 132-136, 138, 143, 148
UNCONQUERED (1947), 50
UNION PACIFIC (1939), 50
UPSIDE DOWN (1898), 78
VALLEY OF GWANGI, THE (1969), 169-170
VAMPIRE CIRCUS (1963), 94
VILLAGE OF THE GIANTS (1965), 213, 215, 217, 219
VIRGIN SPRING, THE (1960), 202
VOLCANIC ERUPTION ON MARTINIQUE, A (1902), 24
VOYAGE TO THE BOTTOM OF THE SEA (1961), 181
WAR OF THE COLOSSAL BEAST (1958), 217
WAR EAGLES (1938), 163, 164-165
WAR OF THE WORLDS (1953), 122-125, 218
WAY OUT WEST (1932), 69
WAY WEST, THE (1967), 186
WEREWOLF OF LONDON (1935), 90
WHEN DINOSAURS RULED THE EARTH (1971), 172
WHEN WORLDS COLLIDE (1951), 120-121, 123
WHITE ZOMBIE (1932), 93
WILD, WILD PLANET (1965), 216
WILD BUNCH, THE (1969), 195, 197, 198
WIZ, THE (1978), 177
WIZARD OF OZ, THE (1939), 175, 176-177
WOLF MAN, THE (1941), 90
WOMAN IN THE MOON (1929), 118, 119
WONDER MAN (1945), 70, 90
WONDERFUL WORLD OF THE BROTHERS GRIMM, THE (1962), 174
WRECK OF THE MARY DEARE, THE (1959), 181
YOUNG FRANKENSTEIN (1974), 88

Designed by
Patrick Couratin

The blue-screen traveling-matte process was used to create the exciting scene in Walt Disney's *The Black Hole* in which the heroes flee a giant meteor as it comes crashing down the main corridor of the spaceship *Cygnus*.
Top: The interior of the corridor was actually a twenty-two-foot-long miniature made of plastic and wood. The meteor, in place at the far end of the corridor, was a thirty-six-inch plastic ball.
Center: The actors were filmed separately against a large blue screen. A traveling matte was produced from this shot and used to combine the live action with the background miniature.
Bottom: The final composite as it appears in the movie.

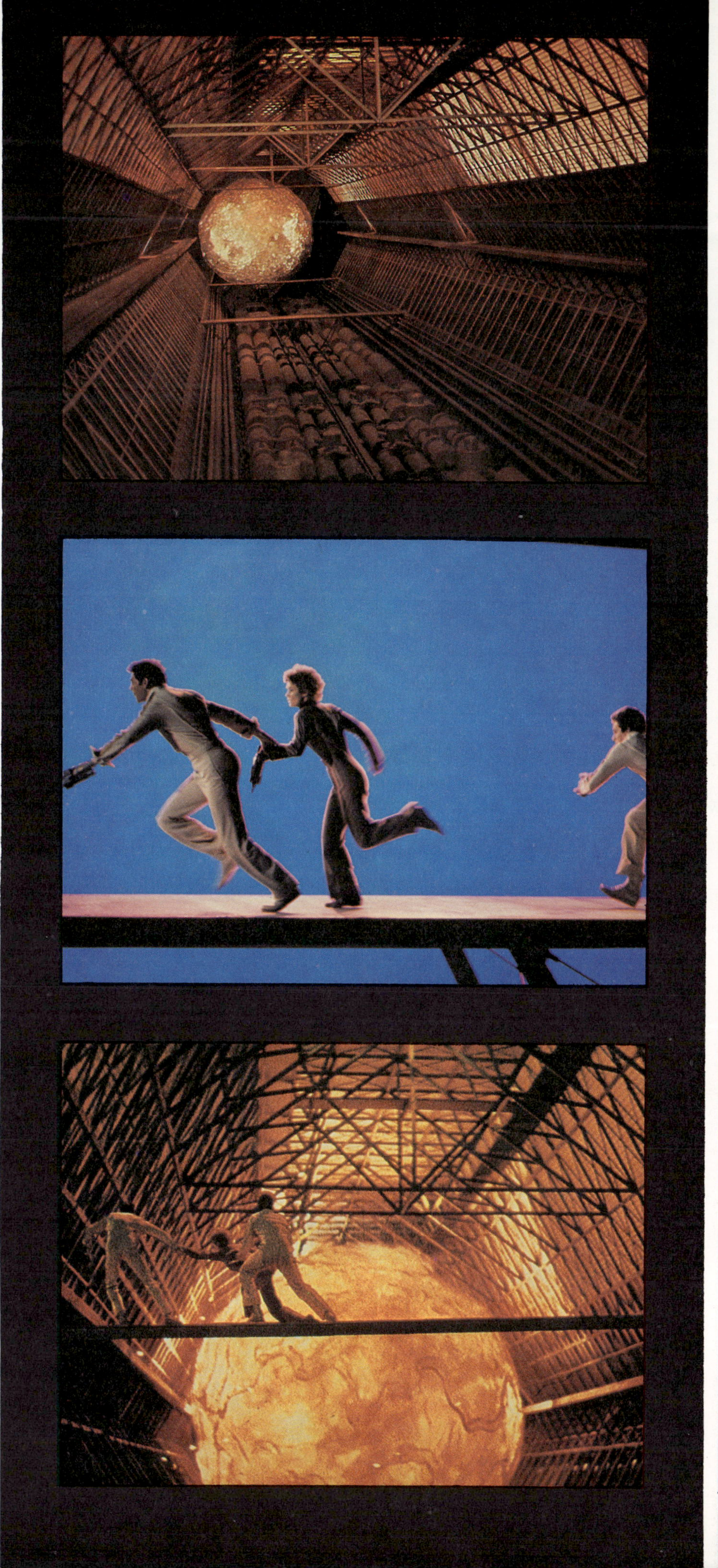

One of Peter Ellenshaw's dramatic preproduction design paintings of the *Cygnus*, the colossal spaceship from Disney's *The Black Hole*.

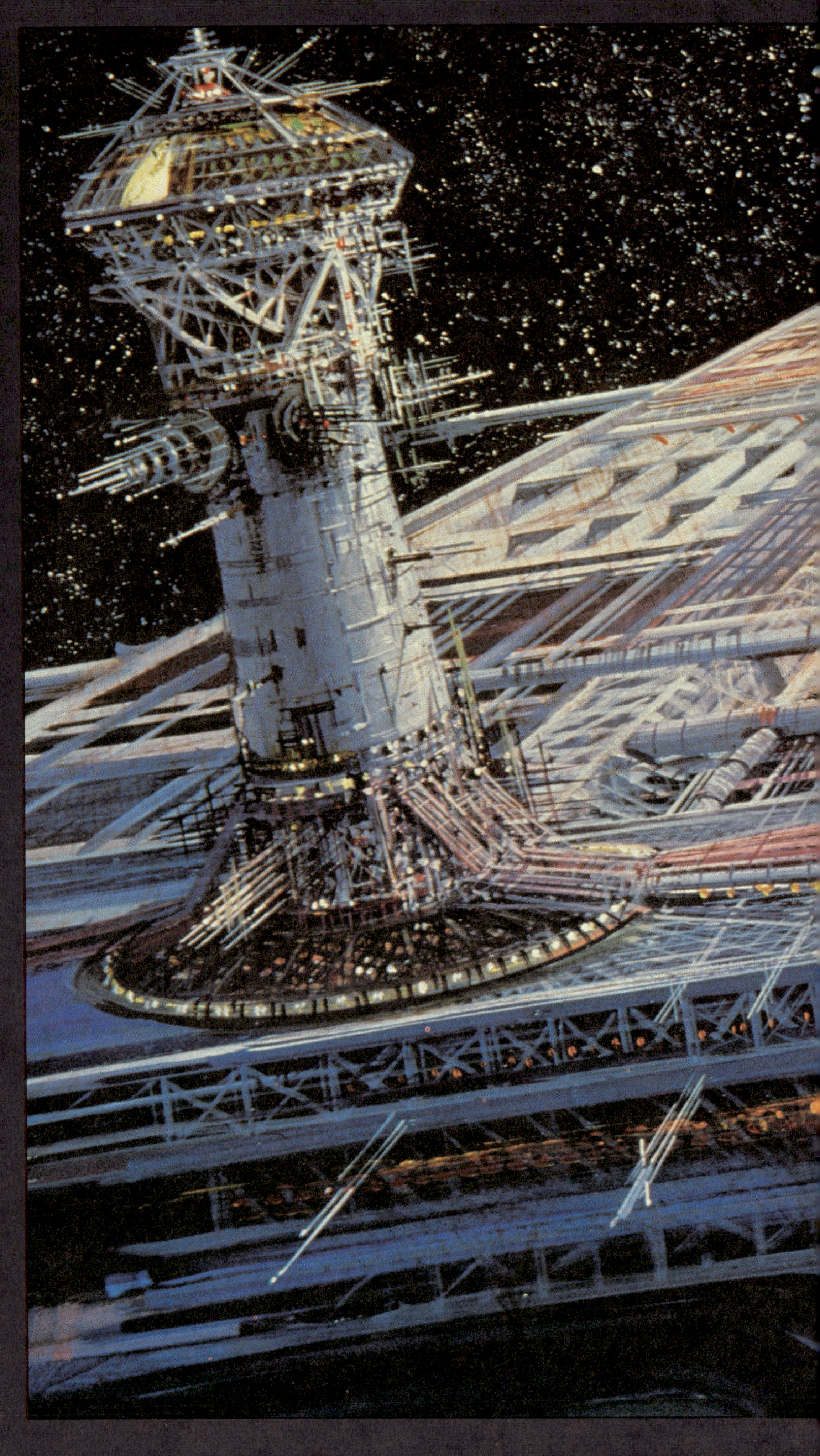

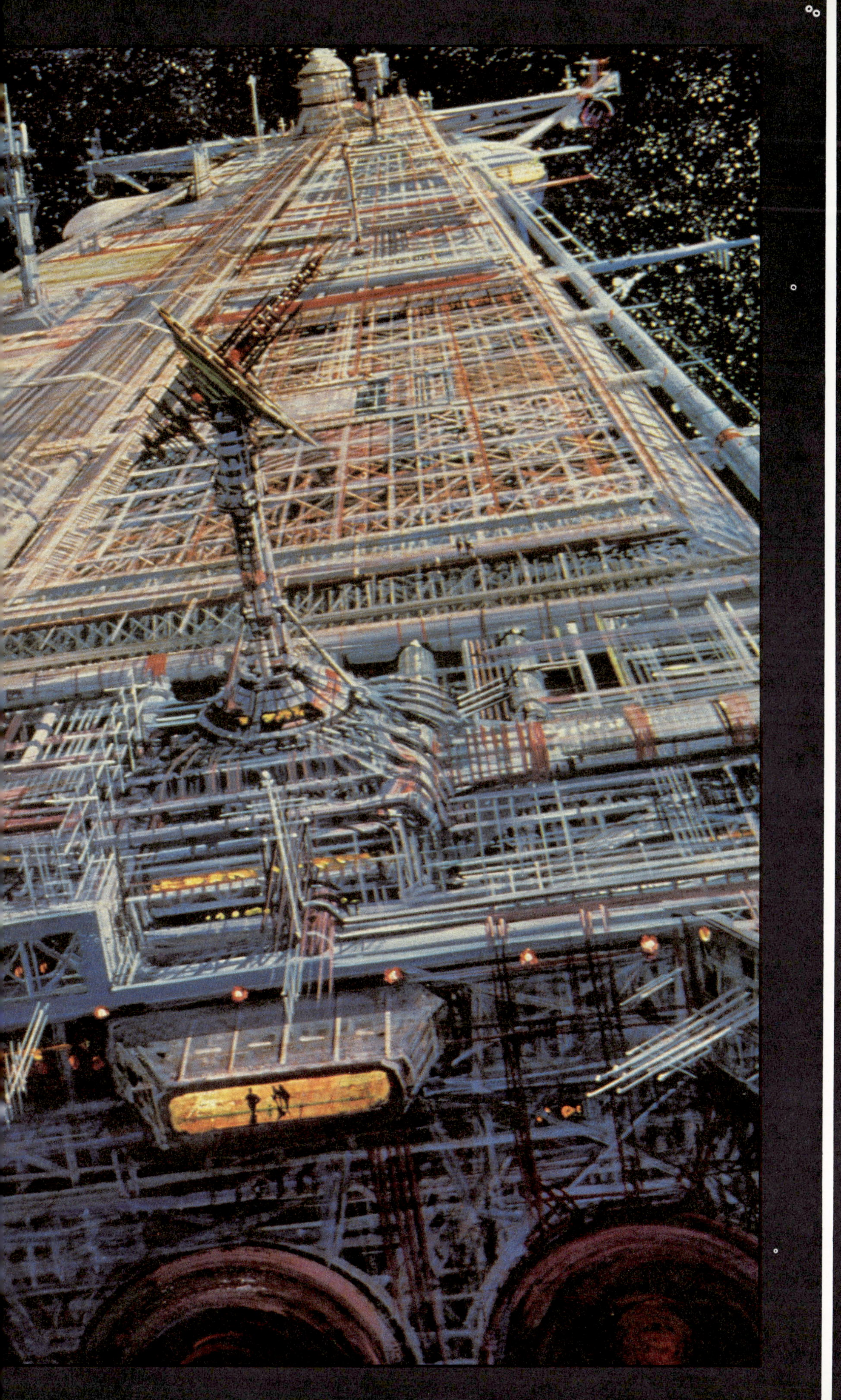

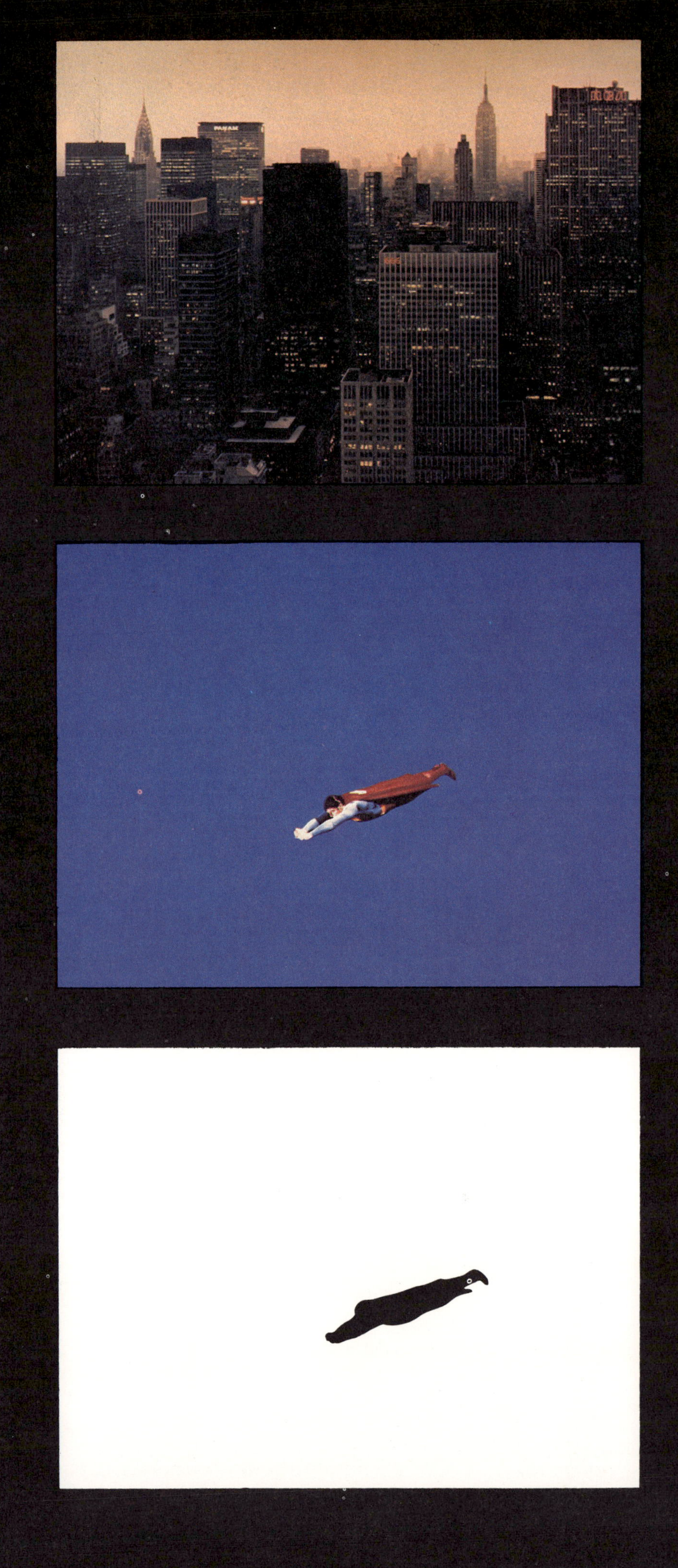

A sequence of pictures illustrating the blue-screen traveling-matte process, one of the methods used in *Superman* to make Christopher Reeve appear to fly. *Top:* The process begins with a background shot of the Manhattan skyline. *Center:* Next, Reeve is filmed separately against a blue background. *Bottom:* From this shot a matte is produced, consisting of an opaque silhouette of the actor against a clear background.

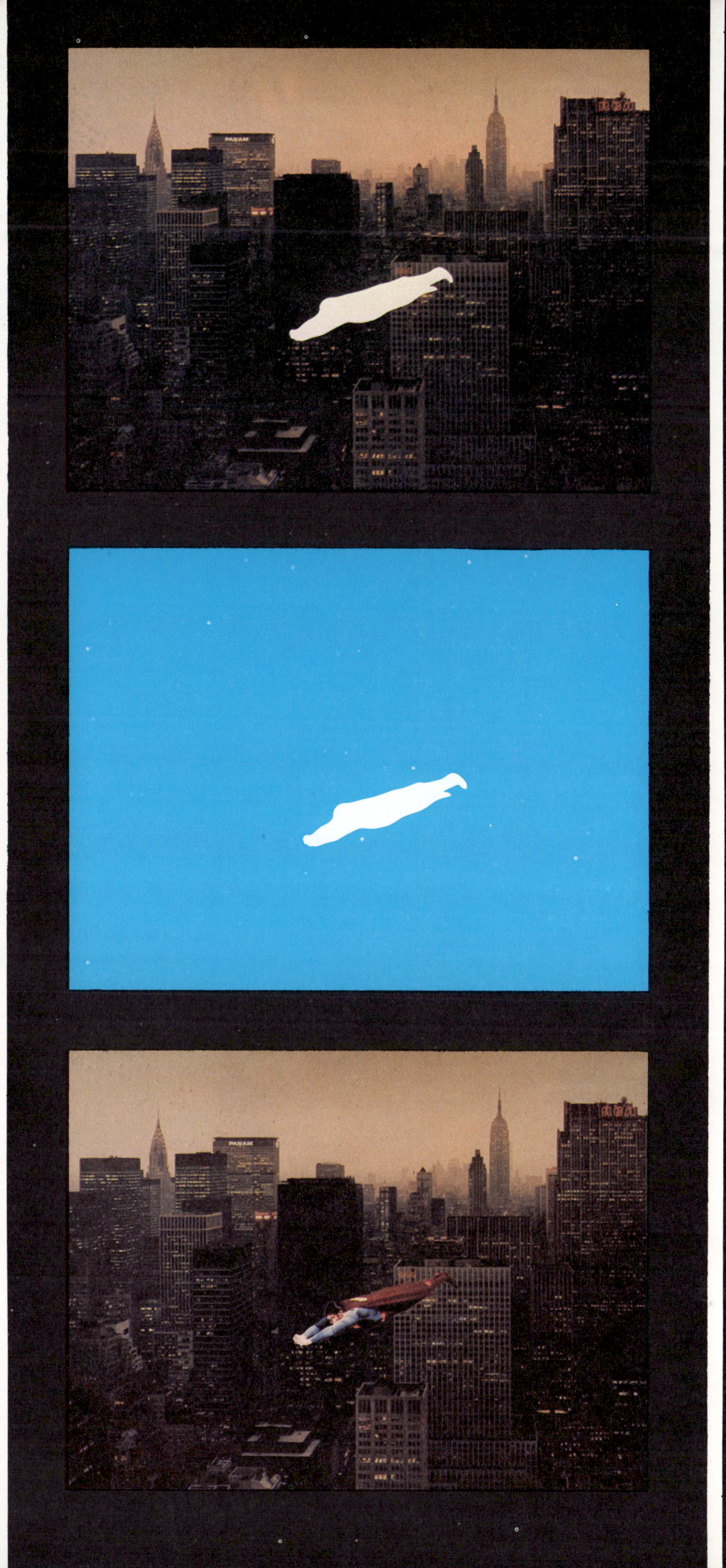

Top: The matte is printed together with the shot of Manhattan to produce a new skyline with an unexposed "hole" in the shape of the actor moving across it
Center: A counter-matte with a completely opaque background is then printed together with the original shot of Reeve. The counter-matte blocks out the blue background, leaving only the image of the actor.
Bottom: This image is then printed into the "hole" in the shot of Manhattan to produce the final composite.

For the horrifying climax of *Maniac* in which the title character has his head torn from his body, make-up/effects artist Tom Savini attached a foam latex replica of actor Joe Spinell's head to a dummy body and filled the neck with animal intestines, Salisbury steak, and tubes to carry artificial blood.

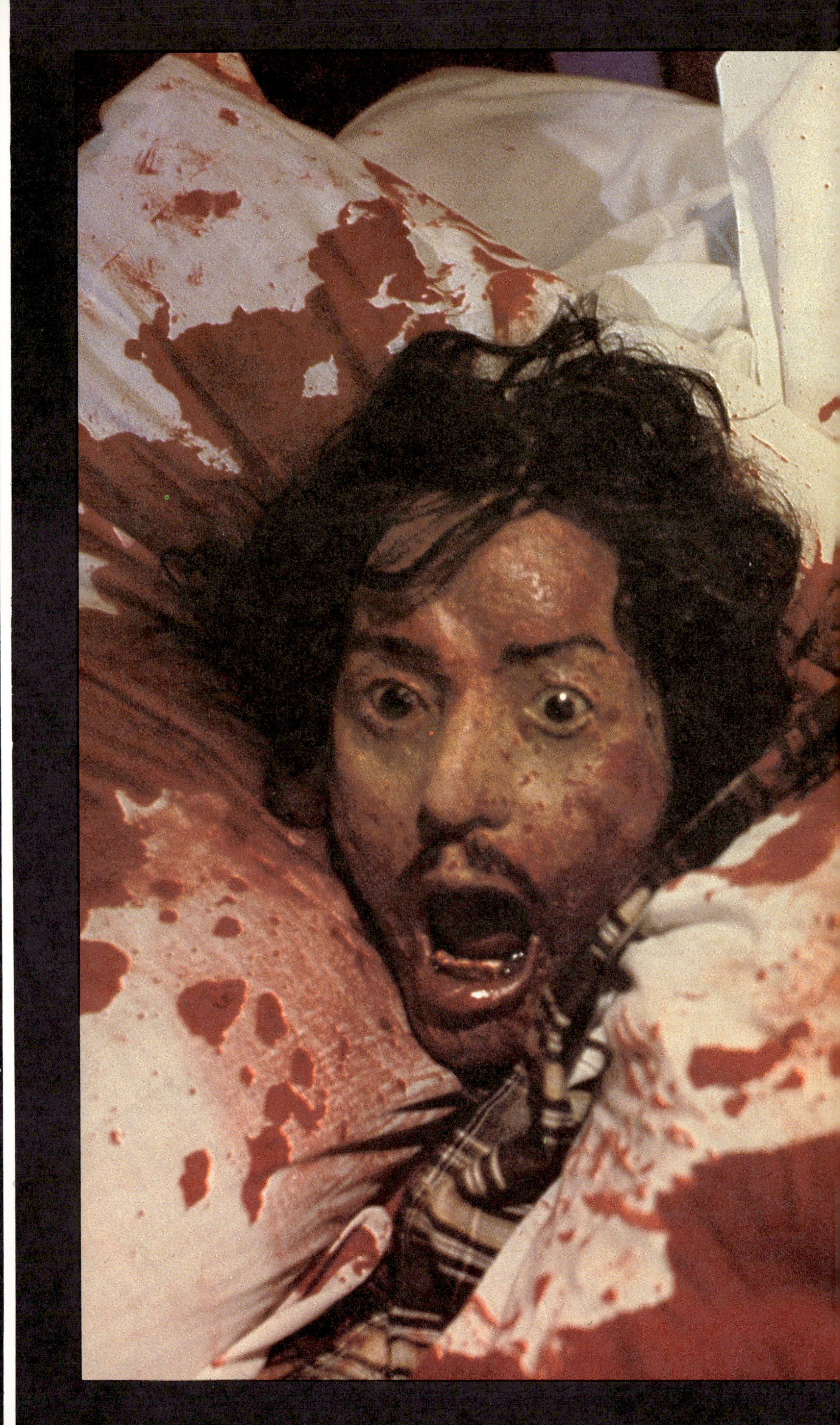

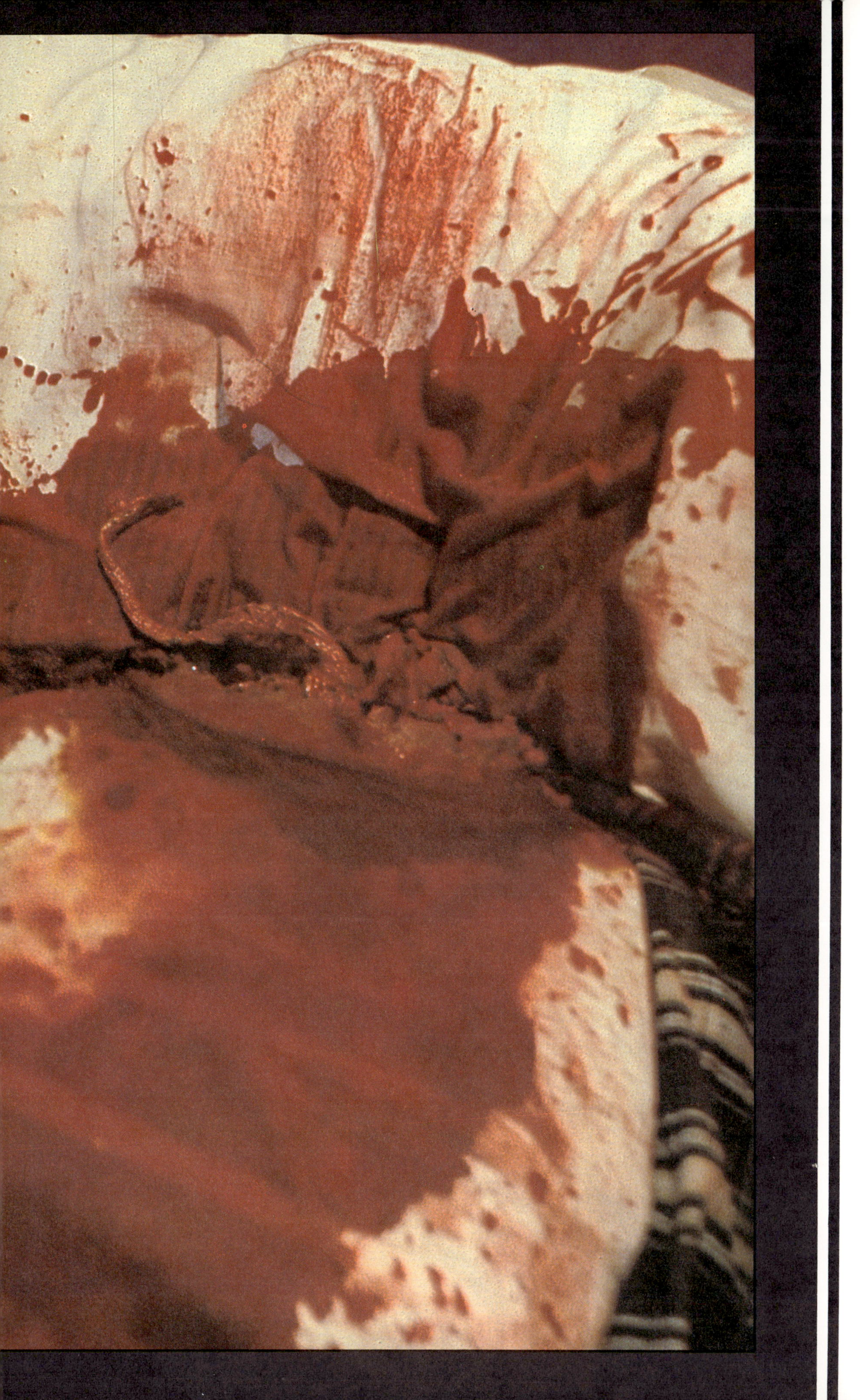

Top: A glass shot setup for *Flesh Gordon.* An eerie painting of a moon, clouds, and distant cliffs was done on a small sheet of glass, which was then positioned between the motion-picture camera and a tabletop model of a castle. The camera filmed the castle through the painting. *Center:* The resulting shot as it appears on screen. *Bottom:* Another castle model, this one from the horror movie *The Evil of Frankenstein.*

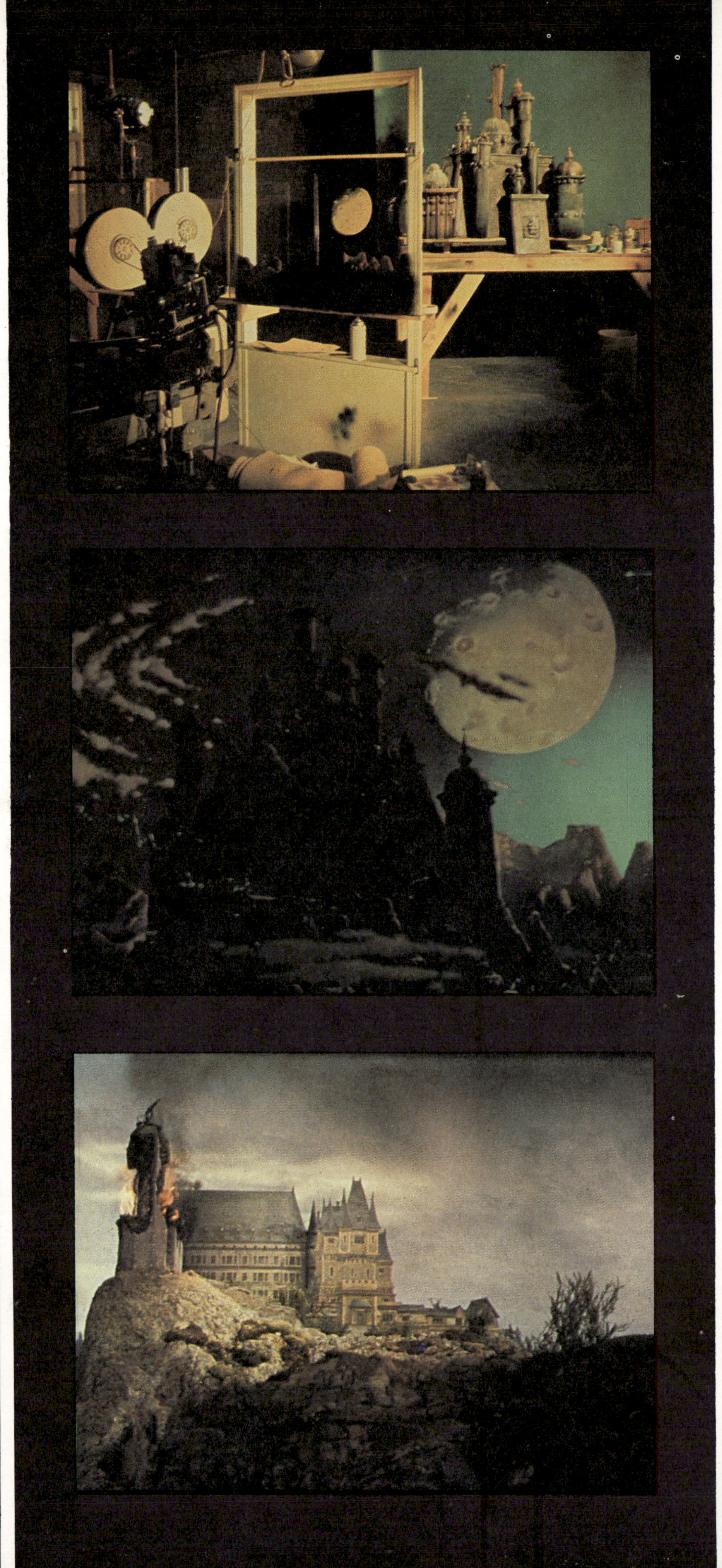